MAXIMUS OF TYRE

The Philosophical Orations

MAXIMUS OF TYRE

The Philosophical Orations

Translated, with an Introduction and Notes, by
M. B. TRAPP

CLARENDON PRESS · OXFORD
1997

Oxford University Press, Great Clarendon Street, Oxford OX2 6DP
Oxford   New York
Athens   Auckland   Bangkok   Bogota   Bombay
Buenos Aires   Calcutta   Cape Town   Dar es Salaam
Delhi   Florence   Hong Kong   Istanbul   Karachi
Kuala Lumpur   Madras   Madrid   Melbourne
Mexico City   Nairobi   Paris   Singapore
Taipei   Tokyo   Toronto
and associated companies in
Berlin   Ibadan

Oxford is a trade mark of Oxford University Press

Published in the United States
by Oxford University Press Inc., New York

© M. B. Trapp 1997

British Library Cataloguing in Publication Data
Data available

Library of Congress Cataloging in Publication Data
The philosophical orations / Maximus of Tyre ; translated, with an
introduction and notes, by M. B. Trapp.
Includes bibliographical references.
1. Philosophy, Ancient.   I. Trapp, M. B.   II. Title.
B588.D572E5   1996   184—dc20   96-21022
ISBN 0-19-814989-1

1 3 5 7 9 10 8 6 4 2

Typeset by Regent Typesetting, London
Printed in Great Britain on acid-free paper by
Biddles Ltd., Guildford & King's Lynn

Acknowledgements

This translation is the product of some fifteen years' engagement with the *Orations* of Maximus, and draws on work done both for my doctoral dissertation (Oxford, 1986) and for my edition of the Greek text (Teubner, 1994). I have accumulated many debts along the way, and am glad to be able to acknowledge them here. Above all, I must thank Donald Russell, who first introduced me to Maximus and who has been an unfailing source of encouragement and wise counsel ever since. He is himself a masterly translator; I can only hope that he will not find my faltering efforts to fall too far short of his standards. Ewen Bowie also has been an outstanding mentor, helper, and friend over the years; in the present context I am particularly grateful for the notes and comments he and Dr B. P. Hillyard produced in examining my doctoral thesis. Professor Jacques Puiggali very generously sent me a copy of his own doctoral dissertation on Maximus; he will be the first to see how much I have learned from it and how heavily I have drawn on it in the present work. Much appreciated gifts of books and offprints have also come from Professors Marian Szarmach and Pieter van der Horst, and Dr Irina Kovaleva. Other forms of assistance, too various to catalogue individually, have been provided by Dr D. P. Coleman, Dr N. G. Devlin, Ueli Dill, Carlotta Dionisotti, Professor A. T. Grafton, Barbara Gygli, Dr J. Kraye, Professor R. G. Mayer, Nicholas Purcell, Professor M. D. Reeve, Professor I. Ševčenko, Professor R. W. Sharples, Professor J. B. Trapp, and Nigel Wilson; my thanks to them all, and to any other helpers and allies whose names ungrateful forgetfulness has temporarily driven from my mind. Among institutions, I am grateful to King's College London for sabbatical leave, and to the British Academy for a grant towards a study-trip to Florence. At the Press, Hilary O'Shea and Enid Barker have seen the project through with warm efficiency; Laurien Berkeley copy-read a knotty text with admirable scrupulousness and sensitivity. In North Finchley, Dr N. G. Devlin and

Master N. W. B. Trapp have provided the most essential support of all.

London
August 1996   M. B. TRAPP

Contents

Abbreviations

ANRW	*Aufstieg und Niedergang der römischen Welt*, ed. H. Temporini and W. Haase (Berlin and New York, 1972–)
D-K	*Die Fragmente der Vorsokratiker*, ed. H. Diels and W. Kranz, 6th edn. (Berlin, 1951-2 and repr.)
DBI	*Dizionario biografico degli italiani*, ed. A. M. Ghisalberti *et al.* (Rome, 1960–)
FGrH	*Die Fragmente der griechischen Historiker*, ed. F. Jacoby (Leiden, etc. 1923-58)
FHSG	*Theophrastus of Eresus: Sources for his Life, Writings, Thought and Influence*, ed. and tr. W. W. Fortenbaugh, P. M. Huby, R. W. Sharples, and D. Gutas (Leiden, 1992)
GCS	*Die griechischen christlichen Schriftsteller der ersten drei Jahrhunderte* (Berlin, 1897–)
Giannantoni	*Socratis et Socraticorum Reliquiae*, ed. G. Giannantoni, 4 vols. (Naples, 1990)
IG	*Inscriptiones Graecae*
Kassel-Austin	*Poetae Comici Graeci*, ed. R. Kassel and C. F. Austin (Berlin, 1983–)
KP	*Der kleine Pauly*, ed. K. Ziegler and W. Sontheimer (Stuttgart, 1964-75)
LIMC	*Lexicon Iconographicum Mythologiae Classicae*, ed. J. Boardman *et al.* (Zurich 1981–)
L-P	*Poetarum Lesbiorum Fragmenta*, ed. E. Lobel and D. L. Page (Oxford, 1955)
L-S	*The Hellenistic Philosophers*, ed. A. A. Long and D. N. Sedley, 2 vols. (Cambridge, 1987)
M-W	*Fragmenta Hesiodea*, ed. R. Merkelbach and M. L. West (Oxford, 1967)
Nauck[2]	*Tragicorum Graecorum Fragmenta*, ed. A. Nauck 2nd edn. (Leipzig, 1889; repr. Hildesheim, 1964)
OGIS	*Orientis Graeci Inscriptiones Selectae*, ed. W. Dittenberger (Leipzig, 1903-5)

ODB	*The Oxford Dictionary of Byzantium*, ed. A. P. Kazhdan *et al.* (New York, 1991)
*PIR*²	*Prosopographia Imperii Romani*, ed. E. Groag, A. Stein, *et al.*, 2nd edn. (Berlin, 1933–)
PMG	*Poetae Melici Graeci*, ed. D. L. Page (Oxford, 1962)
Powell	*Collectanea Alexandrina*, ed. J. U. Powell (Oxford, 1925)
RAC	*Reallexikon für Antike und Christentum*, ed. T. Klauser *et al.* (Stuttgart, 1950–)
RE	*Paulys Real-Encyclopädie der classischen Altertumswissenschaft* ed. G. Wissowa *et al.* (Stuttgart, 1893–1980)
SEG	*Supplementum Epigraphicum Graecum*, ed. J. J. Hondius *et al.* (Leiden, 1923–)
Spengel	*Rhetores Graeci*, ed. L. Spengel, 3 vols. (Leipzig, 1853–6; vol. i rev. 1885–94)
SVF	*Stoicorum Veterum Fragmenta*, ed. H. von Arnim, 4 vols. (Leipzig, 1903–24)
Thesleff	*The Pythagorean Texts of the Hellenistic Period*, ed. H. Thesleff (Åbo, 1965)
TrGrF	*Tragicorum Graecorum Fragmenta*, ed. B. Snell *et al.* (Göttingen, 1971–)
Wehrli	*Die Schule des Aristoteles*, ed. F. Wehrli, 10 vols., 2nd edn. (Basel, 1967–9)
West	*Iambi et Elegi Graeci ante Alexandrum Cantati*, ed. M. L. West, 2 vols., 2nd edn. (Oxford, 1989–92)

Introduction

LIFE, WORKS, AND CONTEXT

THE LIFE

As a historical individual, Maximus of Tyre is scarcely more than a cipher. Only three surviving sources claim to give any direct information about his life and career: Eusebius' *Chronicle* asserts that he 'came to prominence' (*agnoscitur*) in Olympiad 232 (AD 149–52); the brief biographical notice in the *Suda* (one of those taken over from the *Onomatologos* of Hesychius[1]) records that he 'lectured in Rome in the time of Commodus' (who was sole emperor from AD 180 to 191); and the title attached to his *Orations* in the manuscript tradition claims that they were delivered in Rome 'on his first visit'.[2] All three sources agree in describing him as 'Tyrian', though none of them specifies whether this indicates that he was born in Tyre, or whether it means instead that that he was educated there, or scored his first professional successes before a Tyrian public. The *Suda* and the earlier manuscripts agree in calling him a philosopher and a Platonist. At best, only the bare outlines of a possible career seem to be visible: birth *circa* AD 120–5; early recognition, aged 25 to 30, in *circa* AD 150; one or more professional visits to Rome, including one in his sixties during the reign of Commodus, with the original version of the surviving *Orations* delivered either (more probably) then, or (perhaps) on an earlier occasion.[3] On closer examination, however, not even this much turns out to be secure, since the Eusebian date for Maximus' 'recognition' is made suspect by disagreements and obvious errors

---

[1] See Adler (1928–38, vol i, p. xxi), and cf. p. lvi with n. 112 below.

[2] *Suda*/Hesychius s.v.: 'διέτριψε δὲ ἐν Ῥώμῃ ἐπὶ Κομόδου'; Parisinus graecus 1962, fol. 1ᵛ: 'τῶν ἐν Ῥώμῃ διαλέξεων τῆς πρώτης ἐπιδημίας'.

[3] A decision is not helped by the fact that the manuscripts' phrase 'on his first visit' is ambiguous: it could mean either 'on his first rather than second (or third) visit', or 'when he went to Rome, not having visited before'. But this is not the only uncertainty.

in the sources from which it is reconstucted.[4] The only clear biographical testimony is that linking the surviving *Orations* to a visit to Rome, and a period lecturing in Rome to the reign of Commodus.

Attempts have been made to establish something more of an identity and a career, but with little success. Almost nothing can be gleaned from the *Orations* themselves. It is only in *Or.* I that Maximus talks directly about himself, and even there he offers no biographical details. Elsewhere, his claims to have seen with his own eyes the sacred stone of the Arabians (*Or.* 2. 4), the Marsyas and the Maeander in Phrygia (*Or.* 2. 7), and the Dioscuri aiding a ship at sea (*Or.* 9. 7) may well owe more to rhetorical needs than to truthful biography, and in any case reveal little. Nor has the search for other known individuals with whom he might be identified produced any solid conclusions. The best candidate is Cassius Maximus, the dedicatee of books 1-3 of Artemidorus' *Onirocritica*, whom Artemidorus' compliments identify as a Phoenician (*On.* 3. 66), a writer (*On.* 2, proem), and a philosopher (*On.* 2. 70), and whose family is likely to owe its name and its Roman citizenship to the patronage of C. Cassius Longinus, the tyrannicide.[5] The identification is all the more tempting because it supplies a connection between Maximus and the great cultural centre of Ephesus, from which Artemidorus writes. It is certainly better grounded than the match, also canvassed, with the philosophizing Sidonian sophist of Lucian *Demonax* 14,[6] but it is still far from decisive. Not all Phoenicians are Tyrians, and given the uncertainties of dating on both sides, it cannot be guaranteed that Artemidorus' patron and the Tyrian Maximus are even contemporaries. 'Maximus' is, moreover, a common name, even for philosophers.[7]

---

[4] Jerome's version (Ol. 232) pairs Maximus with Arrian, for whom Ol. 232 is far too late an *agnoscitur*. Syncellus (*Ecl. Chron.* pp. 662-3 Dindorf = p. 429 Mosshammer; AD 130) confuses the Tyrian Maximus with the proconsul of Africa Claudius Maximus, before whom Apuleius delivered his *Apology* in AD 158. The Armenian translation (A. Schoene (ed.), *Eusebii Chronicorum Canonum quae Supersunt* ii, p. 168) makes both these mistakes together and seems to be claiming Maximus and Arrian, along with Apollonius and Basilides, as teachers of Marcus Aurelius. All this leaves it unclear where exactly Eusebius himself dated Maximus, let alone whether his dating was correct.

[5] For the identification, see Pack (1963, pp. xxv-vi) and *PIR*[2] ii. 120 (C 509). For Cassius the Liberator, see Rawson (1986).

[6] Suggested by Funk (1907: 180, 686); *PIR*[2] ii. 120 (C 509).

[7] Witness most recently the 'Fl. Maximus philosophus' honoured on the stele from Caesarea Maritima discussed in Burrell (1993).

THE WORKS

It is therefore as the author of his surviving works, rather than as a characterizable individual, that Maximus lives on. As presented in the principal manuscript, Parisinus graecus 1962,[8] these comprise forty-one short discourses, ranging from ninety-nine to 317 lines of Teubner text in length, with an average of 197 lines.[9] They are collectively entitled 'The *dialexeis* of the Platonic philosopher Maximus of Tyre, given in Rome during his first visit',[10] and subscribed 'The philosophical discourses of Maximus of Tyre'.[11] Each individual item bears a further title of its own, and either one or two numerals, as follows:[12]

1.	(–)	On Pleasure, to the effect that even if it is a Good, it is nevertheless not secure (*a*).
	(–)	On Pleasure, to the effect that even if it is a Good, it is nevertheless not secure (*b*).
	(–)	On Pleasure, to the effect that even if it is a Good, it is nevertheless not secure (*c*).
2.	(–)	What is the end of philosophy?
3.	(–)	That it is possible to derive benefit even from external circumstance.
4.	(–)	How might one ready oneself for dealings with a friend?
5.	(I)	That the philosopher's words will prove appropriate to any subject-matter.
6.	(II)	Whether images should be set up in honour of the gods.

[8] On Paris. gr. 1962, see further below.

[9] 99 lines: *Or.* 28; 317 lines: *Or.* 1. These are relatively isolated extremes: the next shortest items are *Orr.* 31 and 19, with 109 and 148 lines respectively, and the next longest *Orr.* 11, 18, and 10, with 297, 284, and 249.

[10] Μαξίμου Τυρίου Πλατωνικοῦ φιλοσόφου τῶν ἐν Ῥώμῃ διαλέξεων τῆς πρώτης ἐπιδημίας, αʹ (= ἡ πρώτη) . . . κτλ. The implications of the recurrence of this title between items six and seven in the sequence of discourses (= *Orr.* 35 and 1) will be discussed below. For the meaning of the word 'διαλέξεις', see below.

[11] Μαξίμου Τυρίου φιλοσοφούμενα.

[12] In the manuscript, the numerals given below in arabic form are minuscule, and those given in roman form are majuscule (uncial). Notice that the two sequences of numerals indicate two different ways of ordering (and numbering) the collections: either thirty-five numbers, with three sets of items sharing the same number (1, 12, 21); or forty-one numbers, with a separate number for each item (but the first six apparentus unnumbered). This translation (like the three most recent editions of the Greek text) follows the latter patterns for reasons explained below, pp. lix–lx.

As will emerge later, the accuracy of these titles is not always beyond reproach, and there are good grounds for concluding that they are editorial additions, rather than the work of the author himself.[13] None the less, they give a good initial impression both of the range of subject-matter dealt with by the *Orations*, and of the manner in which it is approached. It is immediately clear that the interests of the collection are consistently philosophical, but equally that the range of issues covered falls some way short of the whole field of philosophy, as it was understood in the second century AD. Canonically, philosophical doctrine divided into three categories: logic, physics, and ethics. This division had long been standard;[14] close to Maximus' own time it can be seen at work, for instance, in the organization of *Didascalicus* (Exposition of Platonic Doctrine) of Alcinous.[15] Of the three categories, the *Orations* have nothing at all to say about logic, and confine their interests within physics to theology and psychology, with no regard for either metaphysical first principles or natural science. The predominant focus of interest is ethics, which is approached from a number of distinct,

[13] See below, n. 60 and p. lviii. On these grounds I have replaced the manuscripts' titles with my own in this translation. For the Greek wording of the discarded titles, see the introductory notes to the individual orations.

[14] It is first found in Aristotle (*Top.* I. 14, 105^b 19 ff.); see Dillon (1977: 63).

[15] For which, see above all Whittaker (1990) and Dillon (1977: 267–306; 1993). 'Alcinous' is the name attached to the work in the manuscript tradition (almost the whole of which depends, like that of Maximus, on Paris. gr. 1962). J. Freudenthal's conjecture that 'Alcinous' is a scribal slip for 'Albinus', though generally accepted by scholars until recently, now seems to be losing favour, largely thanks to Whittaker (1974: 450–6; 1990, pp. vii–xii).

but complementary, angles: we see not only abstract theoretical topics (e.g. discussion of the nature of the Good), but also questions of personal ethics (e.g. retaliation and friendship), and issues with a civic and political slant, such as the question of farmers and soldiers, or that of the relationship of poets and philosophers to the civic community.

In terms of the general approach to this subject-matter, we register immediately that—again in marked contrast to such scholastic texts as Alcinous' *Didascalicus*—the *Orations* make no attempt to co-ordinate their individual constituents into a sustained or systematic exposition even of their restricted range of subject-matter. Each item (or each set of items, where more than one is devoted to the same topic) is a self-contained discussion of a given question put up for investigation. From this point of view, they are closer to such miscellanies as Plutarch's *Platonic Questions* (Πλατωνικὰ Ζητήματα) or *Dinner-Party Problems* (Συμποσιακὰ Προβλήματα) than to a systematic exposition such as the *Didascalicus*.[16]

Useful though such first impressions are, they leave some large questions unanswered, about form, content, and context. What sort of philosophy is this that the *Orations* contain? Who is it for, at what level of sophistication does it operate, and what is its doctrinal colouring? And what kinds of composition are these short discourses that the manuscript labels *dialexeis*?

THE PHILOSOPHY OF THE *ORATIONS*

Philosophy Made Easy

The only place in the *Orations* where a formal definition of philosophy is offered is at the beginning of *Or.* 26. The definition comes as part of an argument that, as the greatest of divinely inspired poets, Homer must necessarily also be the greatest of philosophers:

When I encounter Homer's stories I am quite unable to praise the man from my own resources, but yet again need him to lend me some of his verses, so as to avoid spoiling my praise by expressing it in mere prose:

---

[16] One might compare also Seneca's *Naturales Quaestiones* and *Epistulae Morales*, though both of those show a rather higher degree of organization in their arrangement. Arrian's *Lectures of Epictetus* (Ἐπικτήτου Διατριβαί), though often comparable to the *Orations* in style and subject-matter, differ in that they are reported by a second party (Arrian) and often include brief narrative frames.

> I praise you, Homer, before all other mortals;
> Your teacher was Zeus' daughter, the Muse, or Apollo.
>
> It is quite improper to suppose the instruction of the Muses and Apollo to be any other than that by which due order is introduced into the soul. What else could that be than philosophy? And how are we to understand philosophy, if not as detailed knowledge of matters divine and human, the source of virtue and noble thoughts and a harmonious style of life and sophisticated habits?[17]   (*Or.* 26. 1)

Both the wording here ('knowledge of matters human and divine'[18]) and the emphasis on philosophy as the 'art of living well' (i.e. no mere intellectual pursuit, but a life-engrossing discipline with marked practical consequences, aimed at producing an orderly, therefore a happy, soul) are entirely familiar—so much so as to count as commonplaces of Graeco-Roman culture of the Hellenistic and Imperial periods. In themselves they give no sense of what might be distinctive of the idea of philosophy espoused and projected by the *Orations*. For that it is more illuminating to resort to the first, introductory *Oration* (which, for reasons that will be discussed below, is the seventh item in the list given above, numbered 5 and (1)). This is the piece in which, in the written text of the *Orations*, Maximus presents both himself and his wares to the new reader, in the person of a speaker coming for the first time before a new audience who are unacquainted both with his eloquence and with any commitment to philosophical values and study. The element of personal introduction will claim our attention later; for now it is the introduction to the name and nature of philosophy that is important.

The first need is to convince the reader or audience of the lecture that this activity—named 'philosophy' by Pythagoras, but known already to Homer as 'Calliope' (*Or.* 1. 2)—is one they should actively desire to participate in. On one level, this task is discharged by an appeal to precisely the same, familiar terms that we have seen invoked in the formal definition in *Or.* 26: philosophy is presented as the shepherd and the guiding light of human life, without which mankind, both individually and collectively, is condemned to chaos and ruin (*Or.* 1. 2–3); to practise philosophy, it is urged, is to develop a potential innate in (almost) all human beings, in virtue of their very human nature (*Or.* 1. 5). This both

---

[17] For this view of Homer, see below, pp. xxiv–xxv, and the introductory notes to *Orr.* 4 and 26.   [18] See note ad loc. (*Or.* 26).

underlines the necessity of the venture, and reassures the diffident about its practicability. But at the same time, there is another level of appeal, to the audience's self-respect as people of taste and culture. Philosophy, it is implied, is not a marginal or a minority pursuit. On the contrary, it is the matter of the most respected of all Greek literary classics, the poetry of Homer (*Or.* 1. 2); and it can draw a cultivated Greek audience far more readily than even that quintessentially Greek event, competitive athletics (*Or.* 1. 4). It is here that something distinctive of the presentation of philosophy in the *Orations* (and thus also of their intended audience) begins to emerge. This is philosophy for the nervous, in need of encouragement, and for those who are as concerned for their image as cultivated Greeks as for the pure (and possibly subversive) light of reason. It is also, it soon emerges, philosophy for those who are liable to be deterred by anything too technical by way of terminology or of formal argumentation:

If you think that philosophy is simply a matter of nouns and verbs, or skill with mere words, or refutation and argument and sophistry, and of time spent on accomplishments like that, then there is no problem in finding a teacher. The world is full of that kind of sophist, and their brand of philosophy is easy to acquire; the quest is soon over. Indeed, I would make so bold as to say that it has more teachers than pupils. But if all that is only a small part of philosophy, and such a part that ignorance of it is disgraceful and knowledge no cause for pride, by all means let us escape reproach by knowing it, but let us not therefore give ourselves airs. If that were justified, then schoolmasters would be people of great account too, who devote their energies to syllables, and spend their time stammering with packs of witless infants. The summit of philosophy and the road that leads to it demand a teacher who can rouse young men's souls and guide their ambitions.   (*Or.* 1. 8)

This is cleverly done: the potential importance of skills of analysis and formal argument is acknowledged, but glancingly, and in such a way as to allow the conclusion that they could at a pinch be neglected in favour of what really matters in philosophical endeavour.

Finally, the audience of *Oration* 1 is reassured that profitable philosophical instruction can come in a large number of different guises, appropriate to the different circumstances of those who stand in need of it, and the varying situations in which they find themselves. Philosophy and the philosophical teacher, like good actors, will adapt themselves to the circumstances of the moment, meeting their audience half-way (*Or.* 1. 1–3); it would be untrue to the variety both of life and of the characters of philosophers themselves to expect them all to conform to a single appearance and style of teaching (*Or.* 1. 9–10). We may read here both a comforting negative ('you do not have to go to a grinding formal course with some austere tutor who looks the part in conventional terms, in order to reap the benefits of philosophy'), and an advertisement ('these *Orations*, to which you are now being introduced, are the real thing, even if they do not immediately sound like what you were expecting as philosophy').

Looking now to the remainder of the *Orations*, it is not difficult to establish that the emphases and the reassuring tone of *Oration* 1 are typical of the collection as a whole. As we have already seen, in surveying the range of topics covered, these are lectures that steer clear of logic, metaphysics, and most of physics, in favour of undemanding theology, psychology, and epistemology, with an overwhelming concentration on ethics. They are also consistently light on technical terminology and formal argumentation. Enough is included for the author to sound the part as an expert in the subject—see, for instance, such passages as the exposition of the *scala naturae* in *Orr.* 9. 3 and 11. 8, of recollection in 10. 4, of natural capacities in 31. 4, or of the nature of God in 38. 6—but this is always done in set-pieces of limited duration, and even within such set-pieces the level of technicality is never as high as one finds in, say, the *Didascalicus*, or the treatises of Sextus Empiricus, or even some passages of Epictetus. Indeed a positive virtue is sometimes made of the avoidance of pedantic precision in such matters, most notably in *Or.* 21. 4:

I beg the pardon of experts in the pursuit of terminology if I call the same thing now 'appetition', now 'desire'. I agree with Plato above all in his freedom over terminology. But if they insist, let love be 'appetition' and not 'desire', and let us draw the distinction in the following manner. . . .

As in *Or.* 1. 8, enthusiasts for precise argument are made to seem in danger of missing the real point. Equally, the encouraging message of *Or.* 1. 2 and 1. 4, that philosophy is an activity that has always been part of the best traditions of Hellenic culture, also spreads through the whole of the remainder of the collection: not so much in the form of explicit declarations, as in the consistency

with which the philosophical teaching conveyed is illustrated by
and integrated with evocations of classical literature and references
to the great periods of the Greek past. This is a topic to which
further attention will need to be given below.

The Audience

It was another commonplace of the culture in which the *Orations*
were composed that philosophical instruction held a particular
importance for the young; not the very young, but rather those on
the threshold of adult life, the *neoi*. As Plutarch explains at the
beginning of the *De Audiendo* (37c–f), the passage from childhood
to adult autonomy was the passage from external control to that
of one's own innate rationality. Philosophy being, precisely, the
pursuit of the values of reason, a new concern for philosophy and
a readiness to undertake some form of philosophical instruction
was therefore a highly appropriate way of acknowledging the
transition, and of establishing that it was being made in a properly
responsible spirit. In Prodicus' famous myth (summarized and
adapted by Maximus at the beginning of *Or.* 14), it was at this age,
'when the young become independent and show whether they are
going to approach life by the path of goodness or by the path of
wickedness',[19] that Heracles had his decisive encounter with Virtue
and Vice. It was at this age that the stereotypical experiences of the
'conversion to philosophy' and the review of the competing philosophical sects took place in the biography of the intellectual.[20] And
it was explicitly to 'lecture to the young' (διαλέγεσθαι τοῖς νέοις)
that philosophers were employed by the cities of the later
Hellenistic and Imperial periods.[21] None of this means that courses
and classes in philosophy were the exclusive preserve of young
adults, ostentatiously parading their new maturity; both the

I am indebted to Koniaris (1982: 113–14) for what follows in this section.

[19] Xenophon *Memorabilia* 2. 1. 21 (in the summary of the Prodican myth that
runs from there to 2. 1. 34).

[20] For which, see above all Nock (1933, ch. 11; 1939). A famous example of
philosophical conversion is provided by the story of Polemo, as told by Diogenes
Laertius (4. 16). Cases of young men reviewing various sects before making their
final choice are provided by Justin Martyr (*Dial. Tryph.* 2–3) and Galen (5. 41–2
Kühn; cf. *PIR*[2] iv. 4–5 (G 24)); Lucian's *Hermotimus*, still questing after twenty
years, and convinced that his conversion is not complete (*Herm.* 1–5, 13) is funny
precisely because he departs so spectacularly from the stereotype.

[21] See e.g. Plutarch *Cicero* 24, with Philostratus *Vit. Ap.* 4. 17 and 31, *SEG* 1.
368 and 6. 725, *OGIS* 339.

interest, and the desire to make a statement about personal values, will regularly have survived into later life too. But young adults were the largest single group to which such teaching could be directed.[22]

There is therefore nothing surprising in the fact that *Oration* I — and, by extension, the whole corpus of the *Orations*—identifies its addressees as 'young men' (*neoi*): once in the reference to the effect of philosophical teaching on 'young men's souls' in *Or.* I. 8, quoted above; and once, still more directly, in the flourish of self-advertisement in *Or.* I. 7: 'Behold, young men, this treasury of eloquence . . . that stands before you . . . '. Not only does this allow us to fit the *Orations* neatly into the general picture of philosophical instruction and its audience just sketched. It also provides us with a context that makes sense of the distinguishing features discussed in the previous section: the reassuring tone, the avoidance of complexity and technical terminology, the concern to integrate philosophical learning with other respected cultural forms. This would be philosophy aimed primarily at first-timers, young men who have had a predominantly literary (rhetorical) education with *grammaticus* and *rhetor*, but who now want at least some brushing of philosophy, so as to complete (and to be *seen* to complete) their education as cultivated and responsible citizens. They know and respect the great classics of the literary heritage, and the great figures of civic history; inevitably, they have acquired some familiarity with the philosophical pantheon too; but they still need to be reassured both that philosophical culture is compatible with their education to date (and the fundamental values of their society), and that they themselves are equipped to understand and to benefit from it.

Further support for this picture of the target audience of the *Orations* can be gleaned from other passages too. The 'advertisement' in *Oration* I. 7, referred to in the previous paragraph, develops the suggestion that the audience may wish to derive other benefits from Maximus' eloquence besides instruction in philosophy: they will be equally useful to those with ambitions to poetic composition, success in the courts, and political power. These suggestions, it turns out, are made with a certain saving irony (see the very end of *Or.* I. 7),[23] but they again make sense

---

[22] For a general account of philosophical teaching in this period, see Clarke (1971, ch. 3).   [23] And cf. Anderson (1993: 139).

as enticements to a young audience, looking forward to various kinds of adult distinction. And in the main body of the *Orations*, the exposition of Platonic theology in *Or.* 11 begins with a revealing preface. Affecting an initial surprise at the demand to have Plato's thought expounded by another, when the dialogues themselves are available to be read, Maximus reconciles himself to it with the thought that *on first reading* they are indeed liable to prove bewilderingly rich, and to need an exegete. This too suggests an audience of beginners, even if the suggestion that they have never before so much as opened a Platonic dialogue sounds more like exaggeration for rhetorical effect than strict realism.

Perhaps disappointingly, no closer characterization of the implied audience of the *Orations* is possible. Just as they are almost wholly devoid of personal details of their author, so too they offer none of their hearers, either as individuals or as a class. The kind of information to be found in Arrian's *Diatribes of Epictetus*, which allows quite a detailed survey of visitors to Nicopolis to be constructed,[24] is unavailable.

Doctrinal Orientation

It would seem natural to ask next about the formal doctrinal affinities of the *Orations*: to which if any of the major philosophical schools of the period—Stoic, Peripatetic, Platonist, Epicurean, Pyrrhonist, perhaps even Cynic—should they (and their author) be assigned? However, this question needs to be approached with more care than it has sometimes received. We need to be prepared to discover that the view of philosophy and its history projected in the *Orations* works on other terms of reference, and that the question has accordingly to be formulated differently, or to be answered on several different levels.

By and large, scholars have been content simply to accept the authority of the manuscript title and the *Suda* and to describe Maximus as a Platonist, and, moreover, to assume that the label Πλατωνικός (not necessarily exactly the same thing as 'Platonist')

---

[24] For which see Brunt (1977). Something more concrete by way of a context might be recoverable if it could be assumed that Maximus' audience were νέοι in the 'official' sense, that is to say members of a formal association of ex-ephebes of the kind studied in Forbes (1933). There is, however, no direct evidence that such associations, as opposed to ephebes (Pélékidis 1962: 266–7; Jones 1940: 224), had any concern with cultural as well as gymnastic and athletic pursuits (Forbes 1933: 51).

is one that he himself would immediately have accepted as appropriate to him.[25] The real situation is more complicated and more interesting.

In the first place, if it is true that the *Orations* are intended for an audience outside the context of formal, systematic, philosophical instruction, then describing them and their author as 'Platonist' is bound to mean something slightly different from the same term used of Alcinous and the *Didascalicus*, or Gellius' mentor Calvenus Taurus, or any of the other scholarchs and καθηγηταί discussed in Dillon's *Middle Platonists* and Glucker's *Antiochus and the Late Academy*.[26] At least as the author of the *Orations* (and we know him in no other identity), Maximus is not a school philosopher offering a systematic course of instruction in philosophical doctrine. If he is a Platonist, it must be in some sense other than that of one committed to the study and interpretation of Plato's dialogues.

But what sense? It is startling to discover that, when one examines him for explicit pronouncements on this score, Maximus never at any point in the *Orations* claims to have any special or exclusive preoccupation with Plato, or to be offering his audience a distinctively Platonic set of approaches to the topics discussed.[27] This absence is symptomatic of a more general characteristic. Along with their avoidance of excessive conceptual complexity, and the technical philosophical terminology of the schools, the *Orations* contrive also to avoid the language of sectarian allegiance. The existence of philosophical diversity of various kinds is certainly acknowledged, but almost never in a way that confronts the audience with the need to choose between mutually incompatible alternative views, assigned to named philosophical sects. The only exception to this rule is made to the disfavour of Epicureanism,

---

[25] So in the title to Soury (1942) Maximus is described as 'platonicien éclectique'. Dillon (1988) protests categorically against the use of the term 'eclectic', as applied to any philosopher of the Imperial period, but remains happy with notion that Maximus courted the label 'Platonist' (1977: 399–400; 1993, p. xii: 'Maximus of Tyre and Apuleius wished to be known as Platonists . . .'). For the ancient sense of Πλατωνικός, covering 'expert on Plato' as well as 'disciple of Plato', see Glucker (1978: 206–25).

[26] Dillon (1977), Glucker (1978, esp. 127–34) on the figure of the καθηγητής.

[27] Too much has been made in the past of the words in *Or.* 21. 4, ἐγὼ γάρ τοι τά τε ἄλλα καὶ ἐν τῇ τῶν ὀνομάτων ἐλευθερίᾳ πείθομαι Πλάτωνι, which are even printed as the epigraph to the whole work in the revised version of Davies's edition (1740). In context, these words are of a purely localized significance, claiming Platonic authority for the author's unpedantic approach to questions of terminology; they are not a general declaration of Platonic faith.

xxiv   *Introduction*

which is regularly abused, along with its founder, and declared incompatible with true philosophy.[28] Otherwise sectarian choice is not an issue, and even the names of the major sects are avoided. Thus in *Or.* 1. 1 and 10, it is diversity of style and delivery, not diversity of doctrine, that is endorsed, and made the basis of Maximus' own appeal to a new audience. When diversity of doctrine is mentioned, and names named, as in *Or.* 29. 7, the names are mainly names of the distant past, rather than those of the founders or upholders of the main contemporary sects, and the whole phenomenon is presented as matter for disapproval and regret.[29] And when real philosophical choices, other than that against the hedonist, atheist Epicureans, are debated, they are never presented as choices between (or even within) formal schools of thought.[30]

It is thus clear that the 'map' of philosophy that the *Orations* seek to present is not one that privileges the sectarian divisions that loom so large in other, ancient and modern accounts of the philosophical culture of the era. The alternative they offer can be discerned if the anti-Epicurean *Orr.* 29–33, just mentioned, are read together with the two discussions of poetry and philosophy in *Orr.* 4 and 26, and the introductory *Or.* 1. On the account that emerges from these lectures, there is indeed one dividing-line that must be drawn: Epicurean hedonism and atheism must be rejected, in favour of a truly philosophical theism, and the pursuit of Virtue through Reason. But once that line has been drawn, then philosophy ought to be seen (as far as can be contrived) not as a diversity of competing sects, but as a single noble tradition, in which all who truly deserve the name 'philosopher' have essentially the same truths to tell (*Or.* 1. 10). This might seem to be a very difficult view to maintain of the contemporary philosophical scene, which gives the impression of having been so firmly divided along sectarian lines (witness, for example, the presentation of philosophers in Lucian's dialogues, and the foundation of the four Imperial Chairs of Stoic, Peripatetic, Platonist, and Epicurean philosophy in Athens in AD 176).[31] Accordingly, when the nature of philosophy is in question, the *Orations* tend to look back with

---

[28] The principal anti-Epicurean sequence is *Orr.* 29–33, but see also *Orr.* 4. 4 and 8–9, 11. 5, 15. 8, 19. 3, 25. 4, 26. 2, and 41. 2.

[29] For which see also *Orr.* 26. 2 and 33. 1.

[30] See above all the discussion of the unity (or otherwise) of the Good in *Orr.* 39–40.

[31] See Jones (1986, ch. 3).

nostalgia to pre-sectarian days: to Plato, and before him to Socrates and to Pythagoras, and still further back, to the times of maximum unity and purity, when philosophical teaching was in the hands of the great early poets, Homer and Hesiod, and Orpheus and Musaeus. All the essential truths about God, the world, and human nature are assumed to be already encoded in those inspired early works, for those who know how to read them correctly (i.e. allegorically: *Orr.* 4. 8–9, 26. 5–9). The subsequent history of philosophy is accordingly presented as largely one of degeneration: the increasing 'sophistication' of human nature has necessitated a move to pedantic precision in place of noble myth (*Or.* 4. 2–5); and individual philosophers have taken to presenting partial truths, or idiosyncratic distortions of the truth, in place of the whole and pure truths of the early poets (*Orr.* 26. 2 and 29. 7). The best of the more recent figures have been those who, like Plato, have pre-served most of both the doctrines and the style of presentation of the early poets (*Orr.* 4. 4 and 26. 3).[32]

Overtly, therefore, Maximus is not a Platonist, because to him philosophical '-isms' are an aberration from what philosophy really ought to be, and has been in more favoured times. He is a spokesman for Philosophy, not for any one narrow sectarian interest.[33] At the same time, however, it is clear that Plato and his doctrines are extremely important to the *Orations*. This is true both of the literary texture, and of the philosophical content. With the sole exception of Homer, Plato's dialogues are the works of Greek literature most frequently quoted from and echoed in the *Orations*.[34] And, once due allowance has been made both for the simplified conceptual level on which the *Orations* work, and for the nature of Platonism in the second century AD, it is clear that, whatever the

[32] This view of the history and development of philosophy is by no means unique to Maximus: cf. pp. xxx–xxxi and 31–3 below.

[33] For an interesting alternative view, see Koniaris (1983), where it is suggested that Maximus should be understood as speaking in a succession of temporary 'personae', Platonist in one oration, Cynic in another, Epicurean in yet another, and so on. This has the virtue of breaking away from an unthinking acceptance of the Platonist tag, but seems unsatisfactory for a number of reasons. First, the whole interpretation depends heavily on a misreading of the dramatic imagery of *Or.* 1. 1 and 10; secondly, the alleged 'personae' are not sufficiently well marked in their respective orations to be recognizable as what they are claimed to be; and finally, as will be suggested below, the philosophical content of the *Orations* is in practice consistently Platonizing, whatever the explicit account of philosophy and his own orientation within it Maximus may give.

[34] See further below, p. xxxv.

overt pose Maximus adopts before his audience, the philosophical formation on which he draws for his discourses is solidly and consistently Platonic.

It is of course undeniable that much of the thought and terminology of the *Orations* cannot be related directly to the dialogues of Plato, or to what can be reconstructed of the unwritten teachings of the early Academy. *Orr.* 8–9, 13, 15–16, and 39–40, for instance, all attack topics which either were only formulated, or at least acquired an enhanced importance, after Plato's death: daimonology, the theoretic ideal, Fate and Free Will, and the nature of the Good. Maximus' use of the topos of the 'flight of the mind' (*Orr.* 7. 5, 8. 7, 9. 6, 10. 1, 3, and 9, 11. 10, 16. 6, 21. 7, 22.5, 26. 1), his occasional acceptance of a bipartite rather than a tripartite soul (*Orr.* 20. 4, 27. 5), and his insistence on the importance of intermediate terms (*Orr.* 4. 6, 10. 9, 24. 3), though all able to claim some Platonic precedent, also owe considerable debts to post-Platonic elaborations. Equally, much matter that he uses derives originally from the work of other sects. The definition of philosophy quoted above from *Or.* 26. 1 began its career among the Stoics. In many places, the argument uses terms and forms of argument of Aristotelian provenance.[35] It has been suggested that *Orr.* 9. 1–4 and 33. 7–8 draw, directly or indirectly, on Posidonius.[36] All that this shows, however, is that Maximus is drawing on an education in the Platonism of the second century AD, rather than that of the fourth century BC. The issues he presents that do not derive directly from the dialogues of Plato are all good Middle Platonic matter, and his Stoic and Peripatetic 'borrowings' are entirely characteristic of the ways Platonists had long felt free to reformulate the Master's ideas in terms drawn from his successors and even his philosophical opponents.[37]

The other general point with which any analysis of Maximus' Platonism must come to terms is the deliberately simplified conceptual level on which he moves, which is so simple that he

---

[35] See e.g. *Orr.* 1. 2, 6. 4–5, 27. 7 and 9, 29. 1–5, and 33. 7, with notes ad locc.

[36] See notes ad locc., comparing Posidonius F 309a, F 400c, F 401, and F 409 Theiler, and Seneca *Ep.* 92. 8–10.

[37] Thus for instance Alcinous' discussion of Plato's conception of Virtue in *Didasc.* 29–30 employs the doctrine of the Mean, and combines the Aristotelian terms διάθεσις and εὐφυΐα with the Stoic προκοπή and ἀντακολουθεῖν; see Dillon (1977: 301; 1993, pp. xxix–xxx, 183–8) and Whittaker (1990: 143–4). For another example of how Middle Platonism could co-opt issues and standpoints from other sects, see the introduction to *Orr.* 39–40 on the Good.

contrives entirely to neglect a good number of importantly and distinctively Platonic doctrines.[38] To give the most striking examples, he does not discuss, or even so much as mention, the theory of Forms; nor does he give any indication that there might be an important distinction to be drawn between a First and a Second God, or between Primary Mind and Cosmic Mind (or World Soul). The closest he comes to the former is the statement in *Or.* 21. 7 that true Beauty resides beyond the physical cosmos; the nearest approach to the latter is the description of the cosmic hierarchy in *Or.* 11. 12, from which the most that can be extracted is a distinction between supreme God, planetary gods, and daimones.[39] It might appear from this list that Maximus was bent on depriving himself of almost all the ideas that establish Platonism as a distinctive philosophical school. In particular, it might seem that in neglecting the Forms and any distinction between a First and a Second God, he is tending towards a philosophical position in which Platonism begins to merge with Stoicism. Such an impression would be wide of the mark. In spite of the simplifications, there is enough distinctive matter in the *Orations* for it to be possible to test them on a number of polarizing issues, and for the results to vindicate their Platonic pedigree. This can be done in cosmology, theology, and ethics.

Three times in the *Orations* (11. 7–12, 10. 9, and 21. 7) we are presented with an unequivocally Platonic 'two-storey' model of reality, comprising both a lower, material cosmos and a higher, intelligible realm from which matter derives what beauty and order it possesses.[40] God is unequivocally, Platonically, transcendent in

[38] With what follows, compare the survey of the 'Dominant Themes of Middle Platonism' in Dillon (1977: 43–51).

[39] Dillon (1977: 400) seems to go too far when he attributes to Maximus a belief in 'God the Father *and his Logos*, which is his agent in the organizing of the universe'. Maximus never speaks of Logos as God's ordering agent, only of his Mind (νοῦς: *Or.* 41. 2).

[40] As often, admittedly, it is left unclear whether we are being invited to envisage a one- or a two-storey model. In *Orr.* 8. 8 and 9. 6, for instance, Maximus speaks only, vaguely, of 'heaven' and 'earth'; in 9. 6 and 37. 8 he uses the terminology of the Platonic beyond (αὐτὸ κάλλος, τὸ τῶν ὄντων πέλαγος), without making it clear whether there is or is not any further realm 'beyond' the fixed stars to which the contemplating soul can 'ascend'. It must also be confessed that, in spite of *Orr.* 10, 11, and 21, Maximus devotes more space and enthusiasm to the beauty and order of the physical cosmos than he does to any higher realm of reality (e.g. *Orr.* 16. 6, 37. 8, 41. 2). Yet such enthusiasm is not incompatible with Platonism; and we nowhere find any explicit statement to the opposite effect, that the cosmos is a single, material unity of the kind postulated by the Stoics.

Orr. 11 and 10. 9; he is never said to be immanent in the Stoic
sense, although most often, as with the issue of the structure of
reality, nothing is said that would settle the matter clearly either
way. In *Or.* 41. 2 God's powers are described solely in terms of his
responsibility for the orderly processes of Nature, but the description stops far short of asserting immanence, and is in any case
directly attributed to the authority of Plato (and Homer) at the end
of the paragraph. Of the human soul, it is clearly implied in *Orr.* 7.
5, 9. 6, 10. 9, and 21. 7 that it will eventually escape from its
alien partner the body, and will then enjoy a conscious and personal immortality. There is no Stoicizing suggestion of any limita-
tion in the duration of its survival as soul, or of any kinship
between its substance and that of the fiery bodies in the heavens.
When analysed, it is found to consist of two parts or three; no
mention is ever made of the eight Stoic faculties. In ethics too, the
cast of thought is Platonic in its general tendencies. Whereas a
Stoic preacher like Epictetus or Aurelius couches his exhortations
in terms of the avoidance of false impressions and the confinement
of ambition to what genuinely lies in a man's power, Maximus'
regular call is instead for effort to control the pleasure-seeking,
chaotic passions that threaten to overwhelm reason in the soul.[41]
Whereas the Stoic characteristically calls for the extirpation of the
emotions, Maximus speaks only of their reduction to order.

If this analysis of the philosophical orientation of the *Orations*
were to be challenged, it could only be on the basis of *Orr.* 5, 13,
and 41—the three in which Guy Soury found enough Stoic
matter to feel justified in describing Maximus as a 'Platonist
eclectic'. All three certainly attack questions that the Stoics more
than any other sect had brought on to the philosophical agenda,
concerning the moral and causal structure of the world, and God's
relation to it; and all three correspondingly contain unusually
strong concentrations of terms and concepts most familiar from
Stoic sources. Thus *Or.* 5, on the futility of petitionary prayer,
paints a stern picture of the tyranny of Fate (§ 5),[42] and lays heavy
emphasis on 'preservation of the whole' as the priority of divine
providence.[43] *Or.* 41, on the Problem of Evil, combines another
assertion of the importance of the preservation of the whole (§ 4)

---

[41] e.g. *Orr.* 27. 5-6, 33. 7-8, 41. 5.
[42] Cf. *SVF* ii. 957 and 997, and Cornutus *Theol.* 12–13.
[43] Cf. e.g. Seneca *Prov.* 3. 2; Epictetus 2. 5. 24; Aurelius 5. 8, 9. 39, 10. 1.

with a series of Stoicizing epithets for God (§ 2),[44] an allegorization of Zeus' nod of assent (§ 2),[45] a defence of cosmic evil as an unavoidable side-effect of the beneficent work of divine Providence (§ 4),[46] and an appeal to the authority of Heraclitus (§ 4).[47] It is, however, in *Or.* 13, on the question of prophecy and human foresight, that the concentration of Stoic material seems to be greatest. A comparison between the cosmos and a military campaign (§ 4), and the statement that it is 'the common home of gods and men' (§ 6), both recall elements in Cicero's account of Stoic cosmology in book 2 of the *De Natura Deorum*.[48] Both the image of the campaign, and the subsequent comparison of the cosmos to a complex machine, might seem more appropriate to the Stoic than to the Platonic cosmos, insisting as they do on order, and on the complex interlocking of many parts into a single whole. The oracle to Laius from Euripides *Phoenissae*, quoted in § 5, was introduced into philosophical discussions by Chrysippus.[49] The allegorization of Homeric μοῖρα and αἶσα as names for Fate likewise begins with Stoic thinkers, [50] as also does the complaint that human beings are far too ready to blame their own wickedness on external Fate, rather than their own innate imperfections.[51] And, finally, Maximus twice speaks as if Free Will were something wholly illusory, in § 4 describing divination as that 'which draws us to follow the guidance of Fate', and in § 8 describing human freedom as no more than the freedom of 'a man in chains who follows his captors of his own free choice'—again, a proposition with which a Stoic would be happy to agree,[52] while a Platonist would indignantly reject it.

The question is whether any of this apparent Stoicizing goes beyond the tendency of Middle Platonism to appropriate for Plato issues and terminology of post-Platonic provenance, into either conscious eclecticism, or (to revert to Professor Koniaris's suggestion[53]) the adoption of a temporary Stoic 'persona' for one or more of the three lectures in question. The most reasonable conclusion

---

[44] Cf. Epictetus 1. 22. 16; *De Mundo* 397a–398b and 400b–410b.
[45] Cf. *SVF* iii. 33.   [46] Cf. *SVF* ii. 1170.
[47] Cf. *SVF* i. 481 and 620, iii. 762.
[48] *ND* 2. 85 and 154; cf. also *SVF* iii. 333–9; Diog. Laert. 7. 138; Musonius 42. 8 ff.; Epictetus 1. 9. 4.
[49] *SVF* ii. 941; Cicero *De Fato* 13. 30.
[50] Cf. n. 42 above.   [51] Cf. Gellius *NA* 7. 2. 12–13.
[52] Cf. *SVF* ii. 975.   [53] n. 33 above.

seems to be that it does not. In all three lectures, the underlying picture of the cosmos is one that insists, in Platonic vein, on the existence of a plurality of independent factors (chance, science, human intellect, etc.), as opposed to the Stoic concept of one single ruling force, called God, or Fate, or Nature. Given this basic orientation, almost all the remaining 'Stoic' material can readily be understood as matter assimilated to the Platonic standpoint that has long since lost any sense of belonging distinctively to its originators. The only item to which this explanation might seem to be inadequate is the apparent denial of human freedom in *Or.* 13, where Maximus does appear to come down on the Stoic side of a substantial disagreement between the two schools. Even there, however, it may be preferable to see inadvertence rather than conscious eclecticism—Maximus (or his source) borrowing for the sake of rhetorical effect what seems to the modern eye a little too much from an alternative ideological position. Whether a second-century eye will have seen anything untoward in this—especially when confronted with Maximus' own blindness to sectarian issues—is very doubtful.

Philosophy and the Times

The philosophy of the *Orations*, thus analysed, is in many ways characteristic of its times. In their general range and style, they offer philosophy for an age in which some acquaintance with the issues, doctrines, and heroes of the philosophical tradition was essential to anyone claiming the status of an educated man.[54] In their choice of a Platonizing standpoint, they provide one instance among many of how broadly and how firmly the revival of dogmatic Platonism that began in the second half of the first century BC, had diffused and consolidated itself by the later second.[55] Equally symptomatic is the irenic picture they offer of true philosophy and its history, that so markedly avoids sectarian strife. By the time the composition of the *Orations*, the manifest and strident disagreements of the major sects had been a matter of anxious concern for several centuries.[56] Various strategies had

[54] See further Clarke (1971, ch. 3), Hahn (1989: 61-99, 137-47), Anderson (1993: 133-43).

[55] Cf. Dillon (1977: 184-340).

[56] See e.g. Diodorus Siculus' unfavourable contrast between the diversity of Greek philosophical doctrines, and the virtuous unity of Chaldaean teaching, in *Bibl.* 2. 28. 3-6.

evolved in response: continuation of sectarian polemic on behalf of one particular school of thought, in the hopes of eventual victory; withdrawal into philosophical or satirical scepticism, on the conviction that if all disagreed so radically, none could be in possession of the truth; and the search for common elements, such as would allow one school to be assimilated to another, and shown to be—despite the polemics—in essential agreement. It is this last tendency, exemplified in the first century BC by the work of Antiochus (assimilating Platonism, Peripateticism, and Stoicism),[57] or in the second century AD by Numenius' attempt to read Plato and Pythagoras as disciples of the more venerable wisdom of Moses and the sages of the East,[58] that gives the *Orations* their cue; though the manner in which they develop the position is admittedly stronger on pious hopes than on hard argument.

The comparison with Numenius, however, also prompts a contrast, in that it can be used to highlight how relatively conservative a view the *Orations* take of the sources of philosophical enlightenment available to the second-century enquirer. As we have seen, the philosophy they offer, though intellectually undemanding, is of a broad scope, comprising a view of the nature of human beings, their place in the overall structure and workings of the world (in particular, their relationship to the Divine), and a set of prescriptions for a good life. By the second century AD it was possible, indeed common, to seek enlightenment over some or all such topics from authorities supposed to speak from beyond the confines of the Hellenic world: from Zoroaster and the Magi, from Brahmins and Gymnosophists, and from the gods and priests of old Egypt. Thus Dio Chrysostom, expounding the nature of the cosmos to his fellow citizens of Prusa in *Oration* 36, tells a myth attributed to the authority of the Magi; Lucian's Menippus seeks the Meaning of Life from the Chaldaean Mithrobarzanes, and his Philosophy records her progress through Brahmins, Ethiopians, Chaldeans, and Scythians, before eventually arriving in Greece; and it is from Egyptian Isis that Apuleius' Lucius achieves his final enlightenment.[59] The *Orations*, by contrast, are wholly innocent of any such exoticism. The only barbarian sage to feature at all is the Scythian

---

[57] See Dillon (1977: 52–113).

[58] Numenius frr. 1a, 8, and 24–8 Des Places; cf. Dillon (1977: 352–79) and Daniélou (1973, ch. 2, esp. 48–68).

[59] Dio *Or.* 36. 39–61, with Russell (1992: 21–2); Lucian *Menippus* 6–7, *Fugitivi* 6–8; Apuleius *Met.* 11.

Anacharsis, in the opening paragraph of *Or.* 25, and his appearance is of the briefest. Otherwise, the serene assumption prevails that all essential truths can be found in the works of sages from the Hellenic mainstream, from Homer to Plato. This is a striking exclusiveness of view, and one to which we shall return later, in connection with second-century Christianity.

RHETORICAL FORM AND LITERARY CULTURE

It is time to return to the question of the literary (rhetorical) form in which the contents of the *Orations* are conveyed. What are these essays or lectures that the *Suda* describes as 'philosophical investigations' (ζητήματα) and the manuscript title as 'talks' (διαλέξεις)?

Structure and Sequence

As already observed, they are short, occupying a dozen pages or fewer of Teubner text each, and requiring considerably less than half an hour apiece to perform aloud. And, as the list of titles given above suggests, each is focused on a single, relatively limited, topic or question. Normally, this topic or question has been explicitly formulated well before the half-way point, but seldom in the very first sentences. The norm is to begin less bluntly, with a famous quotation, or a well-known episode from literature, history, or myth, or a striking image, and only to sharpen the focus once this has done its preliminary work of securing attention and good will. Thus *Or.* 2 begins with a survey of concrete examples of primitive religious forms, before posing the question of the use of images in general in religious worship; *Or.* 5 begins with the story of the prayer of Midas to Satyrus, as a way into the problem of petitionary prayer; *Or.* 12, on the morality of reprisal, begins with some lines of Pindar; *Or.* 13 uses the story of Themistocles at Salamis to introduce the issue of prophecy and human foresight; *Or.* 25 approaches the question of true eloquence through the story of Anacharsis and Myson of Chenae; and so on. In each of the cases cited, a clear formulation of the real issue, to which the introduction points the way, soon follows.[60]

For a more detailed discussion on the subject of this section, see Trapp (forthcoming *a*).

[60] See *Orr.* 2. 1–2, 5. 1, 12. 2, 13. 2, and 25. 2 and 4. It is noteworthy that in a number of cases (*Orr.* 13 and 25 are particularly good examples), the formula-

Once the preliminaries are over, an oration will tend to proceed in a relatively systematic and orderly way, through an identifiable train of argument. Some admittedly aim at a more tightly connected sequence of thought than others, but it is seldom difficult to extract some kind of underlying plan. Thus *Or.* 5, having begun with Midas and Satyrus, and from there formulated its question about the legitimacy of petitionary prayer, lays out a *divisio* of the powers governing the onward march of events, then argues for the uselessness of prayer in each successive domain, before concluding with a description of true, non-petitionary prayer. *Or.* 12, having formulated its question about the legitimacy of reprisal on the back of the quotation from Pindar, examines a series of progressively more satisfactory analyses of the nature of wrongdoing, the last of which answers the question, then turns to a series of confirmatory stories from myth and history. *Or.* 25, beginning with Anacharsis and Myson, surveys and rejects a series of unsatisfactory definitions of eloquence, before explaining what the criteria are that they fail to satisfy, and establishing that only philosophical discourse can answer.[61] This is not to say that the *Orations* are obtrusively formal in their structure; it will indeed be seen that they try hard to avoid the impression of excessive formality. But they do have more by way of an armature of argument than is sometimes supposed.[62]

Care over structure and sequence can also be seen in those instances, six in all, where a single issue is debated over more than one oration. In three instances—*Orr.* 15-16, 23-34 and 39-40— we are presented with a pair of speeches arguing for antithetical positions (over the practical and theoretical lives, soldiers and farmers, and the singleness or plurality of the Good). Each time it is the second of the two cases to be made that prevails (though it is only in *Or.* 16 that an explicit verdict is passed). In the other three instances, the exposition is less formally patterned, and more

tion of the topic given in the body of the oration diverges from that given in its title. This is the single strongest reason for believing that the titles are a later, editorial edition, rather than the work of the author himself: see below, p. lviii.

[61] I have tried to offer a brief analysis of this kind in the introduction to each *Oration*. It will be seen that this has proved easier in some cases than in others (*Or.* 6, for instance, is a difficult case). There are also cases (e.g. *Or.* 13) where it is debatable whether the underlying connections of thought will have been as clear to the original audience as they are to the modern scholar.

[62] See e.g. Koniaris (1982: 102 with n. 35, 114-20), which seems to me to get the characteristic structure of the *Orations* in general, and *Or.* 25 in particular, quite seriously wrong.

linear. *Orr.* 8 and 9 offer a set of preliminary considerations about *daimones*, followed (in *Or.* 9) by a formal account of their nature and place in the scheme of the cosmos. *Orr.* 18–19 begin with the formulation of the problem of Socrates' love-life, and some preliminary manœuvres in his defence (*Or.* 18); this is followed by an exposition of the distinction between virtuous and vicious love, which vindicates Socrates on an everyday level (*Orr.* 19–20); and the sequence concludes with the still deeper vindication which follows from an appreciation of Socratic (Platonic) metaphysics (*Or.* 21). The longest sequence of all begins in *Or.* 29 with an exposition of the general problem of divergent human ends and concepts of happiness. The remaining lectures narrow the issue down to an examination of the distinctive claims of Epicurean hedonism: expounded and provisionally rejected in *Orr.* 30–1; defended by the sect's founder in *Or.* 32; and decisively rejected in *Or.* 33.[63]

Expository Style

The voice which conducts the reader (or hearer) through these sequences of thought is one that seeks to combine intellectual authority (the impression of a sure and comfortable grasp of the philosophical matter involved), with accessibility, liveliness, and cultivation. Language and sentence-structure are relaxed but elegant, observing moderately classicizing (Atticizing) norms in grammatical constructions and choice of vocabulary, and avoiding elaborately periodic sentences, in favour of sequences of shorter clauses, except where more elevated subject-matter calls for a higher tone.[64] Uncouth, or over-precise, philosophical terminology is avoided in the manner already commented on. An impression of engaging spontaneity is given by moments of affected doubt, self-correction, and change of plan.[65] Points of doctrine may be reeled off with a (reassuringly) impersonal professionalism from time to time,[66] but the general presentation is insistently personal, with frequent use of the first-person singular in verbs and pronouns, and facts and doctrines often phrased as declarations of personal belief; and it is enthusiastic in tone, with frequent recourse to exclama-

---

[63] For fuller analyses, see the introductory notes to *Orr.* 8–9, 18–21, 23–4, and 29–33.

[64] For example, in descriptions of God, the cosmic hierarchy, and the Platonic beyond: e.g. *Orr.* 2. 10, 10. 9, 11. 12, 21. 7–8, 41. 2.

[65] See e.g. *Orr.* 27. 3, 28. 3 and 4, 30. 3, 35. 3; cf. Koniaris (1982: 111–13).

[66] See the passages cited on p. xix above, and add *Orr.* 31. 4 and 38. 6.

tion. At the same time, the impression is assiduously given of a speaker keen to reduce the distance as far as he can between himself and his audience, as he steers them considerately but stimulatingly through the lessons he has to teach. They are regularly addressed, individually and collectively, in second-person commands and questions, or co-opted in first-person plural deliberatives and exhortations. Courteous formulae affect to consult their preferences ('Shall we . . .?', 'If you would rather . . .', etc.),[67] and to ease them gently into each new lesson (just as the introductory quotations and anecdotes ease them gently into each new lecture): 'How is it then that Virtue, though it has elements of both theory and practice about it, is still not a science? Follow me as I explain the matter to you like this. The doctrine I will tell you of is not mine; it comes from the Academy . . .' (*Or.* 27. 5).[68] And above all, the level of enthusiasm is never allowed to drop. From the point of view of the *Orations* themselves, this is a combination of style and tone calculated to answer to the demand for the liveliness and inspiration in philosophical teaching that Maximus himself twice makes when discussing the topic of modes of instruction.[69] From the point of view of the modern scholar, it is a version of the style seen also in such authors as Teles and Epictetus, that has come to be known as 'diatribe', but would be better described as 'dialogic' or 'Socratic'.[70]

The Classics: Imitation and Evocation

As in philosophical doctrine, so also in style: the principal point of reference and object of imitation is Plato. Maximus appeals directly to his example over his relaxed attitude to technical terminology in *Or.* 21. 4, but the influence, and the evocation, are far more widespread. Both the main stylistic levels adopted, the Socratic-dialogic and the more elevated tone proper to the glories of God and the cosmos, follow Platonic precedent: the former Plato's portrayal of Socrates in debate, the latter his allegories of higher realms of

---

[67] e.g. *Orr.* 7. 7, 10. 2, 11. 9, etc.

[68] Cf. e.g. 24. 3.

[69] See *Orr.* 1. 8 and 25. 6–7.

[70] Cf. Trapp (forthcoming *a*, n. 100). The style is a development from that constructed for Socrates by Plato, Xenophon, and Aeschines, transferred from dialogue to monologue. 'Diatribe' is a convenient label, but a misleading one in that what it picks out is not recognized as a distinctive form or stylistic level in antiquity, and in that the technical, literary uses of the Greek word διατριβή were entirely different.

reality in the myths.[71] Moreover, it is Plato more than any other classical writer whose vocabulary is echoed in Maximus' choice of words. Karl Dürr's calculation that of some 200 words in the *Orations* traceable to the usage of particular classical authors, some 115 derive from Plato is perhaps unrealistically precise, but it none the less tallies well with the pervasiveness and frequency with which *loci* from the dialogues are echoed and imitated.[72] This is composition that is meant to come across as deeply indebted to the greatest of all philosophical writers, loved and admired for his literary gifts even by those with no interest in his doctrines.[73]

Evocation of the classical literary and cultural heritage in the *Orations* is, however, not confined to Plato. They are quite remarkably full of quotations from great authors, and references to the characters and episodes of myth and history. Individually, these can provide authority for a doctrine or an opinion,[74] clarify and illustrate a line of argument,[75] or simply add an extra layer of elegance to the literary finish. Collectively, they serve to establish the impeccable cultural credentials of both the author and his subject-matter. This is a man who is as comfortably at home with educated culture in general as he is with philosophical learning, and philosophical learning itself is characterized at the same time as an integral part of the great Greek tradition.

Most frequently quarried, by a long way, are the epics of Homer, whom we have already seen is presented in *Orr.* 4 and 26 as a great philosopher as well as a great poet. Characters and episodes from *Iliad* and *Odyssey* parade through the *Orations* in an almost unbroken procession, providing everything from passing illustrations to major topics of discussion in their own right, and a total of 160 lines are quoted in separate passages.[76] Allegorical readings,

---

[71] Compare Dionysius of Halicarnassus' discussion of Plato's stylistic levels: the 'plain style' of which he so approves, and the 'hierophantic' or 'dithyrambic' style which so pains him (*Demosth.* 5–7, repeated with some alterations in *Ep. Pomp.* 2). Cf. also Thesleff (1967: 63–80).

[72] For an attempt to chart these (surely incomplete), see the secondary apparatus and index (s.v. Plato) in Trapp (1994).

[73] Cf. e.g. Dionysius of Halicarnassus *Demosth.* 23, Cicero *Tusc.* 1. 79, Quintilian 10. 1. 81, and for the whole topic of Plato's literary reputation, see Walsdorff (1927).

[74] As for instance with the quotations of Plato *Leg.* 709bc in *Orr.* 13. 7 and Thucydides 1. 2 in 23. 7.

[75] As with the reference to Philoctetes (explicitly labelled as a 'clearer example') in *Or.* 7. 6.

[76] For detailed analysis, see Kindstrand (1973: 45–71, 172–85).

of the kind assumed and sanctioned by the understanding of Homer as philosopher, are frequent, but by no means inevitable. Also quoted or paraphrased—but far more sparingly, in many cases only once or twice each—are Hesiod, Stesichorus, Sappho, Anacreon, Pindar, Epicharmus, Aeschylus, Euripides, Aristophanes, Ariphron, Menander, and Aratus from among the poets, and from the ranks of prose-writers, Heraclitus, Aeschines of Sphettus, Xenophon, Epicurus, Herodotus, Thucydides, and Demosthenes.[77] This is a long enough list to create an impression of literary culture, but at the same time it is hardly an adventurous one. The authors themselves are all standard classics, and with occasional exceptions like the lines of Sappho and Anacreon in *Or.* 18, the quotations chosen from them are hackneyed favourites of philosophical and literary-critical writing. Neither the range of authors exploited, nor the depth of acquaintance claimed with their work, comes anywhere near what one sees in, for instance, Lucian's *Dialogues* or Plutarch's *Moralia*. It is open to question whether this is an indication of the limitations of Maximus' own literary culture, or whether it is rather the result of a conscious decision to tailor the range of reference to the perceived limitations of his audience. The latter is perhaps the more intriguing possibility.

Equally indicative of the desire simultaneously to clarify and to display a mastery of the cultural heritage is the range of mythological and historical reference. In the mythological field, the vast majority of the characters and episodes evoked belong, predictably, to Homeric epic, with Odysseus and Achilles by some way the most frequently named; but Heracles, Orpheus, the Argonauts, Palamedes, Telephus, Cadmus, Pentheus, Amphion, Amphilochus, Laius, Oedipus, Triptolemus, Theseus, Thyestes, Perseus, Neleus, Tlepolemus, Midas, Minos, Daedalus, Salmoneus, Prometheus, Asclepius, the Gorgons, Cecrops, Satyrus, and Marsyas all appear too—often, though not invariably, in roles determined by some particular work of classical poetry.[78] The range of historical reference is still wider, though observing some significant limitations of its own. Over forty passages in the *Orations* make use of characters and episodes from early history, up to the beginning of the Persian Wars, from colonization to the tyrants, and from

---

[77] For the references, see index s.v.
[78] See index, s.v., and footnotes to individual passages.

Sardanapallus to Darius. Another twenty-two refer to events and individuals from the Persian Wars themselves, nine to the Pentecontaetea, thirty-five to the period of the Peloponnesian War, twenty-six to fourth-century history down to the rise of Macedon, eight to Alexander the Great, one to the dissolution of Alexander's empire after his death, and one or two (perhaps) to the Roman period.[79] Two general features of these historical references deserve to be underlined. The first is the pervasive moral colour with which they are so often infused: barbarian monarchs, with the exception of Cyrus, are vicious hedonists; Athenian history from the start of the Peloponnesian War to the defeat of the city in 404 is a sustained illustration of the dangers of unreason and the passions; and so on, in a manner conditioned partly by fifth-century historiography, but still more by fourth-century historians and philosophers. The second striking feature is the carefully classicizing limits observed in the chronology of the references. With only two possible exceptions, there is no reference to any period or event later than the end of the fourth century BC; the intervening five and a half centuries between that point and Maximus' own lifetime are passed over in total, or near-total, silence. The overall centre of gravity sits squarely in the fifth century. This is a view of history that deliberately privileges the great days of Greek political and military history, which are also the subject-matter of the great works of classical historiography.[80]

Kings and generals are by no means the only iconic names to be paraded in the *Orations*. Sages, poets, and artists are invoked too, still further proving the author's grasp of both his own discipline of philosophy and of educated culture as a whole. Socrates and Plato head the list, followed at some distance by Pythagoras and Diogenes—a combination reflecting an even-handed commitment both to philosophy as doctrine and to philosophy as practical virtue. But also named are Pherecydes, Solon, Lycurgus, Aristeas, Epimenides, Anacharsis, Thales, Anaximenes, Xenophanes, Heraclitus, Parmenides, Empedocles, Leucippus, Democritus, Diogenes of Apollonia, Anaxagoras, Gorgias, Prodicus, Protagoras, Hippias, Thrasymachus, Hippocrates, Zopyrus, Theodorus,

[79] The two possible allusions to the Roman period come in *Orr.* 6. 5 (sack of Delos in 69 BC?) and 12. 8 (conquest of Greece?), but neither is certain.

[80] In this respect Maximus' focus corresponds closely to that adopted by sophistic declaimers in their choice of topics, similarly restricted to the great days of Greek achievement: see Kohl (1915), Bowie (1970: 6–9), Russell (1983, ch. 6).

Aeschines, Antisthenes, Aristippus, Xenophon, Aristotle, Zeno, Epicurus, Strato, Chrysippus, Clitomachus, and Carneades; Homer, Hesiod, Archilochus, Sappho, Alcaeus, Tyrtaeus, Telesilla, Stesichorus, Anacreon, Pindar, Aristophanes, Eupolis, and Menander; Connus, Olympus, Ismenias, Phidias, Polyclitus, Zeuxis, Polygnotus, and Mithaecus. The range of reference is once more strikingly classicizing: an overwhelming preference for the names named also by the approved authors (especially Plato), and no mention of any remotely contemporary figure.[81]

The other substantial literary device by which Maximus seeks both to clarify his exposition and to establish his literary culture is his use of imagery. In this domain too it is the sheer quantity of illustrative images employed, rather than any great subtlety in their application, that impresses. Simile and explicit comparison ('just as . . . so . . .') predominate over metaphor, and the terms of the comparison are often spelled out with pedantic exactness. At the same time, the images themselves are chosen with a firm eye to their literary pedigree as well as to their clarificatory power. God is like the sun, a spring, a steward, a craftsman, a king, a legislator, a farmer, a steersman, a doctor, a general, a chorus-master, a guide, and a playwright. The physical cosmos he governs is a stormy sea, a flowing river, a boisterous symposium, a dark cavern, or a prison. The physical bodies of his human subjects are likewise stormy channels, flooding rivers, rotting prisons, monstrous beasts, bolting horses, strife-torn cities, and armies at war. Human Virtue is like health, fertility, civic or military obedience, a well-steered ship, sobriety and wakefulness, while Vice is sterility, disease, anarchy, shipwreck, drunken torpor. Life is like a journey along a road, a military campaign, a voyage by sea, an athletic competition, or a play, and the individual moral agent is correspondingly a traveller, or a soldier, or a steersman, or a swimmer, or an athlete, or an actor. This list by no means exhausts either the range of topics for which images are found, or the sources from which the images are drawn, but it gives an impression of their general quality.[82] Like the references to great names from the Greek heritage, and the quotations from the Classics, these are images that genuflect to tradition, and establish

---

[81] The most recent philosophers to be named, Clitomachus and Carneades, both belong to the second century BC, to the age when Athens was still the philosophical capital of the world.   [82] See index, s.v. Imagery.

their author as its worthy continuator: above all to philosophical tradition, embodied on the one hand in Plato, and on the other in Socratic moral preaching.

The Form

The text of the *Orations* itself provides them with no generic name: Maximus speaks of his own products simply as 'discourses' or 'reflections' (λόγοι or σκέμματα). The article on Maximus in the *Suda* is similarly informal, describing his works as 'investigations' (ζητήματα). The manuscript title, however, does volunteer a formal name: διάλεξις. Though there can be no absolute guarantee that this is a term Maximus himself would have accepted, it seems likely enough: the word was certainly current in the second century, and the senses in which it is attested seem appropriate.

A derivative of the verb διαλέγεσθαι, 'to converse', 'to discuss', 'to discourse', διάλεξις has two applications as a technical term. First, it can designate a philosophical discourse. In this sense it is a near relative of another derivative of the verb διαλέγεσθαι, 'dialectic' (διαλεκτική). The example of Socrates, mediated through Plato and Aristotle, establishes 'conversation', 'discussion', as the proper philosophical mode (as opposed to the non-conversational, 'single-voice' mode of formal oratory), and the name comes to be seen as appropriate to philosophical output in general, even to utterances (and treatises) that have no element of dialogue in them. In its second application, which again depends on the suggestion of informality, the word διάλεξις is used of an element in the repertoire not of the philosopher, but of the epideictic orator, the sophist. In one of the standard forms of sophistic performance in the second century, regularly envisaged, for instance, in the pages of Philostratus' *Lives*, the formal declamation (μελέτη) on a legal or historical theme was preceded by a kind of self-contained, informal prologue, loosely structured, unperiodic in style, and richly decorated with images and quotations. Such prologues, which could on occasion be developed into whole performances in their own right, are legislated for in some detail in Menander Rhetor's *Treatise II* (388. 16–394. 31); and the name for them was either (προ)λαλιά or διάλεξις.[83]

---

[83] For discussion of the form, see Russell–Wilson (1981, ad loc.), Russell (1983: 74–9).

Both of these senses seem to be appropriate to Maximus' products, at least to some degree. In their content, the *Orations* are philosophical discourses, whatever one may think about the level of intellectual commitment and sophistication they display; and in their form, they have the brevity, the suggestions of informality, and the taste for decoration characteristic of the sophistic prologue. It is tempting to conclude that this dual affinity is no coincidence: that we see here the result of a conscious attempt at fusion. A form developed for entertainment is being adapted to carry a more serious subject-matter, while at the same time a newly accessible and—above all—elegant register is being added to the range of possibilities available to propagate philosophical doctrine and values—less austere than the scholastic lecture (but like it in its focus on some single problem or topic for discussion), more polished and cultivated than the lower registers of Socratic preaching, more exciting and easier to follow than dialogue. Whether the innovation is Maximus' own is an interesting question. Given the volume of both oratorical and philosophical activity in the preceding century and a half—of which more shortly—he is more likely to be following an established trend than inventing for himself.

Occasions and Performance

The formal parallel between the *Orations* and an element in sophistic performance presses a question which has so far been kept in the background: that of their own original context. An 'audience' has indeed been identified: of young men on the threshold of adult careers and adult responsibilities who wish to be able to claim some acquaintance with the philosophical heritage as part of their general *paideia*. But it is yet to be asked whether this was ever a genuine audience—a group or groups assembled in odeum, or gymnasium lecture-theatre, or other hired hall, for a live oratorical performance—or whether the *Orations* in fact circulated only as written text, clothed in the stylistic props and costumes of live performance without ever having been performed.

Those props and costumes are certainly on prominent display, throughout the collection, but above all in the first, introductory *Oration*. Here Maximus quite explicitly presents himself as speaker before audience, as much the centre of attention to them as actors or musicians are to a packed theatre (§§ 1–2, 10), or athletes to a cheering stadium (§§ 4, 6): he has 'come before' this audience (§ 7) and stands on 'this podium', modestly calming the supportive exclamations of his admirers (§ 6). The scene evoked is a vivid one, and it is tempting to particularize it further, imagining the kind of setting, in a theatre or a gymnasium, that would give the comparisons with actors and athletes an extra bite: the philosopher urging the superior claims of his wares over those of rival salesmen who compete with him for the same audiences and the same physical space.[84] Yet clearly, nothing in this can establish that such a scene ever took place; it is a perfectly intelligible strategy to construct a wholly fictitious event as a vivid way of introducing a set of discourses for consumption by readers. The text itself offers no proof either way.

The case for supposing that the *Orations* were delivered to an audience, or audiences, must rest instead on the combination of the manuscript title ('Discourses of Maximus of Tyre, given in Rome on his first visit') with the corresponding notice in the *Suda* ('lectured in Rome in the time of Commodus'). These may not be two entirely separate pieces of evidence, but even if they are in some way interdependent rather than mutually supportive, there is no special reason to doubt what they attest. The vivid scenes of *Oration* 1 can be allowed after all to be a reflection of real events in the career of the text, as well as a clever piece of verbal creation. Interesting further questions then arise about the nature, and the location, of these events.

Given all that has been said about Maximus' concern to parade his mastery of the Greek cultural heritage, the Roman setting alleged by the manuscript title might at first sight seem to pose something of a problem: was Rome an appropriate place for such performances, and were the *Orations* as we have them really an appropriate script for Rome? The first question in fact is not a difficult one. By the 180s AD Greek epideictic orators had been performing and finding appreciative audiences in the Imperial capital for well over a century (and even three centuries before a visiting philosopher could shock and enthuse the natives in his own language). Pliny, for instance, gives an appreciative account of series of epideictic 'concerts' by the sophist Isaeus, delivered in Greek, improvised, and following the standard sophistic pattern of

---

[84] Cf. e.g. Dio Chrysostom's awareness of rivals for the same performance-space in his *Alexandrian Oration* (*Or.* 32, esp. §§ 1-13).

προλαλιά ('praefatio') and μελέτη ('controversia');[85] and the pages of Philostratus' *Lives of the Sophists* make it quite clear that Rome provided the sophists with one of their most prestigious stages.[86] The second question, about the suitability of our text of the *Orations* for Roman performance, looks more awkward. The absence of any reference to Rome or things Roman in the *Orations* is remarkable enough, given the time of composition; it becomes still more remarkable if the place of delivery is Rome itself. Also curious, for the same reason, are the references to 'a throng of Hellenes' and 'the theatres of Hellas' in *Oration* 1 (§§ 4, 10); curious enough to persuade one scholar (along with other considerations of a different order) that the manuscript title identified only some of the *Orations* as products of the Roman visit, and that most (including *Or.* 1) were delivered further east.[87] And it might be felt that the references to athletics in *Or.* 1, which sit so well in the context of Greek gymnasium culture, are again inappropriate to a Roman context. None of these worries, however, need be held to constitute an insuperable objection to the evidence of the manuscript title. On the lexical point, it is enough to remember that by the second century the word 'Hellene' could denote a devotee of Hellenic culture as well as an ethnic Greek,[88] and thus would not have sounded so excessively odd to an audience of native Latin-speakers. More generally, one can suggest that a Greek orator performing in Rome might be prized as much for his uncompromising Greekness as for his readiness to accommodate local tastes and local interests; in which case failure to mention Roman history, or reflect details of the Roman scene, would not cause any discomfort either. It is no doubt likely that some or all of the *Orations* we have were performed in cities of the Eastern Empire too, perhaps even composed in the first instance for such performance; but that does not make them positively inappropriate for Roman exposure as well.

Where the attempt to picture the context of Maximus' performances more sharply does run into real difficulties is with the question of the precise circumstances of delivery, the nature of the event that they constituted. Pliny's and Philostratus' reports of sophistic 'concerts', and indications of circumstance in the orations

[85] Pliny *Ep.* 2. 3; cf. Philostratus *VS* 1. 20. The date of Isaeus' visit to Rome must have been some time in the closing years of the first century.
[86] Cf. Bowersock (1969: 28–9, 44–6).
[87] Mutschmann (1917), discussed by Koniaris (1982: 88–102).
[88] Philostratus *VS* 2. 5. 571, etc.

of Dio Chrysostom, Favorinus, and Aelius Aristides, provide us with quite a wide range of possible models, but none of them seems to work at all comfortably for the *Orations*. The heart of the difficulty is the combination of their length—none takes longer than half an hour to declaim, most substantially less—with their independence one from another: even when one resumes the topic of its predecessor, it does so with a definite sense of pause between them.[89] This staccato brevity conforms neither to the model of the substantial oration, as we see it in Dio or Aristides, nor to the pattern of προλαλιά plus μελέτη attested by Philostratus and Pliny. Was each individual item then originally performed together with some more substantial piece, all of which are now lost? But in that case, how would the continuity of such sequences as *Orr.* 19–21 or 29–33 be maintained? Alternatively, did a single 'concert' comprise more than one of the *Orations*? But if more than one, how many each time, and how can the surviving set be arranged into a sequence of approximately equally substantial programmes?

No clear answer seems to be available, and this unclarity might in the end drive us to contemplate a further possibility: not that the *Orations* were never performed at all, but that in performance they had a different shape to that given them in their written version. This would by no means be the only case in classical literature where we have grounds to suspect that the written text is some way from being a verbatim transcript of the original event; but equally, it is difficult to give the suggestion any harder content by pinpointing specific possibilities of compression or redistribution of material in the process from spoken to written. The *Orations* as we have them do not read like epitomes, or like edited highlights in the manner of Apuleius' *Florida*;[90] each has its own identifiable structure, and seems to be complete on its own terms of reference. Nor is it at all easy to unpick the existing divisions between one and another and weave them together into larger wholes. The question of the relation of our *Orations* to any spoken performance, like that of the place of delivery, must remain an open one.

---

[89] e.g. *Orr.* 19.1, with its explicit 'after our rest'; but even where there is no such temporal marker, one might wonder what the point was of dividing the exposition of a topic into two or more parts, if they were in fact to be delivered without a break.

[90] On which, see now Harrison (forthcoming).

Traditions of Philosophical Oratory

Whether the *Orations* came before their public in Rome or in the
cities of the eastern Empire, and whatever the precise form of the
original performances, it remains clear that in composing and
delivering them, Maximus was inserting himself into some well-
established cultural traditions. This holds not only for his role as
an epideictic orator, but also for his more specific identity as an epideictic orator who chose philosophy, rather than myths, historical
episodes, or fictitious legal imbroglios,[91] as his subject-matter. In
the context of the educated culture of the Hellenistic and Imperial
periods, 'philosophical oratory' is not the oxymoron that a reading
of Plato (particularly the Plato of the *Gorgias*) might suggest. The
period in which philosophical and rhetorical study could present
themselves as mutually exclusive forms of education, each claiming sole rights as a route to fulfilment, was a brief one; before long
the two had established themselves as successive phases in a full
education, and the question reformulated as one of the proper
balance between them, rather than of choice. At the same time,
the notion of philosophical modes of delivery as necessarily and
wholly different from the oratorical, developed again by Plato and
by Aristotle, lost much of its force. The topic of the proper style for
the philosopher—the extent to which rhetorical virtuosity required
to be subordinated to higher moral purposes—remained a favourite
point for debate. Maximus' own thoughts on the topic, in *Orr.* 1.
7, 22, and 25, can be compared to the earlier treatments by
Seneca (*Epp.* 40, 75, 100, 115) and Epictetus (3. 21, 3. 23). But
this is an indication that what Plato would have seen as quite
illegitimate compromises between reason and persuasion were now
a regular and accepted phenomenon.

Already in the second century BC, if Cicero is to be trusted (*De Inv.*
1. 6. 8), the rhetorician Hermagoras of Temnos was setting students to debate such θέσεις (*quaestiones infinitae*) as Honour and the
Good, the validity of the senses, and the shape of the world.[92] A century later, Cicero can describe his own re-presentations of Greek
philosophical debates in the *Tusculans* as 'senilis declamatio' (*Tusc.*
1. 4. 7). Against such a background, it is not surprising that, as the
popularity of epideictic oratory, and of school exercises developed

[91] For these characteristic materials for sophistic declamation, see Russell (1983,
chs. 5–6).

[92] Cf. also Theon ii. 125 ff. Spengel ('is the world providentially governed?').

into public entertainment, grew in the centuries AD, philosophical
topics should be among those chosen by speakers as their subject-
matter. From the earlier part of the first century, one can point to
the figure of C. Papirius Fabianus, honourably mentioned by both
the elder and the younger Seneca.[93] And from the later first and
second centuries, there are the great figures of Dio Chrysostom and
Favorinus, and their Latin counterpart Apuleius.[94]

Maximus is not a writer or a performer of precisely the same
kind as any of these three. He lacks Dio's political dimension,
Favorinus' depth of engagement with serious issues in technical
philosophy, Apuleius' breadth of literary output; nor is his own
brand of philosophical oratory identical, either in form, or in range
of subjects treated, or in tone, to theirs. Yet he is in various ways
comparable to all of them. He has subjects in common with all
three: Diogenes, Homer, and the topic of images and concepts of
divinity with Dio;[95] Socratic love, prayer, and Homeric philosophy
with Favorinus;[96] *daimones* and the topics of musical and philosophical versatility with Apuleius.[97] In style, he is closest to
Favorinus;[98] in his keenness to parade his command of the best of
the classical heritage, he recalls Apuleius.[99] These similarities are
not simply a matter of a shared culture. The notion of any direct
links with the Athenian-educated, but Latin-speaking, Apuleius,
may be implausible, but it is hard to believe that Dio and Favorinus
(themselves teacher and pupil) were not among Maximus' models
and his sources of inspiration. The evidence of Philostratus (*VS* 1.
7-8) shows both how high their reputation stood at the end of the
second century, and how firmly they could be identified with the

[93] See esp. Sen. *Ep.* 52. 8-11 and *Brev. Vit.* 10. 1; also *Epp.* 40. 11-12 and 100,
Contr. 2 praef.
[94] For Dio, see Arnim (1898), Jones (1978), Desideri (1978), and Brancacci
(1985: 19-62); for Favorinus, Barigazzi (1966) and Holford-Strevens (1988, ch. 6);
for Apuleius, Tatum (1979, chs. 4-5) and Harrison (forthcoming).
[95] Diogenes: Dio *Or.* 6 (cf. 4), Maximus *Or.* 36; Homer: Dio *Orr.* 12, 53, 56,
Maximus *Orr.* 17 and 26; images and concepts of the divine: Dio *Or.* 12, Maximus
Or. 2. The similarities in treatment are especially striking between Dio *Or.* 6 and
Maximus *Or.* 36, where there seem good grounds for supposing that Maximus is
borrowing directly from Dio (see headnote ad loc.).
[96] Prayer: Favorinus fr. 8, pp. 152-3 Barigazzi, Maximus *Or.* 5; Socratic love:
Favorinus, frr. 19-21, pp. 161-9 Barigazzi, Maximus *Orr.* 18-21; Homeric philosophy: Favorinus fr. 22, pp. 169-70 Barigazzi, Maximus *Or.* 26.
[97] *Daimones*: Apuleius *De Deo Socratis*, Maximus *Orr.* 8-9; musical versatility:
Flor. 4 and *Or.* 1. 2; philosophical versatility: *Flor.* 13 and *Or.* 1.
[98] Analyses in Barigazzi (1966: 27-73), Goggin (1951).
[99] e.g. *Flor.* 9.

combination of philosophical acumen and rhetorical virtuosity. It would be amazing if a philosophical orator of the period did not see himself as to some extent following in their footsteps and trading on the tastes and expectations that they had helped to form.

THE *ORATIONS* AND THE CHRISTIAN APOLOGISTS

As the preceding pages have sought to demonstrate, there can be no mistaking the consistency of purpose with which the *Orations* present themselves as the products of the best Hellenic traditions, both in their choice of subject-matter and of literary form, and in that single-mindedly classicizing outlook that manages entirely (or almost entirely) to neglect the political reality of Rome and the Roman Empire. It is another aspect of this restriction in outlook that—unlike such near-contemporary writers as Lucian and Galen[100]—Maximus in his account of philosophy and philosophical values betrays no awareness at all of the new philosophy, the alternative view of the world, history, man, and the divine, being offered in his day with increasing confidence by the apologists of Christianity.

This is a striking silence. It is clear that the efforts of the Christian propagandists had already made considerable headway towards intellectual and social acceptance—or at least towards becoming a voice that demanded an answer, and could no longer simply be disregarded—by the time the *Orations* were being composed and delivered.[101] Maximus is supposed to have lectured in Rome in the reign of Commodus, in the 180s AD. By then, it was possible for a concubine of that same Emperor, Marcia, to be a Christian, and to have interceded with him on behalf of the Christians of the city;[102] and the preceding decade had seen the production of the first serious, philosophical rebuttal at any length of the Christian philosophy, the *True Account* of Celsus,[103] itself a response to some half a century of increasingly sophisticated and challenging pleading by Christian propagandists.

The hundred years between about AD 120 and 220 saw the development of a new phase in the expansion of the Christian religion from a peripheral Jewish sect to an international faith

---

[100] See Waltzer (1949), Benko (1980).
[101] For general accounts, see Chadwick (1967, chs. 3–4), Grant (1988).
[102] Dio Cassius 72. 4; Hippolytus *Ref.* 9. 12.
[103] For which, see Andresen (1955), Chadwick (1965).

capable of engaging with and winning converts from the old, established cults of the Graeco-Roman world. The process necessarily involved a much closer, and more polemical, engagement not only with pagan religion, but also with the pieties and loyalties of Hellenic and Roman culture in general. Precisely in order to prise converts away from their inherited affiliations, and to set them at a newly detached and critical angle to the culture in which they had been brought up, it was necessary for Christian propagandists to demonstrate their own knowledge of that culture, and to show that their criticism of it was not merely the ignorant abuse of hopelessly uncultivated (and therefore negligible) outsiders. The earliest surviving product of this new attempt to carry the battle on to the pagans' own cultural territory is the *Apology* of Aristides, dating perhaps from the 120s, but more likely from the mid-140s, followed by the *First* and *Second Apologies* of Justin Martyr, Athenagoras' *Embassy*, Theophilus' *To Autolycus*, Tatian's *Oration to the Greeks*, and the *Protrepticus* of Clement of Alexandria, composed some time in the closing decades of the century.[104]

Each of these works has its own individual agenda and emphases, but all are united in their central challenge to the validity of Hellenic religious beliefs and practices and Hellenic ethical values, and the authority of the wise men (poets, prophets, and philosophers) of Hellenic tradition. By reconstructing the history of wisdom and revealed truth they seek to show the Judaeo-Christian revelation of the nature of God, and of his relation to the world and to history, as both chronologically prior to, and more comprehensive in scope than, the teaching of even the oldest and most authoritative of the pagan sages. Similarities between Christian teaching and the words of Greek poets and philosophers, while welcomed as independent confirmation of the truth of the doctrines advanced, are explained away as the result of borrowing, or of partial apprehension in virtue of a shared human rationality of what is known completely only by divine revelation through Moses and Christ. And pagan religious cult, with its whole elaborate, time-honoured apparatus of images and rituals, is reduced to the status of ignorant or self-seeking fabrication, either by manipulative human beings or by malicious demons, seeking (so far successfully) to divert to themselves the worship properly due to the one true God. In pursuance of these arguments, the Apologists

[104] For the chronology, see Grant (1955).

did not have to rely on the resources of the Judaeo-Christian tradition alone; they could arm also themselves with weapons already developed, for different purposes, within Hellenic culture itself. The habit of tracing the history of philosophy back to great sages of early human history, outside the Greek world as well as within it, allowed for the insertion of Moses as the first and greatest of them all, from whom all others had borrowed. The allegorical conversion of the great Greek poets into philosophers, and part of that same history, allowed their worth and authority to be belittled in the same breath. And the readiness of Greek daemonology to explain odd religious cults by reference to gloomy or malicious spirits opened the way to the dismissal of pagan religious cult as a whole as demonic fraud.[105]

There is thus, besides the chronological coincidence with the *Orations*, also a coincidence of aims and of topics of concern, which makes the silence of the *Orations* about Christianity all the more striking. Maximus too is offering his readers a comprehensive philosophical account of the world that claims practical validity as a guide to right living as well as theoretical truth; he too, in the process, discusses the relationship of God to the world of men (*Orr.* 5, 13, 41), the use of images in religious worship (*Or.* 2), the role of *daimones* (*Orr.* 8–9), and the history of poetic and philosophical wisdom (*Orr.* 4 and 26); yet he does all this as a comfortable and untroubled adherent of the old, Hellenic traditions, without the least suggestion that there might now be further, less traditional options available too.

All this gives the *Orations* a double interest for the historian of second-century Christianity, and of its engagement with the cultural world of Hellenism. On the one hand, their bland exclusion of any reference at all to Christian thought is evidence of the distance Christian propagandizing, for all its increasing sophistication and success, had still to travel. Along with many other forms of evidence, they show just how much strength and confidence remained in the old traditions: that audiences in search of ultimate truths were still content to find them wholly within the world-view of classical religion and philosophy.[106] Simultaneously, precisely

---

[105] On all these topics, see above all Daniélou (1973, chs. 1–5), Geffcken (1907, pp. ix–xliii).

[106] For an extensive investigation of this proposition in the religious sphere, see Lane Fox (1986).

because of the way that the topics they address overlap so markedly with the concerns of the Apologists, the *Orations* provide a particularly useful yardstick against which to assess their tactics and plausibility. The aim of the Apologists was to speak to the educated élite of the Graeco-Roman world on their own terms, clothing the Christian message in the forms of argument and the range of cultural reference hallowed by Hellenic tradition. The *Orations*, with their ostentatiously confident mastery of precisely those forms, deployed over a similar range of topics, can illuminatingly be taken as representing the levels of 'cultural fluency' to which the Apologists aspire, and as an epitome of the 'right', culturally sanctioned way to manipulate those counters (*daimones*, allegorical readings of poetry, the history of wisdom) which they sought to appropriate and redeploy in the service of the New.

Above all, perhaps, they can be used to throw light on the achievement of the greatest of the early Christian writers, Clement of Alexandria.[107] For all the efforts of his predecessors to sound at home with the culture they sought to reform, there remains in their works a sense of strain and over-claiming, of a relatively thin and undernourished *paideia* masquerading as something more. Their range of reference to Classical literature and philosophy is narrow, and shows many signs of being second-hand, drawn more from epitomes and handbooks than from direct acquaintance with original texts. And in prose style even the best and most spirited of them, the Syrian Tatian, falls short of a truly convincing finish. Comparison with both the stylistic finish, and the demonstration of *paideia*, in the *Orations* suggests what little favour such products were likely to have found with even a relatively fastidious audience. But when the *Orations* are compared with Clement—the Clement of the *Protrepticus* makes the most economically striking contrast—a very different picture emerges. Both as stylist and as scholar—as *pepaideumenos*, 'man of culture', in the full sense— Clement is not merely Maximus' equal, but easily his superior, in range, depth, and sheer panache. The quality of Clement's work can of course be brought out by the comparison with that of other Christian writers alone, but the addition of the *Orations* to the frame of reference can usefully be made to serve as a further, external check, confirming that his claims to fine writing, and to effective preaching, could stand up before any audience of the day, not only within the narrower circle of Christian believers.

If the preceding argument is accepted, the *Orations* emerge once more as a richly informative document of the culture of their times, now not only by the direct evidence they give of the horizons of educated culture in the later second century, but also indirectly, for the light they cast on developments that they chose—and could still afford—to overlook.

THE PERSONA OF A PHILOSOPHICAL PREACHER

At the beginning of this first half of the Introduction, reasons were given for supposing that almost nothing could be known about a historical individual 'Maximus of Tyre' separate from his surviving works. At its end, we are at least in a position to console ourselves with the thought that, as the author of the *Orations*, he can be given considerable substance even so: the *Orations* themselves are cultural products of a distinct and recognizable kind; and their composer lives in them as an identifiable and analysable persona. It is with this persona that we may conclude.

For obvious reasons, it is displayed in its most concentrated and comprehensive form in the first, introductory *Oration*, which, as we have seen, either reproduces or imitates a speech of advertisement, designed to attract new audiences to a course of philosophical lectures. The composer of such an advertisement necessarily seeks to convince his audience of two things: that they need and want the product on offer, and that he is the man to deliver it. The first half of the lecture (§§ 1–5) is directed to the first of these aims, while the main thrust of the second half (§§ 6–10) is to underline Maximus' own credentials as an instructor. It does so with what is, superficially, a paradoxical blend of vanity and modesty. Maximus is at pains to point out that he is a seasoned and committed speaker whose lectures have been received with acclaim by many audiences (§ 6) and are in themselves masterpieces of oratory that will repay study and imitation for all kinds of purposes (§ 7); but at the same time he insists that what is really important to him is not acclaim, but the winning of converts to philosophical values and philosophical instruction (§ 6). By this second standard, he acknowledges that self-advertisement is inappropriate (§ 7), and that he himself cannot yet boast of success—that now depends on his present audience (§ 6). The persuasive strategy is clear: Maximus' audience are being encouraged to feel that, whether they think of themselves as potential philosophers or not, they have every reason to hear him with respectful attention; and they are having moral pressure put on them to 'save' him from another 'failure', in which his earnest efforts to make converts yield only empty applause. Simultaneously, he himself is being established as a figure of all-round authority and competence (rhetorical as well as philosophical), with a secure grasp of what really matters.

The impression of reliability and competence is reinforced by two further elements, both of which also seek to conciliate and reassure their hearers in other ways too. In § 8 Maximus draws a pointed contrast between true philosophical training, which inspires and guides the young soul like a horse-trainer, and the narrow, pedantic theorizing and disputation of the schoolroom—a contrast which both underlines his own commitment to the essentials of his calling (and consequent superiority over potential professional rivals), and assures his audience that his own 'instruction' will not be full of pedantic and irrelevant technicality. Then in § 9, immediately afterwards, he protests against the (implicitly wide-spread) perception that philosophy is above all the preserve of the poor and humble, on the grounds that Socrates had rich as well as poor pupils (and indeed counted the former more important than the latter), and that the case of Aristippus shows luxury and wealth to be perfectly compatible with philosophy in the instructor too. This both aligns Maximus himself with a great tradition of philosophical teachers, and encourages his audience to cast them-selves as successors to a great tradition of pupils, while at the same time reassuring them that their own means and social status are no obstacle.

Imagery too makes its contribution to the construction of the persona. Not only the comparison of philosophical instruction with the horse-trainer in § 8, but also the image of the musician in § 7, inadvertently and almost imperceptibly training his neighbour's birds to sing in tune, provide reassuring analogies for Maximus himself as gentle and benevolent instructor, as indeed does the much earlier comparison with the piping shepherd, guarding and guiding his flock, in § 3. In fact, the exploitation of this allusive technique pervades the whole oration. Beginning with the very first words of the opening paragraph, the successive images of actor, musician, doctor, shepherd, soldier, and athlete underscore the status Maximus claims both as star performer, commanding his audience's rapt attention, and as committed professional, dedicated to the betterment of those with whom he comes into contact.

All the facets of the persona constructed in the introductory oration can be seen again in the remainder of the collection. Throughout, Maximus underscores his comprehensive expertise and authority, both as a cultivated rhetorical virtuoso and as philosopher: the former in his stylistic fluency and in the easy familiarity with which he evokes the classics of the Greek literary heritage and the great names and deeds of Classical history, the latter both in the moral confidence with which he praises right conduct and castigates vice,[108] and in the sureness with which he parades the names and the doctrines of the great philosophers. He maintains, too, the same ostentatious scorn for those who divert philosophy from its proper moral ends into pedantic theorizing.[109] At the same time, however, the proper philosophical modesty displayed in the opening oration is continued in the care he takes not to place himself on the same level as the great names of the past. His rank, he insists, is that of the expert middle-man, well versed in the doctrines of the greats, and able to expound them clearly and accurately to others, but making no claim to the same kind of authority himself. This can most clearly be seen at the beginning of *Or.* 11, in the surprise he affects at the suggestion that his audience want to hear an exposition of Plato from him, when they can read the Master for themselves, and his insistence that he can operate merely as a humble assayer, cleaning and certifying the pure gold from the Platonic mine (*Or.* 11. 1–2); but it may also be seen, more lightly touched in, on most occasions when he is reporting or expounding the ideas of a named philosopher (e.g. *Or.* 27. 5).

Also sustained throughout is the character of the accessible, conscientious, benevolent instructor, at pains to be both lively and lucid, whose voice has already claimed our attention above. The demand for an inspirational mode made in *Or.* 1. 7 is repeated in closely similar terms in *Or.* 25. 6, and is answered in the fabric of

---

[108] As he himself duly demands of the good (philosophical) orator in *Or.* 25. 6. For some examples, see *Orr.* 3. 8, 5. 7, 6. 6, 12. 6–10, 13. 8–9.

[109] See esp. *Orr.* 21. 4, 27. 8, 30. 1, and 37. 2.

the orations by the avoidance of formal periodic style, and the high proportion of exclamation and apostrophe already remarked. Above all, by frequent use of the devices of engagement—first-person plural exhortations, second-person commands and questions, and the evocation of hypothetical interlocutors—Maximus seeks to infuse elements of (simulated) dialogue into his disquisitions, and to close the gap between speaker and audience.[110] At the same time, we have seen how he ostentatiously avoids erecting barriers of technical terminology—a tendency on which he comments directly, and for which he claims Platonic authority, in *Or.* 21. 4. This does not of course mean that he attempts to avoid sounding like a philosopher. On the contrary, the *Orations* are marked by a carefully calculated proportion of philosophical set-pieces in which the speaker shows off his mastery of a particular cluster of concepts or forms of argument, his ability to 'speak the language' (above, p. xix). The point is that this is always done without recourse to the kind of technical jargon and syntax that is so evident in, say, the *Didascalicus* of Alcinous, the *Placita* of Ps.-Plutarch, or the treatises of Sextus Empiricus. Concern for clarity and accessibility is further evinced by the frequency with which he pauses to comment on the course his argument is taking, to reinforce a point by rephrasing it for a second time, and to (at least affect to) consult the wishes of his audience: that refrain of 'do you want . . .?', 'would you prefer . . .?' The relation between this concern for clarity and the frequency of image and exemplum that is so characteristic of the surface texture of the *Orations* has already been remarked. Thus in *Or.* 7. 6, having used a quotation from Aeschylus' *Philoctetes* to illustrate the tendency of the unenlightened soul to cling to the body in all circumstances, Maximus proceeds to build on this with the words 'I see that the argument has brought me of its own accord to a still clearer illustration of the point I have been trying to impress on you all along,' and introduces Philoctetes himself to prove the superior importance of psychological over physical health. Or again, in *Or.* 21. 5, when an analysis of the difference between 'the pleasant' and 'the good' threatens to become too technical, he hastens to add, 'I mean something like this—for I realize I am drawing a subtle distinction here and need to give you an illustration,' and follows up with the comparable distinction between the enjoyment provided by the

---

[110] On this, see Trapp (forthcoming *a*); and pp. xxxiv–xxxv above.

taste of food and its capacity to nourish. Such passages once again reassure the hearer both of the speaker's concern to instruct without obfuscation, and of his assured command of both literary and philosophical culture.

This pose, like the range of subjects treated in the *Orations*, and the chosen literary vehicle, is not one that is represented in any other surviving document of the age. In this, as in those other respects, attention to Maximus and his products substantially extends and enriches our appreciation of the range of modes and manners available to the educated culture of the high Imperial period.

NACHLEBEN

The first part of the Introduction was concerned with the character and place of the *Orations* in the culture of their own day, as seen from the vantage-point of twentieth-century literary and historical scholarship. There is, however, another story to tell, of other readers and other vantage-points. The *Orations* have been transmitted through the 1800 years since their composition via a series of manuscripts, of which some thirty-five, dating from between the ninth and the sixteenth centuries, still survive; and via about thirty printed editions, dating from between 1517 and 1994.[111] From these manuscripts and printed books, from the comments left in their margins by owners and readers, and from original works by those owners and readers in which they made use of their reading, there is something to be learned about the spirit in which the *Orations* were read, and the uses to which they were put, in the centuries before our own.

FROM THE SECOND TO THE NINTH CENTURIES

Evidence for the transmission of the *Orations*, and for interest taken in them, begins with two documents dating from the ninth and tenth centuries AD: the *Suda*, with its brief entry on Maximus, and

---

[111] For a complete catalogue of these manuscripts and printed editions, with full bibliographical references, see the introduction to Trapp (1994). The figure of thirty-five for the manuscripts includes those which contain only a selection of orations, or excerpts from them, as well as those giving the complete text; the figure for printed editions includes translations and editions of individual orations.

(from the earlier century) the principal manuscript, Parisinus
graecus 1962. Both documents, besides attesting to the availability of the text, and of information about its author, at the time
of their making, offer glimpses of what had been happening in the
preceding six or seven hundred years.

Like so many of the biographical entries in the *Suda*, the article
on Maximus derives from an epitome of the *Onomatologos* or *Pinax*
of Hesychius of Miletus, a guide to distinguished men of learning
and letters composed some time in the last quarter of the sixth
century.[112] It thus testifies not only to Maximus' standing in the
tenth century, but also (and more directly) to his standing in the
sixth: whatever happened to his works between 200 and 575, it
would appear that they had not lapsed into complete obscurity,
and their author was still held to deserve a place in the guidebooks.
The article reads as follows:

Maximus of Tyre, philosopher. Lectured in Rome in the time of Commodus.
'On Homer and the identity of the ancient philosophy to be found in his
work'; 'Whether Socrates did well not to speak in his own defence'; and
other philosophical questions.

The two orations singled out for special mention are clearly the
items we know as *Orr.* 3 and 26. It is intriguing that just these two
should have been chosen in preference to any of the other thirty-
three possibilities, and further food for thought is given by the
observation that the titles Hesychius gives them do not correspond
exactly with those found in the principal manuscript and its
descendants.[113] We are, however, left to guess whether the choice
and the divergence of the titles are the result of personal taste, or
a reflection of some 'edition' of the *Orations* other than that reproduced in the surviving manuscript tradition.

Our other piece of early evidence, the Parisinus, is quite literally
indispensable. As the earliest surviving manuscript copy of the
Orations, the ancestor of all the remainder,[114] it is the pivot on
which almost the whole of our knowledge of Maximus and the

---

[112] See *KP* and *ODB* s.v., with Adler (1928–38, vol. i, p. xxi), and in *RE* s.v.
Suidas, 706–8.

[113] For *Or.* 3, the *Suda*/Hesychius gives εἰ καλῶς Σωκράτης οὐκ ἀπελογήσατο in
place of εἰ καλῶς ἐποίησε Σωκράτης μὴ ἀπολογησάμενος; and for *Or.* 26, περὶ Ὁμήρου
καὶ τίς ἡ παρ'αὐτῷ ἀρχαία φιλοσοφία in place of εἰ ἔστιν καθ' Ὅμηρον αἵρεσις.

[114] See Mutschmann (1913), Schulte (1915), Trapp (1994, pp. xxix–xxxviii,
Koniaris (1995).

Orations turns. Had it not been made, the text of the *Orations* would almost certainly have been lost for ever, and we would know no more of them and their author than is reported by Hesychius and the *Suda*.

The Parisinus was copied in Constantinople, in around 875, as part of a set of eleven codices, containing mainly philosophical works and written in the new minuscule hand, which were first identified as a group by T. W. Allen in 1893.[115] Originally it contained four items, Alcinous' *Didascalicus*, Albinus' *Outlines of Platonism, from the lectures of Gaius* and *Platonic Doctrine*,[116] and the *Orations*: three handbooks of Middle Platonic philosophical doctrine, followed by something more colourful and elegant, but still philosophical in content. At some point—perhaps when the codex was unbound to facilitate the making of a further copy—the two texts by Albinus became lost, and those of Maximus and Alcinous changed places. What now survive are 175 parchment leaves, measuring 245 by 165 mm,[117] carefully ruled and smartly written in the new minuscule script, with the *Orations* occupying foll. 1-145, a list of contents fol. 146, and the *Didascalicus* foll. 147-175. Both the *Didascalicus* and the *Orations* are accompanied by scholia;[118] and, within the latter, the individual items are given their own titles and numbers.

In several ways, the presentation of the *Orations* in the Parisinus, like the notice in the *Suda*, offers glimpses of, or at least prompts questions about, earlier stages in the transmission. There is, in the first place, the question of the company which Maximus' work is made to keep—three Middle Platonic philosophical handbooks. On the one hand, this suggests a view of Maximus too as an author of philosophical as well as (or even, rather than) literary interest. But at the same time it raises the question when such a collection of texts might have been put together in the first place—of the process

[115] See Allen (1893); Wilson (1983: 86-8). The manuscripts are, besides Paris. gr. 1962, Paris. gr. 1807 (the 'Paris Plato'), Paris. Suppl. gr. 921, Laur. 80. 9, Vat. gr. 2197 and 2249, Marc. gr. 196, 226, 246, and 258, and Pal. gr. 398. Four or five scribes only were involved in the making of these codices, but it remains unclear whether they were intended for a single patron or several.

[116] The original contents are listed in a *pinax* on fol. 146ᵛ. For Alcinous, see Dillon (1977: 272-304; 1993) and Whittaker (1990); and for Albinus and Gaius, Dillon (1977: 266-71, 304-6). Cf. also n. 15 above.

[117] A modest format, compared with the much ampler scale of, for example, the Paris Plato.

[118] Transcribed in Whittaker (1990: 154-67), Trapp (1994: 336-45).

by which, and the time at which, the *Orations* ceased to be a text circulating independently in their own right, and became just one item in a larger whole. Given that Middle (as opposed to Neo-)Platonic thought was not of great interest to Byzantine intellectuals, it seems fair to suggest in answer that no date later than the sixth century is really plausible; but equally, any date earlier than that, back to the early third century, must count as possible.[119]

The second feature of the presentation that points back in time is the scholia. Those on the text of the *Orations* are of several different kinds, some in minuscule and some in majuscule characters, alternately drawing attention to out-of-the-way vocabulary and morphology, identifying references, providing background information, noting topics, and summarizing lines of argument (sometimes with the aid of diagrams). Literary quotations are marked out, with separate sigla for hexameter verse, lyric verse, and prose. These appendages are unlikely to be the result of just one campaign of annotation, but instead to represent the accumulation of readers' notabilia and editorial assistance over a considerable period of time. It has been suggested that some or all of the more austerely philosophical marginalia elsewhere in the same manuscript, attached to the text of Alcinous, go back to Alexandrian scholars of the sixth century;[120] if this is so, then there is also a chance that the more obviously philosophical among the scholia to the *Orations* too go back to that same time and milieu.

Thirdly, there is the question of the titles the Parisinus gives to the individual orations. As explained briefly above (n. 60), these quite frequently fail to reflect the actual contents of their respective orations with any closeness, and this observation in turn suggests that they are unlikely to have been the work of Maximus himself (although carelessness, or faulty memory in old age, must remain possible explanations). If they are indeed editorial, rather than authorial additions, then they could have been added at any time from the end of the second century onwards, and their addition gains us another half-glimpse of the process of transmission.

The fourth and final feature of the presentation that seems to preserve the traces of an earlier stage in the transmission is the

---

[119] Cf. Whittaker (1990, p. xxxvii; 1991).
[120] Whittaker (1990, p. xxxvii n. 42).

order in which the *Orations* are presented in the Parisinus. Each oration is numbered, either individually, or as one of a group, but there are two sequences of numbers, not one. One set of numbers, written in minuscule characters, runs in unbroken and coherent sequence from one (*α′*) to thirty-five (*λε′*), beginning with the first item (the first oration on Pleasure) and running through to the last (and counting pairs and sets of orations as one item apiece, so as to reach a total of thirty-five rather than forty-one). This sequence is repeated in the contents list to the *Orations* to be found on fol. 1^r of the manuscript. The other set of numbers, written in majuscule (uncial) characters, is more disjointed. It starts with the seventh item in the collection (on the versatility of philosophical discourse), which it numbers one (*A′*), then continues in sequence, numbering each item separately, even within pairs and sets, as far as the thirty-fifth, which is numbered twenty-nine (*KΘ′*). The next oration, the thirty-sixth, is numbered thirty-six (*Λς′*), and the sequence then runs on to the last item, number forty-one (*MA′*). Only the first six items bear no numbers in this notation.

The implications of this disjointed sequence are most easily seen when the numbers and the oration-titles are set out in a list, as at the beginning of the Introduction: six items at the head of the collection bear no numerals; the sequence of numerals, when it does start, misses six places between items thirty-five and thirty-six. It is immediately tempting to conclude that the unnumbered six items belonged in the gap, and bore the numbers thirty to thirty-five, and that, correspondingly, items seven to thirty-five were previously one to twenty-nine. That this is indeed so, and that the order of orations in the Parisinus was created by a dislocation to some earlier and superior state of the collection, is confirmed when one looks at the contents of the items concerned. If the suggested relocation is made, then the former item seven becomes item one, the introduction to the whole collection; and, as we have already seen, it is indeed a very good introductory piece. At the same time, the old item thirty-five is made to come immediately before the old items one to four (plus five and six). This too works well, as item twenty-nine (as it now becomes) poses the question (about the ends of life) that items thirty to thirty-three set about answering.

There is therefore every reason, in editing (and translating) the *Orations*, to reinstate the order implied by the majuscule numbering, as both earlier and better than the order actually followed by the Parisinus, and summarized in its contents list.[121] And at the same time, we gain our further glimpse of the earlier history of the transmission, and the questions it arouses. At some time between c. AD 200 and c. AD 875, the order of the orations was changed. Was this mechanical and accidental, the result of a few leaves becoming displaced? Or was it a matter of conscious choice, of someone deciding that a set of lectures on the topic of Pleasure and Epicurean philosophy made a weightier and more attractive start to the collection than a rather sophistical piece of protreptic? And is the earlier ordering that of the very first published version of the *Orations*, or itself the product of a reorganization?

It must be admitted that no very coherent picture of the early transmission and reception can be given, on the basis of such scanty and problematic evidence as is now available. Several strands do, however, point to the sixth century as an important stage in the process—the time of Hesychius' dictionary, of Alexandrian scholarly activity of the kind perhaps reflected in the scholia, and of a continuing interest in minor Platonic texts. A hypothetical reconstruction could envisage the making in the sixth century of an uncial manuscript of the *Orations*, together with Alcinous and Albinus, that then survived long enough to become the exemplar for either Parisinus graecus 1962 itself, or its immediate predecessor. This would have the virtue of fitting very comfortably with our general picture of the transmission of Greek texts through the first millennium AD, in which the seventh and eighth centuries are a period of relative neglect, and it is the ninth that sees a revival of both interest and copying activity. It could also be conjectured, within this hypothesis, that the change in the order of the *Orations* took place—accidentally or by design—in the transition from sixth-century uncial to ninth-century minuscule text. No real proof, however, can be offered to substantiate this

---

[121] For all this, cf. Koniaris (1982: 88-102). Puiggali (1983: 13-21) defends the manuscript order, claiming that the two sequences of numerals are 'approximately contemporary'. This is to miss the point: the question is not when each of them was written on the Parisinus (which must indeed have been the same time), but how long each of them had been attached to the collection previously. If there are two sequences of numbers, one corresponding to the actual order of presentation and the other not, then the one that corresponds is almost certain to be the later. The first editor to restore the earlier order in his edition was Hobein (1910): editions from 1557 to 1703 followed the order adopted by Laur. Conv. Sopp. 4 and its descendants (see below, p. lxiii), and those from 1740 to 1840 that of the Parisinus.

piece of guesswork, and other plausible stories could be constructed in its place.

As far as the ninth-century reception is concerned, what little there is to be said must be inferred from the Paris manuscript, and what is known of the context in which it was copied, and from the *Suda*. The picture that emerges is not a very detailed one, nor does it offer any very clear idea of how the work was perceived. From the Parisinus itself, and the *Suda*, it might seem that the *Orations* were being presented and read as a philosophical text: they were at least bound together with other works of philosophy, equipped with scholia summarizing their philosophical arguments and doctrines, and certified as the work of an author identified both by the manuscript and by the biographical guides as a *philosophos*. At the same time, some at least of the marginalia in the Parisinus drew attention to less strictly philosophical aspects of the work: linguistic features, literary quotations, and items of antiquarian lore. The larger group of manuscripts with which the Parisinus is associated is predominantly philosophical in content, but not wholly so. It is thought likely to have been commissioned by a single patron, or for a single destination,[122] but the identity of that patron, or destination, can only be conjectured.[123] It might also be questioned how prominent the *Orations* were, compared to the other texts both in the Parisinus and in the whole manuscript group. They were, after all, just one item among four in the Parisinus, and by no means the largest; and the Parisinus itself— compared, for example, to the Paris Plato (Parisinus graecus 1807)—is a manuscript of modest format. It is therefore quite possible that the *Orations* were not much read; but to the extent that they were, it is likely to have been primarily for their philosophical content.

THE LATER BYZANTINE PERIOD

The subsequent circulation of the *Orations* in the Byzantine period is represented in the surviving record by seven manuscripts, one dating from the thirteenth century and the remainder from the fourteenth, and a brief mention of the author in an essay by

---

[122] Cf. n. 115 above.
[123] Photius and Leo the Philosopher have both been suggested: Wilson (1983: 85–8).

the statesman and scholar Theodoros Metochites (1270–1332). Together they reveal a pattern of continuing interest in the work, but one in which the emphasis seems to be shifting away from a philosophical and towards a more literary appreciation.

The oldest of the manuscripts, Vaticanus graecus 1390, combines the *Orations* with Alcinous' *Didascalicus*, Eustathius Macrembolites' novel *The Adventures of Ismene and Ismenias*, part of Heliodorus' *Ethiopica*, and the works of Synesius, and seems to have been copied in the third quarter of the thirteenth century.[124] It is not clear whether its text of Maximus and Alcinous was taken directly from the Parisinus, or whether there were some intermediate stages. Either way, it shows unmistakable signs of considerable efforts to improve the paradosis: scores of minor slips in the text of the *Orations* have been silently corrected, and many of the scribe's own copying errors are made good either in his own hand, or in that of one of several other contributors; new explanatory glosses, and even a few simple conjectures, have been added in the margins, though as if to compensate, several of the philosophical diagrams have disappeared too.[125] How much of this is new with the Vaticanus itself, and how much it has inherited from earlier exemplars, cannot be determined, which in turn leaves it unclear whether we have evidence of just one episode of interest in the text, or of something more sustained. What is not in doubt, however, is the closeness of the reading and the level of interest required to produce the end-result that can be seen in the manuscript.

Of the other three Byzantine manuscripts containing the full text of the *Orations*, all dating from the fourteenth century, two can be dealt with very briefly. Bodleianus Auct. T. 4. 1 contains only the *Orations*, and is clearly a direct copy of the Parisinus;[126] it bears no interesting marginalia or owner's marks at all. Vaticanus graecus

---

[124] The hand is similar to that on the dated manuscripts Vat. gr. 106 (1251) and 64 (1269). In its present state, the manuscript also contains a number of other texts in different and slightly later hands, which must have been added subsequently.

[125] For the textual corrections, see the apparatus criticus to Trapp (1994); for the differentiation of the different hands involved, Schulte (1915: 6–7, 60–5). It is possible that a number of the missing diagrams have been lost through trimming of the pages, not through failure to copy them.

[126] Its gatherings always begin and end with the same words as the corresponding gatherings of the Parisinus, even when this means leaving blank space at the end of a page—suggesting that the Parisinus was unbound for the making of this copy, and distributed by the gathering to different scribes.

1950 is altogether a larger affair, combining the *Orations* with the *Didascalicus*, the works of Xenophon, Marcus Aurelius' *Meditations*, Aristotle's *De Motu Animalium*, an Epicurean gnomology (the 'gnomologium Vaticanum'), and a paraphrase of Epictetus' *Encheiridion*. In the transmission of the text of Maximus, at least one intermediary exemplar must have intervened between it and the Parisinus, since it has lacunae in several places where the Parisinus is quite clearly legible. It too is wholly devoid of early annotations.

Much more substantial and interesting is the case of the third manuscript of the complete text, Laurentianus Conventi Soppressi 4, which in its original state may have contained the *Orations* alone, but subsequently combined them with the Orphic *Argonautica* and a number of shorter texts. To an even greater extent than Vat. gr. 1390, this manuscript constitutes an attempt at a 'new edition' of the *Orations*. In the first place, the text it presents combines readings distinctive of the tradition from the Parisinus with readings distinctive of that from Vat. gr. 1390, as if two manuscripts (perhaps even the Parisinus and the Vaticanus) had been secured for the preparation of the new copy.[127] Secondly, it offers the orations in a revised order, beginning no longer with *Or.* 1, like the hypothetical original 'edition', nor with *Or.* 30, like the Parisinus and its early descendants, but with *Or.* 11 (on Platonic theology), followed by *Orr.* 12–29, 36–41, 8–10, 4–5, 30–5, 1–3, and 6–7.[128] Thirdly, the heading of the collection is changed, so as to describe Maximus, for the first time, not just as 'philosopher', but as 'sophist and philosopher'. There is also a scattering of new scholia. While the change to the heading suggests a desire to highlight Maximus' literary qualities more strongly, the revision of the order seems calculated to draw attention to his philosophical, and more specifically Platonic philosophical, content.[129]

The existence of this 'new edition' would be interesting enough

[127] Cf. Trapp (1994, p. xxxvii).

[128] By historical accident (see below, p. lxxxii), this is the order also adopted by the first printed edition of the *Orations*, and indeed by all printed editions up until 1740.

[129] *Or.* 11 gets the collection off to an unambiguously Platonic start, after which the sequence is allowed to run on in its old order until the end (*Or.* 41, which is also Platonic-theological in content); then, from the displaced sixteen items, the next most clearly Platonic (*Orr.* 8–10) are picked out, followed by two more of generally similar subject matter (*Orr.* 4–5); then come the pieces shifted from the head of the collection, kept as a clump (*Orr.* 30–5), and finally the remaining odds and ends.

in itself. It is made all the more interesting by the further fact that it can be associated with a known scholar, who may even have been the moving force behind its compilation. The heading to the collection, mentioned above, and the titles to the individual orations are not in the hand of any of the scribes responsible for the copying of the main text; they were instead written into gaps left by the scribes in a hand which can be identified as that of the polymath Nicephorus Gregoras (c.1291/4-1358/61).[130] Now, Gregoras was a pupil and associate of Metochites, who is the only Byzantine scholar of the period to mention Maximus in a surviving treatise. The mention is only a fleeting one—Maximus is simply named as one example among several in support of the thesis that Greek authors from Asia Minor had a smoother style than those from Egypt[131]—but it is enough to establish Metochites' knowledge and favourable opinion of the author, and to suggest where Gregoras might have acquired his own enthusiasm.

However it was acquired, that enthusiasm was clearly substantial, for the presence of Gregoras' handwriting on the Laurentian manuscript is not the only indication we have of an engagement with Maximus on his part. An autograph commonplace book of his, containing excerpts from a whole range of classical and Byzantine authors, survives as Palatinus graecus 129. Among the many authors excerpted into it is Maximus, to the tune of some 102 excerpts, drawn from thirty-two of the forty-one *Orations*.[132] From the text of these excerpts, it is clear that they were taken not from the Laurentian manuscript, but from some other source,[133] which in turn means that, perhaps at different times, Gregoras had access to two separate manuscripts of the *Orations*. The sheer scale

---

[130] I am grateful to Professor Ihor Ševčenko for confirming my own initial impression. For Gregoras, see Wilson (1983: 266-8) and A. M. Talbot in *ODB* ii. 874-5.

[131] *Misc.* 17, p. 128 Müller; discussed by Wilson (1983: 262-3) and Vries-van der Velden (1987: 188-91). For Metochites, see ibid., and A. M. Talbot in *ODB* ii. 1357-8.

[132] These excerpts are all identified in the apparatus to Hobein (1910), with the siglum 'p'. I have noted them briefly, but without giving precise details, in the introductory note to each *Oration* from which they are taken. The manuscript is discussed by Ševčenko (1964). The most excerpted orations are *Orr.* 32 and 18; those wholly neglected are *Orr.* 3, 5, 13, 14, 24, 27, 35, 38, and 39.

[133] For instance, in the excerpt consisting of *Or.* 4. 9, lines 183-6 Trapp, he includes a whole clause omitted by the Laurentian manuscript (and only restored to it in the fifteenth century). From another excerpt, of *Or.* 31. 1, lines 9-14 Trapp, it seems that he was working from Vat. gr. 1390, or a near relative, since he there reads ὅλης with the Vaticanus, not ἄλλης with the Parisinus.

of Gregoras' excerpting makes it difficult to establish any particular direction of interest underlying it. It seems fair to say, however, that his eye fell as much on stylistic and rhetorical felicities as on points of doctrine. The point of making the excerpts will thus have been to provide models and materials for his own writing, rather than to improve his philosophical competence.

Gregoras' rhetorical interest in the *Orations* can be parallelled by another document to survive from this period. Another fourteenth-century manuscript, Vindobonensis philologicus graecus 169, contains (among other items) the so-called *Lexicon Vindobonense*, compiled in the early decades of the century by Manuel Moschopoulos' pupil Andreas Lopadiotes.[134] In the normal manner of such compilations, this guide to classicizing vocabulary and usage borrows heavily from its predecessors, but adds material on its own account from Sophocles, Pherecrates, Himerius—and Maximus. In all, fifty-six entries are illustrated by quotations from the *Orations*, drawn from twenty-four out of the forty-one items, with no particular concentration on one part of the collection rather than another (though twenty of the fifty-six entries are for words beginning with alpha or epsilon). Lopadiotes seems to have quarried the *Orations* with some thoroughness in his desire to add new matter to his lexicon.[135]

Rhetorical and stylistic interest in the *Orations* were, however, not the only avenues of approach to Maximus in the later Byzantine period. We have already seen, in the reordering of the sequence in the Laurentian manuscript, signs of a continuing concern for their philosophical content. This latter trend is also evidenced by one last fourteenth-century manuscript, Laurentianus Mediceus 85.15. Another descendant of Vat. gr. 1390, it contains only 1 to 11 of the *Orations* (foll. 179^v-199), but combines them with Plotinus' *Enneads* (foll. 7-178) and Porphyry's *Life of Plotinus* (foll. 1-7). Here Maximus is returned to the kind of serious philosophical company he kept in the Parisinus in its original form, though here too he seems to be brought in as light relief at the end, rather than as an attraction in his own right.

[134] For Lopadiotes and the *Lexicon*, see Browning's article and bibliography in *ODB* ii. 1251.

[135] The introductory notes to the individual orations below give a general indication of Lopadiotes' borrowings; precise references can be found in the apparatus to Hobein (1910), marked by the siglum 'v'. For the full text of the *Lexicon* see Nauck (1867).

FROM 1400 TO 1517

Exactly how and when the first copies of the *Orations* came across from East to West cannot now be reconstructed, but it must have been within the first couple of decades of the fifteenth century.[136] By the end of the century, five of the eight early manuscripts discussed above were certainly in Italy, and the other three may well have been, and at least a further five complete and two partial texts had either been copied locally or imported.[137] Full texts were available in Florence, Venice, and Rome, and had found readers among both Greek exiles and native Italians, as well as in at least one visitor from north of the Alps.

The earliest indications of a Western diffusion of the *Orations* concern three owners linked by the fact that all were pupils of one or the other of the first great teachers of Greek in Italy, Manuel Chrysoloras and Guarino Guarini. The combination of a library catalogue and marks on the manuscript itself establish that Laur. Conv. Sopp. 4 (Gregoras' manuscript) had moved on to form part of the library of Chrysoloras' Florentine pupil (and Guarino's patron) Antonio Corbinelli, who died in 1425 and bequeathed his outstanding collection of 195 Latin and eighty Greek codices (via an intermediary) to the Florentine Badia.[138] The owner's *ex libris* on fol. 199ᵛ identifies a second surviving manuscript, Laur. Med. 85.15 (containing Plotinus and *Orations* 1–11), as belonging to the the Venetian aristocrat Leonardo Giustinian (1388?–1446), who studied with both Chrysoloras and Guarino and produced translations of three of Plutarch's *Lives*.[139] And a surviving customs pass testifies that a text of Maximus ('Maximus platonicus') was one of forty-three volumes sent in 1445 by the teacher Vittorino da Feltre to his and Guarino's pupil Gian Pietro da Lucca, who was by that time running his own school in Verona.[140] The implication of the list on the pass is that the *Orations* were either the only or the main

---

[136] Laur. Conv. Sopp. 4 takes us tantalizingly close to the point of transition, on both sides. It was certainly in Florence by 1425 (see below), but also bears an anonymous note recording someone's four-year stay in Trebizond between 1384 and 1388 (fol. 139): see Rostagno and Festa (1893: 133–4 = Bandini (1961) ii. 8*).

[137] Counting only manuscripts that still survive: the total would go up if it could be shown conclusively that a number of references in library catalogues and private correspondence relate not to surviving items but to codices now lost.

[138] See Blum (1950) and in *DBI* s.v.

[139] See Oberdorfer (1910), Sabbadini (1922: 78) and Cosenza (1962: ii. 1874–6).

[140] See Cortesi (1980, 1981).

item in their volume, but it is not clear whether this can be identified with any codex now surviving.[141]

None of this, admittedly, allows any very substantial conclusions to be drawn about the level and quality of interest being shown in the *Orations* at the time. It would seem fair to conclude that the educator Vittorino felt them to be of some use to a teacher of Greek (unless he was unloading positively unwanted items on his colleague), but we have no way of knowing whether either of the other two aristocratic owners, Corbinelli and Giustinian, read even so much as a single oration between them. All that can therefore be said with any confidence is that the text was in circulation in Italy in the first half of the fifteenth century and that, for whatever reason, or by whatever accidents, it had found its way into a number of the earliest collections of Greek manuscripts in Italy. As we move towards the middle of the century, however, there is a further case over which a slightly more circumstantial story can be told, and a more definite idea formed of readers' interests.

The first Pope to preside over a serious expansion of the holdings of classical texts in the Vatican Library was Nicholas V (Tommaso Parentucelli, 1397–1455); his Librarian, from 1450 onwards, was Cardinal Giovanni Tortelli. Among Tortelli's surviving correspondence from these years is a letter from an unidentified third party reporting an approach from 'a Greek scribe called Ioannes, in Florence', who had offered to make a copy of 'the forty-one opuscula of the philosopher Maximus of Tyre', and had helpfully included a list of their titles.[142] Tortelli's reply does not survive, but it seems to have been favourable, for the catalogue of the papal library made for Nicholas's successor, Calixtus III (1455–8), by Cosme de Montserrat describes a recently made volume of the *Orations* as the first item in the philosophical class.[143] What is initially striking in this case is that it is the initiative of a Greek scribe, touting for custom, that is responsible for the generation of another copy of the work, not a request from the patron. The list of titles he supplies, however, offering Latin equivalents for the

---

[141] If it is still extant, it would have to be either Bodl. Auct. T. 4. 1, or Ambros. R 25 Sup. (710).

[142] Vat. lat. 3908, fol. 189 (179); see Regoliosi (1966). The order of the titles, starting with 'De deo quis sit Platonis sententia', makes it clear that the scribe in Florence has access either to Laur. Conv. Sopp. 4 (by this stage in the Badia library), or to an apograph.

[143] Fol. 13^v, item 221. See Devreesse (1965: 28).

manuscript's Greek, does something to suggest why his advertisement met with a positive response. A set of works parading a preoccupation with Socrates, Plato, Homer, prayer, religious images, Fate and Free Will, the Problem of Evil, and the Active and Contemplative Lives, was unlikely to have struck the Quattrocento humanist eye as entirely devoid of interest.

Nicholas's manuscript of the *Orations* did not in the event remain for long in the papal collection. It still survives, bearing the Parentucelli arms and written in the distinctive hand of Ioannes Skutariotes,[144] but it now resides in the Biblioteca Marciana in Venice, as Marcianus graecus Z 254 (757). This in turn associates it with another celebrated connoisseur of ancient Greek literature and philosophy, Cardinal Bessarion (1395/1403–72), since it was by his donation that the Venetian republic acquired the bulk of what are now the Marciani graeci. That this manuscript did indeed (if only briefly) pass through Bessarion's hands is confirmed by its presence in the two inventories, of 1468 and 1474, which define the Cardinal's bequest. These inventories also make it clear that it was one of the codices that made up the first instalment, arriving in Venice in 1469.[145] It must therefore have left the papal collection, in circumstances now unreconstructable (theft or gift?), some time in the late 1450s or the early to mid-1460s.[146]

The same inventories further reveal that this was not the only manuscript of Maximus to have belonged to Bessarion. He also owned two others: Marcianus graecus Z 514 (771), which combines a damaged text of the *Orations* with such other items as Sophocles' *Ajax* (with scholia), *Iliad* 1–2 (also with scholia), Philostratus' *Heroicus* and *Imagines*, declamations of Libanius and Aristides, and Pediasimus' *Labours of Heracles*; and a third manuscript, now apparently lost, that seems to have contained the *Orations* alone.[147]

---

[144] For Skutariotes (who names himself in the subscription on fol. 138), see Vogel-Gardthausen (1909: 197), Gamillscheg-Harlfinger (1981, no. 183).

[145] For the story, and the inventories, see Labowsky (1979).

[146] Marc. gr. 258 and 313 are other cases of Papal manuscripts that ended up in Bessarion's library (cf. Labowsky 1961: 160-1)—but did either of them pass as directly from the one library to the other?

[147] This third manuscript is item 534 on the inventory of 1472; the fact that, unlike Marc. gr. 254 and 514, it does not appear on the 1468 inventory shows that it only came into Bessarion's possession after that date. Of the other two, though 254 went to Venice in the first batch of codices in 1469, 514 was one of the 280 retained by Bessarion for his own use during his lifetime.

That the Cardinal's library should have housed such a concentration of texts of Maximus is not surprising, given both his
theological and philosophical background, and his determination,
after 1453, to preserve as much as he could of the Greek cultural
heritage. He does, however, have the distinction of being the first
identifiable owner since Gregoras to have left visible and analysable
traces of his reading, certainly on Marc. gr. 254, and perhaps also
on Marc. gr. 514 as well. The margins of Marc. gr. 254 bear over
thirty notes highlighting points of interest in four separate orations:
Orr. 11 on Platonic theology (fifteen notes), 8–9 on *daimones*
(eighteen notes, of which thirteen on *Or.* 9), and 5 on prayer (one
note)[148]—all topics of a kind readily of interest to a theologian with
marked Platonic tastes. On Marc. gr. 514, the annotation is still
more extensive, attaching not only to *Orr.* 11 (thirty-seven notes)
and 8–9 (thirty-one notes), but also to 34 (on Virtue and
Circumstance, twenty-six notes) and 35 (on Friendship, twenty
notes), and running besides to some eighteen instances of an
abbreviation marking similes and comparisons.[149] Elpidio Mioni,
who first identified Bessarion's hand on Marc. gr. 254, is silent
about this second manuscript, both in his study of Bessarion as
scribe, and in his subsequent catalogue of the Marciani graeci
(Mioni 1985), but I believe there is none the less a good chance
that these annotations too are from the Cardinal's hand.[150] Indeed,
I also suspect that he is responsible for the recopying of some of the
main text in what is clearly a somewhat tattered and repaired
codex.[151] At the maximum, therefore, there would be indications of

---

[148] Foll. 4–6, 90–3, and 103. For the identification of the hand, see Mioni (1976,
1981); and for the location of the notes, see the introductions to the four orations
below.

[149] Foll. 164–8, 185–9, 193–5; the abbreviation is '$\pi a(\rho a)\delta$'.

[150] In addition to the general similarity of the hand, there is at least one case (the
diaeresis in *Or.* 11. 8) where a note on 254 coincides exactly in shape and wording with a note on 514. Is this Bessarion copying or repeating his own note from
a dirtier to a cleaner copy of the text, or Bessarion taking over a note by an older
associate?

[151] *Orr.* 30–3. 3 and 17–29 + 36–41 are missing entirely and 1–2 and 4–5 are
damaged, with blank leaves inserted to fill the gaps; some of the surviving text is
written on stained and worn paper, and some, in another hand, on cleaner paper
of the kind also filling the gaps in *Orr.* 1–2 and 4–5. The best reading of this seems
to be that someone has attempted to repair a badly battered manuscript, by recopying tattered but still legible leaves, and inserting blanks where a countable number
of the originals had been torn away or otherwise made illegible. I am grateful to
Nigel Wilson for the suggestion (made on the basis of a photograph) that the repair-
ing hand may be Bessarion's own.

a very strong and sustained interest in the *Orations* on Bessarion's part, extending both to their philosophical and theological content, and to their literary form, and prompting him both to repair old copies of the text and to acquire (and read) new ones. But even if Marc. gr. 514 is ruled out of the account, there is still the substantial evidence of the annotations on 254, combined with the fact that, even after the Venetian bequest, Bessarion retained not one but two copies of the work for his own collection.

Bessarion's reading of the *Orations* would seem to continue the kind of interest shown in the preceding century by Metochites and Gregoras. A more selective interest, recalling instead the use made of the text by Lopadiotes, was shown by Bessarion's fellow exile and client Michael Apostoles (c.1420-74/86).[152] His *Proverbia*, dedicated to Lauro Quirini († 1480), quotes nine times from the *Orations*, three times for the wording of a (real or alleged) proverb, and a further six for illustrations. All the quotations appeared again in the augmented version of the work later produced by his son Arsenios.[153] Precisely when and where Apostolis did his preparatory reading of the *Orations* is not known, but the manuscript he used seems to have been either the Vaticanus or a close relative.[154]

The cases of Bessarion and Apostoles show how the *Orations* maintained among educated Greeks the place that they seem already to have been accorded in the preceding century. It was, however, in Florence and the last three decades of the fifteenth century that they won their largest and most distinguished readership, among the humanists and Platonists of the Medici circle. Marsilio Ficino, Cristoforo Landino, Angelo Poliziano, Zanobi Acciaiuoli, Cosimo De' Pazzi, Giovanni Pico della Mirandola, and Janus Lascaris can all be shown to have read the *Orations*, and to have been interested enough either to use them as a source, or even to make them an object of scholarly attention in their own right. It may also have been in this milieu that they came to the attention of their first attested reader from north of the Alps, Johann Reuchlin.

Of Pico (1463-94), we know only that he once owned the copy

---

[152] See Vogel-Gardthausen (1909: 305-10), Gamillscheg-Harlfinger (1981, no. 278).

[153] For further details, see the headnotes to *Orr.* 2, 5, 6, 15, 18, 29, 31 and 37, and for the text of the *Proverbia*, Leutsch-Schneidewin (1839-51: ii).

[154] See e.g. *Proverbia* 10. 4, where his text of *Or.* 6. 3, lines 68-9 Trapp follows the Vaticanus rather than the Parisinus, or Laur. Conv. Sopp. 4.

of the text which shows up in a catalogue of his library made four years after his death, under the guise of 'Maximus Teurgus (*sic*), in papyro. no. 82'.[155] This manuscript is now lost (or at best unidentified) and there is no way of knowing when or why Maximus came to Pico's attention. Rather more can be reconstructed in the cases of Ficino and Landino. Both seem to have made the acquaintance of the *Orations* in the later 1460s and 1470s,[156] and although it does not seem possible to establish with any certainty which manuscripts they used, the nature of their interest can be inferred from the material from the *Orations* they reproduce in their own works. For Ficino, Maximus is a useful source of information about Plato and Socrates, cited by name in the introduction to his translation of the *Theages*,[157] and paraphrased at some length in section 7.16 of his commentary on the *Symposium*.[158] For Landino, he is more of a literary model, providing a large part of the structure of the first of the *Disputationes Camaldulenses*, on the Active and Contemplative Lives, and a further set of exempla relating to the same theme at the end of the third *Disputatio*.[159]

Poliziano too seems to have appreciated the *Orations* more as a source of information about antiquity than for any philosophical content, but his quarrying was both more extensive than either Ficino's or Landino's, and, unlike theirs, can be related to a surviving manuscript source: none other than the principal manuscript, Parisinus graecus 1962. Nineteen of the forty-one orations in the Parisinus bear notabilia in a hand that (though not hitherto assigned to him) is clearly Poliziano's, and the identification is put beyond all doubt by the fact that one particular sequence of those notabilia (to the concluding paragraphs of *Or.* 18) can be connected with two other surviving documents to Poliziano's scholarly activities: a set of notes he added to his printed text of the works of Ovid (Bodl. Auct. P. 2. 2), and the script of a series of lectures (on the Ovidian *Epistle of Sappho to Phaon*) given in the Florence Studio in early 1481.[160] The *Orations* annotated by

---

[155] See Kibre (1936: 3 ff. and 127).

[156] Marcel (1956: 11–41), Lohe (1980, pp. x ff.).

[157] Ficino (1551: 8); see the introduction to *Orr.* 8–9 below.

[158] Ficino (1551: 415); Marcel (1956: 260 ff.); and see the introduction to *Orr.* 18–21 below.

[159] Cf. Waith (1960), and see the introduction to *Orr.* 15–16 below.

[160] See the introduction to *Orr.* 18–21 below, with Kubo (1985) and Lazzeri (1971: 5–6, 10–11, 31, 46, and 91). The notabilia are all faithfully reported in the

Poliziano are 8 (*daimones*), 14 (Friends and Flatterers), 15 (the Active Life), 17 (Homer and Plato), 18-21 (Socratic love), 22 (the best form of discourse), 23 (farmers and soldiers), 25 (true eloquence), 26 (Homer), 27 (Virtue), 28 (Freedom from pain), 29 (the End of life), 36 (Diogenes), 39-40 (the Good) and 41 (God and Evil)[161]—a sequence that suggests that this particular reader's attention passed over the opening items on Pleasure, and was only properly caught by the topic of *daimones*, but was thereafter held pretty consistently until the end. The oration most heavily annotated is 18, particularly the final paragraphs on Sappho and Anacreon, which are also the source of the sentences transcribed on to the pages of the printed Ovid (to accompany the *Epistle of Sappho to Phaon*) and quoted in the lectures at the Studio; but 17, 29, and 41 have also received considerable attention. Several further traces of this reading, besides the use in the Ovid lectures, can be found in Poliziano's own work: 8. 1 is quoted in the commentary on Statius' *Silvae*, to explain the reference to prophetic tripods in *Silv.* 1. 2. 247;[162] 29. 1 (along with 32. 3—an item as it happens not marked on the manuscript) is also the source for some information about Sybarites retailed in *Miscellanea* 1. 15.[163]

Besides filling in some details of his scholarly activities, the presence of Poliziano's annotations on the Parisinus also settles a long-standing question about the whereabouts of the manuscript in the closing decades of the fifteenth century. Over twenty years ago, in a preliminary study to his edition of the *Didascalicus* of Alcinous, John Whittaker conjectured the Parisinus to be identical with the parchment manuscript of Maximus mentioned in two catalogues of the Medici library, made in 1490 and 1508/11.[164] The identification of one of the annotating hands on the Parisinus as Poliziano's obviously confirms this conjecture, and the implications that follow from it. However and whenever it arrived in Florence,[165]

apparatus to Hobein (1910), under the anonymous rubrics 'schol. rec.' and 'schol. recent.'.

[161] See Hobein's apparatus, and the introductions to the relevant *Orations* below.

[162] Martinelli (1978: 261-2); there is a cross-reference to this note in the *Fasti* commentary, on *Fast.* 1. 20 (Lo Monaco 1991: 31 n. 93).

[163] Poliziano (1553: 219, 239); I have found no mention of Maximus in *Misc.* 2.

[164] See Whittaker (1974, 1977), Baladié (1975).

[165] Piero De' Pazzi's preface to the printed edition of his brother Cosimo's translation of the *Orations*, published in Rome in 1517 (for which, see Whittaker 1974: 336 ff., and below), alleges that it was brought by Lascaris; this is plausible, but there is no independent proof of it.

the Parisinus was clearly in the Medici library, and available to scholars in the Medici ambit, from some time before 1490 until the second or third decade of the next century.[166] Poliziano's attention seems to have concentrated on just one manuscript, and not to have extended to textual matters as opposed to information content. A fifth Florentine reader, and a close associate of his, Zanobi Acciaiuoli, leaves no indications at all of interest in contents, but clearly devoted a very great deal of energy to reading and correcting the text. Laurentianus Conventi Soppressi 4, Gregoras' and Corbinelli's manuscript, which since before the middle of the century had been available in the library of the Badia, and had been used by Skutariotes in the 1450s to make Pope Nicholas' manuscript, is also covered from end to end with repairs and conjectures in Acciaiuoli's highly distinctive hand. The sheer volume of these interventions prompts interesting questions both about his sources, and about his scholarly methods. They also establish him as an unexpectedly influential contributor to the textual tradition of the *Orations*.

Many of the corrections, indeed the majority, were evidently made without external assistance, by the light of Acciaiuoli's own unaided sense of acceptable Greek and stylistic concinnity, since they can be found in no other manuscript source. They are in general of a high quality, and in many cases anticipate corrections repeated much later, in ignorance of his work, by scholars of the seventeenth and eighteenth centuries. Even where his suggestions do not convince, he is generally right that the text requires attention at the point in question. A substantial minority of his corrections, however, seem to have been imported from another manuscript source; some but not all of these latter are marked with the siglum 'M'. On grounds of availability alone, the other manuscript appealed to is overwhelmingly likely to have been the Parisinus, which is known to have been in the Medici library at the required time, and could easily have been brought together with Conv. Sopp. 4—especially by the man who was successively librarian of the Medicea Pubblica in San Marco, and Vatican Librarian under a Medici Pope. It is therefore tempting to suggest

---

[166] At which time it passed into the library of Cardinal Niccolò Ridolfi, nephew of Giovanni De' Medici (Leo X) and cousin of Giulio (Clement VII): see again Whittaker (1974) and Ridolfi (1929). What exactly happened to the manuscript during the ructions of 1494 is unclear, as it does not feature on the lists made for the city of Florence when the Medici's books were confiscated and stored in San Marco.

that Acciaiuoli's siglum 'M' stands for 'Mediceus', and is precisely an acknowledgement of his use of a Medici manuscript. If right, this is highly intriguing, for it would seem to show that he was attempting—perhaps a trifle tentatively, certainly not wholly conscientiously—a piece of modern philological method: a documented collation in the manner of his colleague and mentor Poliziano.[167]

It would also be interesting to know whether or not Acciaiuoli himself thought of this textual work as preparatory to the making of a translation, especially as the margins and one of the flyleaves of Conv. Sopp. 4 have a small number of Latin equivalents of words and phrases from the _Orations_ scribbled on to them.[168] Whatever his intentions, Acciaiuoli's work was indeed almost immediately so used by another Florentine and Medici intimate, Cosimo De' Pazzi, nephew of Lorenzo De' Medici and archbishop of the city. Pazzi's complete Latin version was finished in time to be presented to Pope Julius II, before the deaths of both dedicator and dedicatee in 1513. It seems now to survive in manuscript in one copy only, but was ensured a wider circulation by being printed in Rome in 1517, through the good offices of Pazzi's brother Piero.[169] It is the combination of Cosimo's own preface with that added to the printed edition by Piero that allows something of the genesis of the translation to be reconstructed.

In the supplementary preface, Piero names both Acciaiuoli and Janus Lascaris as patrons and supporters of the work, but does not specify the precise nature and extent of their assistance. In his own preface, which appears in both the manuscript and the printed version, Pazzi names no names, but does make the revealing complaint that he had difficulty in finding even two Greek texts to work from. One at least of the two can be identified without any difficulty as Conv. Sopp. 4. The thought is already suggested by Piero's mention of Acciaiuoli, and is quickly confirmed by two further considerations: the order in which Pazzi translates the _Orations_,

[167] For a fuller analysis of Acciaiuoli's textual work, see Trapp (forthcoming _b_); a number of his better ideas are recorded in the apparatus to Trapp (1994). Poliziano's techniques in textual criticism are discussed by Grafton (1977; 1983, ch. 1, esp. 24–32). Examples of his collating can be seen, for example, on Bodl. Auct. P. 2. 2. (his printed text of Ovid), fol. 440r, and Leningrad MS 2–627 (his text of Apicius), fol. 9ʳ; cf. Rizzo (1973: 168).

[168] See Trapp (forthcoming _b_).

[169] The presentation copy is Vat. lat. 2196; see Kristeller (1967: 350), Ancona (1914: ii. 770–1 (no. 567); 1950: 27 (no. 7)).

beginning with *Or.* 11 on Platonic theology, which it will be remembered is the ordering that originates with Conv. Sopp. 4; and the numerous places where what Pazzi is evidently translating is not the reading of a manuscript, but one of Acciaiuoli's conjectures.[170] The other manuscript Pazzi used cannot be identified with complete certainty, but is surely highly likely to have been the Parisinus, given both his Medici connections, and the fact that the two had already been brought together by Acciaiuoli. What remains tantalizingly obscure is how closely (if at all) either Lascaris or Acciaiuoli supervised Pazzi's work—above all, whether any of Acciaiuoli's textual interventions were made during the process of translation, as opposed to being already there on the manuscript (perhaps for some time) when it was put under Pazzi's gaze.

Besides being informative about the manuscript resources used, Pazzi's preface also offers a view of how the author himself was regarded—something that does not survive from the hand of any of his other Florentine readers. It is in general a highly conventional performance, but worth consideration for its rarity value at least. An intriguing error (it would be interesting to know whose) swells the meagre biography by conflating Tyrian Maximus with the Maximus of Aelius Aristides *Or.* 4 Lenz-Behr (= 47 Dindorf),[171] thus consolidating his social and intellectual status (as a Roman senator complimented on his eloquence by one of the great figures of the Second Sophistic), and locating his ultimate family origins not in Tyre but in Libya. Style and content are then characterized with predictable enthusiasm, the author being presented as the perfect combination of philosophical acuity with high literary culture and dazzling (but not aggressive or overwhelming) oratorical style:

His orations betray a sublime intellect steeped in the divine ambrosia of Homer and Plato, an admirable enthusiasm to preserve the unified philosophy of olden times, and besides a keen literary talent (positively Horatian, in my opinion), overflowing with resourcefulness, figures, exempla and comparisons, of which it is hard to decide whether it has more in common with the orator or the poet. His judgement is perfect, the depth of his knowledge and competence in all literary forms is immense, his style will admit nothing lax or otiose, and keeps tedium at bay with

---

[170] Cf. Trapp (1994, pp. xl–xlii).
[171] Cf. *PIR*² v. 235 (M 400); *RE* Maximus (27).

brevity, novelty of thought, or varied diction, while both demanding and inviting attentiveness. . . . Also to be numbered among his virtues is a finely-honed and practised power in argument, which thanks to the magnitude of his intellect may escape the vulgar, but which to men of culture and education is clearly discernible; such is the marvellous artistry with which this is built, that it gives no impression of seeking to wrest the hearer's assent from him, but instead aims to educate and to persuade in a spirit of devotion to true wisdom.

Beneath the superlatives, one sees a reading that takes the orator at his own estimation, paraphrasing the overt and covert self-descriptions in *Orr.* 1 and 25, and assimilating them to the conventional compliments of Latin rhetorical criticism. It would be interesting to know how much of this derives from general discussion among the Florentine Platonists, how much is owing to guidance from Pazzi's academic patrons, and how much to his own unaided reflections.

One more name remains to be added to the roll of Maximus' Florentine readers. Janus Lascaris, who we have seen may or may not have been responsible for the arrival of the Parisinus in Florence, and certainly had some hand in the production of Pazzi's translation, also owned his own copy of the *Orations*. Surviving as Harleianus graecus 5760, and written in the hand of Petros Hypselas,[172] it is a copy of Vaticanus graecus 1390, very likely made to Lascaris' own commission, though precisely when and where—given his somewhat *mouvementé* career—cannot be determined. In any event, it is heavily corrected and supplemented in Lascaris's hand; like Acciaiuoli, he found the *Orations* a text worth reading with care, and like him, he deserves a place for some of his corrections in a modern apparatus criticus.

When all the Florentine evidence is assembled, the impression is given of something like a fashion for Maximus among the Medici scholars in the decades between 1470 and 1500, very likely prompted to some extent by Lascaris's salesmanship in the first instance, but subsequently acquiring a momentum of its own. If only for that short period, the combination of Platonic doctrine with a wide range of confident literary and historical reference made this seem a particularly useful text, one both to plunder for one's own use and to recommend to the attention of colleagues.

How closely the first northern reader, Reuchlin, can be associated

---

[172] See Vogel-Gardthausen (1909: 387), Gamillscheg-Harlfinger (1981: 349).

with this pattern is unclear. He certainly studied in Florence, with Demetrius Chalcondyles, in the 1490s, but was also in Milan and (in 1482) in Rome. Given this chronology, there would seem to be good reason for supposing that it was not in fact in Florence that the *Orations* first came to his attention, for the earliest indication of any interest on his part takes the form of a Latin translation of *Or.* 41, on God and Evil, dated 1488, well before his Florentine sojourn.[173] However that may be, it is clear that his enthusiasm for Maximus extended to more than just a single essay in translation. At his death in 1522 he could bequeath to his home town of Pforzheim a manuscript of the *Orations* apparently descending from Vaticanus graecus 1950.[174] He also drew on five other *Orations*—2 (Prayer), 4 (poets and philosophers on the gods), 8–9 (*daimones*) and 10 (recollection)—for various points of information included in his *De Arte Cabalistica Libri Tres*, published in Hagenau in 1517.[175] The topics of the orations thus singled out are at least of the same general kind as we have seen attracting the attentions of the Florentines.

SOME LOOSE ENDS

It will have been clear from what has already been said that the account of patterns of diffusion and interest that can be given for the *Orations* in the fifteenth century is far from complete. Although some readers and some directions of attention can be disentangled, it is often not possible to say how a given reader discovered the text, or what copy he had under his eyes. Equally, not all references in library catalogues can be associated securely with surviving codices, and it is not always possible to be sure where the surviving items were at any given time. This section of the account must end with a few further isolated fragments.

[173] Basel, Universitätsbibliothek E III 15, foll. 299–305; the translation is dedicated to Johannes de Lapide. See Trithemius (1495, fol. 61ᵛ), Kristeller (1990: 64–5).

[174] The existence of this manuscript is attested by the copy of the inventory of Reuchlin's library on Vat. Pal. lat. 1925 (Christ 1924: 3–4, 34 ff., 75 ff.). The case for connecting it with Vat. gr. 1950 rests on the contents: it too joins the *Orations* with the *Didascalicus*, Marcus Aurelius, and Xenophon. It is frustrating not to know where Vat. gr. 1950 was at the time.

[175] See the introductions to the orations in question below. Christ (1924: 76) describes references to Maximus as frequent in Reuchlin's work, so there are no doubt more to be found.

The whereabouts of Vaticanus graecus 1390 through this century are a particularly tantalizing puzzle. We have seen that it is likely to have been used by Apostoles for his *Proverbia*, and by Hypselas to make Harleianus 5760. Besides that, it seems to be the source of two further manuscript texts (Holkhamensis graecus 101 (281), which marries *Orr.* 30–5 with the *Didascalicus* and Libanius *Or.* 17; and Ambrosianus B 98 Sup. (120), which inserts *Or.* 28 into a collection mainly devoted to hexameter poetry), and a set of twenty-two excerpts (from *Orr.* 30–3) copied on to an end-leaf of a text of Aristotle's *Problems*, in a late fifteenth-century hand.[176] One has the sense of a manuscript in circulation, but without the possibility of assigning it to particular places and possessors.

At least one other new manuscript of the whole text of the *Orations* was made in this century, Ambrosianus R 25 Sup. (710), which was copied (like Pope Nicholas's codex) from Laurentianus Conventi Soppressi 4, and which by the 1550s had lodged in Padua;[177] nothing can be reconstructed of its early movements and whereabouts. There is another very large set of excerpts on Neapolitanus graecus 100 which seem to date from this century; and further sequences of *notabilia* in unidentified hands in the margins of Vaticanus graecus 1950 and Laur. Conv. Sopp. 4. The Neapolitan excerpts, which number ninety-five and are drawn from thirty-one of the forty-one orations, show the same kind of interest in the striking thought and the well-turned sentence as was shown a century before by Gregoras.[178] The Vatican and Laurentian marginalia, almost all straight repetitions of names from the text, seem to betray the same kind of concern as Poliziano's, with the *Orations* as a source of information about figures from Classical history, literature, and myth.

---

[176] Parisinus graecus 1865, foll. 4 and 7; the excerpts tally perfectly with passages marked in Vat. gr. 1390, and the same marginal note, in the same hand, appears on Vat. gr. 1390, fol. 85ᵛ, and Paris. gr. 1865, fol. 4ʳ. The Paris manuscript once belonged to Leoniceno (Niccolò da Lonigo, 1428–1524), but the excerpting hand does not seem to be his: see Vat. gr. 1390, fol. 22ʳ, with Mugnai Carrara (1991: 94, 132).

[177] Notes on fol. i mention the name of one Niccolò Londa.

[178] Neap. gr. 100 (II. C. 32), foll. 320 ff. These excerpts, which would probably repay further study, seem to have been drawn either from Paris. gr. 1962, or one of its closer copies, like Vat. gr. 1950 or Bodl. Auct. T. 4 (since at *Or.* 31. 1 (line 9 Trapp) they read ἄλλης rather than (with Vat. gr. 1390 and Laur. Conv. Sopp. 4) ὅλης.

FROM 1517 TO 1600

Manuscript copies of the *Orations* continued to be made through the first half of the sixteenth century: three more from descendants of Vaticanus graecus 1390, and another fourteen from descendants of Laurentianus Conventi Soppressi 4.[179] Together with the older copies already discussed, and some codices now lost, they can be shown to have passed through or come to rest in over twenty libraries, in Italy, Germany, France, and Spain, ranging from those of the Pope and the Fuggers to those of private scholars like Lascaris and Georg Tanner.[180] This was, however, also the period in which the first printed copies began to be produced and to circulate.

The translator of the *Orations*, Cosimo De' Pazzi, had died in 1513, but his brother Piero saw his Latin version through the press in Rome in 1517. The short preface which he added explains the circumstances of publication, and assigns a leading role in the 'recovery' of Maximus to Janus Lascaris, both as the man who brought Lorenzo his manuscript of the *Orations*, and as an

---

[179] From descendants of Vat. gr. 1390: Vindob. philol. gr. 335 (*Orr.* 30-5), Paris. gr. 1837 (30-4), and Bern. 662 (*Orr.* 33-5, 1-15, 30-2). From descendants of Laur. Conv. Sopp. 4: Vat. gr. 236, Angel. gr. 25, Barb. gr. 157, Vat. Pal. gr. 53, Vat. Pal. gr. 386, Monac. gr. 67, Monac. gr. 75, Scor. gr. 26 (R. II. 6), Matrit. gr. 4744 (O 13), Ravennas Cl. 381 (*Orr.* 17, 26, 4, and 13, plus excerpts), Paris. gr. 460, Paris. gr. 1817, Paris. gr. 1837, and Paris. Genov. 3394. A good number of these manuscripts can be attributed to known scribes, and thus something of their time and likely place of origin reconstructed. A more detailed story, concerning Venice, the Vatican, the Imperial Ambassador, and the book-dealer Antonio Eparco, can be pieced together over Vat. gr. 236 and Scor. gr. 26: for the raw materials, see Devreesse (1965: 419 ff.), Legrand (1885, p. ccx ff.), Dorez (1893: 19 ff.); Giotopoulou-Sisilianou (1978: 110 ff.).

[180] Italy: Vatican (Vat. 236, Vat. lat. 2196); Medici library (Laur. Med. 85. 15); library of SS. Giovanni e Paolo, Venice (lost codex; cf. Gesner 1545, fol. 509ʳ); library of Princes of Carpi (Holkh. 101); D. Grimani (lost codex: Pico's); Leoniceno (Paris. 1865; see above); G. F. Torresano d'Asola (Paris. 1817); J. Lascaris (Harl. 5760); N. Ridolfi (Harl. 5760; Paris. 1837, 1865, 1962); P. Strozzi (Paris. 1837, 1865, 1962); George of Corinth (Angel. 25); G. A. Sforza (Angel. 25); F. Orsini (Vat. 1390). Beyond the Alps: A. Arlenius (lost codex, descending from Laur. Conv. Sopp. 4: used by Stephanus for ed. pr.—see below, pp. lxxxii–lxxxiii); J. Reuchlin (lost codex; see above, p. lxxvii); G. Tanner (Vat. Pal. 386); J. J. Fugger (Monac. 67; Monac. 75); U. Fugger (Vat. Pal. 53; Pal. 129); Beatus Rhenanus (lost codex (excerpts) used in revision of Latin translation; see below, p. lxxx); J. Strazelius (lost codex, probably containing only *Orr.* 30-4/5, used by Stephanus); C. de Guise (Paris. Genov. 3394); C. De' Medici (Paris. 1837, 1865, 1962); Bibliothèque royale (Paris. gr. 1817, 1837, 1865, 1962); Diego Hurtado de Mendoza (Scor. 26); Francisco de Mendoza y Bobadilla (Matr. 4744).

enthusiastic supporter of plans for publication.[181] Also reprinted is
the original dedicatory preface composed by Cosimo to Julius II,
already discussed.

What interest the appearance of Pazzi's translation in print
aroused is hard to determine. Though generously sized, the volume
is not particularly elegantly printed, and it contains no aids to
the reader in the form of notes or headings. Copies surviving in
modern libraries are usually devoid of manuscript marginalia, and
do not seem to have been heavily thumbed. It is, however, the fact
that, within two years of this first printed version, a second had
appeared, providing a revised text, a more reflective introduction,
and marginal notes. This revision, by Beatus Rhenanus, was
published by Froben in Basel in 1519.[182] Unlike Pazzi, whose
milieu allowed him to take for granted the interest and worth of
a Platonizing text, Rhenanus felt the need to be more elaborately
apologetic, both in his preface and in his notes. The modern
world would do well, he argues, to take note of such impeccably
Christian sentiments as are urged in *Or.* 12, on the hurtfulness of
retaliation;[183] and in the margins of the translation, he notes
another Christian touch in *Or.* 24. 2. At the same time, he sees a
beneficial example also in the form of Maximus' discourses.
Philosophical declamation, as practised before select and sober
audiences not only by Maximus but also by Apuleius in his *Florida*,
and described by Pliny in his *Epistles*, provides a model that the
rowdy educational institutions of the present day would do well to
imitate.

The third printed version of the *Orations* to be released into the
world was also a translation, and again a mere revision of Pazzi's,
made by one G. Albertus Pictus and published in Paris in 1554,
with a dedication to the royal councillor Antoine Fumée. Although
he had no Greek text to consult, and seems even to be ignorant of
the existence of Rhenanus' version, Pictus claims to have improved

---

[181] Cf. above, pp. lxxiv-lxxv. Pazzi is of course wrong in his claim that the
manuscript Lascaris brought was the first to come to Florence: that distinction
seems to belong instead to Laur. Conv. Sopp. 4. For the full text of Pazzi's preface,
see Whittaker (1974: 337).

[182] In his dedicatory epistle (p. 4), Rhenanus says that he used 'graeca quaedam
excerpta', rather than a complete Greek text, to make his revision. These excerpts
seem now to be lost—there is no sign of them, for instance, in Sélestat—but it has
been conjectured by Sicherl (1978: 42 n. 37a) that they were copied for Rhenanus
from Reuchlin's manuscript by Johannes Cuno.

[183] p. 4 ; cf. also Horawitz-Hartfelder (1886: 133 ff.).

on Pazzi's version as much as could be done without summoning Maximus himself back from the dead.

Pictus' version was the last complete Latin translation of the *Orations* to be published as an item to itself. From this point on full translations appeared only together with the Greek text. Latin translations of individual orations, however, continued to be made up until the closing years of the century, and printed into the next. Arnold Feron's rendering of *Or.* 2 was printed in 1557, along with two orations of Aelius Aristides, Johannes Caselius' of *Or.* 14 in 1587, and again in 1590. John Rainolds, lecturer in Greek and President of Corpus Christi College, Oxford, had completed his translations of *Orr.* 7, 15, and 16 by 1581, even though they were not printed until 1613, with reprints in 1614, 1619, and 1628. It is only at the very end of the century that the first vernacular translation appears: F. Morel's French version of *Or.* 23, printed in 1596 (and followed by *Orr.* 4 and 28 in 1607).[184]

The appearance of the Greek text of the *Orations* in print had to wait for the middle of the century, though had matters turned out only slightly differently, it might have appeared a few years earlier than it actually did. In the early 1550s the Austrian lawyer Georg Tanner, studying in Padua, bought a manuscript of Maximus from a Cretan colleague by the name of Thomas Trivesanos. The manuscript survives, complete with Tanner's ex-libris and the sketch of a possible title-page, as also does a set of letters that passed between Tanner and the Basel printers Bonifacius and Basilius Amerbach between 1554 and 1565. Tanner's plan was for a bilingual edition, in which the Greek text from his manuscript would be printed (by Oporinus, rather than by the Amerbachs) alongside Pazzi's Latin, with the volume dedicated to Archduke Maximilian of Austria, and Tanner himself prominently identified as first editor and benefactor of the world of scholarship. But although, according to his own complaïnts, Tanner sent both manuscript and instructions to Basel, Oporinus never proceeded with the project. The reasons for this are unclear, but may well have had to do with Tanner's haste in sending his text before he had properly marked it up, and his lofty assumption that other people could be left to do the work of adding in the Latin translation.[185]

---

[184] For further details, see Trapp (1994, pp. lii–liv).

[185] For the whole story, see Trapp (1992); Tanner's correspondence is printed by

Whatever the explanation for Tanner's disappointment, it was Henri Estienne (Stephanus) who in the event produced the *editio princeps* in Geneva in 1557.[186] His Greek text was based on a manuscript borrowed from his friend Arnoldus Arlenius (Arnout van Eynthouts), whom he thanks in the preface, while also acknowledging some extra help from another codex borrowed from Ioannes Stracelius (Jean Strazel), 'in paucis tamen λόγοις'.[187] Neither of these two manuscripts of the *Orations* now survives, but it is not difficult to reconstruct their provenance. Stracelius', containing only a few orations, and cited in Estienne's critical notes for passages in *Orr.* 30 and 31, is likely to have contained only *Orr.* 30-4 or 30-5, and thus to have been related to Holkh. 101, Paris. 1837, and Vindob. 335.[188] The main basis for the edition, Arlenius' codex, is quite certain to be a copy of Laur. Conv. Sopp. 4, made some time late in the fifteenth century or early in the sixteenth. The reason for which this can so confidently be asserted is that, in numerous places, the readings which Estienne prints in his edition are ones that can otherwise be found neither in the original state of Conv. Sopp. 4, nor in any other surviving manuscript, but instead reproduce the 'corrections' added to Conv. Sopp. 4 by Zanobi Acciaiuoli.[189] Since Conv. Sopp. 4 itself never belonged to Arlenius, what Estienne borrowed from him must have been a copy, which he would have been in a good position to buy, or have made.

Estienne's preface to his edition is mainly preoccupied with manuscripts and readings (not only in the text of Maximus), and

Stintzing (1879) and Jenny (1982-3), and the manuscript (Vat. Pal. 386) discussed by Canart (1973) and Noailles (1941).

[186] For Geneva rather than Paris as the place of publication, see Reverdin (1980-1); the title-page ('ex officina Henrici Stephani Parisiensis typographi') is intentionally misleading, suppressing mention of Calvinist Geneva without telling a direct lie.

[187] For Arlenius, see Graux (1880) = Andres (1982) and Jenny (1964); and for Strazel, Dionisotti (1983).

[188] Since Estienne's preface also mentions that the manuscript he borrowed contained excerpts from Polybius as well as a text of Maximus, there is a fair chance that it is Vindob. hist. gr. 25, copied in Venice in 1504 and purchased by Strazel in 1536, and now containing the text of Polybius alone.

[189] These tell-tale readings can be seen over and again in the apparatus to Hobein (1910), where divergences between the reading of the *editio princeps* and that of the Parisinus are scrupulously noted. Acciaiuoli thus emerges as a major (unwitting) influence on the vulgate tradition of the *Orations*, from 1557 up until Davies's second edition of 1740. See also Trapp (1994, pp. xlii-xliv).

with pouring Protestant scorn on Cosimo De' Pazzi's prowess as a translator (although, ironically, Pazzi had been closer to good manuscript sources than he was). He has little interest, either in the preface or in the brief textual notes at the end of the volume, in offering any view of the author or of the contents of his work. His description of Maximus is perfunctory, acknowledging him in barely more than a sentence as a Platonist, a refined stylist, and a succesful combiner of the *utile* with the *dulce*. The verdict is in line with those of Pazzi and Rhenanus, but it is expressed with considerably less verve.

The appearance of the *Orations* in print, in the normal way, prompted if not a flood at least a steady stream of textual critical attention: Leopardi, Scaliger, Schott, Canter, and Portus all directed their attention to Maximus, among a host of other newly printed authors all clamouring for the healing hand of conjectural emendation.[190] Otherwise the visible pattern of attention to Maximus follows the lines already laid down in the preceding century, with the *Orations* more likely to be cited for isolated items of information that they happen to transmit, than to be either discussed or imitated in themselves. A characteristically casual and opportunistic example is provided by Pierio Valeriano, who takes over the story of Mithaecus' unsuccessful visit to Sparta (*Or.* 17. 1) in the preface to book 1 of his *Hieroglyphica*, published in Basel in 1556. In two respects, however, one can at least see some longer-term trends at work in the borrowings, one of which seems to begin in this century, while the other continues a pattern already initiated in the century before.

The new trend is represented by Lilio Gregorio Giraldi, who in his study of pagan religion, the *De Deis Gentium*, published in 1548, draws three times on the *Orations* for information about ancient religious practices: on pp. 98–9, for the list of objects of worship given in *Or.* 2. 4–7; on p. 612, for the story of Midas' prayers to Silenus (*Or.* 5. 1); and also on p. 83, for the story of Psaphon and his birds (*Or.* 29. 4), though here it is clear that the story has come to Giraldi via Apostoles' *Proverbia* rather than directly from the text of the *Orations*. Psaphon's birds, indeed, seem

---

[190] Scaliger's, Canter's, and Schott's emendations are reported by Heinsius in his editions of 1607 and 1614, with Scaliger's also appearing in manuscript in his copy of Estienne's edition (Bodl. Auct. K. 5. 12); Leopardi's are in his *Emendationum . . . libri XX* (1568).

to have had quite a fashion, since they also crop up in Georg Pictorius von Villingen's *De daemonum . . . ortu . . . Isagoge*,[191] where Psaphon, along with the Emperor Domitian, is given as an example of of a *pseudotheus*, a demon charged by the Devil with the task of diverting human worship from its proper objects. This use of the *Orations* begins (and no doubt does much to cause) a continuing interest in them as a source for ancient religion, of which further instances will be found below.

The other use found for the *Orations* in this century was as a source of knowledge about Greek lyric poetry and poets. The scholars who mined the *Orations* in this way were pursuing a seam opened up in the previous century by Poliziano, but they seem to have done so without any direct knowledge that he had been there before them. In his printed Ovid and in his Studio lectures on the Ovidian *Epistle of Sappho to Phaon*, Poliziano had pointed to the presence of biographical information about Sappho in the closing paragraph of *Oration* 18, where it is used as part of an argument in defence of the respectability of Socrates' erotic confessions. Since neither Poliziano's Ovid nor his lectures (not printed until 1971) were available to scholars, it must have been quite independently that the same realization was made by Estienne, who printed a long extract from *Or.* 18. 9 in the appendix of new material added to the second edition of his *Pindari Olympia . . . (et) Caeterorum octo lyricorum carmina*, published in 1566.[192] Estienne, however, printed the extract as a single testimonium, and did not take the further step of separating out from Maximus' paragraphs the verbatim quotations from Sappho's poetry which they contain (in some cases, uniquely). This piece of scholarly processing had to wait another two years, for Fulvio Orsini's *Carmina Novem Illustrium Feminarum . . . et lyricorum*, published in Antwerp in 1568. Here, following the standard pattern of his work, Orsini divides Maximus' testimony up into a description of Sappho (*Or.* 18. 7, p. 3), three fragments (all from *Or.* 18. 9: 150 L-P, p. 15; 155 L-P, p. 15; 159 L-P, p. 16), and two testimonia (also from *Or.* 18. 9, on pp. 18 and 22-3).[193] He also drew

---

[191] Published in Basel in 1563, in a volume with the same author's *Pantopolion, De Apibus*, and *De Speciebus Magiae Ceremonialis.*

[192] Estienne had missed this material at the time of the first edition, published in 1560, even though he himself had published his text of Maximus only three years before that. There is likewise no use made of Maximus in the section on Sappho in Michael Neander's *Anthologia Pindarica* of 1556.

[193] Referred to a further nine times in the notes on pp. 285-94.

two fragments of Anacreon, and four testimonia, from *Orr.* 18, 20, 21, 29, and 37,[194] and quoted one additional passage (from *Or.* 37. 5) three times over, as a testimonium to Telesilla, Alcaeus, and Tyrtaeus. This second way of using the *Orations* had an even longer future career than the first: Maximus is still regularly cited in editions of the archaic lyric poets, for precisely the same items as are isolated by Orsini.[195]

FROM 1600 TO 1839

Daniel Heinsius' edition of Maximus, along with Alcinous, Apuleius, and other Platonist and Pythagorean matter, appeared in 1607, followed by a second edition, containing Maximus and Alcinous alone, in 1614. Heinsius reprinted Estienne's text, but collated it against Parisinus graecus 1962, lent to him by Isaac Casaubon from the Bibliothèque royale, and two other manuscripts;[196] in the normal manner of the times, he seems only to have considered alternatives to the vulgate text where it struck him as obviously at fault, so that his edition remains a version of Estienne (and of the tradition from Conv. Sopp. 4), rather than a version based on the Parisinus. His translation makes a more decisive break with Estienne, being substantially rewritten, and his notes are still more of an innovation: besides discussing textual variants, they make a serious effort—the first in print—to analyse the philosophical content of the *Orations*, and relate it to other Platonist texts (like those included in the same volume in the first edition). Both by the nature of his annotation, and by the collocation of the *Orations* with other items, Heinsius offered them again for philosophical attention, in a manner not attempted by Pazzi, Rhenanus, Pictus, or Estienne. But this does not mean that he had no eye for Maximus' literary qualities. Appended to the main body of the work in both the first and the second edition is a short essay of Heinsius' own, in imitation of the styles of Maximus and Apuleius: a 'dissertatio Platonica de pulchro Socratico'.

The next two printed editions of Maximus to appear were simple derivatives from Heinsius. The first, containing the *Orations* alone,

---

[194] Fr. 402 *PMG*, from *Or.* 18. 9, on p. 134; testimonia on pp. 147 (*Or.* 29. 2), 148 (*Or.* 20. 1); 149–50 (*Orr.* 37. 5 and 21. 2–3); cf. also p. 321.

[195] See further the headnote to *Orr.* 18–21, on pp. 158–9 below.

[196] One was a full text borrowed from Marquardt Freher, the other a set of excerpts lent by Sixtus Arcerius; both now seem to be lost.

was published in Paris by Claude Lariot in 1630; the second appeared in Oxford, from the Sheldonian Theatre, in 1677, and joined Maximus with the *sententiae* of Demophilus. Neither contains any exegetic material, though the Oxford edition does at least adjust the text to take account of some of the suggestions made in Heinsius' notes. It was only in 1703 that anything like a new edition appeared, from the hand of John Davies. Though essentially retaining the vulgate text and Heinsius' translation, Davies made his own alterations to the latter, and in the notes he sought to present not only Estienne's and Heinsius' thoughts on the text, but also a good proportion of observations of his own.

The edition of 1703, however, was neither Davies's only nor his most substantial contribution to the study and diffusion of the *Orations*. He continued to work on the text of Maximus, accumulating a much more substantial set of annotations, with a view to producing a second edition. In the process he came to the welcome realization that there was more manuscript evidence than had not yet properly been used by editors: not only in the Parisinus, which had been employed only in a subsidiary role by Heinsius, but also, lying conveniently to hand, Harleianus 5760, once Lascaris's and now in England in the Harleian collection.[197] Besides their interesting alternative readings, these codices (of which the Parisinus at least was clearly both old and authoritative) also presented their contents in a different and more attractive order. Davies died before he could himself complete the project of a new edition, taking account both of his own further work, and the new data from the Harleianus and the Parisinus, but it was taken up and carried through by John Ward and the Society for the Encouragement of Learning.[198] When the revised edition finally appeared in 1740, it not only presented the 'new' order of contents, and a text now purged of (among other things) Zanobi Acciaiuoli's *rifacimenti*; it also incorporated a set of further textual notes contributed by Jeremiah Markland, which have a good claim to being the single

---

[197] See Wright (1972: 286). It is presumably more likely that Davies consulted the manuscript in the time of Edward Harley, second Earl of Oxford (1689-1741), rather than in the time of Robert, the first Earl (1661-1724). The Harleian manuscripts were not bought for the nation until 1753.

[198] For the story, see Ward's preface, pp. 3-5 and 9-11. Davies had completed the draft of a preface in Mar. 1728, and died in Mar. 1732; the *Orations* were the Society's first publication, suggested by Dr Richard Mead, to whom Ward's preface is addressed. Ward himself (1679?-1758) was Professor of Rhetoric at Gresham College from 1720 onwards.

most significant contribution to the textual criticism of the *Orations* ever published.[199]

The remaining eighteenth-century edition is a kind of third version of Davies, supervised by J. J. Reiske, and appearing in Leipzig in 1774-5. Besides repositioning the editorial matter as footnotes rather than endnotes, Reiske added in a number of highly acute textual suggestions of his own, taken from notes he had made some twenty years before. His preface is marked by a striking lack of enthusiasm both for the task—undertaken when he claimed to be 'exhausted with slaving over Plutarch'[200]—and for the author. All previous editors had presented Maximus as the ideal blend of improving subject-matter with delightful style;[201] Reiske brands him impatiently as a quibbling sophist, who betrays the gravity of his subject-matter with an ill-judged levity of style.[202]

One more Latin translation appeared in the first half of the seventeenth century, a version of *Or.* 13, on prophecy and Fate, included by Hugo Grotius in his collection *Philosophorum Sententiae de Fato et de eo quod in nostra est potestate*, posthumously published in 1640. F. Morel, who had published a French translation of *Or.* 23 in 1596, followed it with versions of *Orr.* 4 and 28 in 1607. Complete translations into French then followed, at intervals, from N. Guillebert (1617), J.-H.-S. Formey (1764), and J.-J. Combes-Dounous (1802), with excerpts from Formey (*Orr.* 23-4, on farmers and soldiers) also being published in J.-F. Dreux du Radier's *Temple du Bonheur* (1769). Piero De' Bardi's complete Italian version was published in 1642, and C. T. Damm's German in 1764

---

[199] pp. 652-727 (with Davies's notes, in larger type, on pp. 497-644). Markland had made his own notes on Davies's first edition in the summer of 1739 and revised them in the light of the second thoughts he found in the proofs sent him by Ward. Besides his comments on individual passages he also contributes an argument, now long superseded, for supposing that the *Orations* went through two editions in antiquity (pp. 648-51), and a rather better-founded discussion of improvisation and the travelling orator, in which he compared Maximus to Lucian, Aristides, and Apuleius (pp. 651-2).

[200] 'Defatigatus in ergastulo Plutarcheo'—a reference to the preparation of his complete edition of 1774-82.

[201] Even Markland (p. 652): 'Nihilominus utilissimum et saepe repetita lectione dignum esse hunc Auctorem existimo, cum propter Rerum et Quaestionum, de quibus disserat, momentum et gravitatem; tum ob eximias Ipsius dotes, Ingenii Acumen et Amoenitatem simul, Inventionem felicissimam, Eruditionem diffusissimam. Utinam multo plures huiusce generis antiquos Scriptores haberemus.'

[202] Preface, pp. iv-v; cf. Hobein (1910, pp. ix-x). Between Reiske's edition and that of Friedrich Dübner there was only one more, another adaptation of Davies's second, produced in Vienna in 1810 by Neophytos Doukas.

(with a third edition in 1845).[203] English readers had to wait for Thomas Taylor's two-volume rendition of 1804.[204] Before that, however, Henry Vaughan had made an English version of *Or. 7* (diseases of body and soul), from Rainolds's Latin, and included it in his *Olor Iscanus* of 1651;[205] and George Benson had translated *Or.* 5 (prayer) for his *Two Letters to a Friend* (1737) and *A Collection of Tracts* (1748).

The general impression given by a survey of editions and translations is of a respectable, but far from overwhelmingly large, circulation for an author who was 'on the curriculum', worth keeping in print, as good an exercise yard as any for textual scholarship, and available for exploitation when the need arose, but never exactly in the front rank in any respect. The picture that emerges when references to the *Orations*, and exploitations of their contents, are surveyed is of the same kind.

The antiquarian use of the *Orations* as a source for pagan religious practice, begun by Giraldi, continues in Gerard Voss's *De Theologia Gentili et Physiologia Christiana, sive de Origine et Progressu Idololatriae*, published in 1641. The first, four-book edition refers six times to *Or.* 2, and once each to *Orr.* 5, 8, 20, and 29; the augmented, nine-book edition, posthumously published in 1668, adds another six references to *Or.* 2.[206] Two of Voss's references, from the first edition, recur in Lord Herbert of Cherbury's *De Religione Gentilium* (1663), though it is clear that they do not derive from an independent reading of the *Orations*.[207] But it was not only in works of religious antiquarianism that the *Orations* could be found useful. They are also plundered by Franciscus Junius in his two treatises on ancient art, *De Pictura Veterum* (1637), revised and translated as *The Painting of the Ancients* (1638), and the *Catalogus Architectorum* . . . (1694). A dozen times, Junius resorts to the *Orations* for points of psychology, aesthetics, and biography germane to his argument, in *Orr.* 3, 6, 8, 10, 15, 17, 19, 26, 33, 34, and 38.[208]

---

[203] Hobein's reference (p. iv) to a version in Italian and Spanish, published in Venice in 1559, is an error inherited from Schweiger (1830–4); the work in question is the *Dialoghi* of Massimo Troiano.

[204] Reprinted in 1994 as volume vi of a uniform edition of Taylor's works by the Prometheus Trust, Frome.

[205] Along with versions of Plutarch *De Capienda* and *De Morbis*; also from Rainolds; cf. Martin (1957: 115–22).

[206] See the headnotes to *Orr.* 2, 5, 8, 20, and 29, for references.

[207] *De Religione*, 70 (*Or.* 2. 4) and 89 (*Or.* 2. 8).

[208] See headnotes below.

A more philosophical interest is shown by Hugo Grotius and Ralph Cudworth. Grotius' translation of *Or.* 13, in his collection of philosophical theories of Fate and Free Will, has already been mentioned; he also made use of *Or.* 11 in his most popular work of Christian apologetic. In both cases, it is easy to see what it is about the *Oration* in question that has attracted him. Just as Maximus' Platonizing defence of the reality of Free Will appeals to his Arminian allegiances, so the natural theology of *Or.* 11. 5 chimes with his project in the *De Veritate Religionis Christianae*. This work was first composed in Dutch verse, then rewritten in Latin prose, with a first edition in 1627, followed by a second and a third in 1629 and 1640. Maximus does not appear in the first Latin edition, but he does in the second and the third, both in the main text and in the footnote references.[209] It is *Or.* 11 again that chiefly attracts the attention of Ralph Cudworth in his *True Intellectual System of the Universe*, published in 1678. This time, however, it is not only the argument from consensus in § 5 that is in question, but also the exposition of the cosmic hierarchy in § 12, both of which are appealed to twice, with one further separate reference to the depiction of Zeus in *Or.* 4. 9.[210]

Authors of devotional literature too found the *Orations* a useful source, most notably Jeremy Taylor (1613–67), Lord Bishop of Down, Connor, and Dromore, who quotes and refers nine times in his *History of the Life and Death of the Holy Jesus* (1649), *Eniautos* (1653), *The Worthy Communicant* (1660), and *Ductor Dubitantium* (1660). His favoured pieces were *Orr.* 11 and 12, though 2, 14, and 36 are also exploited.[211] The two translations by George Benson (1699–1762), already mentioned, show the continuation of this strand of interest in the following century, and it seems not to have come to an end even then. According to Thomas Clarkson (1760–1846) in his *A Portraiture of Quakerism* (1806), a (somewhat doctored) version of *Or.* 11.5 was one of the texts regularly used by Quaker apologists to prove the partial anticipation of their ideas by the best of the pagans.[212]

A more generalized interest can be seen to be reflected in Robert

---

[209] See headnotes to *Orr.* 11 and 12.

[210] See introductions to *Orr.* 4 and 11.

[211] See introductions to *Orr.* 2, 11, 12, 14, and 36. There is a complete edition of Taylor's works by Heber and Eden (1847–54).

[212] Clarkson (1806: ii. 6, pp. 164 ff.); cf. p. 96 below. I owe this reference to Dr D. P. Coleman.

Burton's use of the *Orations* in his *Anatomy of Melancholy* (1621), and in the entries made in a manuscript commonplace book by Richard Byfield, Rector of Long Ditton, some time between 1657 and 1664. Among the hundreds of quotations from classical literature in the *Anatomy* are a dozen drawn from the *Orations*, concentrating mainly on the topics of diseases of the soul, love, and *daimones*.[213] Burton's notes refer both to Rainolds's translation of *Or.* 7, and to Pazzi's complete version, but he probably used Estienne's edition as his principal source. At any rate, a copy of Estienne is number 1029 in the inventory of his library published by N. Kiessling.[214] Byfield's notebook, which survives as Harleianus 1790, contains excerpts from Ficino's Plotinus, Epictetus, Plutarch's *Moralia*, nine Platonic dialogues, and Timaeus Locrus, as well as from the *Orations*, all preceded by the text of an oration in praise of rhetoric, given by Byfield in Oxford on 3 December 1657. He starts on fol. 66 (65) with ten extracts from *Or.* 11, followed by fourteen from *Or.* 12, nine from *Or.* 13, three from *Or.* 14, and five from *Or.* 15, finishing up with a mere two from *Or.* 16 on fol. 71 (70), where his enthusiasm seems to have given out.[215]

One last curiosity can conveniently be mentioned here, though it is possible that it may belong in strict chronology to the following section. Among the holdings of the library of Corpus Christi College, Oxford, is a copy of Heinsius' first edition of the *Orations*, pressmarked IV. 313a. The flyleaves at the end of the volume bear a number of annotations in ink in a nineteenth-century hand, which a pencilled note on the title page identifies as that of Thomas De Quincey (1785–1859), 'to whom the vol. once belonged'.[216] The inked notes cover both Alcinous' ('Albinus') *Didascalicus* and the *Orations*, and testify to a close reading of both texts, commenting not only on points of vocabulary (e.g. the distinction in meaning between *prosthesis* and *prostheke*, apropos of *Or.* 39. 1), but also on Greek history (apropos of *Or.* 35. 8), and on resemblances between the thought of Maximus and that of more recent figures (apropos of

---

[213] See introductions to *Orr.* 7, 8–9, 11, 18–21, 23–4, and 28.
[214] Kiessling (1988: 195).
[215] For further details, see the introductions to the relevant *Orations*.
[216] The pencilled note is initialled 'S.H.H.', presumably Shadworth Hollway Hodgson (1832–1912), honorary fellow of the college. Comparison with some samples of De Quincey's hand in the illustrations to Lindop (1981) suggests that the identification is correct.

Orr. 11. 9 and 41. 4).[217] The volume unfortunately bears no marks that would help to put a date to De Quincey's reading of the *Orations*.

FROM 1840 TO THE PRESENT

De Quincey's notes are almost the last sign of an interest in Maximus outside the narrow circle of professional scholars, whose exclusive domain he became in the middle and later years of the nineteenth century. Since that time there have been three full scholarly editions. Friedrich (Jean Frédéric) Dübner's,[218] published by A. Firmin Didot in 1840 and reissued two years later, has the distinction of being the first to have been based solidly on the Paris manuscript, which is described on pp. vii–viii of the editor's general introduction, and reported with some fullness in the *relatio critica* that occupies pp. ix–xxii. It was, however, another seventy years before the *Orations* were given the full modern scholarly treatment. Hermann Hobein, a pupil of Wilamowitz's at Göttingen, began his engagement with Maximus with his doctoral dissertation of 1895.[219] His Teubner edition of 1910 is a work of great industry and continuing value, but more distinguished for the thoroughness of its scope than for sureness of judgement. The seventy-page introduction offers a meticulous survey of the surviving manuscripts, and of all known printed editions and translations,[220] but combines this with a bizarre and erroneous reconstruction of the transmission, which, while privileging the Paris manuscript, manages not to identify it as the ancestor of all other surviving copies, and simultaneously misses the importance of Vaticanus graecus 1390 and Laurentianus Conventi Soppressi 4. The text itself is presented with a very full set of supporting material—not only a large apparatus criticus, but also secondary apparatuses recording parallel passages (within and without the *Orations*), scholia and marginalia from the Paris manuscript, and excerpts [221]—and there is a comprehensive

---

[217] For details, see the introductions to *Orr.* 11, 35, and 41.

[218] 1802–67. Dübner came to Paris from Gotha to work on the new Didot edition of Estienne's *Thesaurus Linguae Graecae*, and subsequently naturalized. His Maximus makes a single volume with Theophrastus' *Characters*, the *Meditations* of Marcus Aurelius, the *Discourses* of Epictetus, and the *Tabula Cebetis*.

[219] Hobein (1895).

[220] The list of manuscripts misses only Matr. 4744 (O. 13), the excerpts in Valicell. 182 (xcii), and two peripheral codices from Mount Athos (5736, 6190).

[221] The scholia and marginalia include both the old Byzantine scholia, and

index of names and quotations. Here too, however, the editor's judgement falls short of his industry. Although he is prepared, on the evidence of the double-numbering of the individual orations (above, p. lix), to restore the earlier ordering discernible behind that of the Parisinus (and that of Dübner's and Davies's editions), he otherwise clings to the detail of his 'best manuscript' with an extreme of conservative zeal, not only refusing to emend except in the direst emergency (and then preferably by mechanical addition rather than by any alteration of the transmitted letters), but also preserving the manuscript's punctuation and its idiosyncratic accentuation. Moreover, his erroneous view of the transmission leads him to lumber his apparatus criticus with a large number of wholly redundant readings.

Many of the shortcomings of Hobein's edition were pointed out by its reviewers,[222] and other German scholars soon established the truth about the status of the Parisinus in the tradition.[223] A further edition was clearly needed, but was not immediately forthcoming, in spite of the good intentions of Johannes Geffcken (announced in the sixth edition of Christ-Schmid-Stählin's *Geschichte der Griechischen Literatur*).[224] The gap has only been made good in the last few years, with the appearance of G. L. Koniaris's text from De Gruyter in 1995 and my Teubner in 1994. Koniaris's magisterial, comprehensive, and beautifully produced volume is the fruit of many years' study of the text of Maximus, from his Cornell doctoral dissertation of 1962, up to the cut-off point for his researches in 1988. It gives an exhaustive and minutely detailed account of the Parisinus, and an expanded apparatus that offers grammatical exegesis as well as variants and conjectures. Professor Koniaris's engagement with Maximus has also produced a valuable series of articles, dealing both with textual criticism and with points of interpretation. The Teubner is more modest in scale, and less accurately produced, but differs also in including more information about the manuscript tradition (particularly its later

---

Poliziano's annotations (above, pp. lxxi–lxxii), unrecognized by Hobein, and labelled simply 'man. recent.'. The excerpts include Gregoras's (again unrecognized), those on Neap. 100 and Paris. 1865, and the quotations in the *Lexicon Vindobonense* and Apostolis's *Proverbia* (above, pp. lxiv–lxv and lxxviii).

[222] Above all, Cronert (1913); but note also Theiler (1930) 3 fn. ('[Text] . . . in gänzlich unglücklicher Gestalt gegeben, doch steht das Richtige meist im Apparat.').

[223] Mutschman (1913), Schulte (1915).

[224] Christ-Schmid-Stählin (1934: 769).

stages) and about the contribution of Renaissance scholars to the emendation of the text.[225]

The only attempt to bring Maximus to more general attention in the last century—and that only on a very modest scale—has been that of Hobein's teacher Wilamowitz, who included a truncated version of *Or.* 2 in his *Griechisches Lesebuch* of 1902.[226] Otherwise, the *Orations* have been very much the preserve of the professional, appreciated in a small way as a source for a few fragments of lyric poetry, and for the history of religious attitudes and philosophical doctrines in the period of the high Empire. Such works as those of Geffcken, Nock, Festugière, Daniélou, and Lane Fox on second-century religious culture (pagan and Christian), or Theiler and Dillon on Middle Platonism, make regular use of individual passages, and Maximus is of course given his place in the surveys of later Greek literature, but Guy Soury's study of *Orr.* 5, 13, and 41 (1942), Jan Fredrik Kindstrand's monograph on Homeric quotation in Maximus, Dio, and Aristides (1973), M. Szarmach's monograph and articles (1982–5), G. L. Koniaris's articles of 1982 and 1983, and, above all, J. Puiggali's dissertation of 1978 (printed in 1983), are unusual in their willingness to discuss the *Orations* at the length of more than a couple of pages. Even the general revival of interest in Imperial period Greek writing, which has been such a feature of the scholarship of the last couple of decades, has rather passed Maximus by.[227]

It would be pleasant to think that the appearance of this new translation will do something to bring the *Orations* more frequently into the reckoning, as a work in their own right, as well as as a source of isolated fragments of information. There is good reason to suppose that there is something to be gained thereby. As the second half of the Introduction has attempted to demonstrate, the *Orations* were for over a thousand years—from the sixth to the eighteenth century—a minor but still appreciable element in the shared culture of European intellectuals, read widely enough

[225] A good many conjectures traditionally attributed to scholars of the 17th and 18th centuries—and indeed still so attributed by Koniaris—were in fact anticipated by one or other of the scribes of Conv. Sopp. 4, Janus Lascaris, and Zanobi Acciaiuoli (for whom see above, pp. lxiii, lxxiii–lxxvi). It seems right that they should be allowed to reclaim the credit.

[226] Wilamowitz (1902: i. 2, pp. 338 ff. and ii. 2, pp. 212 ff.).

[227] No mention is made of him in Bowersock (1969), because the biographical details are so scanty; he rates five and a half pages in Reardon (1971), and two and a half in Anderson (1993).

and with enough attention to have left a surprising number and range of traces beyond themselves. In so far as we continue to be interested in the history of that culture, and concerned for the experience of its participants, we should not neglect this part of it. But at the same time, as the first half of the Introduction sought to suggest, the *Orations* should engage us equally as characteristic products of the time of their composition, a window on to the high culture of the Greek-speaking world of the second century AD. Most obviously, they draw special attention to the role of philosophical education, and the value attached to philosophical learning, in that world; but they also, both by their rhetorical form and by their literary texture, offer insights into more general cultural attitudes. In this connection, they hold a special interest for students of second-century Christianity, representing as they do not only the theological and cosmological understanding, but also the cultural values and loyalties, which the second-century Apologists were striving partly to assimilate and partly to challenge. Appreciation of the ease and confidence with which Maximus displays and manipulates the passwords of the educated élite highlights all the more clearly both the nature of the task which the Apologists faced, and the differing strategies they adopted to meet it, as well as offering a means of assessing the kind of impact they may have had on their original audiences. The *Orations* cannot by any stretch of the imagination be claimed as a unique key, either to Imperial period culture in itself, or to the confrontation with Christianity; but since the accidents of history have left them as a unique representative of their kind of composition, they offer an angle of approach not now recuperable from any other surviving document.

A Note on the Translation

The text of the translation follows that of my 1994 Teubner edition, with a small number of divergences, all noted ad locc. I have tried to make it lively, readable, and speakable, and to reproduce in it at least the most marked variations in stylistic register to be found in the original Greek. In translating Maximus' quotations from classical authors, I have generally consulted an existing translation of the author concerned (Richmond Lattimore's Homer being by a long way the most heavily thumbed), but have in most cases made some adaptations of my own. Daggers in the text († . . . †) indicate places where the manuscript reading in Greek is so seriously corrupt that no plausible correction has yet been thought of; angle brackets (⟨ . . . ⟩) indicate editorial additions, and square brackets ([. . .]) editorial deletions. Fuller details of what is at issue in each case can be found in the Teubner *apparatus criticus*.

The headnotes to each individual oration follow a standard format. They begin with a note of the variant numbers borne by the oration at earlier stages in the history of its transmission (tabulated below in The Numbering of the *Orations*. The first number (designated '1962') is that borne in Dübner's edition and Davies's second, which derives from the ordering in Parisinus graecus 1962 (for which see above, pp. xiii–xv); the second (designated 'Laur. Conv. Sopp. 4') is that borne in all printed editions up to and including Davies's first, which derives from the ordering in Laur. Conv. Sopp. 4 (for which see above, p. lxiii). These numbers are followed by the title attached to the oration in the Paris manuscript, with remarks (as appropriate) on its suitability. The main body of the note will then usually divide into three sections: (1) a brief summary of the content or topic of the oration, with an analysis of its rhetorical structure (cf. p. xxxii above) and remarks on its connections with other pieces in the collection; (2) a discussion of the extent to which Maximus' handling of the topic reflects long-standing and widespread traditions of interest and debate, philosophical and other; and (3) a brief survey of later interest in the oration, to be taken together with the relevant pages of the second half of the Introduction.

The footnotes aim both to amplify and to document more precisely what is said in the headnotes, besides identifying references and quotations, and commenting on features of the literary texture (above all, the use of imagery, as discussed on pp. xxxix–xl above).

Of the two indexes, the first identifies not only direct quotations by Maximus, but also passages alluded to more indirectly, while the second covers names and topics both in the text of the *Orations* and in the editorial matter.

The Numbering of the *Orations*

Translation, Hobein, Trapp, Koniaris	Paris. gr. 1962, Dübner, Davies[2]	Laur. Conv. Sopp. 4. Estienne, Heinsius, Davies[1]
1	7	37
2	8	38
3	9	39
4	10	29
5	11	30
6	12	40
7	13	41
8	14	26
9	15	27
10	16	28
11	17	1
12	18	2
13	19	3
14	20	4
15	21	5
16	22	6
17	23	7
18	24	8
19	25	9
20	26	10
21	27	11
22	28	12
23	29	13
24	30	14
25	31	15
26	32	16
27	33	17
28	34	18
29	35	19

Translation, Hobein, Trapp, Koniaris	Paris. gr. 1962, Dübner, Davies[2]	Laur. Conv. Sopp. 4. Estienne, Heinsius, Davies[1]
30	1	31
31	2	32
32	3	33
33	4	34
34	5	35
35	6	36
36	36	20
37	37	21
38	38	22
39	39	23
40	40	24
41	41	25

THE ORATIONS

ORATION 1   The Philosopher and his Teaching

Introduction

= 7 (1962) = 37 (Laur. Conv. Sopp. 4). The manuscript title—ὅτι πρὸς πᾶσαν ὑπόθεσιν ἁρμόσεται ὁ τοῦ φιλοσόφου λόγος, 'That the philosopher's words will prove appropriate to any subject-matter'—matches the opening paragraphs, but is inadequate to the lecture as a whole.

An introductory address, which once headed the written version of the *Orations* (see Introduction, p. lix), and could have been delivered viva voce on any number of separate occasions. In it, Maximus seeks to persuade his audience both that they need philosophical instruction, and that he is the man to provide it. §§ 1–5 develop the first point: philosophical teaching is essential to bring order and stability into the confusion of human life, by directing humanity to the only truly satisfying and worthwhile goal (Virtue); this goal is both practically attainable, and endorsed by the best Greek traditions; in order to realize it, philosophical teaching itself will take many different forms, and present itself on many different occasions. An element of implicit self-advertisement and self-justification is already detectable in this: 'do not look for your philosophical instruction only in a narrowly defined set of situations; occasions like this have their part to play too'. In §§ 6–10 the advertisement becomes open and direct, as Maximus simultaneously boasts of his oratorical skill and challenges his audience to react to his moral message instead.[1] At the same time he seeks to reassure them that his and their (high) social status is no barrier to claiming the title 'philosopher': impressions to the contrary spring from an ignorant misreading of the historical record (§§ 9–10).

Formally, the lecture is unified by three images: the stage, the stadium, and the musician. The first is used at beginning and end, to insist that the individual philosophical teacher must be allowed to teach in a variety of different ways (§ 1), and that legitimate teachers come in a whole range of different guises (§ 10). The

---

[1] A remarkable piece of coat-trailing, most notably in § 7: 'imitation of my skills will benefit you in all kinds of potential careers—although of course it is the pursuit of truth and virtue that really matters'.

imagery of the stadium, in §§ 4-5 and 6, is applied first to urge the superior value (and practicability) of the pursuit of Virtue, then to highlight the speaker's own quest for converts. The musician, in §§ 1-2 and 7, illustrates both the philosopher's necessary versatility, and the ease with which his teaching can be assimilated.[2] As images of performance by specialist(s) to a mass audience, all three sets serve also to draw attention to the status Maximus himself is laying claim to: certainly in moral authority, and perhaps also as a respected and successful oratorical performer.

Generically, the lecture counts as a λόγος προτρεπτικός: an exhortation to embrace sound moral and/or intellectual values, combined with an exegesis of those values, and of the dangers consequent on failure to embrace them.[3] What distinguishes it from other examples of its kind is not only the unusually direct element of self-advertisement already noted, but also the remarkably vague and non-committal concept of philosophy it advances. The pursuit of Virtue is recommended over the pursuit of Pleasure and material satisfaction (§ 5), but the anxious are quickly reassured that the right choice will not commit them to the uncouth, pedantic technicalities of the schools, or to excessive effort of any kind (§ 7). See Introduction, pp. xvii–xix.

There is no sign of any great interest in this lecture on the part of later readers; its displacement from first position in both the main manuscript families will have done it no service in this respect. Gregoras, however, does take four excerpts from §§ 1, 4, 5, and 9, and the compiler of Neap. 100 five, from §§ 5 and 9. There are discussions by Hobein (1911), Koniaris (1983), and Anderson (1993: 138-9).

---

[2] Note also the images of doctor (§ 2), herdsman (§ 3), soldier (§ 3), horse-trainer (§ 8) and trumpeter (§ 8)—all applied to the philosopher and/or his teaching. Also the (partly interlocking) imagery of flowing water (§ 2), disease (§ 2), darkness and error (§ 3), and untamed nature (§§ 2, 7, 8) for the life deprived of philosophy and philosophical values.

[3] Surviving examples of the form include versions by Galen, Clement of Alexandria, Iamblichus, and Ps.-Dionysius (Dionysius of Halicarnassus, ed. Radermacher, vi. 283 ff.); Aristotle's *Protrepticus* and Cicero's *Hortensius* are known only from fragments, and the Emperor Augustus' essay in the same genre only by report (Suet. *Aug.* 85. 1). See in general Hartlich (1889).

Oration

1   I have a question for you. When actors are playing in Dionysus'
theatre, speaking one moment with the voice of Agamemnon, the
next with that of Achilles, or again impersonating a Telephus or a
Palamedes,[4] or whatever else the drama may call for, no one finds
it at all odd or disturbing that the same men should appear now in
one guise and now in another. What then of someone who, while
upholding Dionysiac tradition in the context of entertainment and
the theatre, believes that he has a place in another drama, the
drama of everyday life? This is no drama in iambics, the artful
composition of a poet for a single festival performance; it has no
harmoniously composed lyrics for a chorus to sing. No, by heaven!
It is made from the business of human life, a kind of drama that—
to the philosopher—tells a truer story, and is unbroken in its duration, composed by no lesser a dramatist than God himself. Suppose
the man were to make his entry into this drama and appoint himself the chorus's protagonist. Suppose also that, while respecting
the dignity of the verse, he adapted the character of his speech to
suit the varying nature of the episodes in the plot that God writes
for us. Would anyone be offended? Would anyone think him many-
voiced, possessed like the sea-god Proteus in Homer[5] of an inconstant and multiple character? Or would it be the same as if human
happiness depended on the art and power of music? In that case, I
imagine, given all the different modes which the art comprises, a
man would count as worthless if he was properly trained to play in
the Dorian mode, but fell silent when faced with the need to tune
to the Ionian or the Aeolian.

2   In fact mens' need of songs and tunes and the entertainment
deriving from them is limited. They need instead another, more
vigorous Muse, whom Homer chose to call Calliope,[6] and
Pythagoras Philosophy,[7] and no doubt others by yet other names.

---

[4] Telephus and Palamedes appeared most famously in the (lost) Euripidean
tragedies bearing their names. Achilles and Agamemnon both appeared in the
former, and Agamemnon in the latter; they are also characters in Euripides *IA*, in
which both parts could indeed be played by the same actor.
[5] As encountered by Menelaus in *Od.* 4. 450 ff.
[6] See *Or.* 26. 1.
[7] Pythagoras was supposed to have been the inventor of the word 'philosophy':
cf. e.g. Cic. *Tusc.* 5. 3. 8–9; Diod. Sic. 10. 10; [Plut.] *Placita* 876e; Diog. Laert. 1.
12. There are grounds for supposing that the claim goes back only as far as
Heraclides of Pontus: see Gottschalk (1980: 23–33).

Is it any the less necessary for the devotee of this Muse, and for his words, to be attuned to the production of many different sounds in many different forms, than it is for the ordinary musician? Must he not constantly respect the beauty of the compositions he plays and never allow himself to be stricken by speechlessness? If there were only one period in the long, unbroken passage of time that needs a philosopher's discourse, then there would be no need for the complex and versatile musical harmonies of which I speak, any more than there would be if human affairs maintained a single pattern and an even tenor, never passing from one passion to another, never changing from pleasure to pain or from pain to pleasure, never twisting and turning the individual's purposes this way and that:

> The opinions of mortals who live upon earth are such
> As the day the Father of gods and men brings on.[8]

Change and counter-change is the rule that divine deliberation imposes on human affairs; they are incapable in their very nature of remaining the same from one day to the next. Rivers rising from their ever-flowing springs have each a single name, Spercheius or Alpheius or whatever, but the belief that each is indeed a single, continuous river is the product of an illusion wrought on the sense of sight by the uninterrupted flow, as the process of generation exchanges what follows on for what has passed away.[9] The stock of human fortunes rises and flows in just the same way, as if from an unfailing spring, in a swift rush that baffles the senses. Our powers of reasoning are deceived, as sight was deceived in the case of the river, into calling life a single, uniform phenomenon, when in fact it is a thing of many shapes and forms, changing again and again as chance and circumstance and opportunity dictate. Set over life, however, is Reason, which constantly adapts itself to the circumstances of the moment, like a skilled doctor whose duty is to regulate the indigence and satiety of a body that is not stable, but surges back and forth, in the turmoil of evacuation and repletion.[10]

---

[8] *Od.* 18. 136–7: famous lines, also quoted by, for example, [Plut.] *Cons. Apol.* 104e. According to Cic. *De Fato* fr. 3 (Augustine *CD* 5. 8) the same lines were used by the Stoics to illustrate the power of fate.

[9] Maximus' comparison here distantly recalls Heraclitus' famous dictum about rivers: B12, 49a and 91 D–K. For water as an image of inconstancy, cf. e.g. *Orr.* 5. 9, 8. 7, 10. 5 with n. 16.

[10] For the doctor as an image of philosophical teaching, cf. *Orr.* 4. 6 and 10. 3. He can serve equally well as an image for God and for the good man (e.g. *Or.* 8. 7).

This is precisely what the rational teaching of philosophers can do for human life, adapting its tone to suit the emotions of the moment, so as both to offer consolation in sad times and to enhance the celebrations in times of joy.[11]

3   If life maintained throughout a single structure and a single form, a single style of teaching would suffice. As things are, there is a set time for the bard, singing sweetly to his lyre, when the tables are laden

> With bread and meat, and the waiter draws wine from the bowl
> And pours.[12]

The speaker too has his moment, in the packed court-house, and the poet at the Dionysia, when a chorus is required. But philosophical teaching has no single occasion set aside as its own. It is inseparable from life, as light is from the eye. Who could conceive a function for the eye, if light were once removed? In point of fact, eyesight can function confidently even in the dark; your eyes may only be able to see dimly, but they can still guess which way to lead you through the obscurity.[13] If, on the other hand, one removes the guidance of teaching from life, it disappears into the abyss, down evil, dark, rough roads, with the uncouth barbarians—bandits, ⟨ . . . ⟩,[14] mercenaries and strays—who travel by such paths. If you were to remove a goatherd from his flock and confiscate his flute, you would scatter the flock. What other result will you achieve by depriving the human herd of its guide and marshaller, Reason? You will scatter and destroy a herd which is naturally tame, but has been made recalcitrant by bad rearing, one that needs a civilized herdsman who will not punish its disobedience with whips and goads.[15] Whoever refuses to allow the philosopher to seize every opportunity to speak seems to me to be doing the same as someone who selects a single station from the

[11] Philosophical teaching is here described in terms appropriate to the true friend: cf. Xen. *Mem.* 2. 4. 6 and Plut. *De Ad. et Am.* 49–50.

[12] *Od.* 9. 9–10. For another use of this episode from the *Odyssey*, see *Or.* 22. 1.

[13] The imagery of light and sight distantly echoes Plato's Cave (*Resp.* 514a ff.): cf. *Orr.* 29. 5 and 36. 4, and (more generally) 10. 3, 11. 9, 34. 1.

[14] The text is corrupt at this point; suggestions for the missing occupation include 'libertines' and 'money-grubbers'.

[15] An echo of Plato *Leg.* 777a; the image of the corrupted herd is also Platonic (*Grg.* 516a ff.). The same image is used in a discussion of the role of philosophy in *Or.* 29. 7, and of friendship in *Or.* 35. 2.

whole chancy, fluctuating, unstable business of war, and there confines the versatile soldier who knows how to fight both as hoplite and as archer, and can shoot as effectively on horseback as he can from a chariot.[16]

4   An athlete is at liberty to compete at the Olympic games but ignore the Isthmian. Yet even in his case laziness is reprehensible: the ambitious soul does not allow desire for comfort to dissuade it from completing the whole circuit; it must stake its claim not only in the Olympic olive, but also in the Isthmian pine, the parsley of Argos, and the Pythian apples[17]—even though here it is the soul's cohabitation and partnership with the body which allows it to share the pleasure of winning and of the victory-proclamation, and it does not itself initiate the effort involved. When therefore the effort is really the soul's own, and the competition and the victory the soul's alone, will it then pass up the chance to compete, or stand idle of its own free choice? In this contest the prize is no prize of apples or olive leaves, but one which offers a fairer object of ambition, greater benefit to the spectators, and an easier course to a speaker seeking to convince. The times and places of the contest vary, and are announced without warning. Hellenes[18] throng together, unbidden and of their own free will, not for the pleasure of the spectacle, but in the hopes of acquiring Virtue, which, I believe, is closer kin to the human soul than Pleasure.[19] In other displays, of physical strength and skill, it is patent that almost none of the spectators arrives with the intention of imitating or competing in what they watch. At this kind of contest, it is from the sight of other people's exertions that we derive our pleasure; with, perhaps, the exception of some few servile spirits, there is no one among the many thousands of spectators who actively desires to be one of those dusty figures running, throttling their opponents or being throttled, or raining blows out in the middle of the stadium. But at the other kind of spectacle, I believe, the competitive spirit

[16] For the military image, cf. esp. *Orr.* 5. 3 and 13. 4, with n. 10.

[17] The classic circuit (περίοδος), best known from the titles of the four books of Pindar's *Odes*; victory in all four was rewarded with the coveted title of περιοδονίκης. Cf. Gardiner (1910: 161), Harris (1964, ch. 5).

[18] i.e. people of taste and culture, people who understand and appreciate the Greek cultural heritage, not necessarily only ethnic Greeks; cf. the references to 'the Panhellenic games' and 'the theatres of Hellas' in §§ 6 and 10 below.

[19] Although not amplified here, this antithesis between Virtue and Pleasure is central to Maximus' moralizing: see above all *Orr.* 29–33.

is so much more intense than in its counterpart, and the exertions so much more useful, and the emotions of the spectators so much more engaged, that no one present in his right mind could fail to pray to abandon his role as spectator and become a competitor instead.

5   Why is this? Physical skills and the exertions needed to acquire them cannot be sustained by every physique. Nor is their acquisition at all a matter of volition; they are innate, a natural gift to a small proportion of humanity. You have to be naturally as large as Titolmus, or as tough as Milo, or as strong as Polydamas, or as fast as Lasthenes.[20] If you are weaker than Epeius and uglier than Thersites and smaller than Tydeus and slower than Ajax[21]—that is, if you are a combination of every form of physical inferiority— and still fix jealous eyes on the arena, it is indeed a vain and unrealizable passion that afflicts you. The contests of the soul, on the other hand, have quite the opposite character. It is only a tiny proportion of the human race, one almost never encountered,—that is not naturally endowed for them; for the virtues of the soul are not innate and do not develop of their own accord. Natural endowment merely plays a preparatory role, as if laying down a small foundation for a great wall, or a tiny keel for a tall ship.[22] Alongside our powers of reasoning, God has settled two further faculties, love and hope.[23] Love is like a light and airy pair of wings which lifts the soul[24] and allows it to run unimpeded towards the objects of its desire; philosophers call these wings 'human impulse'.[25] Hopes in their turn have been implanted in the soul to encourage the

---

[20] All celebrated athletes of the 6th and 5th centuries BC. For a similar list (Titolmus, Milo, and Polydamas, but without Lasthenes), see Lucian *Quom. Hist.* 34-5.

[21] Epeius' feebleness: compare the sources quoted in Austin's note on Virg. *Aen.* 2. 264 (showing cowardice and/or humility to have been Epeius's usual characteristics, rather than weakness). Thersites' ugliness: *Il.* 2. 216 ff. Tydeus' size: *Il.* 5. 801. Ajax's slowness: *Il.* 11. 558 ff.

[22] From the 4th century onwards (Xen. *Mem.* 3. 9. 1-3, Arist. *NE* 10. 1179ᵇ 20 ff., *EE* 1. 1214ᵃ 16 ff.) it was a commonplace that the development of virtue required practice (ἔθος, ἄσκησις) and instruction (μάθησις, διδασκαλία) as well as natural endowment (φύσις): see e.g. [Plut.] *Lib. Educ.* 2a; Alcin. *Didasc.* 28; Diog. Laert. 5. 18; Archytas *De Educ.* 3, p. 41. 20 ff. Thesleff; Philo *Vit. Abrah.* 52-4; and cf. *Orr.* 12. 9 and 27. 9.

[23] This passage is discussed by Theiler (1930: 148-51, esp. 150-1).

[24] An echo of the imagery of Plato *Phaedr.* 246a ff.

[25] ὁρμή: a term of Stoic origin (e.g. *SVF* iii. 171), long since taken into the shared vocabulary of philosophy (e.g. Cic. *Off.* 1. 101).

individual's appetitive urges. They are not blind, as the Attic poet describes them,[26] but extremely clear-sighted; they convince the soul that it will achieve its desires in full, and so prevent it from abandoning the struggle. Were it not for hope, the money-grubber would long since have abandoned his money-grubbing, the mercenary his campaigning, the merchant his travels, the bandit his banditry, and the libertine his adulterous liaisons. But this is just what hope does not allow; instead it enjoins empty labours without end, on the money-grubber in the hopes of making his fortune, on the soldier in the hopes of winning his battles, on the sailor in the hopes of making safe landfall, and on the adulterer in the hopes of avoiding exposure.[27] Yet sudden misfortune can seize on each and every one of them: the money-grubber may have his money stolen, the mercenary may lose his life, the merchant may be shipwrecked, the bandit may be captured, and the adulterer may be exposed. Their hopes then perish along with their desires. The reason is that God has not confined any of these things—wealth, pleasure, or any other object of human desire—within rational limits; they are boundless in their very nature. This is clearly why people who pursue such ends only thirst the more when they have taken their fill of them; what they have attained is always less than what they look forward to.[28] But when the soul leads us to an object that is stable, unified, bounded, and defined—naturally beautiful, accessible to effort, apprehensible by reason, pursuable with love, and attainable with hope—then its exertions are blessed with good fortune, victory, and success. This and nothing else is the reason why philosophic spirits flock to the spectacles I have described.

6   I need the image of the athletes again. In ordinary athletic competitions, since there can be only one winner out of many contestants, each might be pardoned for praying that no one else come out into the stadium; for if that happened he could claim the victory himself by a walk-over. But in the games of the soul, victory belongs pre-eminently to the contestant who can summon many others to compete. I wish to heaven some fellow competitor

[26] [Aesch.] *PV* 250.
[27] With this locus on hope, cf. Philo *Praem. et Poen.* 11 (also in the context of an exhortation to philosophy).
[28] Another familiar moralist's point: see Oltramare (1926: 288, theme 78a). Compare also *Orr.* 29. 5 and 33. 4.

might emerge from my audience, to share with me the dust and the exertions of this platform! Then will I win the glory of a victor's wreath; then alone will my name resound in triumph at the Panhellenic games! Until now, I confess, I have remained uncrowned and unproclaimed—shout though you may! What good to me are the many speeches I have made, the continual struggle in which I have engaged? Praise? I have enjoyed enough of that! I have my fine reputation, and am sated with it! The whole point is this: are people going to praise oratory and not practise it, though they have both voice and ears? Are they going to praise philosophy and not practise it, though they have both souls and teachers? The whole business has become like playing the pipe or the lyre, or again like tragedy or comedy at the Dionysia: everyone praises; no one imitates.

7   In fact, here too there is a very great distance between praise and mere enjoyment. Anyone can listen simply for pleasure, but sincere praise necessitates imitation as well; as long as someone feels no urge to emulate, he refrains from praise also. It is not unheard-of for a man of no musical training to acquire the ability simply by listening to the pipe: the tunes so ring in his ears that he gets them by heart, and can hum them back again to himself. It is my prayer that some of you will have the same experience, and perhaps may even come to desire the pipe itself.[29] There was once an animal-lover who kept birds, of the kind that sing pleasantly in that chirping way of theirs, but tunelessly, as you would expect with birds. This man had a neighbour who played the pipe. Every day the birds listened to the neighbour as he practised, and sang in response; the result was that, through listening to him, their singing was moulded into tune with his playing, until finally when the man began to play they would start singing in unison, taking their keynote from him like a choir. My audience are men, not birds; what they listen to over and again is not inarticulate piping but rationally articulated speech which appeals to the intellect, stimulates its hearers, and is made for imitation. Will they answer my song? It is this question that induces me to break the silence I have so far maintained to all about my own merits. I have hitherto said nothing conceited or boastful either in public or in private, but for your sake I am now

[29]   i.e. become philosophical teachers in your own right.

resolved to speak with all the pride and vanity at my command.
Behold, young men, this treasury of eloquence—prolific, complex,
abundant—that stands before you, such as to appeal to all ears
and all characters, proficient in all styles of speech and all forms of
training, lavish and bountiful, unhesitating, unbegrudged, freely
available to all who can receive it. If there is anyone among you
who desires to be an orator, here is a ready flow of words for him,
rich and resourceful, lofty, striking, unhesitant, firm, indefatigable.
If there is anyone who desires to be a poet, let him bring metre
alone from another source; he will find here all the rest of the
poet's stock-in-trade: impressive diction, brilliant and distinguished
style, fertility, mastery of composition, dramaturgic skill, rich
sound, and faultless harmony. Or again, is it political skill you
come in search of? Do you wish to be equipped for assemblies and
the council chamber? You have found what you need: here are
people, council chamber, speaker, persuasion, and power.

But perhaps there is someone who despises all this, and is given
over to love of philosophy and reverence for the truth instead. For
him I furl the sails of my proud speech, and humble myself; I am
not the same man. This is a weighty matter, God knows, and
demands a champion out of the common run, not one who hugs
the ground and is tainted with the ways of the crowd. [8] If you
think that philosophy is simply a matter of nouns and verbs, or
skill with mere words, or refutation and argument and sophistry,
and of time spent on accomplishments like that, then there is no
problem in finding a teacher. The world is full of that kind of
sophist, and their brand of philosophy is easy to acquire; the quest
is soon over. Indeed, I would make so bold as to say that it has
more teachers than pupils.[30] But if all that is only a small part of
philosophy, and such a part that ignorance of it is disgraceful and
knowledge no cause for pride, by all means let us escape reproach
by knowing it, but let us not therefore give ourselves airs. If that
were justified, then schoolmasters would be people of great account
too, who devote their energies to syllables, and spend their time
stammering with packs of witless infants. The summit of philosophy and the road that leads there demand a teacher who can
rouse young men's souls and guide their ambitions. His task is to

---

[30] With this attack on those who privilege theory over the practical acquisition of
Virtue, cf. *Orr.* 21. 4, 27. 8, 30. 1, and 37. 2. At the same time, Maximus is reassuring his audience that they can do philosophy without excessive intellectual effort.

temper their desires with the aid of pleasures and pains,[31] just as horse-trainers do, neither quenching the colts' fire nor allowing them to indulge their high spirits unchecked. Bridle and reins control a colt's spirit, with the skills of horseman and charioteer. What controls the human soul is teaching, which must not be lax or slovenly or casual, but so compounded as both to beguile and to move, allowing its hearers no leisure to analyse its sounds and the pleasures they contain, but compelling them to rise and share its fervour, as they would at the call of a trumpet, sounding now the charge, now the retreat.[32]

9   If this is the kind of teaching needed by those who aim at philosophy, we must seek out and test and select the man who can deliver it, whether he be old or young, poor or rich, obscure or famous. Old age, to be sure, is inferior to youth, poverty to riches, and obscurity to fame. Yet people are more ready to attach themselves to those who suffer from such disadvantages than to those who do not, thus transforming misfortunes allotted by chance into provisions for the road to philosophy. Because Socrates was poor, the poor man will unhesitatingly imitate Socrates. We should count ourselves lucky that the snub-nosed and the pot-bellied don't lay claim to philosophy too! What nobody remembers is that Socrates did not betake himself to the poor alone, but also to the rich and famous and well-born. I imagine he thought that the Athenian state would derive little benefit from Aeschines or Antisthenes[33] practising philosophy [—or rather, that nobody at the time would benefit, but that we in later generations would, thanks to the record they left of his words—],[34] but that if Alcibiades, or Critias, or Critoboulos, or Callias[35] had turned to

[31] This account of the purpose and means of education recalls the Plato of *Leg.* 631e–632a and 653ab.

[32] With this call for an inspirational style, in which moral effect takes precedence over aesthetic pleasure, compare *Orr.* 17. 4 and 25. 6–7. The danger that well-expressed philosophical preaching will fail in its effect precisely because it can be appreciated for its form rather than its content is a widespread theme: Muson. Ruf. ap. Epict. 3. 23. 29 and Gellius *NA* 5. 1. 1–4; Sen. *Ep.* 108. 6–7; Epict. 3. 21.

[33] Aeschines of Sphettus and Antisthenes the proto-Cynic, both famous Socratic successes. Aeschines and his Socratic dialogues are alluded to again in *Orr.* 18 and 22, and quoted from in *Orr.* 6. 6, 18. 4, and 34. 4.

[34] These words blunt the force of Maximus' contrast between the two categories of Socrates' pupils, and should perhaps be regarded as a reader's interpolation.

[35] Famous cases of Socratic failure (cf. esp. Xen. *Mem.* 1. 2. 12 ff.); all are mentioned again several times in subsequent lectures, Alcibiades being a particular favourite: see esp. *Orr.* 6. 6 and 7. 7.

philosophy, none of the famous disasters of the age would have befallen the people of Athens.[36] Nor does merely carrying a wallet and a staff count as imitating Diogenes, as one can surely have these accoutrements and still be more wretched than Sardanapallus.[37] The famous Aristippus, who wore a purple robe and anointed himself with myrrh, was no less continent than Diogenes.[38] If someone managed to make his body fireproof, he would not worry even about throwing himself into Aetna.[39] Similarly, anyone who is well fortified against pleasures can exist among them without their inflaming him or burning him or melting him away.

10   The philosopher must be judged not by appearance, nor by age, nor by social status, but by his mind and his words and the disposition of his soul; for these are the only things that make a man a philosopher. All those other features conferred by Fortune are like costumes at the Dionysia. The beauty of the poetry is one and the same whether it is a prince who speaks or a slave, but external appearances vary according to the needs of the drama. Agamemnon carries his sceptre; the herdsman wears a leather jerkin, Achilles his armour, Telephus his rags and wallet. None the less, the audience listen as attentively to Agamemnon as they do to Telephus, as it is on the verse, not the status of the speakers, that their souls fasten. You must believe that the beauty of philosophical teaching is not multiple or diverse either, but single and coherent. The performers themselves are sent on to the stage of life dressed in the different costumes that Fortune assigns them: Pythagoras in purple, Socrates in his threadbare cloak, Xenophon with breastplate and shield, and the protagonist from Sinope, like Telephus in the play, with staff and wallet. These same externals contribute to the parts they play in the drama, explaining why it was that Pythagoras overawed his audience, Socrates confounded them with his questioning, Xenophon persuaded,[40] and Diogenes

[36] Maximus recurs to this point in *Orr.* 3. 8 and 18. 6.

[37] For Diogenes, see esp. *Or.* 36; Sardanapallus is regularly used as an exemplum of the hedonist: cf. *Orr.* 4. 9, 7. 7 (with n. 22), 15. 8, 29. 1, 32. 3 and 9.

[38] For this view of Aristippus, cf. e.g. Diog. Laert. 2. 75 and 78, with McKirahan (1994: 377–82).

[39] A sideways glance at the suicide of Empedocles: e.g. Diog. Laert. 8. 69; Lucian *Icarom.* 13, *Peregr.* 1, *VH* 2. 21.

[40] Perhaps unexpected, given the reference to Xenophon's military costume in the previous sentence, but in line with his literary reputation: see above all Quintil. *Inst.*

reproached. Happy the actors in this drama, happy the spectators who beheld them! Might we too, even now, not find a poet and a performer, worthy through his grace and eloquence to play to the theatres of Hellas? Perhaps he may come to light, and if he does, he will not go without honour.[41]

ORATION 2   Images of the Gods

Introduction

= 8 (1962) = 38 (Laur. Conv. Sopp. 4). The manuscript title—εἰ θεοῖς ἀγάλματα ἱδρυτέον, 'Whether images should be set up in honour of the gods'—closely echoes Maximus' own formulation of his topic, in § 9.

The first of Maximus' lectures on what may be called broadly theological and/or cosmological themes, showing points of contact with *Orr.* 4–11, 13, and 41. An initial survey of primitive and rustic divine images introduces the question whether sophisticated, urban man will have recourse to such practices too (§ 1). He will, is the reply, but as a concession to the feebleness of human intellect, not as a fundamental necessity either to men or to the divine (§ 2). An extended survey of Greek and foreign ('barbarian') religious images then underlines how widely and how variously this concession has been made (§§ 3–9). The concluding sections return to the initial question and amplify the answer given in § 2, that images used in cult do not embody God's essential nature, but are a useful aid to human worship.

The basically Platonic vantage-point from which Maximus speaks is clear from §§ 2 and 10, with their picture of a transcendent, ineffable God who is the source of all beauty, and who is perceived by the human soul in an act of recollection: compare, elsewhere in the *Orations*, the God of 11. 7–11, 21. 9, and 41. 2; and elsewhere in Middle Platonic writing, Alcinous *Didascalicus* 10 and Apuleius *De Platone* 1. 5. The attitude to religious images Maximus evinces, combining a relaxed acceptance of tradition with

10. 82 ('in labris eius sedisse quandam persuadendi deam', echoing Eupolis on Pericles); and, for other verdicts, *RE* ix(a). 2, 1895–7 (H. Breitenbach).

[41] On the surface, this conclusion exhorts the audience to be on the look-out for a true philosophical teacher in future. However, it also leaves them free to acclaim Maximus himself as that teacher, if they so choose.

insistence on the higher, philosophical truth which reveals the true scope and value of that tradition, is characteristic of the educated culture of his age: compare above all Plutarch *De Iside et Osiride* 377a-383a. Interesting contrasts may be drawn, in one direction with the contemporary rejection of all such reasoning by the second-century Christian apologists (cf. Daniélou 1973: 18-9, and index s.v. idolatry), and in another with the renewed importance attached to images by the NeoPlatonists (cf. Wallis 1972: 106-10, 120-3; Dodds 1951: 283-311). For the issue of images and idolatry in ancient thought in general, see Clerc (1915), de Burries (1918), and Fazzo (1977).

Also relevant to Maximus' handling of his theme is the (originally Stoic) tradition of theorizing about the sources of human conceptions of the divine (see n. 3 below). A generation or so previously, this had famously been exploited by Dio Chrysostom in his *Olympian Oration* (12), which shows many points of contact with the present lecture, and may well have been one of Maximus' sources. (See Blankert 1940: 169-83.)

Considerable interest in the lecture on the part of later readers can be detected. On the Paris manuscript, each new reference to a different national custom, in §§ 3-8, bears a numeral (*A'-IΔ'*); since this is not the scribe's normal practice, it is likely to reflect an earlier reader's marginal annotation. Gregoras takes two excerpts (from §§ 9 and 10), as does the complier of Neap. 100 (from §§ 2 and 10). The *Lexicon Vindobonense* makes two quotations (from §§ 4 and 7); and Apostolis quotes from § 5 to illustrate the proverb κροκοδείλου δάκρυα (*Viol.* 10. 17). J. Reuchlin cites § 2 in his *De Arte Cabalistica Libri Tres* (1517), fol. xxviiᵛ, and L. G. Giraldi draws on §§ 4-7 for his survey of pagan cult practices in *De Deis Gentium* (1548), 98-9. A century later Giraldi's example is followed by G. Voss, who cites the lecture six times in the first edition of his *De Theologia Gentili* (1641), and a further six in the second (1668).[1] Two of these references are then taken over from Voss in Lord Herbert of Cherbury's *De Religione Gentilium* (1663: 70 (2. 4), 89 (2. 8)). Finally, Jeremy Taylor quotes the description of Persian fire-cult in § 4.1 of his *Worthy Communicant* (1653;

---

[1] First edition: i. 13, p. 99: 2. 5; ii. 62, p. 639: 2. 8 (with cross-reference to Voss's *Oratoriae Institutiones* i. 5. 39); ii. 64, p. 649: 2. 4; ii. 79, p. 711: 2. 8; iii. 74, p. 1132: 2. 5; iv. 63, p. 1523: 2. 6. Second edition: ix. 6, p. 224: general ref.; ix. 10, p. 234: 2. 8; ix. 29, p. 276: 2. 1; ix. 34, p. 290: 2. 1; ix. 35, p. 291: 2. 1; ix. 40, p. 304: 2. 1.

Heber-Eden 1847–54: viii. 118). A French translation by A. Feron, in his *Aristidis Oratio, quae persuadere contendat Smyrnaeis, etc.* (Paris, J. Tourner), appeared in 1557; and an edition of the Greek text was included by Wilamowitz in his *Griechisches Lesebuch* (1902: i. 2, pp. 338 ff.).

Oration

1 The gods are helpers to mankind. In reality, all gods succour all men, but the reputations deriving from their several names have promoted the idea that different gods help different groups of human beings; and each group, receiving the benefits appropriate to its own particular sphere, has assigned its own gods separate honours and images.[2] Thus it was that sailors came to dedicate rudders to the deities of the sea on rocks that stand clear of the waves. Thus it is that some shepherds honour Pan by selecting him a tall pine or a deep cave, and farmers honour Dionysus by fixing the trunk of an uncultivated tree in an orchard to make their own rustic image. The sacred places of Artemis are the springs of rivers and hollow valleys and flowery meadows. Zeus too had images assigned to him by the earliest men, in the form of mountain peaks, Olympus and Ida, and any other mountain that reaches up to the heavens. Rivers too we can see to be honoured, either for the benefits that they bestow, as with the Egyptians and the Nile; or for their beauty, as with the Thessalians and the Peneus; or for their size, as with the Scythians and the Ister; or for reasons of mythology, as with the Aetolians and the Achelous; or from national custom, as with the Spartans and the Eurotas; or for ritual reasons, as with the Athenians and the Ilissus.[3] Are rivers then to receive their share of honour, according to the uses made of them by their beneficiaries; and is each of the several crafts, proffering its own distinctive image, to show itself prolific in the

---

[2] A similar point about the unity of the divine is made in *Or.* 39. 5.

[3] For the idea that early man chose purely natural images for divine worship, cf. Dion. Hal. *Ant. Rom.* 1. 38 and Lucian *Sacr.* 10, and compare also § 9 below; Dio *Or.* 12. 61 attributes the habit to barbarians. The belief is clearly closely connected with Stoic natural theology (Cleanthes ap. Cic. *ND* 2. 12–15, Zeno *SVF* i. 246–7, Dio *Or.* 12. 27–37): what is in that theory the most basic source of *ideas* about the divine is also taken as the source of the most primitive *images*. Jewish and Christian tradition, however, rejected even natural images as illegitimate: Philo *Decal.* 54–9; Strabo 16. 2. 35; Athenagoras *Leg.* 16; Clem. *Protr.* 4. 46. 1–2 and 4. 63. 1.

manufacture of divine honours?[4] But if there exists another race of
men who are neither sailors nor farmers, but who are instead of
urban stock and are united in a political community with its laws
and its practices of reason, will this race have no offerings for the
gods and no honours to pay them? Or will they indeed honour
them, but by word of mouth alone, believing that the gods have
no need of images and dedications, for they do not need images
and dedications any more than great men need statues? [2] One
can, I think, compare spoken utterances, which can easily be
articulated without recourse to written characters, be they
Phoenician, Ionian, Attic, Assyrian, or Egyptian; these latter are
merely the symbols human nature has discovered to help it lay
aside its own particular obtuseness and print a permanent record
for the future.[5] In just the same way, divinity in its own nature has
no need of statues and dedications; but humanity, an utterly
feeble species that lies as far from the divine as heaven from earth,
contrived them as symbols through which to preserve the gods'
names and their reputations. People whose memories are strong,
and who can reach straight out for the heavens with their souls
and encounter the divine,[6] may perhaps have no need of images.
But this is a category ill-represented among men, and one could
not hope ever to encounter a whole people mindful of the divine
and able to dispense with that kind of assistance. Just as primary
teachers contrive to help their pupils by sketching faint letters for
them, over which they can guide the movements of their hands,
as reminders to help them to familiarity with the skill of writing,[7]
in the same way it seems to me that legislators invented their own
kind of images for men, as if for a class of children: as symbols of
the honour paid to the gods and as a kind of pathway to recollection.[8]

3   There is no one set of rules governing images, nor one set

---

[4] A first, brief glance at a second source of conceptions of the gods, the arts: cf.
Dio *Or.* 12. 44 (listing line-drawing, coloured drawing, and stone, wood, bronze,
and wax statuary).

[5] An echo of Plato's discussion of writing in *Phaedr.*, esp. 274d–275b.

[6] Another Platonizing touch: cf. § 10 below, and *Or.* 10. 3 and 10.

[7] The image is adapted from Plato *Protag.* 326d.

[8] Legislation was one of the classic three sources of concepts of divinity named
in the so-called 'tripartite theology', along with reason (philosophy) and myth
(poetry): cf. Dio *Or.* 12. 39–40; Scaevola and Varro in Tertullian *Ad Nat.* 2 and
Augustine *CD* 4. 27; Plut. *Amat.* 763bc.

form, nor one single skill or material for their making. The Greeks
(to begin with them) made it their practice to honour the gods with
the most beautiful things the earth affords: pure materials, the
human form, and the precise craftsmanship of the artist. And
indeed the judgement of those who established images in human
form is anything but unreasonable. If the human soul is something
very close to God and like him in its nature, it is surely not
reasonable to clothe what is most similar to it in an entirely
foreign covering.⁹ One needs instead a form that is light and
sufficiently easily moved to make a comfortable garment for
immortal souls, the only body on earth that lifts its head up high,
proud and splendid in its fine proportions, not astounding in its
size, not frightening for its hairy coat, not slow to move because of
its bulk, not smooth and slippery, not hard and resistant, not cold
and creeping, not hot and hasty, not buoyant and aquatic, not
fierce and carnivorous, not herbivorous and weak, but harmoniously blended to perform its proper functions: [frightening to the
cowardly, gentle to the good,]¹⁰ a being equipped to walk in virtue
of its nature, to fly in virtue of its reason, and to swim in virtue of
its skill, an eater of corn and fruits, a worker of the earth, fair in
complexion, well-proportioned, fine-visaged, and finely bearded.¹¹
Such was the body through whose forms the Greeks chose to
honour the gods.

4   As for foreign peoples, all are similarly conscious of God,¹² but
the different races have established themselves different images.
The Persians have fire, a transient image, voracious and insatiable;
to this they sacrifice by heaping it with its own appropriate food,
and as they do so they say, 'Lord Fire, eat.'¹³ These Persians

⁹ For this affirmation of the appropriateness of the human form as an image of
the divine, cf. Dio *Or.* 12. 55–9, Cic. *ND* 1. 46–7 and 76. The idea is again contested by Jewish and Christian thinkers: Strabo 16. 2. 35; Justin *1 Ap.* 9. 1–3; Clem.
Protr. 4. 53. 4–6 and 4. 57. 1–4 (as also within pagan tradition, famously, by
Xenophanes, B 14–16 D–K).

¹⁰ These words are clearly out of place, and should be deleted as an interpolated
marginal note.

¹¹ With this laudatory account of the human physique and faculties, compare
Orr. 36. 1 and 20. 6; it is related both to accounts of the providential construction
of the human frame in the tradition of *Tim.* 69a ff., and to accounts of the distinction between men and animals in the tradition of *Protag.* 320d ff. See further Cic.
ND 2. 140 ff., with Pease (1958, ad loc.), and Philo *Opif. Mund.* 134–47.

¹² Cf. *Or.* 11. 4–5.

¹³ For other references to Persian fire-worship, see Hdt. 1. 131 ff.; Strabo 15. 3.
13–14; Lucian *Jup. Trag.* 42; Clem. *Protr.* 5. 65. 1.

deserve the retort, 'You most witless of all races, to neglect such a quantity of splendid images—the gentle earth, the bright sun, the navigable sea, the fertile rivers, the nurturing air, and the very heavens themselves—and instead to devote your energies solely to the fiercest and sharpest of all elements. The food you supply it is not restricted to wood and sacrificial victims and incense—no, to this image and this god you handed over the whole of Eretria to be consumed, along with the city of Athens itself and the temples of Ionia and the images of the Greeks.'[14]

5   I have fault to find with Egyptian custom too.[15] They honour an ox and a bird and a goat and the nurselings of the river Nile, creatures with mortal bodies and miserable lives, mean to look at, debasing to serve, and shameful to honour. The Egyptians' gods die and are mourned over; in Egypt they can show you both a god's temple and his grave. The Greeks do indeed sacrifice to good men too, but in that case their virtues are honoured while their misfortune is passed over in silence. But among the Egyptians the gods receive as great a portion of lamentation as they do of honour. An Egyptian woman once had a young crocodile as a pet. The Egyptians regarded this woman as the nursemaid of a god and blessed her for it, some of them going so far as to supplicate both her and her nurseling. She also had a child just come to adolescence, of the same age as the god, who had been raised with him and played with him. For a time, while it was still weak, the crocodile was tame, but when it grew up it revealed its true nature, and killed the child. The wretched Egyptian blessed her son for his death, on the grounds that he had been offered as a gift to their domestic god.[16]

6   So much for the customs of the Egyptians. Alexander the Great, after he had conquered the Persians and mastered Babylon and captured Darius, came to the land of India, which, its inhabitants claimed, had hitherto never been trodden by a foreign army, except for that of Dionysus. At that time a war was being fought between two Indian kings, Porus and Taxiles. Alexander captured

---

[14] In the Persian Wars.

[15] For more elaborate descriptions of Egyptian theriolatry, see Hdt. 2. 65 ff. and Diod. Sic. 1. 83–90; and for a similarly polemical attitude, Cic. *ND* 1. 43, 82, and 101 (with Pease 1955, ad locc.); Dio *Or.* 12. 59; Plut. *Is. et Os.* 379d ff.; Lucian *Sacr.* 14–15, Philo *Decal.* 78–80, Clem. *Protr.* 2. 39. 4–5, Athenag. *Leg.* 14, etc.

[16] For the story, compare Aelian *NA* 10. 21.

Porus and made Taxiles his friend and ally.[17] Taxiles showed
Alexander the marvels of the land of India, huge rivers and many-
coloured birds and fragrant plants and other marvels new to Greek
eyes. And among all this he showed him an immense creature, the
sacred image of Dionysus, to which the Indians used to make
sacrifice. This was a snake five hundred feet long, living [in a
hollow place,][18] in a deep chasm, surrounded by a high wall
surmounting the cliffs; the Indians supplied it with sheep and oxen
from their flocks and herds to eat, and it devoured them greedily,
more like a tyrant than a god.[19]

7   The western Libyans inhabit a narrow, elongated neck of land
washed by the sea on both sides; the Atlantic Ocean divides round
the headland of this peninsula and embraces it in its great sea-
swell. The sacred place and image of these people is Atlas. Atlas is
a concave mountain of considerable height, opening towards the
sea as theatres do towards the air; the middle section of the
mountain is a deep glen with fertile soil and fine trees. One can see
fruit on the trees and can look down from the summit as if into the
bottom of a cistern; but it is impossible to descend, for the cliffs are
sheer, and descent is in any case forbidden. The marvel of the place
is this. The Ocean in full flood dashes against the shore, and everywhere else inundates the plain; but over by Atlas the waves rise
up into a peak and one can see the water standing up on itself like
a wall. It neither flows into the hollow of the mountain nor is held
up by the land; instead, the mass of air between the mountain and
the water forms a hollow grove. This is the Libyans' shrine and
deity and sacrament and image.[20]

8   The Celts revere Zeus, and the Celtic image of Zeus is a tall
oak.[21] The Paeonians revere the Sun, and the Paeonian image of
the Sun is a small disc at the top of a long pole.[22] The Arabians

[17] Porus and Taxiles: Strabo 15. 1. 28–9; Arrian *Anab*. 5. 3–20; Plut. *Alex*.
59–60.
[18] Probably to be expelled as a gloss on 'in a deep chasm'.
[19] The Indians' sacred snake appears again in Aelian *NA* 15. 21; Strabo (15. 1.
28) sceptically reports a story told by Onesicratus of monstrous snakes (plural), kept
not by Taxiles, but by his neighbour Abisarus; cf. Stöcker (1979).
[20] Strabo (17. 3. 3) tells a similar story not about Atlas but about a Libyan altar
of Heracles which, although low-lying, is never inundated by the sea.
[21] For trees and groves in Celtic religion, see Chadwick (1970: 146–7), and for
the association between Zeus and the oak, *RE* v, s.v. Eiche, 2027 (F.Olck).
[22] This passage seems to be the only evidence for this cult.

revere a god, but which god I know not; their image, which I have
seen, was a square stone.[23] Among the Paphians it is Aphrodite
who is honoured; their image is like nothing so much as a white
pyramid, of an unknown material.[24] Among the Lycians Mount
Olympus gives out a fire which is not like the fire of Aetna, but
calm and controlled, and it is this fire that serves them as their
shrine and image.[25] The Phrygians who live about Celaenae
honour two rivers, the Marsyas and the Maeander. I have seen
these rivers; they rise from a single spring, which flows down to
the hill, disappears beneath the back of the city, and then issues
forth again on the other side, having divided its waters into two
rivers with separate names. One of them, the Maeander, flows on
to Lydia; the other expends itself there on the plain. The Phrygians
sacrifice to the rivers—some to both, some to the Maeander, some
to the Marsyas—by throwing thigh-bones into the spring and
calling out the name of the river to which they are sacrificing as
they do so; the bones are then carried downstream to the hill,
dipping beneath it along with the water, and those that are offered
to the Maeander never come out in the Marsyas, nor do those
offered to the Marsyas ever come out in the Maeander; and if the
gift is for both of them, they divide it.[26] The Cappadocians have a
mountain as their divinity and sacrament and image,[27] the
Maeotae a lake and the Massagetae the river Tanais.

9   What a mass and what a diversity of images! Some are
brought into being by human skill, some have won affection for
their usefulness, some have won honour for the benefits they con-

[23] The so-called *baitylos*; cf. Clem. *Protr.* 4. 46. 1, Arnob. *Adv. Nat.* 6. 11; *KP* s.v.
Baitylia (1. 806-8; W. Fauth).
[24] Represented on Cypriot coins of the Roman period, and still to be seen in the
Cyprus Museum, Nicosia; cf. Tac. *Hist.* 2. 3, with Heubner (1968, ad loc.); Servius
on Virg. *Aen.* 1. 724.
[25] Cf. Dionysius of Tarsus in Photius *Bibl.* cod. 223, 212b9-12; in Ctesias
(Photius *Bibl.* cod. 72, 46a34-7; Antig. *Hist. Mir.* 166; Pliny *NH* 2. 236: *FGrH*
688 F45 § 20, F45(e)) the volcanic fire is that of Mt Chimaera, and is noted for the
fact that it is to be extinguished with earth rather than water.
[26] A similar story about offerings to the Eurotas and the Alphaeus is told by
Strabo (6. 2. 9). The relationship between the Marsyas and the Maeander is
differently described by Hdt. (7. 26. 3), Xen. (*Anab.* 1. 2. 8), and Paus. (2. 7. 9, cf.
2. 5. 3). The existence at Celaenae of two springs with opposite effects (but nothing
to do with offerings) is noted by Theophrastus (219 FHSG ≓ Pliny *NH* 31. 19).
[27] Presumably Mt Argaeus (Strabo 12. 2. 7) is intended, on the grounds that
it is the region's most notable peak. Huxley (1978) argues that Cappadocian
mountain-worship is a survival of Hittite religious practices.

ferred, some have won admiration for their capacity to astound, some were divinized because of their size, and some have won praise for their beauty. But no race, Greek or foreign, seafaring or landsmen, nomadic or urban, can bring itself to dispense with establishing some kind of symbols for the honour they pay their gods.[28] How then should one resolve our question, whether one ought to make images of the gods or not? If we were legislating for some other foreign race of men who lived beyond our climes and had just recently grown out of the earth,[29] or been moulded by some Prometheus, and had no experience of life and law and reason, we might then need to consider whether this race should be left with its natural images, bowing down before not ivory or gold, nor oak or cedar, nor rivers or birds, but the rising sun and the shining moon and the spangled heavens, and pure earth and pure air, and the elements of fire and water all together—or whether instead we were going to confine them too and compel them to pay their honours through shapes of wood and stone. But if this latter is in fact the shared custom of all mankind, then let us leave established practice undisturbed, accepting the stories told of the gods and preserving their symbols as carefully as we do their names.

10   For God, Father and Creator of all that exists,[30] is greater than the Sun and the heavens, mightier than time and eternity and the whole flux of Nature; legislators cannot name him, tongues cannot speak of him, and eyes cannot see him.[31] Unable to grasp his essence we seek the support of sounds and names and creatures, and shapes of gold and ivory and silver, and plants and rivers and peaks and streams; though desiring to understand him, we are forced by our own weakness to name merely terrestrial beauties after his divine nature.[32] We are like lovers, for whom the sweetest thing of all is the sight of the loved one's form, but who also find pleasure in the recollections stirred by a lyre and a javelin or a seat or a racetrack, or in general by anything that arouses memories of

[28]   Compare the argument from consensus for the *existence* of God or gods (as in *Or.* 11. 4–5).
[29]   In the manner of the Theban or Colchian Spartoi.
[30]   An echo of Plato *Tim.* 41a.
[31]   Compare the similarly Platonizing descriptions of God in *Orr.* 11. 9 and 41. 2; for the idea of divine ineffability, and inaccessibility to the senses, cf. also Alcin. *Didasc.* 10 (164–5), Apul. *De Plat.* 1.5; Whittaker (1990: 100 n. 169, 106 n. 197).
[32]   Cf. *Or.* 11. 11.

our beloved.[33] What point is there in my continuing to enquire into this topic of images and to lay down the law about it? Let men know the race of the gods, let them only know it! If it is the art of Phidias that arouses recollections of God for the Greeks, while for the Egyptians it is the worship of animals, and a river or fire for others, I have no objection to such diversity. Let them only know God, love him, and recollect him!

ORATION 3   Socrates on Trial

Introduction

= 9 (1962) = 39 (Laur. Conv. Sopp. 4). The manuscript title—εἰ καλῶς ἐποίησεν Σωκράτης μὴ ἀπολογησάμενος, 'Whether Socrates was right not to speak in his own defence'—accurately reflects the content of the lecture.

This is the first of a number of orations to take some aspect of the life and thought of Socrates as their starting-point: see also *Orr.* 8–9 and 18–21. In the others, Socrates is used more as a convenient point of entry to a major issue in Platonic philosophy than as a topic of interest in his own right; here, however, he remains the centre of attention throughout. Thematically, the lecture belongs with the group devoted to problems of philosophy and civic life (see Introduction, pp. xv–xvi): compare above all *Or.* 16, in defence of Anaxagoras and the Contemplative Life.

   The writing of defences of Socrates was a popular activity, from the years immediately following his execution in 399 BC through to the fourth century AD. Besides the surviving texts by Plato, Xenophon, and Libanius,[1] we hear also of efforts by Crito (*Suda*, s.v.), Lysias ([Plut.] *Lives of the Ten Orators* 836b, and Cicero *De Oratore* l. 231), Theodectes (Arist. *Rhet.* 2. 23. 13, 1399ᵃ7-11), Demetrius of Phalerum (Diog. Laert. 9. 15, etc. and Plut. *Aristides* 1 and 27), Zeno of Sidon (*Suda*, s.v.) and Theon of Smyrna (*Suda*, s.v.). The premiss on which Maximus bases his own discussion, that Socrates in fact made *no* defence of himself in court, is

[33] An echo of Plato *Phdo* 73d (as also in *Or.* 10. 7).

[1] *Declam.* 1, v. 13-21 Foerster, with translation in Ferguson (1970: 257-89); *Declam.* 2 (*On the Silence of Socrates*: v. 127-47 Foerster, with tr. in Ferguson 1970: 251-7) is a response to an imaginary edict forbidding Socrates to converse during his last days in prison.

unusual; Xenophon's claim (*Apol.* 1 ff.) that he made no effort to *prepare* a defence because he desired to die is not the same thing. The historical accuracy of the premiss was much debated in the first quarter of this century, with many scholars being prepared to endorse it: see Oldfather (1938) for both the issue and earlier literature. It is as plausible, however, to see a neat piece of rhetorical one-upmanship on Maximus' part: how to defend Socrates, while at the same time impugning the legitimacy of everybody else's *Apologies*.

The compiler of Neap. 100 takes three excerpts from §§ 1, 2, and 8; and the *Lexicon Vindobonense* makes one quotation from § 2. Franciscus Junius cites § 1 in *De Pictura Veterum* ii. xiv. 3, and § 3 at the very end of book iii, and both sections in his entry on Zeuxis in the *Catalogus* (Aldrich *et al.* 1991: i. 192, 359; ii. 417, 421).

Oration

1   What a monstrous discrepancy! Of the other crafts and sciences, each and every one is free from the jurisdiction of the multitude. The steersman, when he takes command of his ship and exercises his science according to its own proper principles, is not held to account by laymen; the doctor does not have to put up with his patients reviewing and examining his prescriptions and the cures and regimes he suggests; nor are potters or leather-workers, or the practitioners of still more lowly pursuits than these, answerable to any other judge of their activities than their own craft. But Socrates, whom not even Apollo—he who knows the numbers of the sands and can divine the measures of the sea—[2] could convict of ignorance,[3] has not ceased to this very day to be the object of accusation and investigation; indeed, the succeeding generations of prosecutors and jurors have been still more vehement than were Anytus and Meletus, and the Athenians of his own day.[4] If Socrates had been a painter or a sculptor, like Zeuxis

---

[2]   A description borrowed from Hdt. 1. 47. 3 (see also *Orr.* 11. 6, 13. 3, and 29. 7).

[3]   An allusion to the famous response delivered to Chaerephon at Delphi: Plato *Apol.* 21a.

[4]   The most famous early example is Polycrates' *Accusation*, for which, see Dodds (1959: 28–9) and Chroust (1957, ch. 4). How many other such works followed is unknown: Maximus' statement certainly involves a degree of rhetorical overstatement. For the anti-Socratic tradition in modern times, see Montuori (1981) and Stone (1988).

or Polyclitus or Phidias, the reputation of his artistry would have secured his works general approbation; on seeing such things, people are so far from finding fault with them that they do not even dare to examine them closely, and need no prompting to come out with the praise due to celebrated attractions. But suppose there was a man whose excellence was not a matter of manual skill, as with painters or sculptors, but who had instead, through reason and toil and habituation and simple living and perseverance and self-control and the exercise of all the other virtues, made a harmonious and precisely crafted artefact of his own life; is it not absurd that this man should fail to achieve a sound reputation and the universal praise of all and the unanimous verdict of his jurors, but that instead the most diverse opinions should continue to be expressed on his account?

2   The case now before us is of such a kind. Socrates was indicted by Meletus, brought to court by Anytus, prosecuted by Lycon, condemned by the Athenians, imprisoned by the Eleven, and executed by the gaoler. He disdained Meletus when he made the indictment, he scorned Anytus when he brought him to court, he laughed at Lycon when he spoke, he voted against the Athenians when they condemned him, and he contested their assessment of his punishment when they made it;[5] when the Eleven bound him he proffered them his one body,[6] which was weaker than their many, but kept his soul, which was stronger than all the Athenians put together; he showed no anger towards the gaoler,[7] nor any reluctance in the face of the poison.[8] Instead, the Athenians condemned him against their will, while he died voluntarily: the voluntariness of his action is proved by the fact that though he had the opportunity to fix a fine as his punishment and to steal away into exile, he chose instead to die; the involuntariness of theirs is shown by their immediate repentance—for what more laughable experience than that could a jury have?

3   Do you still wish to consider whether Socrates was correct in this course of action or not? What would your feelings be if someone came up to you and told you of an Athenian advanced in years and of a philosophical bent, poor in fortune but naturally gifted in intelligence, a good speaker and a shrewd thinker, vigilant and

---

[5] Plato *Apol.* 35e–38b.
[6] Cf. Plato *Phdo* 59e.
[7] Plato *Phdo* 116bd.
[8] Plato *Phdo* 117c.

clear-headed, the kind of man to do nothing and to say nothing hastily, one who had reached an advanced age and had won praise for his character from by no means the lowest among the Greeks,[9] and from Apollo among the gods; how when there rose against him, in jealousy and in hatred and in angry hostility towards the Good, Aristophanes from the dramatists, Anytus from the sophists, Meletus from the informers, Lycon from the orators ⟨, and the Athenians from among the Greeks⟩,[10] and when Aristophanes satirized him, Meletus indicted him, Anytus brought him to court, Lycon prosecuted him, and the Athenians passed judgement on him, this man first of all flew into a rage with Aristophanes, took his stand in the midst of the Athenians and satirized him in return, at the Dionysia before a jury of drunkards; how then when he came to court he spoke against his prosecutors and delivered a lengthy oration, a speech of defence most carefully composed to win the jurors over; how he offered a persuasive account of the events at issue, bolstered it with evidence and proof and arguments from probability, called witnesses from among the wealthy and from those whom the jurors of Athens most admired, then in his peroration begged and besought and implored, and perhaps shed a well-timed tear, then finally brought a wailing Xanthippe and his whimpering children to the stand;[11] and how, by doing all this, he won over his jurors, so that they acquitted him and pitied him and released him?

4   Hail the conquering hero! Can one not picture him marching off from the court back to the Lyceum and the Academy and his other haunts, beaming like a man who has just escaped from a stormy sea? And how could Philosophy have borne to have this man return to her? No more than an athletic trainer could bear to see a competitor returning from the stadium after winning his event without sweat and effort, smeared with perfume, without a bruise or wound on his body, and devoid of any mark of valour.[12]
    Furthermore, what reason could Socrates have had for defend-

---

[9] e.g. Alcibiades in Plato *Smp.* 215a–222b; Laches in Plato *Lach.* 181ab.
[10] Alternatively '⟨ and the jurors from among the Athenians ⟩'.
[11] i.e. followed all the standard rhetorical precepts for narrative, proof, and peroration. The reference to Xanthippe and the children echoes Plato *Apol.* 34c, and the rejection of conventional forensic devices in general, *Apol.* 38de.
[12] Compare the imagery of *Or.* 1. 4 and 6, and the doctrine of *Orr.* 34 and 38.
7 'Without sweat' (ἀνιδρωτί) is a technical term for victory by a walk-over.

ing himself before that Athenian jury? Because he thought that
they were just men? They were unjust. Because he thought they
were wise? They were fools. Because he thought they were good?
They were wicked. Because he thought they were well disposed?
They were enraged. Because he thought they were like himself?
You could not find men more dissimilar. Because he thought they
were his superiors? They were his inferiors. Because he thought
they were his inferiors? Who ever defended himself to an inferior?
Moreover, what could he actually have said in his own defence?
That he hadn't been practising philosophy? That would have been
a lie. Or that he had been practising philosophy? That was precisely
what had made them angry. [5] No, you may say, none of that,
but he should have confuted the charges and shown that he
had neither corrupted the youth of Athens nor introduced new
divinities. But what expert can ever persuade a layman in matters
bearing on his expertise?[13] How were the Athenians to understand
what counted as corruption of the young and what as virtue? Or
what his divine mentor was and how it ought to be worshipped?
These are not matters to be dealt with by a thousand jurors
chosen by lot, nor did Solon draft any measure relating to them,
nor did Dracon's revered laws take them into account. Summonses
and denunciations and indictments and prosecutions and judicial
reviews and affidavits and all such things are dealt with in the
Heliaia, like the squabbles that arise in gangs of children over
knuckle-bones, when they steal from each other, doing each other
down and being done down in return. But truth and virtue and
a life of rectitude demand other jurors and other laws and other
orators, of the kind among whom Socrates won his victories and
his wreaths and his reputation.

6   How could an elderly man and a philosopher have failed to
look ridiculous playing knuckle-bones with children? What doctor
ever persuaded his feverish patients that going without food and
drink was a good thing? Who ever persuaded a hedonist that his
aims were worthless?[14] Who ever persuaded the money-grubber
that his object is not a good? To be sure, Socrates would have had
no trouble at all in persuading the Athenians that the pursuit of

---

[13] An echo of one of the topics in Plato *Grg.* (esp. 458e–459c).
[14] A further series of echoes of *Grg.* The philosopher among children: 521d ff.; the
unpersuasive doctor: 456b and 521e–522a; the argument with the hedonist: the
whole exchange with Callicles (NB 527e).

Virtue is not the same thing as corrupting the young, and that knowledge of the divine is not the same thing as irregularity in religious observance. Either they understood all this as well as Socrates did, or he did and they did not. If they did understand, what need was there to explain to people who already knew? And if they did not know, it wasn't a plea in defence they needed, but knowledge. Other kinds of defence are established by producing witnesses and advancing arguments and submitting to cross-examination and offering proof and putting witnesses to torture and other such measures, with the aim of disclosing what was previously obscure in open court. But for virtue and goodness there is only one test, namely the reverence that is shown for them. And since that had been driven from the Athens of his day, what point was there in Socrates explaining himself?[15]

7   To escape death, for heaven's sake, you may say. But if it is of this that the good man should at all costs beware, then the proper course for Socrates, quite apart from defending himself before an Athenian jury, was not to have incurred Meletus' hatred in the first place, nor to have shown Anytus up,[16] nor to have irritated his erring fellow Athenians,[17] nor to have gone around the city as a pungent and implacable chastiser of all and sundry who mixed with men of every rank and craft and occupation and aim and said nothing meek or sycophantic or subservient to anyone.[18] But if before now many a man has scorned death in war, and likewise many a steersman at sea, and if in general each class of expert seeks to die a good death while still practising his science, can it really be that the philosopher should have played the deserter and jumped ship and clung to life, casting away his virtue like a shield in battle?[19] If he had done this, what juror would have applauded him? Who could have endured the sight of Socrates standing humble and cowed in court, with his hopes of life hanging on what he could beg from others?[20] Because that is presumably the form his defence would have taken. Or should he have spoken, saying

[15] The contrast between legal and philosophical procedure is again reminiscent of *Grg.*: see esp. 471e–472c and 473e–474b.
[16] Plato *Meno* 90a–95a.
[17] Plato *Apol.* 30e–31a.
[18] The project described in Plato *Apol.* 21eff ; compare also the description of Socrates in *Or.* 1. 9.
[19] For the idea of the betrayal of philosophical values, cf. *Or.* 33. 3 (Epicurus).
[20] Cf. again *Apol.* 38e.

nothing humble or cowed or submissive, but something noble and worthy of philosophy instead? That is not a defence you are describing to me, but a way to kindle and inflame his jurors' anger. How could such a defence have been acceptable to an imperfect democratic court, grown degenerate from lack of discipline, intolerant of frank speaking, and accustomed to a constant diet of flattery?[21] They could not have borne it any more than a party of rowdy drinkers could have stood a sober individual confiscating their wine-bowl, taking away their flute-girl, removing their garlands, and putting a stop to their drunkenness. It was therefore the safe course Socrates took, in keeping silent where honourable speech was impossible; safeguarding his own virtue and avoiding the anger of his jurors, he left them with the bitter reproach of having condemned him in spite of his silence.

8   It is quite clear that the Athenian jury needed a speech made to it. When a span of seventy years, with its unbroken record of philosophical Virtue, an unerringly wholesome life and pure habits, a career of encounters, friendships, and associations both virtuous and beneficial—when all this could not save Socrates from court and prison and death, was he going to be saved by a water-jar measuring out the short space of time allocated to a speech at law? That would have been impossible; and even if it had been possible, Socrates would not have accepted it. Zeus and the gods, perish the thought! It is as intolerable as the idea of a similar adviser going up to great Leonidas the Spartiate to tell him he ought to retreat a little, and give way before Xerxes' advance, as if before a prosecutor in armour. Leonidas refused that course, preferring to die where he stood with his valour and his arms unstained, sooner than show a barbarian monarch his back and live. What else would a speech of defence from Socrates have been than a turning of his back, an attempt to flee his enemies' blows, cowardice masquerading as prudence? While the people of Athens thought they were condemning him, he held his ground, stood firm before the charge, and conquered. Xerxes too thought he was defeating Leonidas, but it was Xerxes who was conquered as Leonidas died. So it was that when the Athenians convicted him and Socrates died, God and the truth sat in judgement over them.[22] The words of Socrates' indict-

---

[21]   Another echo of *Grg.*: esp. 515c–517a.
[22]   This turning of the tables on the Athenians echoes the thought of *Apol.* 39cd.

ment against them are these: 'The people of Athens have offended in refusing to acknowledge the same gods as Socrates, and introducing other new divinities instead. For Socrates, "the Olympian" is Zeus; for the Athenians, it is Pericles.[23] Socrates trusts the word of Apollo, the Athenians contest it.[24] The people have further offended by corrupting the young—Alcibiades and Hipponicus and Critias and countless others.' What truth there is in this indictment! How just the court and how bitter the condemnation! In return for their blasphemy against Zeus came a plague and war with the Peloponnese. In return for their corruption of the young, Deceleia and the disaster in Sicily and the catastrophe on the Hellespont.[25] Such is God's judgement, such is his condemnation!

ORATION 4   Poetry and Philosophy on the Gods

Introduction

= 10 (1962) = 29 (Laur. Conv. Sopp. 4). The manuscript title—τίνες ἄμεινον περὶ θεῶν διέλαβον, ποιηταὶ ἢ φιλόσοφοι, 'Which produced the better account of the gods, poets or philosophers'?—copies Maximus' own formulation of his topic in § 7.

A lecture arguing for a historical continuity and an identity of purpose between the poetry of Homer and Hesiod and the philosophy of later centuries. The basic thesis is stated with the aid of an analogy with the development of medicine in §§ 1-3, in the course of which the use of myths (allegories) is identified as the central pedagogical device of early poetry; § 4 illustrates the persistence of allegorical technique in subsequent philosophical writing, while §§ 5-6 explain just why myth and poetic form are so valuable to the educator. The essential identity of early poetry and philosophy is reasserted in § 7, and illustrated in § 8 with an exposition of the philosophical import of Homer's account of the

---

[23] Cf. Plut. Peri. 8; Aristoph. Ach. 530.

[24] Another reference to the oracle to Chaerephon.

[25] Successive stages in the defeat of Athens by Sparta in the Peloponnesian war: the fortification of Deceleia by the Spartans, on the advice of Alcibiades (Thuc. 6. 91-3, etc.; cf. Or. 6. 6); the unsuccessful expedition against Syracuse, again promoted by Alcibiades (Thuc. 6. 1 ff.); and the battle of Aegospotami, in 405 (Xen. Hell. 2. 1. 21 ff.).

gods. The lecture ends with an attack on Epicurus, the one 'philosopher' to have turned his back both on allegory and on sound theology (§ 9).

The lecture is closely related to *Or.* 26, which offers a more thorough exposition of Homer's poetry from the same standpoint. The two together may also be seen as belonging to a whole group of lectures that debate questions to do with the identity and value of various forms of discourse and cultural activity: 17 (also on Homer), 22 (the superiority of philosophical discourse over poetry, oratory, and historiography), 25 (true eloquence), and 37 (the value of the liberal arts). At the same time, the lecture's theological content connects it with *Orr.* 5, 11, 13, and 41.

The argument in *Orr.* 4 and 26 draws on two mutually supportive lines of thought, both characteristic of the culture of the Hellenistic and Imperial periods: a belief in the superiority of the philosophy and teaching of the distant past over the decadent products of more recent eras; and a belief that early poetry, to be properly understood, must be read allegorically. The first is discussed by Andresen (1955: 252-6) (comparing Maximus and Plutarch), Joly (1973: 23-38) (in connection with Justin Martyr), Daniélou (1973: 48-68) (Clement), and Ridings (1995) (Clement, Eusebius, and Theodoret). Within pagan tradition, this approach can be seen as a reaction to the diversity and polemizing of modern philosophy, and an attempt to recover the supposed intellectual harmony of a better age—another form of the nostalgic primitivism one sees also in the encomium of Diogenes in *Or.* 36; for Christian thinkers, it could be adapted to provide a welcome means of challenging the authority of pagan culture. The names of Posidonius (cf. Sen. *Ep.* 90) and Antiochus are often mentioned in connection with the development of this cast of thought, but it is not clear that it can realistically be characterized as the invention of any limited set of individual thinkers.

The practice of allegorical reading, which goes back at least as far as the fifth century BC, was equally well entrenched and widely diffused in the culture of Maximus' day. It too could serve a number of different purposes: not only (as here) a 'defensive' vindication of the claims of myth and poetry to serious attention, but also (like accounts of early man) the construction of an authority-conferring pedigree for modern philosophical theory. Historically, the practice had been most notably developed by Stoic thinkers (whose reading of Homer has duly left its mark on the present lecture), but it had long since ceased to be the property of any individual sect or school. Any doctrines could be read into or extracted from the chosen authoritative text: witness, for instance, Philo Judaeus' and Numenius' Platonizing of the Pentateuch, or Plutarch's of the myth of Isis and Osiris. See Tate (1927, 1934), Buffière (1956, 1962), Pépin (1976), Lamberton (1986), Lamberton and Keaney (1992), Most (1989), Dawson (1992), and Daniélou (1973: 40–68).

Gregoras takes five excerpts from this lecture (from §§ 6, 8, and 9), and the compiler of Neap. 100 three (from §§ 5 and 6); the *Lexicon Vindobonense* makes three quotations (from §§ 1, 2, and 7). J. Reuchlin summarizes Maximus' analysis of poetic myth and quotes from § 5 on fol. xxvii^v of his *De Arte Cabalistica* of 1517. R. Cudworth refers to § 9 in the first part of his *True Intellectual System* (1678; 2nd edn. rev. T. Birch (London, 1743), I. 4. xxvi, pp. 444–5). A French translation of the lecture, along with *Or.* 28, was published in Paris in 1607 by F. Morel.

Oration

1 Human beings are terribly contentious. Not only do they quarrel about constitutions and political power and about the evils that afflict us all; they have even extended this habit to those most peaceable of all pursuits, poetry and philosophy. Now, 'poetry' and 'philosophy' are two names for what is, in reality, a single thing, differing within itself only to the extent that, as one might hold, day is distinct from the light of the sun falling on the earth, or the sun in its course over the earth is distinct from day. Such is the relationship between poetry and philosophy. What is poetry if not a more venerable form of philosophy, composed in metre and mythological in expression? What is philosophy, if not a younger form of poetry, less formal in composition and more lucid in expression? If then these two differ from each other only in age and in superficial form, how ought one to understand the difference in what the two kinds of composer—poet and philosopher—say about the gods?

2 Could we perhaps say that this present enquiry of ours is like someone comparing medicine in its original form with the modern

form that treats the patients of today, and examining the weak and strong points of each? Asclepius would inform this enquirer that other arts and sciences remain unaffected by the passage of time: where the need remains constant, the response does not vary either. The science of medicine, however, is constrained to adapt to the physical constitutions of its patients, which do not constitute a stable and clearly defined factor, but are modified and changed by the diets that go with different styles of life; different treatments and therapeutic regimes, adapted to the dietary habits of the moment, must be devised for different eras. 'So do not think', Asclepius would continue, 'that my famous sons, Machaon and Podalirius, were any less skilled in the art of healing than those who have set their hands to it subsequently, and thought up their various clever cures. At the time my sons were working, the bodies that their arts had to treat were not degenerate and over-sophisticated and completely enervated; as a result they found them easy to cure, and their function was a simple one:

> Cutting out arrows, and smearing on soothing drugs.[1]

But as time went on the human body slipped out of the control of this archaic form of medicine, fell prey to a more sophisticated style of living, and developed flaws in its constitution, with the results that we now see: medical science has itself had to become more sophisticated, and to exchange its former simplicity for something more complex.'[2]

3   Come now, following Asclepius' example, let the poet and the philosopher together defend their pursuits to us. The poet, for his part, would be absolutely outraged if anyone were to suppose that Homer and Hesiod—or come to that Orpheus or anyone else of that era—[3] were in any way less clever than Aristotle of Stagira or Chrysippus of Cilicia or Clitomachus of Libya,[4] or any other of those

---

[1] *Il.* 11. 515.

[2] This censorious account of the development of medicine echoes Plato *Resp.* 405c ff.; the parallel with the increasing sophistication of philosophical teaching is also found in Sen. *Ep.* 95. 14 ff. (cf. *Ep.* 90).

[3] Musaeus and Linus are likely to be the others alluded to: see Diog. Laert. 1. 3–5; Clem. *Strom.* 1. 14. 59. 1; 5. 4. 24. 1–2. On the poetry attributed to Orpheus, see Burkert (1985: 296–301), West (1983).

[4] The pupil of Carneades and head of the sceptical Academy, who died in 110/9 BC; see Glucker (1978, index s.v.). He is the most recent philosopher to be named in the *Orations*.

wise and prolific thinkers whose discoveries have benefited us all. No, the poet would insist, Homer and Hesiod were as skilled—and skilled in the same ways—as those others, if not more so. We saw how, in the case of bodily constitutions, those of older times, nourished by a good regimen, were easy for doctors to treat, while subsequent developments necessitated a different sort of medicine. It is just the same with the human soul. In former times, because of its uncomplicated nature and its so-called naïvety, what the soul needed was a gentle and artistic kind of philosophy which would guide it and control it by the use of myths, just as nursemaids keep children in hand by telling them stories.[5] Subsequently, however, souls became shrewder and more mature.[6] Infected by suspicion and daring, they started to examine the old stories, until unable to endure their subtle indirectness any longer, they stripped and unwrapped philosophy from its old finery and converted it into bare doctrine. However, these philosophical doctrines of today are in essence no different from the myths of the past, except in their form of composition. What descend to us via the whole philosophical tradition are doctrines about the gods that have their origin in a far more distant era.

4   Epicurus I exclude from consideration both as a poet and as a philosopher,[7] but all others have adhered to one and the same course. Except, that is, if you think that Homer had actually encountered the gods firing arrows[8] or conversing with each other[9] or drinking,[10] or doing any of the other things he says about them.

---

[5] For this picture of the historical and pedagogical function of myth, compare Strabo I. 2. 3 and 8, and [Plut.] *De Vit. et Poes. Hom.* 92.

[6] For the idea of human development from naïvety to shrewdness, cf. Sen. *Const. Sap.* 2. 2.

[7] Epicurus is disqualified as a philosopher because of his doctrines (both the denial of divine Providence, as in § 10 below, and his privileging of Pleasure as the proper end of human life, cf. *Or.* 33. 3); he is disqualified as a poet because of his rejection of traditional mythology (§§ 9-10 below), and perhaps also because of the frequently remarked uncouthness of his polemical style: see Diog. Laert. 10. 8; Plut. *Non Posse* 1086e-1087a; Cic. *ND* I. 93; and compare also Cic. *De Fin.* I. 5. 14, where Epicurus' prose style is compared unfavourably with those of Plato, Aristotle, and Theophrastus. For other incidental swipes at Epicurus, see *Orr.* 11. 5, 15. 8, 19. 3, 25. 4, 41. 2; and for a sustained attack on his doctrine of Pleasure, *Orr.* 29-33.

[8] Apollo in *Il.* I. 48-52.

[9] *Il.* I. 493 ff.; etc.

[10] The text is uncertain at this point: 'drinking' or 'getting drunk' is attractive, because it gives another reference to *Iliad* I (584 ff.), but 'taking counsel' (e.g. *Il.* 4. 1ff.) is also possible.

Nor should we believe that Plato had actually encountered Zeus holding the reins and riding in a winged chariot, with the host of the gods drawn up in eleven squadrons,[11] or the gods celebrating the marriage of Aphrodite in Zeus' palace, on the day when Resource and Poverty secretly made love and produced Eros;[12] nor should we think that he actually saw Pyriphlegethon and Acheron and Cocytus and the rivers of water and fire flowing back and forth,[13] or Clotho and Atropos, or that spindle rotating with its seven separate motions.[14] Consider also the poetry of the man from Syros, with his Zeus and Chthonie and their love, and the birth of Ophioneus, and the battle of the gods and the tree and the robe.[15] And remember Heraclitus with his 'dying immortals, undying mortals'.[16]

5 Allegory is ubiquitous, among both poets and philosophers. I admire these older authors' reverence before the truth more than I do the outspokenness of the moderns; the most seemly vehicle for topics which our human frailty does not allow us to see clearly is myth. For my part, if the present generation have seen more deeply than our forebears, I congratulate them on their achievement; but if instead, with no gain in understanding, they have merely converted allegory into explicit doctrine, I am rather afraid that someone may arrest them for profaning mysteries that ought not to be revealed.[17] What else is the point of a myth? It is a doctrine concealed beneath adornments of a different kind, like the statues that priests of the mysteries have clothed in gold and silver and robes, so as to make their appearance the more impressive.[18] Given the boldness of its nature, the human soul tends to think little of what is close to hand, while it admires what is distant. Divining what it cannot actually see, it tries to hunt it out by the power of reason; failure simply intensifies its keenness in the chase, while success means that it loves what it has found as if it were its own handiwork.

---

[11] *Phaedr.* 246e; cf. Trapp (1990: 148–51, 172).
[12] *Smp.* 203bff.   [13] *Phdo* 111cff.   [14] *Resp.* 616cff.
[15] Pherecydes: see A 11 and B 2 and 4 D–K; Kirk *et al.* (1983: 50–71).
[16] A paraphrase of the first half of B 62 D–K (cf. Lucian *Vit. Auct.* 14); the second half of the fragment is quoted in *Or.* 41. 4.
[17] For the comparison between poetry, philosophy, and mystery cult, cf. Dio *Or.* 36. 32–5.
[18] Boyancé (1955) suggests Maximus may here be referring specifically to Orphic mystery cult: cf. Macrobius *Sat.* 1. 18. 22 (= *Fr. Orph.* 152 Abel); *Suda* s.v. Ὀρφεύς.

6   It was their realization of this truth that led the poets to invent the device by which they play on the soul in their discussions of the gods: namely, the use of myths, that are less clear than explicit doctrine, yet more lucid than riddles, and occupy the middle ground between rational knowledge and ignorance.[19] Trusted because of the pleasure they give, yet mistrusted because of their paradoxical content, they guide the soul to search for the truth and to investigate more deeply.[20] What has for the most part gone unnoticed is that these men, with their cunning designs on our attention, are really philosophers. They may be called poets, but that is only because they have accepted a reputation for crowd-pleasing skill in place of one for something less congenial.[21] A philosopher is a difficult and unpleasant thing for most people to listen to, just as a rich man is an unpleasant sight to paupers, a prudent man to the profligate, and a hero to cowards: vices cannot abide virtues preening themselves in their midst. A poet on the other hand makes more soothing and popular listening; he is cherished for the pleasure he gives, while his virtues go unremarked. When doctors are faced with patients who make problems about taking their medicine, they immerse their bitter drugs in pleasant food and thus conceal the unpleasantness of the cure. In just the same way, the philosophy of the distant past covertly entrusted its message to myths and metre and poetic form, blending the unpleasantness of its teachings with a coating of entertainment.[22]

7   So do not ask whether it is the poets or the philosophers who have produced the better account of the gods. Call a truce and arrange a ceasefire between these pursuits, for it is in fact about just the one single and coherent art that you are enquiring. If you use the name 'poet' you are also saying 'philosopher'; if you use the name 'philosopher' you are also saying 'poet'. You are after all equally content to use the name 'hero' of Achilles, going to war

[19] The position assigned to δόξα in Plato *Resp.* 476e ff.
[20] For this idea of the usefulness of myth, cf. Plut. *De E* 385d; [Plut.] *De Vit. et Poes. Hom.* 92; Sallustius 3. 4; Julian *Or.* 5. 170a etc.; Clem. *Strom.* 5. 4. 24. 1–2 and 6. 15. 126. 1. The general idea is in circulation at least as early as Aristotle (*Met.* 1. 2. 9–10, 982^b).
[21] The same contrast, in very similar language, is drawn by Strabo, 1. 2. 8 *ad fin.*
[22] A familiar comparison, also drawn in *Or.* 25. 5; it is best known from Lucret. 1. 936–50, but see also Plato *Leg.* 659e–660a; Xen. *Mem.* 4. 2. 17; Dio *Or.* 33. 10; [Plut.] *Lib. Educ.* 13d; Julian *Or.* 8. 243cd.

with his poetic shield of gold,[23] and of Ajax, even thought the shield he carried was made of oxhide.[24] Their virtue makes both their shields equally heroic and impressive; in this respect at least, gold has no edge over hide. So it is with our concern here. For 'gold' read 'metre and poetry', and for the lowlier material read 'prose'. It is not to the gold or the oxhide that you should be directing your attention, but to the virtue of its user.[25] Let a man only speak the truth, though he may speak as a poet, in myths and in verse, and I will follow him in his allegories and scrutinize his myths, and will not allow his poetry to distract me. Let a man only speak the truth, though he may speak in prose, and I will listen to him, and be grateful for the accessibility of what I hear. But if you deprive either of them, poet or philosopher, of the truth, then you rob the poem of its poetry and turn philosophical doctrine into myth. If there is no truth then you should give no credence at all either to the poet's myth or to the philosopher's doctrine.

8   Epicurus, for example, has his doctrines, but they are far odder than any myth. So much so indeed that I am more prepared to accept what Homer said about Zeus, weighing the souls of his two heroes—

The one of Achilles, the other of man-slaying Hector—[26]

on golden scales, holding up the balance with his right hand. Inclining together with that right hand, I see the Fate that governs man:

nothing I do shall be vain nor revocable
Nor a thing unfulfilled when I bend my head to assent to it.[27]

Yes, I can see what happens when Zeus nods his assent,[28] for it is by this agency that the earth keeps its station, and the sea covers it, and the air surrounds it, and fire flies upwards, and the heavens revolve, and animals are born, and trees grow. Human virtue and human happiness are likewise products of Zeus' nod of assent.[29]

---

[23] *Il.* 18. 478 ff. and 19. 373 ff.
[24] The σάκος ἑπταβόειον of *Il.* 7. 219–25, etc.
[25] For the thought, compare *Or.* 1. 10.
[26] *Il.* 22. 211. This passage was also quoted by Chrysippus (Σ *Il.* 22. 212), *presumably* in the context of a discussion of Fate.   [27] *Il.* 1. 526–7.
[28] *Il.* 1. 528–30, allegorized also in *Or.* 41. 2; see Schwabl (1976).
[29] Zeus is thus identified with Fate and Providence; the allegorization is originally Stoic (cf. Chrysippus in Cic. *ND* 1. 39–41), but fits comfortably with Middle Platonic doctrine too. Cf. also [Plut.] *De Vit. et Poes. Hom.* 114.

I understand Athena too, now standing beside Achilles and turning aside his anger and tugging him back, now assisting Odysseus 'in all manner of toils'.[30] I understand Apollo, archer-god and god of music and poetry; I love his harmony and fear his archery. Poseidon shakes the earth with his trident, Ares brings the ranks of armies together in battle, Hephaistos plies the trade of the smith—but not for Achilles alone;[31] he finds his place and his activity wherever there is need of fire. This is what the poets say, and this is what the philosophers say too; simply change the terminology and you will discover the resemblance and realize what they are discussing. Call Zeus the supreme and venerable Mind which all things follow and obey.[32] Call Athena Intelligence,[33] Apollo the Sun,[34] and Poseidon the cosmic Breath that pervades land and sea, preserving their stability and harmony.[35]

9   Take any other examples you choose; in every case you will find a full stock of names on the side of the poets, matched by a full stock of reasoned concepts on the side of the philosophers. As for Epicurus, are there any myths to which his doctrines can be compared? What poet is there as idle and careless and ignorant of the gods as he is?

The immortal neither toils itself nor causes toil for others.[36]

What kind of myth could I ever find to express that? How could I depict a Zeus of that nature? What would he be doing, what would he be planning, what pleasures would he be enjoying? Zeus does indeed drink in Homer too, but he also makes speeches and conceives plans, just as measures for the affairs of Asia flow from the Great King, and measures for the affairs of Greece flow from the Athenian Assembly. The Great King conceives plans for Asia, for

[30] Il. 1. 193 ff.; Od. 13. 301 and passim.
[31] Another reference to the shield of Achilles, Il. 18. 478 ff.
[32] Cf. nn. 26–9 above, with Diogenes of Babylon fr. 33 (SVF iii).
[33] Compare Heracl. Alleg. 17–20, Chrysippus in Philodemus De Piet. 15 (= Diog. Bab. fr. 33, SVF iii), Cornutus Theol. 20, 35. 7 Lang, Justin Apol. 1. 64; cf. Buffière (1956: 280 ff.). In Or 26. 8, where Od. 13. 301 is again quoted, Athena is identified with Virtue; in Or. 8. 5, she is an instance of a helpful daimon.
[34] Cf. Heracl. Alleg. 6; [Plut.] De Vit. et Poes. Hom. 102; Diog. Bab. fr. 33; etc.
[35] Cf. Chrysippus in Cic. ND 1. 40 and Diog. Bab. fr. 33. In those Stoic sources Poseidon is the πνεῦμα pervading the sea alone. Maximus seems to be adapting the idea in a Middle Platonic direction, making Poseidon the immanent World Soul and removing Zeus to the transcendent intelligible realm.
[36] Epicurus κυρία δόξα (Master Doctrine) 1.

Greece plans are conceived by the people of Athens. The steersman looks out for his ship, the general for his army, and the lawgiver for his city. Steersman, general, and lawgiver all labour to ensure the safety of ship, army, country, and household.[37] Who then, Epicurus, takes thought for heavens and earth and sea and all the other divisions of the cosmos? What steersman? What general? What lawgiver? What farmer? What householder? Not even Sardanapallus was entirely idle. Shut inside the doors of his palace, reclining on his couch of beaten gold in the midst of his harem, he nevertheless took thought for the safety of Nineveh and the happiness of the people of Assyria.[38] Are you going to maintain that Zeus is still more idle in his pleasures than Sardanapallus? What an incredible myth! How utterly unbecoming to the poet's harmonies![39]

ORATION 5   Prayer

Introduction

= 11 (1962) = 30 (Laur. Conv. Sopp. 4). Manuscript title: εἰ δεῖ εὔχεσθαι, 'Whether one ought to pray'.

A sermon on the futility of petitionary prayer. §§ 1–2 set out an allegory of ordinary (materialistic) prayer, backed up by a series of celebrated instances from Herodotus and Homer. § 3 explains how such appeals imply a fundamentally mistaken view of the divinity to which they are addressed, and §§ 4–7a how, when the totality of factors conditioning human fortunes is surveyed, no role at all can be found for petitionary prayer. § 7b, returning to the territory of § 3, declares that if material goods are to be pursued at all, it should be through the efforts of the individual alone. However (§ 8, mirroring §§ 1–2), the only truly valuable pursuit is the cultivation of Virtue (philosophy); those who indulge in this (the few true

---

[37] A trio of standard images for authority and control (whether, as here, of God, or of reason, or of the virtuous man): cf. *Orr.* 8. 7, 13. 4 (with n. 11), 14. 4, 15. 2 and 5, etc. They have a Socratic resonance: cf. e.g. Xen. *Mem.* 1. 7. 1–3, 3. 3. 9.

[38] The argument here demands a slightly more positive portrayal of Sardanapallus than is the norm: contrast *Orr.* 1. 9, 4. 9, 15. 8, 29. 1, 32. 3 and 9.

[39] With this attack on the Epicurean denial of divine Providence, compare Cic. *ND* 2. 73 ff.; for the denial itself, see *ND* 1. 18 ff., Lucret. 5. 156 ff.

philosophers) do indeed pray, but their (legitimate) prayers are not petitionary.

The way the argument is developed, into a discussion of the relationship between God and the world, and of the different factors conditioning the march of events, connects this lecture closely with *Orr.* 13 (on prophecy and foresight) and 41 (on the problem of Evil): see Soury (1942, esp. ch. 2). For the same reasons, it is also one of those lectures that most clearly prompts discussion of Maximus' philosophical orientation: see Introduction, pp. xxvii–xxx, and *Or.* 5 nn. 18–20 below.

The topic of prayer was much discussed in ancient philosophical writing. There are many isolated references in Plato's dialogues, and it is the main subject of the pseudo-Platonic *Second Alcibiades.* Aristotle wrote a περὶ εὐχῆς, of which only a single fragment survives, and further contributions were made in the Hellenistic period: see Schmidt (1907) and von Severus (1972) for references and discussion. It would be particularly interesting to know what relationship, if any, Maximus' lecture bears to the lost περὶ εὐχῆς of Favorinus (Barigazzi 1966: 152–3). Comparisons may also be drawn with subsequent Neoplatonic theorizing, above all with Proclus *Comm. in Tim.* 2. 64a–66a (2. 207. 21–214. 12 Diehl), who summarizes previous treatments by Porphyry and Iamblichus (cf. Wallis 1972: 70, 109–10): while the positive part of Maximus' argument (§ 9) resembles the Neoplatonists' emphasis on prayer as a means of assimilation to the divine, his absolute rejection of petition goes substantially beyond anything they say. Equally, Maximus' discussion may be compared with contemporary and subsequent Christian treatment of the same topic: above all Clement *Stromateis* 7. 7. 35. 1–49. 7 and Origen *On Prayer* (ed. Koetschau, *GCS Origenes*, ii (1889), 295–403; tr. Jay 1954, with notes). The brief discussion in Aurelius 9. 40 also allows some comparison with contemporary Stoic accounts.

Early interest in the contents of the lecture on the part of readers is evidenced by the presence in the margins of Paris. gr. 1962 of a number of scholia, copied at the same time as the main text: they give a schematic summary of contents at §§ 3 and 4, and mark new sections of the argument at the beginning of § 5, and the beginning and middle of § 7 (see the apparatus to Hobein 1910, ad locc., or Trapp 1994, app. 1). The compiler of Neap. 100 takes three excerpts (from §§ 4 and 5); the *Lexicon Vindobonense* makes

two quotations (from §§ 1 and 2); and Apostolis quotes from § 1 to
explain the proverb Μίδου χρήματα (*Proverbia* 11. 67). One of
Bessarion's two manuscripts, Marc. gr. 254, bears a *notabile*
(ποδαπὴ ἡ εὐχὴ καὶ πῶς δεῖ εὔχεσθαι) in the Cardinal's hand at the
beginning of § 9. L. G. Giraldi refers to Maximus' version of the
story of Midas and Satyrus in his *De Deis Gentium* of 1548 (p. 612,
citing Maximus 'in sermone xxx'), and his lead is followed by
G. Voss in his *De Theologia Gentili* of 1641 (i. 21, p. 158). G. Benson
published an English version in 1737 in his *Two Letters to a Friend*,
which was reprinted in 1748 in *A Collection of Tracts*.

Oration

1   A Phrygian once, so the story goes, an idle sort and a lover of
money, captured the bibulous deity Satyrus by mixing wine with
the spring he used to go and drink from when he was thirsty.[1] This
foolish Phrygian made a prayer to his divine captive, and his
prayer consisted of precisely the kind of request you might have
expected the one to make and the other to fulfil: that his land and
his orchards and his crops and his meadows with all their flowers
should turn to gold. Satyrus duly granted his request.[2] But when
his land had been turned to gold, famine gripped the people of
Phrygia. And Midas, lamenting his wealth, sang a palinode to
his prayer,[3] praying no longer to Satyrus, but to the gods and
goddesses instead, for the return of his previous poverty—that
poverty which had been so readily and abundantly productive and
had allowed his crops to grow—and for the gold to afflict his
enemies instead. But for all the loud protestations with which he
uttered this prayer he came no closer to having it answered.[4] I
commend this story not only for its charm but also for the truth
towards which it directs us. For what is it but an allegory of the
misguided prayers of foolish men,[5] who repent the very moment

---

[1] Cf. Xen. *Anab.* 1. 2. 13; Paus. 1. 4. 5. In other versions of the story (Ovid *Met.*
11. 85 ff.; Hyg. *Fab.* 191. 4) Satyrus (or Silenus) is captured by peasants and taken
to Midas. See Bömer (1980: 259-63).
[2] In some versions what Midas gets from Satyrus/Silenus is instead the statement
that death is the best fate that can befall a human being: see e.g. Cic. *Tusc.* 1. 114,
Arist. *Eudemus* fr. 6 Ross.
[3] For the phrase in this connection, cf. [Plato] *Second Alcib.* 142d.
[4] In most versions of the story Midas is allowed to wash off his golden touch in
the river Pactolus: e.g. Ovid *Met.* 11. 127-45.
[5] The topic of [Plato] *Second Alcib.* 141a ff. (cf. n. 3 above).

they gain what they have been praying for? The hunting and capture of Satyrus and the wine are the story's way of symbolizing the fact that when by deceit or by force men obtain what they pray for, but not what they truly desire, they attribute the gift to the gods, even though it was not from the gods that they received it. God does not distribute evils;[6] they are rather the gift of Chance, coming blindly from their unreasoning source like the cheery greetings of drunkards.

2   What about the Lydian, who showed himself a still greater fool than our Phrygian?[7] Did he not pray to Apollo to conquer the Persian Empire, and shower the god with gold like a venal despot? And when repeated messages came to him from Delphi, telling him that

> In crossing the Halys Croesus will destroy a great empire,[8]

did he not seize on the prophecy with joy, cross the Halys, and destroy the great empire of the Lydians? I can hear prayers in Homer too: the Greek, for instance, who prays,

> Father Zeus, let Ajax draw the lot, or the son of Tydeus,
> Or the king of rich Mycenae himself

—a prayer which Zeus indeed granted:

> Out from the helmet leapt the lot which they desired,
> The lot of Ajax.[9]

When Priam offered prayers for his homeland, with daily sacrifices to Zeus of oxen and sheep, Zeus left them unfulfilled.[10] But to Agamemnon he 'promised and consented' that he should invade another country

> And having sacked strong Troy should sail away.[11]

Apollo to begin with did nothing to defend Chryses against the wrong done to him, but when Chryses spoke his mind and reminded the god of the savour of the thigh-bones he had burned,[12]

---

[6] A fundamental truth for Platonists (and Stoics): cf. *Or.* 41. 2–3; Plato *Resp.* 379c–380c, *Tim.* 30a; Hierocles ap. Stob. *Ecl.* 2. 87, ii. 117. 27 ff. Meineke.
[7] Croesus, in Hdt 1. 50 ff.   [8] Hdt. 1. 53. 3.
[9] *Il.* 7. 179–80 and 182–3.   [10] *Il.* 4. 31–49.   [11] *Il.* 2. 112–13.
[12] *Il.* 1. 35–42; cf. Lucian *Sacr.* 3, where the episode is held up as an example of a prayer made in the wrong spirit.

then he launched his arrows at the Greek army, bombarding them and their mules and dogs for nine days on end.[13]

3   What is this, you most excellent of poets? Is the god greedy and venal, no better than the mass of mankind?[14] Are we to accept the verse in which you say that

the gods themselves are pliant?[15]

Or on the contrary is God unbending and stern and implacable? Change of mind and repentance are after all unbecoming to a good man, let alone to a god.[16] Consider the pliant individual who is given to changing his mind: if the change is from worse to better, then his original decision was defective; if on the other hand the change is from better to worse, then the change itself is defective. But God and deficiency are incompatible. Or again, consider someone praying. Either he deserves to obtain what he has prayed for, or he does not: if he does deserve it, then he will obtain it even if he does not pray for it; if he does not deserve it, then he will not obtain it even if he does pray. If a man is worthy but neglects to pray, he is not rendered unworthy by that neglect; if he is unworthy of something, but prays to obtain it, his prayer alone cannot make him worthy. Quite the reverse: the worthy recipient is made still more worthy by his refusal to importune; the unworthy individual, who does importune, merely adds a further reason to be considered unworthy. To the former we attribute modesty and confidence: confidence in his certainty that he will obtain his deserts, modesty in his calm acceptance even when he does not. To the other we attribute folly and wickedness: folly in that he prays, wickedness in that he is not held worthy of a response. What if God were a general, and a baggage-handler asked him to be posted as a hoplite, while his trained hoplite took a rest? Would he not insist on the needs of sound strategy, leaving the baggage-handler to handle baggage and posting the other back among the hoplites? Yet a general is susceptible to ignorance,

---

[13] *Il.* 1. 43–52.

[14] Cf. again Lucian *Sacr.* 1.

[15] *Il.* 9. 497, a statement with which Platonist thinkers in particular were unhappy: Plato *Resp.* 364b ff., *Leg.* 905d; Hierocles ap. Stob. *Ecl.* 1. 3. 53, i. 34. 13–35. 2 Meineke; Iamb. *Myst.* 8. 8.

[16] An opinion widely subscribed to: Sen. *NQ* 2. 36; Hierocles ap. Stob. *Ecl.* 1. 3. 53, i. 34. 15–21 Meineke.

bribery, and deception. Not so God; for which reason he will not grant anything to those who pray, if they do not deserve it, nor will he refuse to grant blessings to those who deserve them, even if they do not pray.[17]

4   Of all the things which men pray to obtain, some are under the control of Providence, some are enforced by Destiny, some are at the mercy of fickle Fortune, and some are regulated by Science. Providence is God's work, Destiny the work of Necessity, Science the work of man, and Fortune the work of blind Chance. It is to the supervision of one or another of these four factors that the raw material of life is allocated. What we pray for must therefore be attributed either to divine Providence, or to destined Necessity, or to human Science, or to the vagaries of Fortune.[18]

If our objects are to be attributed to Providence, what place is there for prayer?[19] If God exercises Providence, then either he exercises it on behalf of creation as a whole and takes no thought for particulars (as kings keep cities safe by the operations of law and justice, but do not extend their concern to every last detail),[20] or alternatively the operations of Providence can be tested in particulars too. What then are we to say? Do you want God to care for creation as a whole? Then do not importune him; he will not

---

[17] Cf. Clem. *Strom.* 7. 7. 41. 5 and 7. 12. 73. 1-6.

[18] There are similar (but not identical) lists of factors conditioning events and human fortunes in [Plut.] *Placita* 885cd, Sextus *Pyrr. Hyp.* 1. 237, Stob. *Ecl.* 1. 5. 15-16, i. 45. 25-47. 16 Meineke, Diog. Laert. 3. 96. Doctrinally, Maximus' list implicitly endorses the Platonic perception that other factors than a single, all-embracing Destiny have a real influence on the march of events, as against the Stoic insistence that Providence and Destiny are one, and that Chance has no real existence (e.g. Sen. *NQ* 2. 45). The same project is followed out more fully in [Plut.] *De Fato*, Alcin. *Didasc.* 26 and Apul. *De Plat.* 1. 12 (cf. also Plut. *Quaest. Conv.* 740c): see Dillon (1977: 166-8, 208-11, 294-8, 320-6). Quite what distinction Maximus himself intends here and in §§ 4-5 between Providence and Destiny remains obscure.

[19] Divine Providence, and its concern for the interests of the whole over those of individual parts, is also discussed in *Or.* 41. 4. It is best known as a Stoic topic: see e.g. *SVF* ii. 1169, 1171, 1174, 1176, 1181, 1184; Aurelius 5. 8; and Cic. *ND* 2. 73 ff. Platonists, however, could claim an interest on the strength of such texts as *Tim.* 29d ff., *Leg.* 903b, and *Resp.* 420b-21e, and produced their own treatments: Philo *De Prov.*(Armenian tr.) 2. 99, [Plut.] *De Fato* 572f ff., Apul. *De Plat.* 1. 12.

[20] For the question and the comparison, compare [Plut.] *De Fato* 569d-570a; Alcin. *Didasc.* 26; Philo *De Prov.* 2. 44 and 54. The idea that divine Providence concentrates on great matters to the exclusion of small is Stoic in origin (Cic. *ND* 2. 167, Epictetus 1. 12. 2), but by this period had become common property (e.g. Justin *Trypho* 1. 47).

listen to you if what you ask militates against the preservation of the whole. What would happen if the limbs of the body gained voices, and if when one of them grew tired of being operated on by the doctor in the interests of the body as a whole, they prayed to Medicine not to be destroyed? Would not Asclepius reply to them like this: 'Miserable creatures, it is not for the whole body to be ruined to serve your interests; it is for you to perish in order that it should be saved.'[21] Precisely the same is true of creation as a whole. The Athenians suffer from the Plague, the Spartans suffer earthquakes, Thessaly is flooded by tidal waves, and Aetna erupts.[22] You may call such breakings-up 'destruction', but the true doctor knows their cause; he disregards the prayers of the parts and preserves the whole, for his concern is for creation at large. Although God's Providence does in fact extend to particulars as well. But prayer is out of place there too, being like a patient asking his doctor for food or medicine on his own initiative: if it is efficacious, the doctor will give it unasked; if it is dangerous, he will withhold it even when asked. To sum up: nothing that falls under the heading of Providence is to be requested or prayed for.

5   What about the things that are controlled by Destiny? Here too prayer is completely and utterly ridiculous. One has still less chance of persuading a tyrant than one does a king, and Destiny is a tyrant, unbending and supreme. Bridling its herd of human charges, it drags them on by force and compels them to follow where it leads,[23] as Dionysius did to the Syracusans, or Pisistratus to the Athenians, or Periander to the Corinthians, or Thrasybulus to the Milesians. In a democracy persuasion and prayer and assiduity and entreaty all have some efficacy of their own; but in a tyranny brute force reigns supreme. In the heat of battle a Homeric hero may cry,

Take me alive, son of Atreus, and take appropriate ransom![24]

But what ransom can we offer to Destiny, to free ourselves from the chains of its compulsion? What gold? What service? What

---

[21] For the imagery, compare Sen. *Prov.* 3. 2; Epict. 2. 5. 24; Aurelius 5. 8.

[22] The same list of events is cited in the service of the same argument in *Or.* 41. 4. All are well known from the classics: Thuc. 2. 47. 3 ff.; Hdt. 9. 35 and Thuc. 1. 101. 2; Hdt. 7. 130. 2; Thuc. 3. 116. 1 + Pindar *Pyth.* 1. 20 ff. + [Aesch.] *PV* 366 ff.

[23] Another echo of originally Stoic imagery: *SVF* ii. 975; Sen. *Ep.* 107. 11; cf. *Or.* 13. 8.   [24] *Il.* 6. 46.

sacrifice? What prayer? Not even Zeus could find an escape; he could only lament,

> Ah me, that it is destined that the dearest of men, Sarpedon,
> Must go down under the hands of Menoetius' son Patroclus![25]

What god can Zeus pray to for his son's life? Thetis too cries out,

> Ah me, the sorrow, the bitterness in this best of child-rearing![26]

Such is Destiny, Atropos, Clotho, and Lachesis, the inflexible spinner of human fortunes that governs our lives in their different courses.[27] How then could anyone offer prayers to implacable Destiny?

6   Nor again can one pray about matters governed by Fortune— still less so in this case than in others. There can be no way of conversing with a mindless despot in circumstances devoid of planning, judgement, and sober instincts, where authority is exercised instead by rage and impulse, by irrational dispositions and mad appetites and successive waves of desire.[28] Such is Fortune: irrational, impulsive, improvident, deaf, and unpredictable, swirling and changing like the tides of the Euripus,[29] and defying the best efforts of helmsmen to steer a steady course.[30] Given this, what prayer could one make to something so unstable, mindless, imponderable, and savage?

After Fortune it remains to speak only of Science. But what carpenter, secure in the possession of his craft, prays to make a good plough? What weaver, secure in the possession of his craft,

[25] *Il.* 16. 433-4. Maximus chooses to ignore the fact that, in the lines following these, Homer implies that Zeus could in fact have overruled fate, but refrains because he is unwilling to incur the disapproval of the other gods.

[26] *Il.* 18. 54; both this and the preceding pair of lines are quoted together by Plato in *Resp.* 388cd, in his attack on the bad moral effects of Homeric poetry. Zeus' tears remained an extremely popular talking-point in discussions of traditional religion: Cic. *De Div.* 2. 25; Heracl. *Alleg.* 42. 1-5; [Plut.] *De Vit. et Poes. Hom.* 111; Josephus *Apion* 2. 245; Sextus *Pyrr. Hyp.* 1. 162; [Justin] *Cohort.* 2; Clem. *Protr.* 4. 55. 3.

[27] The Fates had been allegorized in this way by Chrysippus, *SVF* ii. 913-14; cf. also [Plut.] *De Fato* 568e.

[28] There is a distant echo here of Plato's depiction of the tyrannical individual in *Resp.* 571a ff.

[29] A favourite image of inconstancy, with the Platonic authority of *Phdo* 90c; cf. *Orr.* 10. 5, 28. 3, 41. 3.

[30] With this negative description of Fortune (required by the argument), contrast the more positive picture given in *Or.* 40. 5.

prays to make a good cloak? What blacksmith, secure in the possession of his craft, prays to make a good shield? What hero, secure in the possession of his bravery, prays for courage? What good man, secure in the possession of his virtue, prays for happiness?[31]

7   What then is there that one might properly pray to the gods for, that depends neither on Providence nor on Destiny nor on Science nor on Fortune? Is it money you are asking for? Do not importune the gods; there is nothing noble about what you ask. Do not importune Destiny; what you are asking for does not come within the province of Necessity. Do not importune Fortune, for Fortune does not give to those who ask. Do not importune Science, for Menander tells you that

> Crafts do not prosper into old age, unless
> The man who plies them loves his money.[32]

Are you a good man? Then change your ways, give in to your evil impulses,[33] get on with the job. You will make your money keeping a brothel or trading, or by piracy or villainy or perjury or informing or bribery. Is it victory you are asking for? Something you can win in war with the help of mercenaries, and in court with the help of an informer? Is it goods you are after? Something you can get from a ship and the sea and following winds? The market is open, the objects of your desire can be bought; why then importune the gods? Put any worries about your unworthiness to one side, and you will prosper even if you are a Hipponicus; you will be victorious even if you are a Cleon; you will win your case even if you are a Meletus.[34] But if you venture on prayers to the gods, then you are indeed entering a meticulous and implacable court; God will never stand for you praying for what ought not to be prayed for, nor will he give you what ought not to be given. He

---

[31] With this distinction of the proper provinces of human enterprise and divine assistance, compare *Or.* 13. 4 below, with n. 12. This is yet another Socratic theme (Xen. *Mem.* 1. 1. 6–9).

[32] Menander fr. 408 Koerte, from the *Hymnis*.

[33] The text is corrupt at this point, though the general sense is not in doubt.

[34] A characteristic sequence of exempla drawn from classical history and literature: Hipponicus is known from Andocides (1. 115; and 130 for his wealth) and Thucydides (3. 91. 4), and was a popular butt of comic poets (Cratinus fr. 492 Kassel-Austin); Cleon is of course the demagogue, victorious at Pylos (Thuc. 4. 27–41), and Meletus the successful prosecutor of Socrates (Plato *Apol.* 19bc, etc.).

oversees the prayers of each and every one of us, a stern auditor
and inspector, and he reviews your words against the standards of
what is truly best. You will not get round him by bringing your
appetites to the stand as if in court, wailing piteously, crying out
'have mercy', pouring showers of dust over their heads, perhaps,
and reproaching the god

> if ever I roofed over a pleasing temple for you.[35]

God says, 'Do you ask for some good purpose? Take what you ask
for, if you deserve it; if that is your condition, you have no need
to pray, for you will receive even if you are silent.'

8   But Socrates, you object, went down to the Piraeus to pray to
the god[36] and encouraged others to do the same, and his life was
full of prayer.[37] Yes, indeed; and what is more Pythagoras prayed
and so did Plato, and all others who were granted the privilege of
conversing with the gods. But you believe the philosopher's prayer
to be a request for what he does not have, whereas in my opinion
it is a conversation or discussion[38] with the gods about what he
does have, and a demonstration of his virtue.[39] Or do you think
that Socrates really prayed for riches or for power over the
Athenians? Far from it! It was indeed to the gods that he prayed,
but it was from himself, with their blessing, that he received his
virtuous soul, his serene career, his irreproachable life, and his
cheerful death—those amazing, 'god-given' gifts. If someone asks
the earth for a peaceful voyage, or the sea for a good harvest, or
a weaver for a plough, or a carpenter for a cloak, he goes away
balked and frustrated and empty-handed. O Zeus, Athena, and
Apollo,[40] you who watch over the ways of men, it is pupils who
are philosophers that you require, pupils who will receive your
science in strong souls, and yield a fine and happy harvest in their

---

[35] *Il.* 1. 39; cf. note 12 above.

[36] Plato *Resp.* 327a.

[37] e.g. Plato *Smp.* 220d, *Phaedr.* 279bd, [Plato] *Second Alcib.* 143a; Xen. *Mem.* 1.
3. 2.

[38] An echo of Plato *Smp.* 203a; cf. also *Leg.* 716d and Clem. *Strom.* 7. 7. 39. 6
and 7. 12. 73. 1. The conception of prayer as a species of commercial request is
criticized by Plato in *Euthyphr.* 14ce.

[39] The analysis is tendentious; prayers in Plato are (and are defined as) petitionary: see esp. *Leg.* 801a, and [Plato] *Defin.* 415b. For prayer as petition in
Clement, see *Strom.* 6. 9. 78. 1, 6. 12. 101. 4, 7. 7. 41. 3-4, and 7. 12. 73. 1.

[40] The same triad as in *Od.* 4. 341.

lives.[41] But this form of husbandry is rare; it makes its appearance with difficulty and belatedly. Yet human life cannot dispense with this small, rare flame, as it appears now in one body now in another, any more than sparks of light can be dispensed with at dead of night.[42] The element of good in human nature is not great, yet it is this sparse element that time and again preserves the whole. If you deprive life of philosophy, you have removed from it the living, breathing spark that alone knows how to pray. So too if you deprive the body of its soul, you cause the body to freeze into immobility; if you deprive the earth of its crops, you emasculate the earth; and if you deprive the day of the sun, you extinguish the day.

ORATION 6   Knowledge

Introduction

= 12 (1962) = 40 (Laur. Conv. Sopp. 4). The manuscript title—τί ἐπιστήμη, 'What is knowledge?'—compresses Maximus' own statement of theme at the end of § 1.

The topic of this lecture, the definition of ἐπιστήμη, is that of the *Theaetetus*, but there are no obvious reminiscences of Plato's dialogue (except perhaps to the extent that both begin with a suggested definition that privileges the role of sense-perception). Commentators (Zeller 1923: 220; Puiggali 1983: 329, 334) have detected a lack of conceptual clarity and deficiencies in the sequence of thought in Maximus' treatment, but his exposition can be defended to *some* extent. § 1 poses the question, and 2–3 reject an initial suggestion that ἐπιστήμη is to be identified with organized perceptual experience. §§ 4–5a flirt briefly with the possibility that it is equivalent to the results achieved by abstract reason, before settling for a more inclusive definition: that it is the combined perfection of all three of the higher faculties, perception, practical reason (φρόνησις) and intellect. §§ 5b–6, using the metaphor of the 'laws' of intellect, praise the superiority of intellectual attainment, but in such a way as to suggest that moral excellence too will

---

[41] The image echoes *Phaedr.* 276b ff.; cf. Trapp (1990: 165–70).
[42] Compare the description of the search for the human Good in *Or.* 29. 5–6.

necessarily follow from it. It is here that the main incoherence lies, as the third element, perceptual excellence, is lost to view, and with it the 'inclusive' definition of knowledge that Maximus seemed to wish to recommend. § 7, rather than returning to the lecture's initial theme, follows on to a brief consideration of some literal laws that (virtuously) conform to the 'laws' of intellect. The lecture is incomplete as it now stands, but the missing portion need not have contained very much more.

Thematically, *Or.* 6 belongs with the five pieces that follow, all of which in one way or another involve discussion of the faculties of the human soul, and adopt a manifestly Platonizing standpoint. *Or.* 6 too Platonizes, though in a less immediately obvious way: see nn. 3 and 15 below and Introduction, pp. xxvi–xxviii. The subject-matter also overlaps with that of *Or.* 27.

Gregoras takes one excerpt from this lecture, from § 2; the *Lexicon Vindobonense* makes two quotations (from §§ 1 and 2); Apostolis quotes twice from § 3, to explain the proverbs γέρανοι λίθου καταπεπτωκότος (a false connection) and κραδίην δ' ἐλάφοιο (also dubious) in *Proverbia* 5. 35 and 10. 4. Franciscus Junius in book II (i. 3) of the English version of his *The Painting of the Ancients* (1638) combines a reference to the opening paragraphs with a quotation from Julian *Or.* 7, on the human impulse for knowledge.

Oration

1   What is the characteristic that distinguishes man from beast? And what is it that distinguishes god from man? In my opinion, men are superior to beasts in knowledge, and inferior to gods in wisdom: god is wiser than man, man more knowledgeable than beast.[1] 'Do you then take it that "knowledge" and "wisdom" are different things?' No, by Zeus, any more than I take it that life is different from life; but in this case, granted that the attribute of life is shared by mortal creation with the immortal, the shortness of a human life-span nevertheless separates the two, even though they participate equally in the basic quality 'life'. The life of a god is eternal; that of a man ephemeral. Imagine eyes that had the power to see eternally, to project an unblinking gaze and to receive the incoming rays of light without interruption; imagine that they had no need of eyelids to shelter them, nor sleep to rest them, nor night

[1] For the positioning of man between beasts and God, cf. *Or.* 41. 5.

to bring them peace. The faculty of sight would be something those eyes shared with normal vision, but the two cases would differ in the degee of continuity involved. In precisely the same way knowledge, though a shared quality, nevertheless differs in its human and divine manifestations.[2] Divine knowledge we will perhaps consider on some future occasion; for now let us turn our attention to what is most familiar to us. What are 'understanding' and 'knowing' and 'learning' in human terms, along with all the other similar expressions we use when we attribute a contemplative disposition to the soul?

2   Are we perhaps to give the name 'knowledge' to anything that is gradually assembled by the operations of sense-perception and given the name 'experience', then presented to the soul and stamped with the seal of reasoned thought?[3] Let me give you an example of the kind of thing I mean. The first men, before they had ever seen a boat, began to long for some means of visiting distant peoples. Need drew them on, but the sea stood in their way. They saw birds flying down out of the sky and swimming; they saw flotsam carried buoyantly along on the surface of the waves, even the occasional tree-trunk, carried down by a river into the sea. People followed: either someone was swept away against his will, started to move his arms and legs, and so swam to safety; or perhaps he went in voluntarily, in play.[4] The first result, once experience had gathered all these instances together and con-

---

[2] Compare the contrast between divine and human intellect drawn in *Or.* 11. 8–9, which also uses the analogy of different kinds of sight. The image of ever-active eyes is used in a different connection in *Or.* 34. 1.

[3] The image of the seal used here recalls not only Plato *Theaet.* 191cd, but also the Stoic definition of φαντασία (Zeno: *SVF* i. 141; Cleanthes: *SVF* i. 484; contested by Chrysippus: *SVF* ii. 55–6). The suggested definition of knowledge recalls not only Arist. *Met.* 1. 1, 981ᵃ 5–7 (cf. Sextus *Adv. Log.* 1. 224), but also the standard Stoic definition of ἐπιστήμη (Zeno ap. Diog. Laert. 7. 47 = *SVF* i. 68; cf. Sextus *Adv. Log.* 1. 151, Clem. *Strom.* 2. 2. 9. 4, Philo *Congr.* 140); compare also Julian *Or.* 6. 189d. The account of early human history and discoveries that follows recalls such Epicurean discussions as Epicurus *Ep. Herod.* 75, Lucret. 5. 1152–5, and Diog. Oen. fr. 10 Chilton.

[4] The ideas of need, of the imitation of natural processes, and of accidental discovery all feature prominently in the Epicurean texts cited in the previous note (where, however, they share a function not reproduced by Maximus, of offering alternatives to divine intervention): see Lucret. 5. 1452 (with Bailey 1947 and Costa 1984, ad loc.), 1091 ff. (domestication of fire), 1241 ff. (use of metals), 1361 ff. (artificial propagation of plants), 1379 ff. (music); also Diog. Oen. fr. 10, col. i. 1–11.

structed the notion of a voyage, was a lowly kind of raft, an improvised 'ship' made from pieces of buoyant material lashed together.
But gradually[5] perception and reason, advancing in step, attained
a sufficient degree of sophistication to allow the invention of a
concave vessel powered by oars and sail, driven along by the wind
and steered with rudders, and to entrust the responsibility for
its safe-keeping to the single, distinct science of navigation.
Furthermore (to give a second example), it is said that in the
distant past the science of medicine was invented in the following
manner. If someone fell sick, his relatives would carry him to a
well-frequented thoroughfare and set him down there. People
would then come up to him and enquire as to the nature of his
pain, and if anyone had suffered from the same malady, and then
been helped by some kind of food, or by cautery or surgery or by
going without liquid, they would severally suggest these to the
sufferer, on the basis of their own previous sickness and cure.[6] This
whole process, of exploiting the similarities between different
patients' sufferings to gather together a record of measures that
had proved helpful, little by little, with its accumulating series of
encounters, produced a science. Carpentry and metal-working and
weaving and painting were all discovered in the same way, each
and every one of them being guided to completion by the light of
experience.[7]

3   Very well; are we then to define knowledge as a habituation of
the soul to any given human function or activity? Or does this
capacity extend also to brute beasts? Perception and experience are
after all not distinctive of man; beasts too perceive and learn from
experience, which would give them also a claim to knowledge.[8]
Cranes migrate from Egypt in the summer because they cannot
stand the heat, stretching out their wings like sails and flying

[5] Cf. again Lucret. 5. 1453: ('usus et . . . experientia) . . . paulatim docuit
pedetemptim progredientis'; also Diog. Oen fr. 10, col. i. 14 and col. ii. 10-11.

[6] A process originally described by Herodotus (1. 197), in his account of the
Assyrians. Among later authors, Strabo attributes it in one place to the Assyrians
(16. 1. 20) and in another to the Egyptians (3. 3. 7), while Plutarch, like Maximus,
speaks generally of 'the ancients' (Lat. Viv. 1128e).

[7] Metal-working: Lucret. 5. 1241 ff.; weaving: Diog. Oen. fr. 10, col. i. 4–col. iii. 3.

[8] The intellectual (and moral) capacity of animals was already a point for dis-
cussion in Plato's time: Laches 196e–197c; nearer Maximus' own time, note Plut.
Soll. An. (Mor. 959a ff.) and Brut. An. (Mor. 985c ff.). For the whole issue, see
Sorabji (1993, chs. 1–7).

through the air on a straight course for the land of the Scythians. But the crane is an ungainly bird; with its ponderous body, long neck, light tail, slender wings, and branching legs it tends to wallow around in flight like a ship in a storm. Realizing this, from perception or experience, no crane leaves the ground without first picking up a stone in its beak to ballast it as it flies.[9] Deer swim across from Sicily to Rhegium in summer in search of crops and fruit, but the length of the crossing makes the business of holding their heads above the water very tiring. They alleviate their exhaustion like this. Swimming in single file they follow each other like an army advancing in column; each one as it swims rests its head on the rump of the animal in front, and when the leader of the formation grows tired, it moves round to the tail, so that each time a different animal takes the lead and a different one brings up the rear[10]—just as on campaign Xenophon brings up the rear and Cheirisophus leads.[11] Thus these creatures too can lay claim to acquaintance with generalship and tactics.

4   Perhaps then the truth is that though perception and experience are not distinctive of man, reason is; knowledge would then be nothing other than the secure operation of reason, following a consistent path as it searches out related phenomena, separating dissimilars and assembling similars, placing together what belongs together and moving apart what does not, dividing up what is jumbled, bringing order to confusion and harmony to discord.[12] Such is precisely the case with arithmetic and geometry and music, and whatever other disciplines approach their deliberations and settle them by the pure light of reason, without recourse

[9] This story about the crane is also told by Aelian, NA 2. 1 and 3. 13; other creatures said to use stones in a similar manner are bees (Arist. Hist. An. 626^{b}24, Virg. Geo. 4.191–6, etc.) and sea-hedgehogs (Plut. Soll. An. 979ab). Cranes were also said to use stones to help keep themselves awake (Plut. Soll. An. 967bc, Pliny NH 10. 59), and to fly in close formation, resting on each other in the same manner as the deer Maximus goes on to mention (Cic. ND 2. 125, with Pease (1958, ad loc.); Plut. Soll. An. 967ab; Oppian Hal. 1. 620–5). Such stories are more often used to demonstrate the workings of divine providence (Cicero, Aelian) than to make points about the definition of knowledge.

[10] The story about deer is also told by Aelian (NA 5. 56, mentioning crossings from Cilicia to Cyprus and Epirus to Corcyra), Pliny (NH 8. 114, Cilicia to Cyprus) and Oppian (Cyn. 2. 217–32).

[11] See Xen. Anab. 3. 2. 36–8, 3. 4. 38, 4. 1. 6, etc.

[12] A rhetorically amplified description of the procedure of διαίρεσις, as set out by Plato in Phaedr. 265de; cf. Or. 11. 8.

to any physical procedures.[13] And yet, you may say, it is not these that Homer cites as the most respected disciplines, and he is a venerable authority who surely deserves our credence. The only men he admires as wise are

> The seer, or the healer of ills, or the craftsman in wood,

and the 'inspired bard'.[14] What splendid even-handedness! The seer is wise and the carpenter is wise too, so too are Apollo and the doctor, and Asclepius wins the same respect as Phemius! It may be that though Homer may award honours to the different disciplines according to the order of their discovery rather than their usefulness, we should not proceed in the same manner. Let us instead say this. The human soul, which is the acutest and most mobile of all things, is a compound of the mortal and the immortal. In virtue of its mortal component it falls into the same category of nature as the beasts, in that it exercises the faculties of nourishment, growth, movement, and perception; but in virtue of its immortal component it unites with the divine, in that it is capable of thought, reasoning, learning, and knowledge;[15] and in so far as its mortal and its immortal characteristics meet, the area of overlap is given the general name of 'prudence', a phenomenon intermediate between knowledge and perception. The function of the soul, *qua* irrational entity, is perception; *qua* divine entity, intellect; *qua* human entity, prudence.[16] Perception accumulates experience, prudence reasoned reflection, and intellect surety; and it is to the harmonious combination of *all* these factors that I give the name 'knowledge'. If an analogy is needed to illustrate the point, let perception be compared to the manual labour of carpentry, intellect to geometry, and prudence to the science of the architect, which occupies an intermediate position between geometry and carpentry, being a species of knowledge when compared with carpentry, but at the same time inferior to geometry in surety.[17]

---

[13] There is perhaps a faint echo of Plato *Grg.* 450be (cf. Dodds 1959, ad loc.).

[14] *Od.* 17. 384–5.

[15] Compare the analysis of the soul and its faculties in *Or.* 11. 7–8. Talk of a bipartite soul, together with an ascending scale of faculties, has a decidedly Aristotelian ring to it: *Protrep.* fr. 6 Ross, *NE* 1. 13. However, it is unlikely that Maximus would have felt himself, or have been seen by a contemporary, as adopting a distinctively Peripatetic, as opposed to Platonist, position: see Rees (1957); Dillon (1977: 102, 174–5); Introduction, pp. xxv–xxviii.

[16] This again seems to echo Aristotle, *NE* 1. 13.

[17] More Aristotle: *Met.* 1. 1, 981ᵃ30–ᵇ6.

5   Knowledge,[18] prudence, and experience each have control over
a different range of human capacities. Experience, which deals with
fire and iron and many other kinds of material, uses the productive
resources of the arts and crafts to satisfy the everyday needs of life.
Prudence, which takes command of the passions and subjects them
to rational control, has the role of a science when compared to
experience, but falls short of true science in so far as it adapts itself
to the nature of the unstable and disharmonious matter with
which it has to deal.[19] Intellect, by contrast, is both the most
precious and the most authoritative of the soul's faculties, like law
in the state.[20] Only this is no law written on wooden tablets, or
inscribed on stone slabs, or ratified by decrees, or passed by the
vote of an assembly, or acclaimed by the people, or reviewed by a
court of law, or established by a Solon or a Lycurgus. No, this is
an unwritten law; its legislator is God, its respect owes nothing to
popular vote, and its authority is subject to no review. Indeed, it is
the only true law; the others, though they bear the name, are mere
fancies, misguided, false, and fallible.[21] Under those human laws
Aristides suffered banishment, Pericles was fined, and Socrates was
put to death; by this divine law Aristides was a just man, Pericles
a virtuous man, and Socrates a philosopher. Those laws produced
democracy and courts of law and assemblies and the impulsive
masses and venal demagogues, with blows of fortune and disasters
of every kind; this law produces freedom and virtue, a life immune
to pain and a happiness that nothing can diminish. Under those
laws courts assemble, triremes are manned, expeditions dispatched,
lands devastated, seas fought over, Aegina depopulated, Deceleia
fortified, Melos destroyed, Plataea captured, Scione enslaved, and
Delos razed;[22] under these laws it is Virtue that is assembled, it is

---

[18] Confusing, given that in the previous paragraph it has been suggested that
'knowledge' is the name for the successful operation of *all three* faculties; Maximus
would have done better to say 'intellect' here.

[19] This assessment of the relative status of φρόνησις combines an echo of Arist.
NE 6. 5 (esp. 1140ᵇ1–4) with a Platonist emphasis on the unruly, disruptive nature
of the passions (e.g. *Resp.* 588b ff.).

[20] Cf. *Or.* 11. 12, where the position of God (supreme Intellect) in the cosmos is
also compared to that of law in a state.

[21] The idea of a superior, unwritten, divine law is a venerable one: Heracl. B 114
D-K, Soph. *Antig.* 450–8, etc. Its development here owes a good deal to Stoic precedent: cf. Cic. *De Rep.* 3. 33 (= *SVF* iii. 325).

[22] Aegina: Thuc. 2. 27; Deceleia: Thuc. 7. 19–20; Melos: Thuc. 5. 116; Plataea:
Thuc. 3. 52 ff.; Scione: Thuc. 5. 32. A good example of how 5th-century history
and its historians are reread to provide moral exempla (cf. *Or.* 12. 7 for this

the soul that is filled—and with learning; households are well managed, cities enjoy good laws, land and sea are at peace—there is nothing sinister, inhuman, or barbaric; all is filled with peace and the laying-down of arms, with knowledge and philosophy and the pursuit of learning.

6   How the one set of laws outstrips the other in authority! How much gentler the one set of lawgivers than the other! He who subjects himself to true law is free and well provided for, and need have no fear of ephemeral laws and irrational jurors. Should men transgress these laws with criminal violence, it is not through condemnation by the people of Athens that their punishment comes— they are not led away by the Eleven or brought hemlock by the executioner—but from within themselves, from their own home-grown and voluntary wickedness:

> Through their own mad folly it is that they perish.[23]

It was through transgression of this law that Alcibiades came to grief, not when the Athenians recalled him from Sicily, nor when

> The Heralds and the Eumolpidae called curses on his head,[24]

nor when he went into exile from Attica. Those were trivial measures, a condemnation easy to shrug off: even in exile Alcibiades was mightier than those who stayed behind, winning honour in exile among the Spartans, fortifying Deceleia, obtaining the friendship of Tissaphernes, and taking command of the Peloponnesian armies.[25] The true trial of Alcibiades carried far greater weight; it was heard under a more venerable law and before a more venerable jury. It was when he left the Lyceum

particular set). The reference to Delos is problematic. Delos was famously *purified* (Thuc. 1. 8), but not destroyed; however, to emend the text to read 'is purified' (καθαίρεται for καθαιρεῖται) produces an odd conclusion to the list. A possible solution (suggested by Dr R. G. Mayer) might be to suppose that the reference is to the sack of the island by pirates in 69 BC; but the context does seem to demand a 5th-century event.

[23] *Od.* 1. 7; cf. the quotation of *Od.* 1. 33–4 in *Or.* 41. 4. The use of the line in this connection goes back to Chrysippus (*SVF* ii. 999), cf. also [Plut.] *De Vit. et Poes. Hom.* 120.

[24] An anonymous quotation found also in the *Suda*, s.v. ἐπηράσαντο and Εὐμολπίδαι. For the episode, cf. Plut. *Alcib.* 22 and 33.

[25] Cf. Thuc. 6. 88 ff.; 7. 19 ff.; 8. 45 ff.; Plut. *Alcib.* 23–4. Alcibiades' use here as a moral exemplum follows the precedent set by Plato (*Smp.*; cf. [Plato] *First* and *Second Alcib.*) and Aeschines (see next note).

under Socrates' condemnation and was banished by philosophy that Alcibiades truly went into exile and was truly damned.[26] A bitter condemnation indeed, an implacable curse, a wretched exile! So it was that a simple appeal to the Athenians could bring about his physical restoration. But Philosophy and knowledge and Virtue remain forbidden and implacably opposed to those they have once expelled. Such is knowledge, such ignorance.

7   I am also prepared to award the name of knowledge to the laws of Minos, taught by Zeus in a nine-year period and learned by Minos to bring happiness to the people of Crete.[27] The virtue of Cyrus I call regal knowledge—the knowledge that Cyrus learned, but Cambyses and Xerxes did not. Cyrus ruled the Persians as a shepherd does his charges, preserving and nurturing his flock, fighting the Medes, conquering the Babylonians, and allowing no wild and savage wolf to get among the sheep. But Cambyses, then Xerxes after him, turned from good shepherds into wicked wolves, ravaging the flock and straying from the path of knowledge.[28] The laws of Lycurgus I call knowledge inspired by the Muses . . .[29]

[26] Both here and in 'even in exile . . . stayed behind' Maximus is quoting or para-phrasing the *Alcibiades* of Aeschines of Sphettus (frr. 1 and 8. 42–3 Dittmar = 42 [fr. 1] and 50 [fr. 9] Giannantoni).

[27] As most famously described at the beginning of Plato's *Laws* (624ab); cf. also [Plato] *Minos* 319bc, quoting *Od.* 19. 178–9; Strabo 10. 4. 8 and 16. 2. 38; and *Orr.* 37. 1 and 38. 2. In *Or.* 38. 2 Maximus follows Plato and Strabo in asserting that Minos' conversations with Zeus took place every nine years; here he seems to envisage something different (unless the phrase 'in a nine-year period' should in fact be taken to mean 'on a nine-year cycle').

[28] Cyrus' position as an exemplary monarch was established by Herodotus (1. 107 ff.), Antisthenes (Diog. Laert. 6. 2 and 16, cf. Epict. 4. 6. 20; frr. 84–7 Giannantoni) and Xenophon (*Cyrop.*; cf. Cic. *Ad Quint. fr.* 1. 1. 23); see further Höistad (1948: 73–94). The direct contrast between Cyrus and his successors follows Plato *Leg.* 694a ff. and Dio *Or.* 29. 5 (but note also Hdt. 9. 122). The image of the ruler as shepherd is Socratic (e.g. *Resp.* 440d, *Leg.* 735b, *Grg.* 516a, *Polit.* 274e ff.), but simultaneously echoes the Homeric ποιμένα λαῶν (discussed in Xen. *Mem.* 3. 2); its application to Cyrus harmonizes both with his reputation for φιλανθρωπία (Due 1989: 163 ff.) and with the story that he was a foundling brought up by a herdsman (Hdt. 1. 107 ff., with Murray 1990). See also *Orr.* 15. 8 and 24. 7.

[29] For the notion that Lycurgus' constitution fostered a devotion to the Muses, see Plut. *Lycurg.* 21 and *Inst. Lac.* 238b. The end of the lecture is certainly missing, but it is hard to be sure how much has gone. Maximus has drifted away from his initial project (of defining knowledge) into moralizing about the pursuit of virtue, and thence into a survey of virtuous constitutions. The parallel of, for example, *Or.* 13 suggests that he may not have felt a need to return to his starting-point in order to achieve a satisfactory conclusion.

ORATION 7   Diseases of Mind and Body

Introduction

= 13 (1962) = 41 (Laur. Conv. Sopp. 4). The manuscript title—πότερα χαλεπώτερα νοσήματα, τὰ τοῦ σώματος ἢ τὰ τῆς ψυχῆς, 'Which illnesses are the more harsh, those of the body or those of the soul?'—accurately summarizes the topic.

Another 'psychological' lecture. Though the accent is now more on moral psychology than on epistemology, points of contact with both the previous and succeeding lectures can easily be found: with the picture of the disordered soul offered here, compare Or. 6. 4–5 on the potential confusion held in check by φρόνησις; and with the vision of escape from the body in § 5, compare Orr. 9. 6, 10. 10, and 11. 10.

Maximus returns to the topic of physical and mental sickness from another angle in Or. 28. The existence of a brief (and incomplete) declamation by Plutarch on the same theme (Mor. 500b–502a) helps to show how commonplace it was. Maximus' treatment draws heavily on the imagery of the Gorgias, the Phaedo, and the Republic, blended with allegorized heroic myth (Philoctetes and Odysseus) and a moralized version of fifth-century history and politics. In its stress on the superiority of the soul, and the folly of attaching importance to the body and its concerns, it shares territory both with philosophical protreptic and with consolation-literature.

Gregoras takes three excerpts from this lecture (from §§ 4, 6, and 7), and the compiler of Neap. 100 five (from §§ 3, 5, 6, and 7); the Lexicon Vindobonense makes three quotations (from §§ 4 and 5). The lecture was translated into Latin, along with Orr. 15 and 16, by John Rainolds, President of Corpus Christi College, Oxford, at some time before 1581; the translation was printed, together with versions of Plutarch's De Morbis Animi et Corporis and De Capiendo, in Rainolds' Orationes Quinque of 1613, and reprinted in Orationes Duodecim in 1614, 1619, and 1628 (see Binns 1990, ch. 13, esp. 235–6). Working from Rainolds's Latin, Henry Vaughan translated the two Plutarchan essays and Or. 7 into English for his Olor Iscanus of 1561. Robert Burton, also working in this instance from Rainolds, quotes from or refers to the lecture three times in the

Anatomy of Melancholy (1621: 1. 4. 1. 1, 2. 2. 6. 1, and 3. 2. 2. 1; Faulkner et al. 1989–94: i. 434, ii. 100, iii. 61).

Oration

1   There is an old song that takes the form of a prayer:

> Good health, most venerable of the blessed gods,
> May I dwell with you for the rest of my days.[1]

Let me ask the composer of the song how he understands the nature of this good health that he calls to dwell with him in his prayer. I suspect that it is indeed a divine thing and one worth praying for, not something that would casually and for no good reason have been thought worthy of a song and have continued to be sung about. But if it is indeed what I suspect it to be, let Reason herself answer us on the poet's behalf.

There are two components in the human compound, body and soul. Were it the case that the soul was naturally immune to sickness, then clearly our song would represent a prayer of the body, since it would be the body that by its nature fell prey to sickness and stood in need of good health.[2] But in fact the truth is that both body and soul, though most excellently blended by nature, are none the less tormented by the wayward violence of their constituent parts, and when one element within them gains the upper hand, like the people or a tyrant in a state, it hinders the others and damages their balance. 'Sickness' is our name for both forms of encroachment, sickness of soul and sickness of body.[3] But although in itself each of our two components has an equal need of good health, they are not of equal value when compared one with the other. Given all this, which of the two is it the balance and security of which deserves to be called 'the most venerable of the blessed gods'? In the interests of considering the sickness of each part by comparison with its opposite, and so establishing

---

[1]   Ariphron of Sicyon, *Paean to Health*, fr. 813. 1–2 *PMG* ; quoted in its entirety by Athen. (701f–702b), and extremely popular (see Lucian *De Lapsu* 6, and Page's apparatus).

[2]   The text is corrupt at this point: 'stood in need of good health' is conjecture.

[3]   In this form, the analogy, and the imagery of sickness of soul, is indebted to Platonic precedent (see esp. *Resp.* 444ce, *Grg.* 464a ff., 475c, etc.), but its use neither begins nor ends with Plato: see Democritus, B 31 and 187 D-K; Chrysippus, *SVF* iii. 421–30; Philo. *Virt.* 162; Plut. *Prof. in Virt.* 81f–82a; Dio *Or.* 27. 7 ff.; Epictetus 3. 22. 72 (with Billerbeck 1978: 137).

which is the greater evil for humanity, let me set out the whole
issue like this.

2   Man is a compound of soul and body, the former ruling and
the latter subordinate, like ruler and ruled in a state of which both
are equally parts, in spite of their differing roles.[4] Which of these
two constituents is it that must be in a bad condition for harm to
come to the state? In a democracy the people may fall sick, but as
long as Pericles, the good leader, remains healthy, he can compensate for the people's sickness.[5] But should Dionysius in Syracuse
fall sick with the disease of tyrants, his people's own health is
insufficient to protect them.[6] Are you prepared to compare the body
to a people, and the soul to their ruler? Think then, and put the
analogy to work. The people are more numerous than the ruler;
the body too is bulkier than the soul. The people are impetuous;
so is the body. The people as a mass consist of many parts, speaking with many voices and prey to many passions; the body too
⟨ . . . ⟩.[7] The people are a compound of a variety of dissimilar
constituents; the body too is compounded of a variety of dissimilar
constituents. The people are a creature swift to anger, vehement in
its desires, dissipated in its pleasures, spineless in grief, and harsh
in its rages, exactly like the passions of the body, which is itself
desirous, impetuous, hedonistic, and impulsive. But let us also
compare ruler with ruler. The ruler in a state is the most authoritative, most respected, and the strongest element; the soul in a
human being is the most authoritative, most respected, and the
strongest element. A ruler is by nature the most prudent and
rational of beings, and the same goes for the soul. A ruler acts on
his own authority; so does the soul. All this being the case, the
sickness of which of the two constituents is it that bears the more
harshly on the human individual and on the state? Is it not the

---

[4] Another Platonic comparison, echoing the city-soul analogy of *Resp.*, but again
not the sole property of Platonists (e.g. Arist. *Protrep.* fr. 6 Ross). Cf. *Orr.* 16. 4–5
and 27. 6–7.

[5] It is above all the Thucydidean portrayal of Pericles, particularly in his speech
in 2. 60–4, and the subsequent authorial verdict on his whole career (2. 65), that
makes Pericles available for the role Maximus here assigns him; cf. also Plut. *Peri.*
15 and 34.

[6] Dionysius is chosen as the antitype to Pericles because of his place in Plato's
biography: see [Plato] *Epist.* 7; Diog. Laert. 3. 18–23; Apul. *De Plat.* 1. 4. Cf. also
Orr. 15. 9, 24. 4, 36. 6.

[7] Only the precise wording of the phrase or clause missing here is in doubt, not
the sense.

superior element, when it falls sick, that causes more pain to the whole organism? When the people sicken but the ruler remains healthy, it is at least in a free state that they suffer. But when the ruler sickens, the state is enslaved. To sum the matter up: the soul is more valuable than the body; the good of the more valuable element is the greater good; what is opposite to the greater good is the greater evil; the health of the soul is a greater good than the health of the body; therefore sickness of the soul is a greater evil than sickness of the body. Bodily health is the product of Science, while health of the soul is the product of Virtue; the soul's sickness is moral turpitude, while that of the body is misfortune; moral turpitude is voluntary, misfortune involuntary; involuntary evils are matter for pity, voluntary evils for hatred; what is pitied attracts help, what is hated, punishment; what attracts help is limited in its ill effects, what is punished is worse.

3   Then again, consider health in both cases. The one kind needs nothing, the other everything; the one brings happiness, the other ⟨misery⟩; the one has no taint of evil, while the other is constantly at risk of stumbling into vice; the health of the soul is eternal, secure, and immortal, that of the body ephemeral, unstable, and mortal. Look also at their sicknesses. Physical sickness is an easy matter for medical science to dispose of; sickness of soul is difficult even for the laws to remove. Physical sickness pains the sufferer and makes him the more inclined to accept treatment; sickness of soul destroys the sufferer and sets him to despise the laws; the gods help the former, but hate the latter; physical sickness starts no wars, whereas all the many wars of history have come about through sickness of soul; no one suffering from a physical sickness gives false evidence, or robs tombs, or commits acts of piracy, or indulges in any other major form of wrongdoing, ⟨whereas . . . ⟩;[8] physical sickness causes pain to the sufferer, while sickness of soul causes pain to those around him too.

4   You may gain a clearer appreciation of what is being said from the following political analogy. The democratically governed city of Athens, under the leadership of Pericles, was at its zenith in the size of its population, the extent of its empire, its financial strength, and the abundance of its generals, when the Plague struck; starting

---

[8] '⟨whereas sickness of soul is at the root of all such offences⟩' would give the appropriate sense.

from Ethiopia, advancing through the territory of the Great King, and coming to rest in Athens, it ravaged the city.[9] Coinciding with the onset of this malady came war with the Peloponnese. As the land of Attica was laid waste and the city worn down, as its citizens perished and its power withered away—in short, as the city's body failed—one man, the great Pericles, remained unafflicted and healthy, and thus, like the city's soul, was able to steady it and set it on its feet and inspire it to resist both the Plague and the war. Now consider the second analogy. When the Plague was over and the people had recovered and their power was at its height, then it was that the ruling element in the city fell prey to a terrible disease of its own, one verging on madness, which seized the masses too and forced them to share their leaders' sickness.[10] Did not this people fall victim to the same madness as Cleon, the same sickness as Hyperbolus, the same infatuation as Alcibiades, and in the end follow the demagogues into dissolution, failure and defeat, as each of them called the wretched city down his own path,

> Come hither, dear bride, and witness wondrous works?[11]

Alcibiades points to Sicily, Cleon to Sphacteria, others to yet other lands and seas, as if pointing a feverish man towards springs and wells of water. Are these your wondrous works, you miserable creatures? Ruin and destruction, crowning misfortune, sickness inflamed? Such is the power of sickness of the soul compared to sickness of the body. The body may become sick and disturbed and waste away, but if you set a strong soul over it, it can make light of the disease and scorn its suffering, just as Pherecydes on Syros scorned his: as his flesh wasted away, his soul stood firm and waited for its release from this useless covering in which we are all enfolded.[12]

5   Indeed, I am inclined to say that noble souls do not even feel regret to see the body perish.[13] You might compare the case of a

---

[9] This account of the geographical spread of the Plague closely echoes Thuc. 2. 48. 1–2.

[10] It is again Thucydides' analysis of Pericles' successors in 2. 65. 10–11 that allows Maximus to make this exemplary use of them. Cf. n. 5 above.

[11] *Il.* 3. 130.

[12] For the stories of Pherecydes' death, see Diog. Laert. 1. 118, Diod. Sic. 10. 3–4, and Plut. *Comm. Not.* 1064a, *Non Posse* 1089f, and *Sulla* 36; for his status as an authority on the immortality of the soul, Cic. *Tusc.* 1. 38.

[13] For the sentiments and the imagery of this whole paragraph, compare Plut. *De An.* frr. 177–8. The emphasis on death as a release, and on the folly of clinging to

prisoner who can see the wall of his prison rotting and crumbling and waits for release and freedom from his place of confinement, so that he can step from the deep and murky dark in which he has hitherto been buried, and look up to the high skies and glut himself on the bright light of day.[14] Or do you believe that a man who has disciplined and trained his body with unceasing effort would be upset to find his clothing splitting and tearing around him, rather than hurling it away gladly and exposing his free and naked frame to its kin, the pure and unencumbered air? For what other role do you think this skin of ours and our bones and flesh play in relation to the soul? They are nothing but short-lived cloaks,[15] flimsy and tattered rags, liable at any time to be pierced by steel, or melted by fire, or devoured by disease. The good soul, which has been trained and disciplined with constant effort, sets no store by them and longs to strip them off as quickly as it can. The celebrated remark made about Odysseus applies also to the virtuous man afflicted by bodily disease:

What a thigh the old man can produce from under his rags![16]

But the wretched soul that is earthed into the body like a sluggish creature in its burrow[17] loves that burrow and wishes never to be parted from it or to have to crawl out of it. As it burns, the soul burns too; as it is torn to pieces, the soul is torn too; as it is racked by pains, the soul is racked too; as it cries out, the soul cries out too.

Oh my foot, shall I be rid of you?

cries Philoctetes. Cut it off, man, and stop shouting and abusing your most loyal friends and disturbing the land of the Lemnians!

Oh healer death![18]

the body, also bring Maximus into territory shared with consolation literature: see Kassel (1958: 75 ff.).

[14] The imagery of imprisonment and of escape into the bright light of day recalls Plato's Cave (*Resp.* 514a ff., esp. 515c–516b); cp. also *Orr.* 9. 6, 10. 10, and 11. 10 for similar imagery of escape. The idea of the body as a prison is venerable and widespread: Plato *Grg.* 493e, *Phdo* 82e; [Heracl.] *Ep.* 5; *Corp. Herm.* 13. 7; Philo *Leg. All.* 3. 21; *Ebr.* 101; *Quis Heres* 85.

[15] An echo of Cebes' analogy of the weaver and the cloaks in *Phdo* 87b ff.

[16] *Od.* 18. 74. For the adventures of Odysseus as an allegory of the embodied soul, cf. *Or.* 11. 10 and Buffière (1956: 461–4) (adding Plut. *Tranq. An.* 476ab).

[17] For the image, cf. Philo *Quis Heres* 85.

[18] Aesch. *Philoct.* frr. 254 and 255. 1. For contemporary interest in the play, see

If you say this in the belief that you will be exchanging one misfortune for another, I refuse to accept the validity of your prayer. But if you believe that death is indeed a healer that will free you from misfortune and from an insatiable, disease-ridden beast, then your belief is quite correct. Pray on and invoke your healer!

6 I see that the argument has brought me of its own accord to a still clearer illustration of the point I have been trying to impress on you all along. In those days there were—were there not?—ten thousand bodies in the army of the Achaeans,

As many as the leaves and flowers that appear in their season,[19]

all free from disease, healthy and strong and fit. Yet in ten years they achieved nothing—not Achilles with his swift pursuit, not the stalwart Ajax, not the deadly Diomedes, not Teucer and his arrows, not Agamemnon with his councils of war, not Nestor and his oratory, nor Calchas with his prophetic art, nor Odysseus with his wiles. The god spoke to them:[20] 'You fine and noble sons of the land of Greece, you toil and chase in vain, your archery and your councils are useless. You will find no other way to capture this city until there comes to your aid a mighty soul in a body that is sick, a body that stinks and limps and is eaten through with disease.' They obeyed the god and brought from Lemnos a healthy soul in a sick body to be their ally.

7 Now, if you please, consider the opposite case, of a sick soul in a healthy body. Picture a soul sick with the disease of Pleasure, wasting and withering away.[21] What can be done with the patient? What help is the body to a soul in that condition? Sardanapallus sickens;[22] do you not see how the malady spreads to his body too?

Dio *Or.* 52, with Luzzatto (1983). Quotation of fr. 250 in Plut. *Tranq. An.* 476b, and of 255. 1 in [Plut.] *Cons. Apol.* 106cd, suggests specific passages had been taken into philosophical use substantially before Maximus: cf. Wilamowitz (1899: 201 n. 164). The impression is reinforced by Cicero's use of Philoctetes in *Tusc.* 2. 19, 2. 33 (quoting Accius' *Philoct.*), and 2. 44.

[19] *Il.* 2. 468.

[20] In Apollod. *Epit.* 5. 8 the god's mouthpiece is named as Calchas; in the *Little Iliad* and in Soph. *Philoct.* 604–13, he is Helenus.

[21] Compare the pictures of the hedonist in *Orr.* 31. 5 and 33. 5–7. There are faint echoes in what follows of Plato's depiction of the tyrannical man in *Resp.* 571aff.

[22] The degeneracy of Sardanapallus is described in Diod. Sic. 2. 23, and his death in 2. 27. 2. For his use as a moral exemplar, cf. *Orr.* 1. 9, 4. 9, 14. 2, 15. 8, 29. 1, 32. 3, 32. 9; Aristotle (*Protrep.* fr. 16 Ross) seems to have been influential in conferring the role on him in the first place.

The wretch submits to depilation and cosmetics, his eyes melt, until eventually, unable to withstand his affliction, he perishes in the flames. Alcibiades sickens; a hot, fierce fire devours him, confusing his mind to the verge of madness and sending him on a ceaseless quest, from the Lyceum to the Assembly, from the Assembly to the sea, from the sea to Sicily, thence to Sparta, then to the Persians, from the Persians to Samos, from Samos to Athens, then to the Hellespont again, and all over.[23] Critias sickens; his disease, which is destructive and incurable, takes many forms and proves intolerable to the whole city of Athens.[24] Yet all of these men have bodies that are sound and healthy: Sardanapallus is dainty, Alcibiades is handsome, Critias strong. But this is indeed a hateful health. Let Critias fall sick, to prevent him becoming a tyrant. Let Alcibiades fall sick, to prevent him leading the Athenians against Sicily. Let Sardanapallus fall sick, for it is better for him to be prostrated by disease than by Pleasure. Or rather, to perdition with anyone thus subjected to an unceasing flow of vice! Creeping diseases when they attack the body are always on the advance, devouring and destroying some new part of the healthy residue and savagely resisting attempted cures, until medical science succeeds in excising the seat and basis of the infection. In just the same way, when a man's soul festers and rots with a devouring disease that is forever advancing its depredations and seizing whatever lies next in its path, then the bodily faculties must be excised and taken away from it, as if one were taking away a robber's fists, a roué's eyes, a glutton's tongue.[25] Because if you try to arrange for jury, prison, and executioners to deal with the disease, it will be off again before you can act, and will steal a march on you. Vice can be impossibly quick, when once it has invaded a man's inner character and can feast with unbridled licence and unchastened daring on the rotten matter it finds there.

[23] Maximus here borrows from the *Alcibiades* of Aeschines of Sphettus (fr. 1 Dittmar = 42 [fr. 1] Giannantoni); cf. *Or*. 6. 6.

[24] Critias is linked with Alcibiades as one of the failures among Socrates' pupils: cf. *Orr*. 1. 9, 3. 8, 18. 6, 21. 3, and 22. 5.

[25] For the imagery of moral surgery, cf. e.g. Plato *Grg*. 475d, 480c; Epict. 3. 22. 73.

ORATIONS 8-9   Socrates' Daimonion

Introduction

= 14-15 (1962) = 26-27 (Laur. Conv. Sopp. 4). The manuscript title—
τί τὸ δαιμόνιον Σωκράτους, 'What was Socrates' divine sign?'—is accurate.

After two lectures devoted to the powers and experiences of the embodied soul, the focus now shifts to the nature and role of those disembodied souls known to philosophical cosmology as *daimones*. The particular case of Socrates' famous divine sign (*daimonion*) provides the point of entry, as his erotic experience will to the discussion of Love in *Orr.* 18-21, but the bulk of the discussion is more general. §§ 1-6 of *Or.* 8 constitute a leisurely introduction, arguing that the ubiquity of daimonic powers, in the operation of oracles and in Homer's poetry, ought to make Socrates' individual *daimonion* entirely unproblematic, *provided* that one has a clear conception of the daimonic to start with. The remainder of *Or.* 8 (§§ 7-8) begins the business of providing such a conception by sketching the general providential role of *daimones*, and the features of human life that make that role necessary. This is explicitly marked as preliminary (§ 7 *init.*); it is left for *Or.* 9 to provide hard details of the *daimones*' nature and status. §§ 1-4 establish that, as beings combining the qualities of immortality and susceptibility to emotion (πάθος), *daimones* are an indispensable constituent in the cosmic hierarchy, without which its harmony and coherence would be in jeopardy; §§ 5-6a then enlarge on their immortality, and §§ 6a-7 on their emotions, and consequent diversity of function. The lecture ends with some notable examples of daimonic apparitions, balancing the list of celebrated oracles at the beginning of *Or.* 8.

Ever since the foundational work of Plato (*Smp.* 202d-203a) and the early Academy (*Epinomis* 984b ff.; Xenocrates frr. 15, 23, 25 Heinze), *daimones* had been an important part of Platonic cosmology and religious theory. The closest formal parallel to Maximus' two lectures is Apuleius' *De Deo Socratis*, which also casts its (still fuller) exposition of the basic theory as an explanation of the specific case of Socrates' *daimonion*; but see also Philo *De Gigantibus* 6-18, *De Somniis* 1. 134-5, 141-2; Plutarch *De Defectu Oraculorum* 414e ff., *De Genio Socratis* 588b ff. and (esp.) 589f ff., *De*

Facie 942cff., *De Iside et Osiride* 360d ff.; Alcinous *Didascalicus* 15; Apuleius *De Platone* 1. 11-12; [Plutarch] *Placita* 882b; Chalcidius *Comm. in Tim.*, p. 170. 6-177. 12 W; Porphyry *De Abstinentia* 2. 37. For modern discussions: Heinze (1892: 78-123); Andres (1918); Beaujeu (1973: 183-247); Dillon (1977: 31-3, 46-7, 90-1, 171-4, 216-24, 287-8, 317-20); Boeft (1977); Brenk (1986). Maximus' discussion provides the fullest surviving development of the notion that *daimones* are an indispensable rung in the hierarchy of living beings in the cosmos, but otherwise contains nothing not amply paralleled in the other sources, and at several points side-steps difficulties or refinements which they take into account.

The Platonist credentials of the lectures are effectively established by the choice of topic: although Stoics too had ideas about *daimones*, the construction and diffusion of elaborated theory was a distinctively Platonic preoccupation. If further confirmation is required, it can be found in the assumption of the soul-*daimon*'s immortality (*Or.* 9. 2 and 5), and in the description of its perception of transcendent, essential Beauty once free from the encumbrance of the body (9. 6). The fact that §§ 1-5 of *Or.* 9 contain so much that recalls Aristotelian (and to a much lesser extent, Stoic) precedent merely testifies to the extent to which Middle Platonism had absorbed vocabulary and forms of argument from outside the strict confines of the Academy. See Introduction, pp. xxvi-xxviii.

There are many signs of interest on the part of later readers, from the earliest detectable stage down to the seventeenth century. The contents of §§ 3, 4, and 5 of *Or.* 9 are all summarized in diagrammatic scholia on Paris. gr. 1962. Gregoras takes five excerpts from *Or.* 8 (from §§ 1, 2, and 7) and one from 9 (from § 1), while the compiler of Neap. 100 takes one from 8 and two from 9 (from 8. 3, 9. 5, and 9. 7). The *Lexicon Vindobonense* makes three quotations from 8 (from §§ 2 and 6). On the older of Cardinal Bessarion's two manuscripts of the *Orations*, Marc. gr. 514, there are eighteen notes in the margins to *Or.* 8 and eleven on *Or.* 9 (foll. 185^v-188^r, on *Or.* 8. 1, 3, 6, 7, 8; foll. 188^r-189^r, on *Or.* 9. 1, 2, 3, 4, 5), in a hand that is very likely to be his own; and on Marc. gr. 254, certainly in his hand, there are five notes on *Or.* 8 and thirteen on *Or.* 9 (fol. 90^r, all five notes on *Or.* 8. 8; foll. 91^r-93^v, at least one note on each paragraph). Ficino (1551) lists Maximus with Hermias and Apuleius as authorities on Socrates' *daimonion* in the introduction to his translation of the *Theages*; Poliziano notes the catalogue of oracles in *Or.* 8. 1 (Paris. gr. 1962, fol. 45ᵛ); and Reuchlin, like Ficino, gives Maximus' name as one of several transmitters of (Pythagorean) demonology in the *De Arte Cabalistica* (fol. xliii(bis)ʳ) Robert Burton makes four references to the two lectures in the *Anatomy of Melancholy* (1. 2. 1. 2, 3. 4. 1. 2-3, and 3. 4. 1. 5; Faulkner *et al.* 1989-94: i. 175, 180, iii. 343, 371-2), and Gerard Voss one to *Or.* 8 in the *De Theologia Gentili* (i. 7, p. 94: general reference to *Or.* 8). Francisus Junius uses *Or.* 8. 6 in his entries on Phidias and Polyclitus in the *Catalogus* (Aldrich *et al.* 1991: ii. 299, 319).

Oration 8

1   You seem surprised that Socrates should have enjoyed the company of a benevolent prophetic *daimonion*, which was his constant companion and an all but inseparable element of his mind— even though he was a man pure in body and blessed with a virtuous soul, meticulous in the conduct of his life, a shrewd thinker, an eloquent speaker, pious towards the gods, and holy in his dealings with men. Why is it that this surprises you, when you are not in the least surprised that a whole host of other people should have dealings with the daemonic realm every day, not only to discover what they themselves should do or not do, but also to prophesy to others, in public and in private:[1] a woman chosen at random from among the Delphians at the Pythian oracle;[2] a Thesprotian at Dodona; a Libyan in the temple of Zeus Ammon; an Ionian at Claros; a Lycian in Xanthus; a Boeotian at the shrine of Ismenian Apollo?[3] Do you assume the difference to be that the Delphic prophetess sits on a tripod and is filled by a daemonic

[1] The connection of *daimones* with oracles is standard: Plato *Smp.* 202e; Apul. *De Deo Socr.* 6. 133; Plut. *De Facie* 944cd and (above all) *De Def.* 415aff. Maximus' question here echoes Xen. *Apol.* 12-13.
[2] Cf. Plut. *Pyth. Or.* 405c for the humble status of the Pythia. For the oracle's operations, Fontenrose (1978, ch. 7).
[3] Dodona and Ammon: Parke (1967, chs. 1-7 and 9); Claros: Parke (1985, chs. 7-9); Apollo Ismenius (Thebes): e.g. Pindar *Pyth.* 11. 1, Hdt. 8. 134, cf. Farnell (1896-1909: iv. n. 185). The reference to Xanthus is puzzling: Apollo's most celebrated Lycian oracle was at Patara (Parke 1985: 186-93), on the *river* Xanthus, but not in the town of Xanthus; Maximus is perhaps simply assuming that Lycian Apollo's main oracle must have been in the region's principal town. On the continued vigour and popularity of oracles in the second century, Lane Fox (1986, ch. 5).

spirit before she utters? That the Ionian priest has to draw water
from a spring and drink it before he enters his prophetic state? That
those 'unwashed' individuals who tend the tree at Dodona and
'sleep on the ground'[4] are said by the Thesprotians to learn their
prophecies from the tree? [2] In the shrine of Trophonius (this
too is an oracular site in Boeotia near the city of Lebadeia, sacred
to the hero Trophonius) anyone who wishes to encounter the
daimonion must put on an ankle-length linen robe and a red cloak,
grasp two loaves in his hands, and descend on his back through a
narrow opening; then, having seen and having heard, he returns
to the surface with his oracle, his own prophet.[5] There was also, I
believe, an oracular cave in Magna Graecia in Italy, beside the lake
called Avernus, with attendants called 'leaders of shades' from the
nature of their work. Anyone wishing to consult this oracle came
to the place, prayed, made sacrifice, poured libations, and then
called up the shade of one or another of his ancestors or family.
There would come to meet him a ghostly image, only dimly visible
and indistinct, but with the power to speak and to prophesy; he
would consult this ghost about the matters he wished to have
settled and then go on his way.[6] I believe that Homer knew about
this oracle, but that when he included it in the wanderings of
Odysseus he allowed himself the poetic licence of moving it away
from the Mediterranean sea.[7]

3   If these stories are true, as indeed they are (some of the oracles
remain to this day exactly as they were, clear traces remain of
others to show how they were tended and revered),[8] then it is
astonishing that, on the one hand, no one finds them at all strange
or out of the ordinary, or tries to dispute them, and everyone is

[4] These epithets for the Dodonan Selloi follow Homer, *Il.* 16. 235.

[5] The oracle of Trophonius and its colourful procedure were much described:
Pausan. 9. 39. 4 and Plutarch's lost *On the Descent to the Oracle of Trophonius*
(Lamprias catalogue, 181); it provides the setting for the vision of Timarchus in
Plut. *De Genio* 589ff. and for an exploit of the hero in Philostr. *Vita Apollonii* 8.
19-20; Lucian has fun with it in *Dial. Mort.* 10.

[6] The νεκυομαντεῖον of Avernus was described by Ephorus (*FGrH* 70 F134 =
Strabo 5. 4. 5) and exploited by Virgil (*Aen.* 6. 236-263); Strabo implies it was
defunct by his day. Paradoxographic writers ([Arist.] *Mir. Ausc.* 102, Antig. *Hist.
Mir.* 102, citing Timaeus) dwell on the properties of the lake rather than the
oracle.

[7] Homer *Od.* 11. 13ff. Maximus here echoes the scholarly discussion of the
physical location of Odysseus' wanderings known chiefly from Strabo 1. 2 (but cf.
also Crates in Geminus *Elements* 6. 9-31).

[8] Cf. again Lane Fox (1986, ch. 5).

content to take long tradition as evidence of truth, visiting oracles to put their questions, trusting what they hear, acting on what they have taken on trust, and respecting the oracles whose advice they have acted on; but at the same time, if a man of great nobility of character and the most moral upbringing, a true philosopher supremely blessed by fortune, is judged worthy by God of intimacy with the daemonic, this does strike people as amazing and incredible—as also does the fact that this particular *daimonion*, though entirely adequate to the individual, chose not to give oracles to the Athenians, deliberating over the troubles of Greece, or to the Spartans, consulting about their campaigns, or to prospective competitors at the Olympics, wondering about their chances of victory, or to defendants at law about their chances of conviction, or to money-lovers about their chances of making a fortune, or indeed about any of the matters over which men daily importune the gods for no respectable motive.[9] In fact it is quite likely that Socrates' *daimonion* too was perfectly capable of settling such questions, given its prophetic powers—any doctor who can treat himself can also treat others,[10] and the same holds for carpenters and cobblers and any other skilled profession you care to name. What was distinctive about Socrates was that he conversed with the divine in his mind, and used his conversation with his *daimonion* to order his own life well; this in turn enabled him to deal with others in an appropriate and irreproachable manner.[11]

4 So far so good. 'I quite accept', someone will say, 'that Socrates was judged worthy of conversation with his *daimonion* because of his virtuous character and noble nature. But what I still want to know is what his *daimonion* actually was.' I will gladly answer you, sir, if you will first tell me whether you believe that there is such a thing in nature as a race of *daimonia*—alongside gods, men, and beasts[12]—or not. It would be wholly ridiculous to ask what Socrates' *daimonion* was if you had no idea about them at all. You would be like an islander who had never seen or heard of horses

---

[9] See Fontenrose (1978: 245 ff.), for a survey of enquiries and responses from Delphi.

[10] The wording here echoes the reference to the *daimonion* in Plato *Phaedr.* 242c5.

[11] Contrast Xen. *Apol.* 13 and *Mem.* 1. 1. 4–6, where it is claimed that Socrates did sometimes pass on advice from his *daimonion* to his friends. Plut. *De Genio* 580e records an occasion when such advice was ignored, to the friend's cost.

[12] A first reference to the idea of a natural hierarchy (*scala naturae*), which is to be important in *Or.* 9: see §§ 1–4, with notes.

and who, on learning that the king of Macedonia had something called Bucephalas, which was tame enough for him to ride, but unmountable by others, asked what Bucephalas was. His informant would be at a loss how to explain things to him clearly, given that he had no acquaintance with the species 'horse'.[13]

5 Here is another point.[14] Have those people now expressing doubts about Socrates' *daimonion* never read Homer's story about Achilles, about how, when he made a speech to the assembled army and quarrelled with Agamemnon and drew his sword as if to strike him, he was restrained by a *daimonion?* Homer calls this *daimonion* 'Athena'. For it was she, he says, who appeared to him in his anger,

> And standing behind Peleus' son caught him by his fair hair.[15]

He mentions this same Athena in connection with Diomedes too, saying that

> She took away the mist from his eyes, that before now
> Was there, so that he might well recognize the god and the mortal.[16]

Or again, take the case of Telemachus, about to meet a king and an older man, and feeling embarrassed and helpless. His companion says to him,

> Telemachus, some things you yourself will think of for yourself,
> Others the daimonion will suggest to you.[17]

And he gives his reason for hoping for help from the *daimonion*:

> For I do not believe
> That you were born and bred without the blessing of the gods.[18]

And in another case Homer says,

> The white-armed goddess Hera put the thought into his head.[19]

---

[13] For the story of Alexander and Bucephalas, cf. Plut. *Alex.* 6; Arrian *Anab.* 5. 19. 4–6; Q. Curtius 6. 5. 18; and Anderson (1930).

[14] With this reading of Homer's gods, contrast that of *Orr.* 4 and 26, which makes them physical elements and moral qualities rather than *daimones* subordinate to the supreme God. Other sources are more concerned with the equation between *daimones* and the gods of religious cult: e.g. Plut. *De Def.* 417a ff., Apul. *De Deo Socr.* 14; see Buffière (1956: 521–40); MacMullen (1981: 78–83); and, for the Christian co-option of the idea, Daniélou (1973: 31–5, 47, 49, 427–441).

[15] *Il.* 1. 197.　　[16] *Il.* 5. 127–8.　　[17] *Od.* 3. 26–7.

[18] *Od.* 3. 27–8.　　[19] *Il.* 1. 55.

And in another,

> To Tydeus' son Diomedes Pallas Athene
> Granted strength and daring.[20]

And in another,

> She made his limbs nimble, feet and hands above.[21]

6   You can see just how many men have had dealings with the daemonic realm. Have I your consent to leave Socrates to one side for the moment and instead ask Homer, 'What do you mean by all this, noblest of poets?'

Socrates' *daimonion* was a single entity with a single nature, individual to him. It called him back when he tried to cross the river, it postponed his affair with Alcibiades,[22] it ⟨ . . . ⟩[23] when he decided to defend himself in court, and offered no opposition when he chose to die.[24] But Homer's daemonic power is not a single entity, nor one that associates with just one individual in only one set of circumstances for only trivial purposes. It takes many forms and intervenes on many occasions, under many names, in many shapes, and with many different voices. Do you accept this to some degree, and believe in the existence of Athena, Hera, Apollo, Strife, and all the other Homeric *daimones*?[25] Please do not assume that I am asking whether you believe Athena to be exactly as Phidias sculpted her, in keeping with the dignity of Homer's verses, as a beautiful virgin, tall and grey-eyed, girt with the Aegis and armed with helmet, spear, and shield; nor yet that I am asking whether you think Hera to be as Polycleitus represented her for the Argives, white-armed, with ivory forearms, fair of face and dress, regally enthroned on gold;[26] nor yet whether Apollo is as the painters and sculptors depict him, as a naked youth with a short cloak fluttering

---

[20] *Il.* 5. 1–2.

[21] *Il.* 5. 122.

[22] Incidents recorded in Plato *Phaedr.* 242bc and *First Alcib.* 103a.

[23] How the lacuna should be filled depends on whether Maximus is thought to be following Plato *Apol.* 40b (where it is said that the *daimonion* did not hold Socrates back in making his defence) or Xenophon *Apol.* 4 (where it is claimed that it did).

[24] Cf. again Plato *Apol.* 40bc.

[25] Note that the supreme god, Zeus, is not named in this list; he is the one Homeric divinity who is not a mere *daimon*.

[26] For other ancient accounts of Phidias' Athena and Polycleitus' Hera, see Pollitt (1990: 56–8, 78).

behind him, an archer, his legs parted as if running.[27] That is not what I am asking, nor do I think you are so dull as not to guess the truth and convert these allegories into their real meaning.[28] What I wish to know is whether you believe that these names and forms hint allegorically at real daemonic powers, which assist certain favoured mortals both in their dreams and in waking reality.[29] If you think that there is no such power, then you must take issue with Homer, and deny the efficacy of oracles, and mistrust voices from above, and disregard dreams, and leave Socrates alone. If on the other hand you take these phenomena to be neither incredible nor impossible, but still wonder about Socrates, then I will change my ground and ask you whether you think that Socrates was unworthy of a share in the daemonic, or whether you think that what is possible in other cases failed to come about in his. And yet, if you grant the general possibility, you must grant it in his case too; and you cannot deny that Socrates was worthy. If, therefore, the thing is possible and Socrates was worthy, your only course is to stop arguing about Socrates and turn instead to the more general question of what *daimones* are.

7   This is a topic about which I must speak to you again on a subsequent occasion.[30] For the moment I would ask you to embrace the following belief, as a kind of preliminary purification before you are initiated into the doctrines that are to follow. Namely, that the gods have assigned Vice and Virtue to men as if to contestants in a stadium, the one as the reward for a wicked nature and an evil mind, the other as the prize for a good mind and a strong nature, when it wins through in virtue of its nobility. It is these latter individuals that the divine wishes to stand by and to help in their lives, holding a protecting hand over them and caring for them.[31] One man it preserves by means of prophetic utterances, another by

---

[27] Cf. *LIMC* ii. 1 (1984), pp. 192–5 with ii. 2, pp. 188–9 (illus. 67, 75–6, 78–9a), 324 (209) and 276 (1079).

[28] With the scornful view of artistic representations as a guide to the nature of the divine adopted here contrast *Or*. 2. 3 and Dio *Or*. 12. 39–83.

[29] A point taken up in more detail in *Or*. 9. 7 below.

[30] In *Or*. 9; the wording, however, leaves it unclear how long a gap (or whether any gap) is envisaged between the delivery of the two lectures.

[31] For this view of *daimones* as the agents of divine Providence, cf. [Plut.] *De Fato* 573a, Apul. *De Plat*. 1. 12. 206, *De Deo Socr*. 5–6. Unlike Plutarch (*De Def*., following Xenocrates) and Apuleius, Maximus seems not to envisage malicious *daimones* as well as helpful ones (though cf. n. 42 below).

sending flights of birds, another by dreams, another by chance utterances,[32] another by sacrificial portents. Human nature is too feeble to be able to achieve everything by rational calculation, since in this life we are surrounded by a thick, dark mist and live confused by the din and the turmoil of the ills which afflict us here.[33] What traveller is so swift and sure-footed as never to fall foul of a concealed chasm along his way, or a hidden palisade or a cliff or a ditch? What helmsman is so good and so skilful at keeping his course that he makes his crossing without ever encountering heavy tides and storms and tearing winds and turbulent skies? What doctor is so skilled that he is never baffled by an unnoticed and unsuspected disease, as different symptoms arise from different causes and hamstring his professional judgement? What man is so good that he can pass through his whole life safely and without stumbling—like the diseased body, the treacherous voyage, the scarred and pitted road—and not have need of a divine steersman, or doctor, or guide in the course of it? Virtue is a fine thing; it is resourceful and efficacious in the extreme. But it blends with another element that is flawed and dark and full of obscurity, an element both blind and unstable, which men call Chance. Chance sets itself up as rival to Virtue, opposing and contesting her operations and often confounding them. When clouds spread across the sky and conceal the sun's rays from beneath, the sun itself keeps its beauty, but becomes invisible to us. It is in just the same way that the onset of Chance obstructs Virtue; in other respects Virtue retains her beauty, but she is overshadowed and walled in on entering the obscuring cloud.[34] It is in cases like this that men need God to aid them, fight for them, and stand by them.

8   God himself, settled and immobile, administers the heavens and maintains their ordered hierarchy.[35] But he has a race of secondary immortal beings, the so-called *daimones*, which have

[32] i.e. κληδόνες, utterances which (thanks to divine manipulation) mean something important to one who overhears them that was not envisaged by their speakers.

[33] For this Platonizing view of the chaos and confusion of earthly (embodied) life, cf. *Orr.* 9. 6, 10. 10, and 11. 10. The images that follow, of the road, the sea-voyage, and the body (with the purposeful traveller, the helmsman, and the doctor figuring either the philosopher (the virtuous man) or God) are among those most frequently used in the *Orations*: see e.g. *Orr.* 1. 2, 4. 9, 13. 4, 15. 2 and 5, 30. 1–3, 39. 3, 40. 4.

[34] For the image (although differently employed), cf. Sen. *Ep.* 92. 17–18.

[35] Compare the pictures of God and the cosmos given in *Orr.* 11. 12 and 16. 6.

their station in the space between earth and heaven.[36] These *daimones* are inferior in power to God, but superior to men; they are the gods' servants and men's overseers, more closely related than men to the gods, but more closely concerned than the gods with men.[37] The mortal realm would indeed be separated from the immortal and from any sight or dealings with the heavens by a great intervening gulf, were it not for the harmonizing effect of these *daimones*, who bind and connect human beings to divine beauty in virtue of their kinship with both.[38] Just as, although Greeks and foreigners are separated by their inability to speak each other's language, they are still connected and enabled to deal with each other by interpreters, who take in what each side says and ferry it over to the other; just so, the race of *daimones* is held to have dealings both with gods and with men.[39] It is they who speak to men and appear to them, threading their ways through the midst of this realm of mortal nature and giving help in those matters in which men are compelled to appeal to the gods. They make a numerous swarm:

> Three times ten thousand they are, roaming over the fertile earth,
> Immortal, servants of Zeus.[40]

Some heal diseases, some dispense advice to the perplexed, some reveal what is hidden, some assist the craftsman in his work, some the traveller on his journey; some inhabit cities, some the country-side, some the seas, some the dry land. Different *daimones* are assigned homes in different human bodies: one Socrates, another Plato, another Pythagoras, another Zeno, another Diogenes.[41]

[36] The standard location for *daimones* since Plato *Smp.* 202d; cf. e.g Plut. *De Def.* 416c, Apul. *De Deo Socr.* 6, Ocellus Lucanus *Nat. Univ.* 3. 3.

[37] This will be explained in more detail in *Or.* 9.

[38] The emphasis on the connecting functions of *daimones*, preventing the cosmos from separating into two halves, is again standard: Plato *Smp.* 202d; Plut. *De Def.* 415a; Apul. *De Deo Socr.* 4–6.

[39] The comparison with interpreters is Platonic: *Smp.* 202e; [Plato] *Epin.* 984e; cf. Plut. *De Def.* 416f, *Is. et Os.* 361c.

[40] Hesiod *Op.* 252–3, another crucial text for later *daimon*-theory: see M. L. West's apparatus ad loc.

[41] The idea *seems* to be that *daimones* only inhabit the bodies of particularly dis-tinguished individuals (the δαιμόνιοι, cf. *Or.* 10. 10), but the reference is too brief to be very clear. Does Maximus mean that the whole souls of these philosophers were *daimones* (cf. Apul. *De deo Socr.* 15), or that they had *daimones* in them as well as their souls, or does he have in mind the picture of an external intellect 'tethered' to the person, as Plutarch depicts in the myth of the *De Genio* (591cf; cf. Plato *Tim.* 90ac)? The general idea of a personal daimonic supervisor was of course widespread

Some are terrifying,[42] some benevolent; some concern themselves with politics, others with war. They have as many different characters as men do.

> For indeed the gods, in the guise of strangers from abroad
> Taking all manner of forms, visit the cities of men.[43]

Show me a wicked soul, however, and I will show you a soul which has no daemonic inhabitant or overseer.[44]

Oration 9

1   Why not question the *daimones* themselves? They are benevolent towards men and well accustomed to giving their replies through human bodies, just as the pipe-player Ismenias used his skill to produce notes from his pipe.[1] Let us phrase our question like this, in the words of Homer's Odysseus:

> Are you a god or are you a mortal?
> If you are one of the gods, who dwell in the wide heavens,

Then we need say no more, for we know all about you.

> But if you belong to the race of mortals who dwell on earth,[2]

are you really of such a nature as to share our human emotions and our faculty of speech? Do you belong to the same species as we do? Is your span of life the same? Or is the truth that, though you spend your time in the regions of the earth, in your own nature you belong to a higher order?

Daimones (I must reply on their behalf, since they command me to do so) are not beings of flesh and bone and blood, or any other

in both philosophical and non-philosophical thought: e.g. Plato *Phdo* 107d, *Resp.* 617e; Menander *Epitrep.* 1091-9 and fr. 714; cf. Rohde (1925: 514-15 n. 44).

[42] Perhaps a reference to the idea (particularly associated with Xenocrates) that there exist morose, or even malevolent, *daimones*: see Plutarch *Is. et Os.* 360e ff., *De Def.* 419a; also Philo *Gig.* 16. It is more likely, however, that Maximus is simply referring to the function of *daimones* in terrifying and punishing the wicked.

[43] *Od.* 17. 485-6, widely quoted and important for discussions of divine justice and providence, whether mediated through *daimones* or not: e.g. Plato *Resp.* 381d, *Soph.* 216c; Philo *Somn.* 1. 233; Clem. *Strom.* 4. 155. 3

[44] Cf. the end of the speech of Theanor in Plut. *De Genio* 594a.

[1] For the 4th-century aulos-player Ismenias, see also Plut. *Peri.* 1, *Demetr.* 1, *Reg. et Imp. Apophtheg.* 174 f., *Fort. Alex.* 334b, *Quaest. Conv.* 632c, and *Non Posse* 1095 f.

[2] *Od.* 6. 149-50 and 153, also used to frame a question (about the nature of Fate) in *Or.* 13. 8.

constituent that can be dispersed or dissolved or melted or made to fall apart. What are they then? Let us begin to consider what nature *daimones* must have like this. What feels no emotion is the opposite of what does feel emotion; what is mortal is opposite to what is immortal; what has no perceptions is opposite to what does; what has soul is opposite to what does not. Everything that has a soul must show a combination of two properties drawn from this list: it must be either emotionless and immortal, or immortal and emotional, or emotional and mortal, or irrational and capable of perception, or ensouled but incapable of emotion.[3] It is in this way that Nature contrives a gradual and systematic descent from the most precious down to the least.[4] If you remove any of the stages, you will cut Nature in two. In exactly the same way, it is the middle note in a musical scale that unifies the two extremes; by supporting the transition from the highest notes to the lowest by means of those in the middle of the scale, it renders it harmonious both for the ear to hear and for the hand to play.

2   You must believe that the same situation obtains in Nature as does in the most perfect of scales, taking God to occupy the position marked 'emotionless and immortal', *daimones* that marked 'immortal and emotional', men that marked 'emotional and mortal', animals that marked 'irrational and capable of perception', and plants that marked 'ensouled but incapable of emotion'. For the time being we may leave all other classes of creature to one side. But since we are considering the nature of *daimones*, whom we have said constitute a middle term between man and God, we must ask whether it is possible to remove them from the system, while still preserving the terms to either side. Is God immortal but emotional? No, he is immortal and free from emotion. What about man? Is he mortal but free from emotion? No again, he is mortal and emotional. What then will become of the combination of immortality with susceptibility to emotion? There has to exist a being that combines the two, superior to man but inferior to God,

---

[3] i.e. God, *daimon*, man, animal, plant. This classification of the orders of living beings has an Aristotelian feel to it: cf. *NE* 1. 7, 1097ᵇ33 ff., 1. 13, 1102ᵃ23 ff., *De An.* 2. 2–3.

[4] An enunciation of the so-called Principle of Continuity, important in Scholastic philosophy and best known in Linnaeus' formulation, 'natura non facit saltus'. It is again Aristotelian in origin: *Hist. An.* 8. 1, 588ᵇ4 ff., *Part. An.* 4. 5, 681ᵃ ff. For the principle in Neoplatonism, see Wallis (1972: 131) and more generally, Lovejoy (1936: 55–8, 88–9, 246, etc.), Cf. also §§ 3–4 below.

if there is going to be any relationship between the two extremes.[5]
If two things are separate in their natures, then all association
between them is precluded, unless there is some common term that
is receptive to both.

3   Here is an analogy for what I am trying to say.[6] We are
familiar with an element called fire, which is dry and hot; 'hot' is
opposite to 'cold', and 'dry' to 'wet'. We are also familiar with an
element called water, which is cold and wet. It is impossible for fire
to turn into water, or water into fire: for cold cannot become heat,
nor wetness dryness. Yet Nature has managed to moderate the
enmity of these two elements, in the following way. She has given
them a kind of intermediary in the form of the element air, which,
taking heat from fire and wetness from water, thus combines the
two and establishes a connection between them. Change and
progression from fire to air can take place in virtue of the shared
property of heat, and from air to water in virtue of the shared
property of wetness. To take a second case, air is warm and wet,
while earth is cold and dry. Dryness and wetness are opposites, as
are cold and heat. Air could never change to earth, had Nature not
given this pair of elements too a further element, water, which
takes wetness from air and cold from earth, and thus regulates and
connects the two of them. You may survey the whole system concisely if you sum it up like this. Each of the four elements is made
up of a pair of properties, each of which has its opposite. By
taking away one of the properties of any given element and joining it to another of those available, you bring it about that any two
adjacent elements are separate from each other in half their nature
and united in the other. In this way opposed elements, although
they cannot meet, nevertheless are associated to some degree: fire
and air share heat, air and water share wetness, water and earth
cold, and earth and fire dryness. In just the same way, in the case
we are concerned with, God shares the property of immortality
with *daimones*, *daimones* share susceptibility to emotion with
men, men share perception with animals, and animals share the
possession of a soul with plants.

---

[5] The principle that continuity depends on shared terms again goes back to
Aristotle: *Met.* 10. 1069ᵃ5 ff.; it was first applied to the case of *daimones* and their
intermediate status by Xenocrates: Plut. *De Def.* 416d = Xenocrates fr. 23 Heinze;
compare also Apul. *De Deo Socr.* 13.

[6] Yet another Aristotelian echo: *De Gen. et Corr.* 330ᵃ30–ᵇ13, 331ᵃ7–332ᵃ2.

4   If you want another example, consider the organization of the body. Here too Nature makes no sudden leaps; here too intermediates are needed to ensure a coherent composition. Hair and nails are softer than bone, slenderer than muscle, drier than blood, and tougher than flesh. To sum it all up, wherever there is harmony and order—in sounds, in colours, in flavours, in bodies, in rhythms, in shapes, in emotions, and in speech—there must be intermediate terms. This being so, if God is emotionless and mortal, while man is mortal and emotional, then necessarily the intermediate term between them must be either emotionless and mortal or immortal and emotional. Of these two alternatives the former is impossible: mortality and imperviousness to emotion could never be combined in a single compound.[7] We must therefore conclude that *daimones* are beings susceptible to emotion and immortal, sharing their immortality with God and their susceptibility with men.

5   It is now time to explain the sense in which *daimones* are both immortal and susceptible to emotion. Let us look first at the question of immortality.[8] Everything that perishes does so either by being transformed, or by dissolving, or by melting, or by being cut down, or by being broken up, or by changing. Either it is dissolved, as mud is dissolved by water; or it is broken up, as the earth is broken up by a plough; or it melts, as wax melts in the sun; or it is cut down, as plants are cut down with iron tools; or it is transformed and changed, as water changes into air and air into fire. If, then, *daimones* are to have an immortal nature, they must not be subject to being dissolved, split up, transformed, broken, changed, or cut down; if anything like this could happen to them, they would lose their claim to immortality. And in any case, how could they suffer any such thing, if they are really souls which have shed their bodies?[9] The entity which, for the duration of its stay, staves

[7] They can be, and are, in plants: § 2 above. Maximus' attempt at a neat argument by elimination will not work, even on his own terms.

[8] *Daimones* are not inevitably held to be immortal: the discussion in Plut. *De Def.* 418dff. depends on the idea that they can die.

[9] The identification of *daimones* with once-embodied human souls is another point over which opinions could differ. Apuleius distinguishes three different categories of *daimones* in *De Deo Socr.* 15–16: embodied souls, souls that have left their bodies, and 'pure' *daimones* who have never been embodied and never will be (to which latter category he wishes Socrates' *daimonion* to belong). Plutarch seems sometimes to be thinking of them as permanently disembodied (e.g. *Is. et Os.* 361b) and sometimes as ex-humans (e.g. *De Genio* 593dff.): see Dillon (1977: 216–24).

off destruction from the body (which is naturally perishable) is hardly likely to perish itself.[10] In the partnership of soul and body, it is the body which is held together, and the soul which does the holding. Just assume (*per impossibile*) that something else holds the soul together. What on earth might this be? Could anyone imagine a soul within a soul? When a series of items is held together one by the next, it is inevitable that the sequence should come to an end with some item which holds something else together but is held together by itself. Otherwise one would be faced with an infinite regression.[11] You might compare the case of a ship in a heavy sea, moored to a distant rock by means of a whole series of cables; each cable is held steady by the next, but the whole interconnected sequence ends with the rock, which is firm and steady in itself.

6   It is just the same with the soul, which holds the body together as it wallows in the stormy swell of life, mooring it and steadying it as it is shaken and pounded.[12] But when these sinews of ours grow weary, along with the breath and all the other cables which, as it were, have so far tethered the body to the soul, then the body perishes and sinks into the deep, while the soul, holding itself firmly together, swims free on its own.[13] Such a soul, as it makes the crossing away from the earth, becomes a creature of the air, and is given the name *daimon*. The transition is like one from a foreign country to Greece, or from a lawless and strife-torn city ruled by a cruel tyrant to a peaceful and law-abiding city ruled by a benevolent monarch, and seems to me to bear a very close likeness to the picture painted by Homer, when he tells of Hephaestus modelling two cities on the golden shield of Achilles.

[10]   The thought is that of *Phdo* 105b ff.; the vocabulary in what follows (particularly the use of the verb συνέχει, 'holds together') recalls Aristotle (see next note) and Stoic thinkers (e.g. Posidonius fr. 149 Edelstein-Kidd, *SVF* ii. 441, 716).
[11]   The argument here recalls Arist. *De An.* I. 5, 411^{b}6–14, which had clearly remained a standard and celebrated piece of reasoning about the soul: cf. Nemesius *Nat. Hom.* 70. 6–7.
[12]   For the image of the stormy sea of embodiment, cf. *Orr.* 11. 7–8 and 10–11 and 21. 8 (and see next note). Maximus takes his cue from such Platonic passages as *Phdo* 90c and 109 and *Resp.* 611e; cf. e.g. Plut. *De Gen.* 591e, *De Exil.* 607de; Philo *Quod Omn.* 24, *Sacr.* 13; Numenius fr. 13, Porphyry *Vita Plotini* 22.
[13]   For the imagery of swimming free, cf. *Or.* 11. 10, Numenius fr. 33, Plut. *De Gen.* 593d ff., and Porphyry *Vita Plotini* 22; as 11. 10 makes clear, the prototype swimmer is Odysseus in *Od.* 5; cf. Buffière (1956: 386 ff.), Dillon (1981: 183).

In one of them weddings were being celebrated and the people were
    feasting;[14]

and there was dancing and singing and torch-lit processions. In
the other—war, strife, robbery, fighting, shouting, moaning, and
groans. Such is the difference between earth and the heavens: the
heavens are peaceful, full of the singing and the dances of the
gods;[15] the earth is pervaded with tumult and toil and discord. It is
only when the soul sheds the body, leaving it behind on the earth
to rot away in its own time and manner, and makes the transition
from here to there, changing from man to *daimon*, that it can at
last see the sights truly intended for it with unclouded eyes, no
longer confined by the flesh of the body, no longer confused and
perplexed by a multiplicity of different shapes and colours and
obstructed by the misty air, but able to see Beauty itself with its
own eyes and to rejoice in it.[16] It feels pity at the thought of its past
existence, and congratulates itself on what it has now achieved.
But it also feels pity for its kindred souls who are still confined to
the region of the earth. Moved by its benevolent urges, it desires
to rejoin their company and to lend them a hand when they
stumble.[17] God has therefore given such souls the task of patrolling
the earth and involving themselves with men of all different types
and stations and minds and skills, helping the good, avenging the
victims of injustice, and punishing wrongdoers.

7   Not all *daimones* perform all functions, however; now too, as
in life, each is given a different job.[18] It is here that we see the role
of that susceptibility to the emotions that marks them off from
God.[19] They do not want to rid themselves entirely of the natures
that were theirs when they lived on earth. Asclepius continues to

[14] *Il.* 18. 491; on allegorizations of the shield of Achilles and its decoration, see
Buffière (1956: 156–65), Hardie (1985).
[15] Cf. *Orr.* 16. 6, 37. 5, 41. 2.
[16] For this vision of the flight of the soul, cf. *Orr.* 10. 2, 10. 10, 11. 10, 16. 6,
and 26. 1, with Jones (1926) and Festugière (1949: 444–58). The Platonic basis
for the topos is provided by such texts as *Phaedr.* 246d ff., *Phdo* 82d ff. and 109a ff.,
Theaet. 173a, and *Resp.* 514a ff.
[17] Compare above all Plut. *De Genio* 593d–594a; cf. also *Asclepius* 28. In this
sympathetic role, *daimones* bear a distant family resemblance to Plato's Guardians,
redescending into the Cave to help the prisoners still bound there (*Resp.* 516c ff.).
[18] Cf. Apul. *De Deo Socr.* 6 (without, however, the explicit connection between
diversity of function and manlike emotion that Maximus draws).
[19] Cf. Apul. *De Deo Socr.* 12–14, connecting the *daimones*' differing emotional
states with the different forms of worship they demand, not their differing functions.

heal the sick, Heracles to perform mighty deeds, Dionysus to lead the revels, Amphilochus to give oracles,[20] the Dioscuri to sail the seas, Minos to dispense justice, and Achilles to wield his weapons. Achilles dwells on an island in the Black Sea opposite the mouth of the Ister, where he has a temple and altars. No one would go there of his own free will, except to offer sacrifices; and it is only after offering sacrifices that he will set foot in the temple. Sailors passing the island have often seen a young man with tawny hair, clad in golden armour, exercising there. Others have not seen him, but have heard him singing. Yet others have both seen and heard him. One man even fell asleep inadvertently on the island. Achilles himself appeared to him, raised him to his feet, took him to his tent, and entertained him; Patroclus was there to serve the wine, Achilles played the lyre, and Thetis and a host of other *daimones* were present too.[21] According to the people of Troy, Hector remains on the site of his former home, and can be seen sweeping over the plain, flashing with light.[22] I myself have never seen either Hector or Achilles, but I have seen the Dioscuri, in the form of bright stars, righting a ship in a storm.[23] I have seen Asclepius, and that not in a dream.[24] I have seen Heracles, in waking reality.[25]

---

[20] At Mallus in Cilicia: Lucian *Philops.* 38, *Alex.* 19, *Deorum Conc.* 12.

[21] For this description of the temple of Achilles on the White Isle, and apparitions there, see above all Philostr. *Heroicus* 54–5. 4, Arrian *Periplus* 21–33, and Paus. 3. 19. 11; cf. Rohde (1925: 565–7 n. 102). Hero cult fitted very neatly with *daimon*-theory, as heroes had themselves traditionally constituted a subordinate class of higher power. Hesiod's myth of the Races (*Op.* 109–201) was a particularly useful text for those wishing to make a connection between the two classes of being: see Plut. *De Def.* 415ab, *De E* 390e, [Plut.] *Placita* 885b.

[22] For Hector's continuing presence in the Troad, see Philostr. *Heroicus* 19, Lucian *Deorum Conc.* 12.

[23] For this famous function of the Dioscuri, cf. e.g. Alcaeus fr. 34, *Hymn. Hom.* 33, Theoc. 22. 8–22, etc.

[24] A special favour, also enjoyed by Antiochus of Aegae (Philostr. *Vit. Soph.* 2. 568) and Proclus (Marinus *Vit. Procl.* pp. 79–80). Ordinary mortals only 'saw' Asclepius while incubating in his temple: cf. Lane Fox (1986: 151–3, 161–2) for the practice in the 2nd century.

[25] For the whole topic of 'seeing the gods' in this and other periods, see Lane Fox (1986, ch. 4).

ORATION 10   Learning and Recollection

Introduction

= 16 (1962) = 28 (Laur. Conv. Sopp. 4). The manuscript title—εἰ αἱ μαθήσεις ἀναμνήσεις, 'Whether learning is Recollection'—seems at first sight to echo Maximus' own formulation of the issue in § 3, but gets the emphasis wrong: 'What is Recollection?' would be closer.

Another 'psychological' lecture, on a central point of Platonic epistemology, thematically linked both with *Orr*. 8–9 and with *Or*. 11 (compare especially 10. 9 with 8. 8, 9. 6, and 11. 10). Maximus begins and ends his exposition with accounts of the soul's flight, both in philosophical contemplation and after release from the body at death (§§ 1–3 and 9). In between, in no very conscientious order, he explains the process of recollection, and its implications for our understanding of the soul's nature.

Maximus' Platonic sources are obvious: principally (though not only) *Meno* 80d–86b; *Phaedo* 72e–77a; *Theaetetus* 149a–151d; *Phaedrus* 246a–249d and 276b–277a. Equally clearly, his presentation is influenced by subsequent developments within the Platonic tradition, aimed at combating the epistemologies of rival schools of thought, above all the Stoics and the Peripatetics. Characteristically, however, he does not indulge in open polemic: neither the anti-Stoic account of the germination of seeds in § 4, nor the (anti-Stoic and) anti-Peripatetic insistence that the involvement of the body in mental processes makes Recollection impossible in § 5, is explicitly marked for what it is. For other ancient summaries of the Platonic doctrine, see Cicero *Tusculanae Disputationes* 1. 56–8 and Alcinous *Didascalicus* 25. 177. 45–178. 12, with discussion in Dillon (1977: 98–9 (cf. 91–6) and 290–2).

Early interest in the lecture is testified to by the presence of substantial scholia on §§ 3, 4 (two), and 7: see Hobein (1910, ad loc.) or Trapp (1994, app. 1). Gregoras takes three excerpts, from §§ 1, 5, and 8; the *Lexicon Vindobonense* makes four quotations, from §§ 1, 2, 4, and 5. Reuchlin makes Maximus his authority for the story of Pythagoras and the shield of Euphorbus, and quotes the inscription from § 2, on fol. xxxv^r of the *De Arte Cabalistica*. Franciscus Junius quotes the account of recollecting and the association of ideas from §§ 6–8 (omitting the Homeric quotations) in the third book of *On the Painting of the Ancients* (III. i. 1 and vii. 7: Aldrich *et al.* 1991: i. 198, 302–3).

Oration

1   There once came to Athens a Cretan by the name of Epimenides, bearing a tale hard to credit if taken at face value.[1] He said that he had lain for many years in a deep sleep in the cave of Dictaean Zeus and that in his dreams he had encountered the gods themselves and conversed with them, and that he had encountered Truth and Justice too. This kind of mythological fiction was, I think, Epimenides' riddling way of saying that life on earth for the human soul is like a lengthy dream of many years' duration. He would have been still more convincing had he cited Homer's lines about dreams in support of his own account. For Homer of course says that there are two gates for 'feeble dreams', one made from ivory and the other from horn; dreams that pass out through the gate of horn are true and trustworthy, the others are treacherous and deceptive, and convey no truth to the soul about the waking world.[2] It was the selfsame message that Epimenides' account—call it a myth or a true description as you wish[3]—sought to convey. Our life in this realm is simply and truly a dream; the soul, buried in the body and overwhelmed by stupor and repletion, perceives reality with the dim approximation of one dreaming. The dreams that come to the souls of the majority come through the gates of ivory; but should there be a pure and sober soul, little fuddled by the stupor and repletion of this world, then it is surely reasonable to suppose that the dreams which it encounters come through the

---

[1] For Epimenides, see Diog. Laert. 1. 109–15; D-K i, 27–37. The phrase 'hard to credit at face value' both alerts the reader to the fact that Epimenides' story is to be interpreted allegorically, and echoes the most famous line of his poetry (fr. 1). The connection Maximus draws between him, Pythagoras, and Aristeas, as individuals with striking things to say about the powers of the soul, is a familiar one: cf. e.g. Pliny *NH* 7. 52. 174–5, Clem. *Strom.* 1. 21. 133, Tatian *Or.* 41. It may go back to the work of Heraclides Ponticus: Bolton (1962, ch. 7), but see also Gottschalk (1980, ch. 2 and pp. 98 ff.). Dodds (1951: 140–5) discusses the three sages together as instances of the spread of shamanistic ideas in archaic Greece.

[2] *Od.* 19. 562–7, a much discussed and imitated passage: see the scholia and Eustath. ad loc., Plato *Charm.* 173a; *Anth. Pal.* 7. 42. 1–2; Horace *Odes* 3. 27. 39–42; Virg. *Aen.* 6. 893–8.

[3] Perhaps an echo of Plato *Grg.* 523a.

gates of horn, and are clear and distinct and close to the truth.[4] Such was the sleep of Epimenides.

2   Pythagoras of Samos was the first among the Greeks to dare to say that his body would die, but that his soul would up and fly away, ageless and immortal, because it had also existed before its sojourn here.[5] Men believed him when he said this, and they believed him when he said that he had already lived on earth once before in another incarnation, when he had been Euphorbus the Trojan. The grounds for their belief were these. Pythagoras came to a temple of Athena, in which there were many dedications of different kinds, including a shield of Phrygian design, shabby with age. 'I recognize that shield,' he said. 'It was taken from me by the man who killed me in the battle at Troy all those years ago.' Astonished by his words, the people of the place took the dedication down, and there indeed was the inscription, 'Dedicated to Pallas Athena by Menelaus, from Euphorbus.'[6]

If you wish, I can tell you yet another tale. There was a man from Proconnesus whose body lay prostrate, still animate, but faintly and in a fashion not far removed from death.[7] At the same time, his soul, escaping from his body, travelled through the air like a bird, surveying all beneath it—land and sea, cities and races of men, events and natural phenomena of every kind; then, re-entering his body and raising it up again, it used it like an instrument, to expound the different sights and sounds it had experienced in different nations of the world.

3   What is it that Epimenides and Pythagoras and Aristeas are all trying to hint at? Can their theme be anything other than the freedom of the good man's soul from the pleasures and sufferings of the body, when by escaping from the tumult of the physical world and turning its intelligence in on itself, it re-encounters pure Truth, free from imperfect images? This does indeed resemble a

---

[4] For the use of the imagery of dreaming and drunkenness to describe the experience of the embodied soul, cf. *Orr.* 11. 7, 16. 6, and 21. 7; Philo *Abr.* 70; Plut. *Is. et Os.* 362b, 382–3; Alcin. *Didasc.* 14; *Corp. Herm.* 1. 1; Plotinus 4. 8. 1; Proclus *In Remp.* 2. 351 Kroll. The Platonic precedents are such passages as *Resp.* 533c, *Tht.* 201d–202c, and *Phdo* 79c.

[5] For Pythagoras as the first thinker to maintain the immortality of the soul, cf. *Or.* 27. 5; Porph. *Vit. Pyth.* 19; Diog. Laert. 8. 14.

[6] For the story, cf. Diog. Laert. 8. 4–5 and 45; Porph. *Vit. Pyth.* 27; Iambl. *Vit. Pyth.* 14.

[7] For Aristeas, see Bolton (1962, esp. ch. 7 and pp. 207–14).

beautiful slumber, full of vivid dreams; it does indeed resemble a lofty soaring of the soul, not over mountain peaks in the misty and turbulent lower atmosphere, but beyond this in the heights of the calm ether, as peace and tranquillity escort it serenely to truth and revelation.[8] But what is the nature of this process, and what is the most appropriate name to bestow on it? Should we call it 'learning', or should we adopt Plato's terminology and call it 'recollection'? Or should we use both names, 'learning' and 'recollection', of the one phenomenon? Whatever the answer, the phenomenon itself resembles what can happen to the eye. The eye never ceases to possess the faculty of sight, but from time to time some mischance allows a mist to cover and embrace the organ and so block off its contact with the outside world. When medical science comes to the rescue, its task is not to implant sight in the eye, but rather to remove the blockage so as to uncover it and restore its outward passage. You must understand that the soul too has a kind of sight, the natural function of which is to discern and understand reality. The misfortune of physical embodiment covers it over with a thick mist, which confounds its powers of vision, removes its precise discernment, and quenches its native brightness.[9] Reason, coming to the soul like a doctor, does not bring and implant understanding, like something the soul did not already possess; instead, it reawakens the understanding it does possess, but which is dim and constrained and torpid.[10]

4 Just as the science of midwifery brings helping hands to pregnant women, and with its arts supports the growing embryo, eases the pangs of labour, brings the child safely into the light once it has reached its term and soothes the mother's pains, so too Reason plays midwife to the pregnant soul burdened with the pangs of labour. But many souls miscarry, either through the incompetence of their midwives, or through the intensity of their pains, or through the dullness of their seed. Few indeed and far between are the souls that are successfully delivered of clear and well-articulated offspring that faithfully preserve the likeness of

[8] For this association of the inward turn (ἐπιστροφή) with the flight of the soul, compare Or. 11. 10 (with notes ad loc.); cf. also Or. 9. 6, with n. 16. Theiler (1930: 41–2) sees echoes of the thought of Antiochus here, as also in §§ 4 and 6 below.

[9] For the idea of the impairment of the soul's functions by embodiment, cf. Phdo 66a, 79c.

[10] Both the imagery of the eye and its application echo Plato Resp. 518d. The idea of a slow reawakening is also found in Meno 85c.

their progenitors.[11] 'Intellection' is the name for the soul's conception; its labour pains are 'perception' and its delivery 'recollection'.
Souls all conceive because that is their nature, labour as a matter
of habit, and give birth through reason.[12] Well then, just as it is
impossible for anything to grow except from a seed, or to grow into
anything other than what the nature of the seed determines (man
is ⟨necessarily⟩ born from man, ox from ox, olive tree from olive
tree and vine from vine), so too, if the soul achieves understanding of some truth, the seeds thus planted in it must themselves be
true. If they existed at any time, then they always existed; if they
always existed, then they were and are immortal.[13] This is exactly
what happens in the acquisition of knowledge: the flowering and
coming to fruit of seeds planted in the soul.[14] And as for what men
call ignorance, what else could that be than a failure of seeds to
germinate?

5   If then the soul is an entity of the same kind as the body, a
mortal element that disintegrates and perishes and rots, I have
nothing creditable to say about it, any more than I have anything
creditable to say about the body itself, an ephemeral and precarious
creature, unstable, unreliable, bewildering, and impulsive. If that is
the soul's nature, then knowledge, recollection, and learning are
all equally impossible for it; it could no more retain a piece of
knowledge than wax melting in the sun retains the imprint of a
seal, if it is really only a physical entity.[15] All physical bodies are in
a state of flux, and surge rapidly this way and that like the Euripus,
as their tides now rise from infancy to youthful vigour, now fall
and decline from youthful vigour to old age.[16] But this is not the

[11] Maximus here reproduces the imagery of *Theaet.* 149a-151d (with perhaps
some help also from *Phaedr.* 276b-277a).
[12] For the role of perception in the process of recollection, cf. *Phdo* 73cd, Alcin.
Didasc. 25. 178. 1-12.
[13] Cf. *Meno* 86ab. Maximus here manages only a superficial appearance of
logical rigour.
[14] Cf. again *Phaedr.* 276b-277a. Stoics too used the image of seeds, but for
different purposes (the creative principles contained within God, e.g. *SVF* ii.
1027); it is tempting to conclude that Maximus is here drawing on a more explicitly anti-
Stoic account which had pointedly reclaimed the image for its Platonic application.
For a possible parallel for such an appropriation, see Alcin. *Didasc.* 25. 178. 8-12,
with Dillon (1977: 291-2).
[15] The image echoes *Theaet.* 191c and 194cff. and Arist. *De Mem.* 450ª30-ᵇ6;
like Maximus, Aristotle in the latter passage uses the image in a discussion of ways
in which a memory-trace may *fail* to be imprinted.
[16] For the image of the Euripus, cf. *Or.* 5. 6; and for this manner of talking about

kind of thing Pythagoras or Plato divined the soul to be, nor Homer before them, who gave souls the power of speech and prophecy even in Hades.[17]

Homer also, I think, makes a bard say,

> I am self-taught, and the gods granted me the gift of song.[18]

A true statement: the soul is precisely a self-taught entity, well provided by the gods with knowledge, as part of its essential nature. Other creatures are certainly self-taught with respect to their own proper functions. Who can say who taught lions their bravery, or deer their powers of escape, or horses their speed? The race of birds is self-taught too, using their native skills to build nests in the tops of trees; spiders manufacture their own thread to hang their nets in the air; snakes make their own lairs and fish their holes, and a whole series of other animals have their own native skills to keep their species in existence.[19] Is then man, the most intelligent of all creatures, to acquire his knowledge from some external source? In that case he will never acquire it at all. Knowledge must come either by discovery or by learning,[20] both of which are ineffectual means if there is no basis of innate knowledge to support them. How can someone who makes a discovery do anything with it if he does not know what it can be used for?[21] To take a Homeric example, a landsman coming across a steering-oar

> Will say you bear a winnowing-fan on your noble shoulder.[22]

And when someone learns something, he clearly cannot learn from someone who does not know. But if he learns from someone who does know, then I will ask this teacher of his for the source of *his*

---

the body and human fortunes, *Orr.* 1. 2, 8. 7, 30. 2-4. Aristotle, who does think of memory as dependent on physical condition, singles out the young and the old in *De Mem.* 450^{b}7 ff. and 453^{b}7 ff. as possessing weak memories in virtue of their more precarious physical state. Given the apparent double echo of Aristotle at this point (cf. previous note), it seems likely that Maximus is here himself consciously attacking the Peripatetic conception of memory, or drawing on such an attack by someone else.

[17] Cf. (perhaps) *Meno* 100a.
[18] *Od.* 22. 347, also quoted in *Or.* 38. 1.
[19] This list of animal accomplishments derives ultimately from Stoic arguments for divine Providence: see Cic. *ND* 2. 121-7 with Pease (1958, ad loc.); and cf. *Orr.* 6. 3, 20. 6, 31. 4.
[20] A conventional antithesis: *Theaet.* 150d; *Phdo* 85c, 99c.
[21] A faint echo of *Meno* 80d.
[22] *Od.* 11. 128.

knowledge. Did he discover what he knows, or learn it? If he discovered it, then I repeat the same question: how could he do anything with his discovery if he did not recognize it? If on the other hand he learned from someone else, then I have the pleasure of questioning that someone else in his turn. Where will this process of interrogating our sequence of teachers and pupils come to an end? Sooner or later the chain of reasoning will bring us to someone who did not learn but discovered for himself, to whom we will have to address the same old question all over again.

6   It is at this point that the light of reason can bring us the solution we are seeking. What else are the soul's powers of discovery, self-generated, natural, and innate as they are, than true opinions aroused to consciousness? What is knowledge if not the name we give to the awakening and organization of those opinions?[23] If you wish, you may picture the process in question in the following way too, in terms of a mob of soldiers milling around out of formation. Or rather, let us take Homer's picture of a camp in the deep calm of night, when the whole of the rest of the army lay sound asleep in its ranks.

> But no sweet sleep held Agamemnon, son of Atreus,
> Shepherd of the host;[24]

Striding up to each man in turn and rousing and posting him to his station,

> First he ranged the mounted men with their horses and chariots,
> Then stationed the brave and numerous foot-soldiers behind them
> To be the bastion of battle, and drove the cowards to the centre.[25]

You may take it that the same kind of process unfolds within the soul. Black night and deep sleep shroud its thoughts; reason, in the role of general or king or whatever else you like to call it, strides up to each of them and rouses it and sets it in its proper station. The name for this sleep is 'forgetfulness', the process of rousing is 'recollection' and the guarding and preservation of what has been set in order is 'memory'. Recollection takes place as the soul gradually hunts down one detail after another in sequence and is

---

[23] *Meno* 85c, 86a.
[24] *Il.* 10. 3-4.
[25] *Il.* 4. 297-9. Maximus' use of a military comparison in this connection is perhaps influenced by Arist. *An. Post.* 2. 100ª3-100ᵇ5.

led on by each new one to the next[26]—a process exactly the same as what takes place in everyday recollecting.

7   Demodocus at the Phaeacian banquet sings

> Of the strife of Odysseus and of Peleus' son Achilles;[27]

Odysseus, present in person, hears the song, recognizes its subject, and weeps. Is it not reasonable that his soul, seizing hold of such a starting-point, should have made its way back to all that happened in that distant place, and that while his body stayed where it was, drinking with the Phaeacians, memory should have carried his soul back to Troy, reckoning up all it had seen in the meantime, moved by a small initial impetus to survey a great tract of its experiences? Many a lover before now has seen a lyre and been reminded of the boyfriend who used to play it;[28] recollection is a nimble faculty, easily stirred to action. Bodies that are easily moved need a hand to set them in motion, but retain the motion over a great distance once they have received the initial impetus. In just the same way, once the mind has received the small stimulus to its memory afforded by the senses, it advances great distances in recollection. Every thing and every event that the soul encounters, I believe, is a term in some sequence or another: either chronologically, as night follows day, and old age succeeds youth, and spring succeeds winter; or emotionally, as love is inspired by beauty, anger by insult, pleasure by good fortune, and pain by disaster; or topographically, as

> Pharis and Sparta and Thisbe with its many doves;[29]

or in order of command, as in

> Leitus and Peneleus were leaders of the Boeotians,
> With Arcesilaus and Prothoenor and Clonius;[30]

or in order of power, as in

> Father Zeus, let Ajax draw the lot, or the son of Tydeus,
> Or the king of Mycenae rich in gold himself.[31]

---

[26] *Meno* 81cd.
[27] *Od.* 8. 75.
[28] *Phdo* 73d. The ensuing discussion of reminiscence by association of ideas is inspired, at some remove, by *Phdo* 73d-74a and Arist. *De Mem.* 451ᵇ12 ff.
[29] *Il.* 2. 582.   [30] *Il.* 2. 494-5.
[31] *Il.* 7. 179-80, also quoted in *Or.* 5. 2.

8   When the senses, situated as they are in the vestibule of the soul, catch hold of some starting-point and transmit it to the mind, the mind in its turn seizes hold and discerns the remainder of the sequence, passing on through the terms that follow in chronological order, or in order of command, or place, or rank, or power. If a man flicks the throwing-strap on a long, light hunting-spear, he transmits the motion thus imparted to the whole length of the shaft right up to the point; similarly, anyone who gives a shake to one end of a long, extended cable finds the movement transmitted to the whole as it runs along to the end. In just the same way the mind needs only a small initial impetus to conceive of phenomena in their entirety. A naturally gifted individual, who is swift in his pursuit of Virtue, finds within himself the starting-point from which he journeys on, gathering together and pondering in his memory the sights his mind has seen. The less talented need a Socrates, who teaches no doctrines himself, but whose thorough questioning and cross-examination leads them to articulate truths as they answer him.[32] How is it possible for someone to give answers if he does not already know them—unless perhaps one were to maintain that when a man walks while being led by the hand by another he is not really walking?[33] But what difference is there between the guide and the questioner, or between the man walking in the one example and answering in the other? In each of these two pairs one party provides the effort for himself, while the other keeps him on course. But in neither case is the man who is being guided *learning* how to walk, or the man answering questions *learning* how to answer; the former *walks*, because he has the ability required; the latter *answers*, because he has the knowledge required. The contribution made by the other party in each case is the provision of a steadying hand.

9   Just as the body is naturally constituted to walk, so the soul is naturally constituted to think. If it is immortal (as indeed it is), then surely it follows necessarily that its knowledge and concepts concerning the world should always have been in it. But the soul is enmeshed not in one level of existence but in two, the one pure and bright and immune to untoward disturbance, the other a turbid and disorderly confusion of every kind of random happen-

[32]   *Meno* 84cd.
[33]   The comparison is perhaps inspired by *Meno* 84a.

ing. In the former realm the soul is overwhelmed in obscurity and suffers from a kind of heavy-headedness, for all the world like that of drunkards whose souls are inflamed by excessive drinking to the point of madness. Yet at the same time it does still have the power to take a grip on itself, so as neither exactly to stumble nor yet to think clearly, but still to remain in the no man's land between ignorance and reason. But when the soul escapes from this lower realm to the higher, as if abandoning the land of the Cimmerians for the brightness of the upper air, freed from flesh and desires, diseases and disasters, then at last reality becomes accessible to its sight and its understanding, as it joins the gods and their offspring beyond the outermost vault of the heavens, pursuing its circling course as a member of the divine host led and commanded by Zeus.[34] Then it remembers reality, though now it is forced to recollect;[35] then it advances with confidence, though now it stumbles. The sturdy soul that has drawn a good *daimon* as its protector holds out against the tumult in this lower realm too,[36] freeing itself as far as it can from association with the body and stirring its recollections of those other sights and sounds. This is what poets are hinting at when they call Memory the mother of the Muses, 'Muses' being their name for the many forms of knowledge, a holy band, Zeus' handiwork, brought to birth and set in order by Memory.[37] Let us honour the Muses, let us honour Memory.

ORATION 11   Plato on God

Introduction

= 17 (1962), = 1 (Laur. Conv. Sopp. 4). The manuscript title—τίς ὁ θεὸς κατὰ Πλάτωνα, 'Plato on the identity of God'—faithfully echoes Maximus' own formulation of the topic at issue (at the end of § 2).

[34] Another 'flight of the soul'; cf. § 3 above, with n. 8; *Orr.* 9. 6, 16. 6. From 'then at last reality . . .' onwards, Maximus is echoing the myth of *Phaedr.*, esp. 246e–247e.

[35] 'Remembers' here means 'has a knowledge that it has never lost'—a better state than that of having lost the knowledge and needing to recover it again; the point is a favourite with Philo: *Leg. All.* 3. 91; *Congr.* 39–40; *Mut. Nom.* 100–2.

[36] For the protecting *daimon*, cf. *Orr.* 8–9, esp. 8. 8.

[37] For the importance of memory in the constitution of knowledge, see above all Arist. *Met.* 1. 1, 980ᵃᵇ; cf. also *Or.* 6. 2–3.

This lecture continues the cosmological-theological theme of *Orr.* 2 and 5-10; the thematic connections with 8-9 (the cosmic hierarchy) and 10 (the human soul's ascent to knowledge of transcendent realities) are particularly close. The core of the lecture (§§ 7-12) is an exposition of the (Middle) Platonic doctrine of God as supreme, transcendent Intellect and the incorporeal source of all Beauty, combined with an exhortation to the listener-reader to cultivate such awareness of his nature as he can. This is preceded in §§ 1-6 by an elaborate prologue, in which Maximus establishes first the propriety of consulting expositions of Platonic doctrine, rather than simply referring back to the works of the Master himself, and then—as propaedeutic to specifically Platonic theology— the universality of belief in a supreme and unitary God of some kind or another. Considerable care is taken to ensure overall symmetry and thematic coherence between and within the two main divisions of the lecture. The whole is framed by references to God and his subordinate *daimones*; the prologue by images for Plato's pre-eminence as a source of enlightenment (sun, gold-mine, oracular spokesman). Moreover, the relationship depicted in §§ 7-12, between God the source and the beauty and order of the physical world deriving from him, parallels that implied in § 1 to hold between Plato and his (inferior, derivative) interpreters.

Comparison with chapter 10 of Alcinous' *Didascalicus* shows Maximus to be drawing heavily in §§ 7-11 on contemporary school Platonism, both for his concepts (not only the idea of a transcendent, incorporeal deity, but also the 'three ways' of apprehension—analogy, eminence, and negation) and his terminology: see above all Festugière (1954: 95-115); also Daniélou (1973: 340-3), Dillon (1977: 282-5), and Whittaker (1990: 22-6, and 100-8). Indeed the similarity in sequence of thought to Alcinous' chapter (extending also to § 6[1]) suggests the possibility of a common source. In other ways too the lecture stands squarely in well-established traditions of theological discussion: note above all the juxtaposition of the argument from universal consent with the argument from universal harmony in §§ 4-5 (as also in Plato *Leg.* 885e-886a, Cic. *ND* 2. 2. 4-5 and Sextus *Math.* 9. 60-122); and the distinction of different sources of conceptions of divinity in § 3

---

[1] Maximus' elaborate comparison with Odysseus on his vantage-point in § 6 makes the same point about the difficulty of the venture as Alcinous does with his reference to Plato (*Ep.* 7. 341c) at the very beginning of *Didasc.* 10.

(with which compare Dio *Or.* 12. 39 ff. (with Russell 1992, ad loc.) and the whole tradition of 'tripartite theology'). For further discussion of the Middle Platonic theological background, see Daniélou (1973: 106–27); Dillon (1977: 45–9; 1986: 214–29).

The remarkable history of subsequent interest in this lecture begins in the fourteenth century, with the making of Nicephorus Gregoras' manuscript, Laur. Conv. Sopp. 4.[2] Up until then *Or.* 11 does not seem to have enjoyed any special status in the collection: it was not privileged by its position, and did not bear any significant marginalia in the early manuscripts. With Conv. Sopp. 4, however, it moved to the head of the collection. This reorganization presumably rested (at least in part) on a view of Maximus as particularly interesting for his Platonism and his theology. Whatever the intention, the move certainly ensured that he and the lecture attracted that kind of interest in the future—most notably from Cardinal Bessarion in the fifteenth century and from a sequence of northern European (principally English) divines in the seventeenth. In both of Bessarion's two manuscripts *Or.* 11 is singled out for special attention: fifteen separate notes cluster round § 8 and the beginning of § 9 on fol. 4^r of Marc. gr. 254, thirty-seven are appended to §§ 1, 3, 5, and 7–11 on foll. 193^r–195^v of Marc. gr. 514; the former are certainly, the latter perhaps in Bessarion's own hand.[3] The seventeenth-century story begins with Robert Burton's *Anatomy of Melancholy* (1621), which quotes (in Pazzi's Latin) from §§ 4–5 and 6.[4] The second and third editions of Hugo Grotius' *De Veritate Religionis Christianae* (1629 and 1640) respectively refer to and quote § 5.[5] Jeremy Taylor twice draws on § 5, in his *History of the Life and Death of the Holy Jesus* (1649) and *Ductor Dubitantium* (1660).[6] Richard Byfield's autograph notebook, written in or after December 1657, contains ten excerpts from §§ 5–12.[7]

---

[2] Gregoras also copied five excerpts, from §§ 1–2, 6–7, 9, and 12, into his commonplace book. The compiler of Neap. 100 took just one, from § 5; and the *Lexicon Vindobonense* quotes from §§ 5 and 8.

[3] See Mioni (1976, 1981–5). The hand is not exactly the same in both cases, and Mioni declines to attribute it to Bessarion in the case of 514. However, some of the notes on Maximus are identical in both cases: if Bessarion did not make both himself, he had at least studied the other set.

[4] *Anatomy* 3. 4. 1. 2–3 (Faulkner *et al.* 1989–94: iii. 343, 355, 375).

[5] 2nd edn. i. 16 (p. 30); 3rd edn. i. 16 (p. 27) with text and translation on p. 275.

[6] *History* pref. 28 (Heber-Eden 1847–54: ii. 23); *Ductor* 2. 1. 27 (ix. 291).

[7] Harleianus 1790, foll. 66 (65) ff. The last excerpt bears the title 'Deus est fons omnis pulchritudinis'.

Ralph Cudworth in his *True Intellectual System of the Universe*
(1678) refers four times, to §§ 4–5, 10, and 12, in his survey of
pagan polytheism in book 1 chapter 4.[8] In this tradition of interest,
the exposition of the argument from universal consent in § 5 seems
to have had a special prominence. It is therefore perhaps not
surprising to find the same passage turning up again, a century
later, in Thomas Clarkson's *A Portraiture of Quakerism* (1806).
According to Clarkson, a (somewhat tendentiously translated)
version of § 5 was one of the texts Quaker apologists regularly
appealed to in order to establish that their doctrines had in part
been anticipated by the Ancients.[9] A rather different interest,
finally, was shown by Thomas de Quincey, who was moved to
compare the comparison between divine and human mind at the
beginning of § 9 with 'Kant's distinction between an *anschauung*
and a discursive act'.

Oration

1   In the case of *daimones* I am prepared to see one account
conflicting with another and can tolerate disagreement. I find
nothing strange, discordant, or unusual in the behaviour of someone who sees fit to debate the existence, nature, and qualities
of the daemonic, with himself or anyone else, given that their
nomenclature is unclear, their nature obscure, and their powers a
matter for dispute.[10] But now that my subject is God, how am I to
proceed? With what beauty of diction can I clothe my thoughts,
what illumination can I provide from pellucid terminology, what
choice poetic harmony can I contrive, so as to expound this new
topic to my own satisfaction or anyone else's? When even Plato,
unsurpassed in eloquence (even in comparison to Homer),[11] is still
unable to carry conviction with his account of God, and people

---

[8] I. 4. xiv, p. 234 (§ 5); I. 4. xxvi, pp. 444–5 (§ 12); I. 4. xxvii, pp. 448–9
(§ 4–5); I. 4. xxxii, p. 517 (§ 10 + 12). All references to the second edition (rev. T.
Birch) of 1743.

[9] *Portraiture*, vol. ii, ch. 6 (pp. 164 ff.). The tendentiousness consists in translating the plural θεοί as a singular and suppressing the (irredeemably polytheistic)
reference to gods (plural) acknowledged on the shores of Ocean.

[10] This seems to be a back-reference to *Orr.* 8–9 and perhaps suggests that
originally the three made a single sequence, without the intervention of what is
now *Or.* 10.

[11] For the comparison, and rivalry, of Homer and Plato, see also *Orr.* 17 and 26,
with notes ad locc.

desire instead to learn of his opinions from some other source, then only a fool would be ready to hazard an account. Unless, that is, when confronted with a thirsty man, we could ignore the pure and mighty river to hand—a river most pleasant to view, most agreeable to drink from and most fertile in its nutritive power[12]— and draw him instead—from a feeble and wholly inferior spring— the bare minimum needed to slake his thirst.[13] This would be like what they say happens with the owl: though blinded by the light of the sun, it nevertheless seeks out firelight in the night-time.[14] If someone who has read Plato's own words still needs some further exposition, if anyone thinks the illumination he provides to be dull, and to lack the required brilliance, then we are indeed dealing with someone blind to the sun's rising, the moon's light, the Evening Star's setting, and the Morning Star's ushering in the day!

2   But wait a moment! I am gradually beginning to form an impression of what such an account might in fact involve. The case is like that of miners for precious metals. They, when they cut into the earth and dig out their gold, are unable to distinguish for them-selves what really is and is not gold, and need others to assay it for them with fire. In my opinion a first reading of Plato's dialogues is just like mining for gold: after the first engagement one needs the assistance of some further technique, which will assay and purify what has been mined, not with fire but with the light of reason; only then can constructive use be made of the gold, once the assaying and purification is done.[15]

If then it is clear where the truth is to be mined, and the mine itself is a generous and bountiful one, but we need some further technique to test the yield, then let us summon that technique to assist us in our present enquiry, as we investigate Plato's teachings about God.

3   If this technique had a voice and were to ask us whether, in

[12] Here, as also in *Or.* 21. 8, the reference may be specifically to the Nile: cf. 25. 7. The river imagery anticipates the description of God as the source of all beauty in § 11 below.

[13] The image of 'drawing from the springs of Plato's wisdom' may also be found in Olympiodorus *Vit. Plat.* 1 and in the anonymous *Prolegomena ad Plat.* 1.

[14] The implied comparison between Plato and the Sun echoes the famous image in *Resp.* 507a–509c. For the owl image (differently used, but still in the context of teaching and understanding), cf. Dio *Or.* 12. 1 and 13.

[15] This use of the image of purifying gold, applied to philosophical study, echoes Plato *Polit.* 303e and [Plato] *Ep.* 2. 314a.

our dispute over Plato, we ourselves have no belief in the existence of a divine element in Nature and no conception of God at all, or whether, while entertaining notions of our own, we imagine Plato to hold different beliefs that contradict them; and if when we replied that we do have notions of our own, it were to demand that we say what we think God is like, what would our answer be? That God is

> Round-shouldered, dark in complexion, with curling hair?[16]

What a ridiculous response, even if you were to offer a more impressive characterization of Zeus—raven brows, golden hair, and heaven shaking at his nod.[17] All such descriptions are surely the conjectures of ⟨painters, sculptors, poets, and⟩[18] philosophers, conditioned by the dullness of human intellect and our feeble incapacity either to see God or to reveal him to others. Each group to the best of its ability offers its own imaginative vision of supreme Beauty.

4   If you were to convene an assembly of these experts and command them all to give their answer about God in the form of a single resolution, do you really think that painter, sculptor, poet, and philosopher would all have something different to say? Certainly not! No more would a Scythian, a Greek, a Persian, or a Hyperborean. In all other matters, to be sure, you would find men voting for different conclusions, everybody in disagreement with everybody else. Not all share the same concept of Goodness, or of Evil, or of Shame, or of Nobility. Laws and customs and notions of justice are borne this way and that, in diversity and discord. Not only does nation fail to agree with nation; city fails to agree with city, household with household, man with man, even individuals with themselves!

> The opinions of mortals who live upon the earth are such
> As the day the Father of gods and men brings on.[19]

---

[16] *Od.* 19. 246: a description of Odysseus' companion Eurybates often quoted by grammarians and others (Aphthon. ii. 46. 20 Spengel; Theon ii. 118. 11 Spendel; Herod. iii. 104. 31 Spengel; Tryphon iii. 201. 3 Spengel; Galen *De Dign. Puls.* 1. 4).

[17] An allusion both to *Il.* 1. 528-30, and to Phidias' celebrated image of the god at Olympia; cf. Dio *Or.* 12. 25-6 with Russell (1992, ad loc.). Maximus allegorizes Zeus' heaven-shaking nod in *Orr.* 4. 8 and 41. 2.

[18] The text is defective here, and more may have gone missing than this minimum supplement supposes: perhaps something like '⟨the contrivings of painters, the images of sculptors, the songs of poets and⟩ the conjectures of philosophers'.

[19] *Od.* 18. 136-7, a celebrated expression of human 'ephemerality', much quoted (e.g. [Plut.] *Cons. Ap.* 104e): cf. Fränkel (1946). See also *Or.* 1. 2 with n. 8 ad loc.

5   In the midst of such conflict, such strife, such discord, there is
the one belief, the one account, on which every nation agrees: that
there is one God who is father and king of all, and with him many
other gods, his children, who share in his sovereign power. This is
what Greek and barbarian alike, inlander and coast-dweller, wise
man and fool all say. Even if you go to the shores of Ocean, there
too they have their gods, rising near to the one people, setting near
to the other.[20] Do you really believe that Plato casts his vote against
all these witnesses and lays down another law, rather than endorsing a verdict and an experience of such unsurpassed beauty and
truth? What is this? 'The sun,' replies the eye. What is this?
'Thunder,' replies the ear. What are these beauties and graces,
these cycles and changes and temperings of the climate, and births
of animals and growth of crops? 'They are all the handiwork of
God,' replies the soul, as it yearns for the craftsman and divines the
presence of his craft. Even if in the course of history there have
been some two or three, a godless, mean, insensitive species, as
errant in their vision and misguided in their hearing as they are
emasculated in soul, as irrational, sterile, and unfruitful as a lion
without spirit or a bull without horns or a bird without wings, yet
this group too will still be able to tell you of God. They know him
without wanting to and speak of him in spite of themselves: even
if, like Leucippus, you remove his goodness; even if, like
Democritus, you add 'community of sensation'; even if, like Strato,
you alter his nature; even if, like Epicurus, you allow him to feel
pleasure; even if, like Diagoras, you deny his existence; even if, like
Protagoras, you declare yourself agnostic.[21]

6   Let us leave these individuals to their own devices, since they
are unable to grasp the truth whole and unimpaired, and must
instead make their way towards it by obscure and devious routes.
But what are we ourselves to do? Are we to abandon our venture,
not even searching for oblique traces of the divine, not even

---

[20] The reference here is to the two races of Aethiopians, living to the far east and
the far west, mentioned in *Od.* 1. 22–4 (lines famously discussed by Aristarchus and
Crates: see Strabo 1. 2. 24); cf. also Philostr. *Vit. Ap.* 2. 18. The gods of these
peoples are the heavenly bodies (cf. *Or.* 2. 9).

[21] i.e. even the strange, apparently agnostic or downright atheistic theories of
philosophers are in fact an acknowledgement of God's existence. See Leucippus A
22 and B 2 D-K; Democritus B 166 D-K; Strato fr. 36 Wehrli; Epicurus κυρ. δόξ. 1
and *Ep. Pyth* (Diog. Laert. 10. 97), cf. Cic. *ND* 1. 2; Protagoras B 4 D-K.

encountering it in the form of images?[22] Yet Odysseus, when he landed in a foreign country, used to climb to a point of vantage and search for traces of the inhabitants:

> Are they ruffians and savages, devoid of justice,
> Or hospitable to strangers, and of god-fearing mind?[23]

Shall we then not have the courage to set our powers of reasoning on some vantage-point high in the soul and look round for traces of God, his location, and his nature? Shall we rest content with a clouded view? Would that I had an oracle of Zeus or Apollo, that gave answers neither indirect nor ambivalent. I would not ask the god about Croesus' cauldron (that most witless of kings and most ill-fated of cooks!), nor about the measure of the sea or the number of the sands.[24] I would have no thought either for all those other portentous questions that men have asked: 'The Medes are advancing; how shall I defend myself?' Even if the god does not advise me, I have my triremes. 'I desire Sicily; how may I capture it?' Even if the god does not prevent me, Sicily is large.[25] Let my answer be about Zeus and let it come clearly from Apollo in Delphi, or from Zeus himself.[26] But who will answer me on his behalf? It is from the Academy that the god's spokesman hails, a man of Attica with the gift of divination. His answer goes like this.

7   The human soul has two cognitive faculties: the one simple, called 'intellect', the other diverse, various, and manifold, called 'perception'. They work together, but their essential natures are distinct. The relationship between these two faculties is paralleled by that of the objects to which they are applied; the intelligible differs from the perceptible as much as intellect does from perception. Of the two objects, everyday acquaintance makes the latter— the perceptible—the more familiar to us; intelligible objects, though unknown to us in everyday experience, are nevertheless more

---

[22] The text is corrupt at this point, but must have said roughly what is translated here.

[23] *Od.* 6. 120-1.

[24] Cf. Hdt. 1. 47. 3 and 1. 48. 2; Croesus' cauldron is mentioned again in *Orr.* 13. 3 and 29. 7.

[25] The allusions are to the Athenian consultation of the Delphic oracle in 480 (Hdt. 7. 140-3) and to the Sicilian Expedition of 415 (Thuc. 6. 8 ff., but without any reference to a consultation of the Oracle).

[26] For the phenomenon of theological oracles in Maximus' period, see Lane Fox (1986, ch. 5).

knowable in their real nature. Let me explain. It is clear that habitual and cumulative experience of animals and plants and stones and sounds and flavours and smells and shapes and colours, inextricably bound up with our day-to-day existence, has conditioned the soul and persuaded it to believe that nothing other than these things actually exists. For its part, the intelligible, which is quite free from any contact with or dependence on such things, is such as to be apprehended on its own, by the intellect; but the intellect, because it has been engrafted into the whole conglomerate of the soul, is pulled this way and that by perception and kept in such a state of confused activity that it is unable to maintain a clear view of its proper objects, to such an extent that it can even be cozened into agreeing with the noisy claims of the senses and believing that nothing exists apart from what can be seen and heard and smelled and tasted and touched. Therefore, just as at a symposium, as rich savours fill the air, and the wine is poured, and flutes and pipes and lyres play, and incense burns, it would take a strong-willed man to stay sober and disciplined—a man capable of taking a grip on himself and chastening himself and diverting his senses;[27] in just the same way, in the midst of the tumult of the senses it is hard to find a sober intellect that can fix its gaze on its own proper objects. Perceptibles, moreover, by their very nature, being the manifold, inconstant congeries that they are, in a constant process of change, form the soul in their own image, so that when it makes the transition to the realm of the intelligible, which is firm and stable, it is so shaken by the swell and the tumult that it is quite unable to see clearly and securely. This is exactly like what happens to people who have disembarked from a ship on to dry land; for is it not the case that they too are physically hardly able to stand upright, as they are still moving and spinning and swaying in the manner they have grown used to at sea?[28]

8   In which of these two realms, then, is God to be located? Surely it must be in the firmer and more stable of them, the one

---

[27] The portrayal of Socrates in Plato *Smp.* seems to lie behind this comparison.

[28] For the crucial Platonic distinction drawn in this paragraph between intelligence and the intelligible, and perception and the perceptible, and for the language used to express it, cf. *Resp.* 507a ff. and *Phdo* 65b ff.; at the same time the phrasing of the distinction between what is more knowable *per se* and what is better known *to us* derives from Aristotle (*An. Post.* 1. 2, 71^b33 ff.; *Phys.* 1. 1, 184^a15 ff.); cf. Theiler (1930: 8).

which is free from all flux and change. For can anything have
stability if God does not lay his steadying hand on it? If you need
some kind of guidance to help you grasp the nature of the whole,
follow reason's lead.[29] Reason will lead you by means of a series of
divisions, performed on entirely familiar kinds of entity, dividing
each in half, then each successive time further dividing the more
precious of the resulting segments, until it arrives at the object of
our present enquiry. Well then: everything that exists can be
divided into the inanimate and the animate. 'Inanimate' comprises
stones and sticks and so on; 'animate' comprises animals and
plants. The animate is superior to the inanimate. The animate can
be divided into the vegetative and the perceptive, of which the
perceptive is superior. The perceptive can be divided into the
rational and the irrational, of which the rational is superior. But a
further division still can be made even within the rational soul,
since this itself is a kind of conglomerate, compounded of the nutritive, vegetative, motive, affective, and intellective faculties. Thus
the selfsame relation that holds between the inanimate and the
animate holds also between the intellective element in the soul and
the soul as a whole; and clearly, the rational element is superior
to the conglomerate of all those other faculties.[30] Where then are
we to place God? In the conglomerate? What an unworthy
suggestion! The only possible conclusion is, so to speak, to take
God up to the acropolis in our argument and to establish him in
the citadel of the supreme commander, intellect. Yet even here I
can see a distinction to be made:[31] because, while there is one kind
of intellect that has the natural capacity to think, even though in
fact it does not think, there is another that does think. Yet even
this latter does not yet rank as perfect intellect, unless you add to

---

[29] What now follows is Maximus' version of the 'way of eminence' (Alcinous'
τρίτη νόησις in *Didasc.* 10. 165. 27 ff.).

[30] This passage again displays a characteristic dependence on scholastic
material. The technique of division (διαίρεσις) harks back ultimately to such Platonic
texts as *Phaedr* 265d ff. and *Soph.*, but had long been a philosophical commonplace:
compare above all the analyses of reality ('id quod est', ὄντα) in Sen. *Ep.* 58. 8–15
and Philo *De Agric.* 139, which are discussed along with this paragraph of *Or.* 11
in Theiler (1930: 4–8). The division of the soul into nutritive, vegetative, motive,
affective, and intellective faculties is originally Aristotelian (e.g. *De An.* 2. 4–5 and
3. 9, *NE* 1. 13), but had also long since become common property (Sen. *Ep.* 58.
14); cf. *Or.* 9. 1.

[31] Again, Aristotelian in its ultimate inspiration (cf. *De An.* 3. 4–5, 429ª10–
430ª25, *Met.* 7.6, 1045ᵇ17 ff.); for the Platonic tradition, cf. Alcin. *Didasc.* 10. 164.
18–20, Plotinus *Enn.* 5. 9. 4. 2–3 and 5. 9. 5. 1–4.

it the further properties of thinking eternally, and thinking all things, and not thinking differently at different times. Thus the most perfect form of intellect is that which thinks all things for ever at the same time.[32]

9   If you like, you may take the following image to illustrate what I am saying.[33] Divine intellect is like sight, while human intellect is like speech: for while the beams of the eye are immensely rapid and gather in an impression of their object all at once, the operation of speech is like a leisurely stroll. Or better, think of a comparison along these lines. Divine intellect, like the entire embracing circuit of the sun, sees the whole surface of the earth at once; human intellect is like the sun's progress as it passes over different parts of the whole at different times.

It is this intellect that our messenger from the Academy reports to us is the Father and Begetter of all. He does not tell us its name, for he does not know it. He does not tell us its complexion, for he has not seen it. He does not tell us its size, for he has not touched it. All these are physical properties, grasped by the flesh and the eye. But the Divine itself cannot be seen by the eye or spoken of by the tongue or touched by the flesh or heard by the ear; it is only the noblest and purest and most intelligent and subtlest and most venerable aspect of the soul that can see it in virtue of their similarity, and hear it in virtue of their kinship, grasping it all at once in a single act of comprehension. So, just as if someone desires to see the sun, he does not seek to grasp it with his sense of hearing; and if someone is passionate for vocal harmonies, he does not pursue them with his eyes—it is sight that is passionate for colours and hearing for sounds—just so what intellect 'sees' and 'hears' is the Intelligible.[34]

10   This is precisely the sense of the Syracusan's riddle,

Mind sees and mind hears[35]

[32] For this concept of the Supreme God, cf. Alcin. *Didasc.* 10. 164. 18 ff., where one sees the same slide from God as supreme Intelligible to God as supreme Intelligence (cf. Festugière 1954: 112–3, 127, 136).

[33] Cf. Alcinous' νόησις κατὰ ἀναλογίαν in *Didasc.* 10. 165. 20–6.

[34] Cf. Alcin. *Didasc.* 10. 164. 13–8, and the exposition of 'negative theology' (νόησις κατὰ ἀφαίρεσιν) in 164. 31–165. 19. This too is characteristically Middle Platonic; the ultimate inspiration is Plato's description of the intelligible world in *Phaedr.* 247c.

[35] Epicharmus B 12 D-K, also quoted by, for example, Plut. *De Fort.* 98d, *De Fort. Alex.* 336b, *De Soll. An.* 961a.

How then does the intellect see, and how does it hear?[36] By bringing to bear an upright, vigorous soul, by fixing its gaze firmly on
that pure light and not falling prey to vertigo, nor sinking back
towards the earth, but blocking off its ears, and turning ears and
eyes in upon itself; by forgetting the groans and lamentations and
pleasures and fancies and honours and dishonours below and
entrusting its guidance to true Reason and vigorous Love—Reason
to instruct it on the correct path, Love to watch over it and to ease
the labours of the journey with its persuasive charm. As the
soul advances thither and distances itself from things below, the
clear radiance of what lies ahead of it, stage by stage, serves as a
prelude to God's true nature. As it advances, it hears of God's
nature; as it ascends, it sees it. The end of the journey is not the
heavens nor the heavenly bodies. For though these are indeed
things of wondrous beauty, in that they are his true and legitimate
offspring, in harmony with supreme Beauty, yet must we go
beyond even these and emerge beyond the heavens, into the region
of true Reality and the peace which reigns there,[37]

> Where winter's weight is never felt, nor is it ever drenched
> In rain . . . but bright and cloudless
> Skies spread all around, suffused with radiant white,[38]

with no fleshly sensations to trouble the view, of the kind that
disturb the wretched soul here down below, laying low such
rationality as it possesses in the general tumult and confusion. For
how could anyone hear the voice of God when he is harassed by
a mob of uncouth thoughts and desires? No more could a man
hear the voice of law and authority in a noisy and tumultuous
democracy.

How can one hear in a great din of men?[39]

---

[36] In what follows Maximus combines two well-established philosophical topoi
(both of ultimately Platonic inspiration): that of philosophical ἐπιστροφή (the turning of the intellect away from the world and its values), and that of the flight of the
mind (Himmelfahrt): for the former, which has already featured in the discussion in
Or. 10. 3, see e.g. Phdo 82d–84b and Alcin. Didasc. 10. 165. 2, with Witt (1931)
and Whittaker (1990: 104 n. 194); for the latter, for example, Phaedr. 246d–247e
and Theaet. 173e, with Jones (1926) and Festugière (1949: 444ff.); and compare
Orr. 9. 6 and 10. 2.

[37] Cf. again Phaedr. 247.

[38] A cento of Od. 4. 566 and 6. 43–5, also employed in Or. 30. 4. Od. 6. 42–5
are similarly used as an image of the divine realm in [Arist.] De Mundo 400a.

[39] Il. 19. 81.

For when it falls into this tumult and surrenders itself to be carried along on an irresistible swell, the soul swims in a sea that is indeed hard to escape, until Philosophy takes it in charge, buoying it up with her teachings as Leucothea did Odysseus with her veil.[40]

11   How then can a man swim to safety and see God? The true answer is that you will see him when he calls you to him. Await that call, for it will come soon! Old age will come, leading you on towards him; and death will come, which the coward laments in his fear at its approach, but which the lover of God welcomes gladly, and with confidence, as it approaches. But if you still desire to learn God's nature even now, how might one explain it? For though God is beautiful, and indeed the most radiantly beautiful of all things, he is not a beautiful body; rather, he is the source from which that body derives its beauty. Nor is he a beautiful meadow; rather, he is the source from which the meadow too derives its beauty. The beauty of a river, and of the sea and of the heavens and of the celestial gods—all this beauty flows from God as if from a pure and ever-flowing spring. In so far as individual things have some share in it, they are beautiful and stable and secure; in so far as they are lacking in it, they are ugly and prone to degeneration and destruction. If this account suffices, then you have seen God; but if it does not, how might one still hint at His nature? For I would not have you think in terms of magnitude or colour or shape or any other modification of matter; but just as, if a beautiful body is hidden from sight by many layers of rich clothing, the lover unclothes it so as to be able to see it clearly, so now you should, by the exercise of reason, strip off and remove this covering that obstructs your gaze, and in what remains you will see the true object of your desire.[41]

12   But if you are not strong enough to see the Father and Creator,[42] then it must suffice for the moment to contemplate his works and to worship his offspring, who are many and varied, far more numerous than the Boeotian poet says.[43] God's divine

[40] *Od.* 5. 333–53. For this allegorical use of Odysseus, see Buffière (1956: 386–8, 461–4), and compare *Or.* 9. 6.

[41] Another touch of 'negative theology'; cf. n. 34 above.

[42] An echo of Plato *Tim.* 41a (but the phrase is so frequently quoted as to rank as a cliché of philosophical theology); cf. *Or.* 41. 2.

[43] Hesiod *Op.* 252–3, another much-quoted line: see M. L. West's apparatus ad loc.

children and relatives are not a mere thirty thousand in number, but countless: the stars and planets in the heavens, and the *daimones* in the ether too.

In order to explain to you what I am saying, I should like to invoke a still more lucid image. Think of a great empire and a mighty kingdom, in which all bow willingly to one soul, that of the best and most revered of kings. The boundary of this empire is not the River Halys or the Hellespont or Lake Maeotis or the shores of Ocean,[44] but the heavens above and earth below: the heavens like the circuit of an impenetrable wall, completely enclosing the universe and shielding all within itself; the earth like a watch-house[45] and a prison for sinful bodies. The Great King himself sits motionless, like the law,[46] bestowing on his subjects the security that resides in him. As his partners in power, he has a whole host of visible and invisible deities, some gathered close round the vestibule of his throne-room, like a king's viziers and close relatives, sharing his table and his hearth, others subordinate to these, and yet others further subordinate to them.[47] Here is a succession, a hierarchy for you to behold, from God above to the earth below.

ORATION 12   Revenge

Introduction

= 18 (1962) = 2 (Laur. Conv. Sopp. 4). The manuscript title—εἰ τὸν ἀδικήσαντα ἀνταδικητέον, 'Whether one ought to repay wrong with wrong'—is accurate (cf. § 2 init.).

A lecture on the ethics of retaliation, belonging to the same group of ethical–civic discourses as *Orr.* 3–4, 14–26, and 35–7. The question at issue is introduced and focused by means of a famous poetic quotation (§§ 1–2a), and answered through an analysis of the concepts of wronging and being wronged (§§ 2b–5): while the

---

[44] The boundaries of Croesus' empire, of Asia (thus of the westward expansion of Darius and Xerxes), and of the inhabited world.

[45] Cf. *Phdo* 62b.

[46] Cf. *Polit.* 294a, 297a; and [Arist.] *De Mundo* 400ᵇ12 ff. (for which see Festugière 1949: 460–518; Lorimer 1925; Reale 1974); compare also *Or.* 13. 4.

[47] With this comparison of God to a (or the) Great King, compare again [Arist.] *De Mundo* 6; cf. also Philo *Op. Mund.* 71; *Spec. Leg.* 1. 18; *Decal.* 61.

bad man commits (or at least attempts) bad action, and cannot himself be wronged, it is impossible for the good man, in any circumstances, either to commit wrong or to be its victim (i.e. he has no desire of his own to do wrong, no wrong can be done him such as to provoke him, and in any case, he can never succeed in inflicting real harm on another). The remainder of the lecture expands on this conclusion, dwelling first on great examples from history of the ills brought about by reprisal (§§ 6–9), then on the exemplary behaviour of Socrates in the face of the wrongs done him (§ 10).

This is another thoroughly Platonizing performance, based on a text from the *Crito* (49bd), full of reminiscences of the *Apology* and the *Gorgias* (for which compare also *Or.* 3), and borrowing the idea for its introductory tag from the *Republic*. Apparently Stoic emphases (especially in §§ 2–3) are simply one more indication of how much originally extraneous material had been drafted into Platonism by the second century. Equally characteristic of Maximus' procedures is the use of archaic and classical history (and the classic authors, Herodotus, Thucydides, and Xenophon) to illustrate his moral message (§§ 6–8): see Introduction, pp. xxxvii–xxxix.

Gregoras takes four excerpts from the lecture for his common-place book (from §§ 1, 2, 5, and 6), and the compiler of Neap. 100 also takes four (from §§ 3, 4, 7, and 8). Beatus Rhenanus singles it out for special praise (for its near-Christian sentiments) in the introduction to his translation (1519),[1] and his lead is followed, after an interval, by Hugo Grotius, who makes one reference in his *De Veritate Religionis Christianae* (3rd edn. 1640, note on p. 392, to IV. 12, p. 140); Jeremy Taylor, who quotes or refers three times in his collected sermons and tracts (*History of the Life and Death of the Holy Jesus* (1649), para. 40; Heber-Eden 1847–54: ii. 31: 12. 9; *The Worthy Communicant* (1660), 4. 4: viii. 142: 12. 9; *Ductor Dubitantium* (1660), III. 2. 18. 4: x. 143: general reference to *Or.*

---

[1] *Maximi Tyrii Philosophi Platonici Sermones* (Basel, 1519), 4: 'Porro norunt Platonicae sapientiae studiosi quam huic perbelle cum Christiano conveniat, quatenus saltem humanae et ethnicae doctrinae cum coelesti commune quiddam habere licet. Quid Christianius, quam illatam iniuriam non retaliare? at nonne hoc docet Plato? Habet sermonem de hac re Tyrius tam sanctum, tam pium, tam Christianum, ut si hic auribus vulgi crebrius inculcetur, facile futurum sperem, ut insanis istis bellorum tumultibus, quibus Christiani inter nos concurrimus, aliquando finis imponatur.'

12); and Richard Byfield, who takes no fewer than fourteen excerpts for his commonplace book (Harl. 1790, foll. 67(66)ᵛ–69(68)ᵛ: excerpts from §§ 3–10).

Oration

1   Is Justice warded by a lofty wall,
          Or does the race of men who live on earth
          Scale it with crooked deceit?
          I am in two minds how to answer truly.[2]

It is all very well for you, Pindar, to debate with yourself over deceit and Justice, comparing gold with bronze; you were after all a poet, skilled in composing songs for choruses and epinician odes for tyrants, and your concern was with the metrical forms of words and with musical harmony and rhythmical sequences. But to the man for whom choruses and songs and the pleasures of music have the same importance as children's toys, and whose real concern is with the metres and rhythms and melodies of the soul,[3] and with proper form in the sphere of actions and of life in general, this question, 'Is Justice warded by a lofty wall?', simply would not occur in the first place. His verdict, rewriting your song, would be this: that

          Justice is indeed a lofty wall,
          And the race of men who live on earth
          Scale it indeed with crooked deceit;

but that Justice remains as insurmountable an object to deceit as the heavens were to the Aloidae. Ossa piled on Olympus and Olympus piled on Pelion did them no good at all;[4] they fell as far short of the heavens as deceit does of Justice. Justice belongs to the class of goods, while deceit belongs to the class of evils; Justice is genuine, deceit a forgery; Justice is strong, deceit is weak; the one is beneficial, the other is not.

2   Would then the man who cares for Justice and is protected by that wall of Pindar's ever choose, if wronged, to take his revenge

---

[2] Pindar fr. 213 Snell-Maehler, a quotation inspired by Plato *Resp.* 365b (where, however, only lines 1–2 are quoted); Cic. *Ad Att.* 13. 38 quotes lines 1–2 and 4.
[3] For this 'music vs. real life' trope, cf. *Or.* 1. 1–2.
[4] *Od.* 11. 305–20.

in kind?[5] And yet, let me see what it is that I am saying here. For it may be that it isn't even permissible for him to be wronged in the first place.[6] If wronging and being wronged are the same kind of thing as hitting and being hit or cutting and being cut,[7] then there is nothing untoward in the same person being both the agent and the victim of wrongdoing. But suppose on the other hand that, although in the one case the same person can by a natural association be both the agent and the victim of the action, wronging and being wronged are in fact much more like seeing and being seen: what has the power of sight is also seen, but what is seen does not in all cases also see.[8] Or rather let us put it like this, that ⟨wronging and⟩ being wronged resemble showing someone to be wrong and being shown to be wrong oneself: it is the man who knows the truth who does the showing, and the man who does not know the truth who is shown up.[9] And just as the ⟨possibility of being shown to be wrong⟩ is not open to the man who knows the truth, and that of showing someone else to be wrong ⟨is not open to the man who does not⟩, so too wronging and being wronged could never be co-predicates of the same individual.

3   Since then the two predicates belong not to the same individual but to different people, and given that the good man and the bad man are not identical, which predicate shall we assign to which individual? Should it be doing wrong to the bad man and suffering wrong to the good man? Or is the position that while doing wrong certainly attaches to the bad man, it is still unclear to which of them suffering wrong attaches? Let us consider the matter like this. Wrongdoing is 'removal of the good'; and what else could the good

---

[5] As conventional, non-philosophical morality would dictate: cf. *Crito* 49b10–11; Dover (1974: 180–4).

[6] The proposition that the good man cannot be wronged is particularly associated with the Stoics: *SVF* iii. 578–80; Sen. *Const. Sap.*, esp. 3–5 and 7 (with Klei 1950, ad loc.). Platonists could, however, claim it on the grounds of such passages as *Apol.* 30c (quoted below in § 8 and perhaps alluded to here too); cf. Apul. *De Plat.* 2. 20. 248.

[7] 'Cutting' and 'being cut' are regularly used as examples in philosophical discussions: cf. *Grg.* 476cd, Ar. *Categ.* 2ᵃ3–4, *De int.* 21ᵇ12–17 (also using the example of 'the visible' and 'being seen').

[8] Arist. *Soph. El.* 166ᵃ9–10 diagnoses the fallacy in the inference that what one sees, sees. Here too Maximus is using well-worn philosophical examples.

[9] The comparison inevitably brings Socrates to mind: perhaps particularly the Socrates of *Grg.* (e.g. 458a—however much he himself would deny 'knowing the truth').

be but Virtue?[10] Virtue, moreover, is inalienable.[11] Therefore, either the virtuous man will not suffer wrong, or wrongdoing is not removal of the good. Nothing that is good can be removed or cast away or seized or plundered.[12] The good man, then, is not wronged, either by ⟨good men or by⟩ bad, since ⟨his virtue⟩ is inalienable. The only conclusions left open are either that no one suffers wrong at all, or that the bad man is wronged by his peers. But the bad man has no share in anything good, and wrongdoing is removal of the good; the man who has nothing to be taken away from him has nothing to be wronged in either.

4   We might suggest therefore that wrongdoing is to be defined not by reference to the removal of anything from the victim, but by reference to the intentions of the perpetrator. A bad man could then be wronged by another bad man, even if he does not possess the good; a good man could be wronged by a bad man even if the good he has is inalienable. I accept this account that connects wrongdoing with the moral defect shown in the intention, rather than with the success of the actual attempt;[13] the law certainly punishes not only the man who does the deed but also the man who intends to do it: the housebreaker who attempts a burglary, even if he is discovered; the intending traitor, even if he does not act. This whole line of argument, taken together, will bring us to the required conclusion. The good man neither commits nor suffers wrong: he does not commit wrong because he lacks the desire to; he does not suffer wrong because his virtue is inalienable. The bad man, on the other hand, commits wrong but does not suffer it: he commits wrong because he is bad; ⟨he does not suffer wrong because he is innocent⟩ of good. Moreover, if Virtue alone and nothing else is good,[14] the bad man's lack of Virtue means that he has nothing to be wronged in. But if other things in addition to Virtue are also good—physical attributes and one's external

---

[10] The question whether Virtue was the sole Good (or the sole determinant of happiness) was disputed within Platonism: both 'Stoicizing' and 'Peripateticizing' tendencies can be seen: Dillon (1977: 44, 73-4, 123-5, 299). Maximus himself confronts the issue in *Orr.* 39-40.

[11] Another Stoic tenet (*SVF* i. 568-9, iii. 238-41; Sen. *Const. Sap.* 5. 4) comfortably assimilable by Platonists (Apul. *De Plat.* 2. 20. 248); cf. also Archytas ap. Stob. *Flor.* 1. 72, i. 30. 5 Meineke.

[12] The wording echoes *Il.* 3. 65 (the gifts of the gods) and 9. 408-9 (life).

[13] Cf. Sen. *Const. Sap.* 7. 4, Juvenal 13. 209.

[14] See n. 10 above.

fortunes and surroundings[15]—then in the absence of Virtue it is better for these things to be absent than for them to be present— with the result that not even thus would the bad man suffer wrong, by being deprived of any of these things he makes such ill use of. Therefore if we define wrongdoing by reference to intention, the bad man commits wrong but does not suffer it † . . . †

5   † . . . †[16] the bad man wishes to commit wrong, he is in fact not able to. His desire sets him either against a man like himself or against his better.[17] But what is his better to do? Is he to inflict a wrong on the bad man in return? Yet the bad man has nothing to be wronged in, since it is precisely the absence of the good that makes him bad. In that case the sensible man will refrain from committing a reciprocal wrong against the bad man both in deed (the other has nothing to be wronged in), and in intention (being good, he has no more desire to do wrong than a pipe-player does to play out of tune). And in general, if doing wrong is bad, then so too is doing wrong in return. The man who does wrong incurs no extra charge of wickedness in virtue of having acted first; instead, the man who returns the wrong puts himself on the same level of baseness by hitting back. If the man who does wrong acts badly, then the man who returns the wrong acts no less badly, even if he is taking revenge for a prior offence. Just as someone who returns a favour to his beneficiary acts no less well for the fact that he was benefited first, so the person who ensures a similar reciprocity in the sphere of harmful action acts no less badly for the fact that he was harmed first.

6   What limit will there then be to the harm done? If the victims of wrongdoing take their revenge, the harm will for ever be trans- ferred from one to the other and perpetuate itself, and one act of wrongdoing will follow another. The same justification by which

[15] The conventional classification: Plato *Leg.* 697b, Arist. *NE* 1. 8, 1098^{b}12, Cic. *Tusc.* 5. 15. 45, etc.; cf. *Or.* 40. 5.

[16] The corruption to the text makes it difficult to reconstruct the precise line of thought. It would make sense to end § 4 with '. . . suffer it.' and to begin § 5 with something like 'If, however, we define wrongdoing in terms of what is achieved, then it appears that, though . . .'; but it is difficult to extract anything like this from the paradosis.

[17] Zanobi Acciaiuoli (Conv. Sopp. 4, fol. 24^v) suggests that something has dropped out of the text at this point ('a statement relating to the (bad man's) like seems to be missing'). This is possible: perhaps 'His like will of course attempt to take his revenge.'

you allow the victim to take his revenge is equally effective in
allowing the right of retaliation to pass back from him to the
original offender; the justification is open to both of them equally.
For God's sake, look at what you have brought about! Justice compounded of wrongs! How far will the mischief go? Where will it
come to rest? Don't you realize that this is an inexhaustible source
of wickedness that you are opening up, that you are laying down
a law that will lead the whole earth into harm? It was just this
principle that brought men the great misfortunes of days gone by,
armed expeditions of foreigners and Greeks crossing to attack each
other, robbing and warring and plundering, and making the
preceding wrong their excuse for each new one. The Phoenicians
kidnap a royal princess from Argos; the Greeks kidnap a foreign
girl from Colchis; then the Phrygians strike again, taking a Spartan
woman from the Peloponnese.[18] It is obvious how ill succeeds ill,
how pretexts for war arise, how wrongs multiply. This same
process brought Greece into destructive conflict with herself too—
self-styled victims of wrongs attacking their neighbours, in
inexhaustible rage and undying anger and lust for revenge and
moral ignorance.

7   But if the victims of wrong could only understand that their
own wrongdoing is the greatest of ills for the perpetrators themselves[19]—worse than war and the razing of their fortifications and
the ravaging of their territory and the imposition of tyranny—then
Greece would not have been overwhelmed with such crushing misfortunes. The Athenians are laying siege to Potidaea.[20] Leave them
be, Spartan; they will repent of it soon enough! Don't imitate them
in their evil-doing, don't lay yourself open to the same reproach! If
you seize the pretext and advance against Plataea, the island of
Melos, your neighbour, is done for; the island of Aegina, your
friend, is done for; the city of Scione, your ally, is done for.[21] By
capturing one city you will only bring about the sack of many. Just
as, when people risk their lives at sea on business, they pay
exorbitant interest on the money they have borrowed, so when
people take revenge in anger they pay an exorbitant interest on the
disasters they inflict. And to the Athenian I say: 'You have

---

[18]   This account of successive abductions is borrowed from Hdt. 1. 1–4.
[19]   A familiar Socratic point: *Crito* 49b, *Grg.* 469b.
[20]   Thuc. 1. 56–65 and 71.
[21]   Maximus uses the same set of episodes in *Or.* 6. 5; see n. 22 ad loc.

captured Sphacteria; give Sparta back her men![22] See sense while your fortunes are good! If you do not you will have the men, but you won't have your triremes.'[23] Lysander may score successes in the Hellespont and Sparta may wax mighty. But keep away from Thebes![24] If you do not, you will have a catastrophe at Leuctra and a disaster at Mantinea to weep over.[25]

8 What a murky and misguided style of Justice! It was for this reason that Socrates refused to grow angry with Aristophanes, or resent Meletus, or take revenge on Lycon, but instead cried out, 'Anytus and Meletus can kill me but they cannot harm me; it is not permitted for a good man to be harmed by a villain.'[26] This is the true voice of Justice; if all spoke in it there would be no tragedies, no dramas on the stage, none of those many varieties of disaster. Just as in the case of bodily diseases it is the creeping varieties that are the recalcitrant ones, demanding a cure capable of halting their advance in its tracks and so saving the rest of the body; so when a first act of injustice afflicts a household or a city, the canker must be stopped if the remainder is to be saved.[27] This is what destroyed the Pelopidae, this is what annihilated the Heracleidae and the house of Cadmus; this is what brought down Persians, and Macedonians, and Greeks.[28] What an unremitting disease it is, afflicting the earth in cycle after cycle down the ages.

9 I would make so bold as to say that if it is possible for one kind of wrongdoing to surpass another, then the person who takes revenge is a worse wrongdoer than the original offender. The latter commits his wrong through ignorance and has his punishment in the censure that follows; but the retaliator, by taking an equal share of guilt, actually frees him from his liability to censure.

[22] Thuc. 4. 1–41, esp. 37–41.
[23] A reference to the Athenian naval defeats at Syracuse (Thuc. 7. 70–2) and Aegospotami (Xen. *Hell.* 2. 1. 15–32); the mention of Lysander in the next sentence also refers to Aegospotami and its aftermath.
[24] Xen. *Hell.* 5. 1. 32 ff.
[25] Xen. *Hell.* 6. 4. 4–15 and 6. 5. 22–32.
[26] A paraphrase of *Apol.* 30c.
[27] For the image, cf. *Or.* 7. 7.
[28] The first four references are straightforward: to the woes of the house of Atreus, the children of Heracles, and the royal house of Thebes in myth, and to the Persian Wars of 490–478. The fifth might be an allusion either to the 'enslavement' of Macedonia by Philip and Alexander (cf. *Or.* 14. 8), or to the dissolution of Alexander's empire after his death (cf. *Or.* 28. 1); the last is perhaps a (heavily) veiled reference to the Roman conquest.

Just as a man who becomes entangled with someone covered in soot cannot avoid staining his own body too, so anyone who sees fit to wrestle and take a fall with an unjust man cannot avoid sharing in his wickedness and becoming defiled by the same soot.[29] When two athletes with the same training and the same ambition compete together, I am entirely happy, since I can see that their natural endowments are comparable, their exercises similar, and the desire for victory equivalent in both cases. But if a good man falls in with a villain, when the two don't come from the same gymnasium, and haven't been trained by the same trainer, or learned the same arts, or been taught the same throws, and don't long for the same wreath and the same victory-proclamation, then their combat moves me to pity; it is an unequal contest. It is inevitable that the bad man will win when he is competing in a stadium where the spectators are criminals and the organizers rogues.[30] In such a situation the good man is a layman and an ignoramus, innocent of suspicion and knavery and all the other tricks of the trade with which villainy fortifies and reinforces itself. The man who has no endowment for it in natural aptitude, in acquired skill, or in habit[31] merely makes himself ridiculous by trying to return wrong for wrong.

10   But, someone may say, it is because of this that the just man is slandered and brought to court and prosecuted and has his wealth confiscated and is thrown into prison and driven into exile and stripped of his citizenship and executed. What then if children, making their own laws for themselves and convening their own court, were to arraign a grown man under their legislation, and then, if he was found guilty, were to vote that he should lose his rights in the commonwealth of children and were to confiscate his childish effects, his knuckle-bones, and his toys:[32] what is it reasonable to suppose a man would do ⟨when condemned⟩ by such a court? ⟨Would he not laugh them to scorn,⟩ votes, condemnations, and all? So Socrates laughed the Athenians to scorn, like children casting their votes and ordering the execution of a man

---

[29] The same image is used by Epict. 3. 16. 3 (cf. *Ench.* 33. 6).

[30] For the athletics imagery, cf. *Or.* 1. 4 and 6.

[31] A version of the conventional triad nature, instruction (knowledge), and practice (habituation): cf. *Or.* 1. 5, with n. 22.

[32] This vision of the good man on trial before a jury of children is developed from Plato *Grg.* 521e ff.

who was in any case condemned to mortality.[33] So too any good
and just man will laugh with free and honest laughter as he sees
wrongdoers eagerly attacking him, convinced that they are achieving something noteworthy but in reality achieving nothing. As
they strip him of his rights he will cry the cry of Achilles:

> I know that I am honoured in Zeus' ordinance.[34]

When they confiscate his wealth he will let it go as if it were his
toys and knuckle-bones, and he will die as if from fever or the
stone, with no resentment towards his murderers.[35]

ORATION 13   Prophecy and Human Foresight

Introduction

= 19 (1962) = 3 (Laur. Conv. Sopp. 4). The manuscript title—εἰ μαντικῆς
οὔσης ἔστιν τι ἐφ' ἡμῖν, 'Whether, given the reality of prophecy, there is
Free Will'—is misleading: the main subject is the compatibility of prophecy
with human *intelligence* (§§ 2–3, 5, 9), rather than with Free Will.

This lecture is the last in the main sequence of Maximus'
cosmological–theological discourses; it has close thematic links
with *Orr.* 5, 11, and 41, and points of contact also with 8–9 and
2. 10: see Soury (1942, esp. ch. 3) for a discussion that underlines
the common ground with 5 and 41, but fails to provide a wholly
satisfactory account of the lecture in itself; also Puiggali (1983:
283–304) for a detailed discussion of doctrinal affinities.

Soury, Puiggali, and Dillon (1977: 400), all follow the manuscript title in reading the lecture as Maximus' discussion of Fate
and Free Will, to be taken together with such texts as Cicero *De
Fato*, [Plutarch] *De Fato*, Apuleius *De Platone* 1. 12, and Alcinous
Didascalicus 26. However, although the question is indeed broached
in §§ 4, 5, and 8, it is subordinated to the lecture's principal
theme, which is the compatibility (or not) of prophecy and human
intelligence (γνώμη). In expounding his picture of a cosmos in which
the onward march of events is conditioned by, and therefore also

---

[33] Cf. Xen. *Apol.* 27.
[34] *Il.* 9. 608. The implicit comparison between the wrong done to Socrates and
Achilles is perhaps inspired by *Apol.* 28bd.
[35] *Apol.* 41d, *Crito* 43bc, *Phdo* 116bc.

predictable by, a number of different entities, Maximus necessarily moves into the same territory as is explored in discussions of Free Will; moreover, he exploits this convergence to engineer his moralizing conclusion in §§ 8–9 (ideas of Fate and arguments from prophecy should not be used as excuses for human wickedness). He begins and ends, however, with a spirited rebuttal of the suspicion that acceptance of the validity of prophecy makes human powers of foresight and prediction otiose. This is as much the territory of Cicero's *De Divinatione* as of his *De Fato*,[1] and might also be connected with the discussion in Xenophon *Memorabilia* 1. 1. 6–9; see further nn. 11 and 12 below.

Like *Orr.* 5 and 41, and for the same reasons, the lecture raises questions about the doctrinal standpoint from which Maximus speaks. Although he is vague or silent over a number of disputed points, and once or twice gives the appearance of endorsing a distinctively Stoic formulation, he is best understood as adhering to a broadly Platonic position. See Introduction, pp. xxvii–xxx and nn. 8, 13, and 22 below.

Later interest in the lecture is patchy. The compiler of Neap. 100 takes two excerpts (from §§ 3 and 7), and Richard Byfield nine (from §§ 2–5 and 8–9, on pp. 69a68)v–70(69)v of Harl. 1790). Hugo Grotius included a complete Latin translation in his *Philosophorum Sententiae de Fato*, posthumously published in 1648.

Oration

1   When the Medes were on the march against Greece, the Athenians consulted the god to find out what they should do in the face of this force of foreign invaders, with its Median cavalry, Persian chariots, and Egyptian infantry, Carian slingers, Paphlagonian javelin-throwers, Thracian peltasts, Macedonian hoplites, and Thessalian cavalry. The Athenians, as I say, consulted the god to find out what they should do with such a menace advancing on their city. The god replied to them that they should fortify themselves with their wooden wall. Themistocles said that, in his opinion, the 'wooden wall' meant their triremes. The

---

[1] Fate and prophecy are of course linked in the Stoic argument that the validity of divination proves the truth of their deterministic world view (Cic. *De Div.* 1. 127, cf. 1. 6), and this argument provides an important part of the background to Maximus' lecture.

Athenians accepted his interpretation and, leaving their city, transferred to the god's 'wooden wall'.[2]

Well now, if the Athenians had declined at that point to consult the god for his advice on this matter, and had turned instead to a prudent man, who had the necessary ability to calculate their available resources and the size of the approaching expedition, along with the scale of the impending danger and the chances of success open to them, can we have any reasonable grounds for supposing that this man's advice would have been in any way inferior to the god's oracle? I believe that he would not even have needed to resort to that riddling and ambiguous reference to a wall, but would have spoken something like this: 'Men of Athens, abandon the stones and buildings of your city to the foreigner, and betake yourselves in full force to the sea instead, children, freedom, laws, and all. The triremes that are there to receive you will be quite sufficient both to carry you to safety and to win the war at sea.'[3]

2   Why is it then that men go to oracles and neglect the advice given by their own kind? Is it because human intellect is precarious and unreliable and suspect and bogus and inconsistent and not universally accurate, whereas the divine is trustworthy because of its superiority, of proven accuracy, and irreproachable in the esteem in which it is held? Divine prophetic powers and human intellect—this is a daring thing to say, but I will say it none the less—are kindred faculties; if anything at all resembles anything else, then there is nothing more similar to divine intellect than human excellence. Cease then to wonder both how autonomous human intellect finds a use for prophecy, and how conversely the validity of prophecy leaves a role for human intellect. These are similar phenomena that you are considering. The object of your questioning and bemusement and worry is one and the same thing, and it is quite possible to settle the whole issue in a proper fashion. Divine intellect does not hit its target every time, nor does human intellect always miss.

---

[2] Hdt. 7. 140–3.
[3] A similar point about the superfluity of the oracle in the face of human intelligence is made by Oenomaus of Gadara, fr. 6. 8–9 (see Hammerstaedt 1988, ad loc.). Cic. *De Div.* 2. 3. 9 suggests that the line of criticism goes back ultimately to Carneades.

3   About human intellect we must speak again later.[4] As for divine intellect, do you really believe that it knows everything from first to last—both the beautiful and the ugly, both the precious and the base? I am at a loss for words; reverence for the divine overcomes me! It is an awesome achievement to know everything—the number of the sands, the measure of the sea—and to be aware of a weird cauldron cooking in Lydia.[5] Obviously God makes his prophecies to all comers, and it is in their interests to learn the truth, even if the enquirer is going to gain a dishonest advantage from his knowledge. What an awfully naïve, meddlesome busybody you take God to be—for all the world like those mountebanks who prophesy to all and sundry for two obols! In my view, it is wrong even for a good man to rush to tell the truth, let alone God. There is nothing so very splendid in telling the truth unless it is conducive to the enquirer's best interests. Thus doctors deceive their patients and generals their armies and helmsmen their crews, and there is nothing very terrible in that. Quite the reverse, indeed: lies have often helped people and the truth has often harmed them.[6]

If then you think that prophecy is anything other than divine intellect, differing from human intellect in precision and certainty alone, then you must realize that you are setting reason in conflict with itself. If in fact the two differ only to the extent that the light of the sun differs from the light of a fire—both being equally forms of light[7]—then by all means bestow your love on the brighter, but do not at the same time slight the one which emerges from the comparison as the dimmer. Imagine instead that this whole universe of ours is a harmony like that of a musical instrument, with God as the craftsman, and the harmony itself beginning from him and spreading through air and earth and sea and animals and plants, then falling into a great disparate mass of natural substances and bringing an end to the strife that rages among them— just as the notes sung by the leader of a choir, pervading the many

---

[4] In §§ 4–5 below.
[5] As Apollo is said to in Hdt. 1. 47–8; the weird cauldron is Croesus'. Cf. *Orr.* 11. 6 and 29. 7, and Parke-Wormell (1956: ii. 23–4) for other references to this famous passage. For the underlying issue, of the scope of divine knowledge and concern, cf. *Or.* 5. 4, with n. 20.
[6] Compare Plato *Resp.* 382c and 389bc, Xen. *Mem.* 4. 2. 17 (of which the latter two passages are also quoted in Stob. *Flor.* 9. 59, i. 198–203 Meineke, and *Flor.* 46. 95, iii. 325 Meineke); cf. also Philo *Cherub.* 14–15, Clem. *Strom.* 7. 53. 1–2. Maximus' point is that the selectiveness of divine truth-telling leaves room for human powers of judgement too.   [7] For the image, cf. *Or.* 11. 1.

voices of the choristers, bring order to their discord.[8] [4] As to the nature of this divine craft, I am unable to describe it to you explicitly, but you will be able to understand its effects from an image of the kind I shall now give you. You have surely before now seen ships being hauled up out of the sea and stones of enormous bulk being moved by all sorts of twistings and rotatings of machinery; as each component transmits its impetus to the next, and one component receives the movement from another, the whole machine is set in motion. It is the whole machine that is responsible for achieving the task, but by means of the collaboration of its individual parts.[9] Call the mechanic God, the machines human powers of reasoning, and the mechanic's technical knowledge the prophetic art which draws us to follow the guidance of Fate. Or if you need a still clearer image, you could imagine God as a general, life as a campaign, man as a hoplite, Fate as the watchword, resources as weapons, misfortunes as enemies, Reason as an ally, Virtue as victory, wickedness as defeat, and prophecy as the skill that can predict future contingencies on the strength of present resources.[10] A helmsman in command of his ship, knowing his tackle, watching the sea, and keeping note of the winds, knows what will result.[11] A general in command of his army, knowing his weaponry, keeping his resources in mind, and watching the enemy, knows what will result. A doctor, seeing his patient,

---

[8] The image of the chorus and its leader is used of the cosmos also in [Arist.] *De Mundo* 399^{b}15 ff. and 400^{b}8. In the *De Mundo*, the physical reality described is a cosmos in which an initial impetus given by God to the outermost sphere of the heavens is transmitted to all the rest; comparison with *Or.* 21. 7–8 suggests that here Maximus is using it instead in a Platonizing vein, to describe the descent (or even 'emanation') of divine beauty and order from the intelligible realm. To talk of Stoic influence (Prächter 1901: 37; Helm 1906: 93–4; cf. Puiggali 1983: 290) seems wide of the mark.

[9] The image again recalls the *De Mundo* (398^{b}11–17), though it is here used for a slightly different purpose. Note how, by introducing the notion of causation (how God and the other factors operating in the cosmos *produce* events, as opposed to how God and men *foresee* them), the image prepares for the entry of the question of Fate into the discussion.

[10] For the image of the campaign of life, compare *Orr.* 5. 3, 15. 8 and 10, 33. 3, 34. 4, 40. 5 (and elsewhere, e.g. Teles 6, p. 53 Hense; Aurelius 2. 17; Epict. 3. 24. 31; Plut. *Prof. in Virt.* 77c; Philo *Ebr.* 99–100).

[11] For the helmsman as an exemplar of foresight, compare Cic. *De Div.* 1. 112 (along with the doctor and the farmer). Such images of benevolent and provident control (along with the charioteer and the lawgiver) are commonplaces of the Socratic tradition: cf. *Orr.* 4. 9, 8. 7; Plato *Protag.* 344d, *Leg.* 905e–906a, 961d ff.; Xen. *Mem.* 1. 1. 9, 1. 7. 1–3, 3. 3. 9, 3. 9. 11.

knowing his profession, and watching the disease, knows what will result. Do you see what a mass of prophets there is, how lucid, how skilful, how successful they are? If human autonomy were an isolated factor, severed from any connection with Fate, then there would be no need for prophecy.[12] But if instead human autonomy is inextricably bound up in the whole system, as much part of Fate as anything else, but only a part,[13] then the necessity of prophecy will be established, though the question of its clarity or unclarity will remain to be discussed.[14]

5 We must also observe both that ⟨human⟩ intellect can foresee events brought about by necessity, and that prophecy can reveal ⟨actions brought about by human Free Will⟩. How does this come about in each case? In the first place droughts and failures in rainfall and earthquakes and volcanic eruptions and changes in climate are not known by God alone, but also by inspired human beings.[15] Thus Pherecydes warned the Samians of an earthquake;[16] Hippocrates warned the Thessalians of an impending plague;[17] Timesios warned the Clazomenians of an eclipse;[18] and so on.

[12] The argument here seems to depend on the thought that it is the regular, uncapricious operations of Fate that make the predictions of prophecy both possible (cf. Cic. De Div. 1. 127) and desirable. If, on the other hand, human decision-making was the only factor conditioning future events, then future events could be satisfactorily foreseen by consulting human agents about their intentions, without reference to oracles and divination. This attempt to define legitimate provinces for both divine and human intelligence has some similarities to the discussion of prayer and skill (τέχνη) in Or. 5. 6, and both passages may bear a distant relationship to Xen. Mem. 1. 1. 9.

[13] The phrasing at this point seems to gloss over what ought to be a very important distinction. The overall picture Maximus seems to want is that of Middle Platonism, in which human Free Will is a genuinely autonomous factor, but his choice of wording here comes close to the Stoic contention that 'Free Will' is only an aspect of a rigid, all-embracing Fate. Maximus' formulation here may be a reflection of the difficulty experienced by Middle Platonists in general in simultaneously asserting the universality of divine control and defending the reality of human Free Will: cf. e.g. the use made in Alcin. Didasc. 26 and [Plut.] De Fato. 569d ff. of the analogy between fate and law, discussed by Dillon (1977: 294–8, and 320–6).

[14] The text and meaning of the final clause of this sentence are unclear.

[15] The same point (and one of the same instances—Pherecydes) in Cic. ND 1. 110–12.

[16] Cf. Diog. Laert. 1. 116.

[17] Cf. Pliny NH 7. 123; Thessalus Presbeuticus (Hippocrates ix. 418 Littré); [Soranus] Vita Hippocratis 7.

[18] For Timesius, the colonizer of Abdera, see Hdt. 1. 168; Plut. Am. Mult. 96b; Praec. Ger. Rep. 812a; Aelian VH 12. 9; Maximus is the only author to mention the prediction of an eclipse.

Secondly, how is it that God divines the actions of human Free Will?

> Do not sow a furrow of children against the will of the gods,

God says:

> For if you beget a child, the child you beget will slay you.[19]

He speaks thus, but he knows that he is advising a man who is a drunken debauchee, and for this reason he predicts the disaster for which Laius may have provided the initial impetus, but of which it is God who discerned the true cause.[20]

> If Croesus crosses the Halys, he will destroy a great empire.[21]

God does not say *that* he will cross the river, but what will happen to him *if* he does.[22]

If you separate divine prophecy and human intellect and unwind them from each other, then you have also destroyed the most elegant of harmonies. [6] Heaven and earth, immortal hearths or vehicles for two kinds of being, form this single shared household of gods and men.[23] The former is the abode of the gods and the children of the gods; the latter is home to men, the gods' interpreters, who are not, as Homer has it, 'sleepers on the ground, with unwashed feet',[24] but look towards the heavens with upright spirits and acknowledge the dependence of their intellects on Zeus. Individual gods are appointed to watch over their several lives; for the gods do haunt the earth, preserving its offspring, though they are not seen, nor do they fire arrows or suffer wounds,

> Since they do not eat bread, or drink the dark wine.[25]

---

[19] Eurip. *Phoen.* 18 and 19. The instance of Laius had been conventional in discussions of Fate and Free Will since Chrysippus, and some or all of *Phoen.* 18-20 are frequently quoted: see Cic. *De Fato* 30; *SVF* ii. 941; Alcin. *Didasc.* 26. 179. 15-19; Lucian *Jup. Conf.* 13; etc.

[20] Maximus again glosses over an important distinction: for the Stoic, Laius' having children in spite of the oracle is itself predetermined, for the Platonist it is not. The way Maximus presents the next example, of Croesus, commits him more clearly to the Platonist line.

[21] Hdt. 1. 53. 3.

[22] This idea of the conditional operation of Fate is standard Middle Platonic doctrine: cf. Alcin. *Didasc.* 26, [Plut.] *De Fato* 569d ff.

[23] The image of the shared home is originally Stoic: *SVF* ii. 528-9, 638.

[24] *Il.* 16. 234-5, on the Selloi of Dodona: cf. *Or.* 8. 1.

[25] *Il.* 5. 341. These individual 'watchers' are *daimones*, cf. *Or.* 8. 8.

Human beings in the meanwhile look up to the heavens, in so far as it is permitted to them to behold Zeus' radiant palace, not lighted, in Homer's words, by golden ornaments and youths bearing torches in their hands,[26] but illuminated by the most perfect fire of the sun and the moon and their companions in the celestial order. It is an army you behold of good generals and indispensable subordinates.[27] Keep this compact in mind and you will see what prophecy is, understand what Virtue is, and recognize the connection and partnership between the two.

7   The life of men that you behold is a journey, made not on the solid ground of the mainland, but by a merchant ship pursuing its course over a broad sea.[28] This ship owes its preservation not only to the skill of the helmsman, but also to opportune winds, the obedient labours of the crew, the manœuvrability of the ship's tackle, and the character of the sea. Pray compare the rational powers of the soul to the tackle and the labours of the crew, the uncertainty of human affairs to the sea and the winds, and the accurate predictions of prophecy to the foresight of the steersman's skill. But if † . . . †,[29] you will hear Plato speak as follows:

The all-controlling agent in human affairs is God, assisted by the secondary influences of Chance and Opportunity. A less stern way of putting it is to add that there must be a third factor to accompany these, Science. For instance, in a storm the steersman may or may not use his science to seize a favourable opportunity; I should say it would be a great advantage if he did.[30]

8   These oracular utterances confuse my spirit, neither impelling me to outright contempt for prophecy, nor permitting me to put complete trust in human reasoning. Just as, among creatures that are at home in two habitats, birds share their flight through the air with beings of the upper regions ⟨but their source of food with

---

[26]   *Od.* 7. 100–2, describing the palace of Alcinous.
[27]   Compare the description of the celestial hierarchy in *Or.* 11. 12.
[28]   For this image of the voyage of life (with the good man–philosopher as helmsman), cf. *Orr.* 8. 7 and 30. 2–3.
[29]   The text is corrupt at this point and no convincing emendation has yet been proposed.
[30]   Plato *Leg.* 709bc. The fact that this passage seems also to be alluded to by Plut. in *Quaest. Conv.* 740c suggests that it may have been in regular use as a proof text in Middle Platonic discussions of Fate and Free Will; see Dillon (1977: 209).

beings of the earth⟩;[31] so too, to my eye, do human beings spend their lives in two realms, in a way that brings both autonomy and necessity together, like the autonomy enjoyed by a man in chains who follows his captors of his own free choice.[32] For these reasons I have my suspicions about necessity, but find it difficult to give the phenomenon a name. If I say 'destiny', I am using a name that has no stable meaning in men's minds. What is 'destiny'? What is its nature? What is its essence?

If you are a god, one of those who dwell in the broad heavens,

then nothing that is terrible can be your handiwork, and human misfortunes do not come about through Fate, since it is not permissible to assign the responsibility for evil to God.[33]

But if you are one of the mortal race, who dwell on earth,[34]

then Elpenor is lying when he says,

It was an evil fate sent by the gods led me astray;[35]

and Agamemnon is lying when he says,

it is not I that am to blame
But Zeus and Fate and the Erinys who walks in darkness.[36]

9   These names too look like evasive euphemisms for human wickedness, as men try to lay the blame for it on divine powers and the fates and the Erinyes.[37] By all means let these beings keep their place in tragedies—I don't begrudge the poets the use of their names—but may it not be that in the drama of life they are just

---

[31] Or perhaps '. . . place of rest . . .' instead of '. . . source of food . . .'; cf. Apul. De Deo Soc. 8. 140.

[32] Another Stoic image (SVF i. 527, ii. 975; Sen. Ep. 107. 11; Aurelius 10. 28. 2), used in what seems (perhaps only momentarily) to be an alarmingly Stoic manner (apparently denying real autonomy to human choice); contrast the insistence on the real independence of human autonomy as a causal factor in [Plut.] De Vit. et Poes. Hom. 120; Alcin. Didasc. 26. 179. 1-19; Apul. De Plat. 1. 206.

[33] For God's innocence of evil, cf. Orr. 5. 1, 41. 2-4. Comparison with 41. 4 suggests Maximus' idea to be the Platonic one that evil is produced by autonomous factors, independent of Fate and divine Providence, not the Stoic one that evils only seem to be evil and in fact happen for the best.

[34] Od. 6. 150 and 153; cf. Or. 9. 1.

[35] Od. 11. 61.

[36] Il. 19. 86-7.

[37] The complaint is familiar from the Stoics, who had particularly strong motives to make it: SVF ii. 1000.

that, mere empty names? The Erinys and Fate and the gods and any other names that there may be for criminal intentions, penned within the soul, trouble Agamemnon,

because he paid no honour to the best of the Achaeans.[38]

They lead Elpenor into drunkenness, they impel Thyestes to offend against his brother's marriage, and Oedipus to murder his father; they lead the informer to the courts, the pirate to the sea, the murderer to his sword, the profligate to his pleasures. These are the well-springs of human misfortune;[39] it is from here that all man's many ills flow, as the fire flows from Aetna and the plague from Ethiopia.[40] The fire for its part flows down as far as the plain, and the Plague halted when it had advanced as far as Athens; but the streams of wickedness are many and unceasing, requiring many oracles and countless prophecies. Who then could fail to learn the truth when he enquires about the consequences of wickedness, the consequences of mistrust, the consequences of intemperance? It was not Apollo alone who foretold them, but Socrates too; that was why Apollo praised Socrates, because he practised the same art as he did.[41]

ORATION 14   Friendship and Flattery

Introduction

= 20 (1962) = 4 (Laur. Conv. Sopp. 4). The manuscript title—τίσιν χωριστέον τὸν κόλακα τοῦ φίλου, 'By what criteria should one distinguish Flatterer from Friend?'—is accurate.

One of two lectures on the topic of friendship, the other being *Or.* 35. §§ 1-2 introduce the issue of Friends and Flatterers by summarizing and then rewriting Prodicus' famous myth of Heracles; §§ 3-4 formulate the question of how to distinguish between them,

---

[38] *Il.* 1. 412.
[39] The message is the same as that of *Or.* 41. 5.
[40] Cf. *Or.* 7. 4 for the combined reference to the Plague and Aetna.
[41] The reference is to Apollo's famous oracle to Chaerephon, cf. Plato *Apol.* 21a; *Orr.* 3. 1, 39. 5. The lecture thus ends with one more assertion of the affinity and the joint indispensability of divine prophecy and human intelligence, to foresee the results that will inevitably follow from the misuse of human autonomy.

and dispose of some unsatisfactorily simple attempts to answer it; §§ 5–6 provide the true answer, on the level of personal relationships, and §§ 7–8 show how the same distinction can be drawn in the wider worlds of politics and the arts and sciences.

The importance, and the difficulty, of distinguishing between true friends and mere flatterers is discussed at much greater length by Plutarch in his *De Adulatore et Amico*; the general position taken is the same as Maximus', but there are no very close similarities of detail between the two discussions. The topic of friendship is of course a major preoccupation in ancient ethics, from Plato *Lysis*, Xenophon *Memorabilia* 2. 4–6, and Aristotle *Nicomachean Ethics* 8–9 onwards. From the fourth century and the Hellenistic period we know of lost treatises by Simmias, Speusippus, Xenocrates, Theophrastus, Theopompus, Clearchus, Cleanthes, and Chrysippus; the major surviving discussions from the two centuries before Maximus (besides Plutarch's *De Ad. et Am.*) are Cicero *De Amicitia*, Epictetus 2. 22, Plutarch *De Amicorum Multitudine*, Lucian *Toxaris*, Alcinous *Didascalicus* 33. 187. 8–20, and Apuleius *De Platone* 2. 13. Everything that Maximus says about the Friend can be paralleled many times over from these texts, and his picture of the Flatterer is entirely conventional as well. For a general discussion of the tradition, see Powell (1990: 1–5, 18–21, 23–4), and for a detailed analysis of the parallels, Puiggali (1983: 411–15).

The compiler of Neap. 100 takes three excerpts, from §§ 2, 3, and 6. Poliziano's interest was aroused by the references to Persian trousers, music, and medicine in § 8, which he noted in the margins of foll. 71ᵛ–72ʳ of Paris. gr. 1962. A separate Latin translation, by J. Caselius, was published at Rostock in 1587 and again at Helmstedt in 1590 (and included in J. A. Acker's *J. Caselii Amoeniora Opuscula*, published in Jena in 1707). Jeremy Taylor quotes from §§ 6 and 7 in the ninth sermon of *Eniautos* (1653; Heber-Eden 1847–54: iv. 107, 109).

Oration

1   In his myth Prodicus brings an adolescent Heracles who is just reaching manhood to two roads, and stations Virtue and Pleasure as guides, one for each: the former an imposing figure, graceful to behold, with a firm step, an elegant voice, a calm gaze, and simple clothing; the latter dainty and heavily made-up, with gaudy

clothes, a bold stare, a mincing gait, and a grating voice. Seeing these two Heracles, like the son of Zeus and the good man that he is, takes his leave of Pleasure and entrusts himself to the guidance of Virtue.[1] Come then, let us too fashion a myth of our own, with a pair of roads and a good man and, in place of Virtue and Pleasure as guides, the Friend and the Flatterer. They too differ in bearing and expression and clothing and voice and gait, the one as pleasant to the eye as can be imagined, the other as truthful. Let us picture one of them grinning and holding out his hand, calling on our man to follow him, full of praise and compliments and prayers and entreaties as he tells him of the extraordinary pleasures to which he will take and lead him, flowery meadows and flowing rivers and birds singing and pleasant breezes and spreading trees and smooth rocks and easy paths and flourishing gardens, pears upon pears and apples upon apples and grape growing on grape.[2] The other guide says little, but what he does say is the naked truth: that the rough part of his road is long and the smooth part short, and that the good traveller must come ready prepared to toil where toil is needed and to regard comfort as a superfluous luxury.[3]

2 If they say this, which of the two will our man believe, and away down which road will he go? Let us reply to the author of the myth that, if the man is some wretched Assyrian, or Strato the Phoenician, or the Cypriot Nicocles, or the celebrated Sybarite,[4] he

[1] Cf. Xen. *Mem.* 2. 1. 21–34. Prodicus' myth was widely imitated and adapted: see e.g. Philo *Sacr.* 20–44, [Philo] *De Merc. Mer.* 2–4, Ovid *Am.* 3. 1, *Tabula Cebetis* (esp 5–7, 9–10, 15–22), Dio *Or.* 1. 64–84, Silius *Pun.* 15. 18–128, Lucian *Somn.* 6–16, Galen *Protrep.* 2–5, Themist. *Or.* 22. 280a–282c; and, for discussion, Joel (1901), Alpers, (1912) and Panofsky (1930). Maximus' adaptation of the myth at the beginning of his lecture serves notice that moral character is to emerge as the decisive difference between Friend and Flatterer (cf. § 5). For Heracles as a moral exemplar elsewhere in the *Orations*, see *Or.* 15. 6, with n. 18.

[2] An echo of *Od.* 7. 120–1; cf. *Or.* 25. 5.

[3] The picture of the two contrasting roads is a (very conventional) development of Hesiod *Op.* 287–92, quoted in Xen. *Mem.* 2. 1. 20, immediately before the summary of Prodicus' myth; cf. e.g. *Tabula Cebetis* 15–16, Themist. *Or.* 22. 280a–282c. For other instances of the image of the road of life in the *Orations*, see *Orr.* 1. 3, 8. 7, 34. 2, 39. 3, and 40. 4.

[4] 'Assyrian' is a veiled reference to Sardanapallus (cf. *Orr.* 4. 9, 7. 7, etc.); for Straton, king of Sidon, held up as an extreme hedonist by Theopompus, and his great rival Nicocles, the ruler of Salamis, see Athen. 12. 531ae (following an account of Sardanapallus in 528f–530c). The Sybarite is Smindyrides, mentioned by name in *Or.* 32. 9: cf. Hdt. 6. 127. 1; Arist. *EE* 1. 5, 1216ª16–17; Athen. 6. 273bc, 12. 511c, 541b.

will take against one of the guides, concluding that he is an inhospitable, unpleasant boor, but he will think that the other is most terribly charming and agreeable and benevolent. So let the good-looking guide take his man and lead him off. For a certainty he will end up leading him to a fiery end, like the Assyrian; or to poverty, like the Phoenician; or to prison, like the Cypriot; or to some other real evil to which men are brought by deceptive pleasure. But if our man is a man like Heracles, he will choose the true guide, the Friend, just as Heracles chose Virtue.

3   Thus ends the myth. Let reasoned argument now take its turn and consider how one might seek to distinguish Flatterer from Friend. Gold is tested by being rubbed against a touchstone; but what test will we find for friendship and flattery? Will it be the end-result that each produces? But if we wait for the end-result, we will have suffered harm before we attain it. We need to make an assessment before beginning our association; if assessment lags behind actual dealings with the person, anyone who has dealings first and then repents can only find it an empty investment.[5] Would you then prefer us to distinguish the Friend and the Flatterer in terms of the pleasure and distress they inspire? Yet a Flatterer when he goes to excessive lengths is extremely distressing and distasteful, while a Friend who is also fortunate is a source of the greatest pleasure. 'Perhaps then we should distinguish them in terms of benefit and harm.' This too is a debatable criterion that you suggest. Even if he does harm you, the Flatterer does so either by damaging you financially, or by winning you over to a life of pleasure; the former, financial loss, is an entirely trivial matter, while the latter, a life of pleasure, is highly enjoyable. In pursuit of Friendship, on the other hand, many before now have made themselves partners in exile, and shared the loss of their citizen rights, and met their deaths.

4   By what criterion then shall we distinguish the Flatterer from the Friend, if we cannot do so in terms of end-result, or liking, or harm? Let us look at each of them separately. Is it the case that the one whose aim in his dealings with us is to be liked is a Friend? That seems entirely reasonable. Moreover, if someone who brings

---

[5] Maximus here echoes a famous dictum from Theophrastus' treatise (538A–F FHSG): cf. Cic. De Amic. 85, Sen. Ep. 3. 2; Plut. Ad. et Am. 49de, Am. Mult. 94b, Frat. Am. 482b.

us pain is an enemy, then our friend would be the one who brings us our greatest pleasure. But that is not in fact how things are. It is the benevolent doctor who causes the greatest pain, and the most scrupulous general, and the most reliable helmsman.[6] Fathers, surely, love their children and teachers their pupils; yet what could be more disagreeable than a father to his child and a teacher to his pupil? Odysseus too certainly loved his companions, since he endured many terrible experiences

> As he strove to stay alive and bring his comrades home;[7]

but when he encountered a debauched and pleasure-loving people who lived like beasts,

> cropping the honey-sweet lotus[8]

(this I take to be Homer's name for Pleasure), and when his companions became ensnared by their luxurious living and had tasted the extraordinary delights of the lotus, he seized them against their will and dragged them crying to the ships. Eurymachus certainly didn't behave in this way towards the suitors, but belonged instead to the other category, that of flatterers, in his readiness to join them in chopping up fat porkers and well-fed goats, and to lap up great quantities of wine with them, and allow them to tumble with the serving-maids at night, and plunder a king's household, and carry through a plot against his marriage.[9]

5   Would you like then to sum up by lining up the Flatterer with Vice and the Friend with Virtue, and forgetting about the criterion of pleasure and distress? Friendship does not entirely fail to bring pleasure, nor is Flattery entirely innocent of causing pain, but there is an admixture of each in each, pleasure in Friendship and pain in Flattery. Mothers and nurses love their babies and try to please them as they look after them, and you are not going to deprive them of their claims to love because of the pleasure they try to give. Agamemnon advises Menelaus

---

[6] The familiar examples of prudent and benevolent authority: cf. e.g. *Orr.* 4. 9, 8. 7, 13. 4.

[7] *Od.* 1. 5.

[8] *Od.* 9. 97 + 9. 94. For the allegorical reading of the visit to the land of the Lotus-eaters, see Heracl. *Alleg.* 70. 3 with Buffière (1956: 378); for the allegorical use of Odysseus elsewhere in the *Orations*, cf. *Orr.* 4. 8, 7. 5, 11. 10, 15. 9, 16. 6, 21. 8, etc.

[9] Cf. *Od.* 4. 628–9, 15. 16–18, 14. 81, 14. 105, 16. 108–10, 18. 325, and 22. 37.

To honour all . . . and not to be haughty in spirit;[10]

you surely don't believe that he is recommending him to indulge in flattery? When Odysseus had emerged from the sea in the land of the Phaeacians and stood up stark naked from his resting-place and met the girls at play and recognized their princess, he compared her to Artemis, and then again to a beautiful tree; yet no one would call Odysseus a flatterer on that account.[11] This is because it is in terms of purpose and function and inner disposition that the Flatterer is distinguished from the Friend. Both a hero and a mercenary soldier fight with weapons, yet nobody treats their activities as the same merely in virtue of their shared mode of operation; instead, one regards their functions as separate in virtue of their differing purposes. The former seeks to defend his own people; the latter hires out his services to anyone who wants them. The former acts voluntarily, the latter for money; the former is trustworthy to his allies; the latter is an object of suspicion even to his friends. [6] You may take it that the Flatterer differs from the Friend in just this way, and that though the two may often coincide with each other in their actions and in the company they keep, they nevertheless differ from each other in mode of operation, in purpose, and in inner disposition. The Friend opens a joint account with his friend in what seems to him to be good—whether painful or pleasant—and shares it with him on equal terms; the Flatterer, following his own individual desires, manipulates the relationship with a view to selfish advantage. The Friend aims for fairness; the Flatterer for his own selfish interests. The Friend aims for equality in Virtue; the Flatterer for gains in pleasure. The Friend seeks a relationship involving the free and equal exchange of views; the Flatterer a relationship of subservience and self-abasement. The Friend desires truthfulness in all dealings; the Flatterer deceit. The Friend seeks to bestow benefits for the future; the Flatterer seeks present pleasure. The Friend requires his deeds to be remembered; the Flatterer requires his villainies to be forgotten. The Friend looks after his friend's resources as if they were joint property; the Flatterer plunders them as if they belonged to someone else. The Friend is both the least demanding of partners in good fortune and the most scrupulously fair of partners in mis-

---

[10] *Il.* 10. 69.
[11] For other uses of this episode, cf. *Orr.* 22. 1–2 and 40. 1.

fortune; the Flatterer is the greediest of partners in good fortune, but the most stand-offish when luck turns bad. Friendship is praise-worthy; Flattery is matter for reproach. Friendship involves fairness and reciprocity between the two partners; Flattery is lame, in that the man who cultivates another for utilitarian motives, because the other has something that he lacks, betrays the inequality of the relationship in so far as he is not cultivated in return. It is bad luck for the Friend when his deeds are not noticed; it is bad luck for the Flatterer when his are. Friendship gains strength from being put to the test; Flattery shatters under examination. Friendship grows over time; Flattery is shown up. Friendship needs no practical justification; Flattery cannot do without it. If there can be such a thing as a relationship between men and gods, the pious man is a friend to the gods, and the superstitious man a flatterer. Blessed is the pious man, wretched the superstitious man.

7   Just as the man who is confident in his own virtue approaches the gods fearlessly, while the man who is humbled by his own villainy approaches full of fear, apprehensive and dreading the gods as he would a set of tyrants, so I think Friendship is sanguine and confident towards men, while Flattery is cringing and apprehen-sive. Tyrants have no friends, and monarchs have no flatterers; and monarchy is more divine a thing that tyranny. If Friendship is equality in character, and villainy is fair and equal neither to itself nor to the good, then the good man is friend to the good man, since he is his equal. But as for the Flatterer, how could he be the flatterer of a good man? He would be seen through. As for being the flatterer of a bad man, if he were his equal, he couldn't be his flatterer, since Flattery cannot tolerate an equal relationship. But if on the other hand he wasn't his equal, he couldn't be his friend.

In the sphere of political constitutions too aristocracy is full of friendship, whereas democracy is crammed with flattery; and aristocracy is superior to democracy. Sparta had no Cleon or Hyperbolus, those evil flatterers of a spoiled people. It is true enough that Callias, a private citizen flattered at symposia, where the rewards of flattery were cups of wine and courtesans and other mean and slavish forms of pleasure, was ridiculed by Eupolis at the Dionysia.[12] But what location could one find in which to ridicule

---

[12] In his play *Flatterers*, quoted from in Plut. *Ad. et Am.* 50d and *Max. cum Princ.* 778e; see frr. 156–90 Kassel-Austin.

the people of Athens, who made up the audience for Eupolis' bantering? In what kind of theatre could this be done? At what kind of Dionysia? And where could one ridicule all that multitude of flatterers whose rewards were not trivial, not confined to the pleasures of food and sex, but made up instead of the misfortunes of the whole of Greece? If the people of Athens had been willing to reject their flatterers and obey Pericles and Nicias instead, they would have had leaders who were their friends rather than their flatterers.[13] [8] If you then move on to look at monarchies, you will see Mardonius and Xerxes, foreigner flattering foreigner, fool flattering fool, miserable slave flattering spoiled master.[14] As a consequence of this flattery Asia is forced into emigration, the sea is scourged, the Hellespont is bridged over, and Mount Athos is excavated. But the end-result of all this effort is defeat and flight and the death of the flatterer himself. Alexander too was flattered by the people of Macedonia; the products of this flattery were Persian trousers[15] and barbarian obeisances[16] and oblivion of Heracles and of Philip and of the ancestral hearths of the Argeadae. What point is there in mentioning tyrannies? Where fear and despotic power choke the subject population it is inevitable that flattery should flourish and friendship be overwhelmed.

Forms of flattery can also be seen in the sphere of the arts and professions, resembling real arts in their outward appearance but differing in their products.[17] Men were exposed to the flattery of a bogus form of music when the Dorians, abandoning the ancestral highland music which they had practised while watching their flocks and herds, and acquiring a passion for pipe-music and dance instead, brought about the simultaneous corruption both of their music and of their moral values.[18] Men were exposed to the flattery of a bogus form of medicine, when they abandoned the healing

[13] As in *Or.* 7. 4, Maximus' reading of 5th-century Athenian history takes its cue (ultimately) from Thuc. 2. 65.

[14] The allusion seems to be to Mardonius' speeches in Hdt. 7. 5 and 9–10.

[15] Cf. Arrian 4. 7. 4, 8. 4, 9. 9; Plut. *Alex.* 45, with Hamilton (1969: 120 ff.); *Fort. Alex.* 329f–330e.

[16] Cf. Arrian 14. 12. 3–5; Plut. *Alex.* 54. 3–6, with Hamilton (1969: 150 ff.).

[17] Maximus here echoes the careful distinction between true τέχναι and deceptive κολακείαι drawn by Plato in *Grg.* 464b ff. (even though the specific examples he cites do not correspond exactly with Plato's own list).

[18] The same story of decline, in almost exactly the same form of words, is told in *Or.* 37. 4. For the idea of the superiority of Dorian music (the Dorian mode), see Plato *Resp.* 399ac, and for that of a decline in music from initial virtue and austerity to modern decadence, *Leg.* 700a–701b.

techniques of Asclepius and the Asclepiadae and reduced science to something indistinguishable from gourmet cookery, a substandard flatterer to substandard physiques.[19] The informer imitates the orator, setting argument against argument, fortifying injustice against Justice and the base against the noble. The sophist imitates the philosopher.[20] He is the most scrupulous imitator of them all. ⟨ . . . ⟩[21]

ORATIONS 15–16   The Active and Contemplative Lives

Introduction

= 21-22 (1962) = 5-6 (Laur. Conv. Sopp. 4).The manuscript titles—τίς ἀμείνων βίος, ὁ πρακτικὸς ἢ ὁ θεωρητικός; ὅτι ὁ πρακτικός and ὅτι ὁ θεωρητικὸς βίος ἀμείνων τοῦ πρακτικοῦ, 'Which kind of life is better, that of action or that of contemplation? That the life of action is better' and 'That the life of contemplation is better than the life of action'—identify the issue under discussion, but do not properly reflect the answer reached in *Or.* 16. 5-6.

A pair of lectures devoted to a further issue in practical ethics and politics which raises questions both of individual choice and of civic organization. *Or.* 15. 1-2 sketch the problem at its broadest (the immense variety of styles of life available to choose from), before narrowing it down to the choice between action and contemplation. The remainder of *Or.* 15 (§§ 3-10) is a speech by an advocate of the active life, seeking to prove the perversity of the contemplative's choice in depriving the state of the benefits of his wisdom (3-5), turning his back on the best examples from history and myth (6), leading a life that fails to realize his potential as a human being (7), neglecting the best examples in philosophical tradition too (8-9), and exposing himself to needless danger into the bargain (9). In *Or.* 16. 1 this quite general attack is particularized as a prosecution of the emblematic contemplative, Anaxagoras, not for

---

[19] The comparison of modern medicine to cookery again echoes *Grg.* 464d; a similar picture of the decline of medicine over time is given in *Or.* 4. 2.

[20] Again, reminiscent of *Grg.*, although there it is strictly speaking with the lawmaker that the sophist is contrasted (465c).

[21] How much has been lost of the end of the lecture cannot be established.

impiety in Athens, but for withdrawal from society in Clazomenae. He makes his defence in §§ 2-3, urging both the personal prudence of his decision (2) and the fundamental dependence of civic life on the very values he has devoted his life to investigating (3). Finally, in §§ 4-6 Maximus passes his own verdict: both styles of life have their place and their value, and can even be combined in a single career; however, both Platonic psychology and reports of the contemplative's experience leave no doubt that Anaxagoras is right, and that his is ultimately the superior choice.

The issue of the two lives is a standard topic, on which philosophers in general were expected to have an opinion: see for instance Alcinous *Didascalicus* 2. 152. 30-153. 24, with Whittaker (1990, ad loc.); Apuleius *De Platone* 2 .23. 253, with Beaujeu (1973, ad loc.); [Plutarch] *Placita* 874f-875a, with Lachenaud (1993, ad loc.); Ps.-Archytas ap. Stob. *Floregium* iv. 206. 18 ff. Meineke (= 41. 19 ff. Thesleff), with Giani (1993, ad loc.); note also Philo's *De Vita Contemplativa*. The history of the debate goes back to the later fifth century BC; central texts include Euripides *Antiope*, Plato *Gorgias* (esp. 484c ff.), *Theaetetus* (esp. 173c ff.), and *Republic* (esp. 471c-541b), and Aristotle *Protrepticus* and *Nicomachean Ethics* 10. 7-8; note also the exchange between Theophrastus and Dicaearchus recorded by Cicero (*ad Att.* 2. 16. 3 = Theophrastus 481 FHSG). For discussion, see Jaeger (1948, app. II) and Carter (1986, chs. 6-7).

Gregoras takes seven excerpts from the two lectures (from 15. 2, 4, and 5, and 16. 2-3 and 4), and the compiler of Neap. 100 another seven (from 15. 5, 6, and 7, and 16. 2, 3, and 6). The *Lexicon Vindobonense* makes four quotations (from 16. 6 and 7, and 16. 1); and Apostolis quotes the proverb αὐτὸ τοῦτο, ἄχθος νέως from 15. 4 (*Proverbia* 4. 34). Given the subject-matter, it is not surprising to find signs of particular interest among the Florentine humanists. Cristoforo Landino imitated and adapted both *Or.* 15 and *Or.* 16 in the first of his *Disputationes Camaldulenses* (devoted precisely to the Active and Contemplative Lives), and *Or.* 16 again in the third (on allegorical interpretations of Virgil).[1] Not long

---

[1] The use of Maximus in the first *Disputatio* is noted in Waith (1960), an article not cited in Lohe's edition (1980). The speech of Lorenzo De' Medici (28. 8-33. 6 Lohe) translates and adapts *Or.* 15. 3-6, while that of Leon Battista Alberti (38. 1—40. 10) draws on *Or.* 16. The reference to the careers of Plato and Xenophon, and the travels of Odysseus, towards the end of the third *Disputatio* (172. 8-18), draws on *Or.* 16. 5-6.

afterwards, Poliziano's attention was caught by the references to Tychius, Mithaecus, Phrynion, Philip, and Cleon in 15. 4, and to Plato, Xenophon, and Diogenes in 15. 8, all of which he noted in the margins of Paris. gr. 1962 (foll. 73^v and 75^v). John Rainolds's translation of both lectures, along with *Or.* 7, completed in or before 1581, was published in 1613, 1614, and 1628 (see Introduction to *Or.* 7). Franciscus Junius refers to 15. 3 (on the pleasure-giving function of the visual arts) in *The Painting of the Ancients* II. x. 2, and to 15. 6 (on the uselessness of Phidias' artistry if not applied to gold and ivory) in II. xi. 6 (Aldrich *et al.* 1991: i. 170, 178). Finally, Richard Byfield takes seven excerpts for his commonplace book, from 15. 1, 3, 5, and 7, and 16. 2 and 3 (Harl. 1790, foll. 71(70)$^{r-v}$).

Oration 15

1   It is hard to find the perfect life, just as it is hard to find the perfect man. When judged by the highest standards of worth, each kind of life contains its own element of imperfection, and it is only variations in the degree of imperfection that make one superior to another. One sees the farmer voicing his envy of city-dwellers, for the elegant and luxurious lives they lead; but at the same time one also sees habituées of the Assembly and the courts, even the most distinguished among them, bemoaning their lot and longing to live with a hoe and a little plot of land. One hears the soldier's envy for the man of peace, and the admiration of the man of peace for soldiers. If one of the gods were to strip each of these men of his present life and aspect and reclothe him in those of his neighbour, like actors in a play, then once again these same people will be found longing for their previous lives and bemoaning the present. So utterly malcontent a creature is man, so querulous and so terribly peevish, with no love at all for what is his own.[2]

2   But what need have we to examine the desires and discontents of the vulgar? No more than we have to consider the desires of brute beasts. It is the philosophers who only too richly deserve either our censure or our pity. Though they pride themselves on

---

[2] The similarity of this opening paragraph to Horace *Sat.* 1. 1. 1–22 has often been noticed (cf. Gercke 1893); it is the result of independent exploitation of the same moralist's conceit, not of any direct borrowing by Maximus from Horace; cf. also Lucian *Icarom.* 12 and 31, *Charon* 15; [Hippocr.] *Ep.* 17.

their wisdom and their *ars vivendi*, and their understanding of reasoned argument, they have yet even now to put an end to the quarrels and the debates that rage both among themselves and with others over which kind of life they ought to betake themselves to and make their own. They are for all the world like steersmen who have made all the right preparations for a voyage—large ship, sound tackle, a mass of equipment, full complement of oarsmen, the security conferred by their science, and a well-stowed ballast— but who, when the voyage itself gets under way, find themselves drifting and uncertain what course to steer, unable to feel confidence in a single one of the many ports that present themselves.[3] Let us dismiss all the others, lives and all—the spineless hedonist, the labourer on the land, the aimless voyager by sea, the mercenary under arms, the Assembly ranter, the habituée of the courts.[4] Just as in physical contests, the weak whose hopes of winning have led them into unreasonable ambition soon give up, while those whose prowess makes them true contenders stand firm and persevere and continue their struggle for victory to the end— just so in this contest of lives, let our other competitors admit defeat and depart disqualified, but let our pair of true contenders, on whom the issue really turns, ⟨the life of contemplation and the life of action,⟩ come forward now to argue their cases.[5] Which of them should be the first to present his arguments to our court? In my opinion it should be the advocate of the life of action, because he is the confident one, bolder than his opponent and well used to appearing before crowds. This is what he has to say.

3   'If as we made our way into the City of Life there were some magistrate or founding father who refused to allow us inside his gates before enquiring of each of us what his job was and what useful contribution each of us came to make to the common good of the city,[6] then I think that the builder would say that he was going to use his science to fit stones together in rows so as to provide the inhabitants with sufficient protection against both summer heat and winter cold; the weaver would say that he was

[3] For the image, compare *Orr.* 13. 7 and 30. 1–2.
[4] With this list of inferior pursuits, compare *Orr.* 1. 3 and 5, 5. 7, etc.
[5] For the imagery of athletic competition, compare *Orr.* 1. 4 and 6, and 12. 9.
[6] The picture of the various professions entering the City of Life seems to echo both the scene-setting of the *Tabula Cebetis* (esp. § 4), and Plato's discussion of the first stages of his ideal state in *Resp.* 369b ff.

going to furnish their bodies with both protection and beauty by
making garments woven together from warp and woof; the
carpenter would say that he was contributing a plough or a couch,
or one of the other products of his science, while the smith would
point to all the artefacts, both military and civilian, that involve
the working of bronze or iron. Luxury goods too we might
reasonably expect our founding father to accept: painters and
sculptors to gladden the eye; perfumers and chefs, excellent craftsmen of scents and flavours; and all those who give pleasure to the
ear with pipe or song or lyre or dance. Yet others will enter our
city to raise laughter, others to entertain us with their tricks,
others to entertain us with their words. In Homer even the beauty
of Nireus had its place, and in an armed camp at that.[7] One might
say that no one comes into Life without a contribution to make.
This man has something of practical utility to offer, that man some
craft or skill, that other some source of enjoyment.

4   Well then: to which of these categories shall we assign the
activities of the philosopher? It is entirely obvious that he does not
seek entry into our community as a useless drone; being a man,
he comes as a companion and a fellow worker in our shared
domain. But what is the physical proof of his fellowship with us?
To which group shall we assign him? To the craftsmen, like
Tychius?[8] To the chefs, like Mithaecus?[9] To the entertainers,
like Phrynion? To the clowns, like Philip?[10] To the demagogues,
like Cleon? Or will we let this character just drift around without
fellows and without a proper home? No: he does have a job of his
own, but we do not yet know what it is. 'I live a life of tranquillity,'
he says; 'I contemplate reality by myself, and I glut myself on
Truth.' Lucky man, to have such leisure! It strikes me that if you
were to board a ship, far from making yourself the steersman, you
wouldn't even be an oarsman, nor one of those who bustle about
and lend a hand in keeping the ship on a safe course, nor yet a
passenger agile enough to haul on a rope or set his hand to an oar

---

[7] Il. 2. 671-4.
[8] Tychius was the maker of Ajax's oxhide shield (Il. 7. 220-3), and is often cited
as the archetypal leather-worker; cf. Hesychius Lexicon, s.v.; [Hdt.] Vita Homeri 107,
366 Allen; Ovid Fasti 3. 824; Pliny NH 7. 196.
[9] Also mentioned in Or. 17. 1; see Plato Grg. 518b with Dodds (1959, ad loc.);
Athen. 3. 112de, 7. 282a, 7. 325f, 12. 516c; Aristides Or. 2. 343 and 426.
[10] A prominent character in Xen. Smp.; cf. Athen. 1. 20b, 14. 614cd; Plutarch
Quaest. Conv. 2. 629c.

in a calm; you would be one of those who just lie about anywhere and let themselves be carried, like mere cargo. Or do you perhaps think that a city has any less need of people to lend a hand in keeping her safe than a ship at sea? Far more need, surely. On a ship you have a small crew and a large cargo; but a city is composed entirely of fellow workers. It is like the human body, which is composed of many parts of many different kinds, and is kept together by the collaboration of the parts in the service of the whole: the feet carry it along, the hands do their work, the eyes see, the ears hear, and so on and so forth.

5 Suppose a Phrygian story-teller were to decide to invent a fable,[11] to the effect that the foot, growing angry with the rest of the body and giving out in the face of all the hard work it had to do in lifting up and carrying such a burden, were to choose an idle, peaceful existence instead; or alternatively, that the teeth, grinding and rendering down food for the benefit of such a mass of flesh, were to do the same. Then suppose, with the parts of the body refusing to look after their proper functions, our story-teller were to ask us, 'If all this were to happen together,[12] can there be any doubt that the man in the fable would perish?' This is exactly what happens in the case of political society too. If each participant were to decide from aversion to hard work to give up contributing and to retreat from the partnership into his own private leisure, what is there to stop the whole system from falling apart and going to ruin? Solid buildings owe their structure and stability and durability to the reciprocal interlocking of the stones from which they are built; if you remove anything at all from the arrangement, you will destroy the whole structure.[13] Do you not think that the whole of human life too owes its preservation to the mutual co-operation of the constituent parts? There are indeed some people whose secession from public action is of no account; the desertion of Thersites would have done no harm to the Greek forces. But the actions of Achilles—he whose rage led him to rest by his tent and

---

[11] The nearest Aesopic parallel is *Fab.* 197; compare also Xen. *Mem.* 2. 3. 18–19, Cic. *Off.* 3. 22, Livy 2. 32. 8–12, Sen. *De Ira* 2. 31. 7, Paul 1 Cor. 12. 12–27, Polyaenus 3. 9. 22. For other examples of Aesopic fables in the *Orations*, cf. *Orr.* 19. 2, 32. 1, and 36. 1.

[12] The text from 'or alternatively, that the teeth . . .' to '. . . were to happen together' is uncertain.

[13] The same comparison is made in Sen. *Ep.* 95. 53; cf. Theiler (1930: 121–2).

relapse into leisure and lyre-playing and song—did indeed overwhelm the army with troubles. If the presence of something
ensures benefits, then its absence necessarily causes harm. In our
present case, what other name can we give to the man who
embraces philosophical speculation and truth and the life of leisure
than that of 'sage' and 'prudent man'? Well then: does the best-
qualified steersman relinquish his seat to the least qualified? Does
the general relinquish his command to those least capable of
assuming it?[14] What is there in the least impressive in knowing the
truth and hoarding a sterile, idle, fruitless treasure in your soul,[15]
if you are not going to derive any benefit from it yourself, nor use
it to benefit others? Unless perhaps the sense of hearing is a fine
thing to have, but not to use in the perception of harmony and
language; or unless the sense of sight is a fine thing to have, but
not to see the light of the sun with; or unless wealth is a fine thing
even if one hoards it uselessly and buries it in the ground.

6   To sum up, what is the good of knowledge ⟨if it is not exer-
cised⟩ towards the proper goals? What use is medical knowledge to
a doctor if he does not use it to cure people? What use is artistic
genius to Phidias if he doesn't apply it to ivory and gold? Nestor
too was a sage, I take it we are agreed; but in his case I can
see the fruits of his wisdom: an army preserved, a city at peace,
obedient sons, a virtuous people.[16] Odysseus was a sage; but in his
case too I can see the fruits, both on land and at sea:

> Many were the men whose cities he saw and whose characters he
>   learned,
> As he strove to stay alive and bring his comrades home.[17]

And to cite yet another case, Heracles too was a sage; but his
sagacity ranged over every land and sea; he was not wise for
his own benefit alone. He it was who exterminated wild beasts,
chastened tyrants, freed the enslaved, laid down the laws of liberty,

[14] The familiar images of knowledge and authority: cf. in general, *Orr.* 4. 9, 8.
7, 13. 4; and, for the specific image of the philosopher as steersman, 30. 1–2.
[15] For the image, cf. *Orr.* 4. 8, 25. 5.
[16] This is the Nestor both of the *Iliad* (esp. 1. 247–84, 2. 336–68; 4. 293–310)
and of the *Odyssey* (bk. 3).
[17] *Od.* 1. 3 + 5 (cf. *Orr.* 22. 5). For Odysseus the sage, see above all Höistad
(1948: 94–102), Buffière (1956: 365–91), Stanford (1963, ch. 9). He and Heracles
appear together as ideals of practical virtue again in *Or.* 34. 7–8 and 38. 7; cf. also
11. 10, 14. 4, 15. 9, 21. 8, 26. 5–6 and 9.

established justice, made laws, spoke the truth, and crowned his words with success in action. If Heracles had chosen to retire from the world and live in peace and take his leisure and pursue a wisdom divorced from action, he would surely have been a sophist not a Heracles, and no one would have dared to call him the son of Zeus.[18] No more does Zeus live a life of ease. If he did, the heavens would long since have ceased revolving, and the earth bringing forth its nourishment, and the rivers flowing, and the seas spreading their waters, and the seasons changing, and the Fates assigning destinies, and the Muses singing. Human virtue and the survival of animals and the growth of crops would likewise have come to an end, and this whole universe of ours would have collapsed back in on itself in confusion. But as things are in reality, Zeus' unwearied efforts, in their unsleeping and unbroken continuity, never abandoning their task nor retreating from their labour, preserve the world and its beauty for ever.[19] This, I assume, is why Zeus sends dreams to admonish those good kings who are called 'Zeus-like' that

> The man of counsel, to whom the people's fortunes are entrusted,
> He of so many cares, should not sleep the whole night through.[20]

7   With all this in view, let our philosopher still decline to imitate Zeus and Heracles, good kings and commanders, and live instead the life of a man born in the wilderness, a solitary life in preference to the life of the herd. This is a life for Cyclopes, not for men! Yet even though for the Cyclopes the earth bore wheat and barley,

> Though they neither planted plants with their hands, nor ploughed,[21]

nevertheless each of them exercised authority over his own children and womenfolk,[22] and did not entirely renounce the active life. The whole point is, can we see such a renunciation as the proper characteristic of anything but a corpse? Certainly, if the life

---

[18] For Heracles as a model of practical virtue, cf. *Orr.* 14. 1 and 8, 19. 1, 24. 2, 25. 7, 32. 7, 34. 8, 38. 7. See in general Höistad (1948: 33–73), Galinsky (1972: 101–8).

[19] For this picture of Zeus as the supreme sustainer of the cosmos, cf. *Orr.* 4. 9, 8. 8, 11. 5, and 41. 2.

[20] *Il.* 2. 24–5.

[21] *Od.* 9. 108.

[22] Cf. *Od.* 9. 114–15, alluded to in the context of a political discussion also in Plato *Leg.* 680bc and Arist. *NE* 10. 9, 1080ᵃ26–9.

of action had no virtue in it, then it would be well enough to abandon it in the pursuit of virtue. But if human virtue consists not in theorizing, but precisely in deeds and co-operative action and a life devoted to the affairs of the state, then these things, in which a man may achieve virtue too, are what we should pursue.

> Evil can be got in droves,

as the Boeotian poet says,

> But in front of Virtue the gods set sweat.[23]

What a splendid contestant it is that seeks the victor's wreath from us without the sweat![24]

8   It may be objected that the devotee of public affairs is exposed to danger—danger of punishment, and plots and envy and exile and death and dishonour. Come now: what if the steersman were to think like this, reflecting that sailing is dangerous, beset by perils and toil, and the great uncertainties of storms and winds? What if the general indulged in this kind of reflection, telling himself that the fortunes of war are unpredictable, that both sides run an equal risk of failure, that danger and death are close at hand?[25] If these lines of thought were followed through, what would there have been to prevent ships vanishing from the surface of the sea, peoples failing to get even within dreaming distance of freedom for want of generals, the whole of human life becoming indistinguishable from the craven, idle, cringing life of worms? This is the life of a Sardanapallus you are describing to me, the life of an Epicurus![26] Let us contrast Sardanapallus with Cyrus, Assyrian with Persian: Cyrus who, though he could have guarded his leisure and lived a life of ease, chose instead to liberate the Persian people, toiling and campaigning and enduring hunger and thirst, never relaxing his efforts either by night or by day.[27] As for Epicurus, there are many you can contrast with him, Greek with Greek: Plato from the Academy, Xenophon from the army, Diogenes from Pontus.

---

[23] Hesiod *Op.* 287 and 289.
[24] Cf. *Orr.* 1. 6 and 3. 4.
[25] Cf. § 5 with n. 14 above.
[26] For the combination of Sardanapallus and Epicurus, cf. *Or.* 4. 9; see also 7. 7, with n. 22.
[27] For Cyrus as a moral exemplar, cf. *Or.* 6. 7, with n. 28.

9 For a friend's sake, an exile and a pauper, Plato confronted a great and mighty tyranny, travelling great distances by land, crossing seas, incurring the tyrant's enmity, suffering exile and danger, all so as not to betray the philosopher's calling.[28] Yet he could surely have remained in the Academy, pursuing his philosophical speculations and feasting on truth. Xenophon was summoned by Proxenus, escorted on his way by Apollo, and by Socrates too, from his long years of leisure and his philosophical reflections, not only to march with ten thousand Greeks, but also to command them and to bring them safely home.[29] Do I need to speak of the exploits of Diogenes? Turning his back on the leisure he might have enjoyed, and going about inspecting his neighbours' doings, he proved himself no lax or idle overseer.[30] Like Odysseus,

Whenever he found some king or eminent man,
He would stand by him and restrain him with courteous words. . . .
But whenever he saw one of the common people and found him shouting,
Then he would beat him with his staff.[31]

Nor did he spare himself, punishing himself and making life hard,

Subduing himself with demeaning blows,
And casting shabby rags about his shoulders.[32]

10 I shall not dwell on the fact that the good man, by living the life of action and not retreating nor standing down in favour of the bad, would both ensure his own preservation and set others on the best path. But by retreating and showing his back, he cannot fail to fill all wicked men with a rash and boorish daring, while sacrificing his own interests at the same time.[33]

---

[28] The reference is to Plato's Sicilian visits, described in [Plato] *Ep.* 7; cf. *Or.* 34. 9.

[29] As described in the *Anabasis*: Proxenus' invitation, Apollo's oracle and Socrates' parting words all come in *Anab.* 3. 1. 4–7; cf. again *Or.* 34. 9.

[30] For the picture of Diogenes (or the Cynic philosopher in general) as the scout and overseer of human moral conduct, cf. e.g. Diog. Laert. 6. 27 and 41; Epict. 3. 22. 25, 77, and 97 with Billerbeck (1978, ad locc.). Maximus gives his own fuller account of Diogenes in *Or.* 36, but cf. also *Orr.* 32. 9 and 34. 9.

[31] *Il.* 2. 188–9 + 198–9; also quoted in *Or.* 26. 5 (where Odysseus' behaviour is compared to Socrates'). These were favourite lines of Socrates (Xen. *Mem.* 1. 2. 58, where his use of them is defended against a malicious distortion by (?) Polycrates).

[32] *Od.* 4. 244–5, also applied to Diogenes in *Or.* 34. 9.

[33] The idea, though not the wording, echoes Callicles' warning to Socrates in Plato *Grg.* 486ac (cf. 508cd).

Where are you running to, turning your back like a coward in the press
of battle?[34]

Stay, hold your ground, stand up to their blows and have no fear!
The enemy's army are cowards, their blows are futile; no one will
stand up to you if you advance, but all will pelt you if you flee, as
the Trojans did to Ajax,[35] as the Athenians did to Socrates, not
letting up until they had shot him down.

How then is one to live in safety in the midst of one's foes (and
there is nothing more inimical to a man's virtue than surrounding
vice)? By crouching down, says Socrates, behind a little wall, and
watching the others fall helpless prey to the storm.[36] Show me a
wall that is safe, Socrates, where I can take my stand and scorn
the blows of the world. If you tell me of a wall like the one behind
which you sheltered yourself, I can see the blows I will suffer there,
all the Anytuses and Meletuses; it is a wall that is anything but
impregnable.'

Oration 16

1   If we were defending ourselves in a lawsuit, we would take
against a juror who didn't allow both sides to make their case on
equal terms, but instead seemed more like a tyrant than a true
juror. Now, although both the voting procedures of the lawcourts,
and the role that pure chance can play in them, are foreign to the
distinctive character of philosophy, we none the less now find
argument contesting argument, friend indicting friend in pursuit of
the truth, in a process of testing that does resemble a kind of court.
Let us then today allow the other argument, and the advocate of
the life of contemplation, to plead his case, taking the stand and
contesting the accusation brought against him just as if he were
before a real court. Let the accusation itself be of this or some very
similar kind:

Anaxagoras is guilty of the following offence:[1] though a resident in the

---

[34] *Il.* 8. 94.
[35] *Il.* 11. 544–74, 15. 726.
[36] Plato *Resp.* 496d.

[1] The identification of the spokesman of the contemplative life is abruptly made,
but otherwise entirely appropriate. Thanks to his fame at Athens (Plato *Apol.* 26d,
Phdo 97bc, etc.), his friendship with Pericles (Plato *Phaedr.* 269e, Plut. *Peri.* 4–6)
and (perhaps above all) the story of his trial (Plut. *Peri.* 32), Anaxagoras had been

land and city of Clazomenae, and participating in the same sacrifices and rituals and laws and upbringing and everything else as the people of Clazomenae, he retreats from them as if from wild beasts, neither attending their assemblies nor coming to join them at the Dionysia, or the courts, or anywhere else; his estates are given over for sheep to graze on,[2] and his hearth is deserted, as he continues in the private pursuit of his own fantastic wisdom, with all its twists and turns.

2   Let this be the accusation; and let Anaxagoras make his defence in something like the following terms.

'I know very well, gentlemen of Clazomenae, that I am very far from doing you any wrong. You have suffered no financial losses at my hands, nor am I doing anything on my account to blacken the reputation of your city in the eyes of Greece. Furthermore, in my personal dealings with each and every one of you I believe I show myself entirely inoffensive and moderate; and as for the established laws of the state and the constitution to which we owe our civic order, there is not one single aspect of them that I hold in contempt. If then, while doing you no wrong in my day-to-day pursuits and my chosen style of life, I am still guilty of an error of understanding, it surely remains for me to be acquitted of the charge of public wrongdoing against the city, and in the context of my own private affairs to find not prosecutors but teachers.[3] I shall tell you about my position without concealment, even though it is likely that the revelation of my ambitions will make me a laughing-stock. I am well aware of the great worth of political power and communal living and conspicuous achievement and the administration of public affairs; I understand perfectly that these valuable activities, when combined with personal virtue and decency, bring their practitioner great rewards, but that when they are not so combined, they have the opposite effect of destroying their practitioners' reputations and bringing them down, because they do not permit their deficiencies to go unnoticed. Positions of power

a model of the contemplative philosopher, and a counter in debates about the contemplative life, since the days of the early Academy: see Arist. *EE* 1215ᵇ6 ff., 1216ᵃ10 ff., and *Protrep.* fr. 11 (p. 45) Ross, with Jaeger (1948: 426 ff.) and D-K 59 A 1–34.

[2]   A famous detail: Philo *Vit. Contemp.* 14, Plut. *Peri.* 16, Cic. *De Fin.* 5. 87, *Tusc.* 5. 114; Philo and Cicero (*Tusc.*) link Anaxagoras with Democritus in this; Horace *Ep.* 1. 12. 12 attributes it to Democritus alone.

[3]   An echo of Plato *Apol.* 26a; the whole of Anaxagoras' 'Apology' is composed with more than half an eye on Socrates'.

illuminate their holders with a bright light, and show them up precisely to the extent that they fall short of the ideal. If someone has
a good mind and a reputation that is both distinguished and secure,
then he will benefit from his office; but if, when he takes it on, he
is deficient in the very qualities it demands, then it is quite
inevitable that one whose abundance of resources is hampered by
an ignorance of the necessary skills should fail miserably. With
all this in mind, I felt that I more than anyone should be wary of
inadvertently exceeding my abilities by entering public life, and so
stumbling and falling. In the same way, if I had been appointed by
you to sing in a choir, I would not have been wrong to refuse to
join it until I could sing in tune. This is why I showed little concern
to see that my estates were in good heart, and devoted myself
instead to my present pursuits, which will bring knowledge to my
soul, like light to the eyes, and so enable me to make the rest of my
journey in safety.[4] This kind of light is to be obtained ⟨ . . . ⟩[5] the
roads that lead to that destination—not nonsensical babbling, nor
the concerns of farmers, nor the pursuits of the market-place, not
the associations of the vulgar, but love of truth and contemplation
of reality and the burning ambition to pursue them. Deciding that
this should be my way, I followed the arguments as they led me
and cast about for the traces of their path.

3   Let that suffice as an account of my personal motives. I shall
now prove that in following this course I am serving your interests
too in the best and noblest way. The preservation of the state does
not depend on well-built walls, or the maintenance of ship-sheds,
or the ships themselves as they sail, or on stoas or groves or
gymnasia or shrines or processions; time will carry all these things
away, if foes and fire and other mischances do not get them first.[6]
What keeps cities safe is harmony and an ordered political constitution. [I agree!][7] Harmony and an ordered constitution are the
product of a disposition to obey the laws; the disposition to obey
the laws is safeguarded by the virtue of those who live under them;
Virtue is the product of the exercise of reason; the exercise of

---

[4] For the image, cf. *Or.* 1. 3.
[5] The text is seriously corrupt at this point, and no convincing emendation has
yet been proposed: '. . . ⟨ by the studies I engage in; these are ⟩ . . .' would at least
give an appropriate sense.
[6] A faint echo of the argument of Plato *Grg.* 517a–519b.
[7] A reader's comment, interpolated into the text; cf. *Or.* 27. 1.

reason is secured by practice, practice by truth, and truth by the leisure necessary to pursue it.[8] There is, there can be, no other tool for the acquisition of Virtue than true reason, by which the soul is quickened and kindled: what it does not know it learns; what it learns it retains; what it retains it puts into practice; and in putting it into practice, it is unerring. This is how I use my time; this is my 'leisure': the pursuit of truth, an art of living, the power of argument, an equipping of the soul, a training in Virtue. If then these things have no contribution to make to any good end; or if, though they do have a contribution to make, they do not themselves come by teaching or training, rather than randomly and by chance,[9] then indeed the whole business is an empty show, and entirely deserves impeachment and prosecution. But if there is no one so mad as to argue such a case, and it is true that there is no other way to acquire truth and sound reason and Virtue and knowledge of law and Justice, than by working at them—any more than one can learn leather-working without devoting time to it, or metal-working without spending one's days by the fire and the forge, or steersmanship without going to sea on voyages—then far from doing wrong in following such pursuits, I would actually deserve prosecution and impeachment if I were to abandon them and let my soul become a sterile sheep-pasture.

Gentlemen of Clazomenae, I have offered you a plea which I believe to be both true and just at the same time. I would ask you, however, not to cast your votes immediately, but to hold back for the time being, and instead become witnesses and spectators of the same sights as I see. If what you learn by this experience convinces you that good can come of it, then I would ask you to acquit me of the charge. If on the other hand you are not convinced, then you will vote in accordance with your own conclusions, but I will even so not be robbed of my good sense in this matter.'

4 If Anaxagoras says this in his own defence, the people of Clazomenae, in all probability, will laugh at him. They will not think his case more persuasive than the charges brought against him, yet he will none the less have told them the truth, even if they condemn him. But what if we could find someone able to play the part of the kind of juror who is chosen not by lot, but by the

___

[8] A careful rhetorical *climax*, followed by a second in the following sentence.
[9] An issue taken up in *Orr.* 27 and 38.

only true criterion for electing a juror, real knowledge? And what if he were to hear a plea that did not assume any prior wrongdoing, or any need to defend a case at law, whether from Anaxagoras in Clazomenae, or Heraclitus in Ephesus, or Pythagoras on Samos, or Democritus in Abdera, or Xenophanes in Colophon, or Parmenides in Elea, or Diogenes in Apollonia, or from any other of those inspired individuals, but rather a case made by someone speaking as if to his equals and attempting to persuade them by philosophical dialectic, speaking words of insight to the insightful, words worthy of trust to the trustworthy, words of inspiration to the inspired? These words would tell us that God assigned the human soul three faculties with their own locations and characters, as if assembling groups of people to found a city.[10] Taking the ruling and deliberative faculty up to the acropolis and establishing it there, he assigned it the function of reasoning and reasoning alone. The second faculty, whose vigour gave it skill in action and the ability to put plans into operation, he connected and conflated with the rational faculty as a subordinate to carry out its commands.[11] To the third faculty, an idle, ill-disciplined, low-grade mass awash with desires and passions and violent arrogance and pleasures of all kinds, he assigned the third place, like an idle, cacophonous, impressionable, and unstable populace.

Since the soul is divided up in this way, internal strife is always liable to afflict the organization of the human constitution, just as happens in a city. The happy city is ruled by monarch, with all its other constituent parts, in accordance with divine law, deferring to the one who is naturally able to lead it. The city which comes second to this one in happiness, assigning the name 'aristocracy' to the rule of the group that combines to hold power, is inferior to the monarchic city, but superior to the democratic city; it is strong

[10] In what follows Maximus summarizes and adapts the city-soul analogy of Plato *Resp.* 369a–449a and 543a–592b (cf. *Or.* 27. 6–7). This introductory sentence is phrased so as to pick up and turn round the challenge issued by the advocate of the practical life in 15. 3. For an alternative version of Plato's psychology, drawing on *Phaedr.* rather than *Resp.*, see *Or.* 20. 4.

[11] This account of the second principal faculty of the soul moves it away from Plato's ἐπιθυμητικόν (*Resp.* 439e ff.) in the direction of Aristotle's idea of a derivatively rational faculty intermediate between the vegetative and the fully rational (*NE* 1. 13, 1102ᵃ26 ff.). In the immediate context, this adaptation is essential if the practical life is to be aligned with a distinct faculty of the soul (§ 5), but it presumably also reflects a more widespread Middle Platonic conflation of Platonic and Aristotelian psychology (for which cf. *Or.* 11. 8).

and vigorous, following the manner of the Spartan or Cretan or Mantinean or Pellenian or Thessalian constitution, but at the same time rather too ambitious and quarrelsome, strife-ridden, interfering, impetuous, and rash. The third form of constitution, which bears the fair-seeming name of 'democracy', but is in fact the rule of the mob, is like the Athenian or Syracusan or Milesian constitution, or any other kind of mass rule, cacophonous, ill-disciplined, and unhomogeneous.[12]

5 Corresponding to these three constitutions, you will find three counterparts in the human soul. To match the deliberative and commanding element that takes no part in action and the work of the hands, there is the contemplative cast of soul; secondly, there is the practical cast of soul, which takes second place in rank and honour; nor is it difficult to see the equivalent of democracy in the individual, since that form of constitution prevails only too frequently in each and every soul. This third candidate we can leave to its own devices and vote out of contention for the prize. But when the other two are compared, the contemplative with the practical, each has its stake in the Good: the contemplative in terms of knowledge, the practical in terms of moral virtue. Which then is to be preferred? Let reason give us the answer: that if we weigh the two contenders on the scales of immediate practical utility, action must be preferred; but if we look at them instead as causes of good outcomes, then contemplation must be preferred.[13] Let us then make our peace with both sides and assign men their capacities and proper forms of life on the criterion of natural disposition, or age, or fortune. Men differ from each other by nature, one being weak when it comes to action, but well-endowed in his soul for contemplation, while another tires easily in contemplation but has all the strength he needs for action. Age too differentiates one man from another. Action belongs to the young. Homer says, and I too am convinced, that

---

[12] This account of better and worse constitutions also diverges from the *Republic* in several respects. The five-term sequence Plato there sets out begins with the rule of the philosopher Guardians, to be called *either* monarchy *or* aristocracy (448d), and descends through four rather than two inferior kinds, timocracy or timarchy, oligarchy, democracy, and tyranny. Maximus' summary is in fact closer to what Plato says in the *Politicus* (301–2).

[13] Similar compromises are declared for by Ps.-Archytas ap. Stob. *Flor.* iv. 206. 18 ff. Meineke (41. 19 ff. Thesleff), Alcin. *Didasc.* 2, Apul. *De Plat.* 2. 23. 253, and [Plut.] *Placita* 874f–875a.

all things are seemly for a young man.[14]

When he is a young man, let the philosopher live a life of action, making speeches, taking part in public life, going on campaign, holding offices. Plato's laborious excursions to Sicily and his efforts for Dion all belonged to the prime of his life; when he grew old he found refuge in the untroubled calm and noble debates and uninterrupted contemplation of the Academy, laying the end of his life to rest in a deep and luxuriating quest for truth. My heart goes out to Xenophon for spending his youth in action, but I praise him too for growing old in the pursuit of reason. Fortune too differentiates man from man, clothing the one in power and the life of action that this necessitates, while wrapping the other in leisure and sweet repose.[15] The former I praise for his steadfastness in the duty he cannot avoid, but it is the latter for whom I have both praise and admiration: admiration for his leisure, praise for what he relates.

6   If someone sails from Europe to Asia to see Egypt and the delta of the Nile, or the tall pyramids or the exotic birds, or the ox or the goat, we admire him for what he has seen.[16] So too if someone travels to the Ister, or sees the Ganges, or can survey with his own eyes the ruins of Babylon, or the rivers of Sardis, or the tombs at Troy, or the sites on the Hellespont.[17] Excursions are also made from Asia to Europe, to see the arts and sciences of Athens, or the pipes of Thebes, or the sculptures of Argos.[18] Homer's Odysseus gained wisdom through his long wanderings, as he

Saw the cities of many men and came to know their character.[19]

The sort of sights Odysseus saw were Thracians, or the savage Cicones, or the sunless Cimmerians, or the Cyclopes who murder strangers, or a woman who administers drugs, or the sights of Hades, or Scylla, or Charybdis, or the gardens of Alcinous, or

[14] *Il.* 22. 71.
[15] For the imagery, cf. *Or.* 1. 10.
[16] On tourism in the ancient world, see above all Friedländer (1922, ch. 7, esp. pp. 423-46 on Egypt and 412-15 on Athens and Thebes). On a smaller scale, Dill (1905: 205-7) and Balsdon (1969, ch. 7, esp. pp. 229 ff.).
[17] i.e. follows a route similar to that of Alexander the Great.
[18] For Athens as the home of the arts, cf. Propertius 3. 1. 1 and 23-30, Cic. *De or.* 1. 13; for the pipes of Thebes: cf. *Orr.* 9. 1 and 29. 1; the reference to the statues of Argos is presumably aimed above all at Polycleitus' Hera (Paus. 2. 17. 4-5, Strabo 8. 6. 10; cf. *Or.* 8. 6).   [19] *Od.* 1. 3.

Eumaeus' hut—mortal, ephemeral, and incredible, down to the last detail. But as for the sights seen by the philosopher, to what can they ever be compared? To a dream, but a truthful dream that travels to every corner of the universe.[20] His body does not move at all, but his soul advances over the whole earth, and from the earth to the heavens: crossing every sea, traversing the whole earth, flying up through every region of the air, accompanying the sun and the moon in their orbits, taking its fixed place in the choir of the other stars, and all but joining Zeus in the administration and disposition of reality.[21] What a truly blessed journey! What a beautiful spectacle! What truthful dreams!

ORATION 17   Homer in Plato's State

Introduction

= 23 (1962) = 7 (Laur. Conv. Sopp. 4). The manuscript title—εἰ καλῶς Πλάτων Ὅμηρον τῆς πολιτείας παρῃτήσατο, 'Whether Plato was right to refuse Homer entry to his republic'—is accurate.

Another 'political' lecture, discussing the place and function of poetry in the civic community: compare *Orr.* 3 and 15–16 (the place of the philosopher); 22 and 25 (the place of philosophical discourse); 38 (the place of the liberal arts); and 4 and 26. The thematic connection with *Orr.* 4 and 26 is particularly close, since they too deal with the poetry of Homer (the latter exclusively and the former to a large extent); but at the same time there is a difference in emphasis. *Orr.* 4 and 26 use allegorical reading to vindicate poetry's role in any and every good community; the present lecture, while allowing Homer's poetry its allegorical import (§ 4), seeks to argue that there are *some* communities where it is nevertheless surplus to requirements. The reason for this divergence is of course Maximus' desire both to praise Homer and to vindicate Plato's notorious decision not to allow his poetry into the ideal state (*Resp.* 377a ff., with the celebrated dismissal at 398a; the second discussion of poetry, in *Resp.* 595a ff., does not enter into the discussion).

---

[20] For the image, cf. *Or.* 10. 1–3 and 9.
[21] For the topic of the flight of the soul, cf. *Orr.* 9. 6, 10. 9, 11. 10–12, 41. 2.

The structure of the lecture is simple: §§ 1-2 use the story of the chef Mithaecus' abortive visit to Sparta to introduce the proposition that states can legitimately differ in their habits and needs, without thereby casting damaging aspersions on what they reject; §§ 3-4 explain how the special character of Plato's state leaves no room for the functions that Homeric poetry can usefully perform elsewhere; § 5 is a coda in which it is pointed out that Plato's state is not unique in this respect, and that, quite apart from the problem over Plato, Homeric poetry should be judged by reference to its usefulness, not its entertainment value.

Plato's attitude to Homer was a major talking-point above all for ancient grammarians, and inspired a whole range of responses, from allegorizing vindications of Homer's moral and intellectual worth (cf. *Orr.* 4 and 26), to satirical attacks purporting to show that Plato was himself guilty of the very faults he censured in others. The main surviving texts to reflect this area of activity are Heraclitus *Allegoriae Homericae*, [Plutarch] *De Vita et Poesi Homeri*, Dionysius of Halicarnassus *De Demosthene* 5-7, and Athenaeus 11. 504c-509e; cf. also [Longinus] *De Sublimitate* 13. 3, with Russell (1964, ad loc.). Among lost works we hear of Dio Chrysostom's *Defence of Homer against Plato* (*Suda* s.v.; cf. Dio *Or.* 53. 3), Aelius Sarapion's *Whether Plato was Right to Banish Homer from his State* (*Suda* s.v.), Aristocles of Messana's *Whether Plato or Homer is the More Valuable* (*Suda* s.v.), and Telephus of Pergamum's *On the Accord of Homer and Plato* (*Suda* s.v.). On all this, see Weinstock (1926). Maximus' contribution is characteristically irenic, seeking to preserve the credit of both the two great cultural icons.

Later interest in the lecture is restrained. Gregoras takes two excerpts, from §§ 1 and 2, the compiler of Neap. 100 only one (from § 5); the *Lexicon Vindobonense* quotes once, from § 1. Poliziano notes the reference to the Sophists and to the Spartan authorities in § 1, the list of national occupations in § 2, and the reference to variation in musical νόμοι in § 5, in the margins of Paris. gr. 1962 (foll. 80ʳ-82ᵛ). Pierio Valeriano cites the story of Mithaecus in Sparta from § 1 in the preface to Book LVII of his *Hieroglyphica* (1556). And Franciscus Junius cites the account of idealizing representations from § 3 in *The Painting of the Ancients*, I. i. 3 (Aldrich *et al.* 1991: i. 13).

Oration

1   There was once a Syracusan sophist who came to Sparta.[1] He
was not an expert in Prodican elegance of language[2] or genealogy
à la Hippias[3] or Gorgianic rhetoric or Thrasymachean immoralism,[4]
or in any other kind of verbal activity either. His special science
consisted instead in the manufacture of a product in which
practical utility and pleasure were combined. By balancing and
mixing and varying flavours and by the application of fire he
was able to make all kinds of foodstuffs, staples and relishes alike,
more attractive than they would otherwise have been. Indeed,
Mithaecus' reputation as a chef stood as high in Greece as Phidias'
as a sculptor. He came, then, to a Sparta that was then the
mistress of the Greek world, with high hopes that in this imperial
city, fortified with nobility and power, his science would win him
a distinguished reputation. The outcome, however, did not live up
to his expectations. The Spartan authorities summoned him and
ordered him to leave Sparta that instant for another land and
another people. Their traditions of hard work, they said, meant
that they required a diet that was nourishing rather than one that
was artificially enhanced; their bodies were unpampered and pure,
and no more in need of a chef than those of lions.[5] He should leave
them for some other place where his science was more likely to win
him a reputation, and where people welcomed practitioners like
him both for their practical usefulness and for the pleasures they
brought. Thus Mithaecus left Sparta, taking his arts with him; but
the other Greeks received him no less enthusiastically for that,
welcoming him in the interests of their own pleasure, rather than
despising him for the rebuff he had received in Sparta.

2   Perhaps I need to summon up some other images to illustrate
my present theme, more imposing than Mithaecus and his skills.
The Thebans practise piping, and pipe-music is a national pastime
of the Boeotians;[6] the Athenians practise oratory, and the study of

---

[1] For Mithaecus, cf. *Or.* 15. 4, with n. 9. Maximus is the only source for the story
of a visit to Sparta.
[2] Apparently a somewhat vague reference to Prodicus' celebrated expertise in
drawing distinctions in terminology: D-K 87 A 13–30.
[3] Cf. Plato *Hipp. Ma.* 285d.
[4] Cf. Plato *Resp.* 336b ff.
[5] For the Spartan diet and physique, cf. Xen. *Lac. Pol.* 2. 5–6 and 5. 2–9, Plut.
Lycurg. 12 and 17.   [6] Cf. *Or.* 16. 6.

the spoken word is the Athenian national art; the Cretans devote
their energies to hunting, mountaineering, archery, and running,
the Thessalians to horsemanship,[7] the Cyrenaeans to chariot-
racing, and the Aetolians to brigandage; the Acarnanians are
specialists with the javelin, the Thracians at skirmishing, and the
islanders at sailing. But if you were to redistribute these activities
differently among them, all you would do would be to deprive
the skills of their legitimacy. What need do mainlanders have of
ships? Or the unmusical of pipes? Or mountain-dwellers of horses?
Or plainsmen of race-tracks? Or hoplites of bows and arrows? Or
archers of shields? Well then, just as in those cases the various
skills are shared out according to terrain or national character or
the affinities of the original practitioners, rather than each item
being evenly distributed, respected by all because respected by
some, or scorned by all because some take against it, and each item
gains its good repute purely from the needs of those who take it
up, what is there to prevent the inhabitants of that fine city whom
Plato nurtured with his arguments and settled under strange new
laws, far removed from common practice,[8] from having theoretical
national customs and practices of their own, with which they have
been brought up from childhood, respected by them because of
their own national needs, but at the same time not scorned by
other peoples because they do not happen to suit them too? If we
were comparing city with city, constitution with constitution, laws
with laws, legislator with legislator, upbringing with upbringing, a
review of the kind suggested would make some sort of sense, as we
tried to establish each community's deficiency. But if on the other
hand one isolates an individual constituent of the whole and
examines it on its own, on the evidence of who practises it and
who does not, then matters are different. Examined in this way,
absolutely all human activities would achieve an equal score of
respect and disrespect and would be left hanging, without a secure
valuation. Diets and medications and regimens and everything else
that has a role to play in satisfying human needs are not always
the same for everyone without exception; it is quite normal for the
same thing to harm one person but benefit another, or delight one

---

[7] The choice of Cretans and Thessalians as examples here owes something to
Plato *Leg.* 625cd.
[8] Plato *Resp.* 369b ff. For the style of this very brief, summarizing reference to
Plato's celebrated ideal state, cf. Lucian *Vit. Auct.* 17 and *VH* 2. 17.

while causing another pain. Function and occasion and overall style of life make each of these things seem different to different people.

3   This being the case, let us now proceed to an entirely impartial investigation of Homer. Let us not ask who loves Plato while scorning Homer, nor who admires Homer while criticizing Plato, because the two are not separated or divided one from the other; it is perfectly possible both to respect Plato and to admire Homer. This is how.

What Plato founds in his treatise is not a Cretan nor a Dorian nor a Peloponnesian nor a Sicilian, nor come to that an Athenian, city. Had he been founding that kind of city he wouldn't have needed just Homer, but Hesiod and Orpheus besides, and all other ancient forms of poetry with the power to enchant and guide the souls of the young, gently mingling sound argument with their habitual pleasure.[9] No: Plato's foundation and his republic are established in purely theoretical terms; he aims for the greatest possible perfection rather than for what might be most practicable[10] —just like those sculptors who bring together beautiful elements from all over, using their art to combine details from many different bodies into one single representation, so as to produce a single, sound, well-constructed, and harmoniously beautiful artefact. You wouldn't be able to find a real body that exactly resembled such a statue, because art aims at what is most beautiful, while the things we encounter and use in everyday life fall short of what art can produce.[11] I suppose that if human beings had the power to sculpt bodies of flesh and blood, then our craftsmen would be able to mix together, in the right proportions, the quantities of earth and fire and everything else that when harmonized and co-ordinated with them constitute our bodily nature, and so presumably produce a body that had no need of drugs and quack remedies and the regimens of doctors. Suppose then that someone heard one of those craftsmen legislating for his theoretical creations and saying that they had no need even of a Hippocrates to heal them, but that they ought to crown the man with wool and

---

[9] For this view of the operation of poetry, cf. *Or.* 4. 3 and 6, with nn. 5 and 20.
[10] Cf. *Resp.* 592ab; but Plato is notoriously uncertain over this point: see also *Resp.* 471c ff. and 540d.
[11] The analogy again echoes Plato, *Resp.* 472de; cf. also Xen. *Mem.* 3. 10. 2.

anoint him with myrrh and send him somewhere else,[12] to win his reputation where sickness made his arts necessary; and suppose that our hearer grew angry with the craftsman for dishonouring the art of Asclepius and the Asclepiadae. Wouldn't he be making a laughing-stock of himself by bringing an accusation against someone who was not rejecting medicine because he scorned it, but because he neither needed it for practical purposes nor welcomed it as a source of pleasure?

4   These—practical utility and the capacity to give pleasure—are the two things that gave Homer and Hesiod, and all other famous poets, their reputation;[13] in neither respect, utility or pleasure, do Homer's verses have anything to offer Plato's state. The practical needs of its inhabitants are satisfied by a meticulously organized upbringing in which their listening is dictated to them, with no scope for independent choice or initiative, nor for the kind of story children might hear from their mothers, cobbled together in mindless chatter.[14] Nothing is left to chance; no kind of literature or form of education or even of play could enter such a city unplanned, so as to create the need for a Homer to give harmonious amplification to established doctrines about the gods, and to inspire the souls of the populace with an admiration to replace their own impoverished imaginings. For this is what a poet's words can do when they fall on ears that have been badly trained; they echo within them and so monopolize them that they have no leisure to be seduced by randomly repeated stories,[15] but instead are forced to the realization that all poetry is allegory, and to interpret the allegories with the grandeur that divinity deserves.[16] But in a community where there is no place for the casual and the low-grade, what need is there of this kind of remedy? The famous Anacharsis was once asked by a Greek whether they had piping in Scythia.

[12] A quotation of Plato's notorious words in *Resp.* 398a.

[13] This idea of the qualities of poetry is best known from Horace *Ars Poet.* 333–4 and 343–4, but is already current in Hellenistic literary theory: see above all Neoptolemus of Parium in Philodemus *Poem.* 5. 13. 8 ff. (with Brink 1971 on Horace *Ars* locc. citt.). Eratosthenes (Strabo 1. 15) notoriously allowed Homer to be an entertainer but *not* an instructor.

[14] An allusion to the whole section of *Resp.* devoted to the cleansing of literature for educational purposes (377a ff.), but with a special echo of 377bc.

[15] For the idea of the capacity of wholesome discourse (prose or verse) to monopolize the attention and preclude irrelevantly 'aesthetic' reactions, cf. *Orr.* 1. 8 (with n. 32) and 25. 6–7.

[16] See *Orr.* 4 and 26, *passim*; and 18. 5.

'We don't even have vines,' was his reply.[17] One form of pleasure calls forth another; they cling together and, once the flow starts, it will go on for ever inexhaustibly. The only way to rescue the situation is to still the source and block off pleasures at their point of origin. But the kind of city Plato founded is forbidden territory to pleasure both of sight and sound; it wouldn't accept poetry even as a source of pleasure, still less as something of practical utility.

5 I will pass over the point that among the races of men there are many cities, not only theoretical constructions, but real states with sound constitutions and law-abiding inhabitants, that have no knowledge of Homer. Sparta, Crete, and the Dorians of Libya all came late to the arts of the rhapsode; but their good name, far from being a late development, rests on a long history of virtue. Why need I mention foreigners? They could hardly be expected to learn Homer's poetry, yet even among foreign peoples you can find forms of virtue that have nothing to do with Homer. Otherwise professional rhapsodes—who are in fact utter fools[18]—would be the most blessed of men for their intimate association with Homer's art. But that is not how things are. Homer's poetry is certainly beautiful, indeed the most beautiful and distinguished of all poetry, worthy to be sung by the Muses themselves. But it is not beautiful for all people on all occasions; there is no one mode and no one time that suits all the strains of music.[19] In war it is martial music that sounds best; at the symposium, music to drink to; among the Spartans, the march; among the Athenians, choral music; in pursuit, the charge; in flight, the retreat. All kinds of music give pleasure, but not all have the same kind of practical usefulness. If then you judge Homer by the criterion of pleasure, you are doing something outrageous: you are opening the way for a whole undisciplined, raving mob of poets all of whom are superior in point of pleasure to Homer's work, and you are denying the man his own real claim to give pleasure. He is indeed a great giver of pleasure, but the beauty of his work is mightier still and leaves us free only to praise it, rather than to enjoy it.[20] 'But though praise is not

---

[17] Anacharsis A 23 Kindstrand, also cited by Aristotle *An. Post.* I. 13, 78^{b}29-31.
[18] Cf. Xen. *Smp.* 3. 6, and Plato's *Ion.*
[19] For the thought, cf. *Or.* 1. 1-2. The needs of the argument here lead Maximus away from the common perception of Homer's extraordinary versatility: e.g. Dio *Or.*12. 65-9, [Plut.] *De Vit. et Poes. Hom.*, and indeed *Or.* 26 below.
[20] Cf. n. 15 above.

identical with enjoyment, yet the two are still compatible.' If you welcome Homer's poetry as a source of pleasure, like piping or lyre-playing, then you are in effect expelling Homer not only from among Plato's nurselings, but also from among Lycurgus' and from among the people of Crete,[21] and from all places and all cities where hard work and Virtue are respected.

ORATIONS 18–21   Socratic Love

Introduction

= 24–7 (1962) = 8–11 (Laur. Conv. Sopp. 4). The manuscript titles are: Τίς ἡ Σωκράτους ἐρωτική αʹ, Ἔτι περὶ ἔρωτος βʹ, Ἔτι περὶ τῆς Σωκράτους ἐρωτικῆς γʹ, Ἔτι περὶ ἔρωτος δʹ —'What was Socrates' erotic science (a)?', 'On Love again (b)', 'On Socrates' erotic science (c)', 'On Love again (d)'.

These four lectures on Love address another ethical topic that has both a personal and a civic dimension, seeking to answer both the question 'how should we as individuals behave?', and the question 'what kind of behaviour (and practitioners) do we want in our community?' Compare in general *Orr.* 16, 17, and 26, and for the focus on the specific case of Socrates, *Orr.* 3 and 8–9; just as 8–9 are presented as a response to one of the two principal charges on which Socrates was tried (the introduction of 'new divinities'), so 18–21 are presented as responding to the other, corruption of the young. There are thematic connections also with *Orr.* 14 (Friendship) and 10–11 (the human soul's perception of transcendent reality; the link here is particularly with the final, Platonic analysis of *eros* offered in *Or.* 21. 7–8).

A set of well-known stories from archaic history (linked also by the theme of tyranny and liberty) introduce the distinction between virtuous and vicious love (§§ 1–3), and thus the thorny question of the amorous talk of Socrates (§ 4–5): is it or is it not the scandalous, and dangerous, thing a hostile critic might take it for? The whole of the rest of the sequence of lectures is a response to this challenge, offering a set of progressively deeper and more satisfactory defences of Socrates' probity. The first move is purely

---

[21] Crete earns its place here because of its exemplary status in Plato *Leg.*; cf. *Orr.* 10. 7 and 37. 1.

(and explicitly) rhetorical, as Maximus points out (*a*) that even Socrates' original critics and prosecutors did not use his love-life against him (§ 6); and (*b*) that he was far from being the first great figure in Greek culture to make love his principal theme (§§ 7-9). The more serious defence begins with *Or.* 19. 1-2, where the real nature (and value) of Socrates' activities in Athens is explained, with the aid of a brief (and preliminary) account of the true relationship between Love, Beauty, and Virtue. There then follows a long excursus, from *Or.* 19. 3 to *Or.* 20. 9, in which the distinction between virtuous (Socratic) love and its vicious counterpart is further explained, in terms of divergent aims, the distinction between τέχναι and κολακεῖαι (20. 2-3), the structure of the human soul (20. 4), and the distinction between generative and non-generative relations (20. 5-9); this is illustrated with an ample set of exempla from history and myth. *Or.* 21, echoing the strategy of the *Phaedrus*, brings a recantation (vicious 'love' does not in fact deserve the name: §§ 1-7) and a return to the defence of Socrates, with an account of the experience of transcendent Beauty that sets his amorous pursuits in their full metaphysical context, and thus finally vindicates him at the deepest level (§§ 7-8).

The heavy dependence of all this on Plato's *Symposium* and *Phaedrus* is obvious: not only in the doctrine of Love presented, but also in expository strategy (the move from a relatively simple distinction between virtuous and vicious love, to a deeper account of underlying metaphysical principles).[1] The debt to the *Phaedrus* is particularly heavy: see Trapp (1990, esp. 161-4). But Maximus also borrows and develops from many other sources too; *Phaedrus* and *Symposium* provide not the whole substance of the lectures but a magnetic core to which other material is attracted, from other Platonic dialogues (*Apol.*, *Grg.*, *Leg.*), from the Socratic writings of Xenophon and Aeschines, from other forms of writing about love, and so on. Moreover, this set of ἐρωτικοὶ λόγοι must be seen in the context of a whole tradition of such works, represented also by Plutarch's *Amatorius*, the pseudo-Lucianic *Amores*, the erotic debate in Achilles Tatius *Leucippe and Clitophon* 2. 35-8, and Favorinus' lost essay *On Socrates and his Erotic Science* (Barigazzi

---

[1] i.e. in *Smp.* the move from Pausanias' distinction between Aphrodite Urania and Aphrodite Pandemus, to the speech of Socrates, and the doctrines of Diotima; and in *Phaedr.* that from the distinction between Lover and non-Lover in Lysias' speech and the first speech of Socrates, to Socrates' Palinode.

1966: 161–9²): see Wilhelm (1902), Szarmach (1982, 1985), Hunter (1983: 109 n. 43), Trapp (1990: 155–64), Foucault (1990: 189–232). Maximus thus presents not only a defence of Socrates, and exposition of Platonic epistemology and metaphysics, and a reflection on the value of the virtuous lover to his society, but also a survey of the history of *eros* as a literary topic.

The interest aroused among later readers is second only to that shown in *Or.* 11 on Platonic theology. Gregoras takes no fewer than sixteen excerpts: eight from *Or.* 18 (§§ 1, 4, 7, and 9, with special attention to 9), four from 19 (§§ 2, 3, and 5), one from 20 (§ 6), and three from 21 (§§ 3 and 8); the compiler of Neap. 100 takes four, all from *Or.* 20 (§§ 6–9). The *Lexicon Vindobonense* makes ten quotations, three each from *Orr.* 18 and 19 (18. 3, 4, and 8; 19. 2 and 4), and two each from 20 and 21 (20. 6–7; 21. 5–6). Apostolis quotes the 'proverb' ἔρως θάλλει μὲν εὐπορῶν, ἀποθνήσκει δ' ἀπορῶν (identified as Διοτίμας ἀπόφθεγμα) from *Or* 18. 9 in *Proverbia* 9. 3. Marsilio Ficino adapted the account of Socrates' activities in Athens in *Or.* 19. 1–2 for the section of his commentary on the *Symposium* entitled 'Quam Utilis Amor Socraticus' (*Comm. in Smp.* 7. 16), combining it with material from Diogenes Laertius 2. 21, and a reminiscence of Virgil *Aeneid* 1. 497. Poliziano noted names and topics throughout the four lectures in the margins of Paris. gr. 1962 (sixty-one items in *Or.* 18, twelve in 19, fifteen in 20, and six in 21), but his attention was particularly taken by the account of Sappho in *Or.* 18. 9, sections of which he transcribed from the manuscript into his printed text of Ovid, to accompany the *Epistle of Sappho to Phaon*, and cited in his lectures on that epistle in the Florence Studio in 1481 (Paris. gr. 1962, foll. 83ʳ-96ʳ; Bodl. Auct. P. 2. 2, fol. 494ʳ: *Ovidii Opera Omnia* (Parma, 1477): see Kubo 1985; Munich Staatsbibliothek Lat. 754, foll. 123ᵛ, 124ʳ, 125ᵛ, 131ʳ⁻ᵛ, 134ᵛ, 148ᵛ: see Lazzeri 1971, esp. 5, 6, 10–11, 31, 46, and 91). Poliziano's lead was followed (unconsciously) by Henri Estienne, who also recognized the interest of 18. 9 for students of Greek lyric poetry, and printed

---

² The four surviving fragments of Favorinus' treatise are reminiscent of Maximus in style, sentiment, and choice of historical and mythological exempla: fr. 19 faults Anacreon for protesting at the cutting of his boyfriend's hair, when time is set to work far more serious damage to his beauty; fr. 20 contrasts the true moral beauty of Socrates with the transient physical beauty of Alcibiades; fr. 21 uses Antilochus, Telemachus, and the drunken Alcibiades as examples of the power of youthful beauty to charm both eyes and ears.

most of it in the appendix to the second edition of his *Pindari Olympia . . . (et) Caeterorum octo lyricorum carmina* of 1560. Estienne did not, however, separate out the direct quotations of Sappho's and Anacreon's poetry from Maximus' text; that final stage in the scholarly processing of *Or.* 18. 9 was performed eight years later, in Fulvio Orsini's *Carmina Novem Illustrium Feminarum . . . et lyricorum* of 1568, which divided the material into fragments and testimonia in the manner of more modern editions (Estienne, *Pindari . . . Carmina*, ii. 438–40; Orsini, *Carmina*, 3 (18. 7), 15, 16, and 18, with notes on pp. 285, 289–90, 290–1, 292, and 293–4, for Sappho; pp. 134, 147–50, and 321 for Anacreon). As the sole source for a number of the quotations used in 18. 9, Maximus has retained his place in editions of the lyric poets ever since, as has his presentation of a 'Socratized' Sappho.[3]

Robert Burton quotes from and alludes to *Orr.* 18 and 19 in *The Anatomy of Melancholy* 3. 1. 1. 1 (with a long paraphrase 18. 5–6), 3. 1. 2. 2 (19. 3), and 3. 2. 3. 1 (18. 4, 19. 4) (Faulkner *et al.* 1989–94: iii. 2–3, 20, 174, 195). Gerard Voss, in his *De Theologia Gentili*, makes one reference to *Or.* 20 (§6: *Theologia*, iii. 63, p. 1067). Franciscus Junius quotes the image of the river and the flowery meadow from *Or.* 19. 2 in *The Painting of the Ancients* III. ix (Aldrich *et al.* 1991: i. 350).

Oration 18

1 A Corinthian by the name of Aeschylus had a child called Actaeon, a Dorian youth of outstanding good looks. A young Corinthian of the house of the Bacchiadae, the ruling family in Corinth at the time, fell in love with Actaeon. When the youth proved chaste and rejected his bullying suitor, the suitor and the other young men of the Bacchiadae went on a drunken revel to Actaeon's house. With all the confidence that drink and political power and love could give them they burst into the house and tried to drag the boy away, while his own people tried to hold him back. As both sides tugged at him he met a violent end in their grasp. Comparisons were drawn between this tragedy in Corinth and another that unfolded in Boeotia, since both of the boys involved

---

[3] See e.g. Test. 20 Campbell. This view of Sappho seems to have entered modern scholarly discussion with F. G. Welcker's essay of 1816, 'Sappho von einem herrschenden Vorurtheil befreyt'; see Parker (1993: 313).

bore the same name; both were destroyed, one by dogs in the hunt, the other by lovers in a drunken frenzy.[4] Periander, tyrant of Ambracia, had a young man of that state as his boyfriend, but since their relationship was immorally constituted, it was a matter of lust not love. Confident in his power, Periander made a drunken joke against the youth, a drunken joke that had the effect of putting a stop to Periander's bullying, and turning the youth himself from a love-object into a tyrannicide.[5] That is how unjust love is punished.

2   Would you like me to give you one or two illustrations of the other species, just love? An Athenian youth had two lovers, an ordinary citizen and a tyrant; the former was a just lover because the two of them were of the same social status; the latter was unjust because of his superior authority. But the youth himself was truly handsome and worthy of love; accordingly, he spurned the tyrant and gave his affection to the ordinary citizen. The tyrant in his rage devised various ways of insulting both of them, culminating in the occasion when he dismissed Harmodius' sister in disgrace as she came to carry a basket in the procession at the Panathenaea. The Pisistratidae paid the penalty for this action, and Athenian liberty thus owed its origins to a bullying tyrant, a courageous boy, a just love, and a lover's virtue.[6] Epaminondas liberated Thebes from Spartan rule with a lover's stratagem.[7] There were many young men in Thebes, and they had an equal number

---

[4] The story is alluded to by Alexander Aetolus, fr. 3. 7–10 Powell (quoted in Parthenius Erot. Path. 14), and told at length by Diodorus Siculus (bk. 8, fr. 10, similarly drawing the parallel with the mythological Actaeon) and Plutarch (Am. Narr. 772ef). There is a political dimension, half-suppressed by Maximus, which connects this story with those of Periander and Harmodius that follow: the rogue Bacchiad was Archias, who had to leave Corinth in consequence of his actions, and became the founder of Syracuse. All three are thus stories of liberation from political tyranny, and as such a very useful preparation to discussion of the case of Socrates (charged with corruption of the young in part because of the subsequent political activities of his 'pupils').

[5] The joke was to ask the boy whether he was pregnant yet: Arist. Polit. 5. 10, 1311ª39–41 (immediately following a reference to Harmodius and Aristogeiton), Plut. Amat. 766ef.

[6] The story is most famously told by Thucydides (6. 54–9), but owes its presence here to its use in Pausanias' speech in Smp. (182c). Plutarch Amat. 760c adds the parallel stories of Antileon and Melanippus, just as Maximus here has added the stories of Actaeon and Periander to the Platonic nucleus.

[7] Again, the reference follows the precedent of Smp., this time the speech of Phaedrus (178e; cf. Xen. Smp. 8. 32).

of handsome young boyfriends. Epaminondas armed these lovers and their beloveds and so mustered a Holy Band of love, a fearsome and irresistible regiment which kept such immaculate formation as to be quite invincible, a regiment such as not even Nestor, that wiliest of generals, formed up at Troy,[8] nor the Heraclidae in their attack on the Peloponnese, nor the Peloponnesians in their attack on Attica. Each of the lovers had to show himself a hero, both because he desired to shine as he fought before the eyes of his beloved, and because he could not refuse to defend what was dearest to him; and at the same time the boyfriends strove to rival their lovers in deeds of valour, just as young puppies run with the older dogs in the hunt.[9]

3   What am I getting at with Epaminondas and Harmodius and those other stories about unjust love? My point is that men have taken a twofold phenomenon, one form of which is a companion of Virtue, while the other consorts with Vice, and given it the single name of 'love', which they apply both to the god[10] and to the sickness. This allows vicious lovers to give themselves airs because they share a name with the god, while at the same time virtuous lovers suffer mistrust because of the ambiguous nature of the phenomenon. Just as, if we had to test silver-assayers, to find out which of them could and could not distinguish pure silver, we would firmly deny the title of expert to the man who accepted the apparent in preference to the real, but would agree that the man who recognized the true product knew his trade; in exactly the same way, let us take the art of love and match it up like a set of coins against the nature of true beauty.[11] If one part of it turns out to involve a form of beauty that is apparent but not real, while another involves beauty both real and apparent, then it will necessarily follow that those who strive after the beauty that is apparent but not real are bogus and illegitimate lovers, while those who pursue the beauty that is both real and apparent are lovers of beauty in the true sense.[12]

---

[8] Cf. *Il.* 4. 293–310; *Or.* 15. 6.

[9] The image echoes Plato *Resp.* 537a.

[10] In speaking of Love as a god rather than a *daimon*, Maximus follows the precedent of Socrates in *Phaedr.* 242d and of Phaedrus, Pausanias, Eryximachus, and Agathon in *Smp.* rather than that of Diotima in *Smp.* 201eff.

[11] For the image, cf. *Or.* 31. 2.

[12] This point will be developed in *Or.* 21. 3 ff.

4   So, if this is the manner in which the lover and erotic discourse should be tested and surveyed, we must nerve ourselves to conduct a thorough investigation of Socrates too. What is the true significance of all those claims that he makes about himself over and over again in his conversations, that he is 'a servant of love' and 'a blank ruler when it comes to handsome young men' and 'a skilled practitioner'?[13] He also records the teachers from whom he learned his skill, Aspasia of Miletus and Diotima of Mantinea;[14] he took pupils in it too, the conceited Alcibiades, the beautiful Critobulus, the exquisite Agathon, Phaedrus the 'inspired', young Lysis and the handsome Charmides.[15] He makes no secret of any of his erotic experiences, neither his emotions nor his actions, but gives the impression of complete and total frankness. He tells how his heart pounded and his body broke out in sweat over Charmides, how he was maddened to fever-pitch like the Bacchants over Alcibiades, how his eyes turned to Autolycus as if to a light in the darkness.[16] When founding a city of the virtuous and laying down laws for the rewarding of war-heroes, he assigned them not garlands or statues (the kind of nonsense that Greek tradition favours), but the right for the hero to kiss the beautiful boy of his choice.[17] What a marvellous reward! And what a picture he gives of Love himself in the myth he invents to describe him![18] Ugly and poor to look at (so like his own condition!),[19] barefoot, sleeping on the ground, scheming, predatory, a bewitcher, a sophist, an enchanter: precisely the jibes that comic poets flung against Socrates himself at the Dionysia. And he said all this all but in the midst of the people of Greece, both at home and in public, at symposia, in the Academy, in the Piraeus, on the open road under a plane tree, in the Lyceum.[20] Of all other matters, theories of

[13] *Smp.* 203c2, 198d; *Charm.* 154b.
[14] Plato *Menex.* 235e, Aeschines Socr. frr. 17 and 29 Dittmar (= 60 [fr. 17] and 66 [fr. 23] Giannantoni); Plato *Smp.* 201d.
[15] Plato *Smp.* 215a ff. (cf. *First* and *Second Alcib.*; Aeschines Socr. *Alcibiades*); Xen. *Smp.* 1. 3, 3. 7, etc. (cf. Plato *Euthyd.* 306d ff.); Plato *Smp.* 198b ff.; *Phaedr.* 234d; *Lys.*; *Charm.*
[16] Plato *Charm.* 155d + *Smp.* 215e; Aesch. Socrat. fr. 11. 11 ff. Dittmar (= 53 [fr. 2]. 22 ff. Giannantoni); Xen. *Smp.* 1.9 (where the narrator is in fact Xenophon, not Socrates).
[17] Plato *Resp.* 468b.
[18] Plato *Smp.* 203c ff.
[19] The point is already implicit in *Smp.*; see Bury (1932, p. lxi).
[20] Academy and Lyceum: Plato *Lys.* 203ab; Piraeus: *Resp.* 327a; plane tree: *Phaedr.* 230b.

Virtue, doctrines about the gods, and all the other topics on which the Sophists prided themselves, he disclaimed all knowledge; the arts of love, however, he made his own, claiming this to be his area of skill and his sphere of activity.[21]

5   What did Socrates mean by these clever remarks, allegorical or ironic as they may be? Let us hear an answer on his behalf from Plato or Xenophon or Aeschines or another of his intimates. I for my part am shocked and amazed at the way he dismissed Homeric poetry and Homer himself from the education of the young in that marvellous republic of his, crowning the poet and anointing him with myrrh,[22] on the grounds of the culpable frankness of his verse, because he portrayed Zeus making love with Hera on Ida, enveloped in a supernatural cloud,[23] and the intercourse of Ares and Aphrodite, along with Hephaestus' net,[24] and the gods drinking and laughing with unquenchable laughter,[25] and Apollo fleeing pursued by Achilles,[26]

a man in pursuit of an immortal god,[27]

and gods lamenting:

Ah me, that it is destined that the dearest of men, Sarpedon

(says Zeus); or again

Ah me, the sorrow, the bitterness in this best of child-rearing![28]

(as Thetis says); and all the other allegorical stories about the gods that Homer told and Socrates found fault with.[29] Yet Socrates himself, the lover of wisdom, the conqueror of poverty, the enemy of pleasure, the friend of truth, can fill his conversations with such slippery and dangerous stories that Homer's allegories seem quite blameless by comparison! Anyone who hears such stories about Zeus and Apollo and Thetis and Hephaestus divines at once that the tale is telling them one thing, but hinting at another. Leaving

---

[21] Plato *Smp.* 177de, *Theag.* 128b, etc.
[22] *Resp.* 377a ff., esp. 398a (cf. *Or.* 17).
[23] *Il.* 14. 292–353, Plato *Resp.* 390bc.
[24] *Od.* 8. 266–366; Plato *Resp.* 390c.
[25] *Il.* 1. 597 ff., 4. 1–4; Plato *Resp.* 389ab.
[26] *Il.* 21. 599–22. 20; Plato *Resp.* 391a.
[27] *Il.* 22. 9.
[28] *Il.* 16. 433 and 18. 54 (cf. *Or.* 5. 6); Plato *Resp.* 388bc.
[29] Cf. *Resp.* 378d.

its surface pleasures to the ear, he joins the poet in his enterprise, rises with him to a higher level of imagination, and collaborates with him in the fashioning of the tale, simultaneously mistrusting and revelling in the licence proper to myth.[30] But Socrates, whom we are told *ad nauseam* is a man of truth, picked a far more dangerous course in his allegories, because of the plausibility of his stories, the power of his descriptions, and the lack of consistency in his actions. There seems to be no comparison between Socrates when he is in love and Socrates when he is being chaste, between the Socrates who is bowled over by beautiful boys and the Socrates whose questioning shows up fools, the Socrates who rivals Lysias in erotic skills,[31] who battens on to Critobulus,[32] who turns up fresh from hunting the beautiful Alcibiades,[33] who is electrified by Charmides.[34] How is all this consistent with the life of philosophy? It certainly doesn't square with his frankness to the people of Athens, or his independence towards the Tyrants,[35] or his heroism at Delium,[36] or his scorn for the jurors, or his path to prison, or his readiness in the face of death.[37] Far from it. If all that he says is true, then he ought to keep it quiet; but if on the other hand he is using shameful words as allegories of virtuous actions, that is a difficult and treacherous course to steer. Hiding good under evil and revealing what is beneficial through what is harmful looks like the work not of someone who wishes to help (because the benefit becomes invisible), but of someone who wishes to harm (because the harm is ready to hand). That, I think, is what Thrasymachus, or Callias, or Polus,[38] or any other of Socrates' philosophical opponents, would have said.

6   Let us come to the rescue of Socrates' case, and waste no time in idle chatter. I feel that though I want to do this, my ability does not match my desire; yet one needs both the desire and the ability. Let us adopt the following course, allowing our argument

---

[30] For this view of poetry, cf. *Orr.* 4. 2 ff. and 17. 4.
[31] Plato *Phaedr.* 234d ff. and *Phdo* 60d.
[32] Xen. *Smp.* 4. 28.
[33] Plato *Prot.* 309a.
[34] Plato *Charm.* 155cd.
[35] Plato *Apol.* 32cd.
[36] Plato *Laches* 181b.
[37] Plato *Apol.*, *Crito*, *Phdo*.
[38] Plato *Resp.* 1, *Grg.*; 'Callias' is perhaps an authorial slip or a scribal error for 'Callicles'.

the same licence as is enjoyed by defendants on trial in a court of law. They are permitted in their own defence not only to deal with the matter with which they are charged, but also subtly to divert the blame on to other more notable individuals, making their own misdeeds seem smaller by the association. We too, then, will delay consideration of whether or not Socrates was right to act as he did, just for the time being. Let us give the following reply to these fierce accusers. You seem to us, gentlemen, to be a more curiously malicious set of prosecutors than any Anytus or Meletus.[39] In their indictment of Socrates for wrongdoing and the corruption of the young, they based their accusation on the fact that Critias had become a tyrant, and that Alcibiades had been guilty of *hubris*, and that he himself made the weaker case into the stronger, and swore by the plane-tree and the dog.[40] Yet these same fearsome accusers made no mention at all of Socrates' love-life. Neither did Aristophanes, that most fearsome of all the accusers,[41] when satirizing Socrates at the Dionysia, make fun of his loves, even though he called him a pauper and a chatterer and a sophist—anything indeed rather than a vicious lover. This side of Socrates, apparently, gave no handle either to prosecutors or to comic poets.

7   Thus it escaped both the theatre and the courts of Athens. In the face of these new prosecutors (who are no more irresistible than the old set), let us begin to contest the issue in the following manner. Interest in amatory topics is by no means unique to Socrates, but far, far older: witness Socrates himself, praising and expressing his admiration for such interests, but denying that he was their inventor. When Phaedrus of Myrrhene gave him a performance of the amatory discourse composed by Lysias son of Cephalus, he claimed that he was not at all surprised to find his breast filled like a pitcher with streams of foreign water, perhaps from the fair Sappho (so he is pleased to call her because of the beauty of her poetry, although she herself was short and swarthy), or perhaps, as he says, from the wise Anacreon.[42] His speech in praise of Love at the symposium he attributes to a woman of Mantinea.[43] But whether the mother of the theory was a

---

[39] Cf. Plato *Apol.* 18bc.
[40] Plato *Apol.* 24bff., Xen. *Mem.* 1.2.12; Plato *Apol.* 19b, etc.; *Phaedr.* 236de; *Grg.* 461a, etc.   [41] Cf. Plato *Apol.* 18d, 19c.
[42] Plato *Phaedr.* 230eff., 235c.
[43] Plato *Smp.* 201dff.

Mantinean or a Lesbian, it is at any rate quite clear that Socrates'
discussions of Love are not unique to him and do not begin with
him either. Let us consider matters in this light, starting from
Homer.

8   It seems to me that Homer was most eloquent and skilled in
weaving both good and bad together in his narrative, so as to
help us grasp the former and avoid the latter. All other topics—
medicine, chariot-racing, military tactics—he dealt with in a
wholly naïve and archaic manner, advising his hearers to bring the
left-hand horse hard in to the turning-post, presenting the sick
with a posset of Pramnian wine, stationing the inferior soldiers
inside the good ones, and separating cavalry from infantry[44]—wise
advice of a kind that modern-day generals and doctors and
charioteers would just laugh at. The territory of Love, however, he
surveys in meticulous detail, covering every act and age and form
and experience, noble and base alike, chaste love, licentious love,
just love, violent love, obsessive love, and gentle love. In this
sphere he sheds his naïvety and becomes an expert practitioner,

> compared to the men of today.[45]

For instance, in the first book, we find two lovers contesting over
a prisoner of war, the one bold and obsessive, the other gentle and
emotional. The former's eyes blaze as he flings threats and abuse
at all and sundry;[46] the latter retreats into inactivity and lies
weeping and fretting and says he is going to sail away—and then
doesn't leave.[47] Then Homer offers us a second allegory of licentious
love, in the person of Alexander, whom he portrays as the kind of
man to leave the battlefield for his bedchamber, an incessant
adulterer.[48] He also portrays just and mutual love, as between
Andromache and Hector: she calls her husband 'father' and
'brother' and 'lover', and all the most affectionate of names; he
says that he cares for her more than for his own mother.[49] Homer
depicted love that is happy to use the ground for a bed in his

---

[44] *Il.* 23. 306–48 (esp. 338); 11. 638–41; 4. 293–310. Maximus' choice of
details here is influenced by Plato *Ion* 537b, 538bc, and 540d ff., and by Xen. *Smp.*
4. 6–7.   [45] *Il.* 5. 304, etc.
[46] Agamemnon: *Il.* 1. 26 ff., 101 ff., etc.
[47] Achilles: *Il.* 1. 169 ff., 306 ff., 348 ff.
[48] Paris: *Il.* 3. 380 ff.
[49] *Il.* 6. 429–30, 450–5.

portrayal of Hera and Zeus,[50] hubristic love in his portrayal of the
suitors, an enchantress's love in Calypso, a witch's love in Circe,[51]
and in the person of Patroclus, finally, a manly love, won by long
toil and preserved till death, between two equally young, handsome, and chaste lovers, teacher and pupil. One grieves and the
other consoles; one sings and the other listens. It is a lover's ploy
too to win the permission to fight that he so desires by crying in a
way that his lover won't be able to resist. The other gives in and
arrays his friend in his own armour, and becomes apprehensive
when his return is delayed, and wishes for death when he dies, and
lays aside his wrath. A lover's too are the dreams and the visions
he has, and his tears, and that final gift of a lock of his hair as his
beloved is buried.[52] Such is Homer's account of love.

9   What do Hesiod's Muses sing of if not the loves of men and
women, and rivers and kings and plants?[53] I will pass over
Archilochus' love, hubristic as it is.[54] But is not the love of the
Lesbian poetess (if one can indeed compare older with more recent)
in fact identical with Socrates' amatory art? It seems to me that
each of them pursued a particular kind of affection, for women in
the one case and men in the other. Both claimed to have many
beloveds, and to be captivated by anyone who was beautiful. What
Alcibiades, Charmides, and Phaedrus were to the one, Gyrinna,
Atthis, and Anactoria were to the poetess of Lesbos.[55] What his
rival professionals Prodicus and Gorgias and Thrasymachus and
Protagoras were to Socrates, Gorgo and Andromeda were to
Sappho.[56] At one moment we find her reproaching them, at
another defeating them in argument and practising a positively
Socratic irony. 'Hello Ion,' says Socrates.

My warmest greetings
To the daughter of the house of Polyanax,

[50] *Il.* 14. 152–353.

[51] *Od.* 1. 144–54, 231–51, etc.; 1. 14–5, 5. 55 ff.; 10. 135 ff.

[52] *Il.* 9. 185–91, 11. 785 ff., 16. 2 ff., 16. 130 ff., 18. 3 ff., 19. 55 ff., 23. 62 ff.,
23. 140–54.

[53] Hesiod *Cat.*, test. p. 3 M-W. The text is uncertain at this point; 'kings' may
well be corrupt.

[54] For this view of Archilochus, built on such poems as the Cologne epode
(fr. 196a) and frr. 30–87 and 119 West, cf. Aelian *VH* 10. 13.

[55] Cf. frr. 29, 8, 49, and 16 L-P.

[56] Cf. frr. 29, 144, 68, and 90 L-P. For a discussion of this surprisingly influential view of 'Sappho the schoolmistress', see Parker (1993).

says Sappho.[57] Socrates says that he did not introduce himself to Alcibiades, though he had long admired him, until he thought that he was old enough for serious discussion;

> You seemed to me still a little, graceless child,

says Sappho.[58] He made sport of the sophist's appearance and manner of reclining;[59] she too speaks of

> Some woman clothed in a rustic dress.[60]

Diotima tells Socrates that Love is no child, but an attendant and a servant of Aphrodite; and Sappho too makes Aphrodite speak in one of her poems of

> You and my servant Love.[61]

Diotima says that Love flourishes at times of abundance and dies at times of dearth; this same point is epitomized by Sappho in her 'bittersweet' and 'giver of painful gifts'. Socrates called Love a 'sophist', Sappho a 'weaver of tales'.[62] Phaedrus drives Socrates into a 'bacchic frenzy' of love; for Sappho, love

> Shook my wits,
> Like the wind in the mountains falling among oak trees.[63]

Socrates upbraids Xanthippe for lamenting over his death; Sappho instructs her daughter that

> It is not right for there to be lamentation in the house of the Muses' servants;
> This would not be seemly for us.[64]

The art of the sophist from Teios was of exactly the same form and manner. He too loved all who were beautiful, and praised them all. His poems are full of Smerdies' hair and Cleobulus' eyes

[57] Plato Ion 530a; Sappho fr. 155 L-P.

[58] Sappho, fr. 49. 2 L-P. The reference to Socrates and Alcibiades may derive from the Alcibiades of Aeschines Socraticus (cf. § 4, with nn. 14–16).

[59] Perhaps a reference specifically to the description of Prodicus in Plato Prot. 315c–316a.

[60] e.g. Plato Protag. 314e ff.; Sappho fr. 57. 1–2 L-P.

[61] Plato Smp. 203e, cf. 178ab; Sappho fr. 159 L-P (Maximus is the sole source for this fragment).

[62] Plato Smp. 203de; Sappho frr. 130. 2, 172, 188 L-P.

[63] Plato Phaedr. 253a; Sappho fr. 47 L-P (for which Maximus is again the sole source).

[64] Plato Phdo 60a; Sappho fr. 150 L-P.

and Bathyllus' youthful beauty.[65] Yet even in these you can recognize his restraint.

> I want to be young with you,

he says,

> For the charm of your character.

Or again, he says that just behaviour is an ornament to love. And I think he also revealed the secrets of his art, when he said,

> Boys would love me for my eloquence;
> I know how to sing charming songs, and speak charmingly too.[66]

This is just what Alcibiades said about Socrates, comparing his personal charm with the piping of Olympus and Marsyas.[67] For heaven's sake, who but Timarchus could find fault with a lover such as he?[68]

Oration 19

1   Let us resume the thread of our discussion of love, like the first stages of a long journey, and after our rest push on to its conclusion, calling on Hermes Logios[1] and Persuasion and the Graces to be our guides. The risks in our enterprise are not small and bear on matters of more than casual significance.[2] Along the path that any discussion of love must follow runs a sheer cliff, which offers only two alternatives: to love well, and travel in safety, or to depart from the path by loving badly, and fall headlong.[3] This was precisely the prospect that so alarmed Socrates, when he found the passion of love rampant throughout all Greece, and above all in Athens, with unjust lovers and cheated youths as far as the eye

---

[65]   Anacreon frr. 357, 359, 366 PMG.
[66]   Anacreon fr. 402 (a)–(c) PMG; Maximus is again the sole source.
[67]   Plato Smp. 215c.
[68]   Demosthenes' ally against Aeschines, and the object of Aeschines' In Timarchum (Or. 1).

[1]   For this epithet of Hermes, as the god of orators and persuasive speech, cf. Lucian Apol. 2, Gall. 2, and Julian Or. 4. 132a; also Horace Odes 1. 10. 1, with Nisbet and Hubbard ad loc. (adding Strabo 2. 4. 2, 104). The earliest passage in which Hermes' connection with speech is directly discussed seems to be Plato Crat. 407e–408a.
[2]   An echo of such Platonic reminders of the importance of the topic under discussion as Resp. 352d.
[3]   For the image, cf. Or. 1. 3.

could see. Though he pitied both parties for what they were going through, he was unable either to put a stop to their excesses by legislation (he was no Lycurgus, Solon, or Cleisthenes, or anyone else entrusted with a ruler's power among the Greeks), or to force them into a better course of action by his own personal authority (it would have required a Heracles or a Theseus or some other mighty chastener to do that), or to persuade them by argument (desire inflamed and pushed near to the point of madness is not a state that listens to reason). So Socrates, unable to bring himself to overlook the young men and their beloveds entirely, or to give up his efforts to rescue them, devised a means of voluntary guidance, of the following kind.

2   I will explain it to you by making up a story in the style of Aesop's fables.[4] A shepherd and a butcher were once making a journey together by foot. Seeing a plump lamb separated from its fellows and wandering away from the flock, they both rushed towards it. At that time animals and men spoke the same language. The lamb asked who each of them was and why he wanted to seize him and lead him away. On learning the truth about each man's profession, he went and put himself in the hands of the shepherd. 'You are an executioner and a murderer of flocks of lambs, but this man will be content if things go well for us.' Be so good as to apply this tale by comparing all the bad lovers to a crowd of butchers, Socrates to a single shepherd, and the boys of Attica to straying creatures who speak the language of human beings in plain fact, not merely thanks to a fabulist's licence. What could this shepherd do when he sees the executioners battening on the boys' youthful charms and racing towards them with all speed? Will he acquiesce and stand idle? That would make him a worse murderer than the executioners themselves! He will start running, then, sharing the chase and joining the other pursuers, but not on the same terms. An onlooker who did not know about his profession and the reason for his pursuit would conclude that he too was racing to destroy the young. But if that onlooker awaits the outcome, he will then praise his speed and imitate his vigour, full of admiration for such a huntsman and congratulations for his

---

[4] Cf. *Orr.* 15. 5, 32. 1, 36. 1. Platonic precedent for inventing fables that Aesop might have told but didn't is provided by *Phdo* 60c; cf. also Xen. *Mem.* 2. 7. 13–14 for explicit comment on the fact that human beings and animals can converse in fables.

quarry. This is why Socrates confessed to loving and to loving everyone; this is why he joined in the chase and pursued beautiful boys, beating his fellow lovers to their prey and forstalling the executioners. He was better fitted than they to hard labour, more skilled in love, and had a surer aim for the capture. As indeed is only to be expected. For the others 'love' was a name for lust adrift in a sea of pleasure; it took its beginning from physical beauty falling on the eyes and flowing through them into the soul (the eyes are Beauty's highway).[5] But Socrates' love, though like theirs in its intensity, differed radically in its desires, being more self-controlled in its pursuit of physical pleasure and more surely aimed at virtuous ends; its beginning was a beautiful soul shining through the body that housed it, as you might conceive of a beautiful river flowing over a meadow: the flowers in the meadow are beautiful enough in themselves, but gain an extra brilliance to the eye from the water.[6] The selfsame effect is worked on a beautiful soul embedded in a beautiful body; it gains extra brilliance from it, and shines out through what encloses it. The grace of a young body is nothing other than a flower of virtue yet to be,[7] a kind of prelude to a yet more graceful beauty. Just as a kind of glow from the sun makes a first appearance over the mountain peaks, and our eyes welcome the sight because of their expectation of what is still to come, so too brilliance of soul sends up a preliminary glow over the surface of the body, and philosophers welcome the sight because of their expectation of what is yet to be.

3   A Thessalian will bestow his affection on a colt, an Egyptian on a calf, and a Spartan on a puppy.[8] But the philanthropist, who loves this other creature, man, is on an entirely different level from an Egyptian farmer, a Thessalian horseman, or a Spartan huntsman. Their affectionate tending brings their respective creatures only toil. But the philanthropic lover tends his beloved with a view to their joint cultivation of virtue; he picks out the most suitable candidates for his attentions; and it is the most beautiful who are

---

[5]   An echo of Plato *Phaedr.* 250b ff. (by this stage something of an erotic commonplace, cf. e.g. Achilles Tatius 1. 4. 4, 1. 9. 4, 6. 6. 4).

[6]   An image in the spirit of *Phaedr.* 250cd, though not copied directly from Plato; for a parallel, cf. Plut. *Amat.* 765e.

[7]   An echo of the Stoic (Chrysippean) definition of physical beauty: *SVF* iii. 718, cf. Plut. *Amat.* 767b.

[8]   For a similar comparison in a similar context, cf. Plut. *Amat.* 767a; see also *Or.* 40. 6.

best suited to expectations of virtue.[9] Beauty, though always the
same beauty, appears differently to the eyes of the wicked than it
does to more law-abiding lovers. A sword too, though always the
same sword, appears differently to the war-hero than it does to the
executioner. Odysseus and Eurymachus[10] look on Penelope with
different eyes. Pythagoras and Anaxagoras look on the sun with
different eyes: Pythagoras sees it as a god, Anaxagoras as a stone.[11]
Socrates and Epicurus pursue virtue in different ways: Socrates as
a lover of true happiness, Epicurus as a lover of pleasure. In just
the same manner, Socrates and Cleisthenes pursue physical beauty
in different ways: Socrates as a lover of virtue, Cleisthenes as a
lover of pleasure.[12]

4   So when you hear that both the philosopher and the wicked
man are in love, do not use the same word to describe their
states.[13] One of them is maddened by the goad of pleasure, the
other is in love with beauty. One of them is sick in spite of himself,
the other loves of his own free will. One of them loves for the good
of his beloved, the other for the destruction of both. The love of the
one produces virtue, that of the other violent excess. Friendship is
the end-result of the one love, hatred of the other. The one love
needs no fee, the other is mercenary. The one is praiseworthy, the
other reprehensible. The one is Greek, the other barbarian. The one
is virile, the other effeminate. The one is stable, the other flighty.
The man who loves with the one love is a friend of God and of
order, full of respect and frankness; he tends his beloved by day
and proudly displays his love, wrestling with him in the gymnasium and running with him on the race-track, driving the hounds
with him in the hunt and joining him in deeds of valour in battle,

---

[9] A (very brief and approximate) summary of the doctrines of *Smp.* 209a ff. and
Phaedr. 253c–257b. The distinction between higher and lower love that follows
echoes the same passage from *Phaedr.* (cf. also 237b–238c) and *Smp.* 180d ff.
(Pausanias).

[10] One of the Suitors: *Od.* 1. 399 etc.

[11] Pythagoras: Diog. Laert. 8. 27 (B 1a D-K); Anaxagoras: Hippol. *Ref.* 1. 8. 6
(D-K A 42), cf. Plato *Apol.* 26d.

[12] The reference to Cleisthenes is puzzling, and is perhaps due to a scribal error
induced by the presence of the name in § 1 above. 'Critobulus' (cf. *Orr.* 20. 8 and
21. 3) would suit better.

[13] In the *synkrisis* which follows, the picture of the wicked lover takes its cue from
Socrates' first speech in *Phaedr.*, esp. 238d–241d, while that of the good lover is
more reminiscent of the speeches of Phaedrus and Pausanias in *Smp.*; compare also
Xen. *Smp.* 8. 12–36.

sharing his good fortune and dying with him when he dies; he has no need of darkness or of solitude to be with him. But the other kind of lover is the gods' enemy, because a sinner; he is an enemy of legal order, because a law-breaker; he is spiritless and abject, bereft of respect, a friend of solitude and darkness and hiding-places, unwilling to be seen anywhere spending the daylight hours with his beloved, fleeing the light of the sun, pursuing the dark and

> mist
> That is no friend to the shepherd, but to the thief[14]

a boon. The one is like a shepherd;[15] the other is like a thief, and prays to go undetected. He knows that he is doing wrong, but in spite of his knowledge is drawn on by pleasure. As in the case of fertile crops, it is the farmer who approaches them with tender care, whereas the thief falls on them to scythe them down and ruin them and tear them up.[16]

5   Can you see a body in flower, ready to bear fruit?[17] Don't defile it, don't besmirch it, don't lay hands on that flower. Praise it, as a traveller once praised a tree:

> such was the young palm-sapling
> I once saw growing by the altar of Apollo.[18]

Spare Apollo's and Zeus' plant, wait for it to bear fruit, and you will win a more just love. This is no difficult feat, reserved for a Socrates, for the philosopher alone. History tells us of a Spartiate[19] who had not been brought up in the Lyceum or trained in the Academy or educated in philosophy who once encountered a foreign youth, but one of extreme beauty, just coming into flower. He fell in love with him—how could he fail to?—but he let his love go no further than his eyes. I have more praise for this Agesilaus for his triumph than I do for the celebrated Leonidas. Love is a far more difficult opponent than the barbarian, and Love's arrows wound more deeply than any Cadusian or Mede. So it was that Xerxes trampled on the corpse of the fallen Leonidas and advanced

---

[14] *Il.* 3. 10-11.
[15] For the image, cf. § 2 above, and *Or.* 6. 7.
[16] For the image, cf. *Orr.* 20. 9, 21. 8, 25. 4-5.
[17] For the image, inspired by *Phaedr.* 276e, cf. again *Or.* 25. 4-5.
[18] *Od.* 6. 162-3.
[19] The story is told by Xen. *Ages.* 5. 4-5.

beyond the Gates;[20] but when Agesilaus' love had advanced as far
as his eyes, it halted there at the threshold of his soul. This is the
greater achievement; I award it the prize. I praise Agesilaus more
highly for this deed than for his pursuit of Tissaphernes, or his
victory over Thebes, or his steadfastness under the lash.[21] The
latter were the results of his physical upbringing and education;
but the former is the work of his soul, a soul trained and lashed
into shape in the truest sense.

Oration 20

1   One Smerdies, a Thracian taken prisoner by Greeks, a youth of
regal status and vain of his appearance, was once taken as a gift
to the Ionian tyrant Polycrates of Samos. Polycrates, delighted with
his present, fell in love with Smerdies. His rival in this love was the
Teian poet Anacreon. From Polycrates Smerdies received gold and
silver and all the other things one would expect a beautiful youth
to be given by a tyrant in love; and from Anacreon he received
poems and encomia and all the things one would expect from a
lover who was a poet.[1] If one were to compare one love with the
other, the tyrant's with the poet's, which of them do you think
would appear the more inspired and divine and worthy to be called
by Aphrodite's name, and to be the work of a god? In my opinion,
the one suffused by the Muses and the Graces would win out over
the one steeped in compulsion and fear. The one resembles a
prisoner of war or a miserable mercenary, the other a free Greek
spirit.

2   It is for this reason, I believe, that true love does not have a
proper home among foreigners. Where the mass of the population
is enslaved and rule is despotic, all the middle ground where equal
rights to speech and status, and sociability, can flourish is
removed.[2] Love, on the other hand, has no worse enemy than compulsion and fear; it is a haughty creature and terribly independent,
more so indeed even than Sparta herself. Love is unique among

---

[20] i.e. Thermopylae, literally the 'Hot Gates'.
[21] Tissaphernes: Xen. *Ages.* 1. 6–38; Thebes: *Ages.* 2. 6–16.

[1] Cf. Anacreon frr. 346, 366, etc. (*PMG*).
[2] The observation takes its cue from Pausanias in *Smp.* 182bc; the encomium of
the effects of love that follows draws both on his speech and on that of Phaedrus
(as also *Or.* 19. 4 above).

human phenomena, when once it forms a pure bond with its object, in having no respect for wealth, no fear of tyrants, no admiration for kings, no desire to avoid imprisonment, and no desire to avoid death. No beast can frighten it, no fire, no cliff, no sea, no sword, no noose; impossible feats become child's play, fearsome adversaries prove easy to defeat, terrors dissolve into trivialities, heavy tasks become as light as air; all rivers can be crossed, all storms weathered, all mountains scaled with ease.[3] Love's boldness is equal to every situation; it scorns every foe and wins every battle. Love is indeed a valuable possession, if this is its nature; I should think that anyone with any sense would pray never to be free of it, if being in love is simultaneously going to make him free and fearless and unerring.

3   Yet I am afraid that love is not like this for everyone without exception. There is a wicked practice that resembles it, dressing itself up in the disguise of noble conduct and preening itself on the resemblance. But this other practice, though it manages to construct a similar external appearance, fails to achieve the same goal. Drug-sellers mimic doctors, professional prosecutors mimic orators, sophists mimic philosophers. In every sphere you find good and evil going together, sharing a substantial common element, but differing either in policy, as the orator differs from the professional prosecutor, or in objectives, as the doctor differs from the drug-seller, or in virtue, as the philosopher differs from the sophist.[4] But policy, virtue, and objectives are things that few people can discern. Whenever, therefore, one has an ambivalent activity with two different forms, whose points of similarity are ⟨obvious, while the points of difference are obscure⟩, it is inevitable that people whose ignorance does not allow them to draw a distinction between the two should connect them in virtue of their similarity.[5] [4] Should we not perhaps pass a similar verdict on Love, taking it to be a shared name that falls into the no man's land between Virtue and Vice and is courted by both sides? It can take on the form of either suitor, whichever it happens to be yoked to, and becomes the name of whichever of the two experiences has called it up.

---

[3] This description of erotic love has been compared, both for style and and for content, with Paul's characterization of Christian ἀγάπη in 1 Cor. 13. 4–7: see Theiler (1930: 150–1 n. 3).

[4] An echo of Plato Grg. 464b ff., cf. Or. 14. 8.

[5] This repeats and refines the point already made in Or. 19. 2.

If the soul is indeed divided into two, as Plato's doctrine holds,[6] and the name of one of the two parts is Reason, while the other is Emotion, then it necessarily follows that if Love is a vice, it must be a kind of irrational emotion. If, on the other hand, it is one of the virtues, then it must be assigned to one of two categories, either that of reason divorced from emotion, or that of emotion intertwined with reason. If Love is an impulse towards friendship, and a desire of one like thing speeding naturally to meet its like and straining to combine with it[7] (which would be a phenomenon of emotion, not of reason), then the supervision of reason will have to be added to this emotion in order to make of it a virtue rather than a sickness. Just as in the case of our bodily constitution, health is a certain non-rational condition of the forces of wetness, dryness, cold, and heat, neatly blended by human artifice and artfully harmonized by Nature—and if you remove anything of the contribution made by Nature or by artifice, you will have upset this non-rational state and driven health away—so it is in the case of Love: even if it enjoys the control of reason it remains an emotional state, and if you remove reason, you will have disturbed its equilibrium and converted it wholesale into sickness.[8]

5   Granted then that Love is a desire of the soul, this desire still needs a bridle, just like a mettlesome horse. If you give the soul its head, exactly as in the Homeric simile,[9] you will have released a greedy horse to gallop its wanton way over the plains, bridleless and riderless as it speeds to other destinations than its normal bathing-place or a man-made race-course. A horse running out of control is a shameful sight to see, just as violently excessive love is a shameful thing to hear about. This is the kind of love that jumps off cliffs, that crosses rivers, that takes up the sword, that ties the

---

[6] For this understanding of Plato's psychology (which builds particularly on *Phaedr.* 246a ff.), cf. *Or.* 27. 5 and see Rees (1957) and Lachenaud (1993: 281 n. 2 on [Plut.] *Placita* 898e); in *Or.* 16. 4, however, Maximus attributes a tripartite analysis of the soul to Plato.

[7] The principle of attraction between like and like is central to ancient discussions of friendship from Plato *Lys.* 214e ff. onwards; for its place in discussions of love, see above all *Phaedr.* 252c–253c, *Smp.* 189c–193c (speech of Aristophanes), and *Leg.* 837a.

[8] This comparison between physical health and virtuous love seems to draw on the comparison of Virtue itself with physical health in Plato *Resp.* 444cd.

[9] *Il.* 6. 506 ff. (describing the amorous Paris leaving boudoir for battlefield), but the Homeric simile here blends with a reminiscence of Plato's description of the dark horse of passion in *Phaedr.* 253e ff.

noose, that assaults its stepmother, that plots against its step-
children, a lawless, manic ⟨irrational⟩ love. This is the kind of love
portrayed on the tragic stage and execrated in myth, packed full
of Furies and lamentation, groans and cries of 'alas!', seldom
successful, but buoyed up beyond its deserts and mercurial in its
various twists and turns, as it strains after physical pleasure and
burns to mingle body with body, clinging in an embrace that is
neither seemly nor lawful nor even truly loving. It is drawn
onwards in a frenzy by rumours of beauty, but is lost in a maze of
ignorance.[10]

6 The opposite kind of love, which from innate desire forms
legitimate liaisons exclusively with generative partners, for the
purposes of the propagation of its kind, and confines itself to the
female, is the ordinance of the gods of Marriage, Clan, and Birth.[11]
It holds sway over the entire animal kingdom. Some seek out
partners spontaneously under the impulse of their own desires in
the breeding season; others are guided by the skilled supervision of
shepherd, goatherd, cowherd, or groom, as each mates his charges
according to their natures, and separates them again, for fear of
excess:

> The firstlings in one place, and then the middlings,
> The babies again by themselves.[12]

But that king of all shepherd's arts that supervises flocks of men
will find no other device to divert excess until we yield willingly to
reason and entrust our souls to the shepherding care of shame and
chastity.[13] Just as Nature gives different animals different forms of
protection,[14] adapted to the preservation of their own particular
kind of life—strength to lions, speed to deer, hunting ability to
dogs, the ability to swim to aquatic species, the power of flight to
inhabitants of the air, and lairs in the earth to reptiles—so too it

---

[10] The germ of this moralizing assault on sensual love is again Platonic, but its
development is more reminiscent of such later set-pieces as Cic. *Tusc.* 4. 68–76 and
Lucret. 4. 1037–287.

[11] This insistence that legitimate physical relations can only be heterosexual
follows the Plato of *Leg.* (836b–837d), rather than the Plato of *Smp.* and *Phaedr.*

[12] *Od.* 9. 221–2.

[13] For the image, cf. again *Or.* 6. 7; there is perhaps also a faint echo of the
description of the supervisory activities of the Guardians in *Resp.* 459de.

[14] Maximus here draws again on Plato *Protag.* 320e ff.; cf. *Orr.* 10. 5, 31. 4, and
41. 5, with notes ad locc.

has a gift for men, though in other respects they lag behind all other creatures. They are physically the most feeble and the slowest runners, unable to fly, bad swimmers, and incapable of digging lairs. But what God gave them, to balance out all the other creatures' abilities, was Reason, to which he subjected the erotic impulse like a horse to a bridle, or a bow to its archer, or a ship to its rudder, or a tool to its craftsman. Reason is at its dullest when not animated by Love; and Love is at its most manic when not obedient to the dictates of Reason. And persuasion is the yoked pair of Love and Reason striving after the Beautiful and hastening towards it with all speed.[15]

He who believes Beauty to be buried in man's physical nature has been deceived into choosing not Beauty but Pleasure. Pleasure is indeed a seductive vice, full of flattering wiles. [7] It was she who sent a Trojan youth, who until then had ranged over Ida tending his cows, but now became weary of home-grown pleasures, down from the mountains to the sea, and set him on a ship, and carried him over to the Peloponnese, an amorous freebooter. There was apparently no other physique of sufficient beauty, Trojan or Dardanian, from the Hellespont or from Lydia, speaking the same language as this lover and raised in the same habits and customs. Instead this sea-crossing reveller, this lover from a dream, came to Sparta and the Eurotas, to wrong his host and corrupt and destroy a Greek marriage. Greedy love! Wrongful dreams! Wicked eyes! This is how Pleasure ushers in a mass of ills! So too the affections of the great Xerxes, who fought the Greeks at Salamis and Plataea, whose rule and whose gaze extended over so many subjects, were not engaged by a tall maiden from India, nor a Mede in a tiara, nor a Mygdonian in a bonnet, nor a Carian warrior-maiden, nor a Lydian songstress, nor an Ionian, nor a maiden from the Hellespont. Instead he lusted after Amestris, his own son's wife.[16] Most wicked of loves, that passes over wholesome food and lights instead on bitter and inedible fare, urged on by the unrestrained licence that does such violence to the power of affection! When you strip the soul of understanding but grant it power, then you give full licence to sin to flow rushing in. But strip Alexander of Priam's authority and the confidence it engenders, and he will remain a

---

[15] Text uncertain.

[16] Hdt. 9. 108 ff. (but in Herodotus' account it is Artaynte, not Amestris, that Xerxes falls in love with).

cowherd and never dream of Helen; strip Xerxes of his power, and does not Amestris lose her charms?

8   The unrestrained tyranny that flourishes when Reason is absent and the eyes fall prey to greed can be found among ordinary citizens too. But if you cancel their licence, Critobulus will cease trying to rub himself against Euthydemus, Callias against Autolycus, Pausanias against Agathon,[17] indeed anyone against anyone. For this reason I bestow my praise on the customs of the Cretans and my censure on those of the Eleans: on Cretan customs for the compulsion they exercise, on Elean customs for the licence they permit.[18] It is a matter of shame for a Cretan boy to be without a lover, but equally it is a matter of shame for a Cretan youth to lay hands on his boyfriend. What a fine balance of chastity and love this custom strikes! I shall pass over the Eleans' customs, but I will tell you about the Spartans'. A Spartiate may love a Spartan boy, but he loves him only like a beautiful statue; many can love a single boy, and one can love many. The pleasure of excessive, violent love cannot be shared with others; but the love of the eyes is sociable to a unique degree and extends to all natures capable of erotic feelings. What could be more beautiful or capable of satisfying more lovers than the sun? Yet the eyes of all love the sun none the less.

9   In Italian Locri there was once a beautiful boy, a noble custom, and some vicious lovers. They were compelled to love by his beauty, and prevented by the law from a vicious indulgence in their love. Goaded on by their passion to attempt excess, they failed to win the boy over (for he was chaste), so instead the poor wretches hanged themselves to the last man. They deserved to die: what reason has a man who cannot even stand up to his eyes to go on living? Someone who sees a statue and praises its beauty doesn't need to hang himself. If a connoisseur of horses sees a horse and praises its looks, but is unable to acquire it, he doesn't need to hang himself. If a farmer sees a beautiful plant growing in his neighbour's field, the sight of it alone is enough for him. If a huntsman sees a good-looking puppy in someone else's hands, the

---

[17] Cf. Xen. *Mem.* 1. 2. 30; *Smp.* 1. 2; Plato *Smp.* 193b.
[18] Cretan customs in love: Plato *Leg.* 836b and Strabo 10. 4. 21; Elean customs: Plato *Smp.* 182b; Xen. *Lac. Pol.* 2. 12–13, *Smp.* 8. 34 (both times unfavourably contrasted with Sparta).

sight of it alone is enough for him. None of these people feels suicidal for lack of possession. Misers love money far more than lovers love bodies, and they long more intensely to be buried with their money than lovers long to be buried with the bodies of their beloved; but none of them feels suicidal if he fails to make money. Nor yet did the king of Persia, the most insatiable and obsessive of money-grubbers, think to hang himself when he failed to get his gold.[19] Though ruler of so great a territory, and lapped in such luxurious pleasures as might easily satisfy a licentious king's desires, he none the less laid plans to rob a tomb, lured on by the rumour that gold had been buried with the corpse. The Great King in his crown turned tomb-robber, but he found no gold. Instead there was an inscription inside on the grave, which read: 'You most greedy of all men, who dare to lay hands even on a corpse in your lust for gold.' The very same thing could be said in Greek to a Greek lover setting out under the impulse of his insatiable desire to vent his lust in physical gratification, drawn on by a rumour of beauty buried in the body. 'You most worthless of all men, you are digging up a corpse; otherwise you wouldn't dare to touch male flesh, a forbidden thing for a man. Such intercourse is immoral, it can have no issue; you are sowing on rocks and ploughing the sands.[20] Transfer your enjoyment to what Nature dictates, turn your eyes to true farming, take your delight in pleasures that bear fruit,

So that your clan in after time may not perish without issue.'[21]

Oration 21

1   The tale is untrue,

says the poet of Himera somewhere in his work, abjuring the earlier song in which he confesses to telling lies about Helen, and accordingly making up for his earlier vituperation with words of praise.[1] I think that I too, just like the poet, stand in need of a palinode in my discussion of Love. He too is a god, no less mighty

[19] This story of Darius robbing the tomb of Queen Nitocris is taken from Hdt. 1. 187. 3-5.   [20] Another echo of Plato *Leg.* 838e; cf. Clem. *Paed.* 20. 9. 4.
[21] *Il.* 20. 303.
[1] Both the quotation (of Stesichorus fr. 192. 1 *PMG*) and its application are borrowed from Plato *Phaedr.* 243ab.

than Helen in his power to inflict punishment on those who sin against him. What then is this 'sin' that I say we have to make up for? A great and grave one, requiring the services of a great poet and priest, if we are to have any hope of placating so stern a divinity, not by presenting him with seven tripods, or ten talents of gold, or Lesbian women, or Trojan steeds,[2] but by erasing one account with another, bad with good and false with true.[3]

2   They say that the famous Teian poet Anacreon was similarly punished by Love. At a gathering of the Ionians in the Panionion, a nurse was carrying a baby. Anacreon, as he lurched along, drunk, garlanded, and singing, bumped into the nurse and the baby, and to add insult to injury, swore at the child into the bargain. The woman voiced no anger against Anacreon, except to pray that this same insolent man would one day praise the child as lavishly as he had then cursed him, or even more so. The god answered her prayer. That child grew up to become Cleobulus, fairest of the fair, and Anacreon made reparation to Cleobulus for one small curse with many words of praise.[4]

3   What is there to prevent us too from making amends today, and offering willing reparation to Love for our wicked tongue? How can it fail to be a sin to say that Love inflames men to commit adultery like Paris, or to break the law like Xerxes, or to act the bully like Critobulus,[5] and in general to make a god responsible for impious actions. Let us consider the matter like this. Is the object of love anything other than beauty? By no means: love would hardly be love at all if it were not love of beauty. Whenever we say that Darius is 'in love' with money, or Xerxes with the land of Greece, or Clearchus with war, or Agesilaus with honour, or Critias with tyrannical power, or Alcibiades with Sicily, or Gylippus with gold,[6] is it because we can see some obvious kind of beauty and give the name 'love' to the attraction towards it, that we say each of them is 'in love with' his respective target, one with one thing and one with another? Far from it. We would indeed be

---

[2] The gifts offered by Agamemnon to Achilles, *Il.* 9. 121–30.
[3] A faint echo of *Phaedr.* 243d.
[4] Cf. Anacreon frr. 357, 359 *PMG*.
[5] *Or.* 20. 7–8 above.
[6] Darius: *Or.* 20. 9; Xerxes: *Or.* 20. 7; Clearchus: Xen. *Anab.* 1. 1. 9, etc.; Agesilaus: *Or.* 19. 5; Critias: cf. *Or.* 7. 7; Alcibiades: cf. *Or.* 6. 6, etc.; Gylippus: Plut. *Lys.* 16–17, *Nic.* 28, *Peri.* 22.

sinning against truth itself, by adorning the ugliest of human
activities with a name that does not belong to them. Where is the
beauty in money, which is the basest of all things? Or in war, the
most impious? Or in tyranny, the savagest? Or in gold, which
causes the greatest conceit? If you mention Sicily or Greece to me,
what you are talking about is hopes of pleasure; beauty does not
enter into it. Nor would it even if you were to bring in the land of
Egypt with its lofty pyramids and its great river, or again Babylon
with its superlative fortifications, or Media with its excellent horses,
or the most fertile land of Phrygia, or Sardis, richest of all in gold.
Each of these is as far from being beautiful as it is from being
pleasant; and yet they are closer to being pleasant to those who
can derive pleasure from them than to being beautiful to those who
cannot derive benefit from them. Because nothing that is beautiful
is harmful or treacherous, or contributes to wickedness, or leads to
unhappiness, or brings you to disaster, or ends in repentance.

4   Well then: we have established that love is love of beauty, and
that the man who loves something other than beauty is in love
with pleasure. With your agreement, we ought to withdraw the
term in the latter case and say that such a man feels 'desire' rather
than 'love', just in case our misuse of language might lead us
inadvertently to confuse not only the word but also the thing itself.
Let 'love' be what is felt for beauty, and 'desire' what is felt for
pleasure. Does the man who *loves* beauty then not *desire* it? Indeed
he does. Love can hardly be anything but a form of appetition.[7] I
beg the pardon of experts in the pursuit of terminology if I call the
same thing now 'appetition', now 'desire'.[8] I agree with Plato above
all in his freedom over terminology.[9] But if they insist, let love be
'appetition' and not 'desire', and let us draw the distinction in the
following manner. If the impulse of the soul is towards apparent
beauty, let this be called 'love', not 'desire'; if it is not, let it be
called 'desire', not 'love'. What then if our sophist turns stubborn

[7] Cf. Plato *Phaedr.* 237d.

[8] For the wording and the thought here, cf. Plato *Protag.* 358a.

[9] This acknowledgement of Plato's lack of concern with consistency over terminology is of a piece with Maximus' declared preference for older, more 'poetic'
modes over the pedantic precision of more recent philosophy: cf. *Or.* 4. 1–3. It is
sometimes (mis)used as evidence that Maximus seeks to present himself as a
sectarian Platonist: see Introduction, pp. xxii–xxv. Plato's freedom from pedantic
consistency is also noted by Arius Didymus in Stob. *Ecl.* 2. 6. 3, ii. 21. 11 ff.
Meineke.

and exploits the qualification 'apparent' to claim that such-and-such a pleasant thing *appears* beautiful to *him*? Are we going to concede that he too is in love? Or again, what if someone looks at real lovers as they experience their impulse towards beauty, recognizes the element of pleasure in their appetite for it, and uses this admixture of pleasure to argue that they too feel *desire* rather than *love*? How are we going to differentiate between these cases? If pleasant things can appear beautiful, and beautiful things are tainted with pleasure, we run the risk of confusing desire and love together. Should we then remove the qualification 'apparent' from *beauty*, so as to prevent pleasure ever taking on its form without our noticing, but stop short of removing it from *pleasure* too? Beauty, which is precious in its very nature, must really be beautiful in order also to be an object of love; but it is enough for pleasure to *seem* to be pleasant without actually *being* so. Since pleasure has its basis in the enjoyment of the experiencing subject, not in its own nature, it is enough for it to seem without being.

5   I mean something like this—for I realize I am drawing a subtle distinction here and need to give you an illustration.[10] I take it that it is impossible for the body to be nourished without food being administered, and the teeth chewing it, and the intestines receiving it, and the whole digestive system doing its work as the nourishment is distributed to the body. They say that in the life of the time of Cronus men drew their nourishment from acorns and pears,[11] and the earth was accordingly reputed to bear fruit of its own accord, because men with this self-produced nourishment had no need to work the land in order to live.[12] If you then add in the chefs and sauces that go with a more elaborate diet, differing from people to people—Sicilian gravy and Sybaritic luxury and Persian titbits—these are all names of different kinds of pleasure. All of them that you care to mention share equally in the power to nourish, but each has its individual way of giving pleasure, the nourishment being a natural process, but the pleasure the result of artifice. If you change the tables round, serving Sicilian cuisine to Persians and Persian to Sicilians, each will continue to nourish

---

[10] For the wording, cf. Plato *Phdo* 87b.

[11] Acorns as primitive food: Virg. *Geo.* 1. 148-9, Varro *RR* 2. 1. 4; acorns and pears: Lucret. 5. 965. Cf. *Or.* 23. 5.

[12] A 'soft' picture of the life of early man, in the manner of Hesiod *Op.* 109-19; contrast such 'hard' accounts as Diod. Sic. 1. 8.

each set of consumers in the same old way, but in the exchange the element of pleasure will be converted through unfamiliarity to distaste. Nourishment, then, takes place through the innate character of what is capable of nourishing, while pleasure comes about through the experiences of a subject accustomed to feel it.

6   Different peoples are accustomed to different things. For instance, Greeks and Persians and Lydians and Phoenicians, and any other people in this category, plant vines and tend them and harvest the grapes and make wine, so as to produce a drink that is not a practical necessity, but none the less gives the greatest pleasure. But the Scythians, for the most part, live on milk, just as those others live on wine, and their drink is sweetened by the bees that weave their hives in oaks and on rocks;[13] others of them, however, refuse to contaminate the pure streams channelled by the Nymphs, and have natural water for their drink; and I believe there is yet another Scythian tribe who drink water, but when they need the pleasures of intoxication, build a fire and burn aromatic herbs on it, and sit in a circle round the fire as if round a mixing-bowl, making merry on the smell as other people do on drink, even getting drunk on it so as to leap up and sing and dance.[14]

7   What is the point of this excursus of mine? It is meant to show you the distinction between beauty and pleasure. With the natural and necessary role of solid and liquid sustenance, I should like you to compare true beauty, which has to *be* and not just to *seem*; and with the variety and artificiality of those differing devices that delight different subjects in different ways, you should compare pleasure, which needs only to *seem*. If this is so, then love becomes a matter of Reason and Virtue and Science: Reason in virtue of the connection with truth and reality; Virtue because of the disposition involved; and Science in its sure aim for the beautiful. Desires are revealed as irrational emotions aiming at irrational pleasures.

Since then the beautiful has truly to *be* beautiful in order to engender love, what kind of thing are we to say it is, and how should we say it acts? Shall I tell you what Socrates divined it to be?[15]

---

[13] Cf. Strabo 7. 3. 7, [Hippocrates] *Aër.* 18, etc.

[14] Maximus here borrows from Herodotus' account of the Massagetae, 1. 202. 2.

[15] What follows is essentially a précis and a paraphrase of the central doctrines of *Phaedr.*

According to him, each human soul long ago had contemplation of true Beauty in its ineffable purity, beyond the reach of physical vision, and may even now recollect it in a kind of dream. Yet in its dealings in this life it cannot see with complete clarity, separated as it is from true Beauty both in place and in status, exiled from the sights it used to enjoy to this earthly region, where it is enveloped in a muddy carapace, as thick as it is impure, confused and imprisoned in a life of turmoil and darkness, overwhelmed in chaos and disharmony.[16]

Essential Beauty, for its part, issuing from that higher realm, descends towards us by slow degrees, growing progressively duller and losing its original intensity as it does so. [8] Just as the great rivers of the world, as they discharge into the sea, keep their currents free from the contamination of the saltier waters around them in their first outflow, and furnish fresh drinking-water to sailors at sea who sail into them, but as they advance further and flow into the open sea and their currents become exposed to wind and waves and swell and current, they become contaminated and lose their original character;[17] in just the same way, immortal and ineffable Beauty, as it begins its descent with the heavens and the heavenly bodies, manages to preserve itself pure and unmixed and uncontaminated, but when it comes to descend beneath the heavens to *our* region of the cosmos, it becomes dull and faint, and our sea-born sailor, who knows his river and remembers its character, can scarcely detect its inflow when he sees it meandering over the earth and combining with foreign matter. But when he *does* encounter it, and recognizes even so much as a trace of it before his gaze, then like Odysseus catching sight of the rising smoke,[18] he leaps and burns and beams and falls in love.

Some portion of this Beauty may find its way into a particularly fair-flowing river or a plant of particularly splendid growth or a specially noble horse, but only in the dullest and most inert form. If there is any of its purer self abroad on this earth, you will find it nowhere but in man—man who boasts the most beautiful and

---

[16] For this vision of embodied life, cf. *Orr.* 9. 6, 10. 9, 11. 7; it draws on the imagery of *Phdo* (79c and 109a ff.) as much as that of the *Phaedr.*

[17] In spite of the reference to 'great rivers', this description best fits just one, the Nile: Hdt. 2. 5. 2, Aristides *Or.* 35. 9–10.

[18] Cf. *Od.* 1. 58, 10. 30. For the adventures of Odysseus as images of the trials and tribulations of the human soul, cf. *Orr.* 7. 5, 10. 7, and 11. 6, with Buffière (1956: 413–17, 461–4, 506–15).

intelligent of mortal bodies, and is endowed with a soul from the same stock as Beauty itself. This is why the rational man, when he sees a statue, praises it for its workmanship, but does not fall in love with the statue itself; when he sees a plant, he praises it for its fruits, but does not fall in love with the plant itself; he praises a river for its placidity, but does not fall in love with the river itself—but when he catches sight of a human being, whose living and rational beauty gives promise of virtue to come, his recollection is stirred and he falls in love—in love ostensibly with the visible form, in actual fact with a far truer kind of Beauty.

That is why Socrates had eyes for physical beauty, and sought out its every manifestation with his keen gaze. None escaped him, whether stealing into the palaestra, or roaming the Academy, or making merry at symposia; like the skilled huntsman he was,[19] he never ceased from using the human form to recollect true Beauty.

ORATION 22   Proper Entertainment

Introduction

= 28 (1962) = 12 (Laur. Conv. Sopp. 4). The manuscript title—Ὅτι πάσης τῆς διὰ λόγων εὐφροσύνης ἡ διὰ φιλοσόφων λόγων ἀμείνων, 'That the enjoyment from philosophical discourse is superior to that from all other forms of discourse'—is only a clumsy summary of the thesis advanced.

A lecture on the superior value of philosophical discourse over history, declamation, and other possible forms of 'entertainment'. As a discussion of the place of philosophy (above all, philosophical *lecturing*), it can be compared with *Orr.* 1 and 25; as a discussion of the relative value of different forms of activity in society, it belongs also with *Orr.* 4, 15-16, 17, 18-21, 23-4, 26, and 37; and as a lecture that at least begins as an exegesis and a defence of Homer, it has common ground with *Orr.* 17 and 26.

§§ 1-2 explain the problem posed by the celebrated remark of Odysseus to Alcinous at the beginning of *Odyssey* 9, and suggest that Homer's real meaning begins to become clear if one assumes a hidden message: that what rational human beings ought to listen to is contentful discourse of some sort, not mere irrational

---

[19] Cf. Plato *Smp.* 203d.

sounds. The remainder of the lecture is a search for the most appropriate and beneficial *kind* of discourse. Oratory (and/or declamation, § 3), the dinner-time entertainments of Persians and Thracians (§ 4), and the masterpieces of Greek historiography (§§ 5–6) are all reviewed and rejected, before Maximus concludes (§ 6) that it is philosophical discourse that best answers to human needs. § 7 is a slightly puzzling coda (see n. 32 below).

Subsequent interest in this lecture has been modest. Gregoras takes one excerpt (§ 5), and the compiler of Neap. 100 two (also both from § 5). The *Lexicon Vindobonense* quotes three times, from §§ 1, 2, and 3. Poliziano, reading on from *Orr.* 18–21, notes names and topics from §§ 4–5 and 7 in the margins of Paris. gr. 1962 (foll. 99ʳ–101ʳ, nine items in all).

Oration

1   Homer tells us how Odysseus, for want of a ship, was sailing on a raft; how, when a storm blew up and the raft was wrecked and he had to swim for it, Leucothea buoyed him up with her veil; how he was washed ashore in the land of the Phaeacians, threw himself on the mercy of a royal princess, was escorted by her to the city, met with a respectful reception from Alcinous, and joined the Phaeacian aristocracy at their feast;[1] and how, after all this, he opened his speech to Alcinous with the following words: 'King Alcinous, it is a fine thing to hear a good bard, inspired in his art as this one is. What more pleasing consummation could there be than a people in good heart, diners in your palace seated in due order and listening to the song, a rich board, and a full wine-bowl?'[2] My question for Odysseus is this: 'Most wise of men, what

---

[1] A précis of Odysseus' adventures from *Od.* 5. 262 to the end of bk. 8.

[2] A paraphrase of *Od.* 9. 2–11. The apparent endorsement of hedonism which these lines contain made them famously controversial. Plato condemned their message in *Resp.* 390ab, Heraclides Ponticus used them (apparently in an account of the view he rejected) in his treatise *On Pleasure* (Athen. 512ad = fr. 55 Wehrli), and it was commonly claimed that Epicurus' doctrine of the supremacy of Pleasure was copied from them (Heracl. *Alleg.* 79, [Plut.] *De Vit. et Poes. Hom.* 150, Σ H *Od.* 9. 28; see Bignone (1936, 1973: ii. 285 ff. for an attempt to reconstruct an exchange between Epicurus and Heraclides over these lines). The standard defences of Homer's–Odysseus' moral probity were that he was here speaking out of politeness, or only of the proper end of *dinner-parties*: see the passages of Heracl. and [Plut.] just mentioned, and Σ QVH on *Od.* 9. 5. Though he shows his familiarity with this line of interpretation in *Or.* 40. 1, Maximus on this occasion pursues the alternative thought that Odysseus' words demand to be read

is your conception of good cheer? A table laden with meat and bread, a full wine-bowl, wine flowing,[3] and on top of this a bard singing the kind of songs that Demodocus sang,

> Of the strife of Odysseus and of Achilles son of Peleus?[4]

Or again, of the hollow horse, into which the best of the Greeks climbed and were carried into the city, then poured out to attack the intoxicated inhabitants and capture the city?[5]

> How is it that this seems to you in your heart to be best of all?[6]

2　This is dismaying praise, most wise Odysseus, for a most vulgar form of pleasure, such as might win the approval of a foreigner recently arrived from Babylon and accustomed to a costly board and wine flowing in abundance and improvised song—dismaying particularly because you claim elsewhere to have scorned the honey-sweet Lotus and the song of the Sirens.[7] Perhaps therefore we may suppose Homer to be hinting at some proposition more respectable than the one his lines seem to advance at first hearing. The fact that when there are lavish supplies of food and wine to be had, he sets the one on the table and pours the other into its mixing-bowl, but keeps his *praise* for the diners who listen attentively to the bard even in the midst of such pleasures, seems to betray a desire to show us a seemly kind of merry-making, the kind a man of good sense might imitate, by transferring his enjoyment from the basest of the senses to the most restrained, from belly to ears. But is even this insufficient, if it leaves the ears indulging themselves aimlessly and unrestrainedly in

> the strains of the flute and the pipe and the din of human voices?[8]

allegorically (for which cf. in general *Orr.* 4 and 26). For yet another approach, see also Arius Didymus in Stob. *Ecl.* 2. 6. 3, ii. 20 32 ff. Meineke where Homer is credited with the first use of the word τέλος as a philosophical term, and faintly praised for having at least realized that the human τέλος has to be something spiritual rather than something material.

　[3] Cf. *Od.* 9. 9-10.
　[4] *Od.* 8. 75.
　[5] *Od.* 8. 499-520.
　[6] Cf. *Od.* 9. 11.
　[7] For the Lotophagi and/or the lotus as an allegory of Pleasure, cf. *Orr.* 14. 4, 30. 2, 39. 3, Heracl. *Alleg.* 70. 3, Σ T *Od.* 9. 89, Julian *Or.* 6. 185a; for the Sirens, less often used in this role, Buffière (1956: 380-6). Both are discussed by Kaiser (1964).
　[8] *Il.* 10. 13.

Do we need some further art to bring order to the ears' enjoyment with its elegant harmonies?

3   What then might we expect such harmonies to be? I personally am very fond of the pleasures of the musical melodies that strike the ear when pipes are blown and lyres plucked, or that come from any other musical instrument capable of furnishing and supplying us with pleasant strains. Yet I am afraid that such melodies, though they bring us a well and skilfully crafted pleasure, have no significant contribution to make to the entertainment of the soul, because they have no meaning and no rational content, and cannot speak to us. If someone wanted to compare the pleasure given by melodies to that given by words, then words would emerge resembling solid food, while melodies would be like the smell: food is exactly what is needed to give nourishment, but the mere smell is both utterly fraudulent as a giver of pleasure and utterly ineffectual as a giver of nourishment. The ears, then, are to be nourished even as they are entertained; we must reject the savours of melody and supply instead the food of words.

Since then it is proper for sophisticated diners to revel in words in preference to anything else, what kind of words should these be that we take and supply them with? Should they be words which reproduce the strife and contentiousness and artifices and battles of the lawcourts,[9] strengthening unjust cases, putting fair faces on foul deeds, perverting the truth, allowing nothing to be sound or sincere or to remain in its natural place—for all the world like slave-merchants, who take on simple uncorrupted bodies that have been raised in free air under the pure sun, then rear them in the shadows and smooth them down, thus ruining the original handiwork of Nature,[10] who clothed them in physiques superior to anything that artifice can produce? This is precisely the kind of result achieved by people who spend their lives on court-cases.

4   Representations of that kind of thing, besides being dishonest, are also unrelievedly gloomy and quite unsuitable for souls that are supposed to be being entertained. For the same reason I withhold my approval from the spectacles with which the Aenianes enter-

[9] This can be taken as a reference not only to the great legal speeches of the past, but also to contemporary declamation: cf. Russell (1983, ch. 2). Maximus has further uncomplimentary things to say about declamation in *Or.* 25. 6.

[10] An echo of Plato *Phaedr.* 239c.

tain themselves over their cups, some as participants and some as spectators.[11] Two men mime a battle, to pipe accompaniment provided by a third; one of them takes the part of a farmer, ploughing, while the other takes the part of an armed bandit, and the farmer too has weapons lying close to hand; when the bandit appears the farmer abandons his team and runs for his weapons; the two of them fall to and fight, striking each other's faces[12] and miming wounds and falls. It all makes a highly unconvivial spectacle. I have more praise for the old Persian custom, through which the Persians won their freedom. The Persians used to reserve their deliberations for the symposium as the Athenians did theirs for the Assembly, though the Persian symposium was the more earnest gathering of the two. At the former, the rule restraining drunkenness simultaneously roused their virtues, pouring good cheer on the soul in measured quantities like oil on fire, so as neither to extinguish their contentiousness entirely, nor to inflame it beyond what was needed;[13] at the latter, those sober demagogues, with no rule set over them to restrain their freedom of speech, danced a far more extravagant dance than any drunkards.[14]

5 Let us leave the ways of the Persians and the Athenians and return again to our topic. Good souls are to be nourished on words, and the argument tells us that these must not be words from the lawcourts. What words should they be then? What about words that will take the soul up to the vantage-point of history and reveal to it the panorama of the distant past?[15] History is indeed a pleasure, for it allows you to travel the world without effort, surveying every country of the globe, being present at every battle in complete safety, gathering up an immense span of time into a brief one, learning of a vast mass of events concisely, Assyrian, Egyptian, Persian, Median, and Greek. At one moment you are in the thick of a battle on land, at the next you are with the navies fighting at sea, at the next you are party to deliberations in the

[11] The story is borrowed from Xen. *Anab.* 6. 1. 7–9.
[12] Text uncertain.
[13] Maximus here embroiders on Hdt. 1. 133. 3–4.
[14] Compare the view of the Athenian assembly and the demagogues adopted in *Or.* 7. 4.
[15] With the praise and subsequent dismissal of history that now follow, compare and contrast Diod. Sic. *Bibl.* 1. 1–5. For the topic of pleasure in historiography, raised in the next sentence, cf. Fornara (1983: 120–34).

Assembly; fighting at sea with Themistocles, in the battle line with
Leonidas, making the crossing with Agesilaus, coming safely home
with Xenophon, loving with Pantheia, hunting with Cyrus, ruling
with Cyaxares.[16] If Odysseus is reckoned wise because he was
versatile and because

> He saw the cities of many men and came to know their character,
> As he strove to stay alive and to bring his comrades home,[17]

then far wiser surely is the man who removes himself from all
danger and devours written accounts instead.[18] He will see
Charybdis, but without suffering shipwreck; he will hear the Sirens,
but without being bound; he will meet the Cyclops, but in a peaceful version. Perseus too may have been fortunate in being winged
and able to fly through the upper air surveying all the countries of
the earth and events within them, but history can fly far faster and
higher than his wings could ever carry him. It takes the soul and
carries it to every quarter of the world,[19] and its guidance is
vigorous and meticulous. It gives us the genealogies of men[20]—

> Croesus was Lydian by birth, son of Alyattes, and king of the nations . . .
>
> First of the line was Dardanus, son of Zeus . . .—[21]

and of cities—

> The city of Epidamnus lies on the right as one sails into the Ionian gulf;
> it is in barbarian territory, inhabited by the Taulantians;. . .
>
> > There is a city, Ephyre, in the corner of horse-pasturing
> > Argos—[22]

[16] i.e. reading Herodotus' *Histories*, and Xenophon's *Agesilaus* (or *Hellenica*),
Anabasis, and *Cyropaedia*.

[17] *Od.* 1. 3 + 5; cf. *Orr.* 14. 4, 15. 6, 16. 6, and 38. 7.

[18] The same contrast, between the perils undergone by Odysseus in the acquisition of his wisdom, and the safety of the armchair reader of history, is also drawn
by Diodorus Siculus in *Bibl.* 1. 1. 2–3.

[19] For the sake of the argument at this point, history is described in terms
Maximus elsewhere reserves for philosophical contemplation: cf. *Orr.* 10. 2 and 9,
16. 6. Compare also [Longinus] *Sublim.* 26. 2, on the psychagogic powers of
Herodotus' narrative (ascribed to his use of the second-person singular).

[20] In what follows, quotations from historians are paired with equivalent lines
from Homer. This procedure is not explained, and seems somewhat superfluous,
given that the discussion is of the value of history, not of Homer.

[21] Hdt. 1. 6. 1 (an extremely common quotation, cf. Hermog. ii. 278. 4 and 17
Spengel; Alex. iii. 39. 21 Spengel; Dion. Hal. *Comp.* 4, pp. 88–9 Roberts; etc.); *Il.*
20. 215.

[22] Thuc. 1. 24. 1 (again, very commonly quoted: Dion. Hal. *Comp.* 4, pp. 88–91
Roberts; Dem. *Eloc.* 199); *Il.* 6. 152.

and of rivers—

Which runs from south to north and flows out into the so-called Euxine
sea; . . .

    Whom the gods call Xanthus and men Scamander.[23]

The human race is ephemeral, quick to wither and perish and slip
away. It is history that preserves its memory, guards its virtues,
and ensures immortal glory for its achievements. It is thanks to
history that Leonidas is not hymned by his Spartan contemporaries
alone, nor Themistocles praised only by the Athenians of his own
day. Pericles' generalship lives on, as also, to this day, does the
probity of Aristides; Critias' punishment and Alcibiades' exile are
still in force. To sum up, historical narratives delight the uninitiated with the pleasures they offer, but also offer the initiate a most
attractive reminder of what he already knows.

6   What more pleasant kind of verbal entertainment for the soul
could one find than this? It is hard to speak out and take issue with
so great and distinguished an array of writers, but speak out we
must and say to them that 'Your compositions are indeed fine and
pleasant to recite, but the good soul seeks something other than
what you have to offer.' What good is the recollection of past misfortunes to the man who has not yet learned how to guard against
them? What advantage did the Athenians gain from the great
Athenian *History*? What advantage did the people of Halicarnassus
gain from the great Ionian *History*? Were the people of Chios any
the happier for the great Chian *History*?[24] If they had separated fair
from foul, suppressing some facts and revealing others, then the
soul might have derived some benefit from the imitation of what
was recounted, just as the eyes can from the imitation of a picture.
But as things are, everything is jumbled together indiscriminately
in their accounts, the bad outweighs the good, and shameful deeds
prevail: the greater part of history is taken up with greedy tyrants
and unjust wars and undeserved successes and wicked deeds and
cruel disasters and tragic situations. Such things are dangerous to
imitate and harmful to remember; the ill luck they bring is unend-
ing. For my entertainment I desire the sustenance of health-giving
words; I need that uninfected food that brought health to Socrates,
Plato, Xenophon, and Aeschines.

[23] Hdt. 1. 6. 1 (again); *Il.* 20. 74.
[24] i.e. from the works of Thucydides, Herodotus, and Theopompus.

7   The human soul experiences desire and fear and pain and
envy, and is prey to many other strange and varied emotions; it is
a bitter and truceless conflict that you can see raging within it. Tell
me about this war, forget about the Persian War; tell me about this
sickness, forget about the Plague.[25] Tell me, whom shall I trust to
lead me and heal me? Leave Hippocrates to look after the body and
Themistocles to command at sea; tell me instead who will be
doctor and general to the soul.[26] If you can find no man, then
resort to the gods. Do not ask them about raiding-parties by land,
or pirates at sea, or cities under siege, or bodies wasting away.
That is insignificant, ephemeral: crops will be ravaged, even if the
Peloponnesians hold off; piracy will flourish at sea, even if the
Athenian navy is not in action; if Philip does not slight your walls,
then Time will do so instead; bodies will continue to waste away,
even if the Plague departs. But human virtue

> cannot come back again, cannot be lifted
> Nor captured again.[27]

It is this that you should ask about, when it is the soul that is being
cut down and pillaged and besieged and racked by disease. You
need an oracle, you need a prophecy; pray to the god:

> Hear me, you of the silver bow, you who stand over Chryse,[28]

hear me, Apollo and Zeus and any other god who can cure a sick
soul,

> if ever it pleased your heart that I built you a temple,
> If ever it pleased you that I burned the rich thigh-pieces.[29]

Apollo will be more ready to answer such a prayer as this than he
was to hear Chryses, since it is not to bring a plague, nor to launch
his deadly arrows, nor to slaughter dogs and men and mules that
you are summoning him.[30] Those are not the works of a musician
god, a wise god, a prophetic god. Homer only gave him that
reputation as an allegory for the rays of the sun that fly through

[25] For the imagery, and the picture of the troubles of the soul, cf. above all *Orr.*
7. 1–4 and 35. 8.
[26] For the imagery, cf. *Orr.* 1. 2, 7. 7, 27. 3, 28. 1, etc. (medicine); 4. 9, 5. 3,
10. 6 (the general).
[27] *Il.* 9. 408–9; cf. *Or.* 12. 3.
[28] *Il.* 1. 37.
[29] *Il.* 1. 39–40.
[30] Cf. *Il.* 1. 43 ff.

the air faster than any arrow and upset the balanced constitution of the body.[31] Let Homer or Hesiod or any other inspired poet there may be sing to me of the god who can cure the sufferings of the soul. That would be a song truly worthy of Apollo, and of Zeus.[32]

ORATIONS 23–4   Soldier and Farmer

Introduction

= 29–30 (1962) = 13–14 (Laur. Conv. Sopp. 4). The manuscript titles are Τίνες λυσιτελέστεροι πόλει, οἱ προπολεμοῦντες ἢ οἱ γεωργοῦντες. Ὅτι οἱ προπολεμοῦντες and Ὅτι γεωργοὶ τῶν προπολεμούντων λυσιτελέστεροι, 'Which are more beneficial to the State, those who fight for it or those who farm? That those who fight for it are' and 'That farmers are more beneficial than those who fight for the State.'

This contrasting pair of lectures debates another civic–ethical issue, to do with the kind of people and activities that the good State should contain and encourage. It is thus comparable (though on a less philosophical level) to *Orr.* 1, 3, 4, 12, 14, 15–16, 17, 18–21, 25, 26, and 37. *Or.* 23 puts the case for supposing that soldiers are of superior value to farmers, arguing successively from the evidence of Homer's poetry (§ 1), the histories of the great Greek and barbarian states (§§ 2–4a), the animal kingdom (§ 4b), divine mythology (§ 5a), and the myth of the golden age (§ 5b), before carrying its assault to the enemy camp with the observation that farming, far from being an alternative to fighting, is in fact one of its most fertile causes (§§ 6–7). *Or.* 24 responds on behalf of farmers and the rustic life: § 1 recapitulates the point at issue, and

---

[31] Text uncertain.

[32] The logic of this final paragraph is slightly obscure. It is clear that Maximus is exhorting his audience to give their attention before all else to the truths of philosophy; and it seems that (as for instance in *Or.* 11. 6 and 26. 1) he wishes philosophical truth to be pictured as a kind of divinely inspired 'oracle', embodied either in the treatises of philosophers or in the inspired allegories of poets. But what is the content of this inspired teaching imagined to be? The beginning of the paragraph seems to envisage an account of the human soul and its passions, but the end calls instead for an account of the divine beings who can reveal that truth. Something has not been fully thought through here, or not articulated sufficiently clearly.

§§ 2–3 examine the terms of reference on which it should be debated; §§ 4–7 then argue that rustic life is superior in inculcating each of the cardinal virtues: self-control (4a), justice (4b), piety (5), wisdom (6a), and—again carrying the attack to the enemy camp at the very end—courage (6b–7). No formal verdict is announced, but it is clear the the second of the two speeches wins.

The philosophical content of the two lectures is not high. Plato is appealed to for a point of ethical theory in *Or*. 24. 3, and it might be argued that the whole debate (rather faintly) echoes the discussion of the first two classes in the ideal state of *Resp*. 373d ff.; otherwise, their affinity (particularly in *Or*. 24) is with such moralizing encomia of rustic life as Xen. *Oecon*. 5. 1–6. 10, Musonius fr. 11 Hense (both cited in Stob. *Flor*. 56 (ii. 334. 11 ff. Meineke), περὶ γεωργίας ὅτι ἀγαθόν), and Themist. *Or*. 30. Michel (1970) argues for contemporary political relevance, but fails to convince (cf. Puiggali 1983: 536–40).

Subsequent interest is muted, but not wholly absent. Gregoras takes six excerpts, all from *Or*. 23 (§§ 2, 3, 5, 6, and 7), and the compiler of Neap. 100 two, both from *Or*. 23. 4. Poliziano notes the reference to Homer in *Or*. 23. 1 in the margin of Paris. gr. 1962 (fol. 101ʳ). Beatus Rhenanus in the marginal notes to his Latin translation (1519) adds contemporary evidence to back up the claim made at the end of *Or*. 23. 7 ('hoc saepe sunt expertae Galliae', p. 58), and commends the sentiment at the end of *Or*. 24. 2 ('Christiana sententia', p. 59). F. Morel published a separate French translation of *Or*. 23 in 1596. Robert Burton refers to the same lecture once in *The Anatomy of Melancholy* (in the preface 'Democritus junior to the Reader'; Faulkner *et al*. 1989–94: i. 45). J.-H.-S. Formey's French translations of both lectures were excerpted from his complete version of 1764 and reprinted in vol. i of J.-F. Dreux du Radier's *Temple du Bonheur* of 1769.

Oration 23

1   Can you tell me who it is in his poems that Homer is pleased to call 'born of Zeus' and 'like the gods' and 'shepherds of the host',[1] and all the other names it is reasonable for a poet to use in

---

[1] 'Born of Zeus': *Il*. 1. 337 etc.; 'shepherd of the host': 2. 243, etc.; 'like the gods': 1. 131 and 19. 155, 2. 623, etc. (although the exact phrase Maximus uses, θεοῖς εἴκελος, is not Homeric).

dignifying human virtue? Are they workers on the land with
mattock and ploughshare, skilled at turning the soil, good at
planting, dextrous harvesters, hard workers in the orchard? Or did
he on the contrary not think their work worth including in his
poetry at all, except in so far as he assigned it to an old islander
who had been thrown out of power by insolent young men and
who used to take his rest in the summer on a bed of leaves piled
up on the ground?[2] His happy individuals, the ones he is pleased
to bestow his praises on, are of another kind, with other activities
and achievements: Achilles in hot pursuit, Ajax fighting in single
combat, Teucer with his bow, Diomedes sweeping the field,[3] and
any other of those experts in the arts of the hero. His poetry is full
of great shields and shining helmets and long spears and fine
chariots and brave men wreaking slaughter and cowards being
slaughtered. He had no other way of praising even Agamemnon,
supreme commander of the combined Greek forces, than by adding
the title 'warrior' to that of 'king', as if this alone could count as
the most regal of activities, when he says that Agamemnon was
'both a king and a noble warrior'.[4] This is significant because
Menelaus was no less a king than Agamemnon, but a weak
fighter,[5] for which reason Homer gave him only a small share of
the eulogies in his poems. Yet how could this same Agamemnon
have surpassed the others in fame if he had stayed in Argos, on his
fine estates there, and farmed them, and made them produce a
richer yield of crops than Egypt? When Odysseus boasts about
Ithaca we hear him say that it is

A rough land, but a good nurse of young men.[6]

In his wisdom he knows, evidently, how superior this crop of
bravery is to wheat or barley, or anything else that the earth
nourishes.

2   But I will pass over Homer. You might become indignant at an
argument that presents you with such a bellicose witness as he is.
Shall I then as my second piece of evidence after him cite the

---

[2] Odysseus' father Laertes, as described in *Od.* 11. 192–5.
[3] Achilles: *Il.* 21. 601 ff., etc.; Ajax: 7. 206 ff.; Teucer: 8. 266 ff.; Diomedes: 5. 1 ff.
[4] *Il.* 3. 179, also discussed by, for example, Xen. *Mem.* 3. 2. 2 (together with a
discussion of the meaning of ποιμένα λαῶν), *Smp.* 4. 6; Dio *Or.* 2. 54.
[5] *Il.* 17. 588–9; cf. Dio *Or.* 2. 39.
[6] *Od.* 9. 27.

customs of Sparta, Athens, Crete, or Persia?[7] You praise Sparta as the state with the best laws of all. When Lycurgus (who I imagine needs no one to praise him: Apollo forestalled us in saying to him,

> I am in two minds whether to declare you human or divine),[8]

when Lycurgus, who was likened to a god by a god, was making laws for Sparta in consultation with Apollo, what kind of constitution was it that he established for his nurselings? Was it a constitution for farmers and stewards, mean and niggling and preoccupied with such minor tasks as theirs? Or did he reserve that for the helots and the servile masses and the Laconian *perioeci*,[9] while the Spartiates, freed from the soil and standing tall, their faces towards freedom, whipped and beaten and trained in hunting and mountaineering and all kinds of other labours, and, when sufficiently schooled in endurance, placed in the battle line with spear and shield, fought for freedom under the leadership of the Spartan code, joining their efforts to Lycurgus' and obeying the god's commands, and so preserved the state? If the Spartans had been farmers, what Leonidas would have stood up for them at Thermopylae? What Othryadas would have fought with such heroism at Thyrea? Brasidas was no farmer; Gylippus did not leave his crops to rescue Syracuse; Agesilaus did not set out from a vineyard to defeat Tissaphernes, and pillage the Great King's lands, and free the Ionians and the Hellespont;[10] Callicratidas did not start from a mattock, nor Lysander from a spade, nor Dercyllidas from a plough.[11] Those are the tools of labourers, of helots; they are what shields are there to protect and spears to fight for; they are what fall into the hands of the victors. It was this martial prowess of the Spartans that pillaged the Athenian countryside and ravaged Argos and captured Messenia;[12] when it began to fade among the

---

[7] The accounts which follow of the histories of the great Greek and barbarian peoples are utterly conventional in their factual content; Maximus' own contribution is the pervasive (and in several places highly tendentious) interpretation of these histories in terms of the contrast between farming and fighting.

[8] Hdt. 1. 65. 3.

[9] Free subjects of Spartan dependencies, as opposed to the enslaved helots; cf. e.g. Thuc. 1. 101.

[10] Leonidas: Hdt. 7. 204 ff.; Othryadas: Hdt. 1. 82; Brasidas: Thuc. 2. 25 etc.; Gylippus: Thuc. 6. 93 etc.; Agesilaus: Xen. *Hell.* 3. 1 etc., *Ages.*

[11] Callicratidas: Xen. *Hell.* 1. 6 etc.; Lysander: *Hell.* 1. 5 etc.; Dercyllidas: Thuc. 8. 61–2; Xen. *Hell.* 3. 1 etc.

[12] Attica: Thuc. 2. 18–23 etc.; Argos: Hdt. 1. 82.

Spartiates, they laid down their weapons and became farmers instead of free men.

3   When was it that the Cretans were free men? When they bore arms, when they practised archery, when they hunted. When did they become slaves? At the same time as they became farmers. When were the Athenians free men? When they fought the Cadmaeans, when they sent out the Ionian colonies, when they gave shelter to the Heraclidae, when they expelled the Pelasgians.[13] When did they become slaves? When the Pisistratidae disarmed the people and forced them to take up farming. Later, when the Persian expeditionary force advanced against them, they abandoned the land and rushed to arms, taking up their freedom again along with their weapons. It wasn't by farming that Cynegirus made Athens free; it wasn't at the harvest that Callimachus expelled the Mede;[14] it wasn't among farmers that Miltiades held his command. Their deeds were the deeds of hoplites, their victory was the victory of fighting men, their freedom was the freedom of victors in war. And when they had to take to the sea, they said farewell to the land and abandoned their hearths to be burned; taking only their weapons, they migrated with them to their ships. The city of Athens and its population of landsmen took to the sea: taking to the sea they fought there, fighting there they were victorious, in victory they won command both of sea and of land. I praise Pericles too for his generalship: by turning a deaf ear to the farmers, and refusing to react to the sight of Acharnae being pillaged, he kept Athens free.[15] For while freedom remains, so too will land and trees and crops.

4   Let us leave the evidence of Greece and move on to that of foreign nations. The Egyptians are farmers, the Scythians are warriors: Scythians are free, Egyptians are slaves. The Assyrians are farmers, the Persians are warriors: the Assyrians live in servitude, the Persians rule. The Lydians were warriors once, but then turned to farming: it was when they were free that they made

---

[13] The standard episodes of early Athenian history. The battle with Thebes over the bodies of the Seven and the reception of the Heracleidae, in particular, are commonplaces of the Funeral Oration: Lysias *Or.* 2. 7–16; [Dem.] *Or.* 60. 8.

[14] Cynegirus (Hdt. 6. 114) and Callimachus (6. 109 ff.) were particularly popular as declamation themes: see Lucian *Rhet. Praec.* 18, Polemo *Declam.* 1 and 2; cf. also *Or.* 34. 9.

[15] Cf. Thuc. 2. 55 ff.

war, and only when they had been enslaved that they turned to farming. Now move on to the animal kingdom: there too you will see freedom and slavery, the life of martial virtue and the life of the soil. The ox ploughs while the horse runs races; and if you change their activities over, you offend against natural order. Cowardly creatures are herbivores, mighty creatures are predators. The deer eats grass, the lion hunts; the jackdaw gathers seeds, eagles are birds of prey; seed-gatherers and herbivores are slaves, while beasts of prey are free. [5] If we are also to admit myths of the gods as evidence, then Zeus and Athena and Apollo and Enyalius,[16] the most regal of the gods, are no farmers. Demeter only turned to farming belatedly, after her long wanderings; Dionysus only belatedly turned to farming after dealing with Cadmus and Pentheus; Triptolemus only belatedly introduced farming after Erichthonius and Cecrops. Furthermore, if we were to turn to the age when Cronus was king, how important would we reckon farming to have been then? Indeed even to this day farming is superfluous. The earth has not yet tired of putting forth crops that need no tending: it produces food in the form of acorns and pears;[17] it produces drink in the form of the Nile and the Ister and the Achelous and the Maeander, and other inexhaustible pitchers pouring pure and sober water. No old Icarius, no Boeotian or Thessalian, is needed to tend these crops: they are tended by the sun itself and by the moon, that warm them, and by the nourishing showers, and by the breath of the winds, and the changing seasons, and the earth that puts them forth—immortal farmers of fertile crops and trees that need no human artifice to aid them. No plague or famine or war can put a stop to this husbandry,

All grow unsown and unploughed.[18]

If you desire Libyan lotus and Egyptian wheat and Attic olives and Lesbian vines, then you pervert the science to the service of pleasure.

6   The core of the issue is the contrast between free and enforced labour, between virtue that is freely chosen and farming that is forced upon us. The contrast is not that between peace and war. If farming really were the kind of thing you are suggesting, then away with war, let us turn farmers! Let everyone throw away his

---

[16] Ares.   [17] Cf. *Or.* 21. 5   [18] *Od.* 9. 109.

spear and turn to the mattock: let him show his heroism on the soil, let him win his victories among farmers! Let us honour the man for the fertility of his land:

He is the victor among men, he is the champion.[19]

The real world, however, is full of conflict and injustice. Desire is everywhere abroad, throughout the whole earth, rousing men's greed, and everywhere armed forces are on the advance against others' lands. People sing the praises of a Peloponnesian woman's beauty; immediately a foreigner from Ida sails in to snatch her away—not a farmer, but one still gentler and more leisured and more peaceful than a farmer, a shepherd and a herdsman.[20] Cambyses conceives a desire for the land of Egypt; his desire starts a war.[21] Darius desires the land of Scythia; the Scythians are plunged into war.[22] Desire passes on to Eretria and Athens, and armed excursions follow in its wake. Eretria is swept clean,[23] fleets sail for Marathon. Xerxes' wife conceives a desire for handmaidens from Sparta, Attica, and Argos;[24] to satisfy a woman's desires an invasion force is prepared, Asia is emptied of its inhabitants, and Europe made to decamp. The Athenians conceive a desire for Sicily, the Spartans for Ionia, the Thebans for the leadership of Greece.[25]

7 What bitter passions for Greece! Where might a man go to farm in safety? Where might he find the 'golden visage of Peace'?[26] What portion of the earth is there that does not have its lovers?

Ascra bad in winter, foul in summer[27]—

let us to Ascra! But Boeotia is rich in poplars. Libya may be far away, but it is rich in flocks. India lies far beyond our frontiers, but even she found a Macedonian lover, who made his way to her through many peoples and many wars.[28] Where can a man turn? Where could one find a safe place to farm? Then

---

[19] It is not clear whether this hexameter line is a quotation or Maximus' own composition.   [20] Paris; cf. Hdt. 1. 3 and *Or.* 20. 7.

[21] Hdt. 2. 1 and 3. 1.

[22] Hdt. 4. 1 and 4. 83 ff.

[23] Cf. Hdt. 6. 31, Plato *Leg.* 698a.

[24] Hdt. 3. 134. 5 attributes this desire to the wife of Darius, not the wife of Xerxes.   [25] Thuc. 3. 86, etc. and 6. 1 ff.; Xen. *Hell.* 3. 1 ff.; *Hell.* 6. 1ff.

[26] These words sound as if they ought to be a quotation or a cliché, but the source is elusive; Euripides (fr. 486 Nauck²) speaks of 'the golden visage of justice'.

[27] Hesiod *Op.* 640.

[28] Alexander the Great; cf. *Or.* 2. 6.

Let each man put a good edge to his spear, and ready his shield,
Let each put good fodder before his swift-footed horses.[29]

Farming is indeed a fine, fine thing, if it can hold its place and find
the energy and the protection it needs. But I am afraid it may be
this very thing, fine though it is, that starts wars and civil strife in
the first place. In the words of a venerable authority,

Where the soil was most fertile, there were the most frequent changes of
population. The land of Attica, at any rate, which because of the poverty
of its soil was free from political disunity, was always inhabited by the
same race of people.[30]

You hear how it is that wars start? Don't be a farmer, man; leave
the land unbeautified and squalid! You are laying the grounds for
civil strife and for war!

Oration 24

1   Let us come to the rescue of the farming population, since it is
with words and not with weapons that the present issue is to be
decided—though if weapons were needed, it might turn out soon
enough that the farmer was in no way inferior to the hoplite. But
that we will consider later.[1] It is with words and not with weapons
that we must arbitrate between our two, and there is no need to
defer to the testimony of Homer, or of anyone else there may
be more eloquent that he. Though if there were a need, we too
would be able to summon another poet from Helicon, no less distinguished than Homer, to criticize the men of today

Who were the first to forge the vicious knife
Of the highwayman, the first to eat the flesh of the ploughing ox.[2]

To approve of such deeds as these could only be the mark of a man
who was a worse enemy to human life than the practice of war
itself, which remains a necessity to be pitied, even when it is not
unjust.

2   Let us consider the matter in the following way. Some men are
just and some are unjust. When men fight, is it the case that just
fight with just? By no means: since their thoughts are in sym-

[29] Il. 2. 382-3.   [30] Thuc. 1. 2. 3 + 5.
[1] § 6 below.   [2] Aratus Phaen. 131-2.

pathy, what need could they have of war? It is therefore the unjust
who fight, either with the just or with their own likes, since they
are at odds both with each other and with the just. The weak also
fight, in search of equality, and the strong in search of advantage.
So far so good; these are the three categories that reasoned discussion unearths for us. The first, the category of the just, maintains a perpetual truce and state of peace with itself, while each of
the other two is in a state of war, one with itself and the other with
the just. It is therefore apparent that war is an enforced necessity
for the just, but a matter of voluntary choice for the unjust. As far
as the unjust are concerned, do we really need to consider them
further? There is no risk that anyone is going to accord them a
share of praise. As for the just, since they fight from necessity
rather than from their own free choice, either to punish injustice
in whatever form, like Heracles,[3] or to defend themselves against
aggressors, as the Greeks did against the Persians, do we think that
these same people would be ready, if they could be freed from the
necessity to fight, to lose their martial prowess at the same time?
Or would they choose to keep both the unwished-for activity and
the need to display such prowess? I believe that they would positively prefer one of these two alternatives, namely the former.
Doctors too, if they are just and love their fellow men, would pray
for their art to die out along with the diseases it exists to treat.

3   Let us then consider whether matters are the same for our
three categories in the case of farming as they are with the
practice of war. Men till the soil, some justly, some unjustly:
justly if they are looking to the utility of their produce, unjustly if
they are looking only to make a profit. In this case too we are not
trying to come to a single verdict that will apply universally to all
possible kinds of farming. Since this activity is also practised both
by the just and by the unjust, just as fighting was common to
both categories, there is a risk that the argument may deceive us
without our realizing it, by trying to compare not farming with
fighting, but just with unjust behaviour. Let us then assume that
both our fighter and our farmer are just men, the one going to war
through the force of necessity, the other forced to farm from
practical need, and let us examine each of them on this basis. But
what is it that I have just said? If justice and honour and praise

---

[3] For this view of Heracles, cf. *Or.* 15. 6, with n. 18.

are all applicable to an equal degree in both cases, then we will have to allow both to emerge the winner. Should we then take justice away from both parties and substitute injustice, and consider the issue on that footing? No: because in that case also an equal share of wickedness on both sides would disqualify both equally from praise. How then might we seek to decide the issue? Shall I tell you? I will. My soul divines that, as Plato opines,[4] there is a certain category of human beings who do not have a secure grasp on Virtue, but have not degenerated entirely into the worst forms of Vice either; they live by right opinion, nurtured and educated in a stable community under sound laws. Let us take this category of men, which is ambivalent and occupies the no man's land between Virtue and Vice, and divide it in two, assigning half to the land and dispatching the other half to fight; and let us consider each group in the light of its own particular activity, to see which is the more readily led in which direction.

4   The greatest human evil is desire. Which is the more effective generator of desire, warfare or farming? Well, the one is insatiable, while the other is thrifty: war is insatiable, farming thrifty. The one, war, has many different forms; the other, farming, has only one. The one is full of uncertainty; the other is stable. What could be more uncertain than the fortunes of war? But labour on the land never changes. War waxes rashest when things are going well; good harvests teach the farmer restraint. If we grant that anger is a difficult companion for a man to live with, and one that needs careful training, then what could be more productive of anger than war and weapons? By contrast, what is more peaceable than farming?

As for the virtues in the strict sense of the term, here is how the two activities stand in relation to them. First of all, in regard to self-restraint. When armed, the strong man becomes more impulsive, while the coward becomes more prone to accident; the bold man becomes more impulsive, the weak man becomes bolder, and the pleasure-lover more unbridled.[5] But when he farms, the strong

---

[4] The same doctrine is attributed to Plato by Alcin. *Didasc.* 30. 183. 31 ff. (cf. Whittaker 1990, ad loc.) and Apul. *De Plat.* 2. 3. 224 (cf. Beaujeu 1973, ad loc.) and 2. 19. 246, and echoed in Philo *Pr. et Poen.* 62–5. It is a construction of Middle Platonism, intended to counter the Stoic claim that anyone who falls short of perfect virtue is vicious. Cf. also *Or.* 38. 6.

[5] Text uncertain.

man becomes more productive, the weak man healthier, the coward safer, and the pleasure-lover more self-restrained.

Again, if you compare the two with respect to justice, it is war that teaches injustice, whereas justice is the lesson of peace. War is greedy and leads to attacks on other people's property, and indeed is at its mightiest when it is committing injustice on the grandest scale and its wicked schemes are flourishing. Among farmers, on the other hand, equal returns are the order of the day, and all relationships with others are conducted on fair terms: you tend a tree, and it gives its fruit in return; tend your wheat-crop, and it flourishes; tend your vine, and it gives good wine; tend your olive, and it blossoms.[6] A farmer frightens no one and is an enemy to no one; he is a friend to all, innocent of blood and slaughter, holy and consecrated to the gods of the harvest and the vintage and the threshing-floor and the ploughing-festival. A farmer will participate in the civic equality of a democracy, but oligarchy and tyranny are hateful to him before all else. Dionysius and Phalaris were not farming's children; both came from the cradle of war.

5   What company could be more suitable for feasts and mysteries and festivals? Does not the hoplite strike a discordant note at the feast, while the farmer is in perfect tune? Is not the former utterly foreign to the mysteries, while the latter is their intimate? Is not the former a terrifying sight at a festival, while the latter is most pacific? It seems to me that it was none others than the farmers who established feasts and divine rituals in the first place: they were the first to establish choruses in honour of Dionysus by the wine-press, the first to establish the rites of Demeter on the threshing-floor, the first to assign the invention of the olive tree to Athena, and the first to make offerings of the fruits of the earth to the gods who had granted them.[7] It would be reasonable for the gods to rejoice more at their offerings than at Pausanias sacrificing his tenth or Lysander dedicating his; those were the first fruits of war, acts of piety based on human disaster. But the prayers of farmers show love for their fellow men; their sacrifices are well-

---

[6] A widely used commonplace: [Arist.] *Oec.* 1. 2, 1343ᵃ28; Xen. *Oec.* 5. 12; Philemon fr. 105; Cic. *De Off.* 1. 48; Virg. *Geo.* 2. 460; Musonius fr. 11 Hense.

[7] For the idea of the rustic origins of religious rites, see Xen. *Oec.* 5. 10, Themist. *Or.* 30. 349b (cf. Prodicus B 5 D-K), Tib. 2. 1. 51 ff. with Smith (1913, ad loc.); cf. also *Or.* 2. 1.

omened and spring from their own labours, with no taint of
calamity or misfortune.

6   If we must also review our men for wisdom, let us enquire
about each of them in the following way. The man wise in war is
an expert in

> drawing up the lines of chariots and spearmen,[8]

that is, in the most disruptive and dismaying matter known to
man. But the man wise in the ways of farming begins his harvest

> When the Pleiades born of Atlas rise before the sun,
> . . . and his reaping when they set.[9]

His thoughts are for the seasons of the year and the course of the
moon and the risings of the stars and the volume of rainfall and
the timing of the winds.

Again, if we must judge our men by physical prowess and
bravery in their labours, the soldier has few opportunities for hard
work, whereas the farmer's are continuous. He is forever out of
doors, a friend to the sun, boon-companion to the snows, sturdy,
barefoot, self-sufficient, sound of wind, quick on his feet, and strong
enough to carry heavy weights.[10] And if there is ever any fighting
to be done, you will find him a soldier trained in genuine exertions,[11] of the kind Darius had a taste of when he advanced on
Marathon. The Athenians of that era had an army that was not
composed of hoplites or archers or sailors or cavalry, but was
scattered about through the demes. They were farmers, and when
the foreign expeditionary force sailed to attack them at Marathon,
they rushed from their fields like the worker-soldiers that they
were, one of them brandishing a mattock, another fighting with a
ploughshare, yet another defending himself with a reaping-hook.
What a splendid husbandman army, full of freedom! You splendid
and noble offspring of the soil and the farm, how I praise you for
your prowess, and for the weapons with which you fought for your
own land, and for the vines over which you had toiled, and for the
olives you had planted! After your mighty deeds you returned
again to the land, farmers returned from the war, farmers turned
conquerors. What a splendid transformation! [7] When the

---

[8] *Il.* 2. 554.
[10] Cf. Xen. *Oec.* 5. 8, 6. 9.
[9] Hesiod *Op.* 383-4.
[11] Cf. Xen. *Oec.* 5. 7, 6. 6-8.

Persians went to war their concubines followed them, so as to make them fight bravely to protect their dear ones.[12] Will a farmer then not fight bravely for *his* dear ones, for the vine as it is lopped, and the olive as it is cut down, and the crops as they are ravaged? If you compare this army with its later developments, you will find a greater host of men, but not a victorious host: hoplites, but hoplites serving for pay, hoplites trained out of the healthy light of the sun, insolent hoplites defeated in Sicily and taken prisoner on the Hellespont.[13] If you bring up the case of Persia, here too it is an army raised on farming that you are talking about. When was it, pray, that the Medes were worsted and the Persians victorious? When the Persians were still farmers, and the Medes made war on them, then Cyrus came to their rescue with an army trained in the harsh terrain of the Pasargadae, soldiers hardened by labour on the land.[14] But when the Persians ceased farming, and forgot the soil and the plough and the sickle, then they threw away their prowess along with their tools.[15]

ORATION 25   True Beauty of Speech

Introduction

= 31 (1962) = 15 (Laur. Conv. Sopp. 4). The manuscript title—Ὅτι οἱ σύμφωνοι τοῖς ἔργοις λόγοι ἄριστοι, 'That words which are consistent with one's actions are best'—quite fails to identify the subject of the lecture, being a mere summary of a preliminary proposition advanced in §2 and soon abandoned; Maximus' own formulations of the topic may be found in §§2 and 4.

This argument that true beauty of speech (or true eloquence) is to be identified with morally improving philosophical oratory is closely comparable in its message to *Orr.* 1 and 22. More generally, as a discussion of a valued activity, it belongs with the group of civic-ethical lectures that also includes *Orr.* 3, 4, 12, 14, 15–16, 17, 18–21, 23–4, 26, and 37.

The structure and sequence of thought of the lecture have

---

[12] Hdt. 7. 83. 2.
[13] In the Athenian defeats at Syracuse and Aegospotami; cf. *Or.* 3. 8.
[14] Cf. Hdt. 1. 125 ff., Plato *Leg.* 695a; for Cyrus, see also *Or.* 6. 7.
[15] Cf. Hdt. 9. 121. 3-4.

caused problems: see the unsatisfactory analyses of Puiggali (1983: 375-84), and Koniaris (1982: 113-20). §§ 1-2a are introductory, suggesting two possible relationships between words and deeds; §§ 2b-3 then make the question at issue explicit (what is to count as true beauty of speech?), and explain that the second preliminary suggestion will not suffice: to be truly beautiful, words must do more than merely match deeds; they must bear some close relationship to the real nature, best interests, and proper virtue of the speaker. §§ 4-5a restate the question in such a way as to transfer attention from speaker to hearer: true beauty can only be recognized by a 'receiver' who has the necessary knowledge and awareness—above all, the ability to distinguish between mere superficial enjoyment and real benefit. It is far too easy to be seduced by mere enjoyment, and so go to ruin, like the sick man who eats delicacies instead of taking his medicine (§ 5b). § 6 then provides the lecture's final, considered response to the question: beauty of speech resides in the truly beneficial words of the inspiring philosophical orator; these alone appeal to and feed man's better nature—and yet they too (§ 7) have a virtuous pleasure of their own.

Gregoras takes two excerpts, from §§ 2 and 7, and the compiler of Neap. 100 three, from §§ 2 and 3. The *Lexicon Vindobonense* quotes once, from § 7. Poliziano noted the references to Myson in § 1, Pythagoras in § 2, Zopyrus in § 3, and the Cimmerians in § 4 in the margins of Paris. gr. 1962 (foll. 107^v-108^v).

Oration

1   There once came to Greece from Scythia one of the foreign population of that region, a sage whose wisdom was not of the wordy or talkative kind. Its kernel was a meticulous life-style, a sound mind, and words that were few and well aimed, resembling not a mercenary skirmisher who dashes recklessly forward,[1] but a hoplite advancing at walking pace and with measured tread. Coming to Athens, he found no hoplites there but many skirmishers, for whose flightiness and timidity he—Anacharsis— had anything but praise. So he went on a tour of the whole of Hellas, hoping somewhere to find a firm and stable wisdom. If he

---

[1] The image echoes Plato *Theaet.* 165d.

succeeded in finding such a thing anywhere else, I cannot say; but
he did discover one good man in a small and insignificant settle-
ment called Chenae. His name was Myson.[2] Myson's forte was to
run his household well, to tend his land with skill, to manage his
marriage chastely, and to bring up his son with honour.[3] His
Scythian visitor was content to search no further for a more talkative kind of wisdom, in the presence of deeds like these, all of which
he inspected minutely. When he had examined them to his full
satisfaction, Myson of Chenae said to him, 'It is for this,
Anacharsis, that for some reason or another men think me wise.
But if these habits make me wise, where on earth will folly finish
up?' Anacharsis was greatly delighted by his Greek host's combination of abundant deeds with sparing words.[4]

2   Pythagoras' discourses too, I believe, were short and concise,
like laws;[5] the lengthy sequence of his deeds, however, saw no
interruption: neither by night nor by day did they let his soul rest,
or allow it to relax into idleness. Just as in musical harmonies the
smallest omission destroys the tune's sequence, so in the harmony
of a human life, if we are not to find it discordant and lived out
haphazardly, there has to be a coincidence of word and deed. Deeds
must not be reduced to the point of complete disappearance, nor
must words overwhelm deeds, as if spilling out of a vessel too
narrow to contain them; the two must be co-ordinated with each
other so as to have the same volume and the same level.

Well then, if a man yearns for this kind of harmony and wishes
his voice to match his deeds, could he therefore preen himself on
the beauty of his speech? Far from it, in my view. Peacocks are the
birds that give the greatest pleasure to look at, but no one would
think them blessed in possessing a beauty which contributes
nothing to their ease of flight, which is after all a bird's strength.[6]
We welcome the song of the nightingale as something pleasant to

---

[2] Listed as one of the Seven Sages in Plato *Protag.* 343a; so also Diog. Laert. 1.
106-8 (immediately following Anacharsis in 1. 101-5).
[3] i.e. he practised a purely domestic, non-political virtue; contrast the more
comprehensive kind outlined in *Or.* 38. 4.
[4] For Anacharsis in general, see Kindstrand (1981) and id. in *Dictionnaire des
philosophes antiques*, i (1989), s.v.
[5] A reference to the Pythagorean ἀκούσματα: cf. Diog. Laert. 8. 34 ff.; Porph. *Vit.
Pyth.* 41; Iamb. *Vit. Pyth.* 82-6; and the other texts cited in D-K i, 58 C 1-6.
[6] The point of the peacock's tail was already a philosophical problem for
Chrysippus: *SVF* ii. 1163.

listen to, but what is pleasant for us is no help to them in their survival.

3   When an eagle shrieks or a lion roars, one can recognize the strength of the creature making the noise from the unpleasantness of the noise it makes. So, if human utterances are no weaker or inferior an indication of the speaker's character than a lion's roar or an eagle's shriek, would it not be worth using our sense of hearing to hunt out whether it is a nightingale that is speaking to us, with its tremulous tongue and evanescent song, or on the other hand an eagle, or some other masculine creature full of spirit? The famous Zopyrus[7] had the skill, simply by setting eyes on someone and becoming acquainted with his physical shape, of recognizing his character and divining the truth about his soul from external appearances. A murky form of divination indeed! What bonds of similarity are there between soul and body? If there is a possibility of establishing a form of divination for the soul that does not depend on such obscure and feeble indications, then we must leave the eyes to deal in colours and shapes and the pleasure and displeasure that they bring, and use the sense of hearing instead to track down the character of the soul. We should not, however, follow the reasoning of the masses, for whom sufficient grounds to praise an utterance are furnished by a fluent tongue, and a rush of words, and Attic diction, and well-constructed periods, and elegant composition. All that is, as the comic poet puts it,

> Small fry . . . and twittering,
> A chorus of swallows, and a disgrace to the art.[8]

4   'So what *does* constitute beauty of utterance?', someone might ask. Do not ask that yet, sir; you will see for yourself when you are capable of it. It is impossible to explain the beauty of the sun to a Cimmerian, or the sea to a landsman, or God to Epicurus; these are not things that can be reported through intermediaries; personal acquaintance is required. As long as knowledge is absent, judgement also must necessarily go astray. All kinds of views are

[7] Cf. e.g. Cic. *Tusc.* 4. 80; Diog. Laert. 2. 45. He was famously supposed to have diagnosed depravity of character in Socrates. Diog. Laert. 2. 105 attributes a dialogue *Zopyrus* to Phaedo.

[8] Aristoph. *Ran.* 92–3, chosen to fit in with the preceding references to the song of the nightingale. With the scorn for empty style expressed here, compare and contrast the line taken in *Or.* 1. 7.

taken by casual passers-by of plants growing in the soil, but it is only the farmer who takes the proper view. One person praises a plant's flowers, another its size or the shade it gives, another its colour; the farmer reserves his praise for the fruit, and for its practical usefulness. If someone approaches an utterance in the manner of a passer-by, then I do not begrudge him praising it for its pleasantness as he passes;[9] but if he belongs to the farming community, then I cannot tolerate his praises until he also tells me the usefulness of what he is praising.

5   Tell me, what fruits do you see in this utterance? What have you gathered from it? What condition are they in? Have you tried them and tested them to see if they are fully formed and capable of generating further fruit? Has your soul put forth any good and fertile growths from them?[10] When pear ripens upon pear, and apple grows on apple, grape on grape, and fig on fig,[11] are words alone to be evanescent in their genesis, infertile in their yield, with no capacity to nourish and no involvement with the soul,

But floating above it along the surface like oil?[12]

That is the kind of farming I wish to hear about; leave your praises to one side. If you remove their usefulness, then my suspicions are aroused about your motives, and I begin to pity the praiser and to find fault with his praise.[13] This is the praise uttered by the wayward portions of the soul, those weak in judgement and prone to deception.[14]

No shame it is for Trojans and well-greaved Achaeans
To have suffered hardship for so long over such a woman as this.[15]

See how wickedness wins praise, and one woman and the pleasure taken in her is exchanged for the griefs of Greeks and Trojans! In our arena too we can find the same kind of encomiast: on encoun-

---

[9] The image of the wayfarer praising a plant or tree recalls both Odysseus' words to Nausicaa in *Od.* 6. 160-7 (also cited in *Or.* 19. 5), and Socrates' to Phaedrus in *Phaedr.* 230b.

[10] The imagery again echoes *Phaedr.*, 276e-277a; cf. *Orr.* 5. 8 and 27. 5.

[11] An echo of *Od.* 7. 120-1 (cf. *Or.* 14. 1).

[12] *Il.* 2. 754.

[13] Compare the discussion of praise and imitation in *Or.* 1. 7.

[14] i.e. the emotional, desiring faculty, πάθος or the ἐπιθυμητικόν as opposed to λόγος; cf. e.g. *Orr.* 16. 4; 20. 4; 33. 7-8.

[15] *Il.* 3. 156-7.

tering wayward words, he fails to recognize their deceptiveness and embraces their sweetness, and is carried silently and gradually away by his pleasure, day by day, just like people on a voyage who fail to secure the winds they need for their proper course, and are instead carried away on a gentle current over a waveless sea, to deserted beaches and treacherous reefs. Then, without his realizing it, he is swept away into ignorance and then into hedonism, destinations more desolate than any beach and more treacherous than any reefs, all the while thoroughly enjoying his drifting, and delighting in the entertainment[16]— just like fever patients who gorge themselves on food and drink against doctor's orders. Comparing one evil (disease) with another (exertion), they prefer to be sick and enjoy themselves, sooner than to exert themselves and be cured. Many a resourceful doctor has before now tempered the bitterness of his cure with a small admixture of something sweeter; but neither Asclepius nor the Asclepiadae are indiscriminate purveyors of pleasure—that is the work of caterers.[17] Wayward words are no more worthy of respect than foods that pander to the belly. If you remove their power to confer benefit and replace it with impulsive, unalloyed pleasure, then you are voting words equal rights and an equal say to encourage indiscriminately all the shameful things that come to the soul via the senses under the escort of pleasure.

6   Let us leave these contenders to their symposia, like the miserable servants of belly and ear that they are. What we need is a style of utterance that stands straight and tall, calling out in a loud voice and raising our souls with it up above the earth and all the earthly sufferings that flow from pleasure and desire and ambition and lust and anger and grief and drunkenness. All these are things that the true orator who allies himself to philosophical argument must rise above. He must not be the sluggish and feeble practitioner of a meretricious art, whose only place is in the courtroom, where he gives his assistance to both sides indifferently. He must prove himself in every place and every role, as a prudent counsellor in the Assembly, a just contender in the courts, a decorous contestant at festivals, and a knowledgeable teacher in

---

[16] For the imagery, cf. above all *Or.* 30. 2.

[17] The comparison recalls Plato's discussion of τέχναι and κολακείαι in *Grg.* 462d ff. and 521d–522a; cf. *Orr.* 3. 6, 14. 8.

the schoolroom. He should not speak only about the long-dead Themistocles, nor in praise of bygone generations of Athenians, nor about a non-existent hero; he should not find himself denouncing adulterers and rapists for crimes of which he too is guilty.[18] He should be free of all such experiences, so as to make himself a candid scourge of wrongdoing. This is the nature of the contestant from a good palaestra; he must be full of words that are free from the taint of flattery, healthily trained, and able to command all who come within range with their persuasiveness and inspirational force.[19]

7   If we are going to need pleasure too to assist this process, give me the kind of pleasure that is roused by the strains of a trumpet, stationed in the midst of an army of hoplites and inspiring their souls with its call.[20] I need the kind of pleasure in an utterance that will preserve its grandeur without the addition of anything shameful; I need the kind of pleasure that Virtue will not refuse to have as her companion.[21] It is inevitable that grace and charm and desire and delight and all such pleasant names should go together with what is naturally beautiful. Thus the heavens are not merely beautiful, but the most beautiful of all sights; so too the sea covered in ships, rich fields of grain, wooded mountains, meadows in flower, and flowing streams. Achilles was the pleasantest of sights to behold (how could he not have been?), but not because of his tawny locks; Euphorbus too, after all, had beautiful hair,[22] but Achilles' beauty was at its most pleasing when illuminated by his martial prowess. Among rivers the Nile is the most pleasing to behold, but not for the volume of its waters; the Ister too flows well. But the Ister is not a fertile river, while the Nile is. ⟨Among gods⟩, Zeus is pleasantest to behold, but I would not dare dismiss the god's virtue and ascribe pleasure to him instead. In the case of

---

[18] A rejection of the topics of historical and legal declamation, for which see Russell (1983, chs. 2 and 6); cf. *Or.* 22. 3.

[19] The ideal form of oratory recommended in this paragraph is the same as Maximus advocates on *Or.* 1 (esp. §§ 7–8).

[20] The wording of Maximus' text is uncertain here, but the general sense is clear: cf. again *Or.* 1.

[21] The problem is familiar: the pursuit of sensual pleasure is vicious, but Virtue and the good life must not therefore be branded unpleasant; a different form of pleasure must be found for them. Cf. e.g. Plato *Resp.* 580d–583a; Arist. *NE* 10. 1–8.

[22] *Il.* 17. 51–2. With all these exempla, compare and contrast the peacock and the nightingale in § 2, with their unproductive beauty.

Phidias' statues, I realize the pleasure they give, but I keep my praise for the skill with which they are sculpted; I understand the pleasure that Homer's poetry can give, but I praise him for his more serious qualities.[23] I do not believe that even Heracles lived out his life without taste and experience of pleasure—Prodicus does not entirely convince me[24]— but there are manly pleasures that console the labours of Virtue, pleasures that do not accrue via the flesh or the senses, but which grow spontaneously from inside, when the soul becomes accustomed to rejoice in noble deeds and words and habits. Thus it was that Heracles rejoiced on his way to the pyre, and Socrates rejoiced as he waited in prison, in obedience to the law. Let us compare Socrates' celebrated cup with Alcibiades': which of them drank with less discomfort, Alcibiades his wine, or Socrates his hemlock?[25]

ORATION 26   Homer the Philosopher

Introduction

= 32 (1962) = 16 (Laur. Conv. Sopp. 4). The manuscript title—Εἰ ἔστιν καθ᾽ Ὅμηρον αἵρεσις, 'Whether there is a Homeric school of philosophy'— does not seem to get the emphasis entirely right: 'That Homer is a philosopher' would be better.

This lecture returns to the topic of *Or.* 4, propounding the same understanding of the role and nature of poetry, but concentrating on the single privileged case of Homer. Like *Or.* 17, it is particularly concerned with the links between Homer and Plato. See the introductions to both *Or.* 4 and *Or.* 17 for further discussion.

The first part of the lecture (§§ 1–3) praises Homer for his universal scope, and claims him as the greatest of all philosophers (1);

[23] Explained further in *Orr.* 4, 17, and 26.

[24] In the myth of Heracles at the Parting of the Ways in his *Horae*, retold by Xenophon in *Mem.* 2. 1. 21 ff.; cf. *Or.* 14. 1. The proposition that Heracles enjoyed his labours is advanced again in *Or.* 32. 7, but there it forms part of an Epicurean argument which Maximus ultimately rejects.

[25] Plato *Phdo* 117c, *Smp.* 213e–214a. For Alcibiades as the antitype to the philosopher, cf. *Orr.* 6. 6 and 7. 7. The combination of exempla in this final paragraph (the natural world, Homeric heroes, Nile and Ister, Zeus, Phidias, Homer, Heracles, Socrates, and Alcibiades) gives a particularly good illustration of Maximus' characteristic range; see Introduction, pp. xxxvii–xxxix.

explains the historical understanding of poetry and philosophy on which the claim relies (2); and insists on the particular closeness of the relationship between Homer and Plato. The second half of the lecture examines Homer's poetry, looking first at his strategy as a teacher (4–5a), then offering a series of allegorical readings to prove the presence in his poetry of ethical, political, theological, and physical doctrines consistent with those of Plato (ethics, §§ 5b–6 and 9b; theology and physics, 7–8; politics, 9a). It would be interesting to know how close a relationship this argument bears with that of Favorinus' lost treatise *On Homer's Philosophy* (for which, see Barigazzi 1966: 169–70).

Gregoras takes three excerpts from the lecture, from §§ 2 and 4; the compiler of Neap. 100 takes five, from §§ 1, 2, 3, 5 and 8. Poliziano noted the points made about Homer in §§ 1 and 4, Homer and Plato in § 3, Hesiod in § 4, and Socrates' philosophical adversaries in § 5, in the margins of Paris. gr. 1962 (foll. 110ᵛ–113ʳ). Franciscus Junius cites the distinction between τέχνη and ἀρετή (for which his translations are 'similitude' and 'symmetrie') from § 5, in *The Painting of the Ancients* III. ii. 8 (Aldrich *et al.* 1991: i. 234).

Oration

1   In Homer's own style I should like to summon a god to my aid as I speak. But which god?[1] The same one as he did, Calliope?[2]

> Tell me, Muse, of a man of many wiles, who wandered
> Far,[3]

but not one who journeyed through foreign lands and crossed rough seas and met with savages. Such are indeed the contents of his stories, but it was with his soul, a light thing that can travel further than any body, that he toured every quarter of the world and saw everything that there was to be seen,[4] all the movements

---

[1] Maximus' rhetorical question here echoes Plato *Phaedr.* 236d.

[2] Compare above all *Or.* 1. 2, where 'Calliope' is said to be Homer's name for philosophy; see also *Orr.* 32. 8, 39. 1, 40. 6. Homer in fact never names an individual Muse in either *Iliad* or *Odyssey*. Calliope is singled out as the principal Muse in Hesiod *Theog.* 79, and appealed to for philosophical inspiration by Empedocles (D–K B 131), but her specific connection with epic poetry is generally reckoned to be an invention of Hellenistic literary scholarship.   [3] *Od.* 1. 1–2.

[4] Compare the descriptions of the 'flight of the soul' in *Orr.* 9. 6, 10. 2 and 10, 11. 10, and 16. 6.

of the heavenly bodies, all that happens on earth, the councils of
the gods, the different natures of men, the shining of the sun, the
dance of the stars, the births of animals, the spreading sea, the
outflows of rivers, changing climates, the secrets of politics, household management, war, peace, marriage, farming, horsemanship,
and seamanship, all kinds of arts and crafts, different languages
and customs, men lamenting, rejoicing, grieving, laughing, fighting, growing angry, making merry, and sailing the seas.[5] When I
encounter Homer's stories I am quite unable to praise the man
from my own resources, but yet again need him to lend me some
of his verses, so as to avoid spoiling my praise by expressing it in
mere prose:

> I praise you, Homer, before all other mortals;
> Your teacher was Zeus' daughter, the Muse, or Apollo.[6]

It is quite improper to suppose the instruction of the Muses and
Apollo to be any other than that by which due order is introduced
into the soul. What else could that be than Philosophy? And how
are we to understand Philosophy, if not as detailed knowledge
of matters divine and human, the source of Virtue and noble
thoughts and a harmonious style of life and sophisticated habits?[7]

2   Once upon a time the kernel of this discipline clothed itself in
all kinds of different guises, so as to be able to guide the souls of
those who encountered it with gentle lessons.[8] Some cast their discourses in the form of rites and rituals, some in the form of myths,
some of music, and some of prophecies;[9] the beneficial element was
common to them all, but the external form varied from person to
person. As time went on, however, men became bumptious in their
wisdom, stripped off these coverings, and revealed philosophy

[5] For this picture of the comprehensive scope of Homer's poetry, cf. Plato *Ion*
531cd, Dio *Or*. 12. 68, [Plut.] *De Vit. et Poes. Hom*. 63 and 74 ff., Quint. *Inst*. 10.
1. 46–51.
[6] Cf. *Od*. 8. 487–8 (Odysseus' praise of the Phaeacian bard Demodocus).
[7] Maximus here embroiders on the standard definition of philosophy as 'knowledge of things human and divine': cf. Alcin. *Didasc*. 1. 152. 5–6 (with Whittaker
1990, ad loc.), Apul. *De Plat*. 2. 6. 228, Philo *Congr*. 79; Quint. *Inst*. 12. 2. 8; Cic.
Tusc. 4. 57 etc.; Clem. *Strom*. 6. 7. 54. 1. The formulation was originally Stoic (*SVF*
ii. 35–6, 1017), but had become common property; Platonists could connect it with
Resp. 486a6 and 593e1–2, *Smp*. 186b2, and *Leg*. 631b7.
[8] Cf. *Or*. 4. 3, and [Plut.] *De Vit. et Poes. Hom*. 92.
[9] Compare the account of different guises taken by sophists given by Protagoras
in Plato *Protag*. 316de.

naked and contemptible, common property within easy reach for all the world to associate with, the bare name of a noble pursuit released to wander amidst wretched sophistries.[10] This is why the poems of Homer and Hesiod, and indeed all the famous inspired poetry of ancient times, now count as mere myth. It is the stories they tell and the pleasantness of their verses and the brilliance of their composition that alone are enjoyed, for all the world like pipe-music or lyre-playing, while the truly noble element in them is overlooked and declared to have nothing to do with virtue.[11] And Homer, who was in fact the first philosopher of all, is banished from Philosophy.[12] Yet from the moment that there came to Hellas the clever ideas hatched in Thrace and Cilicia,[13] and Epicurus' atoms, and Heraclitus' fire, and Thales' water, and Anaximenes' air, and Empedocles' strife, and Diogenes' jar, and all those warring camps of the philosophers, clamouring against each other, the world has been full of mumbled words, as sophists clash with sophists, but there has been a terrible shortage of deeds. And that much-vaunted 'Good', over which the Greek world has divided into its hostile factions, has been completely lost to sight.[14]

3   Those early times, when Homer's poetry still had power, nourished and educated true, noble, and legitimate philosophical offspring. Plato too was a nurseling of Homer's poetry.[15] Even if he abjures him as a teacher, I can see the distinguishing marks and recognize the seeds.

> Such were his feet too, such were his hands,
> The glance of his eye, and his head and hair above.[16]

So true is this that I would make so bold as to say that Plato is more similar to Homer than he is to Socrates, however much he

---

[10] Compare again *Or.* 4. 3, and see the introduction to *Or.* 4 for this view of the decadence of modern philosophy.

[11] Compare Maximus' castigation of wrong attitudes to philosophical teaching in *Or.* 1. 6.

[12] Another echo of Plato's notorious banishing of Homer from the ideal state: cf. *Or.* 17.

[13] Thrace presumably because of Protagoras and Democritus of Abdera, Cilicia as the homeland of Chrysippus (cf. *Or.* 4. 3).

[14] Compare the disapproving account of philosophical diversity in *Or.* 29. 7.

[15] For this view of the affinity of Plato and Homer, cf. Heracl. *Alleg.* 18, and [Longinus] *Sublim.* 13. 3 and Dio *Or.* 36. 27 with Russell (1964, and 1992, ad locc.).   [16] *Od.* 4. 149–50.

may try to escape the one and cleave to the other. Do not assume that it is Plato's language, his vocabulary and his phrasing, that I am comparing to Homer. Those too do indeed flow from the same source and derive from Homer's harmony, as Lake Maeotis does from the Ocean, as the Black Sea does from Maeotis, as the Hellespont does from the Black Sea, and the ⟨Mediterranean⟩ from the Hellespont. No, it is Plato's and Homer's thoughts that I am comparing and finding to be related. I will tell you more about the other topic on another occasion;[17] but for now, let us take the discussion back to Homer's thought, and review it in the proper manner.

4   It seems to me that Homer, when he took up philosophy, with his most inspired of natures and his penetrating wisdom and his extraordinarily wide-ranging experience, chose to publicize it to the Greeks in the form of composition that then stood in the highest regard, namely verse. He did not wish this verse of his to be in Ionian, or pure Doric, or in Attic, but instead to take a form that all the Greeks could share.[18] So, with the thought that he was addressing them all, he combined the whole Greek language together into the form of a poem, and in this way made his verses not only pleasant but also comprehensible to all, as well as gratifying to each group individually. Realizing, furthermore, that the cognoscenti are few in any field, and that the masses usually have to be led by others, he decided against composing a separate kind of poetry for each group, in the way in which Hesiod detailed the genealogies of the heroes separately, starting from their mothers as he listed which was born from whom, while giving his account of the gods in a separate poem [and along with his account a theogony], and his helpful recommendations for human life, the works to be done and the days for doing them, in yet another.[19] This is not how Homer's poetry works; it neither separates everything out nor yet mixes it all indiscriminately together. The

---

[17] A promise not fulfilled in the surviving *Orations*.

[18] The mix of dialects in Homer's poetry is commented on also in Dio *Orr.* 11. 23 and 12. 66, and in [Plut.] *De Vit. et Poes. Hom.* 8–11, though none of these texts explains it in exactly the same way as Maximus does.

[19] i.e. in the *Catalogue of Women*, the *Theogony*, and the *Works and Days*. The bracketed phrase is to be removed, as a reader's addition: it is awkwardly expressed, and spoils Maximus' mannered care to avoid giving the actual titles of Hesiod's poems.

external form of this discourse is dictated by the myths he tells, the story of Troy and the experiences of Odysseus, but combined with them is a lucid theology, an account of political forms, and an account of human virtues and vices and experiences and disasters and successes.[20] Each of these topics has its own individual role in his poetry, as one might conceive of some elaborate musical instrument capable of producing many different sounds, all in harmony with each other. Or rather, think of it like this, if you have ever seen a collection of instruments, a flute being played and a lyre plucked, and a choir singing, and a trumpet too and a pipe and other kinds of instruments with their different names, each of which has been created by its own kind of workmanship, but has been assigned its place beside its neighbours to play just the one common tune.

5 To sum up, Homer's poetry can be envisaged in the following manner. Think of a philosophically educated painter, a Polygnotus or a Zeuxis, who paints with deliberation: his activity too has a twofold aspect, involving both artistic skill and Virtue. His artistic skill allows him to preserve an accurate image of reality in the shapes and colours he portrays; his virtue ensures that it is true beauty he imitates as he arranges his lines into a satisfying pattern.[21] This is how I should like you to think of Homer's poetry, as a twofold phenomenon, set in the form of myth *qua* poetry, but *qua* philosophy composed to promote the pursuit of Virtue and apprehension of the truth. For instance, his poetry portrays a young man from Thessaly and a king, Achilles and Agamemnon, the one impelled by rage into insulting action (Agamemnon), the ′other (Achilles) reacting to the insult with fury—allegories of the emotions, of youth and of authority.[22] Contrast with both of them Nestor, old in years, wise, and skilled

---

[20] i.e. Homer's poetry covers theology (in the Hellenistic schools regarded as part of physics), politics, and ethics: two-thirds of the total scope of philosophy, omitting only logic. Compare again [Plut.] *De Vit. et Poes. Hom.* 92 ff.

[21] This passage, and in particular the unusual use made in it of the word 'virtue' (ἀρετή) is discussed by Pollitt (1974: 148–9); comparing, *inter alia*, Plut. *Fort. Alex.* 335b, he suggests that the term refers to 'the artist's . . . intuitive understanding of the characteristic excellence of his subject' and detects a Platonizing tone in the distinction between the representation of shapes and colours and the imitation of true beauty.

[22] *Il.* 1. 101 ff. Contrast *Or.* 18. 8, where Achilles and Agamemnon are taken as representations of two different kinds of lover.

in speech.[23] Then again, Homer also includes Thersites in his poem, insolent in speech and deranged in mind—a perfect allegory of an insubordinate citizenry.[24] With him too we may contrast another character, a good man and a meticulous leader, moving through the host:

Whenever he found some king or eminent man,
He would stand by him and restrain him with courteous words. . . .
But whenever he saw one of the common people and found him shouting,
Then he would beat him with his staff.[25]

Do you not think that Socrates behaved in exactly the same way, paying genteel compliments to outstanding, regal individuals— Timaeus or Parmenides or any other regal visitor—and listening to what they had to say;

But whenever he saw one of the common people and found him shouting,

a Thrasymachus or a Polus or a Callicles, or any other insolent nuisance, administering a sound verbal beating?

6   Let us return to Homer, and to the Trojans in his poem. Here too you will see Virtue and Vice ranged against each other: Paris the profligate, the sober Hector; Paris the coward, Hector the hero.[26] You can compare their marriages too: admirable versus pitiable; accursed versus acclaimed; adulterous versus legitimate.[27] Consider too how the other virtues are shared out character by character: bravery to Ajax, acuity to Odysseus, courage to Diomedes, good counsel to ⟨Nestor. And as for⟩ Odysseus, Homer presents him to us as such a model of the good life and of perfect virtue, that he actually makes him the subject of one-half of all his poetry.[28] All these, in short, are a concise indication of what ought to receive a much longer treatment.

---

[23]   *Il.* 1. 247 ff.
[24]   *Il.* 2. 212 ff.
[25]   *Il.* 2. 188–9 + 198–9; cf. *Or.* 15. 9, where the lines are applied to Diogenes. Their application to Socrates follows Xen. *Mem.* 1. 2. 58–9.
[26]   For the perception of Paris and Hector as antithetical characters in ancient criticism, cf. *Σ* bT *Il.* 6. 390; the point is developed at length in Griffin (1980: 5–9). For Paris as an example of the wrong kind of lover, see also *Orr.* 20. 7 and 21. 3, and Plut. *Aud. Poet.* 18–19.
[27]   *Il.* 6. 313–529.
[28]   For Odysseus as exemplar of manly virtue, cf. § 9 below, with *Orr.* 4. 8, 11. 10, 14. 4, 15. 9, 34. 7–8, 38. 7, and Buffière (1956: 365–91).

7 If we are required also to produce some examples of Homer's thought about the gods, let us, consistently with the character of our discussion, compare all the rest with Plato's one God, matching the older with the more recent account. Well then, this being the manner in which we must settle the issue, does not Plato too speak of

Great Zeus in heaven?[29]

This Zeus of his rides in a winged chariot and leads the procession of the gods. Homer's leader, Zeus, says,

Now let no female deity, nor male god either,
Presume to cut acros the way of my word, but consent to it
All of you, so that I can make an end in speed to these matters.[30]

Whereupon his chariot is yoked for him and his horses run

Flying-footed, with long manes streaming of gold.[31]

A seaborne chariot is yoked for Poseidon too:

He drove across the waves, and the sea-beasts played in his path.[32]

Hades holds the third position of power in Homer's poem; the whole world in Homer is divided into three. Poseidon drew

the grey sea to dwell in for ever;
. . . Hades drew the lot of mists and darkness,

and Zeus the sky.[33] What a fair and philosophical division!

8 You will also find in Homer the origins and genesis of all kinds of other names,[34] which to the fool sound like myths, but to the philosopher are facts. He portrays the source of Virtue, but calls it Athena, standing beside its possessor

in all kinds of tribulation.[35]

He portrays the source of love, but attributes it to Aphrodite, who possesses the magic girdle and distributes desire.[36] He portrays the

---

[29] *Phaedr.* 246e; cf. *Or.* 4. 4, 10. 9. The quotation was a cliché: see Lucian *Pisc.* 22, *Bis Accus.* 33, *Rhet. Praec.* 26.
[30] *Il.* 8. 7–9. [31] *Il.* 8. 42. [32] *Il.* 13. 27. [33] *Il.* 15. 190–3.
[34] The word 'names' here may be a corruption of something else: perhaps 'activities' (ἐπιτηδεύματα).
[35] *Od.* 13. 301; for this allegorization of Athena, cf. *Orr.* 4. 8 and 38. 6, with Buffière (1956: 280 ff.). [36] *Il.* 14. 188–224.

source of the crafts, but attributes them to Hephaestus, who has control over fire and distributes the skills of the craftsman.[37] In his poetry, Apollo has control over choirs and dancing, the Muses over song, Ares over war, Aeolus over the winds, Oceanus over rivers, and Demeter over the fruits of the earth. Nothing in Homer lacks its god, or is devoid of a master or a first principle; everything is full of accounts of the gods, and the names of gods, and the arts of the gods. If we turn to the elements and their strife, you will see a battle on the Trojan plain, not between Trojans and Greeks, with men killing and being killed and the ground flowing with blood, but a battle between fire and a river, the one swollen and standing tall in an unbroken rushing wave, the other falling on his eddies with a mighty blast, scorching the river's locks and his beauty, his willows and tamarisks and clover and rushes, scorching too his inhabitants and nurselings:[38]

> The eels were suffering and the fish in the whirl of the water
> Who leaped out along the lovely waters in every direction.[39]

This battle would have had no end, had not Hera called a truce and put a stop to it and reconciled the warring elements.[40]

But enough of these allegories. Look to your own human concerns. [9] Here is a kind of constitution that has not been fabricated in the Piraeus or legislated for in Crete,[41] but is presented instead by a philosopher through a heroic tale in verse form. Autonomous rulers, taking counsel; noble champions defending their country; a chaste woman resisting her insolent suitors; a just king welcoming a wandering stranger;[42] a sober man working out his own salvation in the midst of every kind of trial. I can also show you whole states contrasted with each other, modelled by Homer in words and by Hephaestus in gold:

> in the one, a wedding celebration,[43]

with singing and dancing, and kings dispensing justice, and their people following;

---

[37] *Il.* 18. 369 ff.   [38] *Il.* 21. 324 ff.   [39] *Il.* 21. 353–4.
[40] This allegorization of the battle of the gods as a representation of the strife of the physical elements seems to be one of the oldest of all, going back to Theagenes of Rhegium (reported in Σ B *Il.* 20. 67): cf. Heracl. *Alleg.* 52–8, with Buffière (1956: 101 ff.).   [41] In Plato's *Resp.* and *Leg.*
[42] Alcinous, in *Od.* 7. 167 ff.
[43] *Il.* 18. 491.

But around the other city there sat the hosts of two armies.[44]

Even if you mistrust this example, you will find no lack of more truthful accounts. Consider the two island states, that of the Phaeacians and that of the Ithacans. Respect rules in the one, anarchy in the other; in the one, law-abiding nobles, in the other, lawless suitors; in the one they regard their king

like a god as he goes on his way,[45]

in the other they plot against his marriage. Each state of affairs is shown to have its own fitting outcome: in the one case, unbroken joy, lives free from pain, hospitality to strangers, safe sea-voyaging, and a fertile land; in the other, wholesale destruction in the midst of pleasure. Such is the end of Vice and insolence, such the end of licence unrestrained.[46] And do you not see how Odysseus himself is preserved by Virtue, and the courage born of it, as he battles against all kinds of misfortune? For that is the significance of the moly he finds on Circe's isle, and of the veil given him at sea.[47] It is Virtue that rescues him from the hands of Polyphemus, that brings him back safely from the land of the dead, that builds his raft, that wins over Alcinous, that resists the suitors when they pelt him, Irus when he wrestles with him, and Melanthius when he insults him, that brings freedom to his hearth and home, that avenges the insult to his marriage—and that makes him truly 'godly' and 'like the immortals', as Plato maintains the happy man to be.[48]

---

[44] *Il.* 18. 509.

[45] *Od.* 8. 173.

[46] For this political reading of the *Odyssey*, cf. [Plut.] *De Vit. et Poes. Hom.* 175-91, with Buffière (1956: 343-64). The positive attitude adopted here towards the Phaeacians is not the universal norm: contrast, for example, Heracl. *Alleg.* 79, where they are portrayed as the forebears of Epicurus.

[47] Moly (*Od.* 10. 302-6): cf. *Or.* 29. 6; Heracl. *Alleg.* 73; Σ T *Od.* 10. 305; *SVF* i. 526 (Cleanthes). Leucothea's veil (*Od.* 5. 351-3): cf. *Or.* 11. 10.

[48] The final sentence alludes to the standard doxographer's view of Plato's doctrine of the end of human life, as 'likeness to God' (ὁμοίωσις θεῷ): see Alcin. *Didasc.* 2. 153. 5-9 and 28. 181. 19-20 with Whittaker (1990, ad locc.).

ORATION 27   Virtue and Science

Introduction

= 33 (1962) = 17 (Laur. Conv. Sopp. 4). The manuscript title—*Eἰ τέχνη
ἡ ἀρετή*, 'Whether Virtue is a Science'—applies better to the first half of
the lecture than to the second.

With this lecture, the focus shifts from civic and practical ethics to
theoretical ethics: to questions concerning the nature of Virtue and
of the Human Good, the correct choice of ends, and the proper
evaluation of possible means to those ends. These will be the
concerns of all but three or four of the remaining pieces.[1]

As emerges most clearly from the final paragraphs (§§ 8–9), the
real topic of the lecture (somewhat obscured by the title given in
the manuscripts) is the acquisition of Virtue. It is Maximus' version
of the hoary Socratic question of the teachability of *ἀρετή*,
bequeathed to posterity by Plato's *Protagoras* and *Meno*. The
answer he offers is the entirely conventional one that both theoretical learning and practical habituation of the character are
required, and that both must have a favourable natural endowment to build on: i.e. the answer first fully articulated by Aristotle
(*NE* 10. 9) and long since absorbed by Middle Platonism (Alcin.
Didasc. 28; Apul. *De Plat.* 2. 10. 234). What makes the lecture
more difficult to follow than it might be is Maximus' decision to
approach the issue via the question of whether Virtue is a science
(*τέχνη*) rather than by asking directly whether it is teachable, or
how it is to be acquired.

§ 1 establishes the proposition that Virtue is not a science, and
acknowledges how paradoxical it is liable to sound. §§ 2–3 seek to
ease any worry that Virtue is thereby degraded, by explaining the
difference between a science and its (equally prized) product.
§§ 4–7a then offer a closer examination of the nature both of
Virtue and of Science: Science is analysed into three categories,
two of which will be relevant to the cultivation of Virtue (4); Virtue
is explained in terms of Platonic psychology, and the imposition of

---

[1] *Orr.* 28 and 41 clearly belong in the group devoted to questions of the soul, the
cosmos, and the hierarchy of rational beings; *Or.* 34 equally clearly belongs in the
set dealing with civic and practical ethics. *Or.* 37 can be taken almost equally comfortably either with the latter or with the third, 'theoretical' set.

order on the passions by reason (5–7a). Finally, §§ 7b–9 apply these analyses to answer the question of how Virtue is to be acquired. The main point on which Maximus wishes to insist is clear enough—that theoretical learning on its own is not sufficient, since Virtue crucially depends on the *application* of this learning in the control of the passions—but (particularly in § 7) a certain laxity and allusiveness make the detail of his exposition obscure (see notes ad loc.).

Substantial scholia in the margins of Paris. gr. 1962, summarizing and schematizing the contents of §§ 4 and 7, testify to interest (or puzzlement?) among Late Antique readers of the lecture: see Hobein (1910: 323, 328), or Trapp (1994: 345). The compiler of Neap. 100 takes one excerpt, from § 1, and Poliziano notes the definition of τέχνη in § 4 and the anatomy of the soul in § 5 in the margins of Paris. gr. 1962 (foll. 115ʳ–116ʳ).

Oration

1   How could one believe a philosopher who claimed that Virtue was not a science, but something else? It would be difficult for *any-thing* to count as a science if Virtue did not. Unless of course we are going to concede that ploughs and shields and ships and walls are all the products of different sciences, but simultaneously maintain that what sets them to work and controls them, putting the usefulness of each at the disposal of any possessor when he needs it, and co-ordinating the combined benefits of all of them to realize a single aim,[2] is no science at all. It would be awful, worse than awful, for heaven's sake, if potters and cobblers and carpenters all learn with a view to acquiring a science, but philosophers, though learning and having the cultivation of Virtue as their aim, learn it not as a science but as something that can be taught them without the aid of science at all.[3] [Well said!][4]

2   Hold on a minute! That is by no means an inappropriate or an artless exordium of yours. I applaud your 'science', but let me con-

---

[2] Maximus here seems to echo Aristotle's notion of 'architectonic' sciences: see esp. *NE* 1. 1, 1094ᵃ9 ff. (the co-ordination of subordinate sciences by πολιτική).
[3] For the indignant comparison between philosophy and the arts and crafts, cf. *Or.* 3. 1. As there, it strikes a consciously Socratic note (cf. e.g. Plato *Grg.* 491a, *Smp.* 221e, Xen. *Mem.* 1. 2. 37).
[4] A reader's comment, interpolated into the text: cf. *Or.* 16. 3.

sider what exactly you mean its essence to be. You say that it is a science that allows the potter to learn to make pots and the cobbler to cut leather and the carpenter to work wood. This I grant you: each of these craftsmen learns to do what he learns to do through the operation of a science. But the end and purpose of each science is not simply that one person should learn it from another. The passage of knowledge from one to another is brought about by the process of learning; but the proper function of sciences in general is not for science to produce science, but for the potter to produce a jar, the piper a piece of pipe-music, and the general a victory—each of which is something else besides the science, science's product not science itself. For if something is not a science, that does not automatically mean that it is positively *un*scientific: to talk of something being 'unscientific' is to talk of the absence of science, where science is needed; but something produced by a science, yet different from that science, is simply 'not a science'.

3   Am I expressing myself clearly, in your opinion, or should I give you a more lucid explanation, of the following kind? You use the word 'medicine' for one science, and 'sculpture' for another, do you not? And the end and purpose of each is not medicine in the case of medicine and sculpture in the case of sculpture, but a statue in the case of sculpture and health in the case of medicine? Well then, do you think that Virtue is anything other than the health and comeliness of the soul?[5] Consider the matter like this. Start by assigning three separate sciences to three separate sorts of raw material, soul and body and stone; in each case the raw material lacks form, and the sciences, bringing to each its proper configuration, clothe stone in orderly shapes so as to give it the appearance of some recognizable object, the body in harmonious blendings of its constituents so as to produce the proportions that constitute health, and the soul in symmetry and responsiveness so as to produce the adornment of Virtue. If you call any of these outcomes a science, transferring the name of the agent to that of the product because of the kinship between them, you seem to me to be doing the same as if you were to give the name 'sun' to the sun's rays, which are something other than the sun, and not the sun itself.

---

[5] For the analogy, cf. *Or.* 7. 1, with n. 3.

4 Consider what I am saying from both sides of the question: let us examine both what science is, and what Virtue is. Do you take it that a science is anything other than a rational procedure aiming at some end? One kind proceeds through manual effort to manufacture some physical object, which we call its 'product', such as the house produced by a builder, or the ship produced by a shipwright, or the picture by a painter; a second kind of science yields some form of activity, which, however, it does not produce in an entirely disembodied way—victory in the case of generalship, health in the case of medicine, justice in the case of politics; yet a third kind of science is constituted by pure reason, deriving its strength from its own resources without the need for any physical medium and dealing solely with itself, as with the sciences of geometry and mathematics, and all others that have purely intelligible ends involving neither physical process nor physical product.[6] Well then, to which of these three categories of science are we to assign Virtue, if indeed it is a science? To the productive category? Not even you would say that. Perhaps, however, you will hesitate between the practical and the theoretical categories? I do not want to say that either of them is unconnected with Virtue. Rather, I prefer to combine the two and add something else into the bargain, and to say that the compound derived from all of them is distinct from each of its constituent elements; in the same way as, if someone said that the human body is fire or earth or air or, come to that, water, I would say that the body is neither fire nor earth nor air nor water, because the combination of all these ingredients is not the same as any one of the constituents from which it is produced.[7]

5 How is it then that Virtue, though it has elements of both theory and practice about it, is still not a science? Follow me as I explain the matter to you like this. The doctrine I will tell you of is not mine; it comes from the Academy, and is a product of Plato's inspiration and a native of his hearth, which found acceptance

[6] This threefold classification of sciences is a scholastic commonplace, going back to Aristotle (esp. *Met.* 5. 1, 1025^b19-28). Diogenes Laertius attributes it in different places to Plato (3. 84) and to Zeno (7. 90), and it is used also by Sextus (*Math.* 11. 197).
[7] The analogy seems a clumsy one: the body is *composed of* its constituent elements, but—as Maximus is at such pains to insist—Virtue is *produced by* the combined operations of theoretical and practical science.

with Aristotle too. In fact, I can trace it still further back, since I suspect that it came to Athens from Sicily, fine merchandise conveyed to Old Greece by certain Pythagoreans.[8] This is how the theory goes. The human soul is divided in the first instance into two aspects, reason and emotion.[9] When either of these two becomes defective and subject to a disordering motion, this is given just the one comprehensive and wholly discreditable name, Vice. The sources and points of origin of this discreditable state are to be found in the flooding and overflow of one of the two constituents, when the emotions boil up and wash over the soul,[10] bringing confusion to the shoots and growths of reason.[11] Just as rivers in winter spate flood over their proper limits on to the fields that farmers have ploughed and sown, and pose their muddy threat to the survival and the good order of their estates, so too the soul is shaken out of its powers of reasoning by an imbalance of emotion, whereupon unnatural growths of false and defective opinion spring up in it. This is precisely what happens to people when they get drunk: over-indulgence rouses the diseases slumbering within, like reptiles from their lairs, thus throwing the intelligence into confusion and forcing it to speak with the reptiles' voices.[12]

6　If you need a still clearer image, this defective state of the soul can be compared to a species of mob rule, of the kind that comes about when the good element in a city is forced into subjection in its entirety and the mindless rabble begins to assume control, emboldened by the exercise of power without fear of retribution.[13] I take it that it is inevitable that such a city should be a cacophony of competing voices and emotions, devoid of unity and full of

---

[8] The idea that Plato depended for his psychology (and other doctrines) on Pythagoras was widespread: see e.g. Cic. *Tusc.* 4. 5. 10, Apul. *Flor.* 15. 26. His immediate teachers are named by Diog. Laert. as Philolaus and Eurytus (3. 6).

[9] Note the qualification 'in the first instance', which suggests that a second, tripartite division is also allowed for: cf. [Plut.] *Plac.* 898e, where both Plato and Pythagoras are said to regard the soul as primarily bipartite, but secondarily tripartite. For the former, cf. *Or.* 20. 4, with n. 6; for the latter, *Or.* 16. 4.

[10] The picture of the boiling passions echoes Plato *Tim.* 70b.

[11] For the Platonizing imagery of the 'shoots and growths' of reason, cf. *Orr.* 5. 8, 10. 4, and 25. 5.

[12] With this picture of the confused, 'drunken' soul, compare in general *Or.* 10. 9. The image of the beasts within, echoing Plato *Resp.* 588b ff., recurs in *Or.* 33. 5 and 8.

[13] Another Platonic echo, of the city-soul analogy of the *Republic*; cf. *Or.* 16. 4, with n. 10.

desires of every kind, intemperate in its pursuit of pleasure, impossible to restrain in its anger, disproportionate in its distribution of honours, unstable in times of success, and hard to revive in times of disaster. When Pericles is dead and gone, and Aristides is in exile, Socrates condemned to death, Nicias sent off against his will, when Cleon sets his heart on Sphacteria, Thrasyllus on Ionia, Alcibiades on Sicily, and others on other lands and seas, and the idle, disorderly, mercenary, fickle mob shares their desires, it is inevitable that these desires should spawn slavery and disorder and tyranny, and all those other states that men shudder to name. The soul too has its wicked demagogues and its licentious mob, Alcibiadeses and Cleons in droves, who will not allow it to sit at rest and make room for the rational principles within it.[14] This is the nature of evil in the human constitution.

7 Virtue—the real topic of this long discussion of ours—lies in the opposite state of affairs, precisely that brought about by the Spartan constitution, under which the disorderly mob of which we have spoken is subordinated, while the few and the good rule: the latter ensure a security from which the former benefit; the latter command and the former obey; and the joint achievement of both is freedom. Each one needs the other: the rulers need subjects, and the subjects need rulers to keep them safe. It is just the same with a soul that is in a good condition: reason offers security, and the emotions accept it; reason imposes due measure, and the emotions have due measure imposed on them;[15] and the joint achievement of both is happiness.

I should like you please to assign everything that makes up theoretical science to the category of reason, and what is made orderly by theoretical science to the category of emotion: call the former 'wisdom' (which is a *kind* of knowledge), and the latter (which is a *product* of knowledge) call 'Virtue'.[16] If you change the

---

[14] For this use of 5th-century history as a source of moral images, compare *Orr.* 6. 5–6, 7. 4 and 7.

[15] By suggesting that the aim is the moderation rather than the extirpation of the passions, Maximus here seems to be siding implicitly with the 'Peripateticizing' rather than the 'Stoicizing' wing of Middle Platonism: cf. Diog. Laert. 5. 31 (Arist.); Alcin. *Didasc.* 30. 184. 14 ff.; Philo *Leg. All.* 3. 132; Clem. *Strom.* 2. 39. 4; and contrast Apul. *De Plat.* 2. 20. 247. See also Lilla (1971: 99–106), and Dillon (1977: 77–8, 151, 196, 241–2, 302).

[16] This clearly connects with Maximus' earlier insistence (§§ 1–3) that Virtue is the product of a science, not itself a science, but in other ways it does not seem to

names around and call knowledge Virtue, I will ask you what brought it about; because that is what knowledge will be, the producer not the product. Do you call knowledge the science that deals with sciences? I hear what you say. Do you call it knowledge of forms of knowledge? I understand, and I will accept your definition if you will grant me just one trifling concession. Call science the science that deals with sciences, and knowledge the knowledge of forms of knowledge; abandon one of the two elements and I will make my peace with your definition.[17] But if, while keeping knowledge as it is, you remove the emotions and transfer their configuration to knowledge, you are doing just the same as if someone were to keep Phidias' artistry as it is, while removing his material and transferring its name to his artistry.[18] Do you want knowledge to rule over a well-lived life? Let it do so. Do you want reason to rule? Let it indeed be sole ruler,

> since cunning Cronus' son granted it this rank.[19]

But whom does it rule? What subordinates are you assigning to it? Who will put its commands into practice with their labour? The body? Stop this instant and consider what you are doing! You are leapfrogging the chain of command, from the general straight down to the baggage-train. Do you not see the hierarchy? The general, then his lieutenants, and after them the detachment

cohere so well with what he has said previously: (1) he has moved from talking of the product of a τέχνη to talking of the product of an ἐπιστήμη; and (2) he seems to have forgotten his insistence (in § 4b) that Virtue is the joint product of *two* kinds of science, not just one. What one wants him to say at this point is that Virtue is the product both of theoretical knowledge (σοφία) and of practical wisdom (φρόνησις), of which the latter is responsible for transmitting the dictates of the former to the lower division of the soul; otherwise there would seem to be little point in distinguishing between forms of science as carefully as he has in § 4.

[17] Maximus here plays with the definition of philosophy as τέχνη τεχνῶν καὶ ἐπιστήμη ἐπιστημῶν, known also from, for example, Philo *Spec. Leg.* 4. 156, Themist. fr. 5. 300c, and Julian *Or.* 6. 183a. His quibbling might have had a more obvious point to it had he been at pains in the rest of the lecture to distinguish clearly between a τέχνη and an ἐπιστήμη.

[18] i.e. it is as ridiculous to treat knowledge (which is a question of pure intellect) as identical to Virtue (which is a matter of the proper organization of the passions) as it would be to speak of an artist's raw materials as responsible for their own organization into a work of art ('Look what Phidias' gold and ivory have done')— but both the thought and its expression are awkward. For Phidias as the artist *par excellence* in philosophical discussion, cf. *Orr.* 2. 10, 3. 10, 8. 6, 15. 6, 17. 1, and 25. 7, with, for example, Plato *Protag.* 311ce, Arist. *NE* 6. 7, 1141ᵃ10, Cic. *Orator* 2. 8, and Dio *Or.* 12.

[19] *Il.* 2. 204 (with a paraphrase of 203 in the preceding line).

commanders, then the hoplites, the skirmishers, and the archers. The chain of command descends by degrees through the whole army from the greatest to the least.[20]

8   I realize the objection that is going to spring to mind. God governs this whole universe of ours with beauty and artistry and knowledge. Of course he does. What then is his knowledge if not Virtue? If you call God's knowledge Virtue, I will not begrudge you the use of the word. Unlike men, God does not have a soul divided into ruling and subordinate parts; he is of a single nature, pure intelligence and knowledge and reason.[21] But if you transfer the name of the subordinate element to the ruling element in cases where there *is* a combination of superior and inferior, I will tolerate this as a manner of speaking, but I will refuse to grant the substantial point behind it. If you wish, call knowledge a virtue; but don't call Virtue a form of knowledge. This will prove a deceptive and a dangerous thing to say, God knows, if men become convinced that mere qualities of theoretical knowledge and a handful of doctrines can bring Virtue in with them when they enter the soul. If that were true, then sophists would be a truly valuable class of person, those garrulous polymaths stuffed with learning, trading in it, and selling to anyone who asks. They set up an open market in Virtue; roll up and buy![22]

9   If on the other hand, though the theoretical prescriptions for Virtue are clear and accessible, and teachers and doctrines are everywhere, their passage is obstructed from within by rough and savage emotions and bad habits and wicked practices and strange desires and the wrong kind of upbringing, you should reflect as

[20] For this idea of natural hierarchy, and of the indispensability of intermediate stages, cf. *Orr.* 9. 1–4 and 11. 12, with notes ad locc. Maximus' point here (perhaps made too compendiously to be very clear) is that the lower division of the bipartite soul is an essential intermediary between intellect and the body (and thus that Virtue must involve the training of this quasi-rational part of the person as well as the acquisition of purely theoretical knowledge by the rational part).

[21] Since the transcendent supreme God of Platonism is incorporeal (Alcin. *Didasc.* 10. 166. 1; Apul. *De Plat.* 1. 5. 190), he cannot have a lower division to his soul, since such a lower division is by definition tied to the operations of the body. Theiler (1930: 53) compares Cic. *De Fin.* 2. 115, and sees a reflection of the thought of Antiochus.

[22] For the use of the term 'sophist' to dismiss empty theorists with no interest in the practical cultivation of Virtue, cf. *Orr.* 1. 8 and 30. 1. The image of sophists as traders follows Plato *Protag.* 313c and *Soph.* 231d.

follows.[23] The first requirement is a good natural disposition, like the foundation of a wall to be built, followed by an upbringing and habits calculated to preserve that initial disposition. These engender in the soul a feeling of kinship with all that is noble, which grows over time, and matures as you yourself grow older. Finally, to crown the whole process, science must supervene to set the seal of stability on the balance of the emotions.[24] This is what produces a happy soul and a healthy life and right opinions, organized into a harmonious blend. This is what God decrees and what makes a man good, the control of the emotions by reason, and voluntary obedience to the dictates of knowledge. Vice is involuntary,[25] a product of the pull of pleasure.

ORATION 28   The Cure for Pain

Introduction

= 34 (1962) = 18 (Laur. Conv. Sopp. 4). The manuscript title—πῶς ἄν τις ἄλυπος εἴη, 'How one might be free from pain'—takes its cue from the opening sentence of the lecture.

This lecture, which discusses a topic related to that of Or. 7, belongs more closely with the psychological–cosmological group than with the items on either side of it, both of which belong to the group dealing with questions of theoretical ethics. Its positioning is perhaps the result of a hasty assumption based on the title: ἀλυπία is after all one possible answer to the question τί τέλος φιλοσοφίας (the title of Or. 29).

The main thesis of Or. 7—that psychological disorders are more serious than physical—is reasserted at the end of the present lecture (§ 4), to support the conclusion that there can be such a thing as a single, unified, psychosomatic therapy of the kind once practised by the centaur Chiron (§ 1). The core of the lecture

---

[23] The account of moral education which follows is built round the familiar scholastic triad of nature, habituation, and instruction (φύσις, ἄσκησις–ἔθος, διδασκαλία–μάθησις); see Orr. 1. 5 (with n. 22) and 12. 9.

[24] The words 'stability' and 'balance' again hint at the ideal of μετριοπάθεια: cf. § 7 with n. 15 above.

[25] A concluding glance at the central Socratic doctrine οὐδεὶς ἑκὼν ἁμαρτάνει (Plato Protag. 345d, etc.).

(§§ 2-3) is a discussion of the mechanics of pain, both physical and psychological, with special reference to the interaction between the two kinds. The topic is discussed by Plato in the *Timaeus* (81e ff., esp. 86b ff.), but Maximus' treatment is more indebted to the interest shown in it by the Hellenistic schools: see nn. 8 and 11 below.

The lecture is also a notably short one—about half the average length. This is however unlikely to be an indication that it is incomplete, given the obviously symmetrical structure, and the coherence of the argument.

Gregoras takes one excerpt, from § 2, and the compiler of Neap. 100 three, from §§ 2 and 4. Poliziano noted the description of Chiron in § 1 in the margin of Paris. gr. 1962 (fol. 118ʳ), and Robert Burton cites it in *The Anatomy of Melancholy* 2. 2. 4. 1 (Faulkner *et al.* 1989-94: ii. 70).

Oration

1   How might a man achieve freedom from pain in his soul? Do we need a doctor for this too, just as we do in the case of bodily pains, and besides a doctor, a pharmacopoeia and a set regimen finely attuned to the production of health? Who then will this doctor to our souls be? What will his drugs be like? And what form will the regimen he prescribes take? Because of my deep affection for everything old, I do not see any distinction between sciences here, but believe the poets when they say that there was once a man skilled in medicine who lived on Pelion.[1] They call him Chiron,[2] and his science was one that applied to both domains: not only did he train the bodies of those who came to him to a peak of fitness by making them hunt and climb mountains and run and sleep on beds of leaves and eat raw meat and drink from streams;[3] he also trained their souls never to fall short of their bodies'

---

[1] For the 'primitivist' stance, and the view of poetry assumed here, cf. *Or.* 4, esp. §§ 1-3.

[2] Chiron is already in Homer the teacher of Achilles and 'most righteous of the centaurs' (*Il.* 11. 831-2) and a great doctor (*Il.* 4. 219), as he is also in Pindar (*Pyth.* 3. 1 ff. and 61 ff.; *Nem.* 3. 43 ff.; etc.). In later references the emphasis falls more on his pedagogical than on his medical skills: e.g. Plato *Resp.* 391c, *Hipp. Min.* 371d; Xen. *Smp.* 8. 23; Dio *Or.* 58; Lucian *Dial. Mort.* 26. 1.

[3] What Chiron is here credited with is essentially a Spartan regime (cf. *Or.* 23. 2); the one extraneous detail—raw meat—is a nod at the diet supposedly adopted by the young Achilles when under the centaur's care (Apollod. 3. 13. 6).

demands in the quickness of their powers of reasoning and the manliness of their emotions.[4] This was how he gained the reputation of combining the highest skills of the doctor with the highest standards of morality; and the poets gave both names to his one science. If now this science has succumbed to internal conflict, do not let yourself be surprised by the fact, unless you can show me that medicine too is a single, unified science, that it does not take on different forms, each one dealing with a different part of the body, one the eyes, another the ears, and so on, and that it doesn't run the risk of disappearing completely as it divides itself up on every possible occasion into mean and tiny portions; just as they say happened to the Macedonian Empire after the death of Alexander, when it fell into the hands of many individuals, none of whom was thought to deserve power over his whole kingdom.[5]

2   Why then has Chiron intruded into our discussion? Let us consider the matter together, and let me ask whether his presence is not entirely apposite. If you acknowledge the term 'physical pain'—as indeed you do—we see that it takes two forms: the first of which is the one that invades the entire body equally, mingling with pretty well the whole of it and upsetting its natural state, as fire does to iron—indeed, this is precisely what we laymen call 'fire', but the doctors, seeking to be reassuring, have changed the name, thinking that it would seem less frightening to us if it were called 'fever' rather than 'fire'.[6] The other kind of physical pain comes about when it is just one part of the body that contains the origin and source of the sickness, and the disorder, starting from there, drags in and involves the whole of the rest of the body in the pain. The passage of the pain in cases like this from the sick to the healthy part of the body is of the most rapid, as you can discover if you stub your toe: as they say, the pain runs from your toenail to your head in the twinkling of an eye.[7]

---

[4] i.e. he sought to inculcate both theoretical and practical excellence.

[5] This picture of the relative decadence of modern medicine compared to ancient, seen in its increasing tendency to diversity and specialization, again echoes the picture given in *Or.* 4. 1–2, and can also be compared to the view of the history of philosophy advanced in *Orr.* 26. 2 and 29. 7.

[6] πυρετός rather than πῦρ; Varro (*Sat.* fr. 33) similarly derives 'febris' from 'fervor'.

[7] This seems to echo Plato *Resp.* 462cd, both for the specific example, and for the general point that the pain of one part of the body is shared by the whole. The latter point was controversial: contrast Lucret. 3. 147–51.

Do you think that this could happen if the soul were not distributed everywhere throughout the whole body and mingled with
it like light with air?[8] Or rather let us put it like this: just as the
smell of incense is perceptible even to people who are far away,
because it infiltrates the intervening air with its fragrance, or just
as in the case of the eyes colours strike them from a distance
because they also have inscribed their character on the air,[9] so too
you may take it that the soul pervades the whole body, and that
no portion of the body is inanimate. (I except hair and nails from
this, just as I do leaves in the case of trees, as they too are the most
insensitive constituents in their own proper structure, that of
plants.[10]) Such being the relationship of soul to body, the one is
implicated in the discomforts and pleasures of the other, and pain,
though it has a physical cause, is none the less an experience of
the soul.

That is one source of human pain. Here now is the second,
which works the other way round to the first, issuing from the soul
and ending up in the body. When the soul is racked by grief, then
the body too is affected to some degree and pines, sometimes
shedding tears from the eyes, sometimes turning pale all over and
losing weight, as happens with the pains of love and the gnawing
of poverty and the self-neglect occasioned by grief. Passion and
anger and jealousy too arouse pains in the body; indeed there is
not a single discordant motion of the soul that does not.[11]

3   Why have I reminded you of all this? The point is that if
pain can both be dispatched to the body from the soul, and enter
the soul from the body, then it would be reasonable if only one
form of medical skill were required to cure it, just as the Euripus

---

[8] This picture of the relationship of the soul to the body, with its suggestion of
a total blend, has a Stoicizing ring to it: see e.g. Hierocles, *Elem.*, col. 4. 38–53
(= 53 B (5–6) L-S). Epicurean theory would talk of an even dispersal of mobile soul-
atoms, rather than a blend, and Platonism, following *Tim.* 69d ff., would tie the
three segments of the soul to a limited number of bodily organs.

[9] These accounts of smell and sight seem to be too vaguely phrased to recall any
specific theory (or theories) of perception. The statement that colours 'inscribe' the
air is faintly reminiscent of Democritus' concept of ἀποτύπωσις (Theophrast. *De
Sensu* 50 = Democr. A 135 D-K), but that is perhaps coincidental.

[10] Cf. Plato *Tim.* 64c.

[11] Such phenomena were frequently noted in discussions of the relationship
between body and soul, but usually served (as in Nemesius *Nat. Hom.* 32 (*SVF* i.
518), or Lucret. 3. 136 ff.) as evidence of the soul's corporeality.

needs only one form of steersmanship to steer a safe course through it.[12]

Let that suffice as my treatment of this topic. But who can now tell us about the medical skill that is going to banish the ills that assault us from both of those two directions? I for my part am at a loss to know whether I will be able to discover anyone skilled in this science, in the manner of Chiron, of whom we spoke, so as to reap that twofold benefit; I neither trust his contrivances (the task is a great one, more arduous than Ossa and Olympus),[13] nor yet do I entirely distrust them. What might the all-daring soul not devise if it wanted to?

4   Suspended as I am between trust and mistrust, I think I will take the following route to settle the issue, in the face of my inability to know for sure. I suspect that there is indeed just one science, but that it does not work on two objects, soul and body; instead, by dealing directly with the superior element alone, it also cures the other, inferior one. Even as I speak, Socrates' remark to Charmides comes to mind: not exactly his 'Thracian incantation', but the other way round. Socrates says that when the whole is cured, the part is cured too, and that it is impossible for soundness to be restored to the part before it comes to the whole.[14] He is quite right in this, and I agree with him as far as the body is concerned; but I maintain that the reverse is true in the case of the combination of body and soul. If the one constituent in any person is in good condition, then necessarily the whole must be too; it cannot be that one of the two constituents is, while the other is not. The association of better with worse makes the security of the worse depend on that of the better. Or do you think that a man whose soul is healthy takes any account of the onset of pain from wounds or from any other form of physical ill-being? By no means.[15]

This is the kind of medical skill that we must seek out and test for; this is the kind of health that must be supplied and hunted

---

[12] For the Euripus as an image of inconstancy (particularly the inconstancy of matter), cf. *Orr.* 5. 6, 10. 5, 41. 3. Here the channel's distinctive two-way flow (e.g. Strabo 9. 2. 8) makes it an appropriate illustration of the point that pain can itself flow either from body to soul or vice versa.

[13] The reference is to the assault of the Aloidae on the heavens; cf. *Or.* 12. 1.

[14] Plato *Charm.* 155e ff.

[15] The point is argued at length in *Or.* 7.

down, the kind that will be followed by physical relief too, or if not, at least by a disregard for physical suffering.

ORATIONS 29–33   The True End of Life: Virtue or Pleasure?

Introduction

= 35 + 1–4 (1962) = 19 + 31–4 (Laur. Conv. Sopp. 4). The manuscript titles—τί τέλος φιλοσοφίας; (29), περὶ ἡδονῆς· ὅτι εἰ καὶ ἀγαθόν, ἀλλ᾽ οὐ βέβαιον α΄, β΄, γ΄ (30–2), τί τέλος φιλοσοφίας; (33): 'What is the end of philosophy?' (29), 'On Pleasure, to the effect that even if it is a Good, it is nevertheless not secure' 1, 2, 3 (30–2), 'What is the end of philosophy?' (33)—are unsatisfactory. Though they give *some* indication that the five lectures make a connected sequence, they fail to convey its rationale; and the proposition about Pleasure which they highlight is one that the lectures themselves reject (*Or.* 31. 1–2).

A sequence of lectures (of the same overall length as *Orr.* 18–21, but made up of five items, not four) devoted to the question of the Human Good, conceived as a debate between the competing claims of Virtue (perfected Reason) and Pleasure. The whole (allowing for the difference in scale) might be described as Maximus' *De Finibus*: Cicero too presents the essential issue as the choice between Virtue and Pleasure (*De Fin.* 2. 14. 44, 3. 1. 1), and gives a large proportion of his treatise to the exposition and criticism of Epicurean hedonism.

Or. 29 expounds the problem. All human beings pursue Happiness (εὐδαιμονία), but have wildly differing views of where and how it is to be found, as the cases of Sardanapallus, Cambyses, Xerxes (§ 1), Pisistratus, Polycrates, Philip, Alexander (§ 2), humble entertainers (§ 3), the Ionian marksman, and Libyan Psaphon (§ 4) all show. The resulting picture of human aspirations is one of chaos and confusion (§§ 5–6). One might hope for a single, unambiguous answer from philosophy, but in fact philosophers too recommend a wide variety of different ends. Which of them is to be trusted (§ 7)?

Or. 30 redepicts the situation as that of a multiplicity of helmsmen attempting to steer a course over a wide and trackless sea, and all but one failing to reach a safe harbour. Who then is that one reliable helmsman (§§ 1-2)? The first candidate for examination is Epicurus, whose philosophy is compared, in an extension of the nautical image, to a cumbersome pleasure-barge, unable to survive the open sea in rough weather (§ 3). Image then gives way to argument. As a first stage (§§ 4-5) it is urged that, even if Epicurus is right that Pleasure is a good, there is nevertheless something disturbing about its inconstancy (as Penelope's suitors, Paris, Sardanapallus, Polycrates, the Sybarites, the Syracusans, and the Corinthians all discovered to their cost).

The criticism of Pleasure is then pressed home in *Or.* 31. The previous concession, that Pleasure could still count as a Good in spite of its inconstancy (*Or.* 30. 4-5), was misguided (§ 1). Pleasure and the Good must be seen as mutually exclusive alternatives (§ 2). Moreover, a proper understanding of human nature, and distinctive human functions, strongly suggests that Pleasure can *not* be the human good (§§ 3-5).

Or. 32 allows Epicurus to reply. Critics of hedonism are hypocrites (§ 1). The pursuit of Pleasure is basic to all sentient creatures, and its universality is no reflection on its value (§§ 2-4). Virtue itself depends on Pleasure, as is clear from the cases of Achilles, Agamemnon and Hector, Heracles and Dionysus, Socrates and Diogenes, and Sparta and Athens (§§ 5-10).

Or. 33 resumes and concludes the sequence with a decisive rejection of the Epicurean case. In spite of the bewildering diversity of philosophical argument (§ 1; cf. *Orr.* 29. 7 and 30. 1), it is clear that Pleasure and Virtue are radically different values (§ 2; cf. *Or.* 31. 2). In championing Pleasure, Epicurus simply proves himself a traitor to Philosophy (§ 3a). Hedonism is inherently tyrannical and excessive, and a cause of suffering rather than satisfaction (§§ 3b-6). The argument from human nature is decisive: to pursue Pleasure is to reduce youself to the level of animals (§§ 7-8).

The overall argument is thus cumulative rather than linear. The Epicurean case is presented twice (*Orr.* 30. 3-4a and 32), and rejected twice, with a growing degree of decisiveness (*Orr.* 30. 4b-31 and 33)—a structure reminiscent (if only at a distance) of that of the *Phaedo*.

Doctrinally, the lectures are more precise about what they reject than about what they recommend. The rejection of Pleasure as an end is common ground between all the dogmatic sects opposed to Epicurus, and Maximus' positive presentation of the case for

Reason and Virtue says little or nothing that would mark out a distinctively Platonist, as opposed to Stoic or Peripatetic, position. See further Introduction, pp. xxii–xxxi.

Subsequent interest in the lectures has to a large extent been conditioned by the accident of their positioning in the corpus: see Introduction, pp. lviii–lx. The six substantial scholia in the margins of Paris. gr. 1962, drawing attention to the contents of 29. 1, 29. 4, 30. 1, 31. 3, 33. 1, and 33. 7 (see Hobein 1910, ad locc. or Trapp 1994: 337–8, 346), presumably date from a time when the five lectures stood in a single sequence, three quarters of the way through the whole collection. Subsequently, interest focuses most heavily on *Orr.* 30–3, as a result of the promotion of those four lectures to the head of the collection. Gregoras takes twenty excerpts, four from *Or.* 29 (§§ 1, 3, 6, 7), three each from 30 and 31 (30. 2, 3, 4; 31. 1 (twice), 4), nine from 32 (§§ 1, 2 (twice), 3, 5, 6, 7, 8, 9), and one from 33 (§ 1) (see Hobein 1910, ad locc.). The compiler of Neap. 100 takes 24, two from 29 (§§ 6, 7), one from 30 (§ 4), four from 31 (§§ 1 (twice), 2, 4), seven from 32 (§§ 3, 8, 9 (thrice), 10 (twice)), and ten from 33 (§§ 1 (twice), 2, 4 (twice), 5 (twice), 6 (twice), 8) (see Hobein 1910, ad locc.). The excerptor working on Paris. gr. 1865, fol. 4, neglects *Or.* 29 entirely, and takes twenty-one excerpts from the remaining four: four from 30 (§§ 1, 4 (twice), 5), three from 31 (§§ 1, 2, 4), six from 32 (§§ 3 (twice), 4, 8, 10 (twice)), and eight from 33 (§§ 1, 2, 3, 4, 5, 6, 7 (twice)). A paraphrase of 33. 7 also appears on fol. 7^v, and is repeated in the margins of the text of the Aristotelian *Problemata* on fol. 116^v (see Hobein 1910, ad locc.). The *Lexicon Vindobonense* quotes ten times, again from 30–3 only: three times from 30, once each from 31 and 33, five times from 32 (see Hobein 1910 ad loc.). Apostolis quotes from 29. 4 to explain the phrase Ψάφωνος ὄρνιθες (*Proverbia* 18. 48; the phrase seems to be known *only* from Maximus), and from 31. 3 to explain Λέων τὴν τρίχα, ὄνος τὸν βίον (*Proverbia* 10. 61). The first of these quotations is responsible for the story of Psaphon turning up again in L. G. Giraldi's *De Deis Gentium* (1548), p. 83 and G. Voss's *Theologia Gentili* (1641), 3. 16, p. 802, and is perhaps also the source for Georg Pictorius von Villingen in his *De Daemonum . . . ortu . . . Isagoge* (1563), where Psaphon is explained as a malicious demon bent on diverting human worship. Poliziano, reversing the general trend, neglects 30–3 entirely, but notes no fewer than seventeen names in 29. 1–2 and 6–7, in the margins of Paris. gr. 1962 (foll. 120ᵛ–122ᵛ). Franciscus Junius quotes the sentiment that 'there was never any brave thing brought to passe by negligence', from 33. 3, in *The Painting of the Ancients* II. xi. 4 (Aldrich *et al.* 1991: i. 176).

Oration 29

1 The Crotoniate longs for the olive of Olympia, the Athenian for naval victory, the Spartan for victory in a hoplite battle, the Cretan for the hunt, the Sybarite for luxury, the Theban for the pipes, and the Ionian for choral dances;[1] or again, the money-maker longs for gold, the drinker for intoxication, the † cultivated man † for love, the music-lover for melodies, and the orator for speeches.[2] Are we then to find that the creature whom men call 'philosopher' has nothing at all that he longs for? That would be the life of a stone,[3] to say nothing of a seeing, breathing, moving creature with impulses and perceptions and desires. Is the point rather that he does have some objective, but is unable to find any one comprehensive name to describe this thing he longs for? 'Happiness,' the man says. I envy you your naïvety, if you think that the man in the street is going to give up his beloved on your account, rather than replying that it is precisely in pursuit of happiness that one person competes, another drinks, or makes money, or hunts, or farms, or fights, or loves, or sings, or speaks.[4] Or do you think that the notorious Sardanapallus, with his worn-down body and his wasted eyes and his plaited hair, buried in his purple and shut up in his palace and surrounded by his concubines, was in pursuit of anything other than happiness? He certainly didn't choose to be miserable of his own free will.[5] What about the Persian who burned down the holy places of the Egyptians and slandered their river and sacrificed the bull Apis;[6] wasn't he too making for the

---

[1] For this list of distinctive national occupations, cf. *Or.* 17. 2.

[2] 'Cultivated man' (μουσικός) looks like a gloss on 'music-lover' (φιλῳδός) which has expelled the original reading: perhaps 'hedonist' or 'libertine'.

[3] Perhaps an echo of Callicles in Plato *Grg.* 494ab.

[4] Maximus' development of this point reads like an embroidery on Aristotle's presentation in *NE* 1. 4, 1095ᵃ17 ff.

[5] For Sardanapallus, cf. *Orr.* 1. 9, 4. 9, 7. 7 (with n. 22), 15. 8, 29. 1, 32. 3 and 9.

[6] Cambyses: Hdt. 3. 16, 3. 25. 3, 3. 27–9, and 3. 37.

same objective when he did all this? As for Xerxes, it seems to me that he could compete even with Zeus in happiness (that's how firm a grasp I think he had on it) ⟨because . . . ⟩ and because he could have Asia bound to Europe by the transitory bond of ships' hulks drawn up in the shape of a bridge.[7] In Homer Poseidon enjoys equal status;[8] from Xerxes (or so *he* thought) he got a beating and was clapped in irons.

2　Why do I talk of foreign kings? Can't you see Pisistratus the Greek, the Athenian, forever rushing up to the Acropolis, as if he were going to find happiness buried there beside the venerable olive, and quite unable to bear life in retirement whenever he is deposed?[9] Not even the warning from Egypt could persuade Polycrates not to be conceited in his happiness, because he owned the Ionian Sea and a fleet of triremes and a beautiful ring, and had Anacreon for his companion and Smerdies for his boyfriend.[10]

All these rulers look like men who have been deceived by the specious evils of luxury and pleasure. But can you not also hear Homer's praise for the Aeacidae, that they were men

who delighted in war just as in a feast?[11]

What could there be more disagreeable than war? Yet even so this disagreeable object too found lovers of the highest rank. Such, for instance, as Philip of old, who could have stayed in Macedon and lived on the good things amassed by Amyntas and the happiness won by Perdiccas, yet went off elsewhere in search of it, as if it had fled from Macedonia. This evidently was why he made war on the Triballi, attacked the Illyrians, laid siege to Byzantium, slighted Olynthus, deceived the Athenians, made terms with the Thessalians, struck a treaty with the Thebans, captured Elatea, displaced the Phoceans, broke his word, lied, and lost his eye. There was nothing he abjured, no word or deed, no matter what the shame or the ill repute attaching to it.[12] Let us ask Philip: 'What is it that

---

[7] Hdt. 7. 33–4; the lacuna may originally have contained a reference to the whipping of the sea, also mentioned in the next sentence (Hdt. 7. 35).

[8] *Il.* 15. 187–93: cf. *Or.* 26. 7.

[9] A reference to Pisistratus' two separate periods in power: Hdt. 1. 59–64.

[10] Amasis' warning: Hdt. 3. 39–40; for Polycrates, Anacreon, and Smerdies, cf. *Or.* 20. 1.

[11] In spite of Maximus' attribution to Homer, this is Hesiod *Cat.* fr. 206 M-W.

[12] The classic account of Philip's career was that of Theopompus, to which Maximus may refer in *Or.* 22. 6, but the reference here is conditioned at least as much by the presentation of Philip in the orations of Demosthenes (e.g. *Ol.* 2. 5–8).

you stand to gain in return for all your labours, all the risks to your position, and the damage to your eyes? Is it unhappiness you long for?' The question is absurd. Yet it would seem that Philip did not find what he was looking for; happiness evaded him. That is why Alexander, judging Europe devoid of good, turned his back on it and crossed over to Asia, in the suspicion that happiness was buried in Sardis in the gold-dust, or in Caria in Mausolus' treasure-chamber, or in the walls of Babylon, or the harbours of Phoenicia, or the shores of Egypt, or the sands of the Ammonians. It wasn't enough for him for Darius to be put to flight, for Egypt to be captured, for Ammon to declare himself his father, for Babylon to fall; arms and all he pressed on as far as India.[13] Let us ask Alexander the reason for his expedition: 'What do you desire? What is it you long for? What goal are you hastening to?' Will his answer be anything but 'happiness'?

3   Let us leave these kings and potentates. Do you not see what happens in everyday life, how everyone from every quarter hastens towards the same objective, one setting his hand to the soil, another spending his energies at sea, another devoting his time to war, another busying himself with oratory, another marrying, another raising children, another turning robber, another resorting to assault and battery, or to taking bribes, or engaging in adulterous liaisons, or taking service as a mercenary[14]— all of them following treacherous and dangerous paths along the very edges of cliffs and precipices.[15] One might well feel pity for them [; but not if they evade detection].[16] These, however, are people who devote themselves to their chosen lives with energy. What about the idle, aimless masses? Have *they* abandoned their hopes of the good? By no means. If they had, flatterers would not be putting themselves out to pander to the desires of the wealthy, or clowns to hunt out material and techniques for buffoonery and jokes, or contortionists to twist and torture their bodies, nor would anyone else be applying himself to any other device, however vain it might be.

[13] With this account of the career of Alexander, compare *Orr*. 2. 6, 16. 6, and 41. 1.

[14] With this list of misguided occupations, compare *Orr*. 1. 3 and 36. 6.

[15] For the imagery of cliffs and chasms on the road of Life, compare *Orr*. 1. 3, 8. 7, 19. 1, 34. 2, and 39. 3.

[16] The bracketed words look like a reader's comment transferred from the margin into the body of the text.

4   An Ionian once came to the Great King at Babylon, with an
act of outstanding dexterity to show off. Making little round balls
of dough, he threw them from a distance at a spike set upright, so
as to hit its point; and this man clearly felt no less pride in the
sureness of his aim at the spike than Achilles did in his great ash
spear from Pelion.[17] In Libya there was a Libyan called Psaphon,
who longed for a happiness of the most exalted and uncommon
kind: he wanted to be thought a god.[18] So he took a large number
of songbirds and taught them to sing 'Psaphon is a great god,' and
released them back into the mountains. These birds duly sang, and
as time went on were joined by the other birds, once they had
grown accustomed to the song. The Libyans, thinking what they
heard was a message from the heavens, began to sacrifice to
Psaphon, who thus was made their god on the suffrage of the
birds—and by no means inferior, in my view, to the well-known
Persian who did not win the obeisance of his people until he had
been elected to office by a rutting stallion.[19]

5   So true it is that no two things agree in this world of ours:
everyone shares a single desire for the Good, but they make their
way towards it by many and various routes, according to the
different rank and status of the occupation each has been allotted.
Desire for the Good is common to all, but for all that no one man
has more success than any other in achieving this goal. They are
just like people searching for gold and silver in the dark, unable to
secure light to reveal what they are searching for and reduced to
fallible guesswork by weight and touch, bumping into each other
and snapping at each other, not daring to let go in case they
really have something, nor able to cease their labours in case they
have not. Hence there is a tumult of quarrelling and exhortation,
and of the cries of people searching, groaning, chasing, lamenting,
snatching, and being robbed: everyone is calling out and shouting
in triumph, as if they have stumbled on the Good, though no
one actually has it; but at the same time everyone mistrustfully
examines his neighbour's findings to be on the safe side.[20]

[17]   *Il.* 16. 160-4, 19. 387-91.
[18]   In Aelian's telling of the story (*VH* 14. 30) the man's name is Hanno, and the
trick fails to work because the birds revert to their natural song when released. For
yet other versions, see Hippol. *Ref.* 6. 7-8 and *Σ* Dio *Or.* 1. 14; cf. Osborne (1987:
70-2) and Sorabji (1993: 80).   [19]   Darius: Hdt. 3. 85-7.
[20]   For this picture of the darkness and confusion of human life, compare *Orr.* 1.
3 and esp. 36. 4; ceaseless toil in pursuit of (mistaken conceptions of) the good life

6 It is these experiences that make chaos of land and sea, it is these that pack the Assembly and convene the courts, these that fill the prisons and build navies and launch triremes, these that start wars and mount the cavalry on their horses and the charioteers on their chariots and install tyrants on the Acropolis. These are what make men *condottieri* and mercenaries,

> Killing the men, while fire razes their city to the ground,
> And others lead their children and deep-girdled wives into slavery.[21]

Many thousands of other ills besides men suffer, from no other cause than their hopes for the Good and their ignorance. God has breathed expectation of the Good into the human race like a spark of life,[22] but has concealed the Good itself and made it hard to find.

> It was black at the root, but milk-white in its flower.

Homer won't deceive me by the name he uses: I can see his 'moly', I understand his allegory, I know full well how hard this thing is to find

> For mortal men, though the gods know all.[23]

7 As things are now, Apollo is quite happy to tell us humans about a bizarre cauldron boiling among the Lydians,[24] and about the wooden wall and the narrow isthmus,[25] and an impending earthquake,[26] and the onset of war, and the descent of Plague;[27] but what he will not give is that superior oracle that tells us how war may be averted, how I can escape the need for walls, how I can free myself from fear of the Plague.[28] Apollo in Delphi does not reveal this, nor Zeus in Dodona, nor any other god from another land. It is philosophy that tells us. What a noble oracle, what a most beautifully beneficial kind of prophecy! Let me only find

---

is highlighted also in *Or*. 1. 5, and the universal dissatisfaction of human beings with their present pursuits in *Or*. 15. 1. The mining and assaying of precious metals provides images for the search for the Good (or for truth) also in *Orr*. 11. 2, 18. 3, 31. 2, and 40. 4.

[21] *Il*. 9. 593–4.
[22] For the idea and the image of the small but precious spark, cf. *Or*. 5. 8.
[23] *Od*. 10. 304 and 306; for the allegory, cf. *Or*. 26. 9, with n. 47.
[24] Hdt. 1. 48. 2; see *Or*. 11. 6 and 13. 3 (with n. 5).
[25] Hdt. 7. 140–3; cf. *Or*. 13. 1.
[26] Hdt. 6. 98. 3.
[27] Thuc. 2. 52. 4.
[28] For the turn of thought (that the inner peace won through philosophy is more important than the avoidance of external calamity), compare *Or*. 22. 7.

consistency in them, and I will happily accept these prophetic strains. Give me an oracle free from inner strife; what I require is a prophecy that will allow me to live securely if I accept it. Whither are you sending the human race, on what routes, to what destinations? Let there be just one, common to all! But as things are now, I can see many colonies of philosophy, each setting off in a different direction, like Cadmus to Boeotia, or Archias to Syracuse, or Phalanthus to Tarentum, or Neleus to Miletus, or Tlepolemus to Rhodes.[29] It is inevitable that the earth should be shared out place by place, and that different people should inhabit different parts of it. But the Good is one and undivided, bountiful and ample, sufficient to all rational and intelligent creatures, just as the sun alone is the single good of the visible creation, and music alone is the single good of the audible creation, and health alone the good of bodily nature.[30] Among other creatures each has its own single good, species by species, to ensure its survival, and in each case like creatures share a single kind of existence and a single goal with their likes, avians and ambulants and reptiles, creatures rejoicing in an aquatic existence, carnivores and herbivores, fruiteaters, gregarious creatures, tame and wild, horned and hornless.[31] If you change their habits around, you offend against the natural order. But the human herd, that pastures together and is the tamest and most sociable and most rational of all, is split and pulled apart not by vulgar desire or irrational appetites or vain infatuation alone, but also by that most stable of all things, Philosophy![32] Philosophy too creates many peoples and countless

[29] The appropriateness of the comparison depends on the fact that consultation of an oracle was a standard part of the business of dispatching a colony: see Parke and Wormell (1956: 49–51), Fontenrose (1978: 137–44); and cf. *Or.* 41. 1.

[30] For the comparisons, cf. *Orr.* 20. 8 and 39. 2. In *Orr.* 39–40 Maximus presents arguments for and against the proposition that there are higher and lower forms of Good (see the introduction to those lectures). That issue does not seem to be raised here: Maximus' point is rather that since the universal human aim (true Happiness) must be the same for all, variations in philosophical teaching concerning its pursuit are particularly gratuitous and objectionable.

[31] Cf. *Orr.* 10. 5 (with n. 19), 20. 6 (with n. 14), and 31. 4 below. Man's corresponding single dominant attribute is of course reason, the proper exercise of which realizes his distinctive Good—but Maximus keeps the explicit development of this point for later (*Orr.* 31. 3–5 and 33. 7–8).

[32] For the image, compare especially *Or.* 1. 3 (where, however, a more flattering impression of the role of philosophy is given). The diversity of philosophical sects, and their inability to agree, had been a major topic in Greek culture for several centuries, and inspired a wide variety of reaction and comment: see Introduction, pp. xxx–xxxii.

legislators, splitting and scattering the herd, and sending its different members in different directions, Pythagoras to music, Thales to astronomy, Heraclitus to solitude, Socrates to love-affairs, Carneades to scepticism, Diogenes to hard labour, Epicurus to pleasure. Do you see what a crowd of leaders there is, what a mass of watchwords? Which way is a man to turn? Which of them should I accept? Which of their exhortations should I heed?

Oration 30

1 'It is a hard thing to be good,' as the old song goes.[1] But is the point that it is difficult even for a horse to be good by equine standards of excellence, and a dog by canine standards? Or is it rather that while horses and dogs find no difficulty in their own specific goods, and each of them can attain its own particular kind of excellence with ease, provided only that the horse is well broken in by a professional hand, and the dog deftly trained in the hunt, for man and man alone the Good is hard to hunt down, hard to seize, and a source of argument?[2] Is the point that no science has yet been discovered that might train this other species sufficiently to prevent it from furnishing sophists with the grounds for debate and dispute and contention, and from giving up its hopes of attaining its goal, and abandoning its chances of salvation because its expectations have been hamstrung by its inability to assess the arguments, and from scorning learning, and experiencing the same kind of feelings as faint-hearted sailors encountering the sea for the first time.[3] These latter, if surprised by even the gentlest swell, are terrified by the unfamiliar experience, abandon ship without the slightest thought of the science that might preserve them, and by entrusting themselves to the waves perish before the ship itself. It seems to me that the same kind of experience is shared by those who, when they first encounter Philosophy and find themselves

---

[1] Simonides fr. 542. 13 *PMG*, from the poem discussed in Plato *Protag.* 339a ff. (with l. 13 quoted in 339d).

[2] The question continues the line of thought begun at the end of the previous lecture (§ 7).

[3] For the attack on pedantic theoreticians ('sophists'), compare *Orr.* 1. 8, 21. 4, 27. 8, and 37. 2. The nautical imagery introduced here is sustained through the first four paragraphs of the lecture: compare the use of theatrical and athletic imagery in *Or.* 1, but this degree of elaboration is unusual for Maximus. In the text the phrase 'faint-hearted sailors' is a guess: the Greek is corrupt, and no fully convincing emendation has yet been proposed.

in the midst of its many competing voices, cannot endure such
choppy seas about their souls, but instead despair of argument in
the belief that it will never stand still and bring them to anchor in
a secure harbour.[4] [2] Or are you unaware that human opinions
and emotions, and their causes and origins and the factors that
correct and preserve them, with which the philosophers deal and
about which they hold forth every day, are no narrow or simple
thing, like rivers with straight currents, to which you can entrust
your ship and let them carry it downstream on a stable and
reliable course. No: here too we find a great broad sea, more dis-
orientating than any Sicilian or Egyptian waters. Professional
expertise allows its possessors to know the route, find their
bearings from the heavens, and recognize the ports of call, but
none the less they experience the very same failings as do the
majority of helmsmen. Each man aims for knowledge, but most of
them fall short of proper knowing, miss their harbours, and are
carried away, some to harsh reefs, others to soft beaches, or to
the Sirens, or the Lotophagi, or to other races of men made
inhospitable by their wickedness, or godless by their ignorance, or
ruined by hedonism.[5] If, however, there is a good helmsman whose
aim is true, he steers straight for the securest of harbours,

> where there is no need of mooring-ropes,
> Nor of casting anchor-stones, nor of fastening stern-cables.[6]

Who then is this helmsman? To whom shall we go and entrust
ourselves? Do not ask me yet, sir, until you have seen and
examined the others, and first among them this luxurious
and exquisitely pleasant helmsman, in a ship that may be most
exquisitely pleasant to behold from the land, but under sail is never
anything but unserviceable and defective, inefficient in every
function, bereft of tackle, and too feeble to offer any resistance to
the onset of a storm.

3   Since somehow or another our line of argument has fastened

---

[4] Maximus' imagery follows a familiar pattern. The use of the sea here as an
image for intellectual instability (conflicting argument) matches its use elsewhere as
an image for the instability of matter or of human fortunes (e.g. *Or.* 5. 6, 8. 7, 10.
5, 21. 8); the helmsman, besides figuring the philosopher (3. 7, 15. 2), can also
stand for the rational soul (40. 5) or for God (4. 9, 8. 7, 13. 3).

[5] Compare *Or.* 25. 5 for the picture of a gradual drift into pernicious hedonism,
and *Orr.* 22. 2 (with n. 7) and 39. 3 for the allegorical use of the Sirens and the
Lotophagi.   [6] *Od.* 9. 136–7.

on a nautical metaphor, let us not allow it to leave us without
working out the image in detail, by comparing the philosophy of
Epicurus with the royal barge of king † Aeetes.[7] The story is not
an invention of mine. It was only a few years ago that the king of
the barbarians who live inland from Phoenicia—those men

> who know nothing of the sea[8]

and who

> have no thought for aegis-bearing Zeus
> And the blessed gods[9]—

set sail from Egypt on course for Troy. In preparation for his
voyage this godless landlubber of a king had made ready a large
and spacious ship, so as to be able to take all his pleasures with
him.[10] One part of it was a palace, that is to say with the finest of
colonnades, and bedchambers, and cloisters;

> And outside the courtyard, near the entrance, was a great
> Orchard of four acres—[11]

with trees growing there, pomegranates and pears and apples
and vines. Another part of the ship was a bath-house and a
gymnasium, then there was a galley and chambers for the king's
concubines, and a banqueting-hall, and other appurtenances of a
luxurious city. The ship was adorned in many colours delightful to
behold, with large quantities of gold and silver, for all the world
like a coward fitted out in golden armour. As was only natural the
Egyptians were amazed at what they beheld and reckoned its
passenger a lucky man, and I imagine not a few of them prayed to
be taken as crew-members on this delightful ship. When the time
came to put to sea, this great and expensive vessel set forth, and
wallowed away from harbour like a floating island. Other, everyday ships, properly equipped and prepared for useful work, put out
along with her. As long as the breeze was gentle, the royal ship
lorded it luxuriously over the others, and the air was full of the
smell of cooking meat

---

[7] 'Aeetes' is surely corrupt; perhaps 'of a foolish (ἀνοήτου) king.'
[8] *Od.* 11. 122.
[9] *Od.* 9. 275-6.
[10] Maximus draws here on descriptions of the θαλαμηγοί of the Ptolemies,
perhaps particularly that of Ptolemy Philopator's by Callixenus (in Athen. 5.
204 ff.).   [11] *Od.* 7. 112-13.

And the music of flutes and pipes, and the hubbub of human voices.[12]

But when suddenly from clear skies a storm convulsed the heavens and a tearing wind bore down with a great crashing, then they realized the difference between what can be achieved through pleasure and what through science. The other ships, furling their sails, joined battle with the waves, rode the wind, and fought off the storm's attack; but that wretched pleasure-barge was tossed around like a fat man staggering drunkenly, his wits fuddled with wine. The steersman was quite unable to bring his science to bear, and the effeminate rabble of passengers lay where they were, moaning in terror. The storm tore down all those marvellous trappings,

> Hurling many a mighty timber uprooted to the ground,[13]

and breaking up the palace and the bedchambers and the baths, and the wreckage of a whole city washed ashore,

> While they like sea-crows around the black ship
> Floated on the waves.[14]

Such was the end of a foolish passenger and an unserviceable vessel, and of misplaced luxury.

4   Let us return again to the doctrine we invoked this image to illustrate. It would indeed seem that it too commands us to pleasures that are every bit as treacherous as the sea, as we struggle our way not through any short voyage or any journey of a few days' duration, but through the whole span of our lives. Let us allow no argument yet to persuade us that Pleasure is not a good; rather let it strive in the hopes of convincing us ⟨that it is not subject to change⟩.[15] If indeed it is not subject to change, then I will be happy to indulge in it without interruption, and to have no thought for Virtue, provided you can show me a kind of pleasure that is secure and uncontaminated with pain, a kind of pleasure that does not end in repentance, a kind of pleasure that can be praised.[16] But how will you be able to do that? You cannot,

---

[12] *Il*. 10. 13.
[13] *Il*. 9. 541.
[14] *Od*. 12. 418–19.
[15] Both here and at the beginning of the next sentence the text is corrupt, and no certainty is claimed for the version offered.
[16] Precisely what Epicurean teaching promised: Cic. *De Fin*. 1. 17. 55–19. 62.

any more than you can for pain. Nature decreed that men should
never find either of these things in a pure and healthy form; everywhere what is pleasant is mixed with what gives pain, each rolled
up with the other. It is inevitable that he who chooses the one
should immediately partake of the other as well; since they form a
natural pair, each supervenes on the other, taking it in turn to
come into being, and alternating their presence.[17] When the soul is
tormented by this ebb and flow, how on earth could it get a grip
on tranquillity, consorting as it does with 'goods' that have no
stability?[18] This is why I mistrust the sea, even when there is
no wind, even when the waves are still; her calm arouses my
suspicions. If you wish me to trust the stillness of the waves, then
take me and lead me to a safe sea,

> Where winter's weight is never felt, nor is it ever drenched
> In rain . . . but bright and cloudless
> Skies spread all around, suffused with radiant white.[19]

It is the soul's fate too to be subject to such experiences. As long
as it has no steersman to aid it with his skills, it fears a storm even
when it can see calm waters, and when it runs into a storm can
only pray for calm. The life of a man who inclines towards
pleasure and is terrified of pain is fickle and nervous and unreliable, and more unpredictable than any sea.

5   Do you not see the suitors indulging in their youthful
pleasures, wolfing down plump goats, gorging themselves on fat
hogs, listening to the bard, drawing and mixing themselves wine,
playing with discuses and throwing-spears?[20] Who would not think
them fortunate in their pleasure? But the prophet, the man who
knows what is to come, cries

> You wretches, what evil fate is this you suffer? Your heads
> Are swathed in darkness,[21]

disaster lies before you, close at hand.' Close at hand was disaster
for Alexander too, when he stole his marvellous pleasure from

---

[17] Perhaps a reminiscence of Plato *Phdo* 60bc.

[18] Text uncertain: 'by consorting with goods of a securer kind' is also possible.

[19] *Od.* 4. 566 + 6. 43–5, also used in *Or.* 11. 10 to describe God's immaterial
realm beyond the heavens.

[20] See *Od.* 1. 144–54, 4. 621–7, 14. 80 ff.; and cf. *Orr.* 19. 3 and 26. 9 for the
Suitors as negative moral exemplars.

[21] *Od.* 20. 351–2, spoken by the seer Theoclymenus.

the Peloponnese. In no time a Greek expedition was fitted out to reclaim her, bringing countless pains to the pleasure-lover himself, and countless more to his whole city.[22] I will pass over the Assyrian's pleasures, which were quickly overtaken by fire—gold, concubines, and all.[23] And I will pass over, too, the Ionian pleasures of Polycrates, overtaken as they were by a most unseemly death.[24] Sybaris was full of pleasures, but the pleasures perished along with those who indulged in them.[25] Pleasures had a high esteem among the Syracusans, but the Syracusans were chastened by the disasters that followed them.[26] Nor did even the Corinthians ⟨ . . . ⟩.[27]

Oration 31

1   A hateful argument attempted to take the floor and persuade us that Pleasure was the end to be chosen, provided it enjoyed the additional attribute of security[1]—a sophistic and wickedly deceptive argument which, faced with the possibility of examining the nature of Pleasure in itself—where its station is, whether it belongs in the category of goods or the category of evils—simply neglects the enquiry, taking it for granted that Pleasure is indeed a good, and considers instead whether this 'good' is a secure one. But could anyone imagine a good that rocked and swayed? Just as if one were to deprive the earth's globe of its stability and rest, one would surely also deprive it of its being, or if one were to deprive the sun of its motion and its orbit, one would also deprive it of its

[22] For Paris as negative moral exemplar, cf. *Orr.* 18. 8, 20. 7, 23. 6, 26. 6.

[23] Sardanapallus, as in *Or.* 29. 1.

[24] Cf. again *Or.* 29. 2.

[25] Cf. *Orr.* 14. 2, 21. 5, 29. 1, 32. 3 and 10, 37. 4. Sybaris was destroyed by its rival Croton in 510 BC (Hdt. 5. 44-5, 6. 21, etc.).

[26] For Syracusan luxury, cf. *Or.* 32. 10; comparison with *Orr.* 5. 5 and 7. 2 suggests that the 'disasters' referred to are the depredations of the tyrant Dionysius.

[27] The concluding words of the lecture are missing, though what their general sense must have been is clear: the Corinthians too found no permanence in their wealth and pleasures. The reference is likely to be either to the tyranny of Periander (cf. *Orr.* 5. 5 and 18. 1), or the decline of Corinthian wealth and power in the 5th century, rather than to the sack of the city by L. Mummius in 146 BC.

[1] This refers back to *Or.* 30. 4 ('Let us allow no argument yet to persuade us that Pleasure is not a good; rather let it strive in the hopes of convincing us ⟨ that it is not subject to change ⟩'). *Or.* 30. 4-5 went on to argue that Pleasure is inevitably subject to change, whilst (at least theoretically) leaving open the possibility that it might still be a good; that possibility is now to be closed off.

essence; in just the same way, if one were to deprive the Good of its exactitude and its immobility, one would also deprive it of its very nature. For, unlike physical beauty, the Good does not need the passage of time to come into flower. How then could attributing goodness to Pleasure, while at the same time denying it stability, provide a sound basis for discussion? If it is necessary for a good to be secure, then the goodness of Pleasure must disappear along with its security. Which of the two claimants is closer to being convincing—the one who says that Pleasure is a good even if it is not secure, or the one who says that it is not a good unless it is as secure as it can be? In my opinion, it is the latter. It is better to deprive Pleasure of the quality of goodness, while endowing Goodness with security, than to attribute goodness to Pleasure, while at the same time depriving Pleasure of the quality of stability.

2   Since then Goodness is not pleasant in every case, but in every case secure, and Pleasure is not good in all cases, but in all cases insecure, we are left with one of two options, either to pursue Pleasure and scorn Goodness, or to choose Goodness and not pursue Pleasure. I believe that nothing is to be pursued unless it is a good, but things that are not good are pursued in the place of goods because they *appear* good—just as counterfeit coins are acceptable to businessmen not *because* they are counterfeit, but because their similarity to true coin conceals their counterfeit nature. In this latter case assayers use their science to separate the fake from the true, but in the case of the distribution of goods, may it not be that reason can fail to separate from real goods those that are not real but apparent, so that we inadvertently, like bad businessmen, store up treasures of counterfeit goods?[2]

3   What then is to become of our enquiry? What is the form of this review of which I have spoken? Tell me, if someone tried unyoking the ox from his plough and the horse from his chariot, and interchanging their functions by yoking the ox to the chariot and the horse to the plough,[3] wouldn't he be proving himself an offender against the laws of nature, an aggressor against the

[2] Compare the discussion of real and apparent Beauty in *Or.* 21. 4.
[3] For this way of expressing an offence against the natural order, cf. *Orr.* 23. 4 and 29. 7.

animals themselves, an incompetent by the standards of the
sciences, useless for any practical purposes, and ridiculous in his
efforts? What about a still more absurd case than this, if you were
to deprive birds of their wings, and desire them to walk instead of
fly, while at the same time putting wings on man and setting him
to fly through the air like a bird? Wouldn't the exchange make you
a laughing-stock, seeing that not even in myth could Daedalus get
away with contriving such unnatural arts as these, but saw his son
flung from the heavens down to earth, wings and all? They also
tell how a Carthaginian youth captured a newly-weaned lion-cub,
taming it by means of an unnatural diet and removing its spirit by
the application of an illegitimate regimen, until he could put a load
on it and drive it through the city like an ass. The Carthaginians
killed him in disgust at his transgression, reckoning him a tyrant
by nature, though only a lowly private citizen in rank.[4]

4   So just as horses as a species have been assigned the ability to
run fast to ensure their survival, and oxen the ability to work hard,
and birds wings and lions strength and others other qualities, just
so man too has a natural capacity designed to ensure the survival
of the species.[5] This must necessarily be something different compared to all the others, if, being human, men are to survive not
through their strength like lions, nor through speed like horses,
nor to carry burdens like asses, nor to plough like oxen, nor to fly
like birds, nor to swim like fishes. Man too has his own particular
function that allows him to live and survive. Well then: the
various abilities are shared out among the animals, each to each
according to the needs of their existence; their characteristic
behaviour accords with their abilities, their characteristic tools
with their characteristic behaviour, and their individual goods

[4] For the story, cf. Aelian Nat. An. 5. 39, Plut. Praec. Ger. Rep. 799e; both name
the Carthaginian in question as Hanno. According to Plutarch, he was banished,
not executed, for his behaviour, and Aelian mentions no retribution at all.
[5] Maximus here makes fully explicit the argument only sketched in Or. 29. 7
above. For the identification of reason as the distinctive human attribute, parallel to
the various survival-aids of the animal creation—a set-piece whose detail derives
ultimately from Plato Protag. 320d ff., further developed in discussions of Stoic
doctrines of Providence—cf. Orr. 10. 5 (with n. 19), 20. 6, and 31. 6. At the same
time, Maximus is also following, in outline at least, Aristotle's argument from
human function (ἔργον) in NE 1. 7, 1097^{b}24 ff., which, according to Bignone
(1973: ii. 320-4), was also deployed in the Protrepticus. For the whole package,
also in the context of a discussion of Epicureanism, cf. Cic. De Fin. 2. 13. 40.

⟨with their characteristic tools⟩.[6] To put the matter concisely, the good of each creature reposes in the sphere of its native functions, its functions in that of its practical needs, its needs in its ability to provide for itself, its ability in the capacity of its tools, and its tools in the variety offered by Nature. Nature in its manifold abundance can clothe and adorn each species of creature with different weapons to enable it to survive and flourish, some with claws at their extremities, others with strong teeth, others with sharp horns, others with fleetness of foot, others with courage, others with venom. But man she has stripped of these forms of protection and left naked and weak and hairless, the slowest of runners, unable to fly, and the clumsiest of swimmers. Yet at the same time she has breathed into him an invisible spark to ensure his survival, a spark which men call intelligence,[7] thanks to which his continued survival is assured and he can make good the deficiencies in his life, and attend to his physical wants, and combat the aggression of other animals, conquering all and subjecting them to its laws and principles.

5   Ask me about man too; we must examine his good, asking where it resides and what is its nature. I will reply to you as I did about the lion and the bird and all the other creatures. Seek man's good where his characteristic functions are located. Where will I find his functions? Where his distinctive instruments are. Where will I find the instruments? Where that which ensures his survival is. Begin from there. What ensures man's survival? Pleasure? That is a shared attribute you specify, common to all species, and for that very reason I refuse to allow it to be privileged.[8] The ox feels pleasure, and the ass and the pig and the ape. Look where you are stationing the human race, look what partners you are giving it in its goods! But if Pleasure really is what ensures human survival, you must then look for Pleasure's instrument. You will find many, of all kinds: up to and including the eyes and ears, these are

[6] This conjectural restoration is not made with any great confidence: it follows what seems to be the superficial logic of the sentence, but the sentence as a whole, thus reconstructed, does not make the clear-cut argument it seems to be aiming for. Similar feelings arise over the next sentence. This may be a place where Maximus' desire to *sound* technical and philosophical exceeds his ability to deliver philosophical sense.

[7] For the image, cf. *Orr.* 5. 8 and 29. 6.

[8] A standard objection to Epicureanism: cf. Cic. *De Fin.* 2. 33. 109 ff., *Acad. Post.* 1. 2. 6; Plut. *Non Posse* 1091c; cf. Bignone (1973: ii. 320).

respectable instruments, but if you advance further on the paths
of Pleasure, look what instruments they are that you make
responsible for his survival. You have now found your instruments;
look for your activities. Let the tongue gourmandize, let the eyes
melt with staring, let the sense of hearing luxuriate, let the belly
be filled, let the wanton organs have their way! You have found
your activities, you have hit upon your good. Is this survival? Is
this happiness?[9]

Oration 32

1   Aesop the Phrygian composed dialogues and conversations
between animals, in which he made even trees and fishes converse,
one with another and with men too, indiscriminately.[1] But
blended into those dialogues there is always a modest lesson that
hints at some truth. Among the fables he tells is the following. A
lion was chasing a deer. The deer, in her flight, drew away from
him and plunged into a deep thicket. The lion (her inferior in speed
by as much as he was her superior in strength), halted by the
thicket and asked a shepherd if he had seen a deer hiding anywhere. The shepherd said that he hadn't seen her, and as he spoke
he held out his hand and pointed to the spot. The lion leaped after
the wretched deer, while the fox (she is the wise one in Aesop's
fables) said to the shepherd: 'What a coward and a villain you
have turned out to be: a coward towards lions, and a villain
towards deer.'[2]

2   It seems to me that Epicurus too could use this allusive story
of the Phrygian's against the condemner of Pleasure, who is
resolute in his words, but in his sympathies (just like the shepherd
with his hand) inclines towards Pleasure. Who could be so at odds
with himself as willingly to shake off the one thing his human
nature finds most attractive of all? All other things that are

    [9] Compare *Or.* 33. 7–8 below, where what is essentially the same argument is
unfolded for a second time. The pro-Epicurean *Or.* 32 is thus framed between two
emphatic assertions of the claim that it betrays human nature; this certainly makes
the overall message of the sequence of lectures clear, but at some cost in elegance
and economy.
    [1] For other references to Aesop, and uses of Aesopic fable, in the *Orations*, cf. *Orr.*
15. 5, 19. 2, and 36. 1.
    [2] The closest surviving parallels to this fable are Babrius, *Fab.* 50 and Phaedrus,
Appendix Perottina 28 (pp. 372 ff. in Loeb *Babrius and Phaedrus*).

pursued by men are either accepted because discovered by experience, or respected because tried and tested by science, or trusted because examined by reason, or welcomed because they have stood the test of time; but Pleasure, which needs no assistance from reason and is more venerable than any human science, forestalls experience and does not need to wait for the passing of time; human affection for it is overwhelming and as old as the body itself; it is set down, so to speak, as the foundation-stone of the survival of the species. If anyone removes it, all that has accrued must inevitably vanish. Knowledge and reason and the very thing that all harp on about so, intelligence itself, men have assembled for themselves over time, gathering them together through experience, by the gradual enrichment of their perceptual encounters;[3] but Pleasure comes to them naturally and without teaching, and they have it at their disposal from the very start. Pleasure they embrace, pain they strive against; Pleasure ensures their survival, pain destroys them.[4]

3   Is Pleasure really worthless? In that case, it would not come naturally, nor be the most venerable of all the forces that promote our survival. As for the well-worn reproaches that sophists bring against it, Sardanapallus' luxury, and the extravagance of the Medes, and Ionian decadence, and Sicilian gourmandizing, and Sybaritic dances and Corinthian courtesans, all this, and anything yet more elaborate, is not the work of Pleasure, but of artifice and calculation, as men have used their recently acquired abundance of technical resources to break Pleasure's laws.[5] Just as nobody abuses Reason and says that it does not possess natural beauty, even if someone diverts its application to an end that is not naturally noble, so you should not abuse Pleasure either, rather than those who put it to bad uses. Of these two elements in the

---

[3] Standard Epicurean theory: Epicurus *Ep. Herod.* (Diog. Laert. 10. 75), Lucret. 5. 925-1457. For the topic, see also *Or.* 6. 2.

[4] The insistence that Pleasure is so obviously and so naturally basic to humanity as to need no argument is also standard Epicurean doctrine: Epicurus *Ep. Menoec.* (Diog. Laert. 10. 129) and fr. 398 Usener; Cic. *De Fin.* 1. 9. 30. Cf. Bignone (1973: ii. 318-19).

[5] Maximus again reproduces a familiar line of Epicurean argument—Epicurus *Ep. Menoec.* (Diog. Laert. 10. 129-30), Cic. *De Fin.* 1. 11. 37-9—but it is noticeable that he avoids distinctive technical detail: neither the terminology of 'natural' and 'necessary' pleasures, nor distinction between 'static' and 'dynamic' pleasure, nor the claim that beyond a certain point pleasure can only be varied, and not increased, is mentioned.

human soul, Pleasure and Reason, Pleasure when mixed with Reason removes none of Reason's power to compel, but adds greater attractiveness to it; while Reason, when it supervenes on pleasures, increases their tendency to moderation by making them easier to come by, while removing the element of compulsiveness from what is naturally pleasant.[6]

4   'But Pleasure is not unique to man; it is shared with all other creatures too!' What you say—the fact that Pleasure tends to preserve *all* to which Nature has given life—is actually the best guarantee that can be given that it ensures our survival too. Or is it the fact that it is shared that bothers you? What arrogance! It strikes me that you don't welcome the light of the sun either, because it is common property to all eyes,[7] when man alone should have been able to see it, and for this reason you refuse to count light a human good. In that case, neither is the air, though it is breathed in and regulates the body by its passage, nor the rivers' streams, nor the fruit of the earth. If you confine your attention to necessities, they are all shared, and none is the private property of any individual species. This is the category into which I wish you to place Pleasure too, as a shared good tending to promote the survival of the whole of perceiving creation.[8]

5   Since our task is to compare Virtue with Pleasure, I will not abuse Virtue (there is nothing biting or offensive about Pleasure's arguments), but I will say this much: if you deprive Virtue of what is pleasant in it, you will also deprive it of its practicability. No good thing is made the object of choice in the absence of Pleasure; the man who labours virtuously labours willingly because of his affection for Pleasure, present or anticipated. Just as in financial

---

[6] Text uncertain: perhaps 'reproach' or 'excess' rather than 'compulsiveness'. The stress placed here on the moderation of true pleasure is properly Epicurean (Epicurus *Ep. Menoec.*, Diog. Laert. 10. 131-2), but the way the issue is cast as one of an interplay between Pleasure and Reason betrays a more Platonizing frame of mind (thinking in terms of a bipartite psychology of Reason and Emotion; compare the account of the interplay of Reason and Love in *Or.* 21. 6). Maximus' 'defence' of Epicureanism seems not to be as purely Epicurean as a serious defender might have made it. However, the paragraph is printed by Usener in *Epicurea* as fr. 433, and the solidity of its Epicurean credentials is argued for in detail by Bignone (1973: ii. 313-18).

[7] For the sun as an example of a shared good, cf. *Or.* 20. 8 and Sen. *Ep.* 73. 6.

[8] Cf. (again) Cic. *De Fin.* 1. 9. 30.

transactions no one willingly exchanges a talent for a drachma,
unless

> Zeus has stolen his wits,[9]

but such exchanges, however evenly balanced, must benefit the
giver in a manner consistent with the interests of the receiver; just
so in our dealings with hard work, no one labours for love of
labour (what could be less desirable, after all), but instead bargains
his present labours against what a more urbane commentator
might call 'the Good', but a more veracious one would call
Pleasure—because even if you say 'the Good', you *mean* Pleasure;
goodness would hardly be goodness were it not also supremely
pleasurable.[10]

6   I believe this whole argument can be turned around; these
very considerations suffice to prove that Pleasure is more worthy
of choice than all other things, since for its sake men are prepared
to accept death and wounds and labours and countless other
vexations.[11] Even if you assign different names to the various
different forms such ⟨exchanges⟩ take, speaking of 'friendship'
when Achilles willingly accepts death and avenges the dead
Patroclus,[12] or 'kingship' when Agamemnon passes sleepless nights
and plans and fights for his people,[13] and 'defence of the homeland'
when Hector leads the way and fights as his people's champion,[14]
in all of these cases it is Pleasure that you are naming. Just as in
the case of physical illness the patient is glad to be cut and burned
and starved and parched, and willingly accepts all such naturally
unpleasant experiences because he is bargaining them against his
expectation of recovering his health, but if you remove his hopes
of future good, you also cancel his acceptance of his present
sufferings; just so in the field of moral conduct there is a trade-off
between Pleasure and toil, which you call Virtue, but I, while

---

[9] *Il.* 6. 234; cf. *Orr.* 35. 3, 39. 1.

[10] The claim that the pursuit of Pleasure necessitates the cultivation of the
Virtues, but that the Virtues are only worth pursuing because they yield Pleasure,
is again a standard part of the Epicurean case: Epicurus *Ep. Menoec* (Diog. Laert. 10.
132), Cic. *De Fin.* 1. 13. 42–16. 54 and 1. 18. 57–61.

[11] Cf. Cic. *De Fin.* 1. 10. 34–6. This is in fact the last substantial point to be made
in this pro-Epicurean lecture: the remaining five paragraphs do no more than illustrate it from Maximus' usual stock of mythological and historical exempla.

[12] Cf. esp. *Il.* 18. 78–126.

[13] Cf. esp. *Il.* 2. 1–34, 10. 1–24.

[14] Cf. esp. *Il.* 12. 243.

granting that Virtue is present, will still ask you whether the soul would have chosen Virtue if it did not feel some affection for it— and if you grant that there is affection, you grant that there is Pleasure.

7   Even if you change the name and call Pleasure 'delight', while not begrudging you your abundance of terminology, I will still keep my eye on the thing itself, and recognize Pleasure for what it is.[15] Or do you think that the great Heracles, the associate and contestant and intimate of those many amazing labours, who matched himself against wild beasts, who tackled mighty rulers in every region, who vied with savage opponents, who tamed the earth, the purifier, the man who went to Oeta and whose path led to the pyre, did not enter on this course willingly, lead on by pure, immense, and extraordinary pleasures, some accompanying the labours themselves, and others supervening on their conclusion? All *you* can see is his labours; what you fail to see are the pleasures in which he delighted. Heracles rejoiced as he performed these deeds, and performed them for that very reason; he would not have performed them if he had not enjoyed it. Dionysus' pleasures take the form of rituals, all those bands and revels and choruses and pipes and songs—all forms of Pleasure for Dionysus celebrated in the mysteries.

8   Why do I speak of Dionysus and Heracles? Their stories are matters for heroic myth. I will cite Socrates.[16] You burn, Socrates, for Alcibiades, and after him for Phaedrus, and after him for Charmides; you burn, Socrates, and no Athenian beauty escapes you. But confess the reason, and have no fear of disgrace. It is possible to love chastely and still feel pleasure, just as it is possible to love licentiously and still feel pain. If your passion has no pleasure in it, if you love the soul alone and not the body, then fall in love with Theaetetus. You don't, because he was snub-nosed.[17] Fall in love with Chaerephon. You don't, because he was pasty.[18] Fall in love with Aristodemus. You don't, because he was

---

[15] 'Delight' ($\chi\alpha\rho\dot{\alpha}$) is a distinctively Stoic term, denoting the good emotional state ($\epsilon\dot{\upsilon}\pi\acute{\alpha}\theta\epsilon\iota\alpha$) enjoyed by the virtuous person in place of pleasure (*SVF* iii. 431). For the ostentatiously relaxed attitude to terminology, cf. *Or.* 21. 4.

[16] Compare the review of Socrates' amatory activities in *Or.* 18. 4, and the defence of them in the remainder of *Orr.* 18–21.

[17] Plato *Theaet.* 209c.

[18] Cf. Aristoph. *Nub.* 103–4, Eupolis fr. 253 Kassel-Austin, $\varSigma$ Plato *Apol.* 20e.

ugly.[19] Whom then do you fall in love with? Anyone with attractive hair, anyone youthful, anyone delicate, anyone beautiful. I trust your virtue, because your love is just, but I do not mistrust your soul because you take pleasure in your love—any more than I mistrust a body warming by the fire, or eyes illuminated by the sun, or ears enjoying the music of pipes, or Hesiod instructed by the Muses, or Homer made eloquent by Calliope, or Plato drawing his grandeur from Homer.[20] Eyes, ears, bodies, words—all feel the pull of Pleasure.

9   It was Pleasure too that brought Diogenes to his cask.[21] If Virtue also contributed to the same effect in him, why should you rule Pleasure out of the account? Diogenes delighted in his cask as greatly as Xerxes did in Babylon; he delighted in his crust as Smindyrides did in his blood-sauce;[22] he delighted in springs everywhere as Cambyses did in the Choaspes alone;[23] he delighted in the sun as Sardanapallus did in his purple robes; he delighted in his staff as Alexander in his sceptre; he delighted in his knapsack as Croesus in his treasury. And if you compare pleasures with pleasures, it is Diogenes' that emerge victorious. The lives of his rivals are full of pleasure, but everywhere mixed with pain: Xerxes laments in defeat,[24] Cambyses groans over his wounds,[25] Sardanapallus moans as he burns, Smindyrides grieves as he is driven off,[26] Croesus weeps as he is taken prisoner,[27] Alexander

---

[19] According to Plato *Smp.* 173d and Xen. *Mem.* 1. 4. 2, Aristodemus' distinguishing feature was shortness, not bad looks.

[20] i.e. Socrates' love affairs were as innocently natural and as naturally pleasant as the basic pleasures of the senses, and as productive of insight and truth as the more exalted, and more sophisticatedly pleasant, inspiration of other great poets and philosophers. For Hesiod and the Muses, cf. *Orr.* 37. 4–5 and 38. 2; for Homer and Calliope, *Orr.* 1. 2 and 26. 1; for Plato and Homer, *Or.* 26. 3. As in *Orr.* 4 and 26, Hesiod and Homer are here counted as philosophers on the same level as Socrates and Plato.

[21] With this account of Diogenes, compare *Or.* 36. 5–6. His cask, staff, knapsack, open-air life, and simple diet are also described in Diog. Laert. 6. 22–3, 31, and 37; the comparison between his simple contentment and oriental luxury is prominent in Dio's account of him in *Or.* 6.

[22] For Smindyrides the Sybarite, cf. *Or.* 14. 2.

[23] For the Choaspes as the source of the Persian king's drinking-water, cf. *Orr.* 33. 4 and 34. 6.

[24] Cf. Hdt. 7. 45 and 8. 100. 1.

[25] Cf. Hdt. 2. 65.

[26] Sc. by Cleisthenes of Sicyon, having failed (along with Hippocleides) to win the hand of his daughter Agariste: Hdt. 6. 126–30.

[27] Cf. Hdt. 1. 87. 2.

is pained when he isn't fighting. But Diogenes' pleasures are pleasures free from lamentation, free from grief and tears and pain. You call his pleasures labours, because you are assessing Diogenes' life by the defective measure of your own nature. You would feel pain if you behaved like that, but Diogenes felt pleasure. I would indeed make so bold as to say that Pleasure has had no more conscientious lover than Diogenes. He didn't live in a proper home, because managing a household causes headaches; he didn't take a role in public life, because that is a burdensome business; he declined to try the experience of marriage, because he had heard of Xanthippe;[28] he declined to have the experience of raising a family, for he saw the dangers. Liberated from all causes of distress, a free man, without a care, without needs, without pain, he inhabited the whole world as if it were a single house, alone of men living among pleasures that needed no guarding, pleasures subject to no rationing, pleasures in abundance.

10   Let us leave Diogenes, turning our attention to lawmakers instead and examining the constitutions they have established. Do not think that I am going to take us to Sybaris, or tell you about the Syracusans and their extreme decadence, or the hedonistic Corinthians, or the wealthy Chians, or the Lesbians with their outstanding wine, or the Milesians and their exquisite dress-sense. I am going to take us to the foremost states: I am going to take us to Athens, and to examine Sparta. Look: whips and Spartan flagellation, and hunting and running and simple meals and rough bedding; yet I can see the pleasure even in this.[29] Well done, Lycurgus! At the cost of trivial labours you have paved the way for great pleasures; for a small expenditure you have made a great profit; by paying out the labours of a day you have won eternal pleasures in return. What, you may ask, are these Spartan pleasures? A city that needs no walls, that has no fear, that has never felt fire or seen an enemy or foreign shields, that has never heard lamentation or threats. What could be more painful than fear? What could be more grievous than slavery? What more burdensome than compulsion? When you free a city from all this, you bring its citizens many pleasures in return. It was these

---

[28] Cf. Xen. *Smp*. 2. 10.
[29] With this account of Spartan society, compare *Orr*. 19. 5, 23. 2, and 34. 9 with Xen. *Lac. Pol*. 2 and Plut. *Lycurg*. 14–18.

pleasures that nourished Leonidas, that nourished Othryadas, that nourished Callicratidas.[30] 'But these men died.' They died nobly. 'For the sake of what pleasures?' Limbs of bodies are amputated to secure the comfort of the whole.[31] Leonidas was a limb of Sparta, and he died for Sparta's sake; so too were Othryadas and Callicratidas. By the amputation of these small limbs, the pleasures of home were preserved. Why do I need to mention arrangements at Athens? The world of Athens is full of festivals and enter-tainments, as they divide their pleasures up between the seasons, the Dionysia in the spring, the mysteries in the autumn, with different divinities presiding at different times of year, at the Panathenaea, the Scirophoria, the Haloa, the Apaturia.[32] As some fight battles at sea, the others are holding a festival at home; as some fight on land, the others are laughing in the theatre of Dionysus. Not even their wars, the most sombre of events, are devoid of pleasures: roles are found there for Etruscan trumpets and triremes' pipes and marching-songs. Do you see what an abundance of pleasures there is?

Oration 33

1   It is difficult to find a true account. The risk is that through an over-abundance of thoughts the human soul will cease to be able to exercise discrimination. Other sciences as they develop acquire a surer aim for the making of further discoveries, each in its own particular sphere; but when Philosophy reaches its peak of inventiveness, it is then that it is overwhelmed by equally balanced and countervailing arguments.[1] It is like a farmer who, when the quantity of his implements runs into superfluity, finds himself getting a smaller return from his land. Political disputes are settled by casting votes, and by a head-count of jurors, and the wit of the

---

[30] Leonidas: Hdt. 7. 204 ff.; Othryadas: Hdt. 1. 182, cf. *Or.* 23. 2; Callicratidas: Xen. *Hell.* 1. 6 etc.; cf. *Or.* 23. 2.

[31] The surgical image is more commonly used in explanations of the workings of divine Providence, as, for instance, Aurelius 5. 8; cf. *Or.* 41. 4.

[32] The number and regular distribution through the year of religious festivals is a standard topic in panegyric of Athens: cf. Aristoph. *Nub.* 305-10; Soph. *OC* 1006-7, [Xen.] *Ath. Pol.* 2. 9, 3. 2 and 8; Thuc. 2. 38 (in the Funeral Oration), Isocrates 4 (*Panegyr.*) 43-6; Aristides *Panath.* 341, 373-5.

[1] A state of affairs welcomed and actively fostered by Sceptics (cf. Sextus *Pyrrh. Hyp.* 1. 202-4), but worrying to a dogmatist.

orator, and by the hands of the people; but in our case who will sit as juror for us, and by what process of voting will we decide on the truth? Reasoned argument? But there is no argument you can give me to which an answer cannot be found. Emotional response? An untrustworthy juror! A majority vote? The majority are fools. Reputation? It is inferior things that enjoy the higher reputation.[2]

2   This present enquiry of ours, in which Pleasure is contesting and being compared with Virtue, is a case in point. Does not Pleasure, thrusting Virtue aside, triumph in popular repute, enjoy the support of a greater number of witnesses, and hold first place in the scale of emotional reaction? As for the one ally Virtue had left, rational argument, this too is split and divided, and support for Pleasure has been found in it too: fine words are pronounced on Pleasure's behalf, Virtue is belittled, and command transferred from the men's quarters to the women's.[3] Our protagonist shrugs off the appearance of a philosopher, but still lays claim to the name. Relinquish the name too, my man, along with the arguments! You are in error about the very foundations of the matter. Wisdom and Pleasure have nothing at all in common. The lover of Pleasure and the lover of Wisdom are different people; their names, their deeds, their kinds are separate, as Spartan is separate from Athenian, as foreigner from Greek. If while claiming to be a Spartiate and a Hellene and a Dorian and a Heraclid, you still admire Median diadems and barbarian feasts and Persian wagons, then you have gone Persian, you have turned barbarian, you have sacrificed Pausanias.[4] You are a Mede, you are a Mardonius.[5] Relinquish the name along with the nationality.

3   I can stand the majority singing the praises of Pleasure; a lowly soul divorced from rationality is to be pitied for its feelings and forgiven for its ignorance. But Epicurus, because of the name he claims, I cannot bear, nor will I tolerate Philosophy playing the

---

[2] There may be a faint echo of Plato *Grg.* 471e-472c and 473e-474a in this contrast of rhetorical and philosophical modes of argument.

[3] The image echoes a witticism of Diogenes, comparing Sparta with Athens (Diog. Laert. 6. 59).

[4] Pausanias' was a famous case of corruption on exposure to the wealth and possibilities of the East: Thuc. 1. 94-5, 128-35.

[5] For the selection of Mardonius as a particularly degenerate foreigner, cf. *Or.* 14. 8.

wanton, any more than I will tolerate a general who abandons his post and leads his troops in flight, or a farmer who burns his own crops, or a helmsman who plays the coward when confronted with the sea.[6] You must sail, you must take command, you must work the land. These are all occupations full of toil, but nothing fine is won by idleness. If pleasure follows on from noble achievements, then I will allow it: let it follow, but in every venture let it be the Good that takes the lead;

> let there be one ruler,
>   One king,

the one to whom Zeus gave command.[7] If you change the ranking, so that Pleasure leads and Reason follows, you are imposing on the soul a vindictive and implacable tyrant, to which it must play the slave, serving it in all kinds of ways that it is not at liberty to criticize, even if the commands are shameful and immoral. What moderation would Pleasure observe, once it had won full licence to indulge its desires? This is indeed an insatiable tyrant who despises what he has and grasps after what he does not, who is inspired by the prospect of excess, given wings by his hopes, and made wanton by his wealth. This is the tyrant who makes evil rise up against good, who arms wrong against right, and excess against due measure.[8] Real physical need finds no difficulty in satisfying its desires. Is someone thirsty? There are springs everywhere. Is someone hungry? There are oak trees everywhere.[9] Here is the sun, the warmest of cloaks. Here are meadows, the most ornate of sights. Here are flowers, with their natural perfumes. Up to this point need itself may be taken as setting the limits on your pleasures; but if you go beyond this and advance further, you grant pleasures an unstoppable career, and shut out the virtues.[10] [4] It is this that begets greed; it is this that creates tyrants. Pasargadae and Cyrus' cardamom[11] do not provide the king of

---

[6] Three standard exemplars of science and control (often applied to God and to the philosopher, cf. e.g. *Orr.* 4. 9, 5. 8, 8. 7, and 15. 5), here used to underline the depth of Epicurus' betrayal of proper philosophical values.

[7] *Il.* 2. 204–5.

[8] Compare the descriptions of the tyranny of Fate in *Or.* 5. 5 and of Desire in *Or.* 20. 6–8.

[9] Acorns were the food of primitive man: cf. *Orr.* 21. 5 and 23. 5.

[10] As a criticism of Epicureanism, this is misconceived, since the Epicureans too insisted on the need to keep pleasures simple: cf. *Or.* 32. 3, with n. 6 above.

[11] Cf. Xen. *Cyrop.* 1. 2. 8; [Diogenes] *Ep.* 30.

Persia[12] with sufficient scope; the whole of Asia is pressed into service to tend the pleasures of a single man. Media raises Nisaean horses for him,[13] Ionia sends Greek concubines,[14] Babylon raises barbarian eunuchs, Egypt sends arts of every kind, the Indians ivory, the Arabs perfume. The rivers too tend the king's pleasures, Pactolus providing gold, the Nile wheat, and the Choaspes water.[15] Yet not even this is enough for him; he desires foreign pleasures, and for this marches against Europe, pursuing the Scythians, banishing the Paeonians from their homeland, capturing Eretria, sailing against Marathon,[16] and ranging everywhere. How utterly wretched he is in his poverty! Because what could be more impoverished than a man in a constant state of desire? When once the soul has tasted pleasures that go beyond its real needs, it becomes tired of what it used to enjoy and longs for something new. This is the true meaning of the riddle of Tantalus, the incessant thirst of a hedonist, the streams of pleasure advancing and retreating again, the ebb and flow of desires and the bitter pains, the consternation and fears, that contaminate them.[17] When Pleasure is there, he fears that it is going to desert him; when it is absent, he is in anguish that it may not return. Thus it is unavoidable that the man who pursues Pleasure should never cease to feel pain, and fail to register it when he is experiencing pleasure, and live a chaotic life completely lacking in definition.[18]

5   Consider what kind of a tyrant it is you are imposing on your soul, as if you were rejecting Solon and imposing Critias on the Athenians instead, or rejecting Lycurgus and imposing Pausanias on the Spartans. In my desire for freedom it is laws and reason that I need. It is these that will preserve my happiness true and

[12] Darius, as the sequel makes clear; cf. *Or.* 20. 9. The description of his dissatisfaction and insatiability recalls that of Philip and Alexander in *Or.* 29. 2.

[13] Cf. Hdt. 7. 40. 2-3.

[14] Cf. Hdt. 3. 134. 5.

[15] Pactolus: Hdt. 4. 101. 2; Choaspes: Hdt. 1. 188.

[16] Scythians: Hdt. 4. 1 ff.; Paeonians: 5. 12-15; Eretria: 6. 100-2; Marathon: 6. 102ff.

[17] *Od.* 11. 582-92. Maximus' allegorization of Tantalus resembles Socrates' of the Danaids in Plato *Grg.* 493ac. For Tantalus as an image of *l'homme moyen sensuel,* cf. Lucian *Charon* 15 and *Bis Accus.* 21, and for his use by later Platonists as an image of the fallen soul, Buffière (1956: 487-9). Compare also *Orr.* 1. 5 and 29. 5 for the topic of the dissatisfactions of materialism.

[18] As in § 3 above, another ostensibly anti-Epicurean point with which Epicurus would in fact whole-heartedly agree.

unshaken and independent and self-sufficient, rather than degraded and subjected to those human crafts through which I might scrape together and assemble this great benefit, Pleasure—begging not for scraps, by Zeus, like Homer's beggar, nor swords and cauldrons alone,[19] but yet more outlandish things than these: relishes from Mithaecus, wine from Sarambus, songs from Connus, courtesans from Melesias.[20] What measure can be observed in all this? What limit will be set on the happiness that comes from Pleasure? Where will we come to a halt? To whom shall we go and award the prize? Who is this happy, vigilant, hard-working individual whom no pleasure evades or passes by, neither by night nor by day, whose soul stretches out all its senses, like the marine octopus stretching out its tentacles, so as to gather in all pleasures together from every quarter?[21]

6   Let us if it can be done mould an image of this character, a man happy with the happiness of Pleasure, beholding the pleasantest of colours, hearing the pleasantest of sounds, smelling the most pleasant of fragrances, tasting the most elaborate of flavours, warming himself, and enjoying the pleasures of love at the same time. If you allow intervals, and space his pleasures out, and separate his sensations, you will curtail his happiness, because everything that gives pleasure when present brings pain when taken away. What soul could endure such a mob of pleasures flowing into it and bearing down on it, allowing no interval or respite at all? Is it not likely that it would lead a wretched existence, longing for change and yearning for a respite? Pleasure protracted produces pain. And what could be more incredible than a form of happiness that arouses pity? O Zeus and the gods, you fathers and creators of earth and sea, and all the creatures of the earth and sea, what a creature this is you have stationed in this

---

[19] An allusion to the description of the disguised Odysseus in *Od.* 17. 222.

[20] Mithaecus and Sarambus: cf. Plato *Grg.* 518b; Connus: Plato *Euthyd.* 272c. The reference to 'Melesias' is obscure: it has been suggested that the text ought to read 'a Milesian'.

[21] The invitation to picture a wholly gratified person is another commonplace of discussions of Epicurean hedonism: cf. Cic. *De Fin.* 1. 12. 40-1 (pro-Epicurus) and 2. 24. 114 (anti-Epicurus). The comparison of the senses to the tentacles of an octopus follows Stoic precedent: see [Plut.] *Placita* 898ef and 903ab (tentacles = the seven subordinate senses radiating from the ἡγεμονικόν; cf. also Plut. *Non Posse* 1098de, where the tentacles stand for desires). The application to the hedonist works particularly well because the octopus was generally supposed to have a strong appetite: Aelian *Nat. An.* 1. 27 (food) and 6. 28 (sex).

life and this realm! How bold and impetuous and rapacious, impotent to achieve the Good, bereft of function, the plaything of the pleasures that nurture it.

Would that it had never been born, and had died unwed,[22]

this whole race, if it is going to receive from you no greater gift than Pleasure.

7   But surely it does. Let us reply on Zeus' behalf in Homeric style. The gift it receives is intelligence and reason; but its life is a compound of mortal and immortal elements, as befits an animal stationed between two poles, having a body derived from mortal discord, but receiving its intelligence from an outflow of the divine.[23] The function particular to the flesh is Pleasure, that particular to the intelligence is Reason; mankind shares flesh with the beasts, but intelligence is its own distinctive possession. You should therefore seek the human good where the distinctive function of man is to be found; ⟨and the distinctive function where the distinctive instrument is to be found;⟩ and the distinctive instrument where the factor that ensures its survival resides. Begin from that preserving factor. Which preserves which, body soul, or soul body? ⟨Soul body.⟩ You have your preserver. ⟨Now look for the instrument.⟩ What is the soul's instrument? Intelligence. Now look for the distinctive function. What is the proper function of intelligence? The exercise of wisdom. You have your Good.[24] If one were to neglect this portion of man, the portion that exercises wisdom and is loved by the gods, and were eager to cherish the worthless part alone, I mean the flesh, the unbridled, extravagant part loved by Pleasure, what image, or what myth for that matter, could we find to illustrate the resulting form of nurture?

8   Poets tell us that there was once a Thessalian race that lived on Pelion and had strange bodies, with the rear quarters of horses, from the navel down. In such an uncouth conjunction as this it is surely entirely inevitable that human and bestial nature should pasture together: that such creatures should speak like men but

---

[22] *Il.* 3. 40.
[23] For the idea of man as a compound of divine and mortal elements, cf. *Orr.* 7. 5, 9. 6, 10. 9, 21. 7, 36. 1, and 41. 5.
[24] This final appeal to the argument from human nature completes what was begun in *Orr.* 29. 7 and 31. 3–5, and answers the Epicurean 'perversion' of the argument in *Or.* 32. 2–4. Cf. *Or.* 31. 4, with n. 5 above.

feed like beasts, see like men but mate like beasts. Well done, poets and sons of poets, progenitors of an ancient and noble poetry; what a clear allegory you have given us of the bond that binds us to the pleasures![25] When bestial desires overwhelm the soul, they do not alter the external human appearance, but in the actions he performs they reveal their victim as a beast not a man. This is what is meant by the Centaurs, the Gorgons, the Chimaeras, Geryon, and Cecrops.[26] Remove the desires of the belly, and you have removed the beast from man; remove the desires of the privy parts, and you have cut the beast in two! But as long as these desires live in a man and are nourished in him, and he defers to them and tends them, it is inevitable that it should be their impulses that dominate, and that his soul should speak with their accents.

ORATION 34　　The Benefits of Adverse Circumstances

Introduction

= 5 (1962) = 35 (Laur. Conv. Sopp. 4). The manuscript title—Ὅτι ἔστιν καὶ ἐκ τῶν περιστάσεων ὠφελεῖσθαι, 'That it is possible to derive benefit even from external circumstance'—gives a reasonable impression of the contents, though it conceals the thematic link with the lectures immediately preceding.

A further lecture on Ends and the Good Life. Orr. 29–33 have argued that Pleasure is no part of the Human Good; Or. 34 now argues the complementary case that pursuit of the true Good, Virtue, cannot be separated from toil and effort, and, correspondingly, that toil and effort (and the harshness of the world that necessitates it) are no evils. The lecture is thus also, implicitly, a

---

[25] For the idea of poets as teachers by allegory, cf. Orr. 4 and 26.

[26] This gallery of mythical Mischwesen, symbolizing the combination in man of a lower, bestial nature with something higher and more truly human, is inspired by two Platonic passages: the image of the lion, the man, and the many-headed beast (= reason, 'spirit', and appetite, the three divisions of the soul) in Resp. 588c ff.; and the reference to Typhon as a possible image for human nature in Phaedr. 230a (with Centaurs, the Chimaera, the Gorgons, and Pegasus in 229d). For a parallel development of the same kind of material, cf. Sen. Ep. 92. 8–10.

vindication of divine Providence: note particularly §§ 1 and 3, but contrast the more overt theodicy of *Orr*. 38. 7 and 41.

Both the general claim that apparent evils are in fact indispensable tools for the realization of good purposes, and its specific application to the struggle to lead a morally good life, are best known as elements in Stoic thinking: see *SVF* ii. 1152 and 1173 (Chrysippus), with Sandbach (1989, ch. 6); Sen. *Prov*. (esp. 2. 2–7); Epict. 1. 6 (esp. 32–5), 1. 24 (esp. 1–2), and 3. 12. The reality of divine Providence was, however, an equally central tenet of Middle Platonic thinking ([Plut.] *Placita* 884f; Alcin. *Didasc*. 7. 161. 5–6, 12. 167. 12–15; Apul. *De Plat*. 1. 12; cf. *Or*. 5. 4 with n. 19), and the whole package is easily assimilable to a Platonist viewpoint. See further Introduction, pp. xxvi–xxx.

Gregoras takes two excerpts from the lecture (from §§ 1 and 3), and the compiler of Neap. 100 likewise two (both from § 4). The *Lexicon Vindobonense* takes four quotations, three from § 1 and one from § 3. The annotator of Marc. gr. 514 (whether Cardinal Bessarion himself, or a close associate) makes twenty-one notes in the margins of foll. 164ʳ–166ʳ, signalling points of interest in all nine paragraphs of the lecture. Franciscus Junius quotes the statement about colour-contrast from the end of § 5 in *The Painting of the Ancients* iii. iii. 4 (Aldrich *et al.* 1991: i. 242).

Oration

1   It is a terrible thing. On men's behalf the gods have separated good from all association with evil, ruling that each should have nothing to do with the other and distinguishing between their natures, like night and day, and light and dark, and water and fire (if you take any of these and move it towards its opposite, mixing their diverse properties into a single common state, you will destroy what is distinctive of each). Yet men on their own initiative and of their own free will, in pursuit of a happy life, mix together ⟨good and bad in their lives. This is perverse. For who but a fool, were we to allow)[1] him to live in perpetual daylight, without sleep and without the need of repose by night, would grow weary of the sun, because it never withdrew nor retired into the shadows? Wait

---

[1] The text is clearly deficient at this point. The supplement suggested is an attempt to reconstruct an intelligible sequence of thought, but is only one possibility among several.

there. Perhaps I can give an answer † . . . †,[2] to the following effect. If there is some power of human sight capable of enduring perpetual light, and if there is some device whereby the sun can be halted in its circular course so as to stand still above the earth for ever,[3] shedding its light on us like a beacon from a high peak—if this state of affairs could come about, and the sun could stand still, while the eyes could endure gazing at it without interruption, who would be so manic and foolish and ill-starred in his passions as to desire night and darkness and idleness of the eye, and a state of bodily prostration almost indistinguishable from that of a corpse? But if the eyes would sooner be able to endure sleeplessness than the sun stand still, and the sun would sooner stand still than the eyes endure sleeplessness, the point is not that affection for light is something to be prayed for, but that acquaintance with darkness is something indispensable.

2   So it is too with love for the Good. The soul desires Good—how could it not? And it is at war with evil—how could it not be? But it is able neither to attain what it desires in a pure form, nor to avoid a necessary entanglement with what it strives against. I am not at this point talking about a wicked soul (that would mean one entirely evil, with no element of good in it, lacking confidence even in its hopes, and liable to fall at any moment even when enjoying good fortune); I mean a good soul possessed of wisdom. Let us see whether we are to declare that this soul too, when it gets a grip on Virtue, can enjoy an easy course in life,[4] and occupy the summit of felicity without interruption.[5] Or is this impossible for human nature? There are after all many obstacles lying in our path, like ditches and cliffs and pits and walls before a man running swiftly along. In such cases the man who does not know the road and is a weak runner and a feeble jumper and liable to slip as he runs along an edge trips and stumbles and gives up out of cowardice; but the good, trained runner who knows the road runs fast because he is strong, unerringly because he knows his

[2] The Greek text is unintelligible at this point, and no convincing emendation has yet been suggested.

[3] For the *adynaton*, cf. *Or.* 31. 1.

[4] Maximus here quotes a Stoic definition of happiness, cf. *SVF* i. 184 (Zeno), 554 (Cleanthes); iii. 4, 16, 73 (Chrysippus).

[5] For the image of the upward road to Happiness (or Virtue), cf. *Orr.* 15. 7 and 40. 4, along with the pasages cited in the next note.

route, and without stopping because he is well trained. He knows which parts of the route are smooth and secure, and which are broken and interrupted, such that the runner is obliged to traverse them, but would not have chosen to of his own free will.[6]

3   Homer provides an allegorical representation of this feature of human lives:

> Two jars stand on Zeus' threshold,[7]

he says, the one full of evils without any admixture of goods, the other containing a mixture of the two (he never mentions any third jar, with only good things in it, in Zeus' palace). According to Homer, Zeus draws from these two jars and distributes what he draws to the human race: from the one jar, a mighty, forceful stream of ever-flowing evils, full of strife and vengeance and terror and fear, and countless other hateful and unrelieved ills; from the other jar he distributes what Homer would call a mixed stream of goods and ills, but I, though I see the mixture and accept the story, would like to find a fairer name for this better of Zeus' two distributions. It works like this.

4   It is Virtue and Vice in the soul that are the springs that feed Zeus' jars. Vice, sending forth a fierce and rushing torrent, brings chaos and confusion to human life, like the onset of a river in winter spate as it rushes at crops and planted fields, hateful to farmers, shepherds, and travellers alike, sterile, infertile, unprofitable, and dangerous; but the springs of Virtue, if ever they well up in a man's soul, make his whole life fertile and arable and fruitful.[8] Yet the farmer still needs sweat and effort and toil.[9] Not even the

----

[6] For the imagery of cliffs and chasms on the road of Life, cf. *Orr.* 1. 3, 8. 7, 19. 1 and 39. 3.

[7] *Il.* 24. 527; the whole passage runs from 527 to 533. The theology of the lines had been challenged by Plato, in *Resp.* 379cd, on the grounds that the gods can be responsible for good alone (a point Maximus too endorses in, for example, *Or.* 41. 2–3 and 5). Maximus' interpretation here saves Homer's credit by taking the jars as an allegory of the consequences of human moral choice, not of divine dispensation. In this he may well have been guided by Plato's own imitation in *Grg.* 493d–494a, where the contrasting states of soul of the miserable hedonist and the happy seeker after Truth and Virtue are compared to two jars. For Neoplatonic allegorizations of the Homeric passage, cf. Buffière (1956: 458, 554).

[8] For (river or sea) water as an image of confusion, cf. *Orr.* 1. 2, 8. 7, 9. 6, 11. 7 and 10, 30. 1–2, etc.; for farming as an image of the cultivation of Virtue, *Orr.* 5. 8 and 33. 1 and 3.   [9] Cf. again *Or.* 33. 3.

Egyptian places his trust in the Nile alone, nor does he entrust his
seed to the soil until he has yoked his ox to the plough, cut a
furrow, and toiled hard; it is only then that he summons the river
on to his land. This is the manner in which the river is combined
with the farmer's labour, hopes with efforts, and crops with toil;
this is how goods should be combined with ills. If you wish, you
may remove the ill-sounding name, but you must realize that the
realities that underlie it must not be taken away from those who
toil. If you come to a harbour, you will take as your helmsman not
the man who has no experience of storms and has never seen a
wave, but the man who has gained his expertise gradually from
many failures, from the experience of ill fortune. I would also mistrust a general who has succeeded in all his ventures ⟨and would
be readier to trust one who occasionally failed,⟩[10] the kind of
general Nicias would have made for the Athenians if he had
returned safely from Syracuse, or the kind of demagogue Cleon
would have been had he returned from Amphipolis.[11] But when I
see helmsman or general, private individual or ruler, man or city,
enjoy success in all things, I mistrust their luck, as Solon did
Croesus' and Amasis did Polycrates'.[12]

5   Croesus ruled a land rich in horses, Polycrates a maritime
domain patrolled by a fine navy; but none of this was secure,
neither Croesus' land nor Polycrates' sea; Orontes seized
Polycrates, Cyrus seized Croesus,[13] and a mass of ills followed on
the heels of a long period of prosperity. This is why Solon did not
count Croesus happy, because he was wise; this is why Amasis
renounced Polycrates, because he was cautious; this is why I
approve a life that has tasted ills, but only tasted them—

He moistens his lips, but his palate he does not moisten—[14]

a life that possesses Virtue, but exercises it also in the face of
unwanted fortunes. The brightest of colours is the one that the eyes
love, but if you do not set a dark colour beside it, you detract from

[10] Some such supplement as this is needed to preserve an intelligible sequence of
thought. For helmsman and general as images for the virtuous man, cf. e.g. *Or.* 33.
3; and for the point that failures are inevitable in the process of learning a craft or
science, Plato *Grg.* 514e.
[11] Nicias' death at Syracuse: Thuc. 7. 86; Cleon's at Amphipolis: Thuc. 5. 10.
[12] Solon and Croesus: Hdt. 1. 32; Amasis and Polycrates: Hdt. 3. 40.
[13] Polycrates and Oroetes (*sic*): Hdt. 3. 120ff.; Croesus and Cyrus: Hdt. 1. 84 ff.
[14] *Il.* 22. 495.

the pleasure it gives; if you mix harsh fortunes with good, you will find it easier to perceive Virtue and appreciate good fortune.

6   It is indeed thirst that prepares the body to enjoy the pleasures of drinking, and hunger that prepares the body to enjoy the pleasures of eating, and night that prepares the eyes to enjoy the pleasure of looking on the sun; yet men desire night in succession to day, and hunger in succession to repletion, and thirst in succession to drunkenness, and if you deprive them of the variation, you turn their pleasure into pain. So the story goes about Artoxerxes, king of Persia, who at one time, because of the long years of peace and the uninterrupted course of his pleasures, failed to realize his own good fortune; Asia prepared him his dinner, the fairest of rivers furnished his drink, the skills of countless craftsmen engineered his comforts. But when war came to him from the sea, ten thousand Greeks and their accomplished commanders, he fled in defeat to a bare hilltop, where he rested for the night, and it was here that the wretched man felt thirst for the very first time, where there was no Choaspes or Tigris or Nile, no drinking-cups, and no cupbearers. He had to be content to accept from the hand of a Mardian a simple leather flask of brackish water. Then it was that the wretched man realized the true point of thirst and the true pleasure of drinking.[15]

7   Will it then be impossible to have too much good fortune, though one can have too much pleasure? I believe it will be possible, and in a form more painful than any repletion felt over food and drink. Inactivity is intolerable to Achilles, silence to Nestor, and absence of risk to Odysseus. Achilles I take it could have lived in peace, and ruled over the Myrmidons, and farmed the land of Thessaly, and looked after old Peleus;[16] Nestor could have ruled in peace in Pylos, and grown old in tranquillity; Odysseus could have stayed at home by Neritus with its fair trees, in the land that rears fine sons,[17] or at the end of his wanderings have stayed with Calypso in her shady and well-watered cave, waited on by the

---

[15] Cic. *Tusc.* 5. 97 tells the same improving story of Darius III Codomannus, the opponent of Alexander. Maximus prefers to tell it of a monarch with connections with his heroes Xenophon and Agesilaus. For the picture of Eastern luxury, cf. esp. *Orr.* 32. 9 and 33. 4.

[16] Cf. *Il.* 9. 356–400 (Achilles' reply to Odysseus in the Embassy) and 24. 540–2 (Achilles to Priam).

[17] Cf. *Od.* 9. 21–7 (Odysseus to Alcinous); *Od.* 9. 27 is quoted in *Or.* 23. 1.

Nymphs, ageless and immortal.[18] But he rejected an immortality that came at the cost of inactivity, and the loss of all opportunity to exercise his virtue in action. It is inevitable that he who takes on the life of Virtue, when confronted with human fortunes, should often have cause to cry out,

> Bear up, my heart, you have endured worse before now![19]

8   Who would remember Odysseus, if you deprived him of his sufferings? Who would remember Achilles, if you deprived him of Hector and the Scamander and the 'twelve cities by the sea' and eleven on the mainland?[20] Men had no other reason for taking Heracles and making him son of Zeus, apart from his association with trial and tribulation. If you deprive him of wild beasts and tyrants, and his journeyings up and down, and all those terrors he faced, then you slight his virtue.[21] At the Olympic and Pythian games you cannot win the olive-crown or the apples by competing on your own, and you need an opponent in order to be proclaimed victor; in the stadium of life and the contests that are fought out there, what opponent could a good man have apart from experience of tribulation?[22]

9   Come, let us summon the contestants to the stadium. Let Socrates come from Athens to fight against Meletus and the prison and the poison; let Plato come from the Academy to fight against an angry tyrant and a wide sea and great dangers.[23] Let another Athenian contestant step forward too, to fight against Tissaphernes and his broken oath, Ariaeus and his plotting, Menon and his treachery, and the king of Persia's assaults.[24] Summon me also the athlete from Pontus: let him too fight a lusty contest against hateful opponents, poverty and obscurity and hunger and cold.[25] I approve of his exercises too:

---

[18] Cf. *Od.* 1. 13-15, 5. 57 ff. and 203 ff.

[19] *Od.* 20. 18.

[20] Scamander: *Il.* 21. 136 ff.; cities: *Il.* 9. 328.

[21] For this use of Heracles, cf. *Or.* 38. 7 and Epict. 1. 6. 32-5.

[22] For the imagery of the games, and the insistence on the importance of effort, cf. *Orr.* 1. 4 and 6, 3. 4, and 12. 9; and Epict. 1. 24. 1-2.

[23] In the voyages to Sicily described in *Ep.* 7; cf. *Or.* 15. 9. This set-piece encomium of Plato, Xenophon, and Diogenes as exemplars of virtuous effort has much in common with *Or.* 15. 9.

[24] Xenophon, in the *Anabasis*; cf. again *Or.* 15. 9.

[25] For Diogenes, cf. *Orr.* 15. 9 (again), 32. 9, and 36. 5-6.

He humbled himself with shaming blows,
Casting mean tatters about his shoulders,[26]

and by this means won an easy victory. For such deeds I crown
these men, and proclaim them victors in their virtue. But if you
deprive them of their struggles against hostile fortune, you strip
them of their crowns and banish them from the contest. Deprive
the Athenians of their dash to Marathon, and the casualties they
suffered there, and Cynaegirus' hand, and Polyzelus' catastrophe,
and Callimachus' wounds,[27] and you leave them with nothing of
note except their incredible myths of Erichthonius and Cecrops.
This is why Sparta remained free for the longest period of any state,
because the Spartans did not relax even in times of peace: see their
whips and Laconian flagellations, the cultivation of ills that they
combined with their virtues![28]

ORATION 35   Friendship

Introduction

= 6 (1962) = 36 (Laur. Conv. Sopp. 4). The manuscript title—Πῶς ἄν τις
πρὸς φίλον παρασκευάσαιτο, 'How might one ready oneself for dealings with
a friend?'—does not match the contents of the lecture particularly well.

A second lecture on the topic of friendship, for which see the introduction to the first, Or. 14. Whereas Or. 14 focused on the distinction between the true Friend and the mere Flatterer, Or. 35
develops the proposition that true Friendship is impossible without
moral Virtue (a proposition which both underlines the value of
friendship and explains its scarcity). The positioning of the lecture
at this point in the corpus, among the pieces dealing with theoretical ethics, rather than, like Or. 14, among those dealing with
practical ethics and politics, is at first sight surprising. Enough of
the lecture, however, is expressed in terms of the choice of Ends
(especially the reference to 'likeness to Zeus' in § 2, and the call to

---

[26] Od. 4. 244-5, also quoted in 15. 9, in the same context of praise of Diogenes'
practical virtue.

[27] Standard topics both in panegyric of Athens and in historical declamation: cf.
Or. 23. 3 with n. 14.

[28] Cf. Orr. 19. 5, 23. 2, and 32. 10.

philosophical values in §§ 7–8) to make the juxtaposition with *Orr.* 29–33 comprehensible; and the scornful attack mounted on contemporary degeneracy sits well next to that in *Or.* 36. 1–2.

§§ 1–2a establish the initial proposition that friendliness is next to godliness; the implication, that the pursuit of Friendship is identical to the pursuit of Virtue, becomes progressively clearer as the lecture unfolds (see esp. §§ 6 ff., with n. 23). §§ 2b–3 dilate on the moral failings by which humanity falls short of divine standards of friendliness, and §§ 4–5 on the consequent scarcity of examples of true Friendship in history. §§ 6–7 return to the question of moral failings, and the inner and outer factors responsible for them; § 8, in conclusion, identifies Philosophy as the sole means both to Virtue and to Friendship.

The lecture is almost entirely neglected by scholiasts, excerptors, lexicographers, and paroemiographers. The only early exception is provided by the annotator of Marc. gr. 514, Bessarion or a close associate, who makes twenty notes in the margins of foll. 166^r–168^r, drawing attention to points of detail in all eight paragraphs. Rather later, Thomas De Quincey's attention was attracted by the implication in § 8 of 'a regular armistice proclaimed under faith and guarantee of Greece at the Periodic Games', which he noted on the back flyleaf of his copy of Heinsius' edition (Corpus Christi College, Oxford IV. 313a).

Oration

1   Can you tell me who it is that Homer is pleased to call 'like to the gods' and 'godly' and 'equal to Zeus in wisdom'? Who else but his heroes, Agamemnon and Achilles and Odysseus, and all the others who qualify for a share of his praises?[1] What then if he compared them not to Zeus, but either to Machaon the doctor, or Calchas the seer, or Nestor the horseman, or Mnestheus the tactician, or Epeius the carpenter, or Nireus the fair?[2] Would you not be able to tell me the reason for the comparison if I asked you? Or is it that you discern the resemblance in these latter cases, but in the former, though you know *that* the heroes are like Zeus, and

---

[1] Maximus here uses exactly the same introductory device as at the beginning of *Or.* 23.

[2] Machaon: *Il.* 4. 193–219; Calchas: *Il.* 1. 68–100; Nestor's horsemanship: *Il.* 2. 336, 23. 306–48, etc.; Mnestheus as tactician: *Il.* 2. 552–5; Epeius: *Od.* 8. 492–3, cf. *Or.* 1. 5; Nireus: *Il.* 2. 671–4.

you praise the poet who made the comparison for his discernment, you are ignorant of the point of resemblance itself? Come then, I will explain matters to you on Homer's behalf, speaking less ornately than he, 'for I am no poet'.[3] I do not believe that he calls Zeus 'father of gods and men' because he descended from the heavens, now in the form of a bird, now in the form of gold, using different disguises on different occasions, and made love to mortal women,

> First begetter of the race of glorious kings.[4]

That would give Zeus few children indeed! No; it was because he attributed to him the responsibility for the existence and the survival[5] of these races that he called him 'father', which is the most venerable of all the names that express affection.

2   Well then, that is how things are with Zeus himself. Do you think the case is any different with those who are like to Zeus? Or don't you see that not even Salmoneus was compared to Zeus by poets, even though he hurled thunderbolts (or so *he* thought) and imitated the crash of thunder and the flash of lightning?[6] In behaving like this Salmoneus actually resembled Thersites imitating Nestor.[7] How then are men to become similar to Zeus?[8] By imitating those preservative and affectionate and paternal qualities of his.[9] It is here that one sees the resemblance between divine and human Virtue, which among the gods is called 'right' and 'justice' and various other mystic and majestic names, and among men, 'friendship' and 'favour' and various other pleasant and human names.[10] Humanity falls short of divine Virtue in various respects,

---

[3] An echo of Plato *Resp.* 393d.

[4] Hesiod *Cat.* fr. 1. 6 M-W.

[5] Cf. the description of God in *Or.* 11. 12.

[6] For the story, see Hesiod *Cat.* fr. 30. 1-23 M-W, Apollod. 1. 9. 7, Virg. *Aen.* 6. 585-94.

[7] In *Il.* 2. 212 ff. Thersites' intervention can indeed be seen as a grotesque parody of Nestor's attempted mediation between Achilles and Agamemnon in bk. 1; Maximus is presumably drawing on a grammarian's observation.

[8] A gentle echo of the Platonist formulation of the End of human life, 'likeness to God' (Alcin. *Didasc.* 28. 181. 19 ff., Diog. Laert. 3. 78, etc.; cf. Plato *Theaet.* 176b1-2); see also *Or.* 26. 9.

[9] There is an allusion here to the cult titles Zeus Philios and Zeus Soter.

[10] An echo of those Homeric passages in which the divine and the human names for some place or creature or person are distinguished: *Il.* 1. 403-4, 14. 291, 20. 74; *Od.* 10. 305, 12. 61.

including the scope of its affections: human nature does not extend its warmth to all like beings, but just like herds of cattle, it is intimate only with its own immediate group; indeed one must be happy if it is intimate even with all of that.[11] But as matters now stand, in a single herd under the guidance of a single shepherd, you can see many conflicts and disputes as they butt and bite each other,[12] and only a few flickerings gathered laboriously together to make a small sum of friendship.[13] Food, drink, clothing, and other physical necessities men procure by bargaining, and by exchanging them for bronze and iron and (impressive substances!) gold and silver; yet they could dispense entirely with the skills of the miner, and obtain all such things from each other without effort, regulating their dealings by the fairest of all measures, with the person in need obtaining what he needs from the man who has it, while the man who has a surplus to dispose of gains from the taker, in an exchange that could not be faulted.[14]

3   Homer reproaches Lycian Glaucus for giving gold and accepting bronze in return, and exchanging the worth of a hundred oxen for the worth of nine;[15] but if they had set the value of these things to one side and measured the exchange by the intentions of the participants, the deal would I take it have been a fair one. But as things are now the world is full of commerce and trading and harsh dealing, in the market-place and at sea and on land, abroad and in town, locally and overseas, and land and sea are turned

[11] For the image of the human herd, cf. *Or.* 1. 3, with n. 15. Maximus' words also recall expositions of the Stoic doctrine of οἰκείωσις: see esp. Hierocles 11. 14–18 and in Stob. *Flor.* 84. 20, iii. 126. 11 ff. Meineke (= frr. 57D and 57G L-S).

[12] Cf. Plato *Grg.* 516a.

[13] The scarcity of true friendship is a familiar topos: cf. Cic. *De Fin.* 1. 20. 65; *De Am.* 15. 79; Sen. *De Ben.* 6. 33. 3; Plut. *Am. Mult.* 97b; Dio *Or.* 74. 28. The classic exceptions are Theseus and Peirithous, Achilles and Patroclus, and Orestes and Pylades (Cic. *De Fin.* and Dio locc. citt.); of these Maximus mentions only the second pair, but adds Harmodius and Aristogeiton.

[14] This would be equivalent to a return to the primitive state of humanity, before the invention of metallurgy and coinage: cf. *Or.* 36. 1–2, Posidonius in Sen. *Ep.* 90. 12 (cf. 36 ff.), Lucret. 5. 1113 ff., 1240 ff. For barter as an indication of virtuous simplicity, cf. the Euboean peasants in Dio *Or.* 7. 43 ff., with Vischer (1965); and for Maximus' own 'primitivist' preferences, cf. *Orr.* 4. 1–3, 26. 2, 28. 1. The importance of mutual benefit is stressed in the description of the 'first city' in Plato *Resp.* 369c (to which, however, coinage is soon admitted, 371b).

[15] Glaucus' famous exchange of armour with Diomedes (*Il.* 6. 232–6) was a proverbial case of a bad bargain: cf. *Orr.* 32. 5, 39. 1, and 40. 1. For other discussions and uses of the episode, cf. Arist. *NE* 5. 9, 1136ᵇ9–12, Σ *Il.* 6. 234, Julian *Ep. Themist.* 260ab and *Ep.* 64. 387c.

upside-down, as men hunt out what has never before been hunted, and unearth what has never been seen, and pursue what is far away, and procure what is scarce, and bury treasures and fill vaults and pile up hoards.[16] The reason for all this is a mistrust of friendship, and a lust for gain, and a fear of want, and evil habits, and a desire for pleasure, by all of which friendship is hounded and buried and sunk,[17] barely preserving itself in weak and feeble traces. Through a dearth of anyone to practise it, if this most sociable and open and generous of all feelings makes an appearance anywhere in Greek or foreign lands, it is instantly celebrated, and accorded the status of a myth, and its reality is debated. And this is not in the least surprising.

4   There came to Asia a Greek armada of a thousand ships, bearing an army comprising the flower of Greek manhood, who encamped and lived together, while for a period of ten years their barbarian enemies resisted them. The fame of their deeds, enshrined in Homer's poetry, can tell us of no example of true comradeship in all that great army over all those many years, bar only one, between a young man of Thessaly and a man of Locri, a friendship than which nothing in Homer is more pleasant to hear, more inspiring to Virtue, or more glorious for posterity to remember.[18] If you look at the rest of Homer, it is all battle and anger and threats and wrath, and their consequences, groans and lamentation and death and destruction and ruin. I believe there is also a story from Attica revered for the friendship it attests, which is celebrated in many Athenian histories. This story alone is worthy of Athena and of Theseus, as it tells of a fair and just friendship between two good men, which gave the two of them a single sword against a tyrant, a single watchword, and a single death.[19] After that there was no friendship in Attica; all was diseased and rotten and treacherous and corroded, full of envy and anger and boorishness and greed and ambition.

---

[16] A highly conventional denunciation; cf. Solon fr. 13. 43 ff., Tib. 1. 1. 1 ff. and 1. 3. 35 ff. with Smith (1913, ad locc.), and Maximus' own catalogues of misguided human pursuits in *Orr.* 1. 5, 5. 7, 15. 1, and 36. 6.

[17] Another commonplace: cf. Cic. *De Am.* 20 and 63, Themist. *Or.* 22. 266a.

[18] In Plato *Smp.* 180ab Achilles and Patroclus are described as lovers, but they are more often used as one of the few classic cases of friendship; cf. n. 13 above and Aeschines *Or.* 1 (*In Timarch.*) 133 ff.

[19] For Harmodius and Aristogeiton, cf. *Or.* 18. 2.

5 If you move on to the rest of Greece, you will find an abundance of sombre tales, man in conflict with man, city with city, nation with nation: not only Dorians with Ionians alone, or Boeotians with Athenians, but Ionians with Ionians, Dorians with Dorians, Boeotians with Boeotians, Athenians with Athenians, Thebans with Thebans, and Corinthians with Corinthians, enemies who share the same race and the same home, everyone attacking everyone else, although they live under the same sun and the same skies and the same laws, and speak the same language and live on the same land and eat the same fruits and are initiates of the same mysteries; they are protected by a single wall and a single city as they wage war and make peace, swear and break oaths, make and change agreements, and welcome the smallest of pretexts for the greatest of harm. When friendship drops out of people's minds, any cause is immediately sufficient to rouse anger and cause turmoil, just as, when a ship's hold is emptied of ballast, even gentle impacts can make it rock and slew it round.

6 How then might a man who loves friendship equip himself so as to achieve it? It is hard to speak out, but it must be done:

As there are no trustworthy oaths between men and lions,
Nor have wolves and lambs spirits that can be brought to agreement,[20]

⟨so⟩ the attraction of friendship cannot operate between one man and another so long as visions of gold and silver dance before his eyes. Even if you divert your gaze from this, your fortitude is not enough to produce friendship, for you will once more be troubled by the youthful charm of a boy or the beauty of a woman. Even if you close your eyes to that, 'fair of face is the people of great-hearted Erechtheus'[21] and proclamations in the Assembly and the glory they bring, an agile thing with wings to carry it over the whole world. Even if you scorn this, you will not be able to scorn the court; even if you scorn that, you will not be able to scorn the prison; even if you can bear imprisonment, you will not be able to scorn approaching death.[22] You must turn your back on many pleasures and face up to many labours in order to win a possession

---

[20] *Il.* 22. 262–3.
[21] A quotation from Plato *First Alcib.* 132a, which itself echoes *Il.* 2. 547.
[22] i.e. cultivating true friendship is as hard (the same thing) as cultivating true virtue, and is liable to lead to the same reward at the hands of unregenerate humanity as was meted out to Socrates.

that is equal in worth to all pleasures and compensates for all toils, a possession more valuable than gold, more enchanting than youthful beauty, more secure than reputation, more real than honour, a possession sought for itself, that offers itself freely, that is praised without partiality, that even if it brings grief and trouble gladdens the practitioner with the recollection of its cause.[23]

7   This possession is a rarity. But its counterfeit is ready at hand in every conceivable form, in the swarming bands of flatterers, grinning and fawning and bearing friendship on the tips of their tongues, not led on by good will but forced by need, mercenaries not friends.[24] There can be no respite from this evil, until they hold friendship ⟨ . . . ⟩.[25] So indeed it is, but most people do not appreciate the reciprocal exchange, either in private or where the state at large is concerned. If they did then they would long since have disarmed themselves and dispensed with the sciences of general and armourer, and the assembling of mercenaries, and the giving of watchwords, and the building of forts, and the ⟨planting⟩ of camps, and have willingly accepted a peace treaty from Zeus himself, who does not announce his truces in Olympia or on the Isthmus, but cries aloud from heaven:

'Hold hard, friends, and leave me alone, loving you as I do,[26]

to save you and not sit idly by as you injure each other.' But as things now are they sign temporary treaties, of a mere thirty years, and so secure an ill-defined and imperfectly reliable respite from ill, until some other pretext supervenes and throws everything into turmoil again. Yet even if they do lay down their arms and keep the peace, there is another war that descends on the soul, a war that is not public but private, fought not with iron nor with fire, nor bringing navies or cavalry, but bare of weapons, making no

---

[23] Again, the description tends to assimilate Friendship to Virtue. For the familiar point that true friendship is only possible between the good, cf. Plato *Lys.* 214ce, *Resp.* 332a, *Leg.* 837a; Arist. *NE* 8. 1, 1155^{a}31 and 8. 7, 1156^{b}7 ff.; Cic. *De Am.* 18; Sen. *Ben.* 7. 12 .2 and *Ep.* 81. 12.

[24] For the figure of the Flatterer, cf. *Or.* 14. For practical need as the basis of inferior forms of friendship, cf. Arist. *NE* 9. 9, 1169^{b}3 ff. and Cic. *De Am.* 26, with Powell (1990, ad loc.).

[25] The text is deficient at this point, and no fully satisfactory emendation has yet been proposed. Something like '⟨to be something that necessarily involves *mutual benefit*⟩' is presumably required.

[26] *Il.* 22. 416, but the picture of Zeus calling from the heavens also echoes the famous protreptic cry of [Plato] *Clit.* 407ab (on which see Slings 1981, ad loc.).

use of iron or fire; it ravages and besieges the soul, filling it with envy and passion and anger and abusiveness and countless other ills.[27]

8 Which way is a man to turn? What truce can one find, what Olympian or Nemean armistice? The Dionysia and the Panathenaea at Athens are fine festivals, but they celebrate them in a state of mutual hatred: this is a war you are telling me of, not a festival. Fine too are the Gymnopaediae and the Hyacinthia and the dances at Sparta; but Agesilaus envies Lysander, and Agesipolis hates Agis, and Cinadon plots against the kings, and Phalanthus against the Ephors, and the Partheniae against the Spartiates.[28] I will not trust the festival until I see that its celebrants are friends. This is the true rule and form for a truce, directed by the law-giving of God; friendship will never be seen if it is not secured, however many treaties are cemented, however many times the enactments of Olympia and the Isthmus and Nemea are recorded. The proclamation, the truce, must go within to the soul itself. As long as the war in the soul is waged bitterly and implacably, the soul will remain friendless, hostile, and sullen. This is what is meant by the Poenae, by the Furies;[29] this is the source of dramas and tragedies! Let us pursue a truce, let us call on Philosophy to aid us! Let her come, let her make peace, let her proclaim it!

ORATION 36   Diogenes and the Life of the Golden Age

Introduction

= 36 (1962) = 20 (Laur. Conv. Sopp. 4). The manuscript title—*Εἰ προηγούμενος ὁ τοῦ κυνικοῦ βίος*, 'Whether the Cynic life is to be preferred'—though echoing the wording of §6, makes only an approximate match with the contents of the lecture.

---

[27] For the comparison between inner and outer 'wars', cf. *Or.* 22. 7.

[28] Agesilaus and Lysander: Xen. *Hell.* 3. 4. 7 ff.; Cinadon: Xen. *Hell.* 3. 3. 4 ff.; Phalant(h)us and the Partheniae (cf. *Or.* 29. 7): Arist. *Polit.* 5. 8, 1306ᵇ27 ff. (followed by references to Lysander, Agesilaus, and Cinadon). The rivalry between Agesipolis and Agis seems to be an *ad hoc* invention.

[29] For the allegory, cf. *Or.* 13. 9.

Another contribution to discussion of Happiness and the Good Life, answering the question posed at the end of *Or.* 29 with an encomium of one remarkable individual. Diogenes has already been held up for admiration twice, in *Orr.* 15 and 34, as an instance of virtuous effort in the face of harsh circumstances. Here the emphasis changes, as he is presented as a man who, by the choice of a simple existence, avoided such harshness altogether, and lived instead the kind of life lost to other humans with the end of the Golden Age. § 1 describes the origins and life of the Golden Age with the aid of a Platonic-Aesopic fable, and § 2 the misery and degeneracy of the present; §§ 3–4 compare the two, and imagine the outcome of an invitation to choose between them. § 5, drawing on both pictures, presents Diogenes as one who lived the older form of life in the midst of the newer, and § 6 asserts his consequent superiority over all others, whether ordinary mortals, philosophers, or princes.

Diogenes as disciple and practitioner of the simple life, and as critic from that vantage-point of luxury and pretension, is a familiar figure in philosophical and satirical writing: see above all Diogenes Laertius 6. 20–81; [Diogenes] *Epistles* (in Malherbe 1977: 14–21, 91–183); Epictetus 3. 22; Dio *Orations* 6 and Lucian *Vitarum Auctio* 8–11 (and for use and discussion of Cynic values in general, Lucian *Fugitivi*, [Lucian] *Cynicus*; Julian *Or.* 6; cf. Dudley 1937, esp. chs. 3, 5–6, and 8). Also familiar is the use of the Golden Age as an image of ideal simplicity and virtue (see the texts cited in n. 4 below), though no surviving work makes the connection with Diogenes as clearly and explicitly as Maximus. That aspect apart, there seems to be a particularly close relationship between Maximus' presentation of the Cynic in § 5 and that of Dio in *Or.* 6 (see nn. 24–34 below); either the two are both indebted to a common source now lost, or Maximus is borrowing from and précising Dio. For other examples of praise for the simple life and values of the past, cf. *Orr.* 4. 1–3, 17. 1, 26. 2.

Gregoras takes two excerpts from the lecture, from §§ 1 and 5; Poliziano notes the presence of a fable in § 1, and the references to Hesiod, Diogenes, and Xenophon in §§ 1, 5, and 6, in the margins of Paris. gr. 1962 (foll. 123ʳ–127ʳ). Jeremy Taylor cites §§ 5–6 in Sermon 15 of *Eniautos* (Heber-Eden 1847–54: iv. 183).

Oration

1   I should like to invent you a fable in the manner of the sage of Lydia. The speakers in my fable will not be the lion and the eagle, or creatures still dumber than they, like oak trees.[1] Instead it will go like this.[2] Zeus existed, and heaven and earth; the heaven was populated by the gods, but the creatures of the earth, mankind, had yet to be brought into the light of day. Zeus called Prometheus and commanded him to colonize the earth with creatures of a double nature, 'almost on a level with us gods in intelligence, and let their bodies be agile and upright and well-proportioned, tame in aspect, dexterous in physical activities, with a steady gait'.[3] In obedience to Zeus, Prometheus created man and populated the earth. And men, when they had come into existence, led an easy life. The land furnished them with all the nourishment they needed, with its grassy meadows and tree-covered hills and a rich supply of all the fruits that the earth is wont to bear without any interference from farmers; the Nymphs too furnished pure wells and clear rivers and the rich and bountiful springs from which all other waters flow. In addition to this the warmth of the sun enfolded their bodies and gently comforted them, and breezes blowing from the rivers in the summer season cooled them. Living as they did off the rich resources that came to them of their own accord, there was nothing they needed to fight over. I believe that the poets too come very close to this story of ours when they speak allegorically of a similar kind of life lived under Cronus, king of the gods, a life that knew no wars and no iron weapons, that was peaceful and had no need of garrisons, where nothing was fought over, a healthy life that lacked for nothing; it would seem that 'the golden race' is Hesiod's teasing term for this era.[4]

2   Let me now dismiss this fable of mine and convert it into a

---

[1]   For the reference to Aesop and his fables, cf. *Orr.* 15. 5, 19. 2, and 32. 1.

[2]   Maximus' fable is inspired in part by Protagoras' in Plato *Protag.* 320c ff., but rapidly develops in a rather different direction.

[3]   With this complimentary account of the human form, compare *Or.* 2. 3; and (in the context of discussions of divine Providence) Xen. *Mem.* 1. 4. 11-12, and Cic. *ND* 133, 140, and 150 ff., with Pease (1958, ad locc.).

[4]   Hesiod *Op.* 109-26. The preceding description is a highly conventional piece of 'soft' primitivism: cf. Aratus *Phaen.* 108-14, Virg. *Geo.* 1. 125-8, Tib. 1. 3. 35-48 with Smith (1913, ad loc.), Ovid *Met.* 1. 89 ff. with Bömer (1969, ad loc.), Sen. *Ep.* 90. 35-46, etc.; and Lovejoy and Boas (1935).

proper, reasoned argument,[5] which as it advances can draw a comparison between the two lives, earlier and later—whether 'iron' or something else is your favoured term for this later form of life, in which men have divided the earth up into lots and have each carved out of it separate portions, surrounding them with enclosures and walls;[6] and entwining their bodies in soft wrappings, and palisading their feet in pieces of leather,[7] and cramping their necks, their heads, or their fingers with gold, in a form of bondage speciously redeemed by its good reputation and good looks;[8] and building shelters and adding inner and outer doors and porches;[9] and importuning the earth, mining and digging and excavating;[10] and not allowing the sea to rest in peace either, but building warships and passenger vessels and merchantmen to assault it;[11] and not holding off from the air either, netting flocks of birds with lime and snares and all manner of contrivances; nor yet holding back from tame animals because of their weakness, or from wild animals from fear, but gorging themselves on blood and guts and gore of every kind;[12] forever inventing something new to serve their pleasure and spurning what is stale and old; pursuing pleasant experiences and entangling themselves in painful ones; grasping after wealth, forever convinced that what they have is inferior to what they do not, and that what they have acquired is less than what they look forward to; fearing want, but unable to satiate themselves; fearing death, but taking no thought for life; cautious of disease, but disinclined to refrain from unhealthy pursuits; suspicious of others, but inclined to plot against their neighbours; terrible against unarmed opponents, cowards in the face of armed men; hating tyranny, but desiring to be tyrants themselves; censuring shameful behaviour, but unable to refrain from it themselves; admiring good luck, but not Virtue; pitying misfortune, but not refraining from evil deeds; daring when luck is

[5] For the explicit turn from μῦθος to λόγος (for which *Protag.* 324d provides a convenient Platonic precedent), cf. *Or.* 14. 3.

[6] Cf. e.g. Tib. 1. 3. 43–4, Ovid *Met.* 1. 136.

[7] The detail already looks towards Diogenes: cf. Dio *Or.* 6. 15.

[8] Necklaces, crowns, and rings as fetters sounds like a good moralist's conceit, but I have so far failed to find parallels.

[9] Cf. Ovid *Met.* 1. 121–2, Sen. *Ep.* 90. 41–3; and, for Diogenes, Dio *Or.* 6. 8.

[10] Cf. Ovid *Met.* 1. 137–40, Sen. *Ep.* 90. 45, and *Or.* 35. 2.

[11] Cf. Tib. 1. 3. 37–40, Ovid *Met.* 1. 132–4, etc.

[12] Cf. Aratus *Phaen.* 130–2 (of which 132 is quoted in *Or.* 24. 1); Ovid *Met.* 15. 75–142 with Bömer (1986, ad loc.).

on their side, hard to restore to equanimity when things are going against them; thinking the dead supremely happy, but clinging to life themselves; hating life, but fearing to die; censuring war, but unable to keep the peace; humble when slaves, but bold when free; impossible to restrain under a democracy, cowering abjectly under a tyranny; desiring children, but despising them once they have got them; praying to the gods as if they could aid them, despising them as if they were impotent to punish; fearing them as if they do punish, but perjuring themselves as if they did not exist.[13]

3   When such conflict and dissension obtains in this second form of life, to whom shall we go and award the victory? Which of the two shall we say is the simple life, untroubled by external circumstance, and secure in the possession of its freedom? And which shall we say is not simple, but constrained and pitiable and loaded with painful circumstances? Come, let a representative of each present himself before the arbitration of Reason;[14] and let Reason question both of them, beginning with the former of the two, that naked, homeless, craftless one, the citizen and inhabitant of the whole world.[15] Let Reason confront him with the second life and its ways, and ask him whether he would prefer to remain with his previous diet and his previous freedom, or whether he would like to adopt the pleasures of the second kind of life, along with its pains? Then let the second representative come forward; let our judge confront him with the earlier style of life and its freedom, and let him ask whether he chooses to keep his own ways, or whether he will change and migrate to that other peaceable, unconfined, wantless, pain-free existence. Which of our two men will prove the deserter? Which will change his abode? Which will be willing to exchange one life for another? [4]   What man is so witless and ill-starred in his passion and so wretched that, for love of minor and ephemeral pleasures and disputed goods and uncertain hopes and ambivalent prosperity, he would refuse to change his ways and migrate to certain happiness? And that knowing that he will free

---

[13] A veritable library of moralist's topics: for some parallels, see the list of Senecan topics in Oltramare (1926: 263–92,) and compare *Orr.* 1. 5, 5. 7, 15. 1, 29. 3 and 5.

[14] For the image, compare *Or.* 15. 2 (the representatives of the practical and the theoretic lives).

[15] Another anticipation of Diogenes: cf. § 5 below, Epict. 3. 22. 22 and 47, Diog. Laert. 6. 63.

himself of many times as many ills, which, mixed up as they are
in the second style of life, must inevitably surround its living with
hostile circumstances, making it wretched and wholly miserable?

Accordingly, I would be inclined to present the following image
for the two lives. That splendid, complicated existence is like a
harsh prison full of wretched men confined in a dark recess, laden
with heavy fetters on their feet and heavy rings round their necks
and their hands tied in rough bonds, filthy and choking and
lacerated and groaning; over time, as they have grown accustomed
to their condition, they have engineered forms of diversion and
entertainment for themselves in there, sometimes getting drunk in
their prison and singing confusedly and gorging themselves and
having sex, stuffing themselves unrestrainedly on anything they
can get, through fear and mistrust and their awareness of the misfortune that presses on them. Thus in each prison a visitor would
hear groans and song, lamentation and jubilation together.[16] As for
the other form of life, I would compare it to a man living in the
pure light of day, with no bonds on his hands or feet, able to move
his neck in any direction he wishes, gazing towards the sun and
seeing the stars, able to distinguish night from day, and to wait for
each season of the year in turn, and to feel the breezes and to
breathe in the pure and free air, freed from all those pleasures
within along with his bonds, not getting drunk, nor having sex,
nor gorging himself, nor groaning, nor crowing in triumph, nor
singing, nor lamenting, nor filling himself with any more than he
needs to live off, with his light and modest digestion.[17]

Which of these two pictures should we reckon the happy one?
Which of these two lives should we feel sorry for? Which should
we choose? The one in the prison, that mixed and obscure life,
lured on by harmful, pitiful pleasures,

Where rose the groans and the prayers of men,[18]

taking their pleasures and lamenting in the same breath? Heaven
forbid, poor soul.

---

[16] An image, like that in *Or.* 29. 5, clearly inspired by Plato's allegory of the Cave
(*Resp.* 514a ff., esp. 514a–515c and 516cd; cf. Gaiser 1985 and see also next note).
For the idea of life as imprisonment, also heavily indebted to Platonic precedent
(*Phdo* 62b, *Crat.* 400c), cf. *Or.* 7. 5, Dio *Or.* 30. 11 ff. and [Lucian] *Cynic.* 5.

[17] Cf. again Plato *Resp.* 515e–516c (the description of the released prisoner outside the Cave); and (for the Cynic preference for simple eating) Dio *Or.* 6. 12.

[18] *Il.* 4. 450.

5 Leave these images and their stories and turn to a man who
lived his life not under the reign of Cronus, but in the midst of this
present race of iron, liberated by Zeus and by Apollo. This man was
neither an Athenian nor a Dorian, the product neither of Solon's
upbringing nor of Lycurgus' education (the creation of virtues is
not the work of places or laws), but a native of Sinope in Pontus.
Counselled by Apollo,[19] he freed himself from all oppressive
circumstances[20] and, releasing himself from their bonds, travelled
freely about the world,[21] like a bird with the gift of reason, fearing
no tyrant, constrained by no law, troubled by no constitution,
untormented by the duties of rearing children, confined by no
marriage,[22] neither detained by the need to farm nor incommoded
by the obligation to serve as a soldier, nor carried this way and
that by the demands of trade.[23] He laughed to scorn all men and
their occupations,[24] as we do small children when we see them
playing intently with their knuckle-bones, hitting each other and
being hit back, snatching and having their own toys snatched.[25] He
himself lived the life of a free and fearless king,[26] not sojourning in
Babylon for the winter nor imposing on the Medes in the summer-
time, but moving according to season from Attica to the Isthmus
and from the Isthmus back to Attica.[27] His palaces were temples
and gymnasia and groves,[28] his treasure the richest and most
secure and the least plotted-against of all, the whole earth and its
fruits and the springs that are born of the earth, more abundant

[19] In the famous oracle advising him to 'alter the currency' (παραχαράσσειν τὸ
νόμισμα): Diog. Laert. 6. 20–1, cf. Dudley (1937: 20–2).
[20] What is distinctive of Diogenes is the *completeness* of his freedom from oppressive circumstances (περιστάσεις): cf. *Or*. 32. 9 and Diog. Laert. 6. 22. The standard
moralists' line is rather that, though unavoidable, they should not be allowed to
upset one's equanimity and should be turned to moral advantage instead: *Or*. 34;
Tabula Cebetis 38; Teles περὶ περιστάσεων (pp. 52–4 Hense); Epict. 1. 6. 30–6, etc.;
Aurelius 1. 15.
[21] A very similar phrase is used of Diogenes in [Diog.] *Ep*. 34. 3.
[22] For Diogenes' freedom from political involvement (his 'cosmopolitanism'), and
from wife and children, cf. *Or*. 32. 9, [Diog.] *Ep*. 47, Epict. 3. 22. 47 and 67–9,
Lucian *Vit. Auct*. 9, Diog. Laert. 6. 38 and 63.
[23] Standard examples of laborious activity (cf. *Or*. 33. 3), and of greed, all of
course absent from the Golden Age (e.g. Ovid *Met*. 1. 123–43).
[24] For Diogenes as mocker and satirist, cf. e.g. Dio *Or*. 6. 21, [Diog.] *Ep*. 47, Diog.
Laert. 6. 24.   [25] For the comparison, cf. *Or*. 3. 5.
[26] The adjectives are pointed; actual monarchs are not free and fearless: Dio *Or*.
6. 35ff.
[27] The same habit is described at greater length in Dio *Or*. 6. 1–7.
[28] Cf. Dio *Or*. 6.14.

than any drink from Lesbos or Chios.[29] He was a friend and an intimate of the open air, like the lion;[30] he made no attempt to run away from the seasons Zeus sends, or to work against him by creating artificial heat in the winter and desiring cooling measures in the summer.[31] So well attuned was he to universal Nature that his style of life made him healthy and strong; he lived into extreme old age without need of drugs or iron or fire or Chiron or Asclepius or the sons of Asclepius, or seers to prophesy to him, or priests to purify him, or magicians to recite spells over him.[32] When Greece was at war and everyone was attacking everyone else,

> Who just now bore sorrowful war against each other,[33]

he alone observed a truce, unarmed among warriors under arms, at peace with all amidst the fighting throng.[34] Criminals and tyrants and informers alike left him alone, because he could show up the wicked not with sophisticated arguments, which is the most painful way to be shown up, but by confronting deeds with deeds on each new occasion, which is both the most useful and the least aggressive way. This is why no Meletus or Aristophanes, no Anytus or Lycon, arose to persecute Diogenes.

6   How then could this life of Diogenes', which he chose of his own free will, which Apollo granted him, which Zeus approved, which all men of sense admire, fail to be preferable? Or do we think that 'circumstance' is anything other than the performance of activities that the agent has not freely chosen?[35] Ask the man who has married, 'Why do you marry?' 'To have children,' he replies. Ask the man who is raising a family why he had it; he wants heirs. Ask the man who serves in the army; he wants profit. Ask the farmer; he wants crops. Ask the money-maker; he wants affluence. Ask the politician; he wants honours. Most people miscarry in their

[29] Cf. Dio Or. 6. 12–13.
[30] Cf. Dio Or. 6. 14 and 26–7. The point is that human beings should live more like animals; the lion is specified as the animal *par excellence*.
[31] Cf. Dio Or. 6. 10.
[32] Cf. Dio Or. 6. 8, 22–4.
[33] Il. 3. 132.
[34] Cf. Dio Or. 6. 60.
[35] Somewhat elliptical phrasing. The full train of thought is: 'Diogenes' life is preferable, because free from oppressive circumstances; oppressive circumstances are indeed an evil because they are forced upon us by the wrong choice of ends, not voluntarily chosen for themselves.' Cf. § 5 above, with n. 20, and Or. 35.

pursuit of these wants and achieve the opposite result to the one they desire; good fortune is something they can pray for, but not achieve by rational planning or science.[36] Every man who chooses these objectives has to live through a life beset by circumstance, and to endure labours that are neither voluntary, nor yet accepted in ignorance of those goods that truly deserve choice in their own right. Which of them could one say is a free man? The demagogue? He is the slave of many masters. The orator? He is the slave of stern jurors. The tyrant? He is the slave of his intemperate hedonism. The general? He is the slave of the uncertainties of fortune. The voyager by sea? He is the slave of an unstable science. The philosopher? Which one do you mean? I admire Socrates along with the rest, but I hear him say, 'I obey the law and go willingly to prison and willingly take the poison.'[37] Socrates, do you see what you are saying? Do you do this willingly, or are you making a seemly stand against a fate you would not yourself have chosen? What law is it that you obey? If it is Zeus' law, then I praise its maker. But if it is Solon's, how is Solon superior to Socrates? Let Plato too answer me on philosophy's behalf, and tell me whether nothing caused him consternation—not Dion's exile, nor Dionysius' threats, nor the Sicilian and Ionian seas, which he was forced to sail this way and that. And if I turn to Xenophon, here too I see a life full of wanderings and uncertain fortune and forced campaigning and unwilling command and speciously disguised retreat.[38] These are the hostile circumstances that I declare were escaped by the life that made Diogenes superior to Lycurgus and Solon and Artoxerxes and Alexander,[39] and freer even than Socrates—for he was brought before no court, confined in no prison, and praised for something other than his misfortunes.

---

[36] Compare and contrast the accounts of ordinary, unregenerate human striving in Orr. 1. 5 and 5. 7.

[37] i.e. above all the Socrates of Crito and Phdo.

[38] Compare the accounts of Plato and Xenophon in Orr. 15. 9 and 34. 9: there they and Diogenes were equals, each exemplifying practical virtue with the same degree of excellence; here the rationale of the argument demands their subordination. Notice also the shift in emphasis, from recommending Diogenes as an example of virtuous effort, struggling with hostile circumstances, to the present picture of a man who contrived to escape from them entirely.

[39] The comparisons, with the (named or unnamed) king of Persia and with Alexander, are commonplace: e.g. Dio Or. 6. 5–7 and 35 ff., Epict. 3. 22. 60; Dio Or. 4, Diog. Laert. 6. 32.

ORATION 37 Virtue and the Liberal Arts

Introduction

= 37 (1962) = 21 (Laur. Conv. Sopp. 4). The manuscript title—Εἰ συμβάλλεται πρὸς ἀρετὴν τὰ ἐγκύκλια μαθήματα, 'Whether the Liberal Arts have a contribution to make to the cultivation of Virtue'—correctly identifies the topic.

A lecture which could as well have stood much earlier on in the collection, along with others posing the question 'What kinds of pursuit ought we to cultivate ourselves and welcome into our communities?' (e.g. Orr. 3, 4, 15–16, 17, 22, 23–4 and 26). Its actual location has presumably been influenced by the phrasing of the title, in terms of means to the end of Virtue, which suggests a connection with, for example, Orr. 27 and 38.

§§ 1–3 recall the educational recommendations made by Plato in the Republic and, above all, the Laws, defend the role he accords to the liberal arts in the face of sceptical objections, and offer a brief catalogue of the arts themselves. The remainder of the lecture then expands on just two, music and geometry, explaining how the former conduces to excellence of character (§§ 4–7a), and the latter to excellence of intellect (§§ 7b–8).

The issue of the relevance of general culture (a liberal education) to the pursuit of Virtue was a perennial, bequeathed to posterity above all by the two Platonic texts from which Maximus starts. The two other substantial discussions to survive from the Imperial period are Philo's De Congressu and Seneca's Epistle 88, but there are many other briefer treatments too (cf. n. 12 below). For general discussion, see H. Fuchs in RAC v. 365–98 and Hadot (1984: 63–100, esp. 95–6, and 295–6).

Gregoras takes two excerpts, from §§ 5 and 6, and Apostolis quotes the 'proverb' καὶ δρῦς μαινὰς ἐγένετο from § 6 in Proverbia 9. 49.[1] Fulvio Orsini uses the description of Telesilla, Alcaeus, Tyrtaeus, and Anacreon from the end of § 5 as a testimonium four times over in his Carmina Novem Illustrium Feminarum . . . et lyricorum of 1568 (pp. 52, 110, 149, 220).

---

[1] The text Apostolis quotes is in fact corrupt, and his proverb consequently a phantom (albeit one accepted also by Erasmus in his Adagia). The correct reading (accepting conjectures by Scaliger and Markland) is probably: τοῦτο ἄρα δρῦς καὶ μελίας ἐλέγετο ἄγειν.

Oration

1   In the discussion Socrates held in the Piraeus with interlocutors knowledgeable in public affairs, he constructed with his
arguments, as if in a play, a representation of a good city and a
good constitution. He made laws, saw to the education of the
young, and trained watchers for his city, entrusting the bodies and
souls of his citizens to intellectual studies and physical training,
and appointing good trainers, specially selected, to supervise both,
like the leaders of a herd, for whom his name was 'Guardians'.[2]
This foundation was a theoretical exercise, not, as some of our less
cultivated friends might imagine, a waking reality.[3] This was
simply the form philosophy used to take long ago, like oracles.[4]

If you wish, I will pass over Socrates. Let us instead summon the
Athenian Stranger to reply to us, since I can hear him too conversing in Crete, ⟨on the way to⟩ the cave of Dictaean Zeus, with
Megillus the Spartan and Clinias the Cretan, founding a Dorian city
and giving it a law-code, so as to persuade the Cretans to add the
arts of the Muses to their cultivation of manly courage, and tame
their spirits with the Muses' melody, thus ensuring that there
should be no deficiency or incompleteness in their Virtue,[5] but that
it should on the one hand prepare them to bear up nobly in the
face of external conflict and endure hardship and die holding their
ground, and on the other should offer its nurselings no opening at
all for the civil war that can rage within, in the soul.[6]

2   What do you mean by this, Athenian Stranger? Is the goal for
us human beings so specialized and complicated a matter and so
hard to grasp, so obscure and so replete with lengthy study, that
we couldn't achieve it except by humming and strumming and
protracting geometrical lines this way and that, and exhausting
ourselves in such pursuits, as if our aim were quite other than that

---

[2] Plato *Resp.* 327ac and 369a–427c. The image of the herd echoes the description of the Guardians as watchdogs in 375a–376c.
[3] Cf. *Or.* 17. 3, with n. 10.
[4] For the idea of philosophical doctrines as 'oracles', cf. *Orr.* 11. 6, 22. 7, 29. 7,
and 41. 3. The point of the comparison is that philosophical doctrines are both
divinely inspired, and require an intelligent interpreter: both ideas which are
central also to the argument for treating ancient *poetry* as philosophy (allegorical,
and divinely inspired by Apollo and the Muses: *Orr.* 4 and 26).
[5] Plato *Leg.*, esp. 624a–632d.
[6] For the idea of the war within the soul, cf. *Orr.* 22. 7 and 35. 7.

of becoming good men[7]— an attainment which when put into practice is something high and noble, close to divine Virtue, and not difficult to achieve for anyone who is once willing to yield to the promptings of what is fine, and set his face against what is shameful? The Athenian Stranger replies that in the case of a city too a so-called law, without the obedience of those it applies to, is an empty formula; it needs a population that obeys it willingly. The population of the human soul is large and impulsive; but when once it gives way and accepts the law and follows where it commands, then the result is that best of all constitutions for the soul, which men call Philosophy.[8]

3   Come, let Philosophy step forward in the character of a law-maker, bringing order to a disorganized and erring soul as if to a people; and let her call to her assistance other arts too. Not mere mechanical arts, God forbid, that involve manual labour and contribute only trivial benefits to our lives,[9] but, in the first place, the art that will make the body into an obedient vehicle to the soul and a vigorous minister in the execution of its commands, to which she gives the name gymnastics; then the art that articulates the soul's conceptions, to which she gives the name rhetoric; then the

goodly nurse and nurturer of young minds,[10]

which she calls poetry; then the guide to the nature of number, which she calls arithmetic; then the tutor of reasoning, which she calls logic; finally, let her summon geometry and music, that pair of helpers[11] and confidants to philosophy, and give to each its own share in her labours.[12]

---

[7] Another swipe at pointless and over-refined theorizing: cf. *Orr.* 1. 8, 21. 4, 27. 8 and 30. 1.

[8] Though the words are attributed to the Athenian Stranger of *Leg.*, the imagery is that of *Resp.*; cf. *Orr.* 7. 2 and 16. 4–5.

[9] For the distinction between banausic and liberal arts, cf. Plato *Resp.* 522b, Xen. *Oecon.* 4. 2–3, Arist. *Polit.* 8. 2, 1337^{b}8 ff., Clem. *Strom.* 1. 26. 3.

[10] Fr. adesp. 305 *TrGrF*.

[11] The word used here (ξυνερίθω) echoes Plato *Resp.* 533d and *Leg.* 889d.

[12] The list of seven liberal arts that Maximus gives here is not quite that of later convention: poetry (= grammar), rhetoric, logic (= dialectic), arithmetic, geometry, music, and gymnastics, but no astronomy. Astronomy, however, is subsequently seen to be subsumed partly under music (§ 5) and partly under geometry (§ 8). The inclusion of Gymnastics, following Plato *Resp.* 376e and 403c ff., is paralleled by Philostr. *Gymnast.* 1 (poetry, rhetoric, philosophy, geometry, astronomy, music, gymnastics), but the idea is pointedly rejected in Sen. *Ep.* 88 (grammar, geometry,

4   I will perhaps expound on the other arts on another occasion. For the moment let us assemble and deliver a proper account of music, which is the most venerable of intellectual pursuits. Music is a fine accomplishment not only for the single individual, but also for those whole cities and nations who happen by the grace of the gods to have it as their national custom. Mark well that I am not referring to the kind of music produced by pipes and song and choruses and strings, which appeals to the soul on an irrational level and is prized for its pleasantness to the ear.[13] Through its affection for this kind of music, it would seem, human error, drawn on by the appearance of pleasure, allowed its passion to pervert the purity of true music, which has now faded away and vanished from our midst, divesting itself of that healthy beauty it boasted of old, and deceiving us like the beauty of a courtesan that is not natural but comes from her make-up box. Without realizing it, we are living with a pale imitation of music, neither possessing nor even knowing that true Muse from Helicon, Homer's beloved, Hesiod's teacher, Orpheus' mother.[14] This perverted form, which has gradually insinuated itself into our experience, has dragged our souls down a slippery slope in both our public and our private existences.[15] Thus it was that the Dorians of Sicily, abandoning that simple mountain music that they played as they tended their flocks

---

astronomy, music, but no gymnastics, § 18). The positioning of music in the list, next to geometry, suggests that it is here meant as the scientific study (harmonics, cf. *Resp.* 530d–531c); the ensuing discussion, however (§§ 4–7), draws heavily on descriptions of the more elementary music-making that trains the character (*Resp.* 398c–400c, *Leg.* 664b–671a). For other lists of the liberal arts, see Philo *Congr.* 15–18 and Apul. *Flor.* 20 (grammar, rhetoric, dialectic, geometry, music), and *Tabula Cebetis* 13 (poetry, rhetoric, dialectic, arithmetic, geometry, astronomy, music).

[13]   For this dismissal of the low form of music that gives only sensuous pleasure, cf. *Or.* 22. 3. In what follows, Maximus distinguishes between two forms of higher music: the divine music of the spheres, which is an expression of superhuman wisdom and perfection (§ 5); and that human 'music' exemplified by the great tradition of Orpheus, Amphion, Homer, Hesiod, Lycurgus, Themistocles, Pindar, Tyrtaeus, Telesilla, Alcaeus and Anacreon, but now lost, which trains the human soul to virtue. This latter seems not merely continuous with but identical to ethical philosophy, just as in § 8 geometry is to come to look identical to theoretical philosophy: this is awkward, in so far as § 3 has described the two as 'helpers' of philosophy, rather than constituent parts.

[14]   Calliope: cf. *Orr.* 1. 2 and 26. 1–2.

[15]   For the topic of the degeneracy of modern music, and the bad moral effects that follow, see Plato *Leg.* 700a ff. and [Plut.] *De Mus.* 1131f, 1136bc, and 1140bd; in *Resp.* 398c–400c Plato rejects some musical modes for their moral tendencies, but without telling any story of degeneration over time.

and herds, and falling in love with the pipe-playing of Sybaris and
taking up the kind of dancing to which the Ionian pipe compelled
them, became what might more euphemistically be called less
sensible, but most truthfully utterly depraved.[16] Old-style music for
the Athenians consisted of choruses of boys and men, workers on
the land in their villages, fresh from harvesting and ploughing with
the dust of toil still on them, singing improvised songs; gradually,
however, this degenerated into an art that pandered to an
insatiable appetite for gratification on the stage and in the theatre,
and thus paved the way for political corruption among them too.[17]
But the true harmonies, sung by the chorus of the Muses under
the leadership of Apollo Musegetes, preserve the individual soul,
preserve households, preserve cities and ships, and armies.[18]

5   If we believe Pythagoras, as we ought, the heavens make
music too. They are not struck like the lyre or blown like the pipe;
instead the revolutions of the divine and musical bodies they
contain, in their symmetry and balance, produce a supernatural
sound. The beauty of this song is known to the gods, but
unperceived by us humans, because of their superiority and our
deficiency.[19] I think that Hesiod too gave an allegorical account of
this when he spoke of 'most holy Helicon', and the sacred dances
there, and their leader, whether one chooses to give the name
Helius, or Apollo, or any other to that most radiant and musical of
fires.[20] As for the human form of music that revolves about the
soul, what else can it be but a means of training the soul's
emotions, soothing its violent and impulsive element, and conversely rousing and inciting what is too relaxed and feeble in it?[21]
It is skilled at tempering grief and calming anger and restraining

---

[16]   The same example, and the same wording, is used also in *Or.* 14. 8.

[17]   For this account of degeneration in Athens, cf. Plato *Leg.* 700a ff. and [Plut.]
De Mus. 1140d f.

[18]   Precisely the role attributed to philosophy in *Or.* 16. 3; cf. [Plut.] *De Mus.*
1140bc. For Apollo and the Muses as patrons of philosophy, cf. e.g. *Or.* 26. 2.

[19]   For the music of the spheres, cf. Plato *Resp.* 617bc and Cic. *Somn. Scip.* 5.
10–11, and (for the attribution to Pythagoras) Arist. *De Cael.* 2. 9, 290b, [Plut.]
De Mus. 1147a, Porph. *Vit. Pyth.* 30. The explanation given here of its
inaudibility to human ears is that also given by Porphyry, as opposed to the alternative referred to by Cicero and Aristotle (that it has ceased to register through
familiarity).

[20]   Hesiod *Theog.* 1–8, etymologizing 'Helicon' as a derivative of the verb ἑλίττειν.

[21]   Cf. Plato *Resp.* 398c ff., *Leg.* 652a ff.; [Plut.] *De Mus.* 1140b ff. and 1145e ff.

passion, good too at chastening desire and healing pain and moderating infatuation and alleviating misfortune, a good companion at the sacrifice, a good fellow at the feast, a good general in war, skilled in good cheer at festivals and revelry at the Dionysia, and reverence at rituals, skilled too at introducing moderation into the constitution of the state.[22] Thus it was that the custom of playing the pipe, and the poetry Pindar sang to its accompaniment, tamed the savage Boeotians, and the elegies of Tyrtaeus roused the Spartans, and the lyrics of Telesilla the Argives, and the songs of Alcaeus the Lesbians. Thus it was, too, that Anacreon tamed Polycrates for the Samians, moderating his tyranny with the love of Smerdies and the locks of Cleobulus and the beauty of Bathyllus and with Ionian song.[23]

6   If we need to go even further back in time than this, the famous Orpheus was son of Oeagrus and of Calliope herself, and lived in Thrace on Mount Pangaeus. This region was inhabited by the Odrysian Thracians, a mountain tribe of brigands; yet these Odrysians willingly followed Orpheus as their leader, charmed by his beautiful singing. This then is the meaning of 'moving oaks and ashes': people compared the base manners of the men he charmed to inanimate objects.[24] Then there was another noble lyre-player who lived in Boeotia.[25] This man did not, as the story has it, move stones with his art (how could singing build a wall?); what he did do was to surround Thebes with an impregnable fortress by using marching and manoeuvring tunes to form the young men of Boeotia into a phalanx. Similarly, Lycurgus engineered the same kind of wall for the Spartans by setting the pipe to lead them in their battles; and they fought obediently in the manner of a chorus.[26] Or again, it was with this same pipe that Themistocles embarked the population of Athens on to ships; to its strains some rowed while others fought, and both parties were victorious, and

---

[22] Compare the descriptions of philosophical discourse in *Orr.* 1. 2–3 and 25. 6.

[23] The precedent for this survey of beneficial poets is provided by Plato's discussion of Tyrtaeus in *Leg.* 629a ff.; compare [Plut.] *De Mus.* 1146bd. For Telesilla in this role, cf. Plut. *Mul. Virt.* 245cf, and for Alcaeus, Horace *Odes* 1. 32. 5, [Acro] on id. 2. 13. 28, Quint. *Inst.* 10. 1. 63. For the reference to Anacreon (a still more unlikely figure in this context), cf. *Orr.* 18. 9, 20. 1, and 21. 2.

[24] For the allegory, cf. Horace *Ars Poet.* 391–3; Dio *Or.* 53. 8; Quint. *Inst.* 1. 10. 9. Orpheus is an example of an early philosopher poet also in *Or.* 4. 3.

[25] Amphion: Horace *Ars Poet.* 394 ff.

[26] Cf. Plut. *Lycurg.* 22; [Plut.] *De Mus.* 1140c.

the goddesses of Eleusis added their voices to the choir.[27] This is
how those victory monuments came to be set up; this is the source
of those Spartan and Athenian trophies, won both at sea and on
land, with their noble inscriptions; this is the choral competition
that the Spartans won under the tutelage of Leonidas.

7   Why need I say more, or extend my remarks about music any
further? She is a good fellow worker in peacetime, a good comrade
in time of war, a good fellow citizen in the community, a good
nurse of the young. Hearing is the swift one among the senses,
rapidly conveying what it has learned to the soul, and compelling
the soul to speak and to move in conformity with the impressions
it transmits. So it is that unmusical and discordant souls, which
surrender to any appearance of pleasure, could never come to
participate in the right melodies, and instead give the name 'music'
to their own pleasure, not through any resemblance in the end-
result, but because of the shared preoccupation with tunes—just as
if one were to give the name of medicine to an art which, divorced
from any connection with health, none the less tried to prove itself
in the deployment of the same drugs as true medicine uses.[28]

In just the same way, most people only admit geometry, which
is in fact the noblest part of philosophy, as a low-grade activity
aimed at low-grade ends, restricted to apparent practical necessity,
such as measuring out land and setting up walls; they approve
of all its contributions to the manual crafts, but they see no
further.[29] But this is not the true state of affairs. Far from it! The
land would be none the less satisfactorily inhabited even if poor
farmers ceased measuring it out into portions. That ought to count
as the least significant of all geometry's applications. Its true
function is to act as a kind of drug to clear the sight of the mind,
and to endow it with great strength for the contemplation of
universal Nature.[30] Most people are ignorant of this application,
just as the landsman who sees a ship in a harbour and, admiring
the ingenuity with which it is built, puts it to work inside the
harbour, manipulating all its tackle, in the belief that this is the
ship's true use. [8] I should think that Athena, who invented this

[27] Cf. *Or.* 13. 1 and 23. 3 (Themistocles and Salamis), 39. 2 (piping on the
trireme); the reference to the Eleusinian goddesses echoes Hdt. 8. 65.
[28] i.e. this inferior form of music is a κολακεία; cf. *Or.* 14. 8 with n. 17.
[29] e.g. Sen. *Ep.* 88. 10–13.
[30] Plato *Resp.* 526c ff.

creation,[31] would say to him, 'Can you see the broad and infinite sea, spreading over the surface of the earth and connecting its furthest points, which up till now you have never heard of or had any hope of visiting? Each man used once to know one place only, as reptiles know only their own lairs. There was no possibility of friendship or intercourse and association and exchange, until I invented you this device. This vehicle will take off like a bird and fly to any land. If you do not believe me, try it and see.' The very same might be said about geometry, but by which of the gods? That same Athena?[32] 'Look hither: do you see this fine and varied spectacle above your head, stretching round the earth in a ring and revolving about it, filled with stars, bearing the sun, containing the moon? You do not know what it is, though you think that you both see it and know. But landlubber though you are, my man, I will lead you up there, by building you a flying craft and entrusting you to the care of Geometry. She will at first ferry you around within the harbour, getting you accustomed to endure the journey and not grow dizzy and be overcome with cowardice in the face of the open sea. Then, taking you out of the harbour, she will lead you on up to the pure and open sea of reality,[33] to the place

> where stand the house
> And dancing-floors of early-born dawn, and the rising-place of the sun[34]

and the rays of the moon and of the other perfect bodies. But as long as you have no sight of these things you will remain with no stake or share in happiness.'

---

[31] A reference to Athena's role in the building of the Argo: Ap. Rhod. *Arg.* 1. 18–19, Apollod. 1. 9. 16, and (for the Argo as the first ship) Catullus 64. 11.

[32] In her role as the goddess of the arts and sciences, and an allegory of Intellect: cf. *Orr.* 4. 8 and 26. 8.

[33] An echo of Plato *Smp.* 210d (the open sea of pure Beauty). For other examples of nautical imagery applied to philosophical endeavour, cf. *Orr.* 11. 7 and 30. 1.

[34] *Od.* 12. 3–4.

ORATION 38   Virtue and Divine Dispensation

Introduction

= 38 (1962) = 22 (Laur. Conv. Sopp. 4). The manuscript title—*Εἰ γένοιτό τις θείᾳ μοίρᾳ ἀγαθός*, 'Whether one might become good by divine dispensation'—is reasonably apposite.

A further lecture on the human Good and the means to its attainment, with particularly close connections with *Orr.* 27 and 34: to the insistence in *Or.* 27 on the need for human effort in disciplining the passions, it adds a complementary insistence on the role of benevolent divinity in creating the necessary external conditions; with *Or.* 34 it shares the reading of those apparent hardships as providentially ordained to aid the quest for Virtue.

§§ 1-4a demonstrate the consistency and pervasiveness of claims to enjoy divine assistance, from Homer's inspired poets to Socrates in his dealings with his young interlocutors. § 4b formulates the resulting question: given that all these goods are claimed to flow from divine benevolence, does Virtue too, the greatest of all goods, derive from the same source? §§ 5-6a answer in the affirmative, arguing on the basis of God's self-sufficiency, omnipotence, and benevolence, that if (as is manifestly the case) he is responsible for *some* goods, then he must also be responsible for the greatest of them. §§ 6a-7 then explain how God's gift of Virtue operates, in terms of the struggle between virtuous and vicious tendencies within the individual soul, and God's provision of suitable external circumstances for the suppression of the one and the cultivation of the other.

Several of the main emphases of the lecture, on the providential role of hardships, and on the need for moral effort in the pursuit of virtue, are more familiar from moralizing in the Stoic tradition than from Platonism. They are not, however, in themselves distinctively Stoic, and the lecture's fundamental proposition, that Virtue is indeed a divine gift, can equally well be referred back to Platonic precedent, in such texts as *Meno* 99e and 100b and *Resp.* 492a-493a. Moreover, the description of human nature at the end of § 6 seems careful to avoid the extreme Stoic view that all degrees of Vice are equal.

Franciscus Junius cites the description of Epimenides' mental powers from § 3 in *The Painting of the Ancients* I. i. 7 (Aldrich *et al.* 1991: i. 18–19).

Oration

1   Talking to Telemachus in the character of Nestor, Homer has this to say about him:

> I do not think it was
> Without the favour of the gods that you were born and reared.[1]

The same poet also uses the epithet 'godly' for all good men because, as I understand him, they were good not through the exercise of human skill, but by the work of Zeus. Furthermore, I suspect that the verses he sings about Demodocus, though applied to him, were actually composed to refer to his own condition. The verses go something like this:

> The Muse loved him exceedingly, and gave him good and ill:
> She took away the sight of his eyes, but granted him sweet song.[2]

I agree with him about his song, but I do not agree about his fortune; that is not a gift appropriate to a Muse. Demodocus too is unconvincing when he says of himself:

> I am self-taught, and the gods granted me my voice.[3]

How can you be 'self-taught', my most excellent of bards, when you received your voice from the gods, who are the most unerring of teachers? Demodocus can give only the same reply as rich men who have inherited their fortunes from their fathers might to those who make their own money, that their wealth is home-produced, not scraped together through the skill and labour of others.

2   Or again, what are we to think of Hesiod? That when he was shepherding his flocks on Helicon in Boeotia and came upon the Muses singing and they reproached him for his shepherd's trade and presented him with a branch of laurel,[4] he was immediately transformed from a shepherd into a poet and began to sing, just as

---

[1] *Od.* 3. 27–8, also quoted to similar effect in *Or.* 8. 5.
[2] *Od.* 8. 63–4.
[3] *Od.* 22. 347, spoken in fact by Phemius on Ithaca, not Demodocus in Scherie. Cf. *Or.* 10. 5, where the same line is quoted more approvingly.
[4] Hesiod *Theog.* 22–34.

they say the Corybants become possessed and ecstatic whenever they hear a pipe?[5] Far from it. I believe instead that Hesiod was hinting at the natural origin of his art when he assigned responsibility for it to the chorus of the Muses, just as if someone who had become a blacksmith without professional training were to go and make Hephaestus responsible for the natural origin of his craftsmanship. What about the Cretans? Do you not think that it was because they were finely organized by King Minos and admired him for his Virtue that they declared Zeus to be his teacher, saying that there was a cave of Zeus there on Ida, which Minos visited once every nine years to converse with him and learn the science of politics from him?[6] For that is what the Cretans say.

3   There was also at Athens a man of Eleusis called Melesagoras. According to the Athenians his wisdom and prophetic craft came not through the learning of any formal science, but by divine dispensation, through possession by the Muses.[7] There also came to Athens another man, a Cretan called Epimenides; though unable to name his teacher, he was none the less sufficiently skilled in matters divine to rescue the city of Athens when it was riven by plague and strife, by offering propitiatory sacrifices. His skill in this respect did not come from any normal process of learning; it was, he explained, a lengthy slumber and a dream that taught him.[8] There was also once a philosopher in Proconnesus called Aristeas. His wisdom was at first regarded with mistrust, because he could produce no teacher for it. Eventually, therefore, he invented an explanation to counter this mistrust. He said that his soul was in the habit of leaving his body and flying straight up to the bright sky, making a circuit of both Greek and foreign lands, along with all their islands and rivers and mountains. The far point in his soul's excursion was the land of the Hyperboreans, and it surveyed systematically all laws and civic customs, types of landscape and variations in climate, expanses of sea and mouths of rivers; what is more, the view it then had of the heavens was much clearer than from below on earth. Aristeas was more convincing when he

---

[5] A Platonizing reference: *Crito.* 54d, *Euthyd.* 277d, *Smp.* 215e, *Ion* 533e.

[6] Plato *Leg.* 624a–625b; cf. *Or.* 6. 7.

[7] For the somewhat murky figure of Melesagoras (or Amelesagoras), see Jacoby *FGrH* 330; his *Atthis* is referred to by Antig. *Mirab.* 12, Clem. *Strom.* 6. 26. 8, Hesychius (s.v. ἐπ' Εὐρυγύῃ ἀγών), and the scholiast on Eurip. *Alc.* 1.

[8] For Epimenides, cf. *Or.* 10. 1, with n. 1.

said this than Anaxagoras or the celebrated Xenophanes,[9] or any other exegete of the nature of reality. Men did not yet understand clearly about his soul's peregrinations, nor about the nature of the 'eyes' with which it saw all, but believed that the soul had literally to travel abroad if it was to give a wholly true account of all things.[10]

4 Shall we now dismiss Aristeas and Melesagoras and Epimenides and the allegories of the poets as pure myth, and turn our thoughts towards the philosophers, those inhabitants of the Lyceum and the noble Academy? They are no spinners of myths, or speakers in riddles, or lovers of marvels, but ⟨communicate⟩ in everyday language and familiar patterns of thought.[11] ⟨Let us question⟩ their leader first in some such way as this:[12] We often hear you insisting, Socrates, that you honour knowledge more than anything else, as you recommend the young each to a different teacher. After all, you encourage Callias to send his son to Milesian Aspasia's, a man to an establishment run by a woman; and you yourself, at your advanced age, go to her as a pupil.[13] Nor is she enough for you: you assemble together expertise in love from Diotima, in music from Connus, in poetry from Evenus, in farming from Ischomachus, and in geometry from Theodorus.[14] About these statements of yours, whether ironic or straightforward, I am quite happy, however other people may receive them. But when I hear you conversing with Phaedrus or Charmides or Theaetetus or Alcibiades, I begin to suspect that you do not attribute everything to learned knowledge, but instead believe that innate ability is a more fundamental instructor

[9] For Anaxagoras and his use as a philosophical paragon, cf. *Or.* 16. 1–3, with n. 1; the presence beside him here of Xenophanes is less expected (perhaps prompted by his fame as the supposed founder of the Eleatic school, e.g. Clem. *Strom.* 1. 64. 2).

[10] For Aristeas, cf. *Or.* 10. 2 with n. 7.

[11] For the contrast between the allegorists of old, and the explicit teaching of more modern philosophy, cf. *Or.* 4. 1–3. Here, however, Maximus draws the dividing-line between the two groups earlier in time (Plato counts—at least in part—as an 'ancient' in *Or.* 4), and takes a rather more dismissive line towards myth and allegory.

[12] With this survey of Socratic procedure, compare *Orr.* 18. 4–5 and 9, and 32. 8.

[13] Maximus here draws on Aeschines Socraticus, fr. 17 Dittmar (= 62 [fr. 19] Giannantoni); cf. also Xen. *Mem.* 2. 6. 36 and *Oec.* 3. 14.

[14] Cf. Plato *Smp.* 201d ff.; *Euthyd.* 272c; *Apol.* 20bc; *Phdo* 60d ff.; Xen. *Oecon.* 6. 17 ff.; Plato *Theaet.* 143d ff.

for human beings. This is what you were getting at when you said in so many words somewhere in your conversations, 'my association with Alcibiades was the gift of divine providence';[15] or again when you call Phaedrus 'godly one',[16] and when you made a prediction in your conversation about the very young Isocrates.[17] What do you mean by this, Socrates? If you like, I will leave you be and turn to your friend from the Academy, who recorded all those discussions in writing. Let him give an answer to our earnest enquiry, whether good men can become the good men they are by divine dispensation. I am not talking about poets, so do not produce me the name of Hesiod, nor seers, so do not speak to me of Melesagoras, nor purifiers, so do not tell me about Epimenides. Take the name of his science away from each of them, and replace it with the kind of Virtue that good men show in distinctively human activities, the skilful management of a house, and the honourable management of public affairs in the state,[18] and tell me about *this* kind of Virtue: can anyone acquire it by gift of the gods rather than by the exercise of a human science? Or shall I leave you too alone, and will reason itself give me its own answer, man to man as it were, in the following confident manner:

5   'You fool, what nonsense is this? Do you really think that the finest of human goods can instantaneously be derived from human science, but only with the greatest difficulty from divine Virtue? Yet at the same time you would not be prepared to say that the arts of the seer and the priest and the poet, and purifications and prophecies, were equal in worth to Virtue, even taken all together. Do you then think that *they* enter human souls by some divine inspiration, but that Virtue, which is a rarer phenomenon than they are, is the work of human science? You certainly seem to have a high opinion of the value of the divine, if its provision of worthless things is good and bountiful, but it proves impoverished when it comes to something better! I am arguing that if God accomplishes each of these things, then he must necessarily also accomplish the better result. It is not the case that, as a worker in

[15] Another borrowing from Aeschines Socraticus, fr. 11. 2–3 Dittmar (= 53 [fr. 12] Giannantoni).
[16] Plato *Phaedr.* 234d.
[17] Plato *Phaedr.* 278e–279b.
[18] A formulation of human excellence that owes as much to conventional as to philosophical values; cf. Plato *Protag.* 318e–319a, Xen. *Mem.* 1. 2. 48, etc.

bronze could not educate a carpenter, and the farmer knows nothing of helmsmanship, and the helmsman nothing of medicine, all of them being simultaneously knowledgeable in one science and ignorant of another, so God too remains within the perimeter of a single skill. The point is that if anything does come from him, it would count as a separate measure of science in relation to the capacities of the human soul, but as a part of the whole in relation to the sum of divine knowledge. You should be prepared to find that, if God is able to share out and distribute such things as these, he is far more able and willing to distribute Virtue. [6] Consider the matter like this. I assume you must account God the most perfect and self-sufficient and powerful of all things, in such a manner that if you remove anything from him, you will damage him as a whole.[19] If he is not perfect, he is not self-sufficient; if he is not self-sufficient, he is no longer perfect; if he is neither self-sufficient nor perfect, how can he be strong? But if he is self-sufficient and perfect and strong, then in his perfection he wishes good things, in his self-sufficiency he possesses them, and in his strength he has the power. If then he has the will, the resources, and the power, what is there to prevent him giving? He who has but does not give lacks the will; he who wishes but does not have lacks the power; but if he has and wishes, how can he fail to give? Therefore if he possesses the Good, he possesses the most perfect thing, and the most perfect thing is Virtue; therefore he gives what he has.[20] So there is no need to fear that any other good might come to men from some other source than God.

But if there is no other good for men that does not come from the gods, what is the manner in which *Virtue* comes from God? The human race, as a species, has a dual nature, combining predispositions on the one hand to Virtue and on the other to Vice.[21] Of the two, Vice needs some force to chasten it, and Virtue some force to preserve it. A bad nature, if it finds a good overseer in the form of law and habituation, secures freedom from distress for its

[19] For the doctrines of divine perfection and self-sufficiency, cf. Plato *Resp.* 381bc, Alcin. *Didasc.* 10. 164. 31–3, Apul. *De Plat.* 1. 5. 190. The argument that follows stands in a tradition descending from Plato *Leg.* 10. 901bff.; cf. Sharples (1995: 6–7).

[20] This has the sound of a stock argument for divine benevolence and omnipotence: cf. Cic. *ND* 1. 2. 3; Julian *Or.* 4. 142cd.

[21] For the idea of the two tendencies inherent in the constitution of the human soul, cf. e.g. *Orr.* 27. 5, 41. 5, and Apul. *De Plat.* 2. 3. 222–5, with Beaujeu (1973, ad loc.).

neighbours, while itself profiting not from any share of the Good, but at least in a reduction in harm. The best natural dispositions of the soul, which are fought over by, and tethered in the no man's land between, supreme Virtue and extreme Vice, need God to fight with them, and to help them to bring the scales down firmly on the better side. The slide towards shame is the work of native weakness, which works deceptively on the pleasures and desires even of good souls, and drags them down to the same paths as the bad.[22] [7] You can hear Zeus himself say,

> How mortals do accuse the gods!
> They say that evils come from us, when they themselves
> By their own misdeeds suffer griefs beyond their lot.[23]

But about good men you will not hear him say any such thing, rejecting the blame, and renouncing concern. Quite the reverse:

> How then could I forget Odysseus the godlike, he whose
> Heart and whose proud spirit are beyond all others forward
> In all hard endeavours, and Pallas Athene loves him?[24]

Who would deny that Odysseus is good by divine dispensation, when Zeus remembers him, and Athena cares for him, and Hermes guides him, and Calypso loves him, and Leucothea saves him?[25] If he was good, as indeed he was, because

> He saw the cities of many men and came to know their character

and

> Suffered many griefs in his heart as he voyaged by sea,[26]

how can the testing-grounds that gave him both the reputation for goodness and the reality not have been brought his way by divine dispensation? God surrounded him with many opponents: from among foreign nations the Trojans, from the Greek army the

---

[22] For this view of the factors operating on ambivalent human nature for good and ill, cf. *Orr.* 24. 3, with n. 4, 27. 9, and Alcin. *Didasc.* 1. 152. 23-6 with Whittaker (1990, ad loc.). Earlier examples of the same way of thinking include Plato *Resp.* 491e, 518e-519a and Xen. *Mem.* 4. 1. 4.

[23] *Od.* 1. 32-4; cf. *Or.* 41. 4, with n. 27.

[24] *Il.* 10. 243-5.

[25] Hermes: on Circe's isle, providing Odysseus with moly, cf. *Orr.* 26. 9 and 29. 6. Leucothea: giving him her magic veil to keep him afloat, cf. *Orr.* 11. 10. and 26. 9. Calypso's love is not elsewhere used as a proof or an allegory of the gods' providential care. For Odysseus as the model of the good man, schooled by adversity, cf. esp. *Orr.* 15. 6 and 34. 7 (both times with Heracles); and for the whole argument that hardships are a sign of divine favour and Providence, Sen. *Prov.* 2. 2-7.

[26] *Od.* 1. 3-4.

champions Palamedes and Ajax,[27] at home the mightiest and the most depraved of his own countrymen; the most savage of the Cyclopes, the most inhospitable of the Thracians, the most fearsome of enchantresses, the most many-headed of wild beasts, great expanses of sea, harsh storms, frequent shipwreck. And God forced him to be a wanderer and a beggar, wearing rags and in them begging for crusts, wrestling, getting kicked, and made the butt of drunken insults. It was God who in his love subjected him to each of these experiences, not Poseidon in his rage

because he had blinded his dear son,[28]

nor Helius angry about his oxen[29] (may Poseidon never feel such love for a savage man and an inhospitable son, nor Helius such meanness and niggardliness with his oxen); these were the commands of Zeus. Was it not he who also forbade his own son Heracles to live a life of ease and luxury, and dragged him away from the clutches of Pleasure?[29] Hurling Eurystheus instead into Pleasure's grasp, did he not set Heracles against boars and lions and rulers and tyrants and bandits, long journeys and deserts and uncrossable rivers? Or did Zeus have the power to make one night into three, but not to rescue the son he got in that night from the toils that beset his life? He did not *want* to: it is not right for Zeus to will anything other than what is best. This is how Heracles and Dionysus[31] and Odysseus acquired their goodness. And so as not to take you too far from matters in hand, do you think that even Socrates became good by the exercise of human skill, not by divine dispensation? Or is the point that as far as science is concerned, he would have become a stonemason, inheriting the status as son from father,[32] but by God's election he rejected human science and embraced Virtue instead?'

---

[27] The references are to Odysseus' rivalry with Palamedes in wisdom, and Ajax in martial prowess; the stories of how he contrived the death of the former, and defeated the latter in the contest for the arms of Achilles, were told in the *Cypria* (OCT Homer, v. 105 and 124) and the *Little Iliad* (OCT Homer, v. 106).

[28] *Od.* 11. 103; cf. 1. 19–21.

[29] *Od.* 1. 8–9, 12. 374 ff.

[30] Compare the account of Heracles in *Or.* 15. 6 and 34. 8, and contrast that in *Or.* 32. 8.

[31] Linked with Heracles also in *Or.* 32. 8; both wandered far to spread the benefits of civilization.

[32] For the biographical detail, cf. Dio *Or.* 55. 2, Lucian *Somn.* 12, Diog. Laert. 2. 19.

ORATIONS 39–40   On Degrees of Good

Introduction

= 39-40 (1962) = 23-4 (Laur. Conv. Sopp. 4). The manuscript titles—
Εἰ ἔστιν ἀγαθὸν ἀγαθοῦ μεῖζον· ἐν ᾧ ὅτι οὐκ ἔστιν and . . . *ἐν ᾧ ὅτι ἔστιν*,
'Whether there exists one Good greater than another; that there does not'
and '. . . that there does'—are accurate as far as they go.

Two further lectures on the End and the Human Good, operating
on very much the same level of abstraction and generality as *Orr.*
29-33, and arguing opposite theses: the first, that the Good for
man is one and homogeneous, and admits of no degrees; the
second, that there is a hierarchy of distinct goods that jointly constitute the End.

Or. 39 uses the famous episode of Glaucus' exchange of armour
with Diomedes to introduce a contrast between wealth and
property, which do admit of degrees of value, and the true Good,
which does not (§ 1). The natural association of Goodness with
unity (and its complete separateness from all supposed 'goods') is
then illustrated by analogies: with medicine, music, seamanship,
horsemanship, and tactics (§§ 2–3a); the contrast between the
(many) stages of a journey and its single destination (§§ 3a–4);
the difference between the heavens and the lower divisions of the
physical cosmos (§ 4); and the unity of the divine, compared to
that of the sea (§ 5a). The lecture ends with an ironic challenge to
the listener to prefer the 'goods' of wealth, good looks, and good
birth, to the true Good enjoyed by Socrates (§ 5b). *Or.* 40 begins
its reply with a brief defence of Glaucus in the face of Homer's
apparent criticism, followed by a string of instances from Homer's
poetry in which degrees of value are distinguished, in beauty, self-
control, and wisdom (§§ 1–3a); health too is added to the list of
phenomena admitting of degrees (§ 3b). Then, after a brief formal
divisio (§ 3c), it is argued successively that it is not only beneficial
to believe that there are higher and lower degrees of Good (§ 4a),
but also possible (§ 4b), and indeed true (§ 5). The final paragraph
(§ 6) adds a few further cases of gradation (the senses, the gods,
breeding), before ending with a slightly enigmatic flourish on the
subject of that most problematic of all goods, wealth (see n. 28
below).

The philosophical classification of (real and alleged) goods into different categories, and the argument over their relative ranking, goes back to Plato (e.g. *Grg.* 451e and 467e, *Meno* 87e, [Plato] *Ep.* 7. 355b, and the further texts cited in n. 18 below). The specific issue that underlies this pair of lectures—whether the Human Good is Virtue alone, or whether a combination of goods of soul, goods of body, and external goods (goods of fortune) is necessary for fulfilment and happiness—crystallizes somewhat later, as a controversy between Stoics and Peripatetics; then, as a further stage, from being an inter-school issue alone, it also becomes an internal point of debate within Platonism, with some Middle Platonists taking a relatively 'Stoicizing', and some a relatively 'Peripateticizing', line: see Dillon (1977: 44, 70–5, 146–8, 299 (Alcin. *Didasc.* 27), 328 (Apul. *De Plat.* 2. 1. 219–2. 222)). As usual, Maximus' bland and schematic treatment obscures this background entirely: he attributes neither of the two positions advanced to a source, thus leaving it wholly unclear whether he is presenting an argument and a choice between distinct philosophical sects, or an interesting issue that can be argued out within the Platonic family.

Later interest in these lectures is restrained. Gregoras takes just one excerpt, from *Or.* 40. 5, and the compiler of Neap. 100 six (from *Orr.* 39. 4 and 5, and 40. 3, 4, and 6). Poliziano notes the reference to the Eleusinian ἀνάκτορον in *Or.* 39. 3, and in *Or.* 40, an apparent reference to Isocrates in § 4,[1] the references to Fortune in § 5, Homer, Atys, and Hippias in § 6, and the final quotation from the *Hippolytus* also in § 6, in the margins of Paris. gr. 1962, foll. 136^v–142^r.

Oration 39

1　I cannot accept even from Homer that reproach against Lycian Glaucus, when he exchanged his gold armour for Diomedes' bronze, and took the worth of nine oxen in return for the worth of a hundred.[2] A money-maker might be justified in making this accusation,

---

[1] The product of a corruption: ἰσοκράτης τὰ (the reading of the MSS) for εἰς ἀκρότητα (Koniaris, surely correctly).

[2] *Il.* 6. 119–236. For the use of the episode as an illustrative example elsewhere in the lectures, cf. *Orr.* 32. 5 and 35. 3; note also Plut. *Comm. Not.* 1063f, where it comes up in the context of a discussion of Stoic concepts of the Good.

> A ship's captain, from the ranks of traders,
> Who minds his cargo . . .
> And his greedy profits,[3]

but not a poet who claims to be a pupil of Calliope, who is not allowed to praise any shameful deed or find fault with any noble one.[4] It was reasonable for Glaucus, if he was indeed the son of Hippolochus, son of Bellerophon son of Sisyphus son of Aeolus,[5] all good men, on encountering one whom the fortunes of war gave the semblance of an enemy, but their forefathers' hospitality that of a friend, to revive the friendship again and summon back the intimacy of generations gone by, and therefore to measure the exchange in terms of the occasion rather than the worth of the weapons, and not to enter into any calculation about gold and silver like men buying wine from Lemnos,

> Some for bronze and others for shining iron,
> Some for skins and some for whole oxen.[6]

As far as everyday transactions go, the exchange allows for an element of calculation, and in the case of goods of unequal value the inequality between greater and lesser is shown up by the scales. Even with his cloak over his head a man can tell that a talent is many times more than ten minae, and a drachma more valuable than an obol. In holdings of land, according to Herodotus, poor farmers measure their land in fathoms, those more affluent than they in *stades*, and those much more skilled at farming in *schoeni*, like the Egyptians;[7] in holdings of livestock, Dardanus,

Who owned three thousand horses that pastured along the low grasslands,

was better stocked than Polyphemus.[8] But if one rejects considerations of practical utility, and makes the comparison with true goods, I believe that one will find that while the former change their value this way and that as opportunity and custom and pleasure and habit and chance dictate, the Good remains firm, steady, motionless, balanced, open to all, unrationed, generous,

---

[3] *Od.* 8. 162-4.

[4] Because a pupil of Calliope must be a philosopher: *Orr.* 1. 3 and 26. 1.

[5] Cf. *Il.* 6. 153-5 and 196-210.

[6] *Il.* 7. 473-4.

[7] Hdt. 2. 6. 2. A *stade* is c.200 m., a *schoenus* (cable) some 30 or 40 times that length.

[8] Dardanus: *Il.* 20. 221; Polyphemus: *Od.* 9. 233-49, etc.

and lacking nothing, offering no scope for increase and tolerating no deficiency.[9] What increases does so as a result of some addition; but if good is added to good, do not think that the good is any more good for the addition, if it really was good before; on the other hand, if what is used to make the increase was *not* good, you are saying something outrageous, if a greater good is going to be created by the addition of something bad. Again, what is deficient is deficient because of some lack; but if the good was deficient because of the absence of good, ⟨then it was not good⟩ when it was deficient;[10] and if it was deficient in some respect other than goodness, then the deficiency does no harm to its goodness.

2   Why not look at the proposition in the following way too? Is there something that you call physical health? Of course there is. Is there also something that you call disease? Then examine each separately, and answer me. Is not health a state of balance and harmony in bodies, achieved when the opposing elements are brought together in the best possible blend, fire with water, earth with air, and each again conversely with each and all with all? Can this health of yours then be something varied and disparate, rather than simple and stable? When you speak of balance, you necessarily speak of stability: nothing that is balanced is in the habit of shifting to one or other of the extremes; such things have strict boundaries. As for disease, what else is it but a disordering and confounding of the truce within the body that comes about when the elements that were previously in harmony fall on each other, fighting and sowing confusion and harming the body as it is pounded and torn and rocked by them?[11] Is there any way that you can think this war to be something simple and single? If so, the art of medicine would not be worth much! As things really are, the diversity and the cacophony of this war that rages within human bodies, which we call disease, has given rise to a variegated science crammed full of a plethora of different kinds of implements and drugs and diets and regimens.[12] Again, if you turn to music,

---

[9] The Stoic position (with Maximus' usual rhetorical elaboration): cf. e.g. Diog. Laert. 7. 101, Cic. *De Fin.* 3. 34 (*SVF* iii. 72); Sen. *Epp.* 66. 28 and 71. 7. For some reason Maximus avoids stating explicitly that this sole good is Virtue.

[10] The same point is made in Sen. *Ep.* 66. 9; for a similar pattern of argument, see also Cic. *Tusc.* 5. 23 (against Antiochus).

[11] For this (wholly conventional) account of health and disease, cf. *Or.* 7. 1.

[12] Compare the (still more disparaging) attitude to the sophistication of modern medicine manifested in *Orr.* 4. 2 and 28. 1.

there too harmony is one and never grows either greater or lesser than itself, whereas disharmony is multiple and varied and divergent. So too a chorus, when unified, is one in the harmony of its voices, but when not unified, it splits and disperses and scatters and becomes a crowd. So too a trireme, when it is rowed in time to a pipe, brings the many hands of its crew together as they pull in unison; but if you take the pipe away, then you reduce their handiwork to disorder. So too, when a chariot is steered by a driver, it runs straight on a single course with a single impetus; but if you take away the charioteer, you split the team apart. So too an army is unified in its ranks by a single watchword, but if you remove that watchword, then you have dissolved the phalanx into a fleeing rabble.[13]

3   What then is the good of the body? Health. And its ill? Disease. Health is a single thing; diseases are many. What is the good in music? Harmony. And the ill? Disharmony. Harmony is one single thing, disharmony is a plurality. In the case of the chorus too, unison is one single thing, while discord is made up of many different elements. In the case of the trireme the pipe was one, but disobedience created a plurality. In the case of the chariot, the charioteer's skill was one single thing, while lack of skill again resulted in plurality. And what of the keeping of the watchword in the case of the phalanx? That too is one, while insubordination makes diversity. In the nature of unity, then, I see no excesses or deficiencies; it is stable and tolerates no rushing either in flight or in pursuit.[14] But when I find myself dealing with a plurality, then I am able to distinguish different elements with different characters. On a long journey, after all, though the destination is one single place, there are many resting-places along the way. If you are going to Babylon, the Assyrian is closer to the destination than the Armenian, the Armenian than the Lydian, the Lydian than the Ionian, and the Ionian than the islander; but none of them has yet arrived in Babylon, not the Assyrian, not the Armenian, not the Lydian, not the Ionian, not the islander. If you are going to Eleusis,

---

[13] This series of examples of virtuous unity, contrasted with vicious disunity, draws on a familiar set of τέχναι, all frequently appealed to elsewhere in the lectures: cf. e.g. *Orr.* 3. 1, 4. 9, 8. 7, 13. 3 and 4, 16. 2, and (for exactly the same trio used in a very similar way) Xen. *Oec.* 7. 3–10.

[14] For the insistence on the centrality of measure and moderation to the nature of the Good, cf. again Sen. *Ep.* 66. 9.

there is the Peloponnese, then the Isthmus, then Megara; but you are still not an initiate, even if you are in Megara, any more than the Peloponnesian is. As long as you have yet to enter the *anaktoron*, you are not an initiate. You must conceive of life too as a kind of long road, leading to Eleusis or to Babylon, and having as its final destination the palace itself and the *anaktoron* and initiation;[15] but because of the volume of travellers this road is full of people running, jostling, toiling, resting, lying down, turning off, and getting lost. Many and seductive are the byways, and the majority of them lead to cliffs and chasms, some to the land of the Sirens, some to the Lotophagi,[16] some to the country of the Cimmerians.[17] Just one path, narrow and steep and stony, which very few can follow, leads to the road's true destination; only hardy and hard-working souls who long for that place and yearn for initiation, discerning the beauty of the path, follow it through with much toil and sweat. When they arrive, they find respite from toil and suffering alike.[18] What other kind of initiation is there more mystic; what other destination worthy to be striven after? The Good holds the same status among human beings as Eleusis does for the uninitiated. Be initiated, come hither, set foot on this ground, seize hold of the Good, and you will desire nothing greater.

4   But if you give the name of 'good' to things that are *not* by nature good, physical health, and beauty, and gold and silver ornaments, and distinguished ancestors, and political honours,[19] all things better suited to be measured in terms of pleasure than in terms of goods, you profane the mysteries, and sin against the divinity. The kind of 'goods' you seek a share in are like the mysteries celebrated by Alcibiades, that inebriate torch-bearer, that

[15] For the imagery, cf. *Or.* 30. 2 (many helmsmen and many courses on the voyage to philosophical truth); *Orr.* 1. 3, 8. 7, 15. 7, 19. 1, 29. 7, and 34. 2 (variants on the image of the road of life and its pitfalls); Julian *Or.* 6. 184c–185a (many roads to the single truth aspired to by all philosophy); Plut. fr. 178 (the passage from life to death as a journey to initiation); Plato *Grg.* 497c, *Smp.* 210a, *Phaedr.* 249c, and Dio *Or.* 36. 33 (initiation into the truths of philosophy). The *anaktoron* (lit. 'palace') was the shrine in which the Eleusinian mysteries were celebrated.

[16] For the allegorization, cf. *Orr.* 22. 2 and 30. 2.

[17] For the Cimmerians as an image of benightedness, cf. *Orr.* 10. 9 and 25. 4.

[18] An elaboration of Hesiod's hard path to Virtue, that becomes easy at the top (*Op.* 289–92); something very similar can be found in *Tabula Cebetis* 15.

[19] i.e. if you count goods of the body and external goods (goods of Fortune) as true Goods, as well as Virtue: cf. *Or.* 40. 5, with n. 18.

hierophant from a drinking-party, that jesting initiate.[20] But you will not find a true good more sacred than another, any more than you will find one form of beauty fairer than another. If you take anything away from these qualities, ⟨what falls short of being beautiful⟩ ceases to be beautiful, and what falls short of being good ceases to be good. Do you not see the heavens there above your head, and the stars in them, and the bright sky beneath them, ⟨and the earth beneath that⟩? Compare the dimensions of each different constituent. Here is earth's share of the whole, broad and fertile, nourishing both plants and animals; but if you compare it with the sea, it is less extensive, as the sea is less extensive than the air, ⟨and the air is less extensive than the bright sky⟩ and the bright sky than the heavens. Up to this point one finds a sequence of con-stituents, each one exceeding the dimensions of the last and being exceeded by the next; but once you reach that point, you will find that the increase in magnitude comes to a halt, along with that in beauty too. What could be more beautiful than the heavens? What brighter than the stars? What mightier than the sun? What more perfectly ordered than the chorus of the stars? What more precious than the gods themselves?[21]

5   It would seem that men weigh out honours to different gods just as they do to different goods. Who is this? Zeus: let him rule. Who is this? Cronus: let him be imprisoned. Hephaestus: let him work bronze. Hermes: let him be the messenger. Athena: let her weave. ⟨The Dioscuri?⟩: let them accompany the Peloponnesians. They seem to be unaware that all the gods share one set of customs and way of life and character, which knows no divisions and no conflict: all of them rule, all are of the same age, all are

[20] A reference to Alcibiades' alleged profanation of the Mysteries: Thuc. 6. 53 and 60-1, Plut. *Alcib.* 19.

[21] The train of thought in this paragraph is awkward. Maximus is expounding the (Stoicizing) view that the superiority of the Good is a matter of kind, not of degree or quantity (as also in Cic. *De Fin.* 3. 34): no addition to its size can make it any the more good. One part of this is illustrated well enough by the analogy of the physical heavens, as possessing a beauty and a size that cannot conceivably be increased; at the same time, however, mention of the subordinate elements in the cosmos seems to suggest the existence of just the hierarchy of beauty—and thus also, by analogy, of Goods—that Maximus at this point is seeking to deny (cf. n. 23 below). On another point, it is interesting to observe that the description of the cosmos here, unlike say those in *Orr.* 21. 8 and 11. 10, makes no mention of any incorporeal, supercelestial dimension—i.e. it seems more like the cosmos of Stoicism than that of Platonism. This is perhaps deliberate, in a lecture that argues for a Stoicizing ethical perspective.

saviours, living together for all time in equal honour with equal rights of speech; though their names are many, their nature is one. It is through ignorance that we assign the benefits they all confer to individuals, attaching each to a different divine name.²² It is like the divisions of the sea: here is the Aegean, there is the Ionian Sea, the Myrtoan Sea is another, and the Crisaean yet another; but in reality the sea is just one element, with the same origins and the same behaviour, and homogeneous. So too we divide the Good in our imaginations because of our feebleness relative to it, and our own ignorance, although really it is one and like itself and equal in all directions.²³

Callias is rich: lucky man, for the goods he enjoys. But Alcibiades is more handsome than Callias. Let us compare these goods, wealth with beauty. Which of them is worth a hundred oxen? Which is worth nine? Which are we to choose? Which are we to pray for? Will then the Phoenician and the Egyptian pray for Callias' kind of good, the Elean and the Boeotian for Alcibiades'?²⁴ Pausanias is well-born, but Eurybiades has the higher repute.²⁵ Let us compare fame with birth: which is superior? To which shall we go and award the prize? Socrates is a pauper, Socrates is ugly, Socrates is obscure, Socrates is of humble birth, Socrates is undistinguished. How could he fail to be ugly and undistinguished and low-born and obscure and poor, when he was the son of a stone-mason and snub-nosed and pot-bellied, the butt of comic poets, thrown into prison and executed there, where Timagoras too met his end?²⁶ How bereft of goods he was! (I shrink from saying, 'how

²² Cf. *Or.* 2. 1. The conception of the divine as a unity, divided only by human nomenclature, is again more reminiscent of Stoic theology than of Platonic: cf. *SVF* ii. 1021, Cic. *ND* 2. 63 ff.

²³ The connection in thought between this paragraph and the next is again not of the smoothest. In what precedes, Maximus has been insisting on the unity of true Good, even where human beings seem to see a plurality and a diversity. In what follows, we are back (as in § 4) with a sequence of merely *apparent* goods that in fact, in comparison with the true Good, are not goods at all. The two points, that the Good is one and without degrees, and that so-called 'goods' of body and fortune are separated from it by an unbridgeable gap, have not themselves been kept properly separate in Maximus' exposition.

²⁴ For the Phoenician and the Egyptian as examples of hedonists–materialists, cf. *Orr.* 14. 2 and 30. 3; for the Eleans and the Boeotians as admirers of masculine beauty, cf. *Or.* 18. 2 and 20. 8.

²⁵ Eurybiades and Pausanias are mentioned consecutively, and implicitly compared, in Hdt. 8. 2–3.

²⁶ Compare the accounts of Socrates given in *Orr.* 1. 9, 3. 2, and 38. 7. The story of Timagoras' death is recounted in Xen. *Hell.* 7. 1. 33–8.

beset by ills'!) What shall we set against all this? What are we to say? Compare Socrates with his antagonists in their possession of goods. Don't you see that he was bettered by Callias in wealth, by Alcibiades in physique, in rank by Pericles, in fame by Nicias, in the theatre by Aristophanes, and in the court by Meletus? Was it then in vain that Apollo awarded him the palm, and cast his vote for him?[27]

Oration 40

1 Since you blame Homer for reproaching Glaucus over the exchange of arms, should I defend Homer to you, or Glaucus to Homer? The latter, by Zeus: Homer demands my respect before anyone else, to say nothing of a judge like you. This then is what Glaucus has to say:

'If this were a case of one good being less than good, or of one good being less substantial than another, then, Homer, it would have been reasonable of you to blame Zeus for damaging my wits. But over an exchange of gold and bronze, you should not be so ready to blame either Zeus or me so severely. Gold brings no advantage to its recipient, and bronze no disadvantage; both sides of the bargain are equally satisfactory to both parties, since the equality of goodwill in the giving cancels out the disparity between the materials.'[1]

Let Glaucus now take himself out of our way, and let Odysseus, his superior in wisdom, step forward instead, to give us *his* opinion about the possession of goods. Is he not the man who expressed his admiration for the good cheer and the singing in Alcinous' palace, seconded Nausicaa's prayers that she might make a marriage of true concord, and declared Calypso blessed in her immortality?[2] I reckon that if he had visited some other host, not from the ranks of people happy in their enjoyment of song and feasting, or blessed in the harmony of their marriage, but of people who enjoy still greater goods than these, he would have found the right thing to say about them too.

Since you also cite me the case of beauty, as a phenomenon that

---

[27] In his famous oracular response to Chaerephon, mentioned in Plato *Apol.* 21a; cf. *Or.* 3. 1.

[1] The same point is made in *Or.* 35. 3.

[2] *Od.* 9. 2–11 (for which cf. *Or.* 22. 1–2), 6. 180–5, and 5. 215–18.

is confined to just one degree, let me give you a brief answer on this point too.[3] It seems to me that if you were put in the place of the Trojan shepherd, and Hermes came to you on his mission from Zeus, bringing three goddesses for you to judge, and told you to decide which deserved the prize for beauty, then in your delight at Aphrodite (which Paris felt too) you would simultaneously convict Hera and Athena of ugliness.[4] If just one thing counts as beautiful in the sphere of beauty, and just one of the three wins, then the defeated parties must necessarily be ugly! [2] Don't do this, my most fortunate of judges! Be sparing with ugly names, and descend gradually down the scale from the top to the bottom. Then you will stop me quoting Homer to you again, when he talks of white-armed Hera, and rosy-armed Dawn, and grey-eyed Athena, and silver-sandalled Thetis, and Hebe of the fair ankles;[5] you are not going to deprive any of these of their claim to beauty, even if it is only beauty in one particular respect, as long as you wish to speak respectfully of the gods, and to avoid offence as far as you are able. Do you hear him, too, when he tells of a band of huntresses, the nymphs sporting in the mountains, led by Artemis?

> She rises above them all, head and shoulders,

he says, and

> She stands out unmistakably, though all are beautiful.[6]

Are you going to deride Homer for giving Artemis precedence in beauty over the nymphs? Do you also hear him speaking like this about Menelaus' beauty too, when he says that the blood ran down his thigh when he was wounded, then compares the beauty of his thigh to a skilled craftswoman staining ivory with purple to make a cheek-piece for horses?

> So, Menelaus, your shapely thighs were stained with the colour
> Of blood,

he says, and your legs and ankles.[7] But when he comes to praise the beauty of Agamemnon, he has no need of a Lydian or Carian

---

[3] A response to *Or.* 39. 4.
[4] The story of the Judgement of Paris is alluded to in *Il.* 24. 25–30, and was told more fully in the *Cypria* (OCT Homer v. 102).
[5] For the epithets, see *Il.* 1. 195; *Od.* 2. 1; *Il.* 1. 206 and 538; *Od.* 11. 603; etc.
[6] *Od.* 6. 107–8; the whole passage runs from 102 to 108.
[7] *Il.* 4. 139–47; the lines quoted are 146–7.

comparison, nor of ivory decorated with purple by a barbarian woman, but instead compares his head and eyes to Zeus.[8] This makes it quite clear that Agamemnon was the more beautiful: his beauty was beauty of head and eyes, whereas Menelaus' was beauty of thighs and ankles. He who is beautiful in better respects is more beautiful; he who is beautiful in less significant respects may not immediately count as ugly, but is certainly less beautiful. Here is another case. Was not Achilles supreme in the Greek army for youthful beauty, and did not Nireus take second prize?[9] By your criteria, in coming second to Achilles, Nireus was no better than Thersites! Lest our discussion should be confined to beauty alone, Ajax cannot vie with Achilles in bravery, nor Diomedes with Ajax, nor Sthenelus with Diomedes, nor Menestheus with Sthenelus; but no one makes this a reason for depriving Menestheus of his claim to virtue because of Sthenelus, or Sthenelus because of Diomedes, or Diomedes because of Ajax, or Ajax because of Achilles. Here too the progression of virtue does not skip the intermediate characters, but descends gradually, in stages, from the best to the most inferior.[10]

3   Moreover—to get away at last from bodies, in which strength and beauty are combined[11]— if you were to compare Andromache with Penelope, is not each of them chaste and loving, but will you not also give precedence to Penelope—not because you are comparing a Greek woman to a barbarian, but because you give greater weight to superiority in virtue? Nestor counsels Agamemnon. Is this a case of a wise man advising a fool? Or would you not want to insult the king of all the Greeks, the Zeus-born shepherd of the host, with such a slanderous accusation? Yet even so, wise though he was, he needed a wiser counsellor, Nestor.

Do you still find me no more convincing when I talk to you thus about virtues, and show myself willing, in comparing similar items, to assign them to different points on a scale, higher and lower, according to the disparity between them in the degree to which they participate in the quality in question? Perhaps not, since you

---

[8] *Il.* 2. 477–8.
[9] *Il.* 2. 671–4.
[10] For gradual progression as an important structural principle, cf. *Orr.* 9. 1, 11. 12 (macrocosmic), and 27. 7 (microcosmic).
[11] i.e. to conclude the long list of Homeric examples with some more obvious instances of goods of soul rather than goods of body.

think that even health is one single thing. In fact nothing could be less unitary. Bodily constitutions show a far greater spread of variations in striking a healthy balance than do those of the soul. Indeed, matters are quite the opposite to what you suppose: to chase after the summit of perfection in health is to pursue a fugitive thing that neither Asclepius nor Chiron[12] can capture at the first rush. Thus, when the degree of health attainable varies, the man who is content with what he can get is not only more grateful to medicine, but also retains his hopes of ultimately reaching the summit. So it is also in the case of goods. There are three considerations in terms of which this investigation of ours might be settled, one relating to the truth of the matter, another to possibility, and the third to benefit. Let us examine them one by one, reversing the order and beginning with the question of benefit. Let us hold back from granting the proposition that one good can be greater than another is either possible or true, and consider instead whether it is beneficial. Many things that are neither true nor possible have proved beneficial simply because they are believed.

4   Does not the man who stations the good on a pinnacle of perfection, and confines goodness to excellence alone, thereby dig ditches and build walls that block most people's hopes of ever attaining it? But he who allows stepping-stones and pauses along the way, and many upward stages, helps the traveller well along his path in the hopes of attaining moderate success, encourages the man who *has* made progress, with his success, into hoping to finish his journey to the best, and proclaims the man who has arrived at the summit as the best among the good.[13] But doesn't the alternative analysis crown the hero among cowards, and the strong man among utter weaklings, and in general fail to give champions worthy adversaries, or to test true virtues against their likes?

That is enough about benefit; I now move on to consider possibility. Superlative gold is tested not against lead but against less pure gold, silver against silver, and bronze against bronze;[14] indeed as a quite general principle all substances are tested by comparison with what is similar in essence but distinct in degree of

---

[12] Asclepius: cf. *Or.* 4. 2–3 etc.; Chiron: cf. *Or.* 28. 1.
[13] Maximus here picks up the imagery of journeying from *Or.* 39. 3.
[14] For the imagery of assaying, cf. *Orr.* 11. 2, 18. 3, and 31. 2.

superiority. Yet *you* test the Good by setting it against pure Evil.[15]
How can even the smallest of goods then fail to rank as the
greatest in your eyes? Just as the light of a fire at night is brighter
than one that is seen in daylight, because it shows up against the
deep darkness all around it, but the same light is weak and dim in
the sunshine because it has a mightier opponent to contest with;
so too any good, when compared with evil, is greatest and best and
supreme, like a small spark in deep darkness or a little light in the
depths of night; but if you allow it to race and compete against its
like, then you will discover what is truly best. As things now are
you are confusing and obscuring the verdict. Can you not see that
the moon, a star that appears both by night and by day, is bright
by night but dim in the sunlight? By day the sun, which is the best
and mightiest of the heavenly bodies, reigns supreme, but in the
night it is the moon, which is the weakest, that is supreme. So too
the Good: if you plunge it into the darkness and dimness and black
of evil, then even its weakest form reigns supreme; but if you
compare goods with goods, then it is necessarily the most brilliant
that wins out.[16]

5   That is enough about possibility; I now move on to truth.
Should we conceive of human life as anything other than the conduct of an existence in which soul and body and chance combine?
When these three are properly and harmoniously blended, each
attaining the highest pinnacle of its own strength, the resulting
combination is to be given the name of happiness, with the soul
leading like a general, the body obeying its orders like a soldier,
and chance working with him, like his weapons;[17] the combination
of their efforts produces victory.[18] If you remove chance, you

[15] Because, in Stoic theory, the goodness of the Good is not appreciated by contrast with other items of lesser goodness: Cic. *De Fin.* 3. 34.
[16] For the imagery of light and darkness, cf. e.g. *Orr.* 1. 3 (the light of philosophical teaching), 5. 8 (philosophy as a small spark in a dark night), 11. 1 (the
sun of Platonic philosophy versus the dim fire of other philosophers), 11. 9 (the sun
of divine Mind), 13. 3 (the sun of divine Mind compared to the dim fire of human
intelligence), 29. 5 (benighted humanity in quest of the Good), 29. 7 (the Sun compared to the human Good).
[17] For the image of the campaign, cf. *Orr.* 5. 3 and 13. 4; and for a different
evaluation of Fortune, *Orr.* 5. 6 and 8. 7.
[18] i.e. goods of soul, goods of body, and external goods are all elements in full
happiness. For this (Peripatetic or Peripateticizing) sentiment, compare Arist. *NE* 1.
8, 1098[b]9—1. 10, 1101[a]21; Antiochus ap. Cic. *De Fin.* 5. 26–7 and 68. Philo is
ambiguous on this point: in *Quis Heres* 285–6 he seems to endorse the Peripatetic

disarm the soldier; if you take away the soldier, you relieve the general of his command; but at the same time, the soldier is worth more than his weapons, and the general than the soldier. You can do one of two things, honour the general and disregard the rest, or include the others too and pay all equal respect: if you do the former, what use will the general have for his expertise? If you do the latter, what use will expertise have for the general? Let the soul lead, let the body serve in the ranks, let chance join its efforts to theirs. I approve of them all and accept them all, but I will not allow them equal status. Do you not also acknowledge the case of the sea-voyage, where the steersman has command, as the soul does of the body; the ship is under his command, as the body is under the soul's; and the winds blow for it, as chance does for Virtue.[19] If a storm supervenes, and both ship and steersman hold fast, then there is hope of survival, † even if the ship goes straight down or sinks †,[20] thanks to the helmsman's science. But if you start by removing the helmsman, then the ship is useless even if it stays firm, and the blowing of the winds is useless, even if it carries the ship along. This is why in the case of sea and ships and voyages, the steersman is the most valuable element, followed by the ship, followed by external assistance. In the course of this life of ours, the soul is the most valuable element, followed by the body, then thirdly chance; and the goods of the more valuable element are themselves more valuable than those of the less valuable.

6 I would abolish equality also in the case of the senses. Homer was blind, but he could hear Calliope; Atys was deaf, but he could see the sun.[21] Change their conditions round, so that Atys can hear but not see, and Homer can see but not hear. Will Calliope not sing for Atys, and will you not rob Homer of his teacher?[22] I would also remove equality from the gods,[23] since I believe Homer when he says,

---

view, though elsewhere he attacks it (e.g. *Quod Det.* 7; cf. Dillon 1977: 146–8). The explicit formulation of the threefold classification of Goods goes back to Plato (*Grg.* 467e, *Euthyd.* 279ac, *Phileb.* 48e, *Leg.* 743e).

[19] For the image, cf. *Or.* 30. 2.

[20] The text is clearly corrupt, but no convincing emendation has yet been suggested; perhaps the whole clause should simply be excised.

[21] Hdt. 1. 34. 2.

[22] Accepting the change in punctuation (question mark for full stop) suggested by Koniaris (1962: 120).   [23] This picks up *Or.* 39. 5.

All was divided three ways, each was given his standing[24]

—a standing that was not equal, any more than their powers. Heaven is not an equal share compared to the seas, nor the seas compared to Hades. Yet Hades and Poseidon and Zeus are all equally gods and sons of Cronus. After all, Lysander was a Spartiate, but Agesilaus was a Heraclid. I grant families greater or lesser honour according to their virtues. The horse-trainer loves well-sired horses,

> which Zeus of the wide brows granted
> Once to Tros, recompense for his son Ganymedes, and therefore
> They are the finest of all horses;[25]

the hunter too loves well-sired puppies. Will not the lover of human beings, who lovingly raises this other species, also discriminate between its breeds, telling not of Artoxerxes son of Xerxes (that is a cowardly breed you mention), nor Hippias son of Pisistratus (that is a wicked breed you mention), nor Croesus son of Alyattes (a weak breed)?[26] But if you speak of Leonidas and Agesilaus, I recognize their excellence and remember Heracles and praise their noble lineage. Would that I could have seen the stock of Aristides, of Socrates, in Athens! I would have honoured them like Heraclids, like Perseids, like Eupatrids! Do you have praise for flowing rivers, if they rise pure from their springs, and praise for plants whose seeds endure even if their stocks grow old, but not for human nobility, if it rises from Virtue as if from a pure spring, and remains real and uncontaminated?

Up to this point you keep your nerve, and what you say is plausible. But if I ask you about wealth, what do you say? Where do you rank this attribute? In which category? Speak out bareheaded, speak with the voice of the soul! What have you to say about wealth? Is it an evil? Why then are you in love with it? Is it a good? Why then do you try to avoid it? Is it that

> Your tongue swore, but your heart remains unsworn?[27]

Or do you think it is neither a good nor an evil, but occupies an

---

[24] *Il.* 15. 189; the lines immediately following (190–3) are quoted in *Or.* 26. 7.
[25] *Il.* 5. 265–7.
[26] For Artoxerxes, cf. *Orr.* 34. 6 and 36. 6; and for Croesus, 5. 2, 11. 6, 13. 5, 22. 5, 32. 9, and 34. 4–5. Hippias (Hdt. 1. 61, 5. 55 ff., etc.) is not mentioned elsewhere by Maximus.
[27] The notorious line from Euripides *Hippolytus* (612).

intermediate position in no man's land? Keep it as an 'indifferent', advance no further, keep within the limits! If you give it a subtly different name and call it not a good but a 'preferred', then for all the change in name, you are still granting it value.[28]

ORATION 41   God and the Sources of Evil

Introduction

= 41 (1962) = 25 (Laur. Conv. Sopp. 4). The manuscript title is Τοῦ θεοῦ τὰ ἀγαθὰ ποιοῦντος, πόθεν τὰ κακά, 'Good being the work of God, whence comes Evil?'

For this final lecture, Maximus returns to the territory of *Orr*. 5, 8–11, and 13: God, man, the structure of the cosmos, and the place within it of the human soul (cf. again Soury 1942, esp. ch. 4). As a vindication of the goodness and benevolence of a provident God, however, the lecture also has thematic links with *Orr*. 34 and 38.

§ 1 tells the story of Alexander the Great's visit to the oracle of Zeus Ammon, and declares that he missed the chance to ask a truly enlightened question: not about the source of Good in the world, which is obvious (§ 2), but about the far more awkward and pressing problem of the source Evil (§ 3). Homer's authority is invoked to establish that Evil does not come from the gods. Its sources are instead two: alterations to matter, and the freedom of choice enjoyed by the human soul (§ 4a). These are discussed in turn, material change in § 4b and the soul's licence in § 5, before the lecture breaks off, apparently incomplete.

---

[28] 'Indifferent' and 'preferred' are Stoic technical terms (Diog. Laert. 7. 101–5). Two different readings of this final paragraph would seem to be possible. On the first, Maximus is co-opting the terminology to make the point that, even though he has argued that external goods are genuinely Good, he is not advocating the pursuit of wealth (as opposed to a more modest material comfort). On this reading, the paragraph's imaginary interlocutor would be a member of the audience, not committed in advance to any particular philosophical position. On the alternative reading, the interlocutor (as in §§ 1–3) is the Stoicizer of *Or*. 39, and Maximus is teasing him with his school's perceived difficulties, and consequent equivocation, over wealth and all other 'preferred indifferents': cf. (for the terminological problem) Cic. *De Fin*. 4. 72–3, Plut. *Comm. Not*. 1047e; and (for Stoic attitudes to wealth) Plut. *Comm. Not*. 1069a ff.

Like *Orr.* 5 and 13, this is another lecture which raises questions about Maximus' philosophical orientation. Although the psychology invoked in § 5 is clearly Platonic, and the lecture contains direct quotations, as well as more indirect reminiscences, of the myths of *Republic* and *Phaedrus*, the account of divine Providence in the management of the physical cosmos (§ 4b) uses materials of an equally clear Stoic provenance (see notes ad loc.). Above all, the implication that apparent physical Evil is not evil at all, but further proof of divine concern for the cosmos as a whole, seems much closer to Stoic immanentist theology than to the Middle Platonic acknowledgement of matter as an independent principle, on which the imposition of divine order can never be complete (cf. Dillon (1977: 45, 158, 199–208, 280–2, 312–15); note also that Maximus makes no mention of that characteristically Middle Platonic entity, the World Soul). Analysis is not made any easier by Maximus' determined avoidance of conceptual complexity, and thus of doctrinal details that might firmly assign the lecture to one philosophical camp or the other. Nevertheless, it does overall seem plausible to read it as an attempt to reflect a Platonic standpoint. The description of divine Mind in § 2, though not uniquely applicable to the transcendent God of Platonism, is quite compatible with such a reading (and, furthermore, echoes Plato's most famous image for transcendent reality, the Sun); and, as already observed, the lecture ends in § 5 with a psychology that is Platonic both in content and in form, as well as an account of the creation of living creatures that echoes the *Timaeus*. Given this, it is surely plausible to see the 'Stoic' material in § 4 as matter claimed for Platonism, on the warrant of such texts as *Laws* 903b and *Timaeus* 47e–48a, 56c ff. and 69b, rather than a chunk of alien matter embedded in an otherwise Platonic discourse. See further Introduction, pp. xxv–xxx.

For other substantial surviving discussions of the problems tackled in the lecture, see the fragments of Hierocles quoted by Stobaeus in *Eclogue* 1. 3. 54 and 2. 8. 7 (i. 35. 4 ff. and ii. 117. 29 ff. Meineke), Philo *De Providentia* (extant in a complete Armenian translation, rendered into Latin by Aucher, and in several long fragments of the original Greek quoted by Eusebius), Seneca *De Providentia*, Sallustius *De Mundo* 13, and Plotinus *Enneades* 3. 2–3.

Gregoras takes four excerpts from the lecture, from §§ 1, 2, and 3, and the compiler of Neap. 100 one, from § 2. Poliziano notes the topics of Alexander and Ammon, oracles, Zeus, Homer, the Euripus, human suffering, natural disasters, and Vice, as well as the quotation from *Phaedrus* 247a, from §§ 1, 2, 3, 4, and 5, in the margins of Paris. gr. 1962, foll. 142ᵛ-145ʳ. Johannes Reuchlin made a separate Latin translation, which survives on Basel Universitätsbibliothek E III 15, foll. 299-305, and is mentioned in Trithemius' account of Reuchlin in his *Catalogus Illustrium Virorum* of 1495 (fol. 61ᵛ). Thomas De Quincey, finally, saw a similarity between the content of § 4 and the thinking of one of his own contemporaries, observing on the flyleaf of his copy of Heinsius' edition (Corpus Christi College, Oxford, IV. 313a).: 'This is Wordsworth's (*sic*: it is in fact Coleridge's) principle of Similitude in Dissimil.—Dissim. in Similitude.'

Oration

1 They say that Alexander of Macedon,[1] when he came to the shrine of Ammon and Ammon addressed him as his son, believed the god because of what Homer says when he calls him 'father of gods and men'.[2] But on receiving this oracle, he only thought fit to ask one question in return. It was not about putting Darius to flight, or about the battle he was about to fight, or the ills of Greece, or the chaos reigning in Asia; instead, as if he was quite satisfied with everything else, he asked the god where the Nile rises before flowing down into Egypt.[3] Clearly this was the one thing he lacked for complete happiness, and on learning it he would have been content! No he wouldn't, for goodness' sake: not even had he found out not only about the Nile, but also about the Ister, or the Ocean itself—whether it has the character of a river encircling the whole earth, or consists of the origins and sources of our own sea, or is a lake that receives the sun and the moon when they set, or has one of the other identities that the poets divine for it.[4] And this

---

[1] For Alexander, cf. *Orr.* 2. 6, 8. 4, 14. 8, 23. 7, 28. 1, 29. 2, 32. 9, and 36. 6. The visit to the oracle of Zeus Ammon is described in all the main accounts of Alexander: Arrian *Anab.* 3. 3-4 (cf. 4. 9. 9, 7. 8. 3), Plut. *Alex.* 26-7 (with Hamilton 1969, ad loc.), Diodorus 17. 49-51, Q. Curtius 4. 7. 5-30, etc.

[2] As in *Il.* 1. 544 etc.

[3] A talking-point since Hdt. 2. 28-34; it seems to be an *ad hoc* invention of Maximus to make it the subject of Alexander's question to Ammon.

[4] Encircling the earth: *Il.* 18. 607-8; source of all seas (and rivers): *Il.* 21. 195-7, Hesiod *Theog.* 337-70; receiver of sun: Stesichorus fr. 185 *PMG* (Athen. 11. 469e).

when he had the opportunity, leaving the rivers to flow from whatever source God has made them rise from, to go to Ammon, or to the land of the Thesprotians and the oak that grows there, or to Parnassus and the oracle at Pytho, or to the Ismenus and the voice that speaks there, or to Delos and the dances that are danced there, or to any other oracle there may be that speaks to men in Greek or foreign lands,[5] and ask Zeus and Apollo to give one single shared and public oracle to the whole of the human race.[6] This would have been a far more generally beneficial mission for mankind to journey on than that of the Dorians consulting about the Peloponnese, or that of the Athenians consulting about Ionia, or the Corinthians asking about Sicily.[7]

2   Come, let us now imitate those public envoys, sent off to the oracles on behalf of their peoples, and ask Zeus, who is the father and provider of human goods, what their origins and sources are, whence they rise and flow. Or do we in fact have no need to bother the god over this matter, since we are well aware of this provision, and see its origins, and understand the source,[8] and know the Father and Creator[9] for ourselves, the governor of the heavens, the director of the sun and the moon, the leader of the swiftly whirling orbits of the dance of the stars, the steward of the seasons, the regulator of the winds, the creator of the sea, the maker of the earth, the provider of rivers, the nurturer of crops, the begetter of living things, the god of the family, the god of rain, the god of fruitfulness, the paternal god, the fostering god,[10] whose mind, adamantine and unwearying, pervading the whole of creation with extraordinary speed, like the glance of an eye, brings order and beauty to all that it touches, just as the rays of the sun when they fall on the earth illuminate every part of it that they

---

[5] For this list of oracles, cf. *Or.* 8. 1–2.

[6] On the question of 'theological' oracles, cf. *Or.* 11. 6 with n. 26.

[7] Compare the list of colonists in *Or.* 29. 7 (with n. 29).

[8] For the insistence that God is the source of good alone, and that his goodness is manifested in the order of the physical cosmos, cf. *Orr.* 4. 8, 8. 7, 15. 6, 16. 6, and 38. 6; and (for Platonic warrant) *Tim.* 29d–30a. This is standard matter in discussions of divine Providence: Cic. *ND* 2. 73 ff., Hierocles ap. Stob. *Ecl.* 2. 8. 7, ii. 117. 29 ff. Meineke, Sen. *Prov.* 1. 1. 2–4, [Plut.] *De Fato* 572f–573d, etc.

[9] For this echo of Plato *Tim.* 28c, cf. *Or.* 11. 12.

[10] For this list of epithets for Zeus, cf. [Arist.] *De Mundo* 7. 401^{ab}, Dio *Orr.* 1. 39 and 12. 75–6 (with Russell 1992, ad loc.), Aristides *Or.* 43. 29 ff. (with Amman 1931: 100–9), Themist. *Or.* 6. 79d, and Cornutus 9, p. 9. 14 ff. Lang.

reach.[11] I cannot myself tell you of the nature of this touch, but Homer hints subtly at it:

He spoke, the son of Cronus, and nodded his head with the dark brows.[12]

At Zeus' nod the earth took form, and all that is nourished on the earth, and the sea took form and all that is born in it, and the air took form and all creatures that ride in it, and the heavens took form and all that moves in them. This is the work of Zeus' nod.[13] Up to this point I need no oracle I believe Homer, I trust Plato— and I pity Epicurus![14]

3   But to move on to our conceptions of evil, whence did this descend into our world? What are the sources and origins of ill? Where did it begin its advance? From Ethiopia, like the Plague?[15] From Babylon, like Xerxes? From Macedonia, like Philip? Not from the heavens, by Zeus, not from the heavens:[16]

for envy has no place in the company of the divine.[17]

It is here then, here, that I need an oracle. Let us ask the gods: 'Zeus and Apollo, and any other god of prophecy who cares for the human herd, tell us, we beg you, the origin of Evil. What is its cause? How are we to guard against it? How escape its attentions?

There is no shame in running and escaping from disaster.[18]

Or do you not see how many terrors descend like baneful spirits on human life, roaming about the earth and filling it with groans and lamentation of every kind?[19] The human body groans as it laments the diseases that lay siege to it, and the precariousness of its

[11] For the comparison of divine Mind with eyesight and with the Sun, cf. *Or.* 11. 9. Though the latter comparison echoes the image of the Sun in Plato *Resp.* 508a ff., the whole description of divine Mind in this paragraph could in theory be applied as well to the Stoics' immanent divinity as to the transcendent God of Platonism.
[12] *Il.* 1. 528.
[13] With this account of Zeus' nod, cf. *Or.* 4. 8, with n. 28.
[14] A routine dig at the 'atheist', cf. *Orr.* 4. 4 and 8, and 25. 4.
[15] Cf. *Orr.* 7. 4, 13. 9.
[16] An echo of a famous phrase from Demosthenes *Or.* 8. 26, presumably triggered by the preceding reference to Philip.
[17] Plato *Phaedr.* 247a.
[18] A line which seems to conflate *Il.* 14. 80 with *Il.* 12. 327.
[19] With this account of human misery, cf. [Plato] *Axioch.* 366d ff.; Crates as quoted by Teles, p. 38 Hense; [Hippocrates] *Ep.* 17. 47; Lucret. 5. 214–34; Seneca as cited by Oltramare (1926: 287, th. 77a); and, in the context of the debate over divine Providence, Philo *Prov.* (Armenian tr.) 2. 90.

survival, and the uncertainty of life. At what time in its career is
the human body free from hostile attention? At the instant of birth,
torn from the mother's womb, it is wet and slimy and leaky, a
mass of wails and snivels; as it advances and grows to boyish
grace, it becomes manic and ill-disciplined; as it advances to the
full vigour of youth, its burning passions send it rampaging out of
control; and if it reaches old age, it soon dies and is extinguished.
As a lodging for the soul it is of little use, hard to please, wretched
and incapable of work, with no tolerance for rain, wind, or sun,
carping at the seasons sent by the heavens and pitting its efforts
against Zeus. Here is winter; it wraps itself up. Here is summer; it
cools itself down.[20] When full it longs for emptiness, and when
empty for repletion. Like the Euripus,[21] or the ebb and flow of
the tides, it never stands still, is never stable—insatiable, uncon-
trollable, gluttonous, unable to do without clothing, footwear, oint-
ments, drugs, and baths. Many hands and many skills are needed
to look after just one body, though one horse-trainer can tend a
thousand horses, one shepherd as many sheep, and one oxherd as
many oxen.[22] Nor yet is all this attention sufficient. What devices
have men discovered to ward off the attacks of diseases, or to
suspend the rains that fall from the heavens, or to still the earth
when it quakes, or to quench the fire that bursts from the earth?[23]
You can see what a series of ills besets us one after the other, and
how uninterrupted are our perils:

> The earth breeds nothing more feeble than man.[24]

And if you turn to the soul, there too you will see a hoard of
diseases descending on it. If you repel grief, fear creeps in; if fear
goes, anger arises; if anger abates, jealousy takes its place.[25] Our
troubles are close at hand, our ills dwell hard about us, and there
is no fitting respite.'

---

[20] Cf. *Or.* 36. 5 (the contrast between Diogenes and ordinary, dissatisfied, un-
hardened humanity).

[21] For the image, and the condition it expresses, cf. *Orr.* 1. 2, 5. 6, 10. 5.

[22] Cf. *Orr.* 33. 4 (the range of resources needed to maintain the king of Persia)
and, for the unfavourable comparison with the animal kingdom, *Orr.* 17. 1 and 36.
5, with Lucret. 5. 228–34 (cf. Oltramare 1926: 270, th. 30a).

[23] A standard list of physical ills: cf. Philo *Prov.* (Armenian tr.) 2. 90, Hierocles
ap. Stob. *Ecl.* 1. 3. 54, i. 35. 4 ff. Meineke.

[24] *Od.* 18. 130.

[25] For this picture of the soul beset by the passions, cf. *Orr.* 1. 2, 7 *passim*, 27. 5
and 9, 28. 2, 33. 7.

4   What then would Zeus or Apollo, or any other prophetic god, reply to this complaint? Let us listen to the words of their interpreter:[26]

> They say that their ills come from us; but it is by their own
> Misdeeds they bring pains beyond their lot upon themselves.[27]

What then is the cause of these misdeeds? Of the two dwellings constituted by heaven and earth, we must believe that the former has no contact with evil, while the latter is compounded of good and evil both, having the goods that flow down to it from the other, and the evils that arise from its own innate imperfections.[28] These imperfections are themselves of two kinds, those deriving from modifications of physical matter, and those deriving from the licence enjoyed by the human soul.[29] I should speak first about the former.

What you see around you is matter that has been subjected to the efforts of a good craftsman: the element of order in it derives from his science, but if earthly things experience any disharmony in their inability to control themselves, then I would beg you to absolve that science from any blame. No craftsman can form an intention that counteracts his science, any more than a lawmaker can form an intention that is unjust;[30] and divine intelligence is surer in its aim than human science. Just as in the exercise of the crafts, science itself produces some effects directly as it aims for its objectives, while other consequences follow on from its activity, not as effects of the science itself, but as incidental modifications of

[26] For the image, cf. the description of Plato as the gods' 'interpreter' in *Or.* 11. 6, and the account of Homer as an inspired philosopher in *Orr.* 4 and 26.

[27] *Od.* 1. 33–4, lines understandably much quoted in defences of divine Providence: e.g. Chrysippus *SVF* ii. 1000, Hierocles ap. Stob. *Ecl.* 2. 8. 7, ii. 117. 29 ff. Meineke. Maximus has quoted them before in *Or.* 38. 7 (cf. also 6. 6). For early Christian use of the lines, see Daniélou (1973: 105).

[28] The common distinction between the celestial and the sublunary regions of the cosmos: cf. *Or.* 21. 8 for its use elsewhere in Maximus, and Hierocles in Stob. *Ecl.* 2. 8. 7, ii. 117–19 Meineke for its application to the problem of evil. Maximus' wording here continues to leave it unclear whether his picture is that of the Stoic or the Platonic cosmos.

[29] For this distinction, cf. Hierocles ap. Stob. *Ecl.* 2. 8. 7 (κακία . . . ὕλη), Philo *Prov.* (Armenian tr.) 2. 82 ('vel materiae vel naturae immoderatae erroris . . . fetus').

[30] For the comparison with the lawmaker (no more responsible for infringements of his laws than the divine craftsman is for occasional elements of disorder in his products), cf. Chrysippus in Plut. *Sto. Rep.* 1049e (= *SVF* ii. 1125); Philo *Prov.* (Armenian tr.) 2. 82.

matter, like sparks from the anvil and gusts of heat from the furnace, and other modifications of other forms of matter, which are necessary consequences of the work done, but not produced directly by the craftsman himself; of just the same kind is the genesis of those earthly events we call the assaults of human ill. Here too we must believe that the science itself is blameless, and that those effects are so to speak the necessary and natural consequences of the crafting of the whole.[31] What we call evil and ruin, the things we lament over, the craftsman calls the preservation of the whole.[32] His concern is precisely for the whole, and it is necessary for the part to suffer in the interests of that whole. The Athenians are ravaged by the Plague, the Spartans are rocked by earthquakes, Thessaly is inundated, Aetna erupts.[33] When ever did Zeus promise the Athenians immortality? If the Plague goes away, will Alcibiades not lead them against Sicily? When did Zeus promise the Spartans a land free from earthquakes? When did he promise the Sicilians a land without eruptions? These are all parts of larger bodies. You can see then that these events, which you call destruction, judging by the passing away of what is lost, I call preservation, judging by the succession of what follows on. What you behold is change in physical bodies and the alteration of things coming into being, 'a road up and down' in Heraclitus' words;[34] and again

living their death and dying their life; fire lives earth's death and air lives fire's death; water lives air's death and earth lives water's.[35]

What you see is a chain of life and a cycle of change in physical bodies, in which the whole is renewed.

---

[31] For the image of the craftsman, cf. Aurelius 8. 50, Origen *Contra Celsum* 6. 55; and for the underlying doctrine, that such minor untidiness is a necessary consequence of creative activity, and no blemish on the perfection of divine Goodness and Providence, add *SVF* ii. 1170; Philo *Prov.* (Armenian tr.) 2. 79, 100, 102, 104; Aurelius 6. 36, 7. 75.

[32] Cf. *Orr.* 5. 4, with n. 19.

[33] Precisely the same examples are used in *Or.* 5. 4.

[34] Heraclitus B 60 D-K.

[35] Heracl. B 62 (truncated and paraphrased) and B 76 D-K; the first part of fr. 62 is quoted in *Or.* 4. 4, and a different version of fr. 76 is given by Aurelius 4. 46 and Plut. *De E* 392c. Soury (1942: 71) observes that Heraclitus was claimed as a significant precursor by the Stoics; but use of Heraclitean dicta is not enough in itself to prove Stoic orientation: he was also known as one of Plato's inspirations (Diog. Laert. 3. 8).

5 Turn now to the other, innate source of ill, which is conceived and brought to term by the soul's own freedom, and which goes by the name of Vice: the familiar story,

The fault is his who chooses; God is blameless.[36]

Since the earth had of necessity to be rich in plants and living things and creatures of many kinds,[37] but had also to hold confined within itself evils that had been banished from the heavens, God implanted many different kinds of colonies of living beings into this realm of ours, making one primary distinction in their natures: between on the one hand, creatures of many different kinds in their manner of life and varied in their physical constitution, lacking in reason and intelligence, mutually destructive, with no concept of God or share in Virtue, nurtured and guided by the sensations of the moment, strong in body but incapable of the use of reasoning; and, on the other hand, human beings, who to the contrary are of one and the same species and band together, weak in body but mighty in possession of reason, knowers of God, participants in political society, lovers of sociability, acquainted with justice and law and friendship.[38] This race then had to be superior to the whole earthly herd, yet at the same time, obviously, inferior to God.[39] The requisite inferiority was not going to be secured even by death, given that the very thing most people mean by 'death' is in fact the beginning of immortality and the birth of a life to come, when bodies perish in their own manner and time, and the soul is summoned up to its own proper life and place.[40] This then was the kind of inferiority that God invented to differentiate the human from the divine. Mounting the soul on a body of earth, like a charioteer on a chariot, and handing the reins over to the charioteer, he set it free to run, in possession both of the strength of expertise that he provided, and the freedom to abandon that

[36] Plato *Resp.* 617e, another much-quoted dictum: Lucian *Merc. Cond.* 42; Chalcidius *Comm. in Tim.* 164, Hippol. *Ref.* 1. 19. 19, Clem. *Paed.* 1. 8. 69. 1, *Strom.* 5. 136. 4, Justin *Apol.* 1. 44 and 2. 81, Porph. *Marc.* 12 and 24, Plotinus *Enn.* 3. 2. 7. 20, and *IG* xiv. 1196.

[37] By the so-called 'principle of Plenitude': Plato *Tim.* 30c ff., 39e–40a, and (esp.) 41ac; cf. Lovejoy (1936: 48–55).

[38] With this (highly conventional) account of man and beast, and of the contrast between them, cf. *Orr.* 6. 1, 10. 5, 20. 6, 29. 7, 31. 4, 36. 1.

[39] For the (equally conventional) notion of man as an intermediate between beasts and gods, cf. *Orr.* 6. 1 and 33. 7.

[40] Cf. *Orr.* 7. 5 and 11. 11.

expertise.[41] When it mounts the chariot and takes hold of the reins, the happy and blessed soul that preserves its recollection of the God who placed it in its vehicle and ordered it to drive holds fast to the reins, and controls the chariot, and restrains the impulses of the team.[42] They for their part are of every conceivable kind, each straining to run in a different direction, one of them licentious and gluttonous and lustful, another spirited and manic and impulsive, another lazy and sluggish ⟨and . . . ⟩, another mean and humble and pusillanimous.[43] The tearing of the chariot between these conflicting forces confuses the charioteer, and if he fails to control it,[44] it is carried headlong in the direction that the dominant horse pulls, with the whole chariot, charioteer and all, now following the licentious horse into violence and drunkenness and lust and other unseemly and impure pleasures, now the spirited horse into all kinds of ill usage. ⟨ . . . ⟩[45]

[41] The image of the chariot developed here echoes both Plato *Tim.* 41e–42b and, more particularly, *Phaedr.* 246a ff. and 253d ff.

[42] As described in *Phaedr.* 254be and 256ab.

[43] The two horses of the *Phaedr.* (esp. 246ab and 253ce) have become four in Maximus' adaptation, and no longer stand, as in Plato, for the two lower divisions of the tripartite soul ('spirit' and 'desire'). What they do stand for, in terms of a philosophical theory of the lower soul and its faculties, is harder to grasp. They do not correspond to the four basic πάθη of Stoicism; and though they clearly enough represent two vices of excess and two of deficiency (as it were ἀκολασία and θρασύτης versus ἀοργησία and μικροπρέπεια), they do not make a neat set of Peripatetic pairs either. The basically Platonic nature of the picture (with soul and body as entities of radically different kinds) is, however, unaffected. For other descriptions of the soul in the lectures, cf. *Orr.* 16. 4, 20. 4, and 27. 5; and for adaptations of the chariot image of *Phaedr.* elsewhere in second-century Greek writing, Trapp (1990: 148–54 and 172).

[44] Cf. *Phaedr.* 254b, 256c.

[45] The lecture seems incomplete, but how much has been lost cannot be established.

References

ADLER, A. (ed.) (1928–38), *Suidae Lexicon* (Leipzig).

ALDRICH, K., FEHL, P., and FEHL, R. (edd.) (1991), *Franciscus Junius: The Literature of Classical Art*, i. *The Painting of the Ancients, De Pictura Veterum, According to the English Translation* (1638); ii. *A Lexicon of Artists and their Works, Catalogus Architectorum . . . translated from the original Latin of 1694* (Berkeley).

ALLEN, T. W. (1893), 'Palaeographica III: A Group of Ninth-Century Greek Manuscripts', *Journal of Philology*, 21: 48–55.

ALPERS, J. (1912), *Hercules in Bivio*, diss., Göttingen.

AMMAN, J. (1931), *Die Zeusrede des Ailios Aristeides* (Stuttgart).

ANCONA, P. D' (1914), *La miniatura fiorentina* (Florence).

——(1950), *Miniatures of the Renaissance* (Vatican City).

ANDERSON, A. R. (1930), 'Bucephalas and his Legend', *AJP* 51: 1–21.

ANDERSON, G. (1993), *The Second Sophistic* (London).

ANDRES, F. (1918), 'Daimon', *RE* suppl. 3: 267–322.

ANDRES, G. DE (1982), *Catálogo de los códices griegos de la Biblioteca nacional* (Madrid).

ANDRESEN, C. (1955), *Logos und Nomos* (Berlin).

ARNIM, H. VON (1898), *Leben und Werke des Dio von Prusa* (Berlin).

BAILEY, C. (ed.) (1947), *Lucretius: De Rerum Natura* (Oxford).

BALADIÉ, R. (1975), 'Contribution à l'histoire de la collection Ridolfi: la date de son arrivée en France', *Scriptorium*, 29: 76–83.

BALSDON, J. P. V. D. (1969), *Life and Leisure in Ancient Rome* (London).

BANDINI, A. M. (1961), *Catalogus Codicum Manuscriptorum Bibliothecae Mediceae Laurentianae* (3 vols., Florence, 1764–70; repr. 2 vols. with app. Leipzig).

BARIGAZZI, A. (ed.) (1966), *Favorino di Arelate: Opere* (Florence).

BEAUJEU, J. (ed.) (1973), *Apulée: Opuscules philosophiques et fragments* (Paris).

BENKO, S. (1980), 'Pagan Criticism of Christianity during the First Two Centuries AD', *ANRW* 2. 23. 2: 1055–1118.

BIGNONE, E. (1936), 'A proposito della polemica di Eraclide Pontico e di Massimo Tirio contro Epicuro', *Convivium*, 14: 445–50.

——(1937), 'Ancora di Epicuro e di Massimo Tirio', *Convivium*, 15: 345–7.

References

BIGNONE, E. (1973), *L'Aristotele perduto e la formazione filosofica di Epicuro*, 2nd edn. (Florence).

BILLERBECK, M. (1978), *Epiktet. Vom Kynismus* (Leiden).

BINNS, J. W. (1990), *Intellectual Culture in Elizabethan and Jacobean England: The Latin Writings of the Age* (Leeds).

BLANKERT, S. (1940), *Seneca (Epist. 90) over Natuur en Cultuur en Posidonius als zijn Bron* (Amsterdam).

BLUM, R. (1950), *La biblioteca della Badia fiorentina e i codici di Antonio Corbinelli* (Vatican City).

BOEFT, J. DEN (1977), *Calcidius on Demons (Comm. ch. 127-136)* (Leiden).

BOLTON, J. D. P. (1962), *Aristeas of Proconnesus* (Oxford).

BÖMER, F. (ed.) (1969), *P. Ovidius Naso: Metamorphosen 1-3* (Heidelberg).

—— (1980) *P. Ovidius Naso: Metamorphosen 11-11* (Heidelberg).

—— (1986) *P. Ovidius Naso: Metamorphosen 14-15* (Heidelberg).

BOWERSOCK, G. (1969), *Greek Sophists in the Roman Empire* (Oxford).

BOWIE, E.L. (1970), 'Greeks and their Past in the Second Sophistic', *Past and Present*, 46: 3-41; rev. in M. I. Finley (ed.), *Studies in Ancient Society* (London, 1974), 166-209.

BOYANCÉ, P. (1955), 'Théurgie et télestique néoplatoniciennes', *RHR* 147: 189-209.

BRANCACCI, A. (1985), *Rhetorike philosophousa: Dione Crisostomo nella cultura antica e bizantina* (Naples).

BRENK, F. E. (1986), 'In the Light of the Moon: Demonology in the Early Imperial Period', *ANRW* 2. 16. 3, 2068-145.

BRINK, C. O. (1971), *Horace on Poetry*, ii. *The Ars Poetica* (Cambridge).

BRUNT, P. A. (1977), 'From Epictetus to Arrian', *Athenaeum*, 55: 19-48.

BUFFIÈRE, F. (1956), *Les Mythes d'Homère et la pensée grecque* (1956).

—— (ed.) (1962), *Héraclite: Allégories d' Homère* (Paris).

BURKERT, W. (1985), *Greek Religion*, tr. J. Raffan (Oxford).

BURRELL, B. (1993), 'Two Inscribed Columns from Caesarea Maritima', *ZPE* 99: 287-95.

BURRIES, B. DE (1918), *Quid Veteres Philosophi de Idololatria Senserint*, diss., Göttingen.

BURY, R. G. (ed.) (1932), *Plato: Symposium* (Cambridge).

CANART, P. (1973), 'L'unique exemplaire connu de l'œuvre grecque de Thomas Trivisanus', in B. M. Biagiarelli and D. E. Rhodes (edd.), *Studi offerti a Roberto Ridolfi* (Florence), 173-95.

CARTER, L. B. (1986), *The Quiet Athenian* (Oxford).

CHADWICK, H. (ed. and tr.) (1965), *Origen: Contra Celsum* (Oxford).

—— (1967), *The Early Church* (Harmondsworth).

CHADWICK, N. (1970), *The Celts* (London).

CHRIST, K. (1924), *Die Bibliothek Reuchlins in Pforzheim, Zentralblatt für Bibliothekswesen*, suppl. 52 (Leipzig).

CHRIST, W., SCHMID, W. and STÄHLIN, O. (1934), *Geschichte der Griechischen Literatur*, 2. 2, 6th edn. (Munich).

CHROUST, A.-H. (1957), *Socrates, Man and Myth* (London).

CLARKE, M. L. (1971), *Higher Education in the Ancient World* (London).

CLARKSON, T. (1806), *A Portraiture of Quakerism* (London).

CLERC, C. (1915), *Les Théories relatives au culte des images chez les auteurs grecs du IIème siècle après J.C.* (Paris).

CORTESI, M. (1980), 'Libri e vicende di Vittorino da Feltre', *Italia Medioevale e Umanistica*, 23: 77–114.

——(1981), 'Un allievo di Vittorino da Feltre: Gian Pietro da Lucca', in N. Gianetto (ed.), *Vittorino da Feltre e la sua scuola* (Florence), 263–76.

COSENZA, M. E. (1962), *Biographical and Bibliographic Dictionary of the Italian Humanists and of the World of Classical Scholarship in Italy, 1300–1800* (Boston).

COSTA, C. D. N. (ed.) (1984), *Lucretius: De Rerum Natura 5* (Oxford).

CRONERT, W. (1913), review of Hobein (1910), in *Berl. Philol. Wochenschr.* 33/21: 644–8.

CUMONT, F. (1915), 'Les anges du paganisme', *RHR* 72: 159–82.

DANIÉLOU, J. (1973), *A History of Early Christian Doctrine before the Council of Nicaea*, ii. *Gospel Message and Hellenistic Culture*, tr. J. A. Baker (London).

DAWSON, D. (1992), *Allegorical Readers and Cultural Revision in Ancient Alexandria* (Berkeley).

DESIDERI, P. (1978), *Dione di Prusa: Un intelletuale greco nell'impero romano* (Messina).

DEPRÉ, M. (1940), *La Connaissance de Dieu chez Maxime de Tyr*, diss., Louvain.

DEFFREESSE, R. (1965), *Le Fonds grec de la bibliothèque vaticane des origines à Paul V* (Vatican City).

DILL, S. (1905), *Roman Society from Nero to Marcus Aurelius* (London).

DILLON, J. (1977), *The Middle Platonists* (London).

——(1981), 'Ganymede as Logos: Traces of a Forgotten Allegorization in Philo?', *CQ* NS 31: 183–5.

——(1986), 'Plutarch and Second Century Platonism', in A. H. Armstrong (ed.), *Classical Mediterranean Spirituality* (London), 214–29.

——(1988), '"Orthodoxy" and "Eclecticism": Middle Platonists and Neo-Pythagoreans', in J. Dillon and A. Long (edd.), *The Question of 'Eclecticism'* (Berkeley), 103–25.

——(1993), *Alcinous: The Handbook of Platonism* (Oxford).

DIONISOTTI, A.C. (1983), 'Polybius and the Royal Professor', in E. Gabba (ed.), *Tria Corda: Scritti in onore di A. Momigliano* (Como), 179–99.

DODDS, E. R. (1951), *The Greeks and the Irrational* (Berkeley).

——(ed.) (1959), *Plato: Gorgias* (Oxford).

DOREZ, L. (1893), 'Antoine Éparque: Recherches sur le commerce des manuscrits grecs en Italie au XVIe siècle', *Mél. Arch. Hist.* 13: 281-364.

DOVER, K. J. (1974), *Greek Popular Morality* (Oxford).

DUDLEY, D. R. (1937), *A History of Cynicism* (London; repr. Hildesheim, 1967).

DUE, B. (1989), *The Cyropedia* (Aarhus).

DÜRR, K. (1899), 'Sprachliche Untersuchungen zu den Dialexeis des Maximus von Tyrus', *Philologus*, suppl. 8: 1-156.

FARNELL, L. R. (1896-1909), *Cults of the Greek States* (Oxford).

FAULKNER, T. C., KIESSLING, N. K. and BLAIR, R. L. (edd.) (1989-94), *Robert Burton: The Anatomy of Melancholy* (Oxford).

FAZZO, V. (1977), *La giustificazione delle imagini religiose della tarda antichità al cristianesimo* (Naples).

FERGUSON, J. (1970), *Socrates: A Source Book* (London).

FESTUGIÈRE, A. J. (1949), *La Révélation d'Hermès Trismégiste*, ii. *Le Dieu cosmique*, 3rd edn. (Paris).

——(1953), *La Révélation d'Hermès Trismégiste*, iii. *Les Doctrines de l'âme* (Paris).

——(1954), *La Révélation d'Hermès Trismégiste*, iv. *Le Dieu inconnu et la gnose*, (Paris).

FICINO, M. (ed. and tr.) (1551), *Omnia Divini Platonis Opera* (Basel).

FONTENROSE, J. (1978), *The Delphic Oracle* (Berkeley).

FORBES, C. A. (1933), *Neoi: A Study of Greek Associations* (Middletown, Conn.).

FORNARA, C. W. (1983), *The Nature of History in Ancient Greece and Rome* (Berkeley).

FOUCAULT, M. (1990), *History of Sexuality*, iii. *The Care of the Self*, tr. R. Hurley (London) from *Histoire de la Sexualité*, iii. *Le Souci de soi* (Paris, 1984).

FRÄNKEL, H. (1946), 'Man's "Ephemeros" Nature according to Pindar and Others', *TAPhA* 77: 131-45 (cf. *Wege und Formen frügriechischen Denkens* (Munich, 1968), 23-39).

FRIEDLÄNDER, L. (1922), *Darstellungen aus der Sittengeschichte Roms*, 10th edn. rev. G. Wissowa (Leipzig).

FUNK, K. (1907), *Untersuchungen über die Lukians Vita Demonactis*, *Philologus*, suppl. 10 (Leipzig).

GAISER, K. (1985), *Il paragone della caverna: Variazioni da Platone a oggi* (Naples).

GALINSKY, G. K. (1972), *The Heracles Theme* (Oxford).

GAMILLSCHEG, E., and HARLFINGER, D. (1981), *Repertorium der griechischen Kopisten*, i (Vienna).

GARDINER, E. N. (1910), *Greek Athletic Sports and Festivals* (London).

GEFFCKEN, J. (1907), *Zwei griechischen Apologeten* (Leipzig).

GERCKE, A. (1893), 'Die Komposition der ersten Satire des Horaz', *RhM* 48: 41–52.

GESNER, C. (1545), *Bibliotheca Universalis* (Zurich).

GIANI, S. (ed.) (1993), *Pseudo Archita: L'Educazione morale* (Rome).

GIOTOPOULOU-SISILIANOU, E. (1978), Ἀντώνιος ὁ Ἔπαρχος (Athens).

GLUCKER, J. (1978), *Antiochus and the Late Academy* (Göttingen).

GOGGIN, M. G. (1951), 'Rhythm in the Prose of Favorinus', *YCS* 12: 149–201.

GOMPERZ, T. (1909), 'Zu Maximos Tyrios', *WS* 31: 181–9.

GOTTSCHALK, H. (1980), *Heraclides of Pontus* (Oxford).

GRAFTON, A. T. (1977), 'On the Scholarship of Politian and its Context', *JWCI* 40: 150–88.

——(1983), *Joseph Scaliger: A Study in the History of Classical Scholarship*, i. *Textual Criticism and Exegesis* (Oxford).

GRANT, R. M. (1955), 'The Chronology of the Greek Apologists', *VC* 9: 25–33.

——(1988), *Greek Apologists of the Second Century* (London).

GRAUX, C. (1880), *Essai sur les origines du fonds grec de l'Escurial* (Paris).

GRIFFIN, J. (1980), *Homer on Life and Death* (Oxford).

HADOT, I. (1984), *Arts libéraux et philosophie dans la pensée antique* (Paris).

HAHN, J. (1989), *Der Philosoph und die Gesellschaft* (Stuttgart).

HAMILTON, J. R. (1969), *Plutarch: Alexander* (Oxford).

HAMMERSTAEDT, J. (1988), *Die Orakelkritik des Kynikers Oenomaus* (Frankfurt am Main).

HARDIE, P. R. (1985), 'Imago Mundi: Cosmological and Ideological Aspects of the Shield of Achilles', *JHS* 105: 11–31.

HARRIS, H. A. (1964), *Greek Athletes and Athletics* (London).

HARRISON, S. J. (forthcoming), *Apuleius: A Latin Sophist* (Oxford).

HARTLICH, P. (1889), *De Exhortationum a Graecis Romanisque Scriptorum Historia et Indole*, diss., Leipzig.

HEBER, R., and EDEN, C. P. (1847–54), *The Whole Works of the Right Rev. Jeremy Taylor, D.D.* (London).

HEINZE, R. (1892), *Xenokrates* (Leipzig; repr. Hildesheim, 1965).

HELM, R. (1906), *Lukian und Menipp* (Leipzig).

HEUBNER, H. (ed.) (1968), *P. Cornelius Tacitus: Die Historien 2* (Heidelberg).

HOBEIN, H. (1895), *De Maximo Tyrio Quaestiones Philologae Selectae*, diss., Göttingen.

——(ed.) (1910), *Maximi Tyrii Philosophumena* (Leipzig).

——(1911), 'Zweck und Bedeutung der ersten Rede des Maximus Tyrius', in Χάριτες F. Leo *zum 60 Geburtstag dargebracht* (Berlin), 188–209.

——and KROLL, W. (1930), 'Maximus (37) von Tyrus', *RE* 14: 2555–62.

HÖISTAD, R. (1948), *Cynic Hero and Cynic King* (Uppsala).

HOLFORD-STREVENS, L. (1988), *Aulus Gellius* (London).

HORAWITZ, A., and HARTFELDER, K. (1886), *Briefwechsel des Beatus Rhenanus* (Leipzig).

HUNTER, R. L. (1983), *Daphnis and Chloe, A Literary Study* (Cambridge).

HUXLEY, G. L. (1978), '*ΟΡΟΣ ΘΕΟΣ*, Maximus Tyrius 2. 8', *LCM* 3: 71-2.

JAEGER, W. (1948), *Aristotle*, 2nd edn. (Oxford).

JAY, E. G. (tr.) (1954), *Origen's Treatise on Prayer* (London).

JENNY, B. R. (1964), 'Arlenius in Basel', *Basler Zeitschrift für Geschichte und Altertumskunde*, 64: 5-45.

——(ed.) (1982-3), *Die Amerbachkorrespondenz*, ix (Basel).

JOEL, K. (1893-1901), *Der echte und der Xenophontische Sokrates* (Berlin).

JOLY, R. (1973), *Christianisme et philosophie: Études sur Justin et les Apologistes grecs du deuxième siècle* (Brussels).

JONES, A. H. M. (1940), *The Greek City* (Oxford).

JONES, C. P. (1978), *The Roman World of Dio Chrysostom* (Cambridge, Mass.).

——(1986), *Culture and Society in Lucian* (Cambridge, Mass.).

Jones, R. M. (1926), 'Posidonius and the Flight of the Mind through the Universe', *CPh* 21: 97-113.

KAISER, E. (1964), 'Odysee-Szenen als Topoi', *Mus. Helv.* 21: 109-36, 197-224.

KASSEL, R. (1958), *Untersuchungen zur griechischen und römischen Konsolationsliteratur* (Munich).

——(1963), 'Kritische und exegetische kleinigkeiten', *RhM* 106: 298-306.

KESELING, P. (1935), 'Zu Maximus Tyrius or. 17 (Hobein)', *Philologische Wochenschrift*, 7-8: 221-3.

KIBRE, P. (1936), *The Library of Pico della Mirandola* (New York).

KIESSLING, N. (1988), *The Library of Robert Burton* (Oxford).

KINDSTRAND, J. F. (1973), *Homer in der zweiten Sophistik* (Uppsala).

——(1980), 'The Date and Character of Hermias' *Irrisio*', *Vig. Christ.* 34: 341-57.

——(1981), *Anacharsis* (Uppsala).

KIRK, G. S., Raven, J. E., and Schofield, M. (1983), *The Presocratic Philosophers*, 2nd edn. (Cambridge).

KLEI, W. (ed.) (1950), *Seneca: Dialogorum Liber 11: Ad Serenum* (Zwolle).

KOHL, R. (1915), *De Scholasticarum Declamationum Argumentis ex Historia Petitis* (Paderborn).

KOKOLAKIS, M. (1960), *The Dramatic Simile of Life* (Athens).

KONIARIS, G. L. (1962), 'Critical Observations in the Text of Maximus of Tyre', diss., (Cornell).

——(1965), 'Emendations in the Text of Maximus of Tyre', *RhM* 108: 353-70.

——(1970), 'On the Text of Maximus Tyrius', *CQ* NS 20: 130-4.

——(1972), 'Emendations in Maximus Tyrius', *AJP* 93: 424–36.

——(1977), 'More Emendations in Maximus Tyrius', *Hermes*, 105: 54–68.

——(1982), 'On Maximus of Tyre: Zetemata (I)', *Class. Ant.* 1: 87–121.

——(1983), 'On Maximus of Tyre: Zetemata (II)', *Class. Ant.* 2: 212–50.

——(ed.) (1995), *Maximus Tyrius Philosophumena—Διαλέξεις* (Berlin).

KOPIDAKIS, M. (1976), 'Notices sur textes grecs I', *Hellenica*, 29: 344–8.

KRISTELLER, P. O. (1967), *Iter Italicum*, ii (Leiden).

——(1990), *Iter Italicum*, v (Leiden).

KROLL, W. and HOBEIN, H., 'Maximus (37) von Tyrus', *RE* 14: 2555–62.

KUBO, M. (1985), 'Sappho-Ovidius-Renaissance', *Mediterraneus*, 8: 3–51.

LABOWSKY, L. (1961), 'Bessarion Studies III', *Medieval and Renaissance Studies*, 5: 155–62.

——(1979), *Bessarion's Library and the Biblioteca Marciana* (Rome).

LACHENAUD, G. (ed.) (1993), *Plutarque: Œuvres morales XII. 2. Opinions des philosophes* (Paris).

LAMBERTON, R. (1986), *Homer the Theologian* (Berkeley).

——and KEANEY, J. J. (edd.) (1992), *Homer's Ancient Readers* (Princeton).

LANE FOX, R. (1986), *Pagans and Christians* (London).

LAZZERI, E. (1971), *Poliziano: Commento inedito all'epistola ovidiana di Saffo a Faone* (Firenze).

LEGRAND, E. (1885), *Bibliographie hellénique*, i (Paris).

LEUTSCH, E. L. VON, and SCHNEIDEWIN, F. G. (edd.) (1839–51), *Corpus Paroemiographorum Graecorum* (Göttingen; repr. Hildesheim, 1965).

LILLA, S. (1971), *Clement of Alexandria: A Study in Christian Platonism and Gnosticism* (Oxford).

LINDOP, G. (1981), *The Opium Eater* (London).

LOHE, P. (ed.) (1980), *Landino: Disputationes Camaldulenses* (Florence).

LO MONACO, F. (1991), *A. Poliziano: Commento inedito ai Fasti di Ovidio* (Florence).

LORIMER, W. L. (1925), *Some Notes on the Text of Pseudo-Aristotle De Mundo* (Oxford).

LOVEJOY, A. O. (1936), *The Great Chain of Being* (Cambridge, Mass.).

——and BOAS, G. (1935), *Primitivism and Related Ideas in Antiquity* (Baltimore).

LUZZATTO, M. T. (1983), *Tragedia greca e cultura ellenistica* (Bologna).

MACMULLEN, R. (1981), *Paganism in the Roman Empire* (New Haven).

MCKIRAHAN, V. T. (1994), 'The Socratic Origins of the Cynics and Cyrenaics', in P. A. Vander Waerdt, *The Socratic Movement* (Ithaca, NY) 367–91.

MALHERBE, A. (ed.) (1977), *The Cynic Epistles* (Missoula, Mont.).

MARCEL, R. (ed.) (1956), *Ficin: Commentaire sur le Banquet de Platon* (Paris).

MARTIN, L. C. (ed.) (1957), *The Works of Henry Vaughan*, 2nd edn. (Oxford).

MARTINELLI, L. CESARINI (1978), *A. Poliziano: Commento inedito alle Selve di Stazio* (Florence).

MEISER, K. (1909), *Studien zu Maximos Tyrios, Sitzungsberichte der König. Bayerischen Akad. der Wiss., Philos.-philol. Kl.*, Jahrg. 1909, 6. Abh. (Munich).

MICHEL, A. (1970), 'De Socrate à Maxime de Tyr: les problèmes sociaux de l'armée dans l'idéologie romaine', *REL* 47/2 (*Mélanges Durry*): 237-51.

MIONI, E. (1976), 'Bessarione scriba ed alcuni collaboratori', in *Miscellanea Marciana di studi Bessarionei*, Medioevo e Umanesimo, 24 (Padua) 263-318

——(1981-5), *Codices Graeci Manuscripti Bibliothecae Divi Marci Venetiarum: Thesaurus Antiquus* (Rome).

MONTUORI, M. (1981), *De Socrate Iuste Damnato* (Amsterdam).

MOST, G. W. (1989), 'Cornutus and Stoic Allegoresis: A Preliminary Report', *ANRW* 2. 36. 3, 2014-65.

MUGNAI CARRARA, D. (1991), *La biblioteca di Nicolò Leoniceno* (Florence).

MURRAY, O. (1990), 'The Idea of the Shepherd King from Cyrus to Charlemagne', in P. Godman and O. Murray (edd.), *Latin Poetry and the Classical Tradition* (Oxford), 1-14.

MUTSCHMANN, H. (1913), 'Die Ueberlieferungsgeschichte des Maximus Tyrius', *RhM* 68: 560-83.

——(1917), 'Das erste Auftreten des Maximus von Tyrus in Rom', *Sokrates*, 5: 185-97.

NAPOLITANO, F. (1974-5), 'Gli studi omerici di Massimo Tirio', *Annali della Facoltà di Lettere e Filosofia della Università degli Studi di Napoli*, 17: 81-103.

NAUCK, A. (1867), *Lexicon Vindobonense* (St Petersburg).

NOAILLES, P. (1941), 'Deux manuscrits d'humanistes et l'édition des Nouvelles de Justinien et Léon le Sage', *Bulletin de la Société Nationale des Antiquaires de France*, 81-113.

NOCK, A. D. (1933), *Conversion* (Oxford).

——(1939), 'Conversion and Adolescence', in T. Klauser and A. Rücker (edd.), *Pisciculi: Studien zur Religion und Kultur des Altertums*, Ergänzungsband i (Münster in Westfalen), 165-77; repr. in Nock, *Essays on Religion and the Ancient World* (Oxford, 1972), i. 469-80.

OBERDORFER, A. (1910), 'Di L. Giustinian umanista', *Giornale storico della letteratura italiana*, 56: 107-20.

OLDFATHER, W. (1928), 'Socrates in Court', *Classical Weekly*, 31/21: 203-11.

OLTRAMARE, A. (1926), *Les Origines de la diatribe latine* (Geneva).

OSBORNE, C. (1987), *Rethinking Early Greek Philosophy* (London).

PACK, R. A. (ed.) (1963), *Artemidori Daldiani Onirocriticorum Libri V* (Leipzig).

PANOFSKY, E. (1930), *Hercules am Scheideweg e und andere antike Bildstoffe in der neveren Kunst* (Leipzig).

PARKE, H. W. (1967), *The Oracles of Zeus* (Oxford).

—— (1985), *The Oracles of Apollo in Asia Minor* (London).

—— and WORMELL, D. E. W. (1956), *The Delphic Oracle*, ii. *The History* (Oxford).

PARKER, H. N. (1993), 'Sappho Schoolmistress', *TAPhA* 123: 309-51.

PEASE, A. S. (ed.) (1955), *M. Tulli Ciceronis De Natura Deorum I* (Cambridge, Mass.).

—— (ed.) (1958), *M. Tulli Ciceronis De Natura Deorum II* (Cambridge, Mass.).

PÉLÉKIDIS, C. (1962), *Histoire de l'ephébie attique* (Paris).

PÉPIN, J. (1976), *Mythe et allégorie*, 2nd edn. (Paris).

POLIZIANO, A. (1553), *Angeli Politiani Opera* (Basel).

POLLITT, J. J. (1974), *The Ancient View of Greek Art* (New Haven).

—— (1990), *The Art of Ancient Greece*, 2nd edn. (Cambridge).

POWELL, J. G. F. (ed.) (1990), *Cicero: On Friendship and the Dream of Scipio* (Warminster).

PRÄCHTER, K. (1901), *Hierokles der Stoiker* (Leipzig).

PUIGGALI, J. (1980), 'Maxime de Tyr et Favorinos', *Annales de la Fac. des Lett. et des Sci. hum. de l'Univ. de Dakar*, 10: 47-62.

—— (1982), 'Dion Chrysostom et Maxime de Tyr', ibid. 12: 9-24.

—— (1983), *Étude sur les Dialexeis de Maxime de Tyr, conférencier platonicien du IIème siècle* (Lille).

RAWSON, E. (1986), 'Cassius and Brutus: The Memory of the Liberators', in I. Moxon, J. D. Smart and A. J. Woodman (edd.), *Past Perspectives: Studies in Greek and Roman Historical Writing* (Cambridge), 101-19; repr. in E. Rawson, *Roman Culture and Society* (Oxford, 1991), 488-507.

REALE, G. (ed.) (1974), *Aristotele: Trattato sul cosmo per Alessandro* (Naples).

Reardon, B. P. (1971), *Courants littéraires grecs des IIe et IIIe siècles après J.-C.* (Paris).

REES, D. A. (1957), 'Bipartition of the Soul in the Early Academy', *JHS* 77: 112-18.

REGOLIOSI, M. (1966), 'Nuove ricerche intorno a Giovanni Tortelli', *Italia Medioevale e Umanistica*, 9: 123-89.

RENEHAN, R. (1986), 'A New Hesiodic Fragment', *CPh.* 81: 221-2.

—— (1987), 'Some Passages in Maximus of Tyre', *CPh.* 82: 43-9.

REVERDIN, O. (1980-1), 'Livres grecs imprimés à Genève au XVIe et au XVIIe siècle', in J. D. Candaux and B. Lescaze (edd.), *Cinq siècles d'imprimerie genevoise* (Geneva), 209-38.

REYNOLDS, L. D. and WILSON, N. G. (1991), *Scribes and Scholars*, 3rd edn. (Oxford).

RIDINGS, D. (1995), *The Attic Moses: The Dependency Theme in Some Early Christian Writers* (Gothenburg).

RIDOLFI, R. (1929), 'La biblioteca del cardinale N. Ridolfi (1501–1550)', *La Bibliofilia*, 31: 1–23.

RIZZO, S. (1973), *Il lessico filologico degli umanisti* (Rome).

ROHDE, E. (1925), *Psyche*, tr. W. B. Hillis, 8th edn. (London).

ROHDICH, R. (1879), *De Maximo Tyrio Theologo* (Breslau).

ROSTAGNO, E., and FESTA, N. (1893), 'Indice dei codici greci Laurenziani non compresi nel catalogo del Bandini', *SIFC* 1: 129–232; repr. in A. M. Bandini, *Catalogus Codicum Manuscriptorum Bibliothecae Mediceae Laurentianae*, 2nd edn. (Leipzig, 1961), ii, app.

RUSSELL, D. A. (ed.) (1964), *'Longinus': On the Sublime* (Oxford).

——(1983), *Greek Declamation* (Cambridge).

——(ed.) (1992), *Dio Chrysostom, Orations VII, XII, XXXVI* (Cambridge).

——and WILSON, N. G. (edd.), *Menander Rhetor* (Oxford).

SABBADINI, R. (1922), *Il metodo degli umanisti* (Florence).

SANDBACH, F. H. (1989), *The Stoics*, 2nd edn. (Bristol).

SCHMIDT, H. (1907), *Veteres Philosophi Quomodo Iudicaverunt de Precibus* (Giessen).

SCHULTE, F. W. (1915), *De Maximi Tyrii Codicibus*, diss., Göttingen.

SCHWABL, H. (1976), 'Zeus nickt (zu Ilias 1,524–30 und seiner Nachwirkung)', *WS* NS 10: 22–30.

SCHWEIGER, F. L. A. (1830–4), *Handbuch der classischen Bibliographie* (Leipzig).

ŠEVČENKO, I. (1964), 'Some Autographs of Nicephorus Gregoras', in F. Barišić (ed.), *Mélanges G. Ostrogorsky (Recueil de travaux de l'Institut d'É-tudes Byzantines [ZRVI]* 8.2), 435–50.

SHARPLES, R. W. (1995), *World under Management? Details, Delegation and Divine Providence, 400 BC–AD 1200* (London).

SICHERL, M. (1978), *Johannes Cuno* (Heidelberg).

SLINGS, S. R. (1981), *A Commentary on the Platonic Clitophon* (Amsterdam).

SMITH, K. F. (ed.) (1913), *The Elegies of Albius Tibullus* (New York).

SORABJI, R. (1993), *Animal Minds and Human Morals* (London).

SOURY, G. (1942), *Aperçus de philosophie religieuse chez Maxime de Tyr, platonicien éclectique* (Paris).

STANFORD, W. B. (1963), *The Ulysses Theme*, 2nd edn. (Oxford).

STINTZING, R. VON (1879), *G. Tanners Briefe an Bonifacius und Basilius Amerbach* (Bonn).

STÖCKER, C. (1979), 'Indische Schlangengötter in einer Alexandersage', *Würzburger Jahrb. für Altertumswiss.* NS 5: 91–7.

STONE, I. (1988), *The Trial of Socrates* (London).

SZARMACH, M. (1982), 'Ἐρωτικοὶ λόγοι von Maximos Tyrios', *Eos*, 70: 61–9.

—— (1982), 'De significato vocis philosophiae apud Maximum Tyrium', *Maeander*, 38: 199-202.

—— (1983), 'Ueber Begriff und Bedeutung der Philosophie bei Maximus Tyrius', *Concilium Eirene XVI: Proceedings of the Sixteenth International Eirene Conference, Prague 1982* (Prague), i. 223-7.

—— (1984), 'Drei Diatriben des Maximos von Tyros mit Sokrates', *Eos*, 72: 75-84.

—— (1985), *Maximos von Tyros. Eine literarische Monographie* (Torun).

TARRANT, H. (1988), 'Salvation from God in the *De Mundo* and *Numenius*', in D. Dockrill and R. Tanner (edd.), *The Idea of Salvation* (*Prudentia*, 20, suppl.) (Auckland), 24-30.

TATE, J. (1927), 'The Beginnings of Greek Allegory', *CR* 41: 214-15.

—— (1934), 'On the History of Allegorism', *CQ* 23: 105-14.

TATUM, J. (1979), *Apuleius and the Golden Ass* (Ithaca, NY).

TESCARI, O. (1937), 'Per la interpretazione di un passo di Massimo Tirio—Epicuro e la poesia', *Convivium*, 15: 212-14.

THEILER, W. (1930), *Die Vorbereitung des Neuplatonismus* (Berlin).

THESLEFF, H. (1967), *Studies in the Styles of Plato* (Helsinki).

TRAPP, M. B. (1990), 'Plato's Phaedrus in Second-Century Greek Literature', in D. A. Russell (ed.) *Antonine Literature* (Oxford), 141-73.

—— (1991), 'Some Emendations in the Text of Maximus of Tyre, Dialexeis 1-21 (Hobein)', *CQ* NS 41: 566-71.

—— (1992), 'More Emendations in the Text of Maximus of Tyre', *CQ* NS 42: 569-75.

—— (ed.) (1994), *Maximus Tyrius: Dissertationes* (Stuttgart).

—— (forthcoming *a*), 'Philosophical Sermons: The "Dialexeis" of Maximus of Tyre', *ANRW* 2. 34. 3.

—— (forthcoming *b*), 'Zanobi Acciaiuoli, Laurentianus Conventi Soppressi 4, and the Text of Maximus of Tyre'.

TRITHEMIUS, J. (1495), *Catalogus Illustrium Virorum* (Mentz).

VISCHER, R. (1965), *Das einfache Leben* (Göttingen).

VOGEL, M., and GARDTHAUSEN, E. (1909), *Die griechische Schreiber des Mittelalters und der Renaissance*, *Centralblatt für Bibliothekswesen*, suppl. 33 (Leipzig).

VRIES-VAN DER VELDEN, E. DE (1987), *Théodore Métochite* (Amsterdam).

WAITH, E. (1960), 'Landino and Maximus of Tyre', *Renaissance News*, 13: 289-94.

WALLIS, R. T. (1972), *Neoplatonism* (London).

WALSDORFF, F. (1927), *Die antiken Urteile über Platons Stil* (Leipzig).

WALTZER, R. (1949), *Galen on Jews and Christians* (Oxford).

WEINSTOCK, S. (1926), 'Die platonische Homerkritik und ihre Nachwirkung', *Philologus*, 82: 121-53.

West, M. L. (ed.) (1978), *Hesiod: Works and Days* (Oxford).

—— (1983), *The Orphic Poems* (Oxford).

Whittaker, J. (1974), 'Parisinus Graecus 1962 and the Writings of Albinus', *Phoenix* 28: 320–54 and 450–6.

—— (1977), 'Parisinus Graecus 1962 and Janus Lascaris', *Phoenix*, 31: 239–44.

—— (ed.) (1990), *Alcinoos: Enseignement des doctrines de Platon* (Paris).

—— (1991), 'Arethas and the "Collection philosophique"', in D. Harfinger and G. Prato (edd.), *Paleografia e codicologia greca* (Alessandria), 513–21.

Wilamowitz, U. von (1899), *Euripides* Herakles, i (Berlin).

—— (1902), *Griechisches Lesebuch* (Berlin).

Wilhelm, F. (1902), 'Zu Achilles Tatius', *RhM* 57: 55–75.

Willing, A. (1909), 'De Socratis Daemonio quae Antiquis Temporibus Fuerint Opiniones', *Commentarii Jenenses*, 8: 127–83.

Wilson, N. G. (1983), *Scholars of Byzantium* (London).

Witt, R. E. (1931), 'The Hellenism of Clement of Alexandria', *CQ* 25: 195–204.

Wright, C. E. (1972), *Fontes Harleiani* (London).

Zeller, E. (1923), *Die Philosophie der Griechen*, 3. 2: *Die nach-aristotelische Philosophie*, ii, 5th edn. (Leipzig).

Index of Texts Quoted by Maximus

This index includes allusions and paraphrases as well as direct quotations; direct quotations are marked with an asterisk; a query following a page number relates to the status, and not the pagination, of the reference.

General Index

In this index, roman numerals refer to pages of the Introduction; italicized numerals indicate references in headnotes and footnotes; a query following a page number relates to the status, and not the pagination, of the reference.

DATE DUE
